MW01502620

# FEDERAL PRISON GUIDEBOOK

## Federal Sentencing and Post Conviction Remedies

**by Alan Ellis and J. Michael Henderson**

# HIGHLIGHTS

This edition of Alan Ellis' popular *Federal Prison Guidebook* contains valuable new practice tips and judicial recommendations on sentencing, and a complete update of the prison directory. You receive these new sections:

**CHAPTER 8: FEDERAL SENTENCING**

§8:50 Advice from the Bench

    §8:50.1 What Judges Want to Know
    §8:50.2 Judges Think We Can Do Better
    §8:50.3 White-Collar Clients
    §8:50.5 Recommendations Judge-by Judge
            §8:50.4.1   Judges Jed Rakoff and Mark Bennett
            §8:50.4.2   Judges Patrick J. Schiltz and Robert N. Scola, Jr.
            §8:50.4.3   Judges Cynthia A. Bashant and Jon D. Levy
            §8:50.4.4   Judges John R. Adams, Otis D. Wright II, Justin L. Quackenbush, and Walter H. Rice
            §8:50.4.5   Judges James S. Gwin, Amy J. St. Eve, and Paul L. Friedman
            §8:50.4.6   Judges James C. Mahan, Mark L. Wolf, Jerome B. Simandle

§8:60 Prison and Sentencing Practice Tips

**PLUS MATERIAL CHANGES IN THE DIRECTORY TO NEARLY EVERY PRISON LISTING!**

**James** Publishing

# We Welcome Your Feedback

Our most useful source of improvements is comments from our subscribers,
so if you have any comments, we would love to hear from you.


James Publishing, Inc.
Attn: Federal Prison Guidebook Managing Editor
3505 Cadillac Ave., Suite P-101
Costa Mesa, CA 92626

www.JamesPublishing.com
(866) 72-JAMES

# ALAN ELLIS'
# FEDERAL PRISON GUIDEBOOK

## FEDERAL SENTENCING AND POST-CONVICTION STRATEGIES

**ALAN ELLIS**

**J. MICHAEL HENDERSON**

James Publishing

Contact us at (866) 72-JAMES or www.jamespublishing.com

Revision Editor
James Publishing
3505 Cadillac Ave., Suite P
Costa Mesa, CA 92626


First Edition,       6/1998
Second Edition,   6/2000
Third Edition,      6/2002
Fourth Edition,    6/2004
Fifth Edition,       6/2006
Sixth Edition,      6/2008
Revision 1,          8/2010
Revision 2,          8/2012
Revision 3,          2/2015
Revision 4,          9/2017


Managing Editor: Julie Anne Ines
Typesetter: Alexandru Oprescu

# ABOUT THE AUTHORS

**Alan Ellis**, past president of the National Association of Criminal Defense Lawyers, is a nationally recognized authority in federal sentencing, prison matters, and post-conviction remedies with offices in San Francisco and New York. He is co-author with J. Michael Henderson of the *Federal Prison Guidebook*; James H. Feldman, Jr. and Mark Allenbaugh of the *Federal Sentencing Guidebook*; Mark Allenbaugh, Jonathan Edelstein, James H. Feldman, Jr., and Karen Landau of the *Federal Post Conviction Guidebook*; and a contributing editor to the American Bar Association *Criminal Justice* magazine for whom he writes a quarterly column on Federal Sentencing. Mr. Ellis has been described as "one of this country's pre-eminent criminal defense lawyers" by *Federal Lawyer* magazine. The United States Court of Appeals for the Ninth Circuit, in a published decision, has identified him as a "nationally recognized expert in federal criminal sentencing." He is a sought-after lecturer in criminal law education programs and is widely published in the areas of federal sentencing, Bureau of Prisons matters, appeals and other post-conviction remedies, with more than 120 articles and books and 70 lectures, presentations and speaking engagements to his credit. He was a Visiting Fulbright Professor of Law, sent by the U.S. State Department, to conduct lectures at Shanghai, China Jiaotong University' School of Law on the protections afforded criminal defendants in America.

**J. Michael Henderson** a federal prison consultant to the Law Offices of Alan Ellis, has over 23 years of experience working with the Bureau of Prisons (BOP). While employed by the BOP, Mr. Henderson had wide-ranging experience in Federal Corrections and Case Management, with expertise in inmate discipline; inmate programs; oversight in two of six Regional Offices for inmate programs, inmate Regional legal appeals, compassionate release applications, and Congressional and Judicial correspondence; Central Inmate Monitoring (special inmate placement and movement); staff training; security classification oversight and prison designations and transfers; and prison facility administration. Additionally, he was an E.E.O. Investigator for the BOP. Mr. Henderson served as the Regional Designator for the Western Region of the United States in the early '90s and again from 1997 until his retirement in 2000. In that capacity, his duties included oversight of the Federal Bureau of Prisons classification of newly sentenced federal offenders in the western part of the United States. Mr. Henderson worked at several prisons, including High, Medium, Minimum and Administrative Security. During his career, Mr. Henderson received numerous awards and recognition for his work. Noteworthy awards include an annual award from the inmate branch of the NAACP at FPC Allenwood, Pennsylvania and the Bureau of Prisons' National Stanford Bates Award for outstanding contributions to improved Case Management. Mr. Henderson is the co-author of the Federal Prison Guidebook.

# ACKNOWLEDGEMENTS

The authors wish to acknowledge Deborah Bezilla, Administrative Assistant to the Law Offices of Alan Ellis for her extraordinary and tireless work on this book and to Mark H. Allenbaugh, who was a significant contributor to Chapters 6, 8 and 11.

# DEDICATION

To my wife, Jie Zheng, who has always been there for me.

— Alan Ellis

# INTRODUCTION

The first edition of the Federal Prison Guidebook was published in 1998. Its purpose, at that time, was to replace the Federal Bureau of Prison's discontinued *Directory of Federal Prisons*, which ceased publication in 1993.

Recognizing that the bench, bar, and public needed to know more about the workings of the Bureau of Prisons, the 2000 edition added substantive chapters. Those chapters have been regularly updated and expanded.

In this 2017-19 edition, the substantive chapters have been expanded with the addition of practice tips and judicial recommendations for more effective advocacy at sentencing.

# SUMMARY CONTENTS

# DETAILED CONTENTS

## CHAPTER 1:
## Prison Programs and Policies

# CHAPTER 2:
## Securing a Favorable Federal Prison Placement

# CHAPTER 3:
## Residential Drug Abuse Program (RDAP)

# CHAPTER 4:
## How To Do Time

# CHAPTER 5:
## Pre-Release

# CHAPTER 6:
# Sex Offenders

# CHAPTER 7:
# Medical Care in the Bureau of Prisons

# CHAPTER 8:
# Federal Sentencing

# CHAPTER 9:
## Direct Appeals

# CHAPTER 10:
## Habeas Corpus: §2255 Motions

## CHAPTER 11:
## Practice Tips

## CHAPTER 12:
## The Mid-Atlantic Region

## CHAPTER 13:
## The North Central Region

# CHAPTER 14:
# The Northeast Region

# CHAPTER 15:
## The South Central Region

§15:10  FCI Bastrop
§15:11  USP Beaumont
§15:12  FCI Beaumont (Medium and Low)
§15:13  FCI Big Spring
§15:14  FPC Bryan
§15:15  FMC Carswell
§15:16  FCI El Reno
§15:17  FCC Forrest City
§15:18  FCI Fort Worth
§15:19  FDC Houston
§15:20  FCI La Tuna
§15:21  FCC Oakdale
§15:22  FTC Oklahoma City
§15:23  FCI Pollock
§15:24  USP Pollock
§15:25  FCI Seagoville
§15:26  FCI Texarkana
§15:27  FCI Three Rivers

# CHAPTER 16:
## The South East Region

§16:09  FCI Aliceville
§16:10  USP Atlanta
§16:11  FCI Bennettsville
§16:12  FCI Coleman—Low
§16:13  USP Coleman Medium
§16:14  USP Coleman I and II
§16:15  FCI Edgefield
§16:16  FCI Estill
§16:17  MDC Guaynabo
§16:18  FCI Jesup
§16:19  FCI Marianna
§16:20  FCI Miami
§16:21  FDC Miami
§16:22  FPC Montgomery
§16:23  FPC Pensacola
§16:24  FCI Talladega
§16:25  FCI Tallahassee
§16:26  FCI Williamsburg
§16:27  FCI Yazoo City I & II
§16:28  USP Yazoo City

# CHAPTER 17:
## The Western Region

# CHAPTER 18:
## Privately Managed Facilities Housing Federal Inmates

# INDEX

(This page intentionally left blank.)

# CHAPTER 1

# PRISON PROGRAMS AND POLICIES

## §1:10   INTRODUCTION TO THE GUIDEBOOK

The *Federal Prison Guidebook* is designed to answer some of the questions that defense attorneys, prosecutors, judges, probation officers, as well as criminal defendants facing incarceration in a federal prison, and federal inmates and their families, may have about the Bureau of Prisons (BOP) facilities.

In this edition, as in our previous editions, we have continued to expand information to include new facilities and updates on most areas of prison life: Education; Library; Vocational/Apprenticeship; Housing; Visitation; Telephones; Fitness/Recreation; Religious Services; Commissary; Mail; and added new Sections on Entering Prison; Counseling/Rehabilitation/Psychology Programs; Staff, Furloughs, Attorneys, Inmate Discipline; Administrative Remedies; Inmate Financial Responsibility Program and Female Offenders. We have also updated information on the Bureau of Prisons' Comprehensive Residential Drug Abuse Program (RDAP) (Chapter Three) and expanded our chapters on "How to Do Time" (Chapter Four) and Practice Tips (Chapter Eleven) and added new information on mental health care. Securing a Favorable Prison Placement (Chapter Two) is completely updated. As in our last edition, this edition also includes a section on lodging and accommodations to give visitors a head start in locating affordable accommodations near each of the 117 federal prison facilities. Each of these sections is briefly introduced below.

### §1:10.1   Entering Prison

Every inmate designated to a BOP institution is required to participate in the Admission and Orientation (A&O) program. See Program Statement 5290.14, Admission and Orientation Program. Staff presentations provide each inmate with written materials describing institution operations, program availability, inmate rights and responsibilities, and the BOP inmate discipline process. After arriving at the designated institution, each inmate receives an introduction to all aspects of the institution and meets with staff from the case management, medical, and mental health units. Later, an inmate is assigned to the Admissions and Orientation Program where he or she receives a formal orientation to programs, services, policies, and procedures of that facility. The program provides an introduction to all aspects of the institution.

The Institution issues clothing, hygiene items, and bedding; and provides laundry services. Inmates may purchase other personal care items, shoes, some recreational clothing, and some food items through the commissary. Civilian clothing (i.e., clothing not issued to the inmate by the Bureau or purchased by the inmate from the commissary) ordinarily is not authorized for retention by the inmate.

Inmates may only possess those items they are authorized to retain upon admission to the institution, items issued by authorized staff, items purchased by the inmate from the commissary, or items purchased or received through approved channels (to include that approved for receipt by an authorized staff member or authorized by institution guidelines). All other items are considered contraband and will be seized and disposed of (destroyed, mailed out of the institution at the inmate's expense, etc.) in accordance with Bureau regulations.

## §1:10.2    Education

Inmates without a GED or high school diploma are required to be enrolled in the Bureau's Literacy Program, in preparation for a GED. Inmates who fail to complete the Literacy Program prior to obtaining a GED are restricted to the lowest pay and are unable to earn the maximum amount of Good Conduct Time. This requirement is not only important for finding work in the outside world, but is also important inside the prison. In order to be considered eligible for enrollment in correspondence courses, college-sponsored programs, vocational training, and apprenticeship programs, inmates must have either acquired a High School Diploma or be enrolled in a Literacy Program. Inmates who are not English proficient to an eighth grade level are required to participate in English as a Second Language (ESL) classes.

Some of the newer prison facilities may not offer college sponsored educational programs, vocational training, or apprenticeship programs. This is usually because the institution's education department hasn't been in existence long enough to implement college-sponsored educational programs or to develop its own vocational and apprenticeship programs. This does not necessarily mean the education department of the institution is poorly run. It takes some time to get programs up and running—in some cases, several years. However, there are many other institutions that have been in existence for quite some time and have well-established programs.

The Guidebook is especially useful in the area of education, vocational, and apprenticeship training because it helps identify the many different programs that exist throughout the BOP and the eligibility requirements that must be met prior to enrollment.

Due to staffing and budgetary constraints in the BOP, educational and vocational programs have been and will continue to be subjected to change. For the time being, we are including the most up to date information as provided to us by the Bureau of Prisons.

## §1:10.3    Vocational/Apprenticeship

Instruction for the vocational training programs is given by either the BOP or local community colleges or technical colleges sponsoring the program. A GED or high school diploma, or concurrent enrollment in the Bureau's Literacy Program, is required for Occupational Training Programs. There is a wide variety of vocational and apprenticeship program offerings throughout the BOP, which can differ between prisons based on the type of prison facility, *i.e.*, security level. Almost all of the vocational programs are paid for by the Bureau of Prisons in some way, either the cost of tuition and/or textbooks and by UNICOR earnings. Vocational/Occupational training information can be found by going to the Bureau web site: www.bop.gov/inmates/custody_and_care/docs/inmate_occupational_training_directory.pdf.

## §1:10.4    Library

Every prison contains a law library. Since the last edition of this Guidebook was published, Bureau of Prisons law libraries for inmates have become electronic libraries, and the old hardbound law books and binders with Bureau of Prisons Program Statements are now on computers. Because of the advance in technology, there are also computers for word processing, which are usually in the inmate housing units, from which printouts can be made at a charge of 15 cents per page, and some law libraries may still have typewriters.

The Guidebook is designed to give readers information about the hours of operation of the prison's law library, the availability of computers and copy machines, whether inmates are responsible for purchasing legal materials (paper, typewriter ribbon, pinwheels, etc.) from the prison's commissary, and the cost of using the prison's copy machine. In addition, the Guidebook is useful in identifying the various resources the leisure library has to offer. In particular, it describes whether the leisure library participates in an inter-library loan program with local public libraries, if it offers a video library, videocassette recorders and/or audio cassette players, or belongs to any book clubs, such as McNaughton Books. Generally, inmates are permitted to receive books directly from the publisher.

## §1:10.5    UNICOR

FPI (trade name UNICOR) employs inmates in a variety of factory, manufacturing, and warehouse work. UNICOR products can only be sold to federal government agencies, and complete product information can be found at www.unicor.gov. Most of the prisons are in the business of manufacturing textiles, electronics, furniture, and metals. Some of the prisons even contain a graphics and services plant or a distribution warehouse. While inmates are paid for their work, pay is generally higher in UNICOR-related jobs, and based on an inmate's experience or seniority. Deportable aliens, however, are excluded from UNICOR employment.

The Federal Prison Industries Program is available at the following facilities:

| Mid-Atlantic Region | North Central Region |
|---|---|
| FCI Ashland, KY - Low | FCI Englewood, CO - Low |
| FCI Beckley, WV - Medium | FCC Florence, CO - Complex |
| USP Big Sandy, KY - High | FCI Greenville, IL - Medium |
| FCC Butner, NC - Complex | USP Leavenworth, KS - Medium |
| FCI Cumberland, MD - Medium | USP Marion, IL - Medium |
| FCI Gilmer, WV - Medium | FCI Milan, MI - Low |
| USP Lee, VA - High | FCI Pekin, IL - Medium |
| FMC Lexington, KY - Med. Ctr. | FCI Sandstone, MN - Low |
| FCI Manchester, KY - Medium | FCC Terre Haute, IN - Complex |
| FCI Memphis, TN - Medium | FCI Waseca, MN - Low |
| FCC Petersburg, VA - Complex | |

Northeast Region
FCC Allenwood, PA - Complex
FCI Danbury, CT - Low
FCI Elkton, OH - Low
FCI Fairton, NJ - Medium
FCI Fort Dix, NJ - Low
USP Lewisburg, PA - High
FCI Loretto, PA - Low
FCI Otisville, NY - Medium
FCI Ray Brook, NY - Medium
FCI Schuylkill, PA - Medium

Southeast Region
USP Atlanta, GA - Medium
FCC Coleman, FL - Complex
FCI Edgefield, SC - Medium
FCI Jesup, GA - Minimum
FCI Marianna, FL - Medium
FCI Miami, FL - Low
FPC Montgomery, AL - Minimum
FPC Pensacola, FL - Minimum
FCI Talladega, AL - Medium
FCI Tallahassee, FL - Low
FCC Yazoo City, MS - Complex

South Central Region
FCI Bastrop, TX - Medium
FCC Beaumont, TX - Complex
FPC Bryan, TX - Minimum
FCI El Reno, OK - Medium
FCC Forrest City, AR - Complex
FCI La Tuna, TX - Low
FCC Oakdale, LA - Complex
FCC Pollock, LA - Complex
FCI Seagoville, TX - Low
FCI Texarkana, TX - Low

Western Region
USP Atwater, CA - High
FCI Dublin, CA - Medium
FCC Lompoc, CA - Complex
FCI Phoenix, AZ - Medium
FCI Safford, AZ - Low
FCI Sheridan, OR - Medium
FCI Terminal Island, CA - Low
FCC Tucson, AZ - Complex
FCC Victorville, CA - Complex

Several different hourly pay rates are available:

| GRADE LEVEL | HOURLY RATE |
| --- | --- |
| Premium #1 | $1.35 |
| Grade #1 | $1.15 |
| Grade #2 | $0.92 |
| Grade #3 | $0.69 |
| Grade #4 | $0.46 |
| Grade #5 | $0.23 |

Inmates who receive above grade four for UNICOR pay must have a high school diploma or a GED certificate.

All federal inmates who are able must work and are paid a small wage, a portion of which some inmates use to make restitution to victims through the Inmate Financial Responsibility Program. Approximately 18 percent of medically able federal prison inmates are employed by UNICOR.

The Guidebook provides information about each prison's UNICOR factory, the type of industry involved, and the number of inmates employed.

### §1:10.6     Counseling/Rehabilitation/Psychology Services

Bureau of Prisons policy now requires all institutions to provide a non-residential drug abuse treatment program (NR DAP). Many institutions also offer Narcotics Anonymous and Alcoholics Anonymous groups, and individual counseling. However, there are 62 prison facilities in the BOP that offer the 500-hour Residential Drug Abuse Program (RDAP), which is designed to counsel inmates intensively regarding drug-abuse issues. The 500-hour drug and alcohol-abuse treatment program is nine-to-12 months long and is found at high-security, medium-security, low-security, and minimum-security prisons. High-security institutions (penitentiaries) also offer the Challenge Program, an intensive residential treatment program designed to facilitate successful living and coping skills through the elimination of drug use and the elimination or management of mental illness. The Challenge Program has two treatment tracks, one for drug abuse and one for mental health illness, and a core program that is common to both. Participants can be referred through staff assessment or self-referral that is followed by staff review, and are housed separately from the general inmate population. The Guidebook provides information about a prison's psychology staff, counseling, and mental health programs available to inmates. The 500-hour Residential Drug Abuse Program (RDAP) is discussed in Chapter 3.

### §1:10.6.1     Bureau Rehabilitation and Values Enhancement (BRAVE) Program

The advantages of successfully completing the BRAVE Program can include a monetary award of $40 for each treatment phase completed, and local institutional awards and privileges.

The BRAVE Program is a cognitive-behavioral, residential treatment program for young male offenders serving their first federal sentence. Programming is delivered within a modified therapeutic community environment; inmates participate in interactive groups and attend community meetings. The BRAVE Program is designed to facilitate favorable institutional adjustment and reduce incidents of misconduct. In addition, the program encourages inmates to interact positively with staff members and take advantage of opportunities to engage in self-improvement activities throughout their incarceration.

The BRAVE Program is a six-month program. Inmates participate in treatment groups for four hours per day, Monday through Friday. As the BRAVE Program is designed to facilitate a favorable *initial* adjustment to incarceration, inmates are assigned to the program at the beginning of their sentence.

Program admission criteria are as follows: medium security male offender, 32 years of age or younger, a sentence of 60 months or more, and new to the federal system.

Program content focuses on developing interpersonal skills; behaving pro-socially in a prison environment; challenging antisocial attitudes and criminality; developing problem solving skills; and planning for release.

Research found BRAVE Program participants had a misconduct rate that was lower than the comparison group, and BRAVE Program graduates had a misconduct rate that was also lower. The BRAVE Program utilizes cognitive behavioral treatment within a modified therapeutic community; these interventions have been found to be effective with an incarcerated population in the reduction of recidivism.

The BRAVE Program is available at the following facilities:

Mid-Atlantic Region                     Western Region
FCI Beckley, WV - Medium                FCI Victorville, CA - Medium

## §1:10.6.2    Challenge Program

The Challenge Program is a cognitive-behavioral, residential treatment program developed for male inmates in penitentiary settings. The Challenge Program provides treatment to high security inmates with substance abuse problems and/or mental illnesses. Programming is delivered within a modified therapeutic community environment; inmates participate in interactive groups and attend community meetings. In addition to treating substance use disorders and mental illnesses, the program addresses criminality via cognitive-behavioral challenges to criminal thinking errors. The Challenge Program is available in most high security institutions.

Inmates may participate in the program at any point during their sentence; however, they must have at least 18 months remaining on their sentence. The duration of the program varies based on inmate need, with a minimum duration of nine months.

A high security inmate must meet one of the following criteria to be eligible to participate in Challenge Program: a history of substance abuse/dependence or a major mental illness as evidenced by a current diagnosis of a psychotic disorder, mood disorder, anxiety disorder, or personality disorder.

The Challenge Program focuses on the reduction of antisocial peer associations; promotion of positive relationships; increased self -control and problem solving skills; and development of pro-social behaviors. The program places a special emphasis on violence prevention. In addition, there are separate supplemental protocols for inmates with substance use disorders and inmates with serious mental illnesses.

The Challenge Program is available at the following facilities:

Mid-Atlantic Region                     South-Central Region
USP Big Sandy, KY - High                USP Beaumont, TX - High
USP Hazelton, WV - High                 USP Coleman I, FL - High
USP Lee, VA - High                      USP Coleman II, FL - High
USP McCreary, KY - High                 USP Pollock, LA - High

North Central Region                    Western Region
USP Terre Haute, IN - High              USP Atwater, CA - High
                                        USP Tucson, AZ - High

North East Region
USP Allenwood, PA - High
USP Canaan, PA - High

The advantages of successfully completing the Challenge Program include a monetary award of $40 per each treatment phase completed, and local institutional awards and privileges.

### §1:10.6.3    Drug Abuse Education

Drug Abuse Education is designed to encourage offenders with a history of drug use to review the consequences of their choice to use drugs and the physical, social, and psychological impacts of this choice. Drug Abuse Education is designed to motivate appropriate offenders to participate in nonresidential or residential drug abuse treatment, as needed; Drug Abuse Education is not drug treatment. Drug Abuse Education is available in all Bureau institutions.

Drug Abuse Education is a 12-15 hour educational course. Class lengths and times are varied to meet the scheduling needs of each institution. Since the goal of Drug Abuse Education is to motivate offenders to participate in treatment, inmates are given the opportunity to participate in the course at the beginning of their sentence, ordinarily within the first 12 months.

Inmates are required to participate in Drug Abuse Education if any of the following criteria are met: their substance use contributed to the instant offense; their substance use resulted in a supervised release violation; a significant substance use history is noted; or a judicial recommendation for substance abuse treatment is noted. Additionally, any inmate may volunteer to take the course.

Participants in Drug Abuse Education receive information on what distinguishes drug use, abuse, and addiction. Participants in the course also review their individual drug use histories, explore evidence of the nexus between drug use and crime, and identify negative consequences of continued drug abuse.

All Bureau facilities offer the Drug Abuse Education Program.

### §1:10.6.4    Nonresidential Drug Abuse Program

The advantages of successfully completing the Nonresidential Drug Abuse Education Program include a monetary award of up to $30 and consideration for the maximum period of halfway house (RRC) placement.

The Nonresidential Drug Abuse Program is a flexible, moderate intensity cognitive-behavioral treatment program. The program is designed to meet the needs of a variety of inmates including: inmates with relatively minor or low-level substance abuse impairment; inmates with a drug use disorder who do not have sufficient time remaining on their sentence to complete the intensive

Residential Drug Abuse Program (RDAP); and inmates with longer sentences who are in need of treatment and are awaiting future placement in the RDAP. The Nonresidential Drug Abuse Program is available in all Bureau institutions.

The Nonresidential Drug Abuse Program is comprised of 90-120 minute weekly group treatment sessions, for a minimum of 12 weeks and a maximum of 24 weeks. Treatment staff may offer treatment beyond the 12 week minimum based upon the treatment needs of the inmate and supplemental treatment services available at the facility.

An inmate must have a history of drug abuse as evidenced by self-report, Presentence Investigation Report (PSR) documentation, or incident reports for use of alcohol or drugs to be eligible to participate in the program.

The Bureau's treatment of substance abuse includes a variety of clinical activities organized to treat complex psychological and behavioral problems. The activities are unified through the use of Cognitive Behavioral Therapy (CBT), which was selected as the theoretical model because of its proven effectiveness with the inmate population.

The Nonresidential Drug Abuse Program utilizes cognitive-behavioral interventions, which have been proven to be effective in the treatment of substance use disorders. The group treatment format used in this program also offers empirically supported benefits from pro-social peer interaction among participants.

All Bureau facilities offer the Nonresidential Drug Abuse Program.

More information about the program can be found at Bureau of Prisons Program Statement 5330.11, Ch. 2, §2.4.8b.

### §1:10.6.5      Residential Drug Abuse Program (RDAP)

See Chapter 3.

### §1:10.6.6      Steps Toward Emotional Growth and Awareness (STAGES) Program

The STAGES Program is a residential treatment program for male inmates with serious mental illnesses and a primary diagnosis of Borderline Personality Disorder. The program uses an integrative model which includes a modified therapeutic community, cognitive behavioral therapies, and skills training. The program is designed to increase the time between disruptive behaviors, foster living within the general population or community setting, and increase pro-social skills.

The STAGES Program is conducted over 12-18 months. Inmates may participate in the program at any time during their sentence. Formal programming is facilitated half-days, five days a week with the remaining half-day dedicated to an institution work assignment or other programming.

Inmates referred to the STAGES Program have a primary diagnosis of Borderline Personality Disorder and a history of unfavorable institutional adjustment linked to this disorder. Examples of unfavorable institutional adjustment include multiple incident reports, suicide watches, and/or extended placement in restrictive housing. Inmates designated to the STAGES Program must volunteer for treatment and be willing to actively engage in the treatment process. Willingness to engage in the treatment is assessed through a brief course of pre-treatment in which the inmate learns basic skills at the referring institution.

The program curriculum is derived from Dialectical Behavior Therapy (DBT) and takes place in a modified therapeutic community. There is also an emphasis on basic cognitive-behavioral skills consistent with other Bureau treatment programs; for example, criminal thinking is addressed through the identification of criminal thinking errors and engagement in pro-social interactions with staff and peers. Program content is designed to prepare inmates for transition to less secure prison settings and promote successful reentry into society at the conclusion of their term of incarceration. Program staff collaborate with community partners to facilitate reentry.

The Stages Program is available at the following facilities:

North Central Region
STAGES Program
FCI Terre Haute, IN - Medium

Secure STAGES Program
USP Florence, CO - High

South Central Region
FPC Bryan, TX - Minimum
FMC Carswell, TX - Med. Ctr.

South East Region
FCI Aliceville, AL - Low
FPC Coleman, FL - Minimum
FPC Marianna, FL - Minimum
FCI Tallahassee, FL - Low

Western Region
FCI Dublin, CA - Low
FPC Victorville, CA - Minimum

More information about the program can be found at Bureau of Prisons Program Statement 5330.11.

### §1:10.6.7    Skills Program

The Skills Program is a residential treatment program designed to improve the institutional adjustment of male inmates with intellectual disabilities and social deficiencies. The program uses an integrative model which includes a modified therapeutic community, cognitive-behavioral therapies, and skills training. The goal of the program is to increase the academic achievement and adaptive behavior of cognitively impaired inmates, thereby improving their institutional adjustment and likelihood for successful community reentry.

The Skills Program is conducted over 12-18 months. Participation in the program during the initial phase of an inmate's incarceration is recommended; however, inmates may participate in the program at a later time. Formal programming is facilitated half-days, five days a week with the remaining half-day dedicated to an institution work assignment or receiving tutorial assistance.

Male inmates with significant functional impairment due to intellectual disabilities, neurological deficits, and/or remarkable social skills deficits are considered for the program. Participants must be appropriate for housing in a low or medium security institution. Inmates must volunteer for the program, have no history of sexual predatory violence, and be no less than 24 months from release when beginning the program.

The Skills Program operates as modified therapeutic communities and utilizes cognitive-behavioral treatments, cognitive rehabilitation, and skills training. The program employs a multi-disciplinary treatment approach aimed at teaching participants basic educational and social skills. Criminal thinking is addressed through the identification of criminal thinking errors and engagement in pro-social interactions with staff and peers. Program content is designed to promote successful reentry into society at the conclusion of their term of incarceration. Program staff collaborate with community partners to facilitate reentry.

The Skills Program is available at the following facilities:

North East Region                          South East Region
FCI Danbury, CT - Low                       FCI Coleman, FL - Medium

More information about the program can be found at Bureau of Prisons Program Statement 5330.11.

### §1:10.6.8     Mental Health Step Down Program

The Mental Health Step Down Program is a residential treatment program offering an intermediate level of care for male and female inmates with serious mental illnesses. The program is specifically designed to serve inmates who do not require inpatient treatment, but lack the skills to function in a general population prison setting. The program uses an integrative model that includes an emphasis on a modified therapeutic community cognitivebehavioral therapies, and skills training. The goal of the Step Down Program is to provide evidence-based treatment to chronically mentally ill inmates in order to maximize their ability to function and minimize relapse and the need for inpatient hospitalization.

The Mental Health Step Down Program is conducted over 12-18 months. Inmates may participate in the program at any point in their sentence. Formal programming is facilitated half-days, five days a week with the remaining half-day dedicated to an institution work assignment or other programming, as participants are able.

Inmates with serious mental illnesses, who would benefit from intensive residential treatment, are considered for the program. Male inmates with a primary diagnosis of Borderline Personality Disorder are referred to the STAGES Program, as opposed to the Mental Health Step Down Unit Program. Program participants must volunteer for the program and must not be acutely mentally ill (i.e., they must not meet criteria for inpatient mental health treatment).

Mental Health Step Down Programs operate as modified therapeutic communities and utilize cognitive-behavioral treatments, cognitive rehabilitation, and skills training. Criminal thinking is addressed through the identification of criminal thinking errors and engagement in pro-social interactions with staff and peers. The programs work closely with Psychiatry Services to ensure participants receive appropriate medication and have the opportunity to build a positive relationship with the treating psychiatrist. Program content is designed to promote successful reentry into society at the conclusion of their term of incarceration, and program staff collaborate with community partners to facilitate reentry.

Mental Health Step Down Programs are available at the following facilities:

Mid-Atlantic Region             South East Region
MH Step Down Unit               Secure MH Step Down Unit
FCI Butner, NC - Medium         USP Atlanta, GA - High

More information about the program can be found at Bureau of Prisons Program Statement 5330.11.

### §1:10.6.9   Sex Offender Treatment Program – Resident

See Chapter 6.

### §1:10.6.10   Sex Offender Treatment Program – Nonresidential

See Chapter 6.

### §1:10.7   Housing

Housing varies from one prison to another. Generally speaking, the higher the prison's security level the more restrictive the confinement. High-security and medium-security inmates are housed in either one or two-man cells or, in the modern-design, medium-security facilities, they are housed in one or two-man rooms. Inmates who are confined at low-security prisons or camps (and in some cases, medium-security prisons) are usually housed in rooms and/or dorms containing two, four, or six-man cubicles. Inmates housed in Administrative-level facilities are housed in cells. All inmates are housed in buildings called "units" which can hold anywhere from 50 to several hundred inmates and, with the exception of units that house inmates in individual rooms, almost all inmates are double bunked. Inmates with "seniority" and "clear conduct" are given priority for single-man rooms or bottom bunks. All housing units also contain television rooms and laundry rooms.

The Directory provides additional information on inmate housing.

### §1:10.8   Smoking

All facilities are now smoke-free. No longer will tobacco products be sold in the commissary. If inmates are caught with tobacco products or items associated with smoking, contraband procedure will apply and be enforced.

### §1:10.9    Fitness/Recreation

All prisons offer some form of fitness and leisure activities. You will find that every prison offers organized sports: softball, flag football, soccer, volleyball, handball, racquetball, and basketball. Most prisons also offer bocce and horse-shoes. In addition, every prison contains a hobby craft center offering a variety of arts and crafts. The crafts differ from prison to prison.

There are two areas in which federal prisons significantly differ from one another: weight equipment and musical equipment. The passage of the Zimmer Amendment in 1996 had the effect of prohibiting the inclusion of weights and electric instruments (*i.e.*, guitars) in all of the new federal prisons added to the BOP since 1996. The Zimmer Amendment also provided for the eventual "phasing out" of weights and electrical musical instruments at the existing "older" federal prisons; that is, weights and electric instruments cannot be fixed or replaced once they break or are damaged. The bottom line is that inmates are not likely to find weights, electric instruments, and in some cases, pool tables at any of the new prisons. However, prisons do offer aerobic exercise equipment and acoustic instruments.

The Guidebook is helpful in identifying various fitness and recreation activities, as well as hobby crafts, that are offered throughout the BOP.

### §1:10.10    Religious Services

Bureau institutions offer religious services and programs for the approximately 30 faith groups represented within the inmate population. All prisons have at least one chaplain. A few have one or two full-time rabbis. Most of the institutions also offer contract rabbi and imam services, a sweat lodge for Native-American services, and volunteers in the community who provide religious services to most faiths.

Inmates are granted permission to wear or retain various religious items, and accommodations are made to facilitate observances of holy days. Bureau facilities offer religious diets designed to meet the dietary requirements of various faith groups, such as the Jewish and Islamic faiths. Religious programs are led or supervised by staff chaplains, contract spiritual leaders, and community volunteers. Chaplains oversee inmate worship services and self-improvement programs, such as those involving the study of sacred writings and religious workshops. Bureau chaplains also provide pastoral care, spiritual guidance, and counseling to inmates.

The Life Connections Program (LCP) is a residential faith-based program offered to inmates of all faith traditions, including for those who do not hold to a religious preference. This program is available to offenders at low, medium, and high security facilities. The goal of LCP is to provide opportunities for the development and maturation of the participants' commitment to normative values and responsibilities, resulting in overall changed behavior and better institutional adjustments. In addition, the participants receive life skills and practical tools and strategies to assist them in transitioning back to society once released from federal custody.

LCP is an 18 month program in which participants attend classes and meetings, Monday through Friday afternoons for approximately four hours per day, as well as evening mentoring sessions and seminars. In addition, the participants participate in their respective faith services and chapel programs during the evening and weekend hours.

Program admission criteria are as follows:
- Low and medium security male offenders within 24 to 36 months of their projected release date.
- High security male offenders with 30 months or more prior to their projected release date.
- Low security female offenders with 30 months or more prior to their projected release date.
- Must not have a written deportation order.
- Must not be on Financial Responsibility Program (FRP) Refuse status.
- Must have met English as a Second Language (ESL) and GED obligations.
- Must receive recommendation from relevant staff (Chaplain, Unit Team, and Associate Warden) and approval from the Warden.

The objectives of the program are to use secular outcome-based objectives that foster personal growth and responsibility, and to correct inmates' relationships with their victim(s) and the community. The program facilitates the practice of one's personal belief system, whether secular or religious, to bring reconciliation and restoration, and to take responsibility for their criminal behavior. In addition, community organizations and volunteers at the inmates' release destinations serve as mentors to assist and support the participants upon their release.

The Life Connections Program is available at the following facilities:

Mid-Atlantic Region
FCI Petersburg, VA - Low

South Central Region
FMC Carswell, TX - Med. Ctr. (Female)

North Central Region
USP Leavenworth, KS - Medium
FCI Milan, MI - Low
USP Terre Haute, IN - High

The Directory provides information about each institution's religious staff and services. Religious programming is led by agency chaplains, contracted spiritual leaders and trained community volunteers. Inmates may participate in religious observances; wear religious items; and have access to religious materials.

More information about Religious Policies and Practices in the Federal Bureau of Prisons is found at Program Statement 5360.09 1:20.

### §1:10.11   Commissary

All prisons contain a commissary. The BOP currently sets a monthly commissary spending limit of $360 which may be increased by $50 during the November-December holiday period. Each prison can set its monthly maximum commissary spending at or below that amount. The monthly maximum spending limit is usually applied to goods that are under $25 in value, which are otherwise known as "non-specialty" items. Specialty items typically include clothing items, shoes, stamps, telephone and photocopy credits. Almost all prison commissaries offer, more or less, the same selection of commissary items.

**Categories and Examples of Products Approved for Sale in the Commissary (from BOP Program Statement 4500.10, Trust Fund/Deposit Fund Manual):**

(1) **Edible Items.** Cookies, crackers, potato and corn chips, doughnuts, candy bars, bagged candy, peanuts, mixed nuts, dry cereal; items not requiring refrigeration before opening, such as tuna fish, sardines, salmon, potted meats, Vienna sausage, sandwich meats (Spam, Treet, etc.), dried beef sticks, chip dips, processed fruit; frozen items (such as pizza, ice cream, yogurt, sherbet, and ice cream novelties), provided that adequate freezer storage is available before sale, sold in such quantities to ensure they are eaten before the need for refrigeration; peanut butter, honey, dry soup mix, bouillon cubes, nutrition bars such as Balance that are not marketed as body-building or weight-enhancing and do not contain unauthorized supplements (bars must have less than 25 grams of protein and carbohydrates in one serving size); sugar-free snacks, such as diet carbonated drinks, instant drinks, and candy. Per BOP policy, institutions must ensure that healthier snacks are available, such as fruit juices, dried fruit, applesauce, fruit snack packs, cup-a-soup, tuna (in water), graham crackers, cheese crackers (low salt), peanut butter crackers (low salt), fig newtons, cracker snacks (low salt, low saturated fat), pretzels (no visible salt), instant oatmeal, rice cakes, bagels, dry roasted nuts (unsalted), granola bars (no coconut), low-fat or fat-free frozen yogurt (plain, lemon, coffee, and vanilla), pudding cups (low-fat or fat-free), and other low-calorie, reduced-calorie or fat-free, low-cholesterol or cholesterol-free, and low-saturated-fat or fat-free snacks.

(2) **Kosher/Halal Shelf-Stable Entrees.** Per BOP policy, the Commissary must make available for purchase, or sell through special purchase, a minimum of four Kosher/Halal-certified entrees. Individual entrees are in sealed bowls suitable for microwaving and contain the Kosher and Halal certification on the label. Inmates are limited to purchasing 14 shelf-stable entrees per Commissary visit, and may not have more than 21 shelf-stable entrees in their possession. However, Wardens may limit the number of entrees stored in inmates' cells to less than 21 for inmates at the ADX Florence, Colorado, or in any special housing unit or hospital, if a limitation is necessary for security and sanitation.

(3) **Beverages and Related Items.** Instant drinks such as coffee, tea, Tang, Kool-Aid, hot chocolate, powdered milk; condiments such as non-dairy creamer and sugar; carbonated drinks such as Coca-Cola, Pepsi-Cola, Royal Crown Cola, and Seven-Up; juices such as apple, orange, grape, pineapple, and grapefruit.

(4) **Postage Stamps.** The Commissary may sell a maximum of five different denominations of stamps. The Commissary may stock pre-stamped international postage envelopes. The Commissary must have sufficient stamp denominations to allow mailing of domestic letters, letters in excess of one ounce but not requiring an additional first-class stamp, foreign mail, packages, registered or certified letters or packages, and any other charges attributable to mail privileges. Ordinarily, the Commissary sells no more than 20 postage stamps (for first-class, domestic, one-ounce mailing), or the equivalent per Commissary visit. An exception may be made where visits are limited to one per week or less, in which case the Unit Manager may authorize additional purchases based on a demonstrated need.

(5) **Radios.** Only clear digital radios (AM/FM) are permitted for sale after current stock is depleted. Radios are battery-operated, receive only AM/FM frequencies, and are equivalent to a Sony Walkman AM/FM (Digital)—that is, a "Walkman"-type radio/receiver that can only be listened to using earphones, has been approved by the Warden, and has performance and characteristics that comply with Federal Communication Commission (FCC) requirements in 47 CFR, part 15, subpart C.

(6) **Watches.** Watches ($100 maximum selling price, no stones, electronically unsophisticated [*i.e.*, cannot send or receive signals]) and watch batteries.

(7) **MP3 Player.** MP3 players may only be ordered from the vendor identified by the Central Office, Trust Fund Branch, to ensure the special security features and interface with TRULINCS function correctly. The players will have many of the normal features deactivated (Micro SDHC slot, microphone, etc.) for security purposes. The players will be programmed with security controls that will link each player to a specific inmate. Once the player is activated it will display that inmate's name and register number.

(8) **Electrical Appliances.** Fans may be sold on a local-option basis where weather conditions dictate and the electrical system can handle them.

(9) **Miscellaneous.** Writing supplies, alarm clocks, word spellers, plastic bowls and cups, hangers, wallets, small purses, athletic and cosmetic bags, tokens for laundry or copy services, and TRUFACS-generated photo vouchers.
  • Playing cards, fingerless athletic gloves, handball gloves, harmonicas, racquet and tennis balls, weightlifting belts/gloves/wraps, and softball gloves.
  • Master Lock Padlock #1525 or equivalent that is keyed V-85 is the only combination padlock permitted.

(10) **Clothing.** The following items may be sold in accordance with restrictions identified in the Program Statement on Inmate Personal Property and that are appropriate for the institution: Athletic supporters, bathrobes (no hoods), baseball caps (no logos), gym shorts, handkerchiefs,

headbands/sweatbands, knee wraps, socks, stockings/pantyhose for female inmates, sweatpants, sweatshirts, T-shirts/sleeveless undershirts, underwear, authorized religious headgear.

(11) **Shoes.** The following may be stocked or sold through the SPO process: Athletic, specialty shoes (*i.e.*, a court, turf, basketball, or running shoe, $100 maximum selling price; casual [such as hushpuppies]; shower shoes; slippers; work shoes [ASTM Standard F2412-05 and F2413-05]).

(12) **Toiletries.** Common items such as soaps, deodorants, hair grooming supplies, shaving supplies, general cosmetics, and other grooming aids.

(13) **Hygiene Items.** Non-prescription drugs and personal hygiene items that are sold over-the-counter in drug and grocery stores may be considered using these examples as guidelines:

- *Dental products.* Toothbrushes, denture brushes, dental bridge cleaners such as Dentu-Creme, toothpaste, unwaxed dental floss, floss threaders, denture adhesive (powder or paste).
- *Miscellaneous products.* Cough drops, mouthwash (non-alcoholic), contact lens solutions, disposable douche, suntan lotion, Magic Shave, wheat germ, artificial sweeteners, Band-Aids, earplugs, analgesic balm, arch supports, corn pads, insoles (Dr. Scholls), lip ointments (such as Chapstick), moisture lotion, medicated rubs (such as Mentholathum, Vicks VapoRub).
- *Personal hygiene products.* Deodorants (such as Right Guard), bar soaps (such as Zest, Ivory, Neutrogena, generic), disposable plastic razors (such as Bic), shaving cream, shaving brushes, combs and brushes, feminine hygiene products (such as Tampax), hair shampoos, hair conditioners, laundry soaps/detergents.

Each inmate is verified by fingerprint before being able to purchase Commissary items.

The inmate sets up a commissary account during the first week upon arriving at an institution. The TRULINCS program, which is discussed separately in this chapter, is for inmates' use; they can check their account balance and purchase telephone and e-mail credits. Inmates are not permitted to possess currency in any amount. It is recommended that inmates who are "self-surrendering" bring some form of money (cash or U.S. postal money orders) with them, so they can establish an account. An inmate's commissary account can otherwise be replenished from outside sources (such as family, friends, etc.), or with the money an inmate earns while employed by the prison. Inmates' families and friends wishing to send funds through the mail must send them to the following address:

Federal Bureau of Prisons
(insert valid committed inmate name)
(insert inmate eight digit register number)
P. O. Box 474701
Des Moines, IA 50947-0001

Acceptable methods for sending funds to inmates are Money Orders, Government checks (Federal, State, County, City), Foreign negotiable instruments payable in U.S. Dollars only, Business checks, Cashier's checks, Certified checks, and Bank Drafts. The deposit must be in the form of a money order made out to the inmate's full <u>committed</u> name and eight digit registration number. The BOP will return funds that do not have this information to the sender. The sender's name and return address must appear on the upper left hand corner of the envelope which contains the money order. No other items may be included in the envelope to the inmate. In the event where funds have been mailed but reported to the sender as not received by the inmate, the sender must initiate a tracer with the U.S. Postal Service.

Inmates' families and friends may also send inmate funds through Western Union's Quick Collect Program. This may be sent as follows:

1. A Western Union agent location with cash; family or friends must complete a Quick Collect Program form; to find the nearest agent call Western Union or go to the website, www.westernunion.com.
2. Using telephone and a credit/debit card: the inmate's family or friends may call the Western Union toll free telephone number.
3. On line using a credit/debit card: go to www.westernunion.com and select "Quick Collect."

For each Western Union Quick Collect transaction, the following information must be provided:

Inmate's committed name
Valid inmate eight digit registration number
Code city: FBOP
State code: BC

**NOTE:** If the inmate's registration number and/or name are inaccurate, funds may not be returned to the sender.

The Guidebook is helpful in providing the reader with information about the commissary's days and hours of operation, the method by which shopping days are assigned, and the monthly spending limit for each institution.

### §1:10.12 Telephone Policy

One of the first things inmates should be aware about telephone usage is that they will not be permitted to use the phone to conduct any business dealings while they are incarcerated. After the inmate signs the TRULINCS agreement, he or she then creates a contact list that will facilitate, among other things, telephone calls. Telephone calls cannot be made until the inmate loads the contact names and telephone numbers into the TRULINCS computer system. While an inmate's contact list can include up to 100 contacts, only up to 30 at any one time can be approved for telephone calls.

Almost all prisons utilize the pre-payment method, known as TRUFONE. The following are standard features of TRUFONE: Inmates are responsible for transferring funds, only in whole dollar amounts, from their Commissary account to their TRUFONE account. Inmates are given written instructions for using the interactive voice response to access their balances. Inmates may also access the cost of the last completed telephone call and the minutes remaining for that month via the telephone. TRUFONE account statements are not regularly provided to inmates. Inmates requesting a statement are charged $3.00 for each 30-day period requested. There is a 3-minute minimum limit on an inmate call, and maximum time limits for each call may be set by the Warden at each institution, usually at 15 minutes. An inmate's calling list is limited to 30 callers and telephone calls are limited to 300 minutes per month. Telephone area codes 700, 800, 900, and 976 are prohibited. The features of this system are standard throughout the BOP. Inmate telephone calls are subject to monitoring. Inmates can arrange for unmonitored calls to their attorneys through their Correctional Counselor or Case Manager.

The Guidebook is useful in identifying whether an institution utilizes the pre-payment method and/or collect call method, and how long it takes inmates to add phone numbers to their caller-approved list.

### §1:10.13    Inmate Mail

An inmate must enter contact list information in the TRULINCS computer system in order to initiate written correspondence. Outgoing mail must be addressed using pre-printed labels, which are printed by the inmate directly from his or her contact list in the TRULINCS computer. Inmates are ordinarily limited to 10 labels per day. Up to 20 First Class stamps can be purchased per commissary visit, and postage stamps are excluded from the monthly spending limit of $360. All incoming mail from family, friends, and other prison inmates (when specifically authorized only) is opened and checked for contraband. Mail from an attorney and on attorney letterhead, bearing the attorney's name and marked "special mail—open in the presence of the inmate," will be opened in the inmate's presence for contraband. Such mail, however, is not copied or read by BOP staff.

All of the prisons accept mail via the United States Postal Service. This includes U.S. Priority mail and Express mail. There are also some institutions that will accept mail sent either via Federal Express, UPS Overnight mail, or another commercial service. It is recommended that the institution be contacted to find out whether the receipt of such mail is permitted. It is also important to note that mail sent overnight does not necessarily mean the inmate will receive it the very next day. In some cases, it may take longer for inmates to receive overnight mail than regular mail via the U.S. Postal Service. It's also recommended that the "mail room" of the prison be contacted to determine the most expedient way to send mail to an inmate. Non-legal mail may only contain enclosures which are in adherence to Program Statement 5265.14, Correspondence. For example photographs must be non-polarized and in adherence to the constraints set forth in the aforementioned Program Statement. In addition other enclosures *i.e.* news articles (not entire publications) may accompany correspondence. More specific detail of these enclosures is determined by the individual facility and its own Program Statement.

TRULINCS has been implemented throughout the Federal Bureau of Prisons to provide inmates with some limited capabilities to send and receive electronic correspondence, without access to the Internet and at no taxpayer cost. Electronic communications have become a standard form of correspondence within most American homes and businesses and can now also serve as a way to keep inmates connected to their families. Strengthening or re-establishing these family ties assists the inmates with their successful reentry into the community and can reduce the possibility that they recidivate. Inmates can only communicate via e-mail with those individuals who agree to such communications, and certain exclusions apply, which are covered in the TRULINCS section of this chapter.

### §1:10.14   TRULINCS Electronic Messaging

The Trust Fund Limited Inmate Computer System (TRULINCS) is a program developed to provide inmates with limited computer access, to include the capability to send and receive electronic messages (e-mail). This program does not allow inmates access to the Internet. Some of the objectives of the TRULINCS program are to provide inmates with an alternative means of written communication and to provide the BOP with a more efficient, cost-effective and secure method of managing and monitoring inmate communication. TRULINCS has been activated in most BOP facilities as of June of 2011. E-mail has become a standard form of communication within most American homes and businesses, and it can now be used to help inmates stay connected with families and friends, which is considered to be essential to rehabilitation and reentry into society.

TRULINCS is available to pre-trial, hold-over detainees, and designated inmates in facilities where the program has been activated. There are individual inmates who may be excluded from the program due to their history of behavior. For example, inmates with a personal history of, or prior offense conduct or conviction for, soliciting minors for sexual activity, or possession/distribution of child pornography through the Internet or other means, are excluded from the program. Likewise, an inmate with a personal history or special skills or knowledge of using computers/e-mail/Internet or other communication methods as a conduit for committing illegal activities will be excluded. As part of the classification process, inmates are reviewed individually for participation in TRULINCS messaging. If there are grounds for exclusion, they will be notified in writing of the findings and advised of their right to appeal the decision.

Upon arrival at a facility with TRULINCS, the inmate will be provided with an Inmate Agreement for Participation in TRULINCS Electronic Messaging Program Form (BP-0934). This form documents the inmate's notice, acknowledgment and voluntary consent to the rules and regulations of the program, which include monitoring of incoming and outgoing correspondence, including transactional data, message contents, and other activities. This includes rejecting individual messages sent to or from inmates that jeopardize the safety, security, or orderly running of the institution or the protection of the public and staff. The inmate will also receive a Personal Identification Number (PIN) and a Personal Access Code (PAC). Both are needed to access TRULINCS and an inmate's telephone contact list. These numbers should be carefully guarded to avoid unauthorized use by others.

All inmates begin the TRULINCS process by creating a contact list. The contact list is very important; it includes telephone numbers, e-mail addresses, account access, and written correspondence. Newly arriving inmates should bring with them information such as name, complete mailing address, telephone number, and e-mail address for desired community contacts. It is preferred that the information be brought with them on a single sheet of paper, as an address book or other bound item may be confiscated upon arrival. Telephone calls and written correspondence cannot be initiated until the contact list has been loaded into the computer system by the inmate. Inmates may have up to 100 contacts on their contact list; however, they are limited to 30 telephone contacts at one time. With TRULINCS, an inmate can manage his or her list instantly, adding and removing individuals from the phone, e-mail, and label contacts as they desire.

Inmates may only exchange electronic messages with persons in the community who have accepted the inmate's request to communicate. The recipient will receive a message indicating a federal inmate seeks to add the person to his or her authorized contact list. If the person in the community consents to receive e-mails, that person is added to the inmate's contact list. The person has the option of approving, declining, or blocking a contact. Inmates may not exchange messages with unauthorized contacts, including victims, witnesses, other persons connected with the inmate's criminal history, and law enforcement officers, contractors, or volunteers. Inmates may communicate with their attorneys, "special mail" recipients, or other legal representatives with the understanding that the messages exchanged are not treated as privileged and will be subject to monitoring.

Ordinarily, inmates are required to place a TRULINCS generated mailing label on all out-going postal mail. There are exceptions, but for the majority of inmates, a label is required in facilities using TRULINCS. These labels are generated from the inmate's individual contact list. The inmates print them as needed, and are limited to no more than 10 labels per day. Again, these labels are for out-going postal mail only and other use is prohibited.

Funding for TRULINCS is provided entirely by the Inmate Trust Fund, which is maintained by profits from inmate purchases of commissary products, telephone services, and the fees inmates pay for using TRULINCS. Inmates are charged by the minute for using TRULINCS electronic messaging and are limited to the number of minutes they may stay on TRULINCS at any one time. For example, an inmate may be limited to 30 minutes of access to TRULINCS, and charged $0.05 per minute. Once the time frame has been exceeded, there would ordinarily be a 30-minute window before access is allowed again. Inmates are also limited to 13,000 characters per e-mail. There are no fees associated with time spent entering a contact list, printing mailing labels, checking account balances, and checking for new incoming messages. Inmates may also print messages at an established per page rate, currently $0.15 per page.

In most facilities, TRULINCS terminals are located in the housing unit and available during open unit times, much the same as telephone hours. This easy access allows inmates the opportunity to manage their contact lists with minimal delay. Print terminals are often placed in a centralized location, such as the library, and only accessed during business hours.

TRULINCS messaging is for the exchange of simple electronic mail only. No attachments, graphics, photos, etc., are allowed. Incoming messages will be blocked and the sender will be notified of the violation. Likewise, unauthorized use of TRULINCS can result in disciplinary action. It is very important that inmates remember these documents are reviewed. Three-way or forwarded messages are not authorized, as well as conducting a business. The use of TRULINCS messaging is a privilege, and as such can be restricted. Sanctions for a violation can include exclusion from the TRULINCS messaging program for a period of time. Inmates are then limited to written correspondence when not authorized for messaging.

Certain sex offenders are denied access to Trulinks. See Chapter 6.

### §1:10.15 Visiting

Shortly after arriving at their designated prison facility, inmates will have to complete and submit an approved-visitor list to their counselors. Only approved visitors will be permitted to visit the inmate. Absent strong concerns by the Warden that would preclude visiting, immediate family members (*i.e.*, mother, father, spouse, children, brothers and sisters) are automatically placed on the approved-visitor list, if their relationship to the inmate is verified in the presentence report (hereinafter "PSR"). Individuals who are not considered immediate family may be approved for visitation after they have submitted the appropriate forms and have been "cleared" by prison staff.

While BOP-wide visiting regulations do exist, each prison facility has local visiting guidelines. Attorneys should always contact the case manager or counselor to make arrangements for legal visits that are not going to be conducted during regular social visiting hours. Unlike pre-trial detention facilities, attorneys cannot simply show up and expect to get in without an appointment.

While the Guidebook is useful in identifying each prison's visiting policy, for current and up to date visiting hours, please check the Bureau's website at www.bop.gov.

Visitors may be subjected to the Bureau's ION Spectrometry screening. The ION Spectrometry device is a minimally invasive method for screening visitors and their possessions for the presence of illegal drugs. A visitor who is requested by prison staff to undergo such screening can refuse, but then he or she will not be able to visit.

Conjugal visitation is not permitted within any BOP facility.

## §1:10.16    Lodging and Accommodations

As a courtesy to our readers, we have continued to include a section to the Guidebook that lists the names and phone numbers of lodging and accommodations near each of the 117 federal prison facilities. The names and addresses were taken from available lists on the Internet. Their inclusion in the Guidebook does not represent an endorsement, but is merely provided to give our readers a head start in locating affordable accommodations that are situated near the prison facility.

For information on the location of a federal prison facility and driving directions to and from the prison to your destination site, log on at www.bop.gov and http://www.mapquest.com to obtain detailed maps of the state, region and city and directions, respectively.

## §1:10.17    Staff

Inmates will often have direct daily contact with Unit staff who will make most of the decisions about their daily lives. These staff (the Unit Manager, Case Manager, and Correctional Counselor) have offices in inmate living units, thereby facilitating inmate access to staff and vice versa. Unit staff are directly responsible for involving inmates housed in their units in programs that are designed to meet their needs. Unit staff receive input from other institution employees (such as work supervisors, teachers, and psychologists) who work with the inmate, and meet with the inmate on a regular basis to develop, review, and discuss their work assignment, appropriate program opportunities, and progress, as well as any other needs or concerns. These regularly-scheduled meetings do not preclude inmates from approaching a member of the unit team or any other appropriate staff member at any time to discuss their particular issues.

Overview authority for Case Management as well as special classification issues such as Central Inmate Monitoring (CIM – Separation, Special Supervision, Broad Publicity, etc..) rests with the institution Case Management Coordinator. If an inmate wishes to informally resolve a classification or program matter, they should first attempt to do so through their Case Manager, and if that is unsuccessful then through the Unit Manager, and if that is also unsuccessful, then contact with the Case Management Coordinator may be appropriate. Inmates are encouraged to first research the issue which they may wish to contest by reading the applicable B.O.P. Program Statement (policy) available in the inmate law library. Bothe the Unit team staff and the Case Manager are under the authority of the Associate Warden of Programs, commonly referred to as the AW(P). The AW(P) is usually present in the inmate dining room during lunch period and is available for inmates to speak with. Again, unless a Unit or Case Management matter is extremely sensitive, inmates should first try to resolve any problems with staff prior to seeing or writing to the AW(P). The Warden is the highest institution authority at stand-alone B.O.P. prisons; at B.O.P. prison complexes, each secure component (High, Medium and Low Security) has a Warden, with a Complex Warden over them. Wardens are also usually available in the inmate dining rooms during lunchtime. At Minimum security satellite camps, the Camp Administrator is directly under the AW(P) and is either in place of a Unit Manager or the Unit Manager. At independent, stand-alone Minimum security camps, the Camp Administrator or a Warden is the top authority. Correctional Officers are supervised by Lieutenants, and disciplinary reports regardless of what staff issues them are referred to Lieutenants for investigation. The Lieutenants are supervised by a Captain, and the Captain in turn is supervised by the Associate Warden of Operations, commonly referred to as the AW(O). The Captain and the AW(O) are usually present in the inmate dining room during lunch time and are thereby accessible to inmates. Like the AW(P), the AW(O) is under the authority of the Warden. Other key staff of whom inmates should be aware are (a) Superintendant or Associate Warden of UNICOR, (b) the Warden's Executive Assistant (who may be the same person as the Camp Administrator at some satellite camps), who is actively involved in public relations and the inmate Administrative Remedy Appeal process (BP-9 appeals to the Warden), and (c) the institution Legal Advisor. These staff, as others referenced in this section, are usually, though not always, available in the inmate dining room during lunchtime. All staff can be contacted by filling out a Form called Inmate Request to Staff Member, commonly referred to in the B.O.P. as a "Cop-Out" request. Additionally, staff can now be contacted electronically.

### §1:10.18 Furloughs

Under limited circumstances, inmates who meet strict requirements are allowed temporary releases from the institution through staff-escorted trips and furloughs. The Bureau permits approved inmates to go on staff-escorted trips into the community to visit a critically-ill member of their immediate family; attend the funeral of an immediate family member; receive medical treatment; or participate in other activities, such as a religious or work-related functions.

A furlough is a temporary authorization for an appropriate inmate to be in the community without a staff escort. Inmates near the end of their sentences who require minimal security may be granted permission to go on trips into the community without escort to be present during a crisis in the immediate family, to participate in certain activities that will facilitate release transition, and to re-establish family and community ties. Furloughs are not very common, and inmates are carefully screened for risk to the community before they are released on a furlough. P.S. 5280.09.

### §1:10.19 Attorneys

Inmates are permitted to contact and retain attorneys. See Retention of Attorneys, 28 C.F.R. pt. 543, subpt. B, and Program Statement 1315.07, Legal Activities, Inmate; Program Statement 7331.04, Pretrial Inmates; and 28 C.F.R. pt. 551, subpt. J, Pretrial Inmates, Access to Legal Resources. Attorney visiting takes place during regular institution visiting hours. Attorney visits for pretrial inmates may be conducted at times other than established visiting hours with the approval of the Warden or designee. Attorneys and, in some cases, their representatives, may generally visit inmate clients in private conference rooms if available, or in other accommodations designed to ensure a reasonable degree of privacy. Attorney representatives, such as interpreters, paralegals, and private investigators, must contact the institution's legal department in advance in order to complete the necessary documentation to be permitted to visit an inmate on behalf of an attorney. Legal visits are visually monitored, as necessary, but are not subject to auditory monitoring. See 28 C.F.R. pt. 543, subpt. B, Visits by Attorneys.

All outgoing special mail from an inmate must be delivered directly to a staff member for further processing. Staff then confirm that the inmate delivering the special mail to be sent out is the same inmate reflected in the return address. Inmates may seal outgoing special mail, before submitting directly to staff for further processing.

Special mail from attorneys must be marked "Special Mail-Open only in the presence of the inmate". In addition, the sender must identify himself or herself on the envelope as a person entitled to invoke the protections of special mail. The sender's return address must reference an individual identified as an attorney, not a firm, e.g., "John Doe, Attorney"; not "Law Offices of Smith & Smith." Incoming special mail is opened in the presence of the inmate and is visually inspected for contraband. Staff may inspect incoming special mail to determine that it qualifies as such, but may not otherwise review its content.

For further information see Legal Resource Guide to the Federal Bureau of Prisons 2014, http://www.bop.gov/resources/pdfs/legal_guide.pdf.

Inmates may place unmonitored telephone calls to their attorneys. See 28 C.F.R. §540.102 and Program Statement 5264.08, Inmate Telephone Regulations. To do so, inmates must specifically request staff assistance to first approve the call, and then place the call on an unmonitored staff telephone. A pretrial inmate may telephone his or her attorney as often as resources of the institution allow. See 28 C.F.R. pt. 551, subpt. J, Access to Legal Resources and Program Statement 7331.04, Pretrial Inmates. To receive permission to place an unmonitored attorney call, an inmate is ordinarily required to establish that his or her communication with attorneys by other means is not adequate. The 300-minute per calendar month limitation does not apply to unmonitored legal telephone calls.

Attorneys may also initiate unmonitored telephone calls with their inmate clients. To do so, the attorney should contact the inmate's Correctional Counselor. Please note that all too often unmonitored calls take place in the Correctional Counselor's office and the staff member is often present. To make sure that the call is, indeed, unmonitored, the attorney should request the counselor to step out of the room during the duration of the call.

## §1:10.20   Inmate Discipline

Pursuant to 18 U.S.C. §4042(a)(3), the BOP administers an inmate disciplinary process to promote a safe and orderly environment for inmates and staff. After arriving at a BOP facility, all inmates receive written notice of their rights and responsibilities, prohibited acts within the institution, the possible range of sanctions for each offense, and the disciplinary procedure.

Violation of a prohibited act carries sanctions corresponding to the severity of the offense. Sanctions may include time in disciplinary segregation, loss of good time credits, and loss of privileges. See 28 C.F.R. pt. 541, subpt. A, and Program Statement 5270.09 Inmate Discipline Program.

Consistent with the minimum procedural protections required by Wolff v. McDonnell, 418 U.S. 539 (1974), the BOP disciplinary process requires that staff provide the inmate with a written cop of the charges, and that the inmate is entitled to be present during the initial hearing. An inmate is not permitted a staff representative nor to call witnesses at a Unit Discipline Committee (UDC) hearing, but the inmate may request a staff representative and may have witnesses appear at the proceeding. An attorney may not represent the inmate at either hearing. Inmates may appeal the decision of the UDS or the DHO through the Administrative Remedy program. See 28 C.F.R. pt. 542, subpt. B, and Program Statement 1330.17, Administrative Remedy Program.

### §1:10.21  Administrative Remedies

The Administrative Remedy Program provides every inmate with the opportunity to seek formal review of a grievance concerning virtually any aspect of his or her confinement, should informal procedures not achieve resolution. See 28 C.F.R. 542, subpt. B, and Program Statement 1330.17, Administrative Remedy Program. The Administrative Remedy Program is also used to appeal Inmate Discipline Sanctions. This program applies to all inmates confined in institutions operated by the BOP, inmates designated to contract RRCs, and to former inmates for issues which arose during confinement. Inmates are obligated to attempt informal resolution of grievances prior to filing a formal request for administrative reemdy. Once a formal request is filed at the institution level ("BP-9"), the Warden of that facility has 20 days to investigate and provide the inmate a written response. If the inmate is dissatisfied with the Warden's response, he or she has 30 days to file a Regional Administrative Remedy Appeal ("BP-10"). Once received in the Regional Office, the Regional Director has 30 days to investigate and provide the inmate a written response. If the inmate is dissatisfied with the Regional Director's response, he or she has 30 days to file a Central Office Administrative Reemdy Appeal ("BP-11"). Once received in the Central Office, the Administrator, National Inmate Appeals, has 40 days to investigate and provide the inmate a written response. After receiving the Administrator's response, the inmate has exhausted the BOP's Administrative Remedy Program.

### §1:10.22  Sentence Computation

For inmates whose offense was committed on or after November 1, 1987, U.S.C. §3624(b) allows 54 days of credit "at the end of each year of the prisoner's term of imprisonment" so long as the sentence is in excess of one year. Thus, defendants sentenced to a "one year" term of imprisonment will actually serve one year without the benefit of any GCT credit. Defendants sentenced to "a year and a day" term of imprisonment, however, can receive credit for satisfactory behavior and thus can actually serve less than one year. This generally computes to **13%** of an inmate's sentence. Sentence credit is awarded for any time spent in official detention prior to the date a term of imprisonment commences provided it was served as a result of the offense for which the sentence was imposed, or as a result of any offense for which the defendant was arrested after committing the offense for which the federal sentence was imposed. Additionally, the time must not have been credited against any other sentence.

After a defendant is sentenced, the Designation and Sentence Computation Center (DSCC) is responsible for determining what periods (or prior custody) may be credited toward the federal term of imprisonment. Defendants on pretrial release no matter how restrictive, such as home confinement, cannot be awarded as prior custody credit.

An excellent article discussing the interaction between federal and state sentences by former Bureau of Prisons' Northeast Regional Counsel Hank Sadowski is contained in the Bureau's Legal Resources Guide, www.bop.gov; Sadowski, "Federal Sentence Computation Applied to The Interaction of Federal and State Sentences," *The Champion* (2014).

### §1:10.23   Inmate Financial Responsibility Program

To assist in the collection of court-ordered financial obligations, the BOP operates the Inmate Financial Responsibility Program (IFRP) in conjunction with the Administrative Office of the U.S. Courts. See Program Statement 5380.08, Financial Responsibility Program, Inmate. All inmates with financial obligations including special assessments, restitution, fines and court costs, state or local court obligations, and other federal obligations, are encouraged to work with staff to develop an individual financial plan.

Participation in IFRP, while voluntary, is tied to eligibility for prison privileges including preferred housing, job assignments, and community activities such as community confinement and furloughs. Participation is also tied to institutional program and custody level changes. Inmates are responsible for making all payments from funds in their inmate accounts, including funds from outside resources and pay from work in the institution, or a combination of the two.

The sentencing court can require inmates to pay fines and special assessments as part of the judgment. If the court either orders that these financial obligations are "due immediately," or if the J&C is silent as to when they are due, then the BOP will collect those fines and special assessments through the IFRP. In the latter case, 18 U.S.C. §3572(d) requires "immediate" payment.

### §1:10.24   Female Offenders

Female inmates are not housed with male inmates. At various sites, female offender units are co-located with male units. However, all housing units and activities are separate. Appropriate programs and services are provided to meet the physical, social, and psychological needs of female offenders.

The BOP provides female inmates with medical and social services related to pregnancy, birth control, child placement, and abortion. See 28 C.F.R. pt. 551, subpt. C, and Program Statement 6070.05, Birth Control, Pregnancy, Child Placement and Abortion. Each female offender having child bearing potential is medically screened for pregnancy upon admission, and is instructed to inform medical staff should she suspect she may be pregnant, so that pre-natal care may be immediately provided. Childbirth typically takes place at a community hospital. While placement of the child in the community is the inmate's responsibility, staff will assist the inmate and work closely with community agencies to effect an appropriate arrangement.

### §1:10.24.1     Mothers and Infants Together (MINT)

The BOP offers a community residential program for pregnant inmates, Mothers and Infants Together (MINT). The MINT program, managed by private social service agencies under contract to the BOP, provides mothers with childbirth, parenting, and coping skills classes. In addition to parenting services, MINT sites offer chemical dependency treatment, physical and sexual abuse counseling, self-esteem building programs, budgeting classes, and vocational and educational programs. It is at the discretion of the inmate's institution housing Unit Team to decide whether to refer the inmate to MINT. A MINT participant may remain at the residential program for a period after birth, to provide an opportunity to bond with her newborn child before returning to an institution to complete her sentence. Prior to the birth, the mother must make arrangements for an appropriate custodian for the child. An inmate is eligible to enter the program if she satisfies the general criteria for furlough eligibility, and is in her final two months of pregnancy. See Program Statement 5280.09, Inmate Furloughs. Designation to the MINT program is in accordance with Program Statement 7310.04, Community Corrections Center (CCC) Utilization and Transfer Procedures.

Pursuant to 28 C.F.R. pt. 551, subpt. C, and Program Statement 6070.05, Birth Control, Pregnancy, Child Placement, & Abortion, the Warden provides each pregnant inmate with medical, religious, and social counseling to aid her in making the decision whether or carry the pregnancy to term or to have an elective abortion. The BOP will assume all costs associated with the abortion procedure only when the life of the mother would be endangered if the fetus is carried to term, or in the case of rape. In all other cases non-BOP funds must be obtained to pay for any abortion procedure. Whether or not the BOP pays for the abortion, the BOP may expend funds to escort the inmate to a facility outside the institution to receive the procedure.

### §1.10:24.2     Resolve Program

The Resolve Program is a cognitive-behavioral program designed to address the trauma related mental health needs of female offenders. Specifically, the

29

program seeks to decrease the incidence of trauma related psychological disorders and improve inmates' level of functioning. In addition, the program aims to increase the effectiveness of other treatments, such as drug treatment and healthcare. The program utilizes a standardized treatment protocol consisting of three components: an initial psycho-educational workshop (Trauma in Life); a brief, skills based treatment group (Seeking Safety); and either Dialectical Behavioral Therapy (DBT), Cognitive Processing Therapy (CPT), and/or Skill Maintenance Group which are intensive, cognitive behavioral treatment groups to address persistent psychological and interpersonal difficulties. The Resolve Program is available in many female institutions. The Bureau is also piloting a gender-specific of the program in a male facility in FY 2014.

In most instances, inmates are expected to participate in the Resolve Program during their first 12 months of incarceration. The full Resolve Program protocol takes approximately 40 weeks to complete; however, scheduling conflicts may extend the length of the program. Inmates also have the option of continuing to participate in the Skills Maintenance Group indefinitely to continue practicing healthy coping skills.

The Resolve Program is for female inmates with a mental illness diagnosis due to trauma. While the Trauma in Life workshop is the first stage of the Resolve Program, other female inmates without a history of trauma may participate in this workshop is the institution resources permit.

The program content focuses on the development of personal resilience, effective coping skills, emotional self-regulation, and healthy interpersonal relationships. These skills are attained through the use of educational, cognitive, behavioral, and problem-solving focused interventions.

The Resolve Program is available at the following facilities:

FPC Alderson, WV - Minimum
SFF Hazelton, WV - Low
FPC Lexington, KY - Minimum

FCI Greenville, IL - Medium
FCI Waseca, MN - Low
FCI Danbury, CT - Low
(Males)

More information about the program can be found at Bureau of Prisons Program Statement 5330.11

## §1:20   GLOSSARY OF BOP INSTITUTION TERMINOLOGY

AD—Administrative Detention—status into which inmates are placed if they are pending classification status, investigation, or possible disciplinary action.

AW—Associate Warden.

Call-out sheet—a form posted daily in the housing unit and/or other bulletin boards which must be read by inmates denoting required appointments for that day.

Census—a formal accountability procedure, where all inmate movement is stopped.

Central File—the folder that contains the official file documentation that the Bureau of Prisons maintains on an inmate, including sentencing information, institutional adjustment and classification documentation, inmate correspondence, visiting list, and telephone list.

CIM—Central Inmate Monitoring—a program designed by the BOP that ensures a higher level of review for inmate movements (such as transfers and furloughs) (note: any inmate classified under the CIM system is notified in writing of such classification and the rational for the classification).

Contraband—anything that is not authorized for issuance to, or retention by an inmate while in a Bureau of Prisons facility.

Cop-out—an inmate's written request to a staff member (BOP Form No. BP-70).

Count—the formal process of accountability for inmates; normally conducted by staff five times per day.

Custody—the rating given to each inmate which has been determined appropriate for supervision while in the Bureau of Prisons. Custody levels are Community (least amount of supervision), Out, In, and Maximum.

DHO—Disciplinary Hearing Officer, a certified disciplinary hearing staff member who can impose, subject to final review by the Warden, disciplinary sanctions of loss of goodtime, disciplinary segregation, and transfer for serious institutional misconduct following the inmate's receipt of a formal Incident Report and following a hearing by the Unit Disciplinary Committee (UDC).

FCI—Federal Correctional Institution—housing low - to medium-security inmates.

FOI Exempt—the documentation contained in the Central File of an inmate which cannot be disclosed to the inmate, based on privacy expectations or sensitivity of investigative information.

FRP (or IFRP)—Financial Responsibility Program (Inmate Financial Responsibility Program)—a program which requires inmates to make regularly scheduled payment on any court-ordered financial obligations while they are confined and in BOP custody.

Furlough—temporary release to the community. An inmate must have Community custody in order to be eligible for furloughs.

Gate Pass—a pass authorized by staff at secure facilities which allows an inmate to work outside the secure perimeter of the institution.

Gig—a deviation from acceptable standards of sanitation or housekeeping within an inmate's assigned living quarters.

Gratuity—the amount of money provided to an inmate upon his/her release or transfer to a halfway house.

Intake Screening—the process of fingerprinting, photographing, search, unit team interview, medical interview, at the time of arrival at a BOP facility.

Lockdown—a formal immobilization by placement in assigned cells, rooms, or dormitories at a BOP facility. Lockdown is routinely imposed each night at an institution, and can be imposed for emergency security matters.

New Law—sentences imposed for offenses that were committed on or after November 1, 1987.

Old Law—sentences that were imposed for offenses that were committed before November 1, 1987.

Program Review—a regularly scheduled in-person review between the inmate and his unit team. Such reviews consider program involvement and participation, Financial Responsibility Program participation, custody and security level, and when applicable pre-release planning.

PSI (PSR)—Presentence Investigation Report. The Report that was prepared by the U.S. Probation Office following sentencing.

Recall—the procedure that allows inmates to return to their assigned housing units early from institution work or study programs, usually to allow for special staff meetings or special holiday observances.

RRC—Residential Reentry Center (halfway house).

Register Number—the eight-digit identification number that was assigned by the United States Marshal Service. This number must accompany all correspondence to an inmate while confined.

Security Level (level)—the classification rating given to each inmate which determines the appropriate facility for confinement. Security level ratings include Minimum (least secure), Low, Medium, High, and Administrative (administrative facilities house pretrial offenders, holdover inmates, and inmate work cadres).

SEG—Segregation—also known as disciplinary segregation, for inmates who have received a formal disciplinary sanction.

Shakedown—an official search conducted by staff of the inmate's person, property, or living area.

Shot—a written Incident Report filed against an inmate by a staff member who believes a violation of institutional rules and regulations has been committed.

SHU—special housing unit—which is comprised of Administrative Detention (AD) and disciplinary segregation (SEG) cells.

SORT—Special Operations Response Team—a specialized team of institution staff members who are highly trained to respond to crisis situations.

Special Purchase—an item that must be purchased as authorized through institutional channels that is not provided by the inmate commissary. A list of such items can be obtained at the institution after an offender has reported for designation.

Transfer Sheet—a printed form which is posted on institution bulletin boards Monday through Friday denoting work assignment changes and living quarters assignment changes (see call out sheet).

TRUFONE—The inmate telephone system.

TRULINCS—Acronym for the Trust Fund Limited Computer System.

UDC—Unit Discipline Committee comprised of member(s) of the unit team certified to hear incident reports and impose limited disciplinary sanctions.

Unit—the living quarters to which an inmate is assigned at an institution.

Unit Team—those staff members which consist of the Unit (housing) Manager, Case Manager, Correctional Counselor, and available education representatives.

UA (urinalysis)—periodical urine testing of inmates of drug screenings.

V-PIN—A security voice-verification feature for inmate telephone use.

Writ—an order issued from the court requiring the presence of an inmate (the BOP routinely follows federal writ orders, but it is within the BOP's discretion whether or not to follow state writ orders).

## ENDNOTES
  • All BOP program statements mentioned in this chapter can be found on the Bureau's web site, www.bop.gov

(This page intentionally left blank.)

# CHAPTER 2

---

# SECURING A
# FAVORABLE
# FEDERAL PRISON
# PLACEMENT

(This page intentionally left blank.)

## §2:10    INTRODUCTION

The Bureau of Prisons has substantially revamped its designation and placement procedure particularly in light of the new medical and mental health Levels of Care. The latter two are more fully described in Chapter 7.

## §2:20    FAVORABLE FEDERAL PRISON PLACEMENT AND DESIGNATION

### §2:20.1    The Federal Prison System

The process of designating a facility for service of a federal sentence has become more complex and involved. Previously, an inmate was assigned a security level and a facility with a corresponding security level was identified and designated. Now, however, in addition to receiving a security level, each incoming inmate receives a presumptive Care Level reflecting the level of medical services he requires and a presumptive Mental Health Care Level based on his mental health status. The assignment of security levels is discussed more fully below, and the assignment of Care Level and Mental Health Level are discussed more fully in Chapter 8. When an inmate has received all three assignments, a facility that meets each of those requirements is identified and designated for service. Thus, if an inmate is classified as minimum security with a Care Level of 2 (chronic but stable) and Mental Health Care Level of 1 (no or minimal need for mental health intervention), he may be placed at most BOP camps. However, if that inmate requires medical Care Level 3, there are very few camps for which he will be qualified.

The information used for these classifications is based primarily on the information contained in the PSR, emphasizing the importance of having full, complete, and accurate information included in that document. In addition to the PSR, judicial recommendations or even medical evaluations ordered by the court to be amended to the PSR are considered. Sometimes, additional medical or mental health records are sought prior to designation.

The federal prison system's institutions are divided into five categories: minimum, low, medium, high (the most secure) and administrative.

Minimum-security institutions, commonly called "federal prison camps," are designed for offenders who do not pose a risk of violence or escape. According to Bureau statistics, approximately 15 percent of all inmates are housed in minimum-security facilities, i.e., prison camps, and in community settings. Most individuals want to be designated to a federal prison camp because of the lack of violence and what they perceive to be better conditions of confinement. Minimum-security institutions have dormitory and room housing, a relatively low staff-to-inmate ratio, and limited or no perimeter fencing. These institutions are work- and program-oriented, and many are located adjacent to larger institutions or on military bases, where inmates help serve the labor needs of the larger institution or base. While inmates are theoretically free to "walk away" from these facilities, few of them do because inmates who escape from prison camps and are recaptured face severe consequences. In addition to being prosecuted for escape, such inmates serve the rest of their time in more secure (and therefore harsher) facilities.

Although prison camp designation is the most common type of minimum-security placement, the BOP also operates minimum-security work cadres at administrative facilities, *i.e.*, Metropolitan Correctional Centers, Metropolitan Detention Centers and Federal Detention Centers, whose primary mission is the detention of pre-trial defendants. Usually, an inmate must be within five years of release to be considered for cadre placement. And, the odds of being so designated increase in the absence of a valid judicial recommendation or in the face of a non-specific recommendation (for example, the Court recommends that the BOP designate someone who resides near a major urban center "at a facility closest to home"). Work cadre placement is fundamentally different than camp placement. Although housed in a segregated unit with other minimum-security inmates, cadre inmates, who are tasked with helping maintain the institution's daily operation, are exposed to a general population of all security levels, including individuals who have been charged with or convicted of very serious offenses—the latter awaiting transfer. Also, environmentally, cadre inmates are confined similar to high security inmates, *i.e.*, in a cell as opposed to an open cubicle; heightened noise levels persist throughout the institution at all hours of the day and night; and inmates cannot walk outdoors or breathe fresh air.

Low-security Federal Correctional Institutions (FCIs) have double-fenced perimeters, mostly dormitory or cubicle housing, and strong work and program components. The staff-to-inmate ratio in these institutions is higher than at minimum-security facilities.

Medium-security FCIs have strengthened perimeters (often double fences with electronic detection systems), mostly cell-type housing, a wide variety of work and treatment programs, an even higher staff-to-inmate ratio than low-security FCIs, and even greater internal controls.

High-security institutions, also known as United States Penitentiaries (USPs), have highly-secured perimeters (featuring walls or reinforced fences), multiple- and single-occupant cell housing, the highest staff-to-inmate ratio, and close control of inmate movement.

Administrative facilities are institutions with special missions, such as the detention of pretrial offenders; the treatment of inmates with serious or chronic medical problems; or the containment of extremely dangerous, violent, or escape-prone inmates. They are capable of holding inmates in all security categories. Administrative facilities include Metropolitan Correctional Centers (MCCs), Metropolitan Detention Centers (MDCs), Federal Detention Centers (FDCs), and Federal Medical Centers (FMCs), as well as the Federal Transfer Center (FTC), the Medical Center for Federal Prisoners (MCFP), and the Administrative-Maximum (ADX) U.S. Penitentiary.

A number of BOP institutions belong to Federal Correctional Complexes (FCCs). At FCCs, institutions with different missions and security levels are located in close proximity to one another. FCCs increase efficiency through the sharing of services, enable staff to gain experience at institutions of many security levels, and enhance emergency preparedness by having additional resources within close proximity.

### §2:20.2    How the BOP Designation Process Works

Following the imposition of a sentence of imprisonment the BOP begins the process of determining the defendant's facility for service of his sentence.

The U.S. Court Clerk uploads the signed Judgment Order into the "E-Designate" system and transmits it to U.S. Probation. Bureau of Prisons Program Statement 5100.08 (Inmate Security Designation and Custody Classification) September 12, 2006. U.S. Probation then adds the Presentence Report and transmits it to the U.S. Marshals. Once the U.S. Marshals receive the documentation electronically, they add their USM-129 Form, upon which the Bureau can determine if any jail time credit should be calculated for time already served, and transmit all documents to the Bureau of Prisons Designation and Sentence Computation Center (DSCC) for classification and designation of the offender. If the Statement of Reasons (SOR) has not been included in the judgment order the Bureau receives, then DSCC staff must make a reasonable effort to obtain a copy by contacting the Court or USPO. This is required to better ensure that the Bureau follows the intentions of the Court when designating a facility, as the SOR may contain information that overrides the Presentence Investigation Report (PSR) and may affect security classification decisions as part of the designation process.

One of several classification teams at the DSCC will handle the incoming documents, according to Court of Jurisdiction. They compute classification scoring and transmit it to one of seven Senior Designators for final review and designation.

Primary responsibility for inmate placement rests with officials at the Designation and Sentence Computation Center (DSCC) in Grand Prairie, Texas, 346 Marine Forces Drive, Grand Prairie, Texas 75051; (972) 352-4400; BOP-CDP/ DSCC@bop.gov. The DSCC consists of 17 classification teams, based upon the district in which the inmate is sentenced and one designation team. Hotel Team is the designation team for the DSCC. The team is comprised of nine senior designators who process all the initial designations as well as other transfers, and eight designators who process transfers. There are also four specialist designators who handle special cases such as RDAP transfers. Designator caseloads are based upon the institution the inmate is assigned. There are also five OMDT designators who assign inmates to BOP medical facilities, if applicable.

| | | |
|---|---|---|
| Alpha<br>District of Columbia<br>D.C. Superior Court | Foxtrot<br>Connecticut<br>Ohio (all districts)<br>Rhode Island | Papa<br>Eastern & Southern California |
| Bravo<br>Maryland<br>Tennessee (all districts)<br>Eastern Texas<br>West Virginia (all districts) | South Dakota<br>Virginia (all districts)<br><br>India<br>Southern Texas | Quebec<br>Massachusetts<br>Montana<br>Nevada<br>Oregon<br>Utah<br>Washington (all districts) |
| Charlie<br>Arkansas (all districts)<br>Kentucky (all districts)<br>North Carolina (all districts)<br>Oklahoma (all districts) | Juliet<br>Western Texas<br><br>Kilo<br>Georgia (all districts)<br>Louisiana (all districts) | Romeo<br>Hawaii<br>Illinois (all districts)<br>Michigan (all districts)<br>Puerto Rico |
| Delta<br>Delaware<br>Idaho<br>Maine<br>New Hampshire<br>New York (all districts)<br>Vermont | Mississippi (all districts)<br>Northern Texas<br><br>Lima<br>Florida (all districts)<br>Guam<br>Northern Marianna Islands<br>Virgin Islands | Sierra<br>Northern California<br>Iowa (all districts)<br>Kansas<br>Nebraska<br>Wisconsin (all districts)<br>Wyoming |
| Echo<br>New Jersey<br>North Dakota<br>Pennsylvania (all districts)<br>South Carolina | November<br>Alabama (all districts)<br>Central California<br>New Mexico | Tango<br>Alaska<br>Colorado<br>Indiana (all districts)<br>Minnesota<br>Missouri (all districts) |
| | Oscar<br>Arizona | |

### §2:20.3    Security Level Scoring and Designation by Designations Staff

The designation of an inmate to a specific institution is governed by Bureau of Prisons Program Statement 5100.08. First, staff at the DSCC "score" the defendant to determine his or her security level. To score an individual, designation staff consider various factors, including:

(a)  court-recommendation, if any,

(b)  voluntary surrender status,

(c)  severity of current offense,

(d)  criminal history category,

(e)  history of violence,

(f)  history of escape,

(g)  detainers, if any,

(h)  age,

(i)  education level (verified high school, enrolled in high school or GED, or no high school), and

(j)  drug/alcohol abuse within the past five years.1

Although most factors the designation staff consider can raise a defendant's score (and potentially the security level), a court order permitting the defendant to voluntarily surrender to the designated institution can actually *lower* a defendant's score by three points. Inmates will not receive the reduction of points for Voluntary Surrender if they voluntarily surrender on the same day they are sentenced or if they are a Supervised Release Violator.

This factor can sometimes make the difference between a defendant being designated to a camp or a low-security institution. Additionally, voluntary surrender spares an individual the unpleasantness of being shackled and trans-ferred via "con air" aboard the U.S. Marshal Service inmate transport aircraft, or bussed. Bussing, known as "diesel therapy" by inmates, can often take weeks. Defense counsel should therefore request voluntary surrender whenever they think there is a possibility that the court will grant it.

Scoring with regard to drug/alcohol abuse and education levels can raise the total security level score by no more than three total points. However, the criminal history category can increase the total by up to 13 points, which could increase security by one or two levels (for example, from minimum security to low or medium security). The age category requires scoring higher points for younger offenders, which can also increase the security classification by one or two levels. The scoring for education and drug/alcohol abuse can result in a total point increase of no more than three points, which primarily impacts those cases that might be borderline between security levels—for example, a minimum-security case scoring at the top of the BOP Minimum security range could be raised to low security with the addition of these points.

Next, the DSCC determines whether Public Safety Factors (PSFs) apply. A PSF that applies to an individual will rule out a prison camp designation—even if he or she would have otherwise qualified for one. Public Safety Factors are so important in the designation process that we have described them in detail below. Public Safety Factors can be waived—but only by the DSCC.

Finally, the DSCC considers whether there are any medical or mental health factors that might affect designation. Medical and Mental Health Care factors utilized in designation and placement are described in Chapter 8. Thus, an inmate is assigned a security level, Medical Care Level, and Mental Health Care Level.

When initially scoring an inmate, the assigned team utilizes a Medical Calculator to determine the screen level. If the inmate is scored as a SCRN3 or SCRN4, he/she will be referred to the Office of the Medical Designator (OMDT) for further review. OMDT then decides what the SCRN level will be after a further review of the documents. If the inmate comes back from OMDT as a SCRN1 or SCRN2, Hotel Team will designate them to an appropriate CARE1 or CARE2 facility. If the inmate is determined to meet the criteria for a CARE3 or CARE4 facility, OMDT will designate them. Assuming that Medical Care Level and Mental Health Care Levels are 1 and 2, the Hotel Team will then make a designation taking into consideration the inmate's release residence, the inmate's determined Security Level, any judicial recommendation and prison population pressures.

### §2:20.4    Public Safety Factors

*Disruptive Group.* A male inmate who is identified in the BOP Central Inmate Monitoring System will be housed in a high-security level institution, unless the PSF has been waived. A "disruptive group" is a prison gang that has been identified by prison staff and certified by the BOP as engaging in illicit activities within the BOP and/or being disruptive to the internal operation of the

BOP. Organized crime groups like La Cosa Nostra, which operate outside the prison environment, are not "disruptive groups" as defined by the PSF, unless they meet these criteria.

*Greatest Severity Offense.* A male inmate whose current term of confinement falls into the "Greatest Severity" range according to the Offense Severity Scale (Appendix A) of BOP Program Statement 5100.08 will be housed in at least a low-security level institution, unless the PSF has been waived.

Greatest severity offenses include:

- Aircraft piracy.
- Arson.
- Assault (serious bodily injury intended or permanent or life-threatening bodily injury resulting).
- Car-jacking.
- Certain drug offenses—but only if the defendant was a manager or owner of large-scale drug activities (*i.e.*, drug activities involving drug quantities in excess of 10 kilograms of cocaine, 31 grams of crack, 250 kilograms of hashish, 620 kilograms of marijuana, 2 kilograms of heroin, 17 kilograms of methamphetamine, 20,000 dosage units of PCP, and 250,000 dosage units of amphetamine, barbiturates, LSD or other illicit drugs). Just because an individual is involved in large-scale drug activity does not mean that the offense is considered "greatest severity." That appellation is reserved for "organizers/leaders," which includes importers, high-level suppliers, growers, manufacturers, financiers, money launderers, aircraft pilots and captains of large boats or ships. For example, in a drug case involving more than 10 kilograms of cocaine or 620 kilograms of marijuana, designation staff will look at the role in the offense portion of the PSR to see if there's any upward adjustment under United States Sentencing Guideline §3B1.1. If not, the offender will generally not be treated as a greatest severity offender. If an individual receives a mitigating role under USSG §3B1.2, he or she will not qualify for the greatest severity PSF. Similarly, if the sentencing judge finds that an individual's guideline offense level should not be enhanced under USSG §3B1.1 for an aggravating role, make sure that the PSR is corrected and/or that the judge issues findings pursuant to Rule 32(c)(1) of the Federal Rules of Criminal Procedure. When it is a close call whether this PSF applies, a finding by the sentencing judge (try getting the government to concede this) and/or a notation on the judgment in the criminal case that the defendant was not part of an organizational network and did not organize or maintain ownership interest/profits from large-scale drug activities will help avoid this PSF.
- Escape from a closed institution or secure custody through the use of force or weapons.
- Espionage, including treason, sabotage or related offenses.
- The use or possession of explosives involving risk of death or bodily injury.
- Extortion by weapons or threat of violence.

- Homicide or voluntary manslaughter.
- Kidnapping involving abduction, unlawful restraint, or demanding or receiving ransom money.
- Robbery.
- Sexual offenses, including rape, sodomy, incest, carnal knowledge, or transportation with coercion or force for commercial purposes.
- Use of toxic substances or chemicals as weapons to endanger human life.
- Distribution of automatic weapons or exporting sophisticated weaponry, or brandishing or threatening use of a weapon.

*Sex Offender.* A male or female inmate whose behavior (current or prior) includes one or more of the following elements will be housed in at least a low-security level institution, unless the PSF has been waived. A defendant need not have a sex-offense conviction for this PSF to apply. For example, if a sex offense was dismissed as a result of a plea bargain, the BOP will apply this PSF if the PSR documents the behavior that triggers it. Any of the following offense elements (or attempts to commit any of them) can trigger the "sex offender" PSF:

- engaging in sexual conduct with another person without obtaining permission (examples include forcible rape, sexual assault or sexual battery);
- possession, distribution or mailing of child pornography or related paraphernalia;
- any sexual contact with a minor or other person physically or mentally incapable of granting consent (examples include indecent liberties with a minor, statutory rape, sexual abuse of the mentally ill, and rape by administering a drug or substance);
- any sexual act or contact not identified above that is aggressive or abusive in nature (examples include rape by instrument, encouraging use of a minor for prostitution purposes, and incest).

Application of this PSF is also required if a defendant's current offense is referenced in the Sex Offender Notification and Registration Program Statement, or if it involves a violation of any of the following statutes: 18 U.S.C. §2241, 18 U.S.C. §2242, 18 U.S.C. §2243, 18 U.S.C. §2244, 18 U.S.C. §2251, or 18 U.S.C. §2252.

*Threat to Government Officials.* A male or female inmate classified under the BOP Central Inmate Monitoring system as a Threat to Government Official will be housed in at least a Low-security level institution, unless this PSF has been waived.

*Deportable Alien.* The BOP now applies this PSF to any male or female inmate who is not a citizen of the United States. This includes all long-term detainees. Application of this PSF requires placement in at least a Low-security facility. It is not to be applied when the U.S. Immigration and Customs Enforcement (ICE) or the Executive Office for Immigration Review (EOIR) have determined that deportation proceedings will not be warranted, or when there is a finding not to deport.

*Sentence Length.* A male offender with more than 10 years remaining to be served will be housed in at least a Low-security facility, unless this PSF has been waived. A male offender with more than 20 years remaining to serve will be housed in at least a Medium-security facility, unless the PSF has been waived. A male offender with more than 30 years remaining to serve (including non-pa-rolable life sentences) will be housed in a High-security facility, unless the PSF has been waived. This rule does not mean that a defendant who receives a 12 year (*i.e.,* 144 month) sentence would necessarily be ineligible for a prison camp. First, the BOP does not look to the *sentence* the defendant received to determine whether this PSF applies—it looks to the time a defendant has left to serve. After expected good-time credit is subtracted, a sentence of 144 months results in approximately 123 months to serve ($144 \times .85 = 122.4$). While this might still leave more than 10 years to serve, if the defendant has already served more than three months in pre-trial confinement, he may have less than 10 years to serve following designation, and may therefore be eligible for a federal prison camp.

*Violent Behavior.* A female inmate whose current term of confinement or history involves two convictions for serious incidents of violence within the last five years will be assigned to at least a Low-security level institution, unless the PSF is waived.

*Serious Escape.* A female inmate who has been involved in a serious escape within the last ten years, including the current term of confinement, will be assigned to the Carswell Administrative Unit, unless the PSF has been waived. A male inmate who has escaped from a secure facility, or has an escape from an open institution or program with a threat of violence will be housed in at least a Medium-security level institution, unless the PSF is waived.

*Prison Disturbance.* This PSF applies to male or female inmates who have been involved in more than one serious incident of violence within an institution and have been found guilty of one or more of certain prohibited acts, such as engaging in or encouraging a riot. Male inmates with this PSF are housed in High-security institutions, unless the PSF has been waived. Female inmates with this PSF will be assigned to the Carswell Administrative Unit, unless the PSF has been waived.

*Juvenile Violence.* This PSF applies to current male or female juvenile offenders with any documented single instance of violent behavior, past or present, which resulted in a conviction, a delinquency adjudication, or finding of guilt. For purposes of this PSF, "violence" is defined as aggressive behavior causing serious bodily harm or death, or aggressive or intimidating behavior likely to cause serious bodily harm or death (*e.g.*, aggravated assault, intimidation involving a weapon, or arson).

*Serious Telephone Abuse.* This PSF applies to male or female inmates who have used a telephone to further or promote criminal activities. An inmate need not have been convicted of this criminal activity so long as it is documented in the PSR or other official report. Not every inmate who has used a telephone to commit a crime will be assigned this PSF. However, some white collar offenders who would otherwise be camp eligible will not be. Defense counsel should consult BOP Program Statement 5100.08 to determine its applicability to a particular individual. An inmate assigned this PSF must be housed in at least a Low-security level institution, unless the PSF has been waived. Any offender who is assigned the Serious Telephone Abuse PSF may also have his or her use of the telephone at Bureau of Prisons institutions restricted.

### §2:20.5    Management Variables

Management Variables (MGTVs) are factors that can trump a defendant's security score or PSF, and are generally imposed by the designator. Management variables include:

- *Judicial Recommendation.* Occasionally, the BOP may rely on a judicial recommendation to apply an MGTV to place an inmate in a higher or lower security level than his or her score would otherwise require.
- *Release Residence.* Occasionally, the BOP will assign an inmate to an institution because it is close to his "release residence," even though the inmate's score would normally require an institution with a different security level. Generally, this MGTV will be applied to assign an inmate to a higher security level institution, although in theory it can work both ways.
- *Population Management.* Sometimes the BOP will place an inmate in an institution with a higher security level because the lower security level institutions for which the inmate qualifies are overcrowded. When it does, it applies this MGTV.
- *Central Inmate Monitoring Assignment.* Some inmates need to be monitored or separated from others. Sometimes these special management concerns limit the options for placement. When this happens, the BOP applies this MGTV to permit placement outside normal guidelines.
- *Medical or Psychiatric.* The BOP will apply this MGTV when an inmate needs medical/psychiatric treatment that is available only in an institution outside his or her security level.
- *Work Cadre.* At secure facilities without satellite camps, the Regional Director may authorize a certain number of work cadre inmates to perform work outside the perimeter of the institution. When such a placement is outside normal security level scoring guidelines, the BOP will apply this MGTV to allow the inmate to participate in the work cadre.
- *PSF Waived.* This MGTV is applied when a PSF has been reviewed and approved for waiver by the DSCC Administrator, and will cause the inmate to be placed at a different security level than if the PSF were as in place.
- *Long-Term Detainee.* Although the BOP assigns security levels to long-term alien detainees at the time of initial classification, these detainees do not receive subsequent custody reviews as do non-alien regular BOP inmates. Therefore, should circumstances warrant a transfer to a lesser or higher security, the BOP assigns this MGTV. This MGTV can only be approved by the BOP Detention Services Branch, Correctional Programs Division, Central Office.
- *Greater Security.* When the Bureau of Prisons believes that an offender represents a greater security risk than the assigned security level

would suggest, it may apply this Management Variable and place the inmate in an institution with a higher security level. The BOP typically applies this MGTV to offenders with lengthy prior arrest records but few convictions, non-violent offenders who have a history of poor adjustment under probation or community supervision, offenders with a history of organized crime involvement, offenders with significant foreign ties and/or financial resources, and offenders who have had disciplinary problems during prior incarceration. Inmates who receive this MGTV are placed one security level higher than their score would otherwise require.

- *Lesser Security.* When the Bureau of Prisons concludes that an offender represents a lesser security risk than his or her scored security level would suggest, it can apply this MGTV to place him or her in an institution outside normal guidelines.

### §2:20.6    Central Inmate Monitoring Information

The Central Inmate Monitoring (CIM) system is an additional classification tool to monitor inmates who present special security management needs. This can include those who have documented needs to be separated from certain other inmates, those who pose threats to Government officials, those who have received widespread publicity, and others whose backgrounds suggest that special supervision is needed in determining prison placement. Pertinent information, especially with regard to inmates requiring separation from specified others, can be communicated to the BOP at the time of initial classification and designation, preferably by the AUSA who prosecuted the case or other Federal law enforcement official involved in the case."

### §2:20.7    After an Inmate Is Designated

Once a designation is made, the information is communicated to the U.S. Marshal. If the individual is not incarcerated, the Marshal is required to inform that person of the designation. Unfortunately, sometimes, this notice is not sent. Hence, it is important that counsel for the defendant keep in touch with the U.S. Marshal to determine the defendant's designated facility. If the inmate is incarcerated at a federal institution, the inmate may be able to obtain that information from a staff member, who can obtain it from the BOP computer system. (Staff members are not required to provide this information to an inmate, but some will.) If the inmate is in a non-federal facility, he or she may not be able to obtain this information from institution staff because it is not privy to the computer used by the BOP and the U.S. Marshal Service. If the inmate is unable to obtain this information, defense counsel may be able to obtain it from the Marshal. (Marshals are not required to disclose that information, but some will.) Unfortunately, under strict BOP policy, the Bureau will not release this information to non-law enforcement agencies or the public, including defense attorneys in most districts.

### §2:20.8    Transfers

Transfers (also known as redesignations) are used to move inmates from one institution to another as needed, with each type of transfer having a specific objective. The following are some of the more frequent reasons for a transfer:

- Institution classification;
- Nearer release;
- Disciplinary/close supervision;
- Adjustment;
- Medical/psychological treatment;
- Temporary transfer;
- Training purposes/program participation;
- Institution Hearing Program;
- Pre-release; and,
- Transfers from RRC's.

The two most common requests for transfer by inmates are (1) institution classification transfers based on a decrease in the inmate's security level and (2) Nearer Release Transfers.

When a decrease in an inmate's security level is indicated, transfer of the inmate to a lower security institution would be considered.

Nearer Release Transfers move the inmate closer to their legal residence or release destination consistent with their security level. Inmates must be considered for a Nearer Release Transfer only after serving 18 consecutive months of clear conduct in a general population. Once the inmate has been transferred within 500 miles of his or her release residence no further referrals will be made for Nearer Release Transfer consideration. Transfers to a facility in an area other than an inmate's legal residence or sentencing district may be considered by the inmate's Unit Team provided that the inmate can provide strong evidence of community and/or family support.

Inmates with an Order for Deportation, an Order of Removal, an ICE detainer for an unadjudicated offense(s) or an ICE detainer for hearing will not be nearer release purposes since they will be returning to the community outside, rather than inside, the United States upon release.

Request for Nearer Release Transfers should be made by the inmate.

The Warden of an institution with a satellite camp may transfer an inmate from the main institution to the camp if the inmate is assigned an appropriate security and/or custody level.

An inmate may travel via "unescorted transfer" from a Low or Minimum security level institution to a Minimum security level institution if the inmate is a Minimum security level inmate and has OUT or COMMUNITY custody. The inmate's family (on the approved visiting list) may provide transportation to the receiving institution only if the inmate is transferring from a Minimum level security institution to another Minimum level security institution and, if approved by the Warden, inmate's family is expected to bear all transportation costs. The inmate must go directly from the sending institution to the receiving institution.

When initially scoring an inmate, the assigned team utilizes a Medical Calculator to determine the screen level. If the inmate is scored as a SCRN3 or SCRN4, he/she will be referred to the Office of Medical Designations (OMDT) for further review. OMDT then decides whether the SCRN level will require further review of the available information. If the inmate comes back from OMDT as a SCRN1 or SCRN2, the latter will be referred back to Designators who will designate the inmate to an appropriate CARE1 or CARE2 facility. If the inmate is determined to meet the criteria for a CARE3 or CARE4 facility, OMDT will designate them.

**ENDNOTES**

- The forms which list these factors (one for male and one for female inmates) are part of BOP Program Statement 5100.08, which can be found at http://www.bop.gov/policy/progstat/5100_008.pdf.
- All BOP program statements mentioned in this chapter can be found on the Bureau's web site, www.bop.gov

# CHAPTER 3

---

# RESIDENTIAL DRUG ABUSE PROGRAM (RDAP)

(This page intentionally left blank.)

## §3:10  INTRODUCTION

The Federal Bureau of Prisons (BOP) estimates that 40 percent of federal inmates have diagnosable, moderate-to-severe substance abuse problems. *See* Stmnt. of BOP National Drug Abuse Coordinator Beth Weinman at the U.S. Sentencing Commission's Symposium of Alternatives to Incarceration, *Prison Programs Resulting in Reduced Sentences* (July 14, 2008) (available at www. ussc. gov/Research/Research_Projects/Alternatives/20080714_Alternatives/ 05_FINAL_PrisonPrograms.pdf). Some form of drug treatment is *mandatory* where drug use contributed to the commission of the offense, where it was the basis for revocation of supervised release or community placement, or where the sentencing court so recommends. Sanctions for failure to complete mandated treatment include pay reduction and community program ineligibility.

The BOP operates three drug abuse programs, the administration of which is governed by 28 C.F.R. §550.10, *et. seq.* and, in turn, BOP Program Statement 5330.11, *Psychology Treatment Programs* (March 16, 2009). The first program is the 12-15 hour voluntary Drug Abuse Education Course offered at all institutions, designed to teach inmates about the consequences of drug/alcohol abuse and addiction by reviewing their personal drug use and the cycle of drug use and crime. The second program is the 12-24 week (90-120 minutes per week) Non-Residential Drug Abuse Treatment (NR DAP), which is targeted to, *inter alia*, those awaiting RDAP, those who do not meet RDAP admission criteria, and those found guilty of an incident report for use of drugs or alcohol. In addition to paying NR DAP graduates $30, BOP policy encourages wardens to consider them for maximum pre-release (halfway house and/or home confinement) placement. The third program is the nine-plus month, 500-hour Residential Drug Abuse Treatment Program (RDAP) for inmates with a diagnosable and verifiable substance abuse disorder.

## §3:20  WHAT IS RDAP?

Through the Violent Crime Control and Law Enforcement Act of 1994, Congress directed that the BOP "provide residential substance abuse treatment ... for all eligible prisoners," defining "eligible prisoner" as one the BOP determines has "a substance abuse problem" and is "willing to participate in a residential substance abuse treatment program." 18 U.S.C. §§3621(e)(1)(C), (e)(5)(B). The BOP's "inpatient" 500-hour residential drug abuse program, in existence since 1989, employs Cognitive Behavioral Therapy (CBT) to treat substance abuse. The "inpatient" component is followed by an aftercare component, which is administered in the community during the final six months of an inmate's sentence.

Experience shows that parties to the federal criminal justice system (courts, probation officers, prosecutors) favor RDAP because it is one of the few avenues for mental health treatment available to inmates not suffering from acute psychological problems. This, in turn, reduces substantially the risk of recidivism and of substance abuse relapse. *See* Pelissier, et al., *Triad Drug Treatment Evaluation*,

65 FEDERAL PROBATION 3, 6 (Dec. 2001). Male inmates who successfully complete RDAP are 16 percent less likely to be re-arrested or revoked than cohorts who went untreated, and male RDAP graduates are 15 percent less likely to use drugs. Female graduates are 18 percent less likely to re-offend or use drugs. *Id.*

Through the 1994 Crime Bill, Congress also incentivized RDAP participation: those *nonviolent* offenders who successfully complete the program while incarcerated (and who have not previously received early release via RDAP) are eligible for release up to one year prior to the expiration of sentence. 18 U.S.C. §3621(e). Importantly, prisoners ineligible for a reduction in sentence under §3621(e) are not precluded from participating in RDAP; the two are not mutually exclusive.

Congress's action had its desired result, especially since RDAP is the only BOP program through which federal prisoners can earn a sentence reduction. An increasing number of inmates seek admission into RDAP annually, with more than 17,000 participating in 2008. *See* Weinman Stmnt., *supra* (approximately 7,000 inmates on waiting list). Since 2009, BOP has employed a sliding scale for §3621(e) reductions tied to sentence length, meaning that not all RDAP participants qualify for the full year reduction in sentence.

## §3:30   ADMISSION TO RDAP

RDAP participation is voluntary. Interested prisoners within 36 months of release may apply by requesting an eligibility interview via a "cop-out" (informal request from a staff member) or a BP-8 (formal request for resolution). The written request serves to initiate the RDAP application and should prompt an interview with either the institution's RDAP Coordinator or a drug treatment specialist (DTS), or, if a prisoner is housed at a facility that does not offer the RDAP, a member of the Psychology Services staff.

To qualify for RDAP, one must, *inter alia*, have at least 24 months or more remaining to serve; present a verifiable, documented pattern of substance abuse or dependence within the 12-month period preceding arrest on the underlying offense; have no serious mental or cognitive impairment precluding full program participation; be halfway house eligible (which precludes participation by removable non-U.S. citizens); and sign acknowledgment of program responsibilities.

### §3:30.1   Diagnosable Disorder

Section 3621 is silent with respect to how determinations about whether a prisoner has "a substance abuse problem" are made. And, while 28 C.F.R. §550.53(b) establishes criteria, in practice Program Statement 5330.11 controls. Staff reviews each program applicant's PSR before scheduling an interview to ascertain whether the applicant meets the diagnostic criteria for abuse or dependence indicated in the *Diagnostic and Statistical Manual of the Mental Disorders, Fourth Edition, (DSM-IV)*. An RDAP applicant's chemical dependency need not be linked to his offense conduct, nor is a judicial recommendation necessary.

There is, however, debate over how much drug or alcohol use is enough. *Compare* P.S. 5330.11 §2.5.8(2)-NOTE ("recreational, social, or occasional use of alcohol and/or other drugs that does not rise to the level of excessive or abusive drinking does not provide the required verification of a substance abuse disorder") *with Kuna v. Daniels*, 234 F.Supp.2d 1168 (D. Or. 2002) (social use of alcohol sufficient to warrant RDAP admission).

In terms of assessing a prisoner's substance abuse history, the BOP places primary reliance on a prisoner's self-reporting to the Presentence Investigation Report (PSR) writer. Whatever is written in the PSR is presumptively valid, and any claim of a disorder that the PSR does not plainly substantiate is treated as suspect. Counsel must, therefore, be attuned to a client's substance abuse history.

Counsel should meet with the client before the presentence interview to fully understand the nature and extent of the client's problem(s) (*e.g.*, illegal drugs, prescribed pharmaceuticals, alcohol, etc.). Prudence also dictates that counsel encourage clients to be fully forthcoming with the PSR writer, that is, not to minimize for fear of embarrassment. Subject to client pre-approval, counsel can foster this conversation by offering the PSR writer an overview during the interview, allowing the writer to follow-up directly with the client as deemed appropriate. Counsel can also provide documentation (*e.g.*, medical records and clinical assessments) from an independent professional (*e.g.*, physician, mental health professional, drug and alcohol counselor) concerning the existence and degree of a client's dependence. Barring that, it is useful to find records that demonstrate the nature and extent of the client's substance abuse difficulties, such as certified copies of DUI judgments, hospital records noting blood alcohol level, and/or a primary physician's treatment notes with entries that substantiate the existence of the problem. If circumstances interfere with or prevent client candor during the PSR interview, counsel should refer clients to qualified independent providers for assessment and treatment as soon as practicable.

Given the §3621(e) incentive, and to ferret out malingering, RDAP eligibility interviews often entail difficult questions designed to determine whether admission is sought in good faith to obtain treatment, or simply to secure a quicker return home. Applicants are routinely asked when they learned about the program and the §3621(e) credit, whether attorneys advised them to exaggerate treatment needs when meeting with probation, and the details of their drug or alcohol use (*e.g.*, when, how often, where, with whom, others' awareness, etc.). Counsel should thus advise clients not to malinger or to overstate their problems, either during the presentence interview or when seeking entrance into the program.

Should the BOP deem a PSR factually insufficient, an inmate might well be refused an interview or found ineligible for services. In that instance, counsel and/or the client may supply "collateral documentation." As set forth in P.S. 5330.11, this "requires documentation from a substance abuse treatment provider or medical provider who diagnosed and treated the inmate for a substance abuse disorder within the 12-month period before the inmate's arrest on his or her current offense." (Emphasis added). This documentation must be sent to and received by the drug abuse treatment staff in the Bureau of Prisons institution. It is not to be sent through the inmate for him or her to provide to the drug abuse treatment staff. If the document is acceptable, the inmate will be referred to the Drug Abuse Program Coordinator for a diagnostic interview.

Multiple convictions (two or more) for Driving Under the Influence (DUI) or Driving While Intoxicated (DWI) in the five years prior to his or her most recent arrest will suffice to show eligibility for the RDAP prgrom.

### §3:30.2    The 12-Month Rule

Although unstated in P.S. 5330.11, the so-called "12-month rule" derives from the BOP's disputed interpretation of "sustained remission," as provided for in the DSM. *See* Weinman Stmnt., *supra*, at 83–84 (2008) ("[W]e use the [DSM], and that's where all the information is regarding what we call court specifiers. Sustained remission is that you have not used drugs for over a year.... Because that's the standard in the [DSM] and that's what we follow."). Thus, no matter the nature or extent of a prisoner's substance abuse problems, if the BOP cannot verify that the individual used to a level rising to the level of a DSM diagnosis in the year prior to arrest, RDAP is denied.

Neither statute nor controlling Code of Federal Regulations provisions provide for the 12-month rule. Furthermore, courts have found that the "DSM-IV does not require documentation of substance abuse or dependency during the 12-month period *immediately preceding either a diagnostic interview, arrest, or incarceration.*" *Mitchell v. Andrews*, 235 F. Supp. 2d 1085, 1090 (E.D. Cal. 2001) (emphasis in original); *see Smith v. Vazquez*, 491 F. Supp. 2d 1165 (S.D. Ga. 2007). A simple hypothetical highlights the unsustainability of the artificial 12-month rule construct. Inmate A was abusing alcohol following his arrest and up to his sentencing in order to self-medicate for the stress he was encountering. Prior to his arrest, he did not have an alcohol abuse problem. He is not eligible for the program. On the other hand, an inmate who was abusing alcohol within one year prior to his arrest and who upon his arrest stopped using alcohol, is still eligible for the program, even though sentencing was delayed by years.

### §3:30.3    The 24-Month Cutoff

As noted, Congress requires that the BOP provide residential substance abuse treatment for each inmate determined to have a substance abuse problem. Moreover, Congress intends that the BOP administer RDAP so as to maximize each eligible inmate's sentence reduction. *See Conf. Rep. to Consolidated Appropriations Act of 2010*, 155 CONG. REC. H13631-03, at H13887 (daily ed. Dec. 8, 2009), Pub. L. No. 111-117, 123 Stat. 3034 (Dec. 16, 2009). However, "[Fiscal Year] 2007 was the first year that the Bureau was unable to meet its mandate to provide treatment for all inmates who volunteer for and are qualified for treatment before they are released from the Bureau of Prisons." Wienman Stmnt., *supra*, at 72. Soon thereafter, BOP eliminated its handful of RDAPs for Spanish-speaking prisoners; in order to participate in the program, a prisoner must now be able to speak and understand English. Through Program Statement 5330.11, promulgated in 2009, the BOP also implemented the 24-month cutoff. BOP then reported compliance with its mandate to Congress. *See* USDOJ-BOP, *The Federal Bureau of Prisons Annual Report on Substance Abuse Treatment Programs Fiscal Year 2010*, at 9 (Dec. 2010) ("In FY 2010, the BOP met the requirement [of the VCCLEA] to treat 100 percent of the eligible prisoner population....").

Program Statement 5330.11 directs that otherwise eligible prisoners must "ordinarily" be within 24 months of release to qualify for admittance to RDAP. There is no known basis for this 24-month cutoff date, which is troubling since, *inter alia*, the program can be completed in as little as 15 months. *See Scott v. FCI Fairton*, 407 Fed. Appx. 612 (3rd Cir. 2011) (citing BOP submissions). Accounting for customary good time credits, the 24-month cutoff means that a defendant with a diagnosable disorder and no pretrial jail credit must receive a sentence of 27.6 months or greater to even be considered for the program. Notably, BOP officials have stated publicly that the 24-month cutoff has shifted to 27 months, which means a sentence of at least 31 months (if the prisoner is ineligible for pretrial jail credit).

Like the 12-month rule, the 24-month cutoff, which is inconsistent with the agency's historic administration of RDAP, is properly seen as arbitrary, capricious, and not meriting *Chevron* deference. Similarly, for those in custody, the rule can be challenged by way of a habeas corpus §2241 petition.

### §3:30.4    Ineligibility

The following categories of inmates are not eligible for the RDAP Program:
(1)  Immigration and Customs Enforcement detainees;
(2)  Pretrial inmates;
(3)  Contractual boarders (for example, State or military inmates)
(4)  Inmates with detainers that preclude halfway house placement.

## §3:40    THE PROGRAM

Once deemed RDAP-eligible, a prisoner is placed on a wait list that is ordered by projected release date (*i.e.*, time remaining to serve, accounting for anticipated good time credit). If housed at an institution that does not offer RDAP, a prisoner will be transferred to one of the 74 programs (64 male, 10 female) at or around the time of expected entrance into a treatment class.

There is a potential that prisoner movement may delay RDAP admission. RDAP-eligible inmates at an institution offering the program are routinely bumped from a class at the last minute when new prisoners arrive with less time remaining to serve. Displacement from a class, which is generally 24-to-27 persons in size, can postpone program participation for several months.

RDAP has two distinct components that must both be completed: the 500-hour "in custody" treatment phase, and the Community Transitional Drug Abuse Treatment Program (TDAT) phase for halfway houses and home confinement.

The residential phase is designed for participants to reconcile their individual substance abuse issues. To this end, they are placed in a segregated housing unit, and institutional assignments (work/school) become part-time and secondary to treatment, recovery and reentry preparation. RDAP participants attend both of the daily 3.5-hour classes, which include course workbooks, homework, and regular group therapy sessions. "The remainder of the day is spent in education, work skills training, and/or other inmate programming." USDOJ-BOP, *State of the Bureau 2009*, at 25.

"RDAP follows the CBT model of treatment wrapped into a modified therapeutic community model where inmates learn what it is like living in a pro-social community." *Id.* Counseling strategies are intended to compel inmates "to identify, confront, and alter the attitudes, values, and thinking patterns that lead to criminal and drug-using behavior." *Triad Drug Treatment Evaluation*, 65 Federal Probation at 3. "Upon completion of this portion of the treatment which lasts nine months, aftercare services are provided to the inmate while he/she is in the general population of the prison, and later at the residential reentry center (RRC)." *State of the Bureau 2009*, at 25. Because the community corrections component of the program is mandatory, prisoners ineligible for hallway house placement (*e.g.*, removable aliens, individuals with serious medical or mental illness) are ineligible for RDAP.

Anecdotal evidence suggests that approximately one-third of RDAP participants fail to complete the program. Tardiness, incomplete assignments and institutional rules violations can all result in expulsion from the program and the loss of any anticipated time credit. Those who reach TDAT are expected to work and prepare for reentry while being subject to added conditions, like group counseling, random urinalysis and a lower violation threshold than other halfway house residents. These demands continue throughout the period of pre-release confinement, including home confinement. As at the institution, a rules violation can result in loss of §3621(e) credit, as well as transfer back to a prisoner's parent institution for the remaining sentence.

## §3:50    THE SENTENCE REDUCTION

The determination as to whether an inmate is ineligible for early release has been the subject of significant controversy. After much litigation, the BOP modified the criteria for eligibility for early release from a sentence for successful completion of RDAP. *See* 28 C.F.R. §550.58; Program Statement 5331.02, *Early Release Procedures Under 18 U.S.C. §3621(e)* (3/16/2009); and Program Statement 5162.05, *Categorization of Offenses* (3/16/2009). This change was intended to exclude violent offenders by the exercise of the implicit discretion placed in BOP by the statute, 18 U.S.C. §3621(e)(2)(B), rather than by definition of the statutory language "nonviolent offense." The authority for determining whether prior offense history or current offense characteristics preclude §3621(e) credit has been moved to the BOP's Designation and Sentence Computation Center (DSCC) in Grand Prairie, Texas.

Bureau policy, which the Supreme Court has upheld, denies early release to persons who have been convicted of a crime of violence—homicide, forcible rape, robbery, aggravated assault, child sexual offense (but *not* possession of child pornography), arson or kidnapping—or a felony offense (1) that has as an element, the actual, attempted, or threatened use of physical force against the person or property of another; (2) that involved the carrying, possession, or use of a firearm or other dangerous weapon or explosives (including any explosive material or explosive device); (3) that by its nature or conduct, presents a serious potential risk of physical force against the person or property of another; or (4) that by its nature or conduct involves sexual abuse offenses committed upon children. *Lopez v. Davis,* 531 U.S. 227 (2001); *but cf. Paulsen v. Daniels,* 413 F.3d 999 (9th Cir. 2005) (program statement violated the Administrative Procedures Act). Inmates with firearm convictions and inmates who have received a two-level adjustment in their drug guideline offense severity score for possession of a dangerous weapon (including a firearm) pursuant to Guideline Section 2D1.1(b)(1) are also ineligible for early release. For information on the specific crimes that would preclude an inmate from an early release, *see* Program Statement §5162.04.

### §3:50.1  Ineligibility

Inmates who have a prior felony or misdemeanor conviction for:
- Homicide (including deaths caused by recklessness, but not including deaths caused by negligence or justifiable homicide);
- Forcible rape;
- Robbery;
- Aggravated assault;
- Arson;
- Kidnapping; or
- An offense that by its nature or conduct involves sexual abuse offenses committed upon minors.

Inmates who have a current felony conviction for:
- An offense that has as an element, the actual, attempted, or threatened use of physical force against the person or property of another;
- An offense that involved the carrying, possession, or use of a firearm or other dangerous weapon or explosives (including any explosive material or explosive devise);
- An offense that, by its nature or conduct, presents a serious potential risk of physical force against the person or property of another; or
- An offense that, by its nature or conduct, involves sexual abuse offense committed upon minors;
- Inmates who have been convicted of an attempt, conspiracy, or other offense which involved an underlying offense listed in paragraph (b) (4) and/or (b)(5) of this section; or
- Inmates who previously received an early release under 18 U.S.C. §3621.

## §3:50.2    Amount of Reduction

The Bureau has implemented a sliding scale for the amount of a sentence reduction: those serving 30 months or less are ineligible for more than a six-month reduction; those serving 31-36 months are ineligible for more than a nine-month reduction; and those serving 37 months or longer are eligible for the full 12 months. See P.S. 5331.02 §10. Additionally, certain sex offenders, in particular individuals convicted of possession of child pornography, are not automatically disqualified from §3621(e) eligibility.

## §3:60    RESIDENTAL DRUG ABUSE PROGRAM LOCATIONS

The Residential Drug Abuse Program (RDAP) is available at the following facilities:

NORTHEAST REGION
FCI Allenwood – Low (PA)
FCI Allenwood – Med (PA)
FCI Berlin (NH)
USP Canaan (PA)
FCI Danbury (CT)*
FCI Elkton (OH)
FCI Fairton (NJ)
FCI Fort Dix 1 (NJ)
FCI Fort Dix 2 (NJ)
FPC Lewisburg (PA)
FPC McKean (PA)
FCI Schuylkill (PA)

SOUTHEAST REGION
FCI Coleman (FL)
USP Coleman II (FL)
FPC Edgefield (SC)
FCI Jesup (GA)
FCI Marianna (FL)
FPC Miami (FL)
FCI Miami (FL)¤
FPC Montgomery (AL)
FPC Pensacola (FL)
FCI Talladega (AL)
FCI Tallahassee (FL)*
FCI Yazoo City (MS)

NORTH CENTRAL REGION
FPC Duluth (MN)
FCI Englewood (CO)
FPC Florence (CO)
FCI Florence (CO)
FPC Greenville (IL)*
FPC Leavenworth (KS)
USP Leavenworth (KS)
FCI Milan (MI)
USP Marion (IL)
FCI Oxford (WI)
FPC Pekin (IL)
FCI Sandstone (MN)
USMCFP Springfield (MO)◆
FCI Terre Haute (IN)
FCI Waseca (MN)*
FPC Yankton (SD)

MID-ATLANTIC REGION
FPC Alderson (WV)*
FPC Beckley (WV)
FCI Beckley (WV)
USP Big Sandy (KY)
FCI Butner (NC)
FPC Cumberland (MD)
FCI Cumberland (MD)
SFF Hazelton (WV)*
FCI Morgantown (WV)
FMC Lexington (KY)
FMC Lexington (KY)◆
FCI Petersburg – Low (VA)
FCI Petersburg – Med (VA)
FCI Memphis (TN)

SOUTH CENTRAL REGION
FCI Bastrop (TX)
FPC Beaumont (TX)
FCI Beaumont – Med (TX)
FCI Beaumont – Low (TX)
USP Beaumont (TX)
FPC Bryan (TX)*
FMC Carswell (TX)*♦
FMC Carswell (TX)*¤
FCI El Reno (OK)
FCI Forrest City - Low (AK)
FCI Forrest City - Med (AK)
FCI Fort Worth (TX)
FCI La Tuna (TX)
FCI Seagoville (TX)
FPC Texarkana (TX)

WESTERN REGION
FCI Dublin (CA)*
FPC Dublin (CA)*
FCI Herlong (CA)
FPC Lompoc (CA)
FPC Phoenix (AZ)*
FCI Phoenix (AZ)
FCI Safford (AZ)
FPC Sheridan (OR)
FCI Sheridan (OR)
FCI Terminal Island (CA)
FCI Terminal Island (CA)♦

CONTRACT FACILITY
RCI Rivers (NC)

KEY
FCI = Federal Correctional Institution
FMC = Federal Medical Center
FPC = Federal Prison Camp
FSL = Federal Satellite Low
MCFP = Medical Center for Federal Prisoners
USP = United States Penitentiary
RCI = Rivers Correctional Institution

* = Female Facility
♦ = Co-Occurring Disorder Program
¤ = Spanish

## ENDNOTES

- This chapter derives, in part, from: A. Ellis and T. Bussert, *Looking at the BOP's Amended RDAP Rules*, CRIMINAL JUSTICE (ABA Fall 2011); T. Bussert and H. Martin, *The Federal Bureau of Prisons* in DEFENDING A FEDERAL CRIMINAL CASE (Sarah Gannett, ed.) (Federal Defenders of San Diego, Inc. 2010); and T. Bussert and J. Sickler, *BOP Update: More Beds, Less Rehabilitation*, THE CHAMPION (NACDL March 2005).
- All BOP program statements mentioned in this article can be found on the Bureau's website, www.bop.gov.

(This page intentionally left blank.)

# CHAPTER 4

# HOW TO DO TIME

(This page intentionally left blank.)

# §4:10   QUESTIONS AND ANSWERS

The following information is from multiple interviews conducted between co-authors of the *Federal Prison Guidebook* Alan Ellis and J. Michael Henderson, supplemented by Phillip S. Wise, retired Bureau of Prisons Assistant Director, Health Services Division.

### §4:10.1   Initial Placement

[Alan Ellis] Q: Will each offender be placed at a particular federal prison of their choice, and close to their family?

[J. Michael Henderson] A: Initial placement of an offender is based upon an initial classification of the individual by the Bureau of Prisons, based on security and medical needs, with consideration for how crowded some institutions are, an offender's specialized program needs, legal residence, and court recommendations. Classification information is obtained from the Presentence Investigation Report (PSR), and so it is essential that the attorney and client ensure that the information is both accurate and complete as to his offenses conduct, prior record, open or pending cases, legal residence, physical and mental health, verifiable education level, and substance abuse, particularly if the offender wants to qualify for the Bureau's comprehensive Residential Drug Abuse Program (RDAP). Each offender is assigned a security level: minimum, low, medium, or high security, based on offense characteristics, sentence, and history. Each offender is also assigned a Medical Care Level (I, II, III, or IV) based on current or anticipated medical requirements, and a Mental Health Care Level, (1, 2, 3, or 4). These levels are discussed further in Chapter 8. The facility nearest the offender's legal residence as reflected in the PSR, that meets the security, medical and mental health requirements, and which has bed space available is generally designated for service of sentence. So, if the offender would like to be placed in a minimum-security camp that houses offenders who are considered medically and mentally stable, for example, but is classified by the Bureau of Prisons as low, medium, or high security, then the offender would not be initially assigned to a camp. Similarly, even if the offender qualifies for a minimum-security camp, but has significant medical and mental health issues, he would not initially be assigned to a camp without the resources to provide for the necessary medical care. Similarly, if an offender knows of a particular federal prison near their home, the offender will not likely be assigned there if his or her initial security level classification or medical care level determined by the Bureau of Prisons are not the same as the security level and care level of the institution. Finally, every new offender should know that the Bureau of Prisons currently houses a very large number of inmates, and can have extremely limited bed-space at some institutions, which can result in an offender's initial placement further from their homes than either they or the Bureau of Prisons would actually prefer. In such cases, a future transfer is a reasonable possibility after 18 months of clear conduct; *i.e.*, no disciplinary infractions, good work evaluations, and participation in the Inmate Financial Responsibility Program (if required).

## §4:10.2    What to Bring

Q: If an offender is granted self-surrender by the court, what should they take to prison?

A: It is usually best to arrive at a federal prison with as few personal possessions as possible because the offender is leaving his or her regular life and lifestyle for a while. Also, minimizing what one brings will lessen the possibility of confiscation by prison staff of unauthorized items, and reduce the amount of personal belongings that are returned or mailed back to the next of kin. That said, the individual should bring no single item worth over $100, meaning no expensive jewelry or wristwatch. A wedding band, if married, is fine, as well as a relatively inexpensive wristwatch and religious medal, if worn. The personal clothing the offender wears when reporting will be returned to the family or friends or attorney. I recommend that the offender report with only a relatively modest amount of money, no more than $360. Such an amount will permit some discretionary spending at the institution commissary and establishing a TRUFONE account to call home, thereby freeing the new inmate from having to rely on, or falling into debt to, other inmates. Caution should always be the watchword, should the new inmate encounter another "more experienced" inmate who "offers" to help purchase or buy something the new inmate cannot otherwise afford. Such offers can have illicit payment return terms that the new inmate is not prepared for, and can be dangerous! Similarly, if a new inmate arrives with a lot of money, other curious inmates can quickly become aware of it, which may result in the new inmate becoming a "target" by other inmates who would like little more than to get some of the new inmate's money.

In addition, we recommend that an offender take a one-month supply of any prescription medication. In all probability, the Bureau of Prisons will have the necessary medications on hand, and your supply will not be required, but if you take a medicine that is not currently routinely used by the Bureau of Prisons, your supply will allow plenty of time to get necessary approvals and pharmacy stock. Understand that any medications you take with you will likely be held for you in the Health Services Department, and dispensed from the pharmacy at "pill line."

Q: Many new offenders ask about how much money they will be able to have in their prison accounts, how much they can spend, and how they can receive money and other materials from their friends and families while they are confined. What is your response and/or advice?

A:   The money new inmates bring with them to prison, as mentioned above, will be used to open an inmate Trust Fund account for them, from which they will be required to pay for their personal telephone calls, postage stamps, and items from the commissary (personal hygiene items, snacks, etc.) which they might want to purchase. This really is the only preliminary information that a new offender needs prior to entering prison. Immediately after their arrival, as noted in the intake process remarks, inmates will have all of the answers governing procedural regulations given them in the prison's Admission & Orientation Inmate Manual. Also, as noted in the remarks about orientation, the new inmate will also receive all pertinent information directly from a staff member from the institution business office and/or commissary. Once armed with not only written information but information from prison staff members who run the Inmate Trust Fund accounts, the new inmate, within only one week or so after arriving, will have all the information needed regarding receiving funds, how they can be spent, and what restrictions and approvals are in place regarding receipt of anything from family or friends.

Q:   How about medications?

A:   The Bureau of Prisons typically prescribes medication via its formulary, which can be accessed via its website (*see* http://www.bop.gov/news/ PDFs/formulary.pdf and http://www.bop.gov/news/PDFs/formulary_ part2.pdf). New inmates can bring prescription (not over-the counter) medicine when reporting to serve a sentence, though it should be understood that all medication will be checked by institution medical staff and confiscated. If a particular medication is in the formulary, new medication will likely be issued to replace it. If medication is not in the formulary, it will be confiscated, and the new inmate will have to see medical staff concerning whether a substitute medication can or will be prescribed. To minimize the risk of disruption in receiving necessary medications, it is highly recommended that individuals with conditions managed by medication, particularly opiate-based medications, which the BOP is generally disinclined to prescribe, provide a copy of the BOP formulary to their prescribing physician(s) well in advance of sentencing to assess the suitability of substituting formulary medications for their existing medications. To the extent a medication can be substituted, it should be before an individual is placed in BOP custody. Similarly, where a formulary medication is not suitable substitution (*e.g.*, due to side effects, interaction with other medications), a letter should be obtained from the prescribing physician, attesting to that fact and efforts that were taken. It is important that an individual's PSR contain accurate information concerning name, purpose and dosage amounts of prescribed medications. In addition to prescription medication, the institution Commissary is required to carry a minimum of 25 over-the-counter medical products for inmate purchase.

Q:   What can a new inmate expect from staff upon arrival at a federal prison?

A: Upon arrival, the offender will be met by either a correctional officer or member of the Receiving and Discharge Department (R & D). A strip search, issue of institutional clothing, photograph, fingerprinting, and inventory of personal property will subsequently be performed in the R & D Department. If the offender arrives after normal working hours or when the R & D Department is not staffed, he or she will be taken to an area where a strip search will be conducted, issued institutional clothing, and likely placed in a secure cell until being processed for intake through R & D.

This process, as well as the R & D process, will be conducted in a very business-like manner, which for new inmates can seem impersonal. However, this is a good time for the new inmate to simply watch, listen, and learn about the staff and what they do.

### §4:10.3    Intake and Orientation

Q: Who are these staff, and what do they do during the intake process?

A: The R & D staff are those who perform the search, fingerprinting, and personal property inventory of the new arrival. A Correctional Counselor or a Case Manager will conduct a brief private interview. A Medical staff member, usually a Physician's Assistant, will conduct a medical screening (at which time the new inmate should report any and all health-related issues for the record, to better ensure proper future treatment if needed while incarcerated).

Q: What is most important for the inmate at this initial intake phase?

A: It is important for the inmate to understand that this is the business of incarceration, and to understand that prison staff members are not trying to be demeaning. It is also wise for the new arrival to listen carefully to any and all questions that the staff members ask, and to answer those questions honestly. If the new inmate does not understand a question, it is entirely appropriate to ask for clarification or meaning. Similarly, the new inmate should read and fully understand any and all forms that are provided, some for the inmate's signature. A failure in this early communication process could lead to potential difficulties at some future point of incarceration. Forms and information relative to telephone use, mail correspondence, and visiting are provided.

Q: Will the new inmate receive written rules and guidance before being placed in the general inmate population?

A: Yes. Upon arrival, each new inmate is given an Admission and Orientation (A & O) handbook, for which they must sign. I cannot overstate the importance of this document and the inmate's receipt of it with signature, because from that moment forward, the inmate will be held responsible for knowing and complying with all of the Bureau of Prisons' institutional rules outlined in it. The A & O handbook is thorough and describes the various institutional departments and staff, schedules for the inmate to follow within the institution, and visiting and correspondence information. The smartest action that a new inmate can take with respect to the A & O handbook is to read it, cover to cover, as soon as possible, and to keep it at hand for future reference.

Q: When does a new arrival enter the general inmate population?

A: Upon successful completion of the intake process. Successful completion means that the institution has received all necessary official documentation from the sentencing court, and from the respective U.S. Marshals and U.S. probation offices. Such documentation includes the Judgment Order, the Presentence Investigation Report, and appropriate U.S. Marshals documents. If such documentation is lacking or incomplete, it may not be possible for staff to allow the inmate to enter the general inmate population. The attorney and/or client should contact the Inmate Systems Management department (records office) at the facility designated prior to arrival to determine if the necessary documentation has been received. Similarly, if during the intake screening process some interviewing staff members identify a potential concern for the new inmate's health or safety, then the individual may not be put in the general inmate population. Finally, in situations where bed space at an institution to which an individual has been designated is very limited, there have been instances requiring that a new arrival be temporarily housed in administrative detention status, in the restricted Special Housing Unit of the institution, until bed space in the open inmate population becomes available.

Q: What is important for the inmate to know if not placed in the general inmate population, and what, if anything, will they be told?

A: It is important that the new arrival understand that most federal prisons do not lock their general inmate population up in isolated cells 24 hours per day, which means simply that inmates in that population are moving about. Given that fact, Bureau of Prisons' staff who are charged with ensuring an inmate's safety cannot and should not place a new arrival in the open inmate population, unless and until they have complete case documentation which, in conjunction with the intake interviews, provides reasonable assurance that the new inmate will not encounter an identifiable and undue risk if housed with the other inmates.

Also, the new arrival's health can be a concern. If, during the intake screening process, medical staff determine that the inmate may have a contagious disease, such as measles, chicken pox, or tuberculosis, that individual will likely be placed in medical isolation until necessary steps to protect him and the other inmates and staff have been completed.

If the new arrival cannot be placed in the institution's general inmate population because of insufficient or unreceived documentation, or for health reasons, he or she will be so informed. If a potential security risk to his or her safety or to the safety of others is identified by staff during the intake process, the new arrival may be given only limited information because such information cannot divulge sensitive or investigative details which the staff has or which the staff may need to pursue.

Q:  What happens when the new inmate is placed in the general inmate population, and what can the new arrival expect?

A:  The inmate will be assigned specific housing and will begin an Admission and Orientation period. The new arrival should expect during this period to meet his or her Case Manager, Correctional Counselor, and Unit Manager, all of whom compose the inmate's Unit Team. These are the key staff members with whom the inmate should become familiar, as they will have primary responsibility for managing almost every aspect of the inmate's case during confinement. The new arrival will also attend formal Admission and Orientation sessions, where staff members from every department in the institution will provide information and answer questions concerning all aspects of confinement.

At some point during the first two weeks, each newly arrived inmate is seen by a qualified medical staff member who takes a medical history and completes a physical examination. This is an excellent time to discuss with the medical provider any existing medical issues, history of treatment, known allergies, and medications. Any mental health issues, particularly those involving medications, should also be discussed with the medical provider at this time.

Q:  What is important for the new inmate during this orientation period?

A:  As mentioned earlier, it is most important for new inmates to read the A & O handbook they are issued. This will lay a foundation for the information that they will receive from several staff members at the Admission and Orientation sessions. Next, it is important for the new inmate to observe and to listen, keeping personal business to himself, rather than carelessly sharing it with other inmates, and to understand his or her own accountability for where to be at any given time in the institution.

Q:  Will the inmate be given a work assignment, what should they know about it, and what if the new inmate decides that he or she is not satisfied with their housing and/or work assignments?

A:  The new inmate may be given a temporary work assignment during the Admission and Orientation period, or may be assigned after completing it. It is important for new inmates to know that the initial work assignment they are given is based solely upon institutional need, rather than the inmate's personal preference. Therefore, they may be assigned what could be perceived as menial work, or work that is uninteresting to them. However, they will receive some monetary stipend for their work, and during the Orientation phase, they will see and hear from staff members about work assignments the inmate might find more interesting, and how to go about applying for those assignments.

With regard to their housing assignment, new inmates may be assigned to quarters with another inmate not of their choosing, and usually to an upper bunk bed. Through routine inmate movement and in meeting other inmates, it may be possible to discuss changing quarters assignments with a member of the Unit Team, usually the Correctional Counselor. Also, through seniority and clear conduct, an inmate can receive preferred quarters within a housing unit.

Q: In addition to quarters and work assignments, what other aspects will the new inmate learn about?

A: The new inmate will be told about how the custodial staff, or correctional officers, conduct their supervision of inmates; disciplinary processes; visiting privileges; mailroom services; sentence computation and earning of good time credit; educational services which include available classes, training, law and leisure libraries, and recreational activities; medical and mental health services; psychology programs; religious services; food service; payment of court-ordered fines and restitution; and release planning and preparation programs.

Q: Can new inmates "learn the ropes" from other inmates?

A: I suppose it may be inevitable for every new inmate to learn something about institutional rules, staff roles, and various aspects of prison life from other inmates. However, caution in this regard is needed because the only things a new inmate can know about another inmate is what the other inmate chooses to tell the new inmate. Potential pitfalls abound, and new inmates who wish to get through the process of incarceration successfully, without negative repercussions, and with an eye toward benefiting from all available programs for which they may qualify, should let the written Bureau of Prisons' regulations be their primary guide, rather than other inmates. Further, in understanding how the Bureau of Prisons' regulations are implemented and actually function, the inmate should rely primarily upon staff for clarification, as well as on information in the inmate law library at the institution. In determining which inmates to seek advice from, new inmates may consider speaking with inmates who work in the education department. Also, in attempting to decide on a possible work assignment, the new inmate can speak to other inmates who work in various departments, keeping in mind that information they receive will not override the information that is provided during the Admission & Orientation process. Finally, an inmate always has the right, throughout confinement, to obtain legal counsel, preferably from an attorney who is familiar with Bureau of Prisons' policies and procedures, and who is experienced in federal inmate-related matters.

## §4:10.4    Solving Problems

Q: What if a staff member seems unwilling to be helpful, is less than responsive to a problem, or does not seem open or straightforward in communicating with the inmate?

A: The inmate almost always has a Case Manager, Correctional Counselor, and Unit Manager available to them for assistance. In addition, every day the inmate goes to eat a meal, there are almost always staff members available to them in the dining area from all institutional departments, including upper management of the institution, which are the associate wardens and the warden. The availability of a wide range of staff members is important because Bureau of Prisons' staff members are human beings, meaning that some will be more effective communicators than others and some will be more thorough and patient than others. So, if an inmate is experiencing difficulty in dealing with a particular staff member, there are multiple other staff members who can address a problem.

Q: So, what if an inmate follows all of the rules and regulations but encounters a situation or has a problem that none of the institution staff, including the warden, can or will resolve?

A: This is likely to be a rare scenario; just because an inmate may not receive an answer to a question, or receive a response that is personally favorable, does not mean that staff have not responded and acted within the scope of Bureau of Prisons' policy. Sometimes, inmates mistakenly believe that because they do not receive action or a response they want, somehow the institution staff has mistreated them. This usually stems from incomplete or inefficient communication, lack of understanding Bureau of Prisons' policies and procedures, and inmates not speaking to all appropriate institution staff who could resolve a given dispute. That said, there is a procedure that is available to inmates, known as the Administrative Remedy Procedures, by which an inmate can request reconsideration of staff decisions and/or formal reviews of staff decisions at levels higher than the level at which the decision was made.

Q: What do the Administrative Remedy Procedures involve?

A: First, the inmate is required to make a meaningful attempt at informal resolution of a dispute. Then, if unsuccessful, the inmate can file an Administrative Remedy form, BP-9, to the warden. If this step fails to resolve the issue for the inmate, the inmate can then file an Administrative remedy form BP-10, to the Regional Office for the region in which the inmate is confined. If that process is unsatisfactory, the inmate may then file an Administrative remedy form BP-11, to the Bureau of Prisons Central Office in Washington. D.C., for the highest level of formal review. One of the most important things an inmate should consider, both in filing an Administrative Remedy complaint and reasonably expecting a positive result from the filing, is whether or not the staff action or decision which is being appealed was made within the authority and parameters of Bureau of Prisons' policies. If it was, there is little a formal review will accomplish, regardless of what other inmates may say. Conversely, review of appeals can involve careful scrutiny by Bureau of Prisons' legal staff as well. So, if a complaint involves a staff decision or action that was not made within the parameters of policy, the action or decision will be rectified for the inmate.

Q: What can an inmate anticipate in terms of maintaining clear conduct and open communication with staff, as you have stressed?

A: An inmate who conducts himself in an above-board manner at all times, in terms of both staff interaction and interactions with other inmates with whom they associate, generally will not attract extra scrutiny or suspicion. The inmate likely will receive favorable consideration for security and custody level reductions when eligible, which can result in placement in a less secure setting with less intense staff supervision and participation in community activities, if eligible. Earlier, I referenced that an offender who is initially assigned to a prison farther from their home than might be preferred could receive a future transfer to an institution closer to their home. It must be stressed that clear conduct is required in order for an inmate to receive such a transfer. Disciplinary action, on the other hand, can result in placement in a more restrictive setting, an upgrade in security level and custodial supervision, loss of good time, greater restrictions on visiting, unfavorable consideration for transfer to a prison closer to the inmate's home, not to mention loss of preferred quarters assignment and loss of eligibility for certain programs.

Q: What about problems with other inmates?

A: If there is a situational conflict or personality clash that is unlikely in the immediate short term to escalate into a physical altercation, then avoidance is always the best practice. For example, if the conflict is with a bunkmate, roommate, or co-worker, the inmate should tell the other person that he will request a bed, room or work assignment change, which he can do through the Correctional Counselor or a work supervisor. It may not seem fair, especially when tempers flare, but it is the best way to conduct one's self above-board and not get into disciplinary trouble. If an inmate encounters a more serious threat or intimidation that is likely to escalate into a serious conflict, or the threat of being hurt, then there are steps that can and should be taken, again, however, with avoidance being the key. As mentioned previously, there are many different staff members with whom an inmate will become familiar and interact on a regular basis. I strongly recommend that an inmate work to develop a positive and respectful working relationship with as many staff members as possible, though not being overly friendly, which can draw adverse reaction from other inmates. Then, if a potentially violent threat arises, the inmate can and should confide in a staff member that he trusts and who knows him. Such a staff member can be anyone—the Unit Officer, the Case Manager, a work supervisor, a Lieutenant, a staff teacher, etc. Every staff member in a Federal Bureau of Prisons facility is considered, first and foremost, to be a correctional worker; their primary jobs, regardless of their specialty area of work, is the institution and inmate security.

Q: Some inmates have court-ordered fines, criminal penalty assessments, or restitution. Will these need to be paid for from the same Inmate Trust

Fund account that is used for personal spending in the institution while the offender is confined? If so, what can the new inmate expect?

A:   Possibly, yes. The payment of court-directed fines or fees will be dependent upon how the court order is written. Some fines and/or fees, for example, might be imposed strictly as a condition of the offender's supervised release, after incarceration. Some court orders do not distinguish. The information is contained in the court's Judgment and Commitment (J & C) order that is also used to impose sentence, and so it could benefit the offender to review that document closely, and with his or her attorney, for any needed clarification. After arrival at a federal prison, institution staff will review the J & C and, if payment is required during confinement, they will discuss payment options with the inmate. When an installment-type of payment plan is needed, the inmate and the Unit team can set up a payment schedule, which can involve regular fixed withdrawals from the inmate's Trust Fund Account. The Bureau of Prisons' term for this is the Inmate Financial Responsibility Program (IFRP), and the new inmate should understand that the Bureau of Prisons is quite serious in its administration of the program, to the point that there can be serious repercussions if prison staff determine that an inmate is not making a meaningful effort at satisfying court-imposed financial obligations. Sanctions that the bureau can impose for failure, which they call refusal, to make measurable progress in a payment plan can include loss of a preferred housing assignment, reduction of pay for an inmate's work assignment, and exclusion from programs for which the inmate may otherwise be qualified, including furloughs and halfway house placement.

## §4:10.5    For Family Members

Q:   What can you tell family members about some prison issues that they might be concerned with? Let's start with visiting.

A:   The new inmate will receive a copy of visiting regulations and forms to send his family, which need to be completed and returned in order to visit. The family must understand that it is imperative for them to answer the questions on the visiting forms accurately and honestly because failure to do so may result in a loss or denial of visiting privileges. For example, a family member who has a prior court conviction of any type, even if given probation, should report it matter-of-factly on the appropriate section of the visiting form. A background check by the Bureau of Prisons will uncover this and if it has been intentionally omitted, may result in denying visiting rights.

New inmates will be given a copy of their approved visiting list, usually by their assigned Correctional Counselor. Families should ensure that they are approved prior to traveling to the prison to visit. It's helpful if the family can prepare for visiting by viewing a federal prison as a serious and controlled setting, and not a place of emotional warmth. There are no private and/or unsupervised visits with family members in Bureau of Prisons' facilities. However, families can be somewhat relieved in knowing that the majority of visiting rooms are open ones, without the glass partitions and telephones for communicating so often depicted in television and movie dramas. Inmates are permitted to kiss and embrace at the beginning and conclusion of a visit. Some facilities even provide outdoor visiting areas when the weather permits. Family members should be prepared for being subjected to search procedures and supervision when visiting. Such scrutiny is necessary because, unfortunately, one of the ways illegal drugs and other types of contraband are smuggled into prisons is by visitors, including family visitors. Therefore, it is recommended that family visitors bring very little with them into the prison, giving nothing to their incarcerated loved one, other than change which can be spent on the inmate at the vending machines in the visiting room. After being cleared into the Visiting Room, family visitors will be expected to conduct themselves appropriately at all times, meaning they should avoid any conduct which might make correctional staff suspicious, especially excessive physical contact. It is important to understand and appreciate the fact that a prison visiting room is a serious setting.

Another important factor that the family should be prepared for is the possibility of early termination of their visit, should the visiting room become crowded. This can and does happen to enable other inmates to receive visits. This can be an emotionally difficult situation for both the inmate and the family, so it's important to remember that early visit termination due to crowding will be an impartial and necessary decision by prison staff. Arguing with prison staff will not improve or change the decision. In fact, in order to maintain visiting privileges, all visitors are expected to comply with prison staff at all times. The Bureau of Prisons holds the inmate accountable if a visitor fails to follow regulations or comply with staff instructions.

Finally, the family should know that while their loved one is serving a sentence in a federal prison, misconduct that results in the receipt of a written Incident Report may be sanctioned by the loss of visitation privileges, even if the misconduct was not related to visiting. The reason for this is because the Bureau of Prisons expects clear conduct, if the inmate is to be permitted full privileges, and because receiving visits is meant to be a motivating factor to help an inmate maintain clear conduct. With this understanding, the family can reiterate the importance of visiting to the inmate. Should the inmate incur misconduct sanctions that include a temporary loss of visitation, rather than being angry at the Bureau of Prisons, the family will be better served by helping their loved one understand that family visitation is a priority and worth clear conduct behavior.

Q: Are family members also subjected to security measures with regard to written correspondence and telephone calls?

A: Family members should clearly understand that telephone calls and e-mails they receive from an inmate are subject to monitoring and recording for security, and that their incoming postal mail will be opened and screened. Therefore, what they say and what they write should always be above board and appropriate. Further, the family also needs to know that an inmate is prohibited under Bureau of Prisons' regulations from conducting a business while confined. So, telephone, e-mail, and written correspondence must not involve such prohibited conduct. Finally, the family should be strongly cautioned against making 3-way, or third-party calls, after the inmate has connected with them telephonically, because this, too, is prohibited by the Bureau of Prisons. Such calls are generally viewed by the bureau as circumventing telephone regulations, which are reasonable, since inmates are allowed a large number of people on their authorized telephone lists, which can be frequently modified.

Q: Since you earlier referenced the disciplinary process, what should the family know about the prison disciplinary process?

A: As already mentioned, the new inmate will receive a full and comprehensive list of Bureau of Prisons' rules and regulations which includes all prohibited acts immediately upon arrival at a federal prison. Therefore, the family should understand that there is usually very little excuse for an offender's claim that they may not have known they were violating a rule. Also, the family should understand that Bureau of Prisons' staff are generally much too busy with daily routines to write disciplinary reports against an inmate simply because the staff member "dislikes" the inmate. In fact, the formal disciplinary process requires an eyewitness staff account of an inmate's prohibited conduct, further investigation by a Correctional Supervisor, and then review with the inmate in person by a Unit Team staff member and, later, if referred by the Unit Team, by a Disciplinary Hearing Officer (DHO). The process leaves very little room for the personal likes or dislikes of a single staff member. The family should realize that the institution's DHO is virtually autonomous as an independent department within the institution. Finally, even if found guilty of an act, the inmate has an appeal process whereby all disciplinary proceedings are reviewed at administrative levels higher than the institution's.

## §4:10.6    Medical Care

Q: What should the family understand about medical care in the Bureau of Prisons?

A: The family should understand that when an offender is sentenced to serve a federal prison term, the Bureau of Prisons must assume all responsibility for medical care. Therefore, their personal doctor will not be able to continue treating the inmate, and neither will the new inmate or family have a choice in selecting a medical provider. Each Bureau of Prisons facility has at least one licensed physician on staff, and most frequently, those physicians specialize in family practice or internal medicine. Many are board certified in their specialty areas, as well. The medical services are extended by use of mid-level providers, usually Physician's Assistants or Nurse Practitioners who will generally provide the initial evaluation of a medical concern. However, if necessary, a physician or specialist from the community will also be available.

As mentioned earlier, it is a good idea to bring a month's supply of any prescription medications if possible. This will ensure an initial supply of your medicine until you are examined by a Bureau of Prisons physician and longer term arrangements are made.

The standard of medical care provided in the Bureau of Prisons is based on the standard of medical care provided in the community, and regular review and accreditation of the medical practices within facilities is required. The Bureau of Prisons policy is to provide medically neces-sary care. This means that any medical care determined by Bureau of Prisons staff to be medically necessary will be provided, but treatment that might be medically appropriate but not always necessary, may not be provided. For example, some hernia repairs or repair of old, existing orthopedic issues that do not significantly interfere with daily living may be deferred.

The medical staffing can vary from one federal prison to another, and offenders whose needs cannot be managed at one might be placed in another, which may mean a move further from their families. Families should be as supportive as possible under such circumstances, know-ing that the health of their loved one should supersede proximity to the family. Also, the family should know that many prison facilities augment their medical care with doctors from the community, usually specialists, on a contract basis. These consulting specialists are avail-able if Bureau of Prisons staff determine that a specialty consultation is required, and any recommendations made by a consulting specialist will be evaluated by a Bureau of Prisons physician for compliance with the agency's scope of service.

Of course, the Bureau of Prisons has some institutions which are strictly for in-patient medical care and surgery, if needed. The hardest part for the family, I believe, is not having a choice in the health care of their loved one during confinement. But focusing on the positives of the Bureau of Prisons' system can help, even if that system is more impersonal to the inmate than private medical practice is. Finally, the family can be assured that each Bureau of Prisons Region has a Regional Health Services Administrator, who is usually open to knowing about serious and significant health care concerns, should an inmate believe medical needs are not being adequately addressed. [*See* Chapter 7, Medical Care in the Bureau of Prisons, for more information.]

### §4:10.7    Unit Management

Q:  How will an inmate interact with BOP staff in prison?
A:  The mission of the Unit Team is to determine an inmate's program needs, monitor the inmate's progress, and encourage positive interaction between inmates, staff, victims, families and the community at large. The offices of most Unit Team members are located directly in or adjacent to the inmate housing unit. The Unit Team consists of a Unit Manager, Case Manager, Correctional Counselor, Unit Officer, and Unit Secretary. There are also assigned Education and Psychology representatives. Each team member has a specific role and works closely with each other. It is imperative inmates develop and maintain a positive relationship with members of their Unit Team. These relationships can make or break a program in no time. Maintaining a positive approach to change and working with the Unit Team toward inmate program goals will help establish a mutual level of respect and understanding. Inmates are expected to work through their difficulties, with the guidance of staff when necessary. However, because Unit Teams have large inmate caseloads to manage, those inmates who insist on consuming larger and disproportionate amounts of staff time tend to alienate both staff and other inmates. Under such circumstances, the relationship between inmates and the Unit Team is not enhanced, and an inmate's ability to get along successfully with other inmates can become problematic. Observing a Unit Team member's "open house" hours of availability, making reasonable requests, and working toward established goals will aid inmates in doing their time with the support of their team.

Unit Manager: The role of Unit Managers is very diverse. They direct and manage the housing unit and its programs. They are responsible for the security, sanitation, and operations of the unit. They also are responsible for planning, developing and implementing programs geared toward the unit's inmate population. They directly supervise the other members of the team and serve as a department head. Unit Managers are often responsible for more than one housing unit and up to 500 inmates. Unit Managers chair Unit Team meetings and inmate program reviews, and oversee disciplinary processes. Unit Managers are accessible to the inmate population and post their hours of availability, known as "open house" hours, and are available in the inmate dining room during meals. They also work some evenings and occasional weekend hours, adding to their accessibility. Unit Managers are often the first line of contact for members of the community, family, attorneys, and other law enforcement agencies who require referral to the appropriate Unit Team member. Inmates are advised to address individual concerns to the appropriate Unit Team member, seeking assistance from the Unit Manager after all other avenues have been attempted. The Unit Manager is also the conduit for contact with the institution's executive staff. Inmates who fail to address issues with the Unit Team first, advising the Unit Manager, and seek redress from executive staff will often be turned back to start at the lowest level.

Case Manager: Case Managers develop, evaluate, and analyze the program needs of inmates. They monitor the progress of individual inmates toward meeting program goals, adjusting as necessary. They coordinate and integrate inmate training programs, develop social histories, and evaluate an inmate's positive and negative behaviors. Case Managers are responsible for evaluating an inmate's security and custody classification and appropriately referring inmates for transfer if their security or custody levels change. Case Managers are also responsible for assisting with release planning through the development of a strong release plan, work and education opportunities, family integration, and finally, halfway house placement. Case Managers rely heavily on the Presentence Report for historical information, as well as the Statement of Reasons in the Judgment and Commitment Order. In sum, Case Managers are responsible for the long-term goal planning, treatment, evaluation, monitoring and release planning of the inmates in their care. They work closely with the U.S. Probation Office, especially during the release phase. Case Managers hold open house hours and are available during evenings and weekends. Case Managers are notoriously busy individuals who dedicate themselves to their ever-changing case load. It is strongly recommended that all issues be presented during regularly scheduled team meetings or during established open house hours. It is important that inmates maintain a positive and honest relationship with their Case Manager. Inaccuracies, stretches of truth and incomplete information can derail a program or a release plan, sometimes resulting in no opportunity for additional referral.

Counselor: Correctional Counselors address the day-to-day issues facing inmates. They assign work, make bed/cell/room assignments, coordinate visiting, and handle any money, phone, mail, or property issues. They monitor sanitation in the housing unit, as well as maintain supplies and materials needed. They coordinate and facilitate appropriate counseling groups on a regular basis, geared toward a self-help topic of interest for the current population. Counselors are an integral member of the Unit Team and have specific input during inmate program reviews. They report on the inmate's sanitation, work performance, participation in the Financial Responsibility Program, and present any educational or vocational issues. Counselors often spend a vast amount of their time in the housing unit, monitoring and observing inmate behavior, as well as addressing sanitation and program needs. Counselors are often the first person an inmate should seek for assistance.

Unit Officer: The Unit Officers work directly for the Correctional Services Department, maintaining the safety and security of the housing unit. They are the primary enforcers of discipline within the housing units. They are also an important part of the Unit Team, providing necessary information about an inmate's behavior, demeanor, and interactions within the unit. They assist with sanitation inspections, bed assignments, and orientation. They, too, can address many of the day-to-day issues that inmates encounter, often in conjunction with the Correctional Counselor. They are welcome to participate in inmate program review meetings and observe other sessions as appropriate.

Unit Secretary: Inmates generally have minimal contact with the Unit Secretary, except during the final release planning phase when travel arrangements are made. Secretaries work directly for the Unit Manager and have specific duties that relate to the overall benefit of the team. Some Secretaries address inmates directly during distribution of legal mail, as a member of the Unit Disciplinary Committee, while conducting census counts, or assisting with correctional duties. As a whole, they are not required to maintain open house hours and are not at the service of the inmates. But, they are a vital part of the team and provide important input during team decisions regarding inmates.

Education and Psychology Representative: Each Unit Team is assigned a representative from the Education and Psychology departments. These assigned individuals are the direct contact for inmates in their departments. They will meet with the inmate shortly after arrival to establish any goals or required program participation. If there are issues requiring further meetings, the unit representative will continue to offer assistance. They often attend program review meetings or provide valuable input for open discussion during the meeting. The Counselor will present any educational information necessary after conferring with the unit representative. As with other staff, Education and Psychology Services have established and posted open house hours, in addition to an emergency contact.

## §4:10.8    Release Planning

Q: How early can an inmate be released?

A: Prior to final release, inmates can become eligible for visits to their homes and communities with social furloughs. To qualify for an unescorted social furlough, inmates must be, and remain classified as, minimum security. Additionally, they must have been assigned to what is known as Community Custody, which is the very lowest supervision assignment in the Bureau of Prisons. The inmate must have maintained clear conduct and otherwise conducted themselves appropriately during confinement, as observed and judged by staff, not according only to the inmate's self-report or accounting (this is important!). Social furlough eligibility is further contingent upon how much time the offender has remaining to serve, since furloughs cannot occur early in the sentence. Initially, there can be one-day furloughs, and subsequently, as the sentence is served, there can be overnight furloughs. The Bureau of Prisons places restrictions on the frequency, and the inmate bears the cost, of social furloughs. Other possible furloughs can be granted under extraordinary circumstances, such as admission to a community hospital or to attend the funeral of an immediate family member, and sometimes for specially defined and regulated legal or religious functions. These are granted on a case-by-case basis, and always require minimum-security classification and clear conduct. Generally, an inmate will not be eligible for a furlough until s/he has been at the facility for 24 months with clear conduct. Finally, is important for every new offender to understand that there is no "entitlement" to unescorted social furloughs while they are serving their sentence, or to halfway house placement before the conclusion of the sentence. With that understanding, there is then the matter of technical eligibility for these programs, and the fact that technical eligibility does not mean an automatic approval in all cases.

Pre-release halfway house placement, known by the Bureau of Prisons as placement in a Residential Reentry Center (RRC, formerly called a Community Correctional Center, or CCC), is a program that is widely utilized for as many inmates as possible. The general time an inmate will be approved for RRC placement will range from 30 days to, in some cases, six months. In extraordinary cases, it may be as much as 12 months. No inmate should consider RRC placement as a means of early release from prison nor a reward for good behavior, nor that a lengthy RRC placement will be likely. The Bureau of Prisons contracts with private agencies for halfway house space, therefore one factor for placement is federal funding (regardless of how many available beds a particular halfway house says it has). Another factor will be the length of time an individual has served, because RRC placement is provided for transition back to community life from confinement, and offenders who serve long sentences generally need greater transitional assistance. Other factors considered by Bureau staff in determining RRC placement for an offender are the nature and quality of family and community ties and the inmate's conduct during confinement. There are some offenders who, because of the crime they committed, will be excluded from RRC placement. However, most offenders will receive the benefit of some RRC placement.

Release planning ultimately begins at the time of initial classification. Staff will continually address release residence, employment opportunities, community support, assistance programs, identification, financial support, and any goals toward reaching a viable release plan. Not every inmate will have a residence to go to, or financial and community support. Very few do, which is why planning as early as possible for release is essential. Inmates are required to complete a six-phase Release Preparation Program (RPP) prior to release. They should enroll in the RPP no later than 30 months prior to direct release to the community or through a Residential Reentry Center (RRC). However, inmates are encouraged to participate in RPP courses throughout their confinement. Inmates serving sentences of 30 months or less should consider immediate enrollment. There are six core topics presented during RPP: Health and Nutrition; Employment; Personal Finance/Consumer Skills; Information/Community Resources; Release Requirements and Procedures; and Personal Growth and Development. It is up to the individual instructor(s) to determine the length and amount of participation. For example, the Employment course may include a mock job fair with prerequisite classes in interview skills, resume writing, etc. Some courses may have an outside guest for a one-hour program. Remember, participation is required and failure to complete RPP may result in exclusion from program participation, which includes a halfway house. Begin early, participate earnestly, and be proactive with your future.

Approximately 13-17 months from release, the Unit Team should discuss Release and Reentry Center (RRC) placement with you. While there are limitations and exclusions, the majority of inmates are reviewed for some time in an RRC, either pre- or post-release. The greater placement lengths should be reserved for those with the greatest need and minimal resources. While viewed by many as an early-out option, RRC placement is restrictive, program-oriented, and under the same disciplinary rules and regulations as an institution. The Unit Team will evaluate the needs of the inmate and make an appropriate recommendation to the Community Corrections' officials. It is only a recommendation; usually a range of days for placement (*i.e.*, 90-120 days). Again, in some cases it can be even as much as six months and in extraordinary situations, as long as twelve months. Once notified of a placement date, travel planning and release procedures will begin.

## §4:10.9    Final Advice

Q:  Do you have any final words of advice?
A:  Let me offer the three most important pieces of advice that I can to the offender who will be going to a federal prison facility for the first time: First, the federal court proceedings and, ultimately, sentencing to prisons, has likely taken a very serious toll on the offender and his or her family psychologically, emotionally, and often financially. When the time for confinement finally arrives, which suspends the individual's freedom and separates him or her from family, it sometimes happens that the offender and/or family will vent frustrations on or toward the Bureau of Prisons. It is important to keep the perspective, however, that

the Bureau of Prisons is not responsible for the current circumstances. Ultimately, it will not be the Bureau of Prisons' responsibility to re-build lives or relationships, although there are prison programs and counseling that can be beneficial. Straight thinking in this regard can empower the offender and family, to help them avoid the non-productive trap of feeling as though they are victims.

Second, the offender would be well-advised to keep important personal information about themselves and their families confidential, period! This does not mean being so secretive as to arouse the suspicions of other inmates. But it should be painfully obvious that there are real criminals in federal prisons, and becoming vulnerable to these criminals will only complicate life for the well-meaning inmates who truly wish to serve their sentences with as little hassle as possible. Well-meaning inmates can be conned, their family's privacy and well-being compromised, and life seriously disrupted, if they are too friendly with the wrong inmates.

Last but not least, humility, clear conduct, and an understanding that federal prison, while offering a variety of programs and activities, may be an experience of some drudgery. There are no "entitlements," which should help the offender appreciate freedom and family even more. With self-reliance and keeping the "big picture" in mind, the offender can focus on the confinement term and returning home and staying out of prison. There is no sounder advice than this.

## ENDNOTES
- All BOP program statements mentioned in this chapter can be found on the Bureau's web site, www.bop.gov

(This page intentionally left blank.)

# CHAPTER 5

---

# PRE-RELEASE

(This page intentionally left blank.)

## §5:10  INTRODUCTION

Pre-release placement refers to the latter stages of a prisoner's sentence, when the Bureau of Prisons (BOP) begins to prepare the prisoner for reintegration into society through designation to a halfway house (also known as Residential Reentry Center (RRC), formerly known as Community Corrections Center) and/or home confinement. The general purpose of pre-release placement is to assist those with transitional needs in establishing a foothold in the community before being discharged from BOP custody. Although the law provides for 12 months' pre-release placement, the norm is no more than six months, with less time afforded those serving shorter sentences and/or possessing greater personal and community resources.

## §5:20  BRIEF HISTORY

The nation's largest correctional system, the BOP traditionally used community-based facilities as places of imprisonment for qualified inmates based on individualized placement and programming needs. In the mid-1960s, following enactment of the Prisoner Rehabilitation Act, the BOP expanded halfway house use for those needing substance abuse treatment and, later, for any prisoner who might benefit from and be safely managed in structured community-based confinement. Then BOP Director Myrl E. Alexander emphasized that reentry support was central to the agency's mission of preparing "our clientele for community adjustment rather than adjustment to probation or to the correctional institution."

Community corrections grew through the 1970s and 1980s, becoming a standard component of the BOP's overall range of placement options. Congress expressly provided for BOP's use of residential treatment centers as places of imprisonment in 18 U.S.C. §§4082(a), (c) and reaffirmed the agency's designation responsibilities in promulgating the Sentencing Reform Act of 1984 (SRA). Through 18 U.S.C. §3621(b), Congress authorized BOP to "designate the place of the prisoner's imprisonment" at "any available penal or correctional facility that meets minimum standards of health and habitability." In 1985, BOP's general counsel issued a legal opinion interpreting the phrase "penal or correctional facility" in section 3621(b) as coincident with "institution or facility" in the former 18 U.S.C. §4082(a).

In 1990, the statutory definition of "imprisonment" expanded to include home confinement when employed at the end of a prisoner's sentence. 18 U.S.C. §3624(c). Shortly after the enactment of §3624(c), which limits home confinement to the final 10 percent of a prisoner's sentence, the BOP issued a written policy statement that announced its intention to "promote greater use of community corrections programs for low risk offenders." The BOP acknowledged that "[t]here is no statutory limit on the amount of time inmates may spend in CCCs [Community Corrections Centers]" and instructed that, "[u]nless the warden determines otherwise, minimum security inmates will ordinarily be referred [for CCC placement at the end of their sentences] for a period of 120 to 180 days."

The Department of Justice's Office of Legal Counsel (OLC) upheld the bureau's analysis and flexible use of CCCs in a 1992 legal opinion:

> There is . . . no basis in section 3621(b) for distinguishing between residential community facilities and secure facilities. Because the plain language of section 3621(b) allows BOP to designate 'any available penal or correctional facility,' we are unwilling to find a limitation on that designation authority based on legislative history. Moreover, the subsequent deletion of the definition of 'facility' further undermines the argument that Congress intended to distinguish between residential community facilities and other kinds of facilities.

USDOJ-OLC, *Statutory Authority to Contract With the Private Sector for Secure Facilities*, 16 Op.OLC 65 (1992).

The BOP discussed its halfway house usage practices in a 1994 report to Congress, explaining that, in keeping with the objective of housing prisoners "in the least restrictive environment consistent with correctional needs," it had created a two-part community corrections model that differentiated between those designated to halfway houses to serve their entire sentences and those placed there in preparation for reentry. The report described a "community corrections component" used for direct commitments that was "sufficiently punitive to be a legitimate sanction, meeting the needs of the court and society, yet allowing the offender to undertake other responsibilities, such as participation in work, substance abuse education, and community service." The prerelease component, on the other hand, was for those nearing the ends of their sentences—ordinarily not to exceed six months—to "assist offenders in making the transition from an institutional setting to the community . . ."

The BOP's view of sanctioned halfway house usage remained constant in all versions of its official written policy statements. The most recent program statement, Program Statement 7310.04, which was promulgated in 1998, provides: "[T]he Bureau is not restricted by §3624(c) in designating a CCC for an inmate and may place an inmate in a CCC for more than the 'last ten per centum of the term,' or more than six months, if appropriate. Section 3624(c), however, does restrict the Bureau in placing inmates on home confinement."

The BOP's pre-release practices remained relatively constant until December 2002, when, as directed by the Justice Department, it implemented a much more restrictive view. The resultant litigation produced a substantial body of case law declaring the policy change unlawful. *See, e.g., Levine v. Apker*, 455 F.3d 71, 77-78 (2nd Cir. 2006); *Woodall v. Federal Bureau of Prisons*, 432 F.3d 235 (3rd Cir. 2005). In the midst of the litigation, the BOP began referring to halfway houses as Residential Reentry Centers (RRCs) while making clear that the name change "will not effect existing facilities . . . [W]e have used the terms halfway house and CCC synonymously for years and now we can add RRC." Stuart Rowles, 48 Community Update: Notes to BOP's Local Partners 1 (May 2006).

Through the Second Chance Act of 2007 (Public Law 110-199, Apr. 9, 2008), Congress restored and expanded historic norms. Congress directed the BOP to ensure that each federal prisoner serve a portion of his term of imprisonment, not to exceed one year, "under conditions that will afford that prisoner into the community. Such conditions may include a community correctional facility." 18 U.S.C. §3624(c)(1).

## §5:30    PRE-RELEASE FOLLOWING
##          THE SECOND CHANCE ACT

Section 3621(b) requires the BOP to consider certain factors when making any designation decision, including pre-release placement decisions. They include offender-specific variables such as "the history and characteristics of the prisoner," "the nature and circumstances of the offense," and sentencing courts' statements concerning a sentence's purpose or facility recommendations. In addition to these statutory factors, BOP personnel must also account for the controlling program statement (Program Statement 7310.04) and operations memoranda. *See* D. Scott Dodrill, *Revised Guidance for Residential Reentry Center (RRC) Placements* (June 24, 2010) (setting forth guiding criteria; *see* §6:40). Other factors thus considered are available halfway house bed space, which is usually at a premium; length of time an individual has served, with a presumption that individuals serving longer sentences have greater need given the amount of time they have been away from the community; the nature and quality of family and community ties, with stronger ties indicating less need; and an inmate's conduct during confinement. In short, pre-release placement, and the programming and community access it provides, is intended to reduce the risk of recidivism, meaning that priority is given to those inmates who present as posing a greater risk to re-offend upon completion of their sentences.

There are some offenders who, because of the crime they committed, will be excluded from pre-release placement. However, most prisoners will receive the benefit of some pre-release placement (RRC and/or home confinement), though not likely the full year that Congress contemplated. The BOP has tended to limit placements to the final six months of a given prisoner's sentence, with a growing emphasis on maximizing home confinement for those prisoners lacking transitional need (*i.e.*, those with a home, financial resources and/or a waiting job). One suggested method to assist a client in receiving the maximum allowable pre-release placement time is to have the court expressly recommend it in the judgment order.

An inmate's release plan, including a decision regarding halfway house or home confinement referral, is to be completed 17-to-19 months prior to his projected release date. That said, release planning begins at the time of initial classification. Usually at a prisoner's periodic program review, staff will address pre-release considerations, including release residence, employment opportunities, community support, assistance programs, identification, financial support, and any goals toward reaching a viable release plan. Not every inmate will have a residence to go to, or financial and community support. Most do not, which is why planning as early as possible for release is essential.

Inmates are required to complete a six-phase Release Preparation Program (RPP) in which they should enroll no later than 30 months prior to direct release to the community or prior to transfer to an RRC. However, inmates are encouraged to participate in RPP courses throughout their confinement. Inmates serving sentences of 30 months or less should consider immediate enrollment. There are six core topics presented during RPP: Health and Nutrition; Employment; Personal Finance/Consumer Skills; Information/Community Resources; Release Requirements and Procedures; and Personal Growth and Development. It is up to the individual instructor(s) to determine the length and amount of participation. For example, the Employment course may include a mock job fair with prerequisite classes in interview skills, resume writing, etc. Some courses may have an outside guest speaker for a one-hour program. Participation is required and failure to complete RPP may result in exclusion from program participation, which includes transfer to a halfway house.

It is a prisoner's Unit Team that prepares his release plan and pre-release package, the latter being sent to the BOP Residential Reentry Manager (RRM), who oversees the judicial district to which the prisoner is being referred, for final approval. For instance, where the Unit Team recommends a period of pre-release confinement, usually a range of days, the RRM is most familiar with available bed space and the transitional needs with which other potential halfway house residents present, meaning the RRM may authorize less time than the institution believes appropriate. Also, issues that can delay the referral and transfer process include the receiving district's Probation Office's inspection of the release residence, the inability to secure a promise to pay for medical care for those inmates lacking health insurance, and resolution of outstanding charges. Once notified of a placement date, travel planning and release procedures begin.

Every halfway house resident is required to maintain gainful employment and to contribute a percentage of their earnings towards the cost of his/her bed. To the extent that a halfway house permits residents to drive their own motor vehicles to work (subject to RRM approval), the resident must be prepared and able to provide a copy of a valid driver's license, automobile registration, and an insurance certificate indicating the resident as a named insured. Similarly, where a cell phone is a necessary tool of employment, the RRM can authorize use, upon receipt of a letter from the employer establishing the need. RRC residents cannot be self-employed nor can they work for family-owned businesses. The strong preference is for residents to work for a business with a permanent location, with a manager amenable to responding to inquiries from the halfway house operator concerning the resident (for example, work site visits, random phone calls).

As time progresses and a resident develops a track record with the halfway house operator, s/he may gain great privileges. Most notably, usually after providing the RRC with two pay stubs (which indicates the importance of finding an employer who pays weekly), a resident will be granted a 'day pass' permitting travel home during daylight hours on a Saturday or Sunday. Assuming all continues to go well, thereafter the resident can expect to begin receiving 'weekend passes' that allow for release from the halfway house from Friday evening to late Sunday afternoon.

For those inmates who do not need the services of a halfway house (*i.e.*, inmates unlikely to be employed in the community, due to factors like retirement or disability), direct commitment to home confinement is authorized for up to ten percent of one's sentence, not to exceed six months. While policy does permit *direct* placement on home confinement, the BOP typically requires that prisoners transition through a halfway house, which can last from a few hours to several days depending on the district and the halfway house. This type of home confinement, unlike home confinement as a condition of pre-sentence release, does not include electronic monitoring.

In closing, we emphasize that while viewed by many as an early-out option (*i.e.*, the end of one's term of imprisonment), pre-release placement is restrictive, program oriented, and subject to the same disciplinary rules and regulations as an institution. Violations of pre-release rules most often result in immediate placement in the local federal pre-trial holding facility, the loss of Good Conduct Time credits, and, depending on the amount of time remaining to serve, transfer back to the correctional institution from which the prisoner was referred.

A listing and a map of Residential Reentry facilities contracted with the BOP can be found at the following web site:

http://www.bop.gov/about/facilities/residential_reentry_management_centers.jsp

## §5:40    REVISED GUIDANCE FOR RRC PLACEMENT MEMO

**U.S. Department of Justice**

Federal Bureau of Prisons

---

*Washington, DC 20534*

June 24, 2010

MEMORANDUM FOR CHIEF EXECUTIVE OFFICERS

FROM:          D. Scott Dodrill, Assistant Director
               Correctional Programs Division

SUBJECT:       Revised Guidance for Residential Reentry Center
               (RRC) Placements

This memorandum provides guidance to staff when making inmates'
pre-release Residential Reentry Center (RRC) placement decisions.
Assessment and decision-making practices are to focus on RRC
placement as a mechanism to reduce recidivism.  Recidivism
reduction results in cost efficiencies, less victimization, and
safer communities.

Our RRC resources are limited and must be focused on those
inmates most likely to benefit from them in terms of anticipated
recidivism reduction.  In other words, our decisions are to be
based on an assessment of the inmate's risk of recidivism and our
expectation that RRC placement will reduce that risk.  Our
strategy is to focus on inmates who are at higher risk of
recidivating and who have established a record of programming
during incarceration, so that pre-release RRC placements will be
as productive and successful as possible.

As Chief Executive Officers, you play a vital role in
implementing the Bureau of Prisons' (Bureau) reentry strategy,
including RRC utilization.  This guidance will assist you in
making RRC placement decisions.

**GENERAL CONCEPTS** - The following general concepts apply to all
RRC placement assessments and decision-making:

**Eligibility vs. Appropriateness** - When making RRC placement
determinations, it is critical that staff understand the
difference between eligibility and appropriateness.  All inmates
are statutorily eligible for up to 12 months pre-release RRC

-1-

placement. Nevertheless, not all inmates are appropriate for RRC placement, and for those who are appropriate, the length of the RRC placement must be determined on an individual basis in accordance with this guidance.

**Individual Assessments Required** – Inmates must continue to be individually assessed for their appropriateness for and the length of pre-release RRC placements using the following five factors from 18 U.S.C. § 3621(b):
   (1) The resources of the facility contemplated;
   (2) The nature and circumstances of the offense;
   (3) The history and characteristics of the prisoner;
   (4) Any statement by the court that imposed the sentence:
       (a) concerning the purposes for which the sentence to imprisonment was determined to be warranted; or
       (b) recommending a type of penal or correctional facility as appropriate; and
   (5) Any pertinent policy statement issued by the U.S. Sentencing Commission.

These individual assessments occur as part of the inmate classification and program review process, with the unit manager holding decision-making responsibility at the unit level. Institution- or region-specific parameters for RRC placement decision-making are prohibited.

**RRC Placements of More Than Six Months** - Regional Director approval of RRC placements longer than six months is no longer required.

**Residential Drug Abuse Program Graduates** – Inmates who successfully complete the institution-based portion of the Residential Drug Abuse Program (RDAP) will continue to be assessed for pre-release RRC placements according to the guidance in the Psychology Treatment Programs policy.

**Coordination Between Institution Staff and Community Corrections Management Staff** - Community Corrections Management (CCM) staff must continue to review referral documents and other pertinent information for every RRC referral. If CCM staff question the appropriateness of the referral or the length of the requested placement, they must communicate these concerns to the referring institution. Differing recommendations will be resolved at the appropriate level within the regional management structure. Under no circumstances should CCM staff unilaterally deny RRC referrals or adjust placement dates, unless these determinations can be linked directly to a lack of RRC bedspace or fiscal resources.

-2-

**Medical and Mental Health Concerns** – When considering RRC placement for inmates with significant medical or mental health conditions, institution staff are strongly encouraged to coordinate release planning with CCM staff and Transitional Drug Abuse Treatment staff (for mental health concerns). If an inmate's condition precludes residential placement in an RRC, and if staff can make appropriate arrangements to secure the community-based medical and/or mental health services these inmates will need, direct placement on home detention should be considered.

**Inmates Who Decline RRC Placement** – If an institution recommends release through a community-based program and the inmate declines, institution staff should counsel the inmate as to the benefits of a structured reentry program. However, if the inmate continues to decline this opportunity, she/he may do so without being subject to disciplinary action.

**Inmates Who are Inappropriate for RRC Placement** – Inmates who, during incarceration, have refused programming or failed to engage in activities that prepare them for reentry may be inappropriate for RRC placement. Similarly, inmates with recent, serious, or chronic misconduct and those who have previously failed an RRC program may be inappropriate.

RRCs provide opportunities for inmates to acquire the support systems, e.g., residence, employment, follow-up treatment, they will need to live a crime-free life, but inmates must be ready to take advantage of these opportunities. If they have clearly demonstrated through their behavior that they are not ready, RRC programming is unlikely to result in behavioral change and would be a waste of the Bureau's resources, as well as place the public at undue risk.

Professional judgment must be exercised, insofar as inmates with some misconduct, or some refusal to participate in programming, may still be appropriate for RRC placement. Staff must exercise their discretion in determining whether an inmate is ready to take advantage of the opportunities and expanded liberty that RRCs offer.

If staff decide not to refer an inmate for RRC placement, the inmate's release should be carefully coordinated with U.S. Probation or Court Services and Offender Supervision Agency (DC Code inmates).

–3–

**Professional Judgment** - RRC placement, in and of itself, is not a reward for good institutional behavior, nor is it an early release program or a substitute for the furlough program. RRC placement and length of placement decisions cannot be reduced solely to a classification score or any other type of arbitrary categorization. While staff assessment and analysis of tools such as the Custody Classification Form (BP-338) and the Inmate Skills Development (ISD) Plan are helpful in establishing broad-based groupings, staff must continue to exercise their professional judgment when making individual inmate RRC placement decisions and be prepared to justify those decisions.

## LENGTH OF RRC PLACEMENT

**General Guidelines**

- **Prospective Application** - Inmates with previously established RRC transfer dates will not be reconsidered under this guidance.

- **90 Days Minimum Placement** – With the exception noted below under the heading of Lower-Risk Inmates, inmates should be considered for at least 90 days pre-release RRC placement whenever possible.

- **High-Risk Versus Low-Risk Inmates** - RRCs are most effective, in terms of recidivism reduction, for inmates at higher risk for recidivism. Consequently, appropriate higher-risk inmates should be considered for longer RRC placements than lower-risk inmates. The BP-338 measures some of the factors that predict risk. Ordinarily, the lower the BP-338 score, the lower the risk; conversely, the higher the score, the higher the risk. Therefore, low-, medium-, and high-security inmates tend to be higher risk than minimum-security inmates.

  Similarly, the ISD tool identifies deficits that may contribute to recidivism. Inmates with a significant number of deficits may be at higher risk for recidivism than those with few or no deficits. When making RRC placement decisions, staff should ensure that the BP-338 and ISD Assessment have been accurately completed. While neither tool can be relied upon solely, they are helpful tools in assessing an inmate's risk level.

–4–

**Lower-Risk Inmates**

- **Consider Home Detention Option** - With the exception of RDAP graduates, institution staff will evaluate minimum-security inmates who have an approved release residence to determine if direct transfer from an institution to home detention is appropriate. If so, this determination will be noted in item 11 of the Institutional Referral for RRC Placement form, and the requested placement date (item 3.b.) will be the inmate's home detention eligibility date. These procedures are to be followed even if this results in a community-based placement of fewer than 90 days.

- If a minimum-security inmate is not appropriate for direct placement on home detention, staff will request an RRC placement of sufficient length to address the inmate's reentry needs.

- CCM staff are to ensure that procedures are in place for the direct placement of inmates on home detention, or after only a brief stay (14 days or less) in an RRC. At a minimum, CCM staff must monitor their minimum-security population weekly and follow up with RRC contractors to ascertain why eligible minimum-security inmates have not been referred for placement on home detention.

**Higher-Risk Inmates** - As previously stated, in terms of recidivism reduction, inmates at higher risk for recidivism stand to benefit most from RRC services. When considering the length of the RRC placement for higher-risk inmates, staff should consider the following:

- **History of Individual Change** - Assess whether the inmate's history of individual positive change during incarceration indicates an ability and willingness to take advantage of opportunities for positive reintegration to the community. Based on that history, staff must predict whether the inmate is likely to respond positively to the highly structured regimen of an RRC, and whether the inmate will avail her/himself of the available RRC opportunities.

- **History of Program Participation** - Assess the inmate's history of successful completion of, or participation in, available programming opportunities during incarceration, including programming which addresses the deficits identified through the ISD System. In particular, determine whether the inmate completed or made satisfactory progress toward completing a program shown to reduce recidivism, such

-5-

as any of the cognitive/behavioral treatment programs
described in the <u>Psychology Treatment Programs</u> Program
Statement, as well as academic and vocational training
programs.

- **Inmate's Community Support Systems** – Assess the inmate's
available community support systems, e.g., housing,
employment, etc.

- **Length of RRC Placement** - Longer RRC placements should be
considered for inmates whose following factors are high:

> Risk for recidivism;
> Demonstrated successful participation in or completion
of programming opportunities; and
> Need to establish community support systems.

Your assistance in implementing these procedures is appreciated.
I look forward to working with you as we seek to effectively
utilize the Bureau's limited RRC resources.

## §5:50 RELOCATION

When an inmate who will have a period of post-release supervision wishes
to be released to a district other than the one in which they were sentenced, the
inmate must initiate a request for supervision relocation through his/her Case
Manager. The request should provide (a) the specific rationale for wanting to be
released to the proposed district, (b) what family and community ties the inmate
has in the proposed release area, (c) how and where they could secure residence
in the release district, and (d) what employment opportunities and/or job skills
they have. If some transitional assistance through pre-release placement in a RRC
(halfway house) will be needed, the inmate should be sure that the Case Manager
includes such information in the relocation request. The request for relocation of
supervision is sent to the U.S. Probation Office in the district where relocation
is being requested, and that office will investigate the proposed release plan.
If the requesting inmate has indicated a residence an available residence upon
release, the U.S. Probation Office can be expected to conduct a home visit at the
proposed address. Upon completion of their review and investigation, the U.S.
Probation Office will either approve or deny the request. It is important that this
process be completed in ample time prior to the time that the Unit Staff prepare
a final RRC placement referral.

## §5:60 THE SECOND CHANCE ACT

The Second Chance Act (SCA) is a piece of legislation signed into law by
President George W. Bush on April 9, 2008. The law had bipartisan support in
both houses of Congress. The law authorized federal funding for state and federal

reentry programs. It also directed – but did not require – the Bureau of Prisons (BOP) to consider giving federal prisoners longer stays in halfway houses, and it authorized funds for a very limited test program for elderly prisoners. The "second chance" act applied almost exclusively to people leaving prison – it did not give shorter sentences to people already in prison.

It requires the Bureau of Prisons to ensure that a prisoner serving a term of imprisonment spend a portion of the final months of that term (up to 12 months) in a community correctional facility—now called a "residential re-entry center"--(halfway house) or in conditions that will afford the prisoner a reasonable opportunity to adjust and prepare for reentry to the community. It clarifies that the BOP may place a prisoner in home confinement for ten percent of the term of imprisonment or six months, whichever is shorter.

The SCA requires the BOP to ensure that, to the extent practicable, a prisoner is considered for halfway house placement or other release preparation conditions for up to twelve months, not just up to six months, as previous law had stated. The SCA does not require the BOP to grant each prisoner 12 months in a halfway house. In fact, the BOP has since stated that while it considers each prisoner individually, the standard amount of halfway house time most prisoners will receive is a maximum of six months, and only in extraordinary cases will a prisoner receive more than six months halfway house time.

## ENDNOTES

- This chapter derives, in part, from: T. Bussert, P. Goldberger and M. Price, "New Limits on Federal Halfway Houses," CRIMINAL JUSTICE (ABA Spring 2006); T. Bussert and H. Martin, *The Federal Bureau of Prisons* in DEFENDING A FEDERAL CRIMINAL CASE (Sarah Gannett, ed.) (Federal Defenders of San Diego, Inc. 2010); and "The U.S. Bureau of Prisons' Pre-Release Program - Getting Out Early," by Alan Ellis and J. Michael Henderson, Criminal Justice (Winter 2017).
- All BOP program statements mentioned in this chapter can be found on the Bureau's web site, www.bop.gov.

# CHAPTER 6

# SEX OFFENDERS

(This page intentionally left blank.)

## §6:10 INTRODUCTION

According to the U.S. Sentencing Commission's 2012 Report to Congress entitled *Federal Child Pornography* Offenses, federal prosecutions of child pornography possession, distribution and production offenses respectively rose from a 16, 61 and 10 in 1992 (a total of 87 child pornography offenses overall) to 904, 813 and 207 respectively in 2010 (for a total of 1,924). Thus, the prosecution of child pornography offenses grew in excess of 2,100% in that period of time—far and away the fastest growing prosecution rate of any of the major offense categories.

Concurrent with an increase in prosecution has been an increase in potential penalties, both statutory and Guideline. Whereas courts have roundly rejected these new sanctions as politically motivated and lacking empirical support, sentencing in sex offense cases presents unique responsibilities and challenges for which counsel must be prepared.

Sex offenders' life in federal prison also differs from their criminal cohorts. From placement to programming to release, incarcerated sex offenders face many more obstacles than others seeking to return to a law-abiding existence in the community.

## §6:20 SENTENCING

The average child pornography defendant is a 42-year-old, white (88.9%) male (98.7%) U.S. citizen (97.7%) with at least a high school diploma (92.1%), though likely at least some college (58.1%), and no prior felony conviction (79.9%). *See* USDOJ, BJS, *Federal Prosecution of Child Sex Exploitation Offenders*, 2006 (Dec. 2007). Greater than 95 percent of such prosecutions result in conviction, overwhelmingly via a guilty plea. *Id.* As is true in most criminal cases, sentencing courts are left to question and understand the factor(s) that contributed to the defendant's offense behavior, though with sex offenses, recidivism concerns are magnified.

One of the first steps defense counsel should take in case involving alleged sexual misconduct is refer the client for a confidential psychosexual evaluation. Similar to a standard mental health evaluation, a psychosexual evaluation assesses an individual's social, familial, education and employment history as well as general psychological make-up. However, such assessments focus further on issues concerning sexual history and development, including victimization, paraphilias, and risk. Obtaining a psychosexual evaluation early in the process not only informs issues concerning a client's alleged misconduct but, looking prospectively, provides a baseline upon which the client can improve during a case's pendency.

Subject to cost and available clinical resources, a recommended course after obtaining an initial evaluation, for which a report is not necessary, is to refer the client for treatment with a confidential, independent provider, that is, with a professional other than the person who conducted the evaluation. Stand-alone treatment provides the benefit of not only enabling the evaluator to view the client both before and after treatment, thereby permitting a more objective assessment of any progress and risk reduction, but it also affords additional insight into the client from a second clinician capable of speaking to the evolution of treatment.

Courts confronted with an Internet sex offense are generally sensitive to the reality that the step from viewing child pornography to sexual contact is enormous, and there is little-to-no empirical support for a causal link between viewing these illegal images and the commission of contact offenses. *See, e.g.*, D.L. Riegel, *Effects on boy-attracted pedosexual males of viewing boy erotica*, 33 Archives of Sexual Behavior 4, 321-23 (2004). Although, in certain cases, pornography may be part of a larger offense process, viewing pornography is not the cause of sexual offending (acting out). *See* R. Bauserman, *Sexual aggression and pornography: A review of correlational research*, 18 Basic Applied Psychology 4, 405-427 (1996); W.L. Marshall, *Revisiting the use of pornography by sexual offenders: Implications for theory and practice*, 6 Journal of Sexual Aggression 1/2, 67-77 (2000). Of particular relevance to federal prosecutions, "the current research literature supports the assumption that the consumers of child pornography form a distinct group of sex offenders." J. Endrass, et al., *The consumption of Internet child pornography and violent and sex offending*, 9 BMC Psychiatry 43 (2009).

One study looking at re-offense rates for adult male child pornography offenders found that while four percent (4%) of child-pornography-only offenders (no prior sex offense convictions) committed a further pornography offense, only one percent (1%) escalated to a contact sexual re-offense. M. Seto and A. Eke, *The criminal histories and later offending of child pornography offenders*, 17 Sexual Abuse: A Journal of Research and Treatment 2, 201-210 (2005). Another study found that "there is some indication to suggest that there is a sub group of internet offenders who pose a risk of repeated internet pornography offending, but not an escalation to contact sex offending.... [B]y far the largest subgroup of internet offenders [including those convicted of making child pornography] would appear to post a very low risk of sexual recidivism." L. Webb, J. Craissati and S. Keen, *Characteristics of Internet Child Pornography Offenders: A Comparison with Child Molesters*, 19 Sexual Abuse: A Journal of Research and Treatment 4, 463 (2007). Finally, after analyzing six years of recidivism data of 231 men convicted of child pornography offenses, the Endrass study, *supra*, found:

> Among the subjects of the present study, only 1% were known to have committed a past hands-on sex offense, and only 1% were charged with a subsequent hands-on sex offense in the 6 year follow-up. The consumption of child pornography alone does not seem to represent a risk factor for committing hands-on sex offenses in the present sample— at least not in those subjects without prior convictions for hands-on sex offenses.

When coupled with a psychosexual evaluation that confirms the isolated nature of a defendant's conduct and low risk to re-offend, the foregoing empirical considerations have contributed to courts regularly rejecting a sex offender's prescribed guideline range in favor of a more rational disposition, one that satisfies 18 U.S.C. §3553(a)'s parsimony requirement. The chart below demonstrates that while, non-government-sponsored below guideline sentences (*i.e.*, non-§5K1.1 departures) have increased since *Booker*, the rates more than doubled from 2006 (20.8%) to 2016 (45.0%) in child pornography cases.

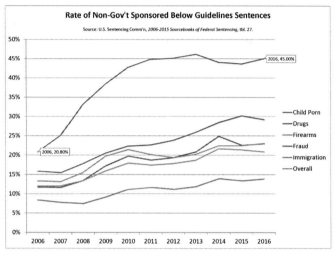

Central to achieving such a result is showing courts why the sex offense guidelines must be rejected. The person perhaps most responsible for leading this charge has been Assistant Federal Public Defender Troy Stabenow. *See* Mark Hansen, *A Reluctant Rebellion*, ABA Journal (June 2009). Attorney Stabenow's memorandum, *Deconstructing the Myth of Careful Study: A Primer on the Flawed Progression of the Child Pornography Guidelines* (available at http://www.fd.org/docs/Select-Topics---sentencing/child-porn-july-revision.pdf), provided the analytical framework on which first district courts and then circuit courts relied when holding the sex offense guidelines unsustainable, on policy grounds. *See United States v. Henderson*, 649 F.3d 955, 962 (9th Cir. 2011) (most amendments to the child pornography guidelines "were Congressionally-mandated and not the result of an empirical study"); *United States v. Grober*, 624 F.3d 592 (3rd Cir. 2010); *United States v. Dorvee*, 616 F.3d 174 (2nd Cir. 2010). Equally as important, the Sentencing Commission effectively corroborated Attorney Stabenow's conclusions concerning the guidelines' deficiencies through its own report and analysis. USSC, *The History of the Child Pornography Guidelines* (Oct. 2009) (available at http://www.ussc.gov/Research/Research_Projects/Sex_Offenses/20091030_History_Child_Pornography_Guidelines.pdf). In 2012, the Commission published a comprehensive follow-up report to Congress entitled Federal Child Pornography Offenders that further corroborates its earlier findings and documents the continuing dissatisfaction the judiciary has with these Guidelines.

## §6:30   BUREAU OF PRISONS

The notion of sex offenders as pariahs in correctional settings is not without foundation. Like the rest of society, prison culture is not immune to condemning those who engage in criminal sexual misconduct, especially in cases involving acting out against children. So too corrections officials approach the management of sex offenders differently than other classes of offenders, both in terms of assessing the risks they pose and the risks that they face.

Whenever there is evidence of sexual misconduct in an inmate's background, regardless of whether it involves the offense on conviction for which the inmate is serving time, the federal Bureau of Prisons (BOP) applies a "sex offender" Public Safety Factor (PSF). This PSF results in an inmate's placement in at least a low-security institution. Sex offenders are disqualified from minimum-security (camp) placement, though many remain eligible for pre-release placement (halfway house and/or home confinement). Most, though not all, sex offenders may be prohibited from using the BOP's inmate electronic mail system (TRULINICS).

Sex offenders are housed in standard general populations. This often tends to be a cause for client concern, especially in child pornography cases, since the standard profile of such individuals is akin to an ordinary "white-collar" client. Experience shows that when other prisoners discover a client's offense of conviction—for child pornography offenders, others in low-security housing—the response is more one of rebuke than reprisal (*i.e.*, it is more likely that the client will be shunned than assaulted).

The Adam Walsh Act has added a wrinkle to sex offender placement. *See* 18 U.S.C. §3621(f). Relying on a set of unwritten criteria that considers both offense of conviction and prior criminal history, BOP officials at the DSCC tap "more serious" sex offenders for placement at one of eight sex offender management programs (SOMPs). By security level, SOMP locations are Low: FMC Devens (MA) (technically administrative, as inmates of all security levels are housed at the FMC), FCI Seagoville (TX), FCI Englewood (CO) and FCI Elkton (OH); Medium: FCI Petersburg (VA), FCI Marianna (FL) and FCI Marion (IL); and High: USP Tucson (AZ). Moreover, experience indicates that due to population pressures, the BOP may employ a management variable to permit the placement of low-security inmates deemed appropriate for SOMP at Medium security institutions. Sex offenders purportedly comprise 40 percent or more of a SOMP location's general population. Aside from that, however, the only characteristic of the "program" that distinguishes SOMP placement from standard institutional placement is the nine-month nonresidential treatment component.

BOP sex offender treatment, be it at a SOMP or at the residential sex offender treatment program (SOTP) at FMC Devens, is voluntary, and prisoners are highly encouraged to avoid it. BOP asserts that its sex offender treatment program "employs a wide range of cognitive-behavioral and relapse prevention techniques to help the sex offender manage his sexual deviance both within the institution and in preparation for release." *See* USDOJ-BOP, *Legal Resource Guide to the Federal Bureau of Prisons* at 29 (Nov. 2008). However, judicial decisions discrediting a "study" of the former SOTP at FCI Butner, North Carolina (since disbanded) highlight the Fifth Amendment and civil commitment concerns attendant to the BOP's approach to treating sex offenders:

> As [one expert] testified, the program is 'highly coercive.' Unless offenders continue to admit to further sexual crimes, whether or not they actually committed those crimes, the offenders are discharged from the program. Consequently, the subjects in this Study had an incentive to lie, despite the fact that participation in the program would not shorten their sentences. Rogers testified that the Study's 'whole approach' is rejected by the treatment and scientific community.

*United States v. Johnson*, 588 F.Supp.2d 997 (S.D. Iowa 2008) (citations omitted); *United States v. Phinney*, 599 F.Supp.2d 1037, 1045 (E.D.Wis. 2009) ("... the Butner studies are flawed. Most significantly, participants risk being kicked out of treatment if they do not admit prior contacts.").

The Adam Walsh Act provided for the civil commitment of sex offenders upon completion of their federal terms of imprisonment. *See United States v. Comstock*, 130 S. Ct. 1949 (2010) (affirming 18 U.S.C. §4248's civil commitment provisions). The BOP weighs information disclosed to corrections and treatment staff when determining whether an individual prisoner should be committed.

In terms of pre-release placement (halfway house and/or home confinement), the BOP does, as a matter of policy, notify local officials about a sex offender's anticipated transfer to or release into the community. *See* BOP Program Statement 5141.02, *Sex Offender Notification and Registration* (12/14/1998); see also 18 U.S.C. §4042(c). Concerns raised by local law enforcement about a particular prisoner's transfer to a Residential Reentry Center (RRC) might bar halfway house placement. For example, law enforcement authorities in a given jurisdiction may classify sex offenders according to their offense and history, if any, of sex offenses. Depending upon the classification level assigned by local authorities, the halfway house, under contract with the BOP, may not accept the offender according to its established criteria. Similarly, zoning ordinances and sex offender registration requirements may interfere with a prisoner's ability to transition to the release residence of his choosing.

Finally, experience shows that halfway house operators subject sex offenders to greater scrutiny. The facilities are quicker to violate a sex offender and return him to his parent institution. This is something about which child pornography offenders who successfully completed RDAP should be particularly aware, as a pre-release violation will likely result in revocation of the potential reduction in sentence available pursuant to 18 U.S.C. §3621(e). *See* Chapter 3.

### §6:30.1    Sex Offender Treatment Program – Nonresidential

The Sex Offender Treatment Program – Nonresidential (SOTP-NR) is a moderate intensity program designed for low to moderate risk sexual offenders.

The program consists of cognitive-behaviorally based psychotherapy groups, totaling 4-6 hours per week.

Inmates are ordinarily placed in the SOTP-NR during the last 36 months of their sentence and prioritized by release date. The typical duration of the SOTP-NR is 9-12 months.

Most participants in the SOTP-NR have a history of a single sex crime; many are first time offenders serving a sentence for an Internet Sex Offense. The program is voluntary. Prior to placement in the SOTP-NR, prospective participants are screened with a risk assessment instrument to ensure their offense history is commensurate with moderate intensity treatment.

The SOTP-NR was designed to target dynamic risk factors associated with re-offense in sex offenders, as demonstrated by empirical research. These factors include: sexual self-regulation, deficits and sexual deviancy; criminal thinking and behavior patterns; intimacy skills deficits; and emotional self-regulation deficits. The program employs cognitive-behavioral techniques, with a primary emphasis on skills acquisition and practice.

Nonresidential Sex Offender Treatment Programs are available at the following facilities:

Mid-Atlantic Region
FCI Petersburg - Medium

South East Region
FCI Marianna, FL - Medium

South Central Region
FMC Carswell, TX - Med. Ctr.
(Females)
FCI Seagoville, TX - Low

North East Region
FCI Elkton, OH - Low

Western Region
USP Tucson, AZ - High

North Central Region
FCI Englewood, CO - Low
USP Marion, IL - Medium

More information about the program can be found at Bureau of Prisons Program Statement 5324.10.

## §6:30.2    Sex Offender Treatment Program – Residential

The Sex Offender Treatment Program – Residential (SOTP-R) is a high intensity program designed for high-risk sexual offenders. The program consists of cognitive-behaviorally based psychotherapy groups, totaling 10-12 hours per week, in a residential treatment unit employing a modified therapeutic community model.

Inmates are ordinarily placed in the SOPT-R during the last 36 months of their sentence, prioritized by release date. The typical duration of the SOTP-R is 12-18 months.

Participants in the SOTP-R have a history of multiple sex crimes, extensive non-sexual criminal histories, and/or a high level of sexual deviancy or hyper sexuality. The program is voluntary. Prior to placement in the SOTP-R, prospective participants are screened with a risk assessment instrument to ensure their offense history is commensurate with high intensity treatment.

The SOTP-R was designed by target dynamic risk factors associated with re-offense in sex offenders, as demonstrated by empirical research. These factors include: sexual self-regulation deficits and sexual deviancy; criminal thinking and behavior patterns; intimacy skills deficits; and emotional self-regulation deficits. The program employs cognitive-behavioral techniques, with a primary emphasis on skills acquisition and practice. The modified therapeutic community model is employed to address pro-offending attitudes and values.

Residential Sex Offender Treatment Programs are available at USP Marion, Il-Medium/High and FMC Devens, MA-Medical Center.

More information about the program can be found at Bureau of Prisons Program Statement 5324.10 available at http://www.bop.gov/policy/progstat/5324_010.pdf.

## §6:40 ARTICLES

### §6:40.1 Child Pornography Guidelines are Ripe for Challenge.

See §8:30.5.

### §6:40.2 Trends and Practices for Representing Child Pornography Offenders at Sentencing.

See §8:30.4.

### ENDNOTES
- This chapter derives, in part, from: T. Bussert and H. Martin, *The Federal Bureau of Prisons* in DEFENDING A FEDERAL CRIMINAL CASE (Sarah Gannett, ed.) (Federal Defenders of San Diego, Inc. 2010).
- All BOP program statements mentioned in this chapter can be found on the Bureau's web site, www.bop.gov.

### ACKNOWLEDGMENTS
**Mark H. Allenbaugh** is a former staff attorney to the U.S. Sentencing Commission, and is currently an executive with Sentencing Stats, LLC (www.sentencingstats.com), a premier data analytical firm providing federal sentencing data and analyses to attorneys and their clients. He is a nationally recognized expert on federal sentencing law, policy, and practice.

(This page intentionally left blank.)

# CHAPTER 7

# MEDICAL CARE IN THE BUREAU OF PRISONS

(This page intentionally left blank.)

## §7:10 BOP HEALTH CARE: WHAT YOU (AND YOUR CLIENTS) NEED TO KNOW

This section focuses on the recently promulgated Bureau of Prisons (BOP) rules on the subject of health care for inmates, the impact the new rules have on the medical care provided to inmates, how an inmate's medical condition may influence in which facility the individual is placed, and how inmates with medical needs will be treated in the federal prison system.

BOP policies are complex and difficult to understand—even defense lawyers find them taxing. Clients and families are more often than not lost in the bureaucratic maze of terminology and regulations, and they turn to their lawyers for explanations. This information is intended specifically for the attorney to give to clients and their families and friends.

### §7:10.1 BOP Medical Classification

There are four levels in the Bureau of Prisons medical CARE level classification system. A provisional CARE level is assigned by the Designation and Sentence Computation Center (DSCC), based primarily on information contained in the Presentence Investigation Report. After arrival at the designated facility, the provisional CARE level is reviewed and a nonprovisional CARE level is assigned by BOP clinicians. These assignments depend on the defendant's physical and medical condition, clinical resources and inmate needs, and his or her ability to function daily without assistance.

**CARE level 1 inmates:** This designation is made by the DSCC. These inmates are less than 70 years of age and are generally healthy, but may have limited medical needs that can be easily managed by clinician evaluations every six months. Examples of such needs include mild asthma, diet-controlled diabetes, and stable HIV patients who do not require medications. Level 1 institutions are located approximately one hour or more from community medical centers since medical care is not often needed.

**CARE level 2 inmates:** This designation is made by the DSCC. These inmates are stable outpatients who require at least quarterly clinician evaluations. Their medical conditions, including mental health issues, can be managed through routine, regularly scheduled appointments with clinicians for monitoring. Enhanced medical resources, such as consultation or evaluation by medical specialists, may be required from time-to-time, but are not regularly necessary. Examples of issues at this level include medication-controlled diabetes, epilepsy, or emphysema. Level 2 institutions have no special capabilities beyond those that health services staff ordinarily provide; however, they are located within one hour of major regional treatment centers (for example, Fort Dix and Fairton, New Jersey), thereby permitting more immediate attention to medical emergencies. Most BOP facilities are classified as CARE level 2 facilities.

**CARE level 3 inmates:** This designation is made by the BOP's Office of Medical Designation and Transportation in Washington, D.C. These inmates are fragile outpatients who require frequent clinical contacts to prevent hospitalization for catastrophic events. They may require some assistance with activities of daily living, such as bathing, dressing or eating, but do not need daily nursing care. Other inmates may be assigned as "companions" to provide the needed assistance. Stabilization of medical or mental health conditions may require periodic hospitalization. Examples of these medical conditions include cancer in remission less than a year, advanced HIV disease, severe mental illness in remission on medication, severe congestive heart failure and end-stage liver disease. Level 3 institutions may be located within Level 4 institutions, that is federal medical centers (*e.g.*, Lexington, Kentucky, FCI Butner, North Carolina FPC Devens, Massachusetts), USMCFP Springfield, Missouri, FMC Rochester, Minnesota, and FMC Carswell, Texas. To date, the only level 3 facilities identified are FCI Butner, North Carolina, FCI Fort Worth, Texas, FCI Terminal Island , California, USP Terre Haute, Indiana, USP Tucson, Arizona, FCI Allenwood-Medium, Pennsylvania, and USP Allenwood, Pennsylvania..

**CARE level 4 inmates:** This designation is made by the BOP's Office of Medical Designation and Transportation in Washington, D.C. These inmates require services available only at a BOP Medical Referral Center (MRC), which provides significantly enhanced medical services and limited inpatient care. Functioning may be so severely impaired that it requires 24-hour skilled nursing care or nursing assistance. Examples include cancer on active treatment, dialysis, quadriplegia, stroke or head injury patients, major surgical treatment, and high-risk pregnancy.

The BOP operates six CARE level 4 MRCs:
- U.S. Medical Center for Federal Prisoners, Springfield, Missouri, provides care primarily for higher security level inmates, and includes a full dialysis unit as well as an inpatient mental health unit.
- FMC Rochester, Minnesota, is affiliated with the Mayo Clinic for complex medical requirements, and includes an inpatient mental health unit.
- FMC Lexington, Kentucky, generally manages lower security level inmates.
- FMC Devens, Massachusetts, includes a dialysis unit and an inpatient mental health unit, as well as the residential sex offender treatment program.
- FMC Butner, North Carolina, includes an inpatient mental health unit and can manage inmates at all security levels. It is the cancer treatment center for the BOP.
- FMC Carswell, Texas, is exclusively for female inmates and is the only FMC available for women. It includes an inpatient mental health unit.

Most federal prisons have a full-time medical staff on hand and/or contract medical staff from the community. A local community hospital provides contract services for inmates who are in need of inpatient care because of a medical emergency. Normally, inmates in need of special medical attention due to complex health problems will be designated to one of the BOP's six major medical centers listed above. With the exception of the federal medical centers, which provide primary and inpatient care, all other BOP facilities provide outpatient care (otherwise known as "ambulatory care"). Most BOP facilities also have one or more contract hospitals in the surrounding community that provide secondary and inpatient care to inmates in "emergency situations" or when an inmate's medical needs cannot be adequately treated by medical staff at the prison facility.

### §7:10.2    Levels of Intervention

The BOP defines its scope of medical services according to five levels of medical intervention:

**Medically Necessary—Acute or Emergent.** Medical conditions that are of an immediate, acute or emergent nature, which without care would cause rapid deterioration of the inmate's health, significant irreversible loss of function, or may be life-threatening.

**Medically Necessary—Nonemergent.** Medical conditions that are not immediately life-threatening but that without care the inmate could not be maintained without significant risk of serious deterioration leading to premature death, significant reduction of the possibility of repair later without present treatment, or significant pain or discomfort that impairs the inmate's participation in activities of daily living.

**Medically Acceptable—Not Always Necessary.** Medical conditions that are considered elective procedures, when treatment may improve the inmate's quality of life. Relevant examples in this category include, but are not limited to, joint replacement; reconstruction of the anterior cruciate ligament of the knee; and treatment of non-cancerous skin conditions (*e.g.*, skin tags, lipomas).

**Limited Medical Value.** Treatment for medical conditions that provide little or no medical value is not likely to provide substantial long-term gain, or is expressly for the inmate's convenience. Procedures in this category are usually excluded from the scope of services provided to Bureau inmates. Examples in this category include, but are not limited to, minor conditions that are self-limiting; cosmetic procedures, for example, lepharoplasty—cosmetic surgery on the eyelids; or removal of non-cancerous skin lesions.

**Extraordinary.** Medical interventions are deemed extraordinary if they affect the life of another individual, such as organ transplantation, or are considered investigational in nature.

It is the policy of the BOP to provide care to inmates when clinicians deem it medically necessary. Those medical interventions that fall into the categories of "medically necessary, acute or emergent" or "medically necessary, nonemergent" are those the agency considers to be medically necessary. Those that fall into the classification of "medically acceptable, not always necessary" are considered elective All interventions not classified as "medically necessary – acute or emergent" must undergo review by a utilization review committee before approval. Those classified as "medically acceptable – not always necessary" are unlikely to be approved and completed based on limited medical resources.

The utilization review committee members include the clinical director, health services administrator, medical trip coordinator, health care providers, director of nursing (if applicable), and a chaplain or social worker.

These committees typically convene every two weeks to consider the nonemergency referrals. The intent of these committee reviews is to establish an initial assessment of priority for recommended interventions and ensures that *no* services that fall outside the scope of those defined in BOP policy are provided.

Although there is no certainty that a utilization review committee will approve a specific recommendation for treatment, as long as the recommended intervention falls clearly within the category of "medically necessary, nonemergent," it is likely to be approved. Those that are within the category of "medically acceptable, not always necessary" are far less likely to be approved by the committee. Some institutions assign an initial priority for approved consultations or interventions using a numeric system (where a priority one requires attention within one week, a priority two requires attention within two to four weeks, and a priority three can be delayed for a month or more), while others use a color code with similar requirements.

In order for an inmate to be seen by a medical specialist, such as a cardiologist or neurologist, outside the facility for a nonemergency condition, an escorted trip must be approved and arranged in advance. The number of correctional officers required for each escorted trip ranges from one to five or more, depending on the characteristics of the inmate involved. Because of staffing limitations, a facility will typically schedule a limited number of escorted trips each day, and generally, the number of inmates requiring such trips exceeds the number approved daily. As a result, Bureau of Prisons medical staff (generally the clinical director) establishes priorities to determine which inmates should fill the limited number of escorted trip "slots" available. These are clinical decisions based on the director's assessment of acuity. Thus, while an inmate may have received medical approval for specialty consultation or intervention, the delivery of that care depends heavily on the number of escorted trips available and the acuity of his or her condition. The likelihood that an inmate will receive regular escorted trips for medical specialist consultation over an extended period of time is diminished in light of these logistical variables. It is most likely that at some point the inmate's care, even if approved by the utilization review committee, will be interrupted as he or she is displaced by an inmate with more acute needs.

It is likely that the Bureau of Prisons will have access to the services of medical specialists that most inmates will require. In larger or higher security facilities, the wait for an approved outside consultation may be extensive, based on limited escort staff. In some instances, medically appropriate nonemergent appointments (specifically orthopedics) have been delayed for up to a year after the initial recommendation for consultation. Should such consultation occur, any intervention or treatment suggested by the medical specialist is considered a recommendation subject to the review and approval of the institution clinical director in compliance with the scope of services defined by agency policy and the national formulary. It is not unusual for an institution's clinical director to decline to pursue a recommendation made by a consulting specialist, particularly if that recommendation includes intervention that is seen as medically acceptable, but not always necessary, or includes a nonformulary medication.

Pretrial or nonsentenced inmates, and inmates with less than 12 months to serve, are ineligible for health services considered "medically appropriate, not always necessary," "limited medical value," or "extraordinary."

### §7:10.3 Primary Care Teams

The Bureau of Prisons has recently implemented Primary Care Provider Teams (PCPT). Under the PCPT model, each inmate is assigned to a primary health care provider who will be responsible for managing the inmate's health care needs. In a nutshell, under the PCPT model, upon arrival at an institution each individual will be assigned to a primary care provider, and during the remainder of the inmate's stay at the institution, he or she will need to complete a request form any time he or she wishes to receive treatment and/or see the primary care provider under circumstances other than a medical emergency.

The PCPT includes a staff physician, mid-level practitioners, and ancillary staff such as pharmacists, radiology technicians, and lab technicians.

The primary health care of the inmates is provided chiefly by the mid-level practitioners (physician assistants, nurse practitioners, or unlicensed foreign medical graduates) under the supervision of a staff physician. Upon arrival at the institution, inmates will be medically screened by one of the prison's medical staff. This process involves an interview and may include a brief physical examination. In addition, any medications the inmate was taking prior to incarceration will be re-evaluated by the prison physician, who will decide whether or not to prescribe the same or a similar medication. Newly arriving inmates on anti-psychotic medication are continued on that medication until reviewed by a psychiatrist. Prison pharmacies in the BOP do not dispense herbal medicines or dietary supplements not FDA approved, nor are they available through the institution commissary. A full history and physical are generally completed within 14 days of arrival at the designated facility.

The staff physicians are generally family practitioners or internal medicine specialists. They control an inmate's access to specialty medical care and review any recommendations made by medical specialists to determine whether they are within the scope of services and policy of the Bureau of Prisons before implementation.

In order for an inmate to receive care or treatment by a specialist, including physical therapy, the mid-level practitioner would have to identify the inmate's medical problem and alert the staff physician who would then decide whether to refer the inmate to a specialist, if one is available.

If the staff physician determines that a referral to a specialist is warranted for a nonemergency condition, such as physical therapy, that referral must be approved by the utilization review committee.

The Bureau of Prisons seeks to obtain medical specialty care for its inmates through contracting with local hospitals. However, contracts with hospitals do not necessarily include services of specialty physicians. In fact, each facility of the Bureau of Prisons uses a variety of procurement practices to establish agreements with both hospitals and individual physicians and other medical specialists for specialty care. The success of establishing those agreements depends on the availability of any particular medical specialist or facility in the community in which the prison is located, the willingness of that provider or facility to travel to the prison and subject him or herself to the security requirements for entrance and the constraints of treating individuals in prison, the willingness of that provider to see inmates in his office/practice/facility, and, increasingly significant, the ability of that specialty provider to obtain medical malpractice insurance when his or her practice includes inmates. The refusal of many malpractice insurers to cover practices that include inmate patients severely limits the number of specialty providers willing to treat inmates. The BOP does not indemnify contract medical specialists who treat inmates.

### §7:10.4    End of Life

The BOP has also implemented a policy to facilitate the creation and implementation of advanced health care directives and Do Not Resuscitate (DNR) orders. Each BOP institution is to have an institution policy supplement covering advanced directives and DNR orders, including a copy of pertinent state laws; a sample standard form for inmate use if available from the pertinent state law; and instructions for inmates to execute advanced directives, including the option of retaining private legal counsel at the inmate's expense. Bureau policy requires the filing of an inmate's executed advanced directives in the inmate's health record. Each institution policy supplement must also provide DNR information that complies with the law of the state in which the institution is located; a statement that DNR orders will never be invoked while an inmate is housed in a general (non-medical) population institution, which means that DNR directives may be implemented only at community health care facilities or BOP medical referral centers; and that copies of valid DNR orders be documented in the inmate's health record.

### §7:10.5    Mental Health Classification

In addition to receiving a classification for security and health care, BOP inmates are now classified based on mental health care needs. Similar to the four medical care levels, all inmates are assigned to one of four mental health levels:

**CARE1-MH:** No Significant Mental Health Care: those who show no significant level of functional impairment associated with mental illness and demonstrate no need for regular mental health interventions; and either has no history of serious functional impairment due to mental illness or if a history of mental illness is present, have consistently demonstrated appropriate help-seeking behavior in response to any reemergence of symptoms.

**CARE2-MH:** Routine Outpatient Mental Health Care or Crisis-Oriented Mental Health Care: those requiring routine outpatient mental health care on an ongoing basis; and/or brief, crisis-oriented mental health care of significant intensity; e.g., placement on suicide watch or behavioral observation status.

**CARE3-MH:** Enhanced Outpatient Mental Health Care or Residential Mental Health Care: those requiring enhanced outpatient mental health care (i.e., weekly mental health interventions); or residential mental health care (i.e., placement in a residential Psychology Treatment Program).

**CARE4-MH:** Inpatient Psychiatric Care: those who are gravely disabled and cannot function in general population in a CARE3-MH environment.

In determining an appropriate mental health care level, an individual's current, recent, and historical need for services is considered, along with consideration of any type of psychotropic medication required. The BOP offers a number of formal, organized psychology treatment programs with specific target populations, admission criteria, and treatment modalities. Many of these are residential programs offered only at select facilities. General psychological services and mental health crisis intervention are available throughout the BOP.

Psychiatric services, including psychotropic medication, are generally coordinated through health services in conjunction with psychology services staff. Psychiatry services may be available either through contracts with a community psychiatrist, or increasingly, through telepsychiatry with a BOP psychiatrist at another location.

## §7:20   LEVEL OF CARE SCORING

When initially scoring an inmate, the assigned team utilizes a Medical Calculator to determine the screen level. If the inmate is scored as a SCRN3 or SCRN4, he/she will be referred to the Office of Medical Designations (OMDT) for further review. OMDT then decides whether the SCRN level will require further review of the available information. If the inmate comes back from OMDT as a SCRN1 or SCRN2, the latter will be referred back to Designators who will designate the inmate to an appropriate CARE1 or CARE2 facility. If the inmate is determined to meet the criteria for a CARE3 or CARE4 facility, OMDT will designate them.

## 7:30   PRACTICE TIP

Since the Bureau of Prisons relies largely on the Presentence Investigation Report in determining the level of care scoring for both, it is important that counsel ensures the accuracy of the information in the PSR particularly as regards medical and physical health and mental health. Counsel should ensure that any necessary documentation and list of medications--type and dosage--are provided to the US Probation Office drafting the PSR.

(This page intentionally left blank.)

# CHAPTER 8

# FEDERAL SENTENCING

## §8:10    INTRODUCTION

Just over 25 years ago, before the Sentencing Guidelines went into effect, a federal judge could, with a few exceptions, sentence a convicted defendant anywhere from probation to the statutory maximum. All that changed when the Sentencing Guidelines went into effect in 1987. The Guidelines were part of a major overhaul of federal sentencing called the Sentencing Reform Act (the "SRA").

The SRA was supposed to correct what some politicians thought were unfair aspects of the old system, such as unexplained disparities in sentences, light sentences for white-collar defendants, and a parole system that made it impossible to know how much time a particular defendant would actually serve. The SRA tried to solve these problems by creating a nearly-mandatory guideline system. Under that system, a sentencing court would use the guidelines to determine a sentencing "range." In most cases, a court was required to sentence a defendant somewhere within that range.

While the mandatory guideline system "solved" some of the things Congress thought were "problems," it created others. Unfair sentencing disparities still existed. Cooperators often received lower sentences than the people they helped convict, even when the cooperators' offense conduct was more serious. A prosecutor's decision of what charges to bring could also create unfair differences in sentences. While white collar defendants no longer received lenient sentences, they received harsh ones instead. In fact, sentences in almost every kind of case became longer under the guidelines.

The mandatory guideline system also had a fatal flaw—it was unconstitutional. Unfortunately, it took nearly 18 years for the Supreme Court to recognize this defect. On January 12, 2005, the Supreme Court ruled in *United States v. Booker* that the mandatory guideline system was unconstitutional. The problem was that under the mandatory guideline system, the maximum sentence a defendant faced was often determined by facts not charged in the indictment or found beyond a reasonable doubt by a jury (or admitted by a defendant as part of a guilty plea colloquy).

The Supreme Court perhaps could have solved this problem by requiring guideline facts to be charged in indictments and proved beyond a reasonable doubt to juries. But it did not. Instead, the Court focused on the parts of the Sentencing Reform Act that gave rise to the constitutional problem. It removed the language from the SRA that required judges to sentence within the guideline range in most cases.

In some ways, sentencing did not change much after *Booker.* Sentencing facts are still not charged in indictments. Sentencing judges still calculate a defendant's guideline offense level and criminal history score. And they still decide the facts necessary to make these calculations by a preponderance of the evidence. What is different is that sentences are not controlled by the guidelines in the same way they used to be. Judges have more flexibility to evaluate cases individually.

Now that the guidelines are no longer mandatory, the most important part of the SRA is the requirement that the sentencing judge impose the sentence that is "sufficient, but not greater than necessary," to fulfill the purposes of sentencing as defined in the statute. In other words, the court must impose the lowest sentence that still meets these goals. What are those goals? Promoting respect for law, just punishment, deterrence, protection of the public, and rehabilitation and treatment of the defendant.

To determine the lowest sentence that meets these goals, the remaining parts of the Sentencing Reform Act require a court to "consider" seven general factors: Two of those factors are the sentencing range suggested by the guidelines and the guideline policy statements. The five other factors a court must "consider" are: (1) the facts concerning the defendant and the offense, (2) the purposes of sentencing, (3) the "kinds of sentences available,"(4) the need to avoid sentences that are unnecessarily higher or lower than those in similar cases, and (5) the "need to provide restitution to any victims."

The sentencing guideline range is only one of seven factors a court must "consider" before it imposes sentence. But often judges treat it as the most important. Many courts still impose most sentences within the guideline range in most cases. But even for courts that are more willing to impose sentences outside that range, the guidelines are still important. They are the starting point for considering a lower or higher sentence. It is therefore still important to understand how the guidelines work.

This chapter is meant to serve as an easy-to-read primer to help the non-lawyer as well as lawyers understand federal sentencing.

## §8:11    AN OVERVIEW OF THE GUIDELINES

When the guidelines are applied to a case, they produce a "range." A range might be 51-63 months, for example. The sentencing range is determined by matching two numbers on a chart known as the "Sentencing Table." One of the numbers is the offense level. The other is the criminal history category. The "offense level" is supposed to reflect the seriousness of the offense. The criminal history category reflects the number and seriousness of the defendant's prior convictions. A sentencing court is *required* to consider this range before imposing sentence. It is therefore important that the court correctly calculate the sentencing range suggested by the guidelines.

### §8:11.1    How the Offense of Conviction
### Affects the Guideline Range

The guidelines measure the seriousness of an offense in two different ways. First, they look to the offense of conviction to determine the offense guideline. This can be critical. For example, a public official who took a bribe might be convicted of accepting a bribe in violation of 18 U.S.C. §201(b), or of accepting a gratuity, in violation of 18 U.S.C. §201(c). Pleading to a gratuity count will result in a lower guideline range because the offense guideline for a gratuity conviction has a base offense level of 9 (11, if the defendant is a public official), whereas a the offense guideline for a bribery conviction has a base offense level of 12 (14, if the defendant is a public official). The higher the total offense level, the higher the sentencing range.

### §8:11.2    "Relevant Conduct"

Selection of the offense guideline is controlled by the offense of conviction. Almost all other guideline decisions are determined by "relevant conduct." "Relevant conduct" looks beyond the offense of conviction to what actually happened. For some cases, "relevant conduct" means what the defendant did to commit the offense, or to prepare to commit the offense, or to try to avoid being caught after committing the offense. In many (if not most) cases, "relevant conduct" includes much more.

The fraud, theft, tax, and drug guidelines use amounts of money or quantities of drugs to measure the seriousness of the offense. In cases like these, "relevant conduct" can include conduct that is not part of the offense of conviction. The guidelines look beyond the offense of conviction to other acts or omissions that were part of the same "course of conduct" or "common scheme or plan."

For example, a defendant convicted on a $1,000 fraud count could end up with a higher guideline range than another defendant convicted on a $100,000 fraud count. If the $1,000 fraud count was part of a "scheme" that included 200 such frauds, the "relevant conduct" would be $200,000. If the $100,000 fraud was not part of a larger scheme, then its "relevant conduct" would be only $100,000. Because the "relevant conduct" for the $1,000 fraud would then be higher than the "relevant conduct" for the $100,000 fraud, it will most likely produce a higher guideline range.

"Relevant conduct" sometimes includes things done by other people. This kind of relevant conduct applies when a defendant worked with other people to commit an offense. The guidelines call it "jointly undertaken criminal activity." A defendant does not have to be charged with a conspiracy for this type of relevant conduct to apply. A defendant does not even have to know the other people, nor does he have to know everything about what they did. Before a defendant can receive a higher guideline level for things other people did, several factors must be present. First, several people must have worked together to commit the offense. Second, the things that someone else did must have been "reasonably foreseeable" to the defendant. In other words, if the defendant had stopped to think about it, would he have been surprised at what the others did? Finally, the things that other people did must have been "in furtherance of the jointly undertaken criminal activity." That means that they must have been done to help accomplish the same overall illegal plan the defendant helped carry out.

For example, if a defendant unloaded one crate from a truck full of marijuana, all the marijuana from the truck could be "relevant conduct." The entire truckload could be "relevant conduct" if three conditions are met. First, other people had to be involved with the offense. Second, it must have been "reasonably foreseeable" to the defendant that the entire truck was filled with marijuana. Finally, unloading the one crate must have been part of an effort to distribute the whole truckload.

"Relevant conduct" does not have to be described in the indictment. It can involve conduct described only in counts dismissed under a plea agreement. *It can even include conduct for which a defendant has been acquitted.* The only limit on how high "relevant conduct" can push an offense level is the maximum sentence allowed by the statute of conviction. No guideline offense level can exceed the limit placed by statute on the counts of conviction.

### §8:11.3    The Guidelines "Sentencing Range"

The guidelines calculate a suggested sentencing range that applies to an entire case. They do not determine suggested ranges for particular counts. Once a court determines a range, the judge must "consider" it, along with the other factors listed in 18 U.S.C. §3553(a), before imposing sentence.

The guidelines tell the judge how to calculate a sentencing range for the entire case. After the court "considers" that range, along with the other §3553(a) factors, it must formally impose sentence separately on each count. If the guideline range is less than the statutory maximum of each count, the guidelines recommend that the court impose the sentences to run concurrently with each other.

The guidelines recommend that a court impose sentences to run consecutively if that is necessary to achieve a sentence within the guideline range. For example, the statutory maximum for one count of conspiring to commit an offense against the United States (18 U.S.C. §371) is five years. If a defendant were convicted on two such counts, the court could impose a guideline sentence of 84 months (seven years) only by running the sentences consecutively. However, if the guideline range was 11 to 15 years, the court could not impose a sentence higher than ten years in all. A court may not exceed the statutory maximum for any count. The total sentence for the case must stay within the total maximum for all the counts.

## §8:12    CHOOSING THE CORRECT GUIDELINE MANUAL

The Sentencing Commission has issued changes to the Guidelines Manual almost every year since the first edition came out in 1987. The changes are compiled into a new version of the Manual on November 1 of every year. The law requires courts to use the version of the sentencing manual in effect on the day a defendant is sentenced. Sometimes, however, the manual in effect on the day of sentencing produces a guideline range that is higher than it would be if the court had used the manual in effect on the day the offense was committed. When this happens, the court must use the manual in effect on the day the defendant committed the offense. This is required by the Constitution's *Ex Post Facto* Clause.

To check whether there is an *Ex Post Facto* problem, the court may have to make two calculations. The court will calculate the range using the manual in effect on the day of sentencing. It will then calculate the range using the manual in effect on the day the defendant committed the offense. The court then compares the two ranges and uses the lower one. A court will not pick one guideline section from one manual and another from the other manual, to come up with the lowest sentence possible. This is called the "one book" rule.

There is one important exception to the "one book" rule. A court will apply a "clarifying amendment" from a later manual, even if it uses an earlier manual. A "clarifying amendment" is a change that explains what an earlier guideline meant. A court will apply a clarifying amendment to an earlier manual, because the amendment does not really change the earlier guideline. It just explains what the guideline meant all along.

## §8:13 APPLYING THE GUIDELINES

### §8:13.1 Step One: Select the Offense Guideline

The first step is to select the offense guideline for each offense of conviction. The offense guidelines are found in Chapter Two of the Guidelines Manual. The Statutory Index lists the offense guidelines applicable to most federal offenses. It can be found in Appendix A to the Manual. If an offense is not listed in the Statutory Index, then the guidelines provide that the "most analogous" offense guideline should be used. If the defendant has a plea agreement that stipulates to an offense that is more serious than the offense of conviction, the guidelines require the court to use the offense guideline for that more serious offense.

### §8:13.2 Step Two: Determine the Base Offense Level

After selecting the offense guideline, the next step is to determine the "base offense level." The "base offense level" is the minimum offense level for a particular offense. It usually does not depend on any of the details of the case. For example, the base offense level for insider trading is Level 8.If a defendant is convicted of insider trading, he will start out with eight offense levels, no matter what happened in the case.

Some offense guidelines set the base offense level based upon an amount of money or drugs. For example, USSG §2D1.1(c) uses drug weight to set the base offense level. In tax cases, the base offense level is at least level 6, but could be higher, depending on the amount of taxes involved. Only drugs or money that qualify as "relevant conduct" are used to set the base offense level.

Sometimes, the base offense level is established by the offense level for an underlying offense. This is true for money laundering cases, for example. If the money laundered is from a fraud, then the fraud guideline sets the offense level for money laundering. Occasionally, a guideline will set a minimum base offense level, but will provide that the offense level of an underlying offense will apply if it is higher. This is true for RICO cases.

### §8:13.3 Step Three: Specific Offense Characteristics

The next step is to see if any "specific offense characteristic" (SOC) applies. SOCs add (or sometimes subtract) offense levels to the base offense level. The

Sentencing Commission lists different SOCs for each offense guideline. For example, in fraud cases, the victim's loss is an SOC. This SOC ranges from no increase in offense level where there is no loss, to a 30-level increase when the loss exceeds $100 million.

It is important to remember that an SOC applies only to the offense guideline in which it is found. For example, a drug offense SOC provides for a two-level increase if a gun "was possessed." Therefore, a defendant in a drug case will receive a two-level increase if a firearm "was possessed." (The defendant does not have to be the person who "possessed" the firearm. He will receive two levels if the firearm "was possessed" by anyone for whose conduct he is responsible.) However, because the "Promoting a Commercial Sex Act" guideline, §2G1.1, has no similar SOC, a defendant in that kind of a case where a gun "was possessed" does not receive an increase in offense level.

### §8:13.4   Step Four: Cross References and Special Instructions

Occasionally, the offense guideline contains a "cross reference" or "special instruction." "Cross references" tell the court to apply a different offense guideline under certain circumstances. For example, USSG §2D1.7 normally applies to sales of drug paraphernalia. Although the base offense level for this offense is normally 12, a "cross reference" requires the court to use the drug offense guideline in some paraphernalia cases, if that results in a higher offense level.

"Special instructions" tell the court how to apply the guidelines in particular situations. Some special instructions relate to the calculation of fines. The price rigging offense guideline has an instruction like that.So does the guideline for use of a firearm during and in relation to certain crimes.Other offense guidelines instruct the court to calculate the guideline offense level as if the defendant were convicted on a separate count for each victim, even though he was not. The guideline for the unlawful production of weapons of mass destruction has that kind of instruction.

### §8:13.5   Step Five: Adjustments Related to the Nature of the Victim, the Defendant's Role in the Offense, and Obstruction of Justice

Next, the Court applies adjustments that have to do with the victim, the defendant's role in the offense, and obstruction of justice.These adjustments are found in Chapter Three, Parts A, B, and C of the Sentencing Guidelines Manual. Unlike the offense guidelines in Chapter Two of the Manual, these adjustments apply to all offenses. For example, USSG §3B1.1 adds between two and four levels based on a defendant's leadership role. This adjustment can be added no matter which offense guideline applies.

There are also adjustments that apply based on the nature of the victim. A defendant can receive additional levels if the victim was especially "vulnerable," for example.Levels are also added if the victim was a government official.An adjustment applies if the victim was "restrained,"or if the offense involved or promoted terrorism.

Role in the offense adjustments can either increase or decrease the offense level. If the defendant was an organizer, leader, manager, or supervisor of at least one other participant, the court must increase his offense level from between two and four levels. The amount of increase depends on the nature of the defendant's role and the number of people involved in the offense, or how extensive the offense was.A defendant's offense level is decreased between two and four levels if his role in the offense was comparatively "minimal," "minor," or somewhere in between.In drug cases, defendants who receive minor or minimal role adjustments also qualify for additional decreases.

The guidelines also call for a role-in-the-offense increase if the defendant abused a position of trust or used a special skill.There is also an upward adjustment if the defendant used someone under the age of 18 to help commit the offense, or to avoid detection or apprehension.

Before the abuse of a position of trust adjustment applies, the government must prove two things. First, the defendant must have held a "position of trust." A "position of trust" is not the same as "being trusted." This adjustment does not apply simply because a victim trusted a defendant. The defendant must hold a *position* of trust. For example, a corporate officer holds a position of trust with respect to his corporation. Second, being in a position of trust must have helped the defendant commit the offense. For example, being a corporate officer might help a defendant steal funds to which he had access because he was an officer.

The use of a special skill adjustment applies to defendants who have "special skills," such as lawyers, chemists, doctors, pilots, and accountants. But having a special skill is not enough to qualify for this adjustment. The special skill must help the defendant commit the offense. A chemist convicted of tax evasion would not receive this adjustment. You don't need to be a chemist to evade taxes. A chemist convicted of manufacturing controlled substances, on the other hand, might receive it. The question would be whether his special knowledge of chemistry helped him commit the offense.

The obstruction of justice adjustment is found at USSG §3C1.1. It is most often applied against defendants who testify falsely in their own defense. Not all defendants who testify receive this adjustment. The Court must first find that they committed perjury. It is a risk that all defendants must consider before taking the stand. The adjustment is also applied to other obstructive behavior, such as destroying evidence, or pressuring or threatening witnesses.

### §8:13.6    Step Six: Grouping

Whenever there is more than one count of conviction, the offense levels for each count or group of counts must be "combined." The offense levels must be combined for the guidelines to determine an offense level that applies to the entire case. There are two ways that the guidelines combine offense levels from different counts to determine the offense level for the case. The first way is by "grouping." The second way is by taking the offense level for the most serious count, and then adding levels to it. The number of levels added to the offense level for the most serious count depends on the seriousness of the other counts.

Counts can be "grouped" if they are "closely related."Several kinds of counts can be grouped. Counts are grouped when their offense levels are largely determined by a quantity of something.For example, if a defendant pleads guilty to two counts of possession of marijuana with intent to distribute, those counts are considered together. The total amount of marijuana from both counts is added up and used to establish the base offense level for the "group." Counts of fraud or tax evasion would group this way.

Counts can also be grouped when their offense levels are not largely determined by quantity. Courts look to a number of factors to make grouping decisions in these kinds of cases. First, a court would look at whether the crimes had the same victim or victims. If they did, the court would look to whether the offenses involved the same acts or transactions. It would also look to whether they were part of a common scheme or plan. If both of these factors were present, the counts would group.Consider a case in which a defendant trespassed on government property and stole something from the government. The defendant was convicted on one count of trespassing on government property and another count of theft of government property. The counts would group because both factors are present. First, the victim of each count is the same—the government. Second, both counts are part of the same scheme—a scheme to steal something from the government. When counts are grouped in this way, the offense level for the group is the offense level for the most serious count.

Counts are also grouped when one count is conduct that is used to determine the offense level for another count.For example, the base offense level for a money laundering count is the offense level for the underlying offense. If the underlying offense is a drug offense, then the money laundering and drug offenses would be grouped. When counts are grouped in this way, the offense level for the group is the offense level for the most serious count.

Some offenses are never grouped together. Some of these crimes are identified in USSG §3D1.2. For example, burglary counts are not grouped, even though their offense level depends on the loss to the victim. USSG §2B2.1 is the burglary guideline. Generally, violent crimes or offenses against persons are not grouped. Assaults, robberies, and sexual offenses are not grouped. Some non-violent offenses also do not group. These include fraudulently acquiring naturalization, citizenship or residency documents, payment to obtain public office, or escape from custody or confinement.

If counts are not grouped, the court will use USSG §3D1.4 to determine a combined offense level. For example, if a defendant was convicted of conspiracy to commit murder, several drug distribution counts, and a bank robbery, not all the counts would group. The drug distribution counts would group with each other, but they would not group with the other counts. The murder and bank robbery counts would not group with any count. The court would therefore calculate an offense level for the drug distribution group. It would also separately calculate an offense level for the murder group and one for the robbery group. The court would then combine these offense levels. Even though there was only one count of robbery and one count of murder, the guidelines think of them as separate "groups" when it combines them.

When a court combines offense levels, it first looks to the offense level for the most serious group. It then compares that offense level to the offense level for each of the other groups. When the offense level for a group is between one and eight levels less serious than the most serious group, the combined offense level will be raised. When a group is nine or more levels less serious than the most serious offense, it does not cause the combined offense level to increase. When a defendant is convicted of more than one crime, and those counts cannot be grouped, the combined offense level is determined solely by the counts of conviction. For example, if a defendant is convicted of four bank robberies, his combined offense level will be based on the four counts of conviction. This is so, even if the government has evidence that the defendant committed nine bank robberies. The court might consider the other bank robberies in deciding whether to impose a sentence that is higher than the top of the guideline range.

### §8:13.7 Step Seven: Acceptance of Responsibility

The last step in calculating the offense level is to determine whether the "acceptance of responsibility" adjustment applies. Defendants who accept responsibility are entitled to at least a two-level reduction in offense level. Sometimes, defendants are entitled to a three-level reduction.

The two-level reduction is most often given to defendants who plead guilty. But pleading guilty is no guarantee. Defendants who plead guilty are sometimes denied credit for acceptance of responsibility. Defendants who try to withdraw their pleas prior to sentencing have been denied the credit. So have defendants who have made statements denying guilt after they pleaded guilty. Defendants who obstruct justice or commit other crimes after pleading guilty are often denied the credit, too.

Sometimes, but not very often, a court will give credit for accepting responsibility to a defendant who went to trial. Defendants who receive this credit after going to trial usually have not disagreed with the prosecutor's version of what happened. Instead, they are people who made only a legal argument at trial that what they did was not a crime.

A defendant is entitled to an additional level reduction for acceptance of responsibility, for a total of three, if he meets three conditions. First, he must have an offense level of 16 or higher. The level is measured right before the credit is applied. Second, he must timely notify the prosecution of his intent to plead guilty, "thereby permitting the government to avoid preparing for trial and permitting the government and the court to allocate their resources efficiently." Finally, a court may grant this third level downward adjustment only if the prosecutor files a motion which states that defendant meets the criteria for the additional level.

## §8:13.8    Step Eight: Criminal History Category

A defendant's guideline range is determined by two factors. The first factor is the offense level. The second factor is the criminal history category. A higher criminal history category means a higher guideline range.

A court calculates a defendant's criminal history category using criminal history points. Defendants receive "points" for prior sentences. The number of points a defendant receives partially depends on the length of each prior sentence. A defendant receives three points for each prior sentence of at least 13 months. A defendant receives two points for each prior sentence of at least sixty days. Otherwise, a defendant receives one point for a prior sentence. A defendant receives two more points if he committed his current offense while he was on probation, parole, supervised release, imprisonment, work release or escape status. The court adds another two points if the defendant committed the current offense when he was in prison. The court also adds up to two more points if the defendant committed the current offense less than two years after he completed a sentence of at least 60 days.

Some sentences are too old to be counted. A sentence of more than 13 months does not count if the sentence was imposed more than 15 years before the defendant began to commit the current offense. There is one exception to this rule. A sentence imposed more than 15 years ago counts if the defendant committed the current offense less then 15 years after he was released from prison on the prior sentence. A similar ten-year rule applies to prior sentences of 13 months or less.

A prior sentence of probation normally counts for one criminal history point. For example, if a defendant was sentence to 30 days in jail and three years' probation, he would normally receive one point. However, if the court later revoked probation and sentenced the defendant to 14 months in prison, he would receive three points.

Some minor offenses never add points. Sentences for hitchhiking, loitering and public intoxication never count. Other sentences only count if the defendant received at least 30 days' imprisonment or one year of probation, *or* if the prior offense was similar to the current offense. Sentences for careless or reckless driving, disorderly conduct, contempt of court, gambling, prostitution and trespassing are treated like this.

A prior sentence that punished conduct that is part of the current offense does not count. In other words, if conduct underlying the prior sentence is "relevant conduct" for the current offense, no points are added. For example, when a defendant is prosecuted in both state and federal court for the same acts, the defendant receives no points for the prior state sentence.

Cases that ended in diversion or deferred prosecution usually don't add points. The exception is cases in which the defendant entered a formal plea of guilty or *nolo contendere.*

Sentences imposed in foreign countries do not count. Neither do sentences for expunged, reversed, or invalid convictions. Sentences that are "set aside" for errors of law, or because the defendants are innocent, do not count. Prior sentences usually do not count if the defendant committed the offense when he was under 18. However, when juveniles receive adult sentences of 13 months or more, they do count as priors. Sentences imposed on juveniles also count if the defendants began their current offenses within five years of completing the juvenile sentences.

There are six criminal history categories. Category I is for defendants with either zero or one criminal history point, representing no to minimal and non-serious prior criminal conduct. Category VI is for defendants with more than 13 points, representing those with numerous and serious prior criminal conduct. Criminal history points affect a defendant's guideline range. A defendant in Category I will have a lower guideline range than will a defendant with the same offense level who is in a higher criminal history category.

Sometimes, a defendant's criminal history score exaggerates or understates the seriousness of his criminal record. A defendant may have a lot of points because of many minor brushes with the law. The high criminal history category may make his priors seem more serious than they really are. In that case, a guideline policy statement suggests that a "downward departure" may be appropriate. Another defendant may have a long criminal history, but few prior sentences that count. This can happen when a defendant has many foreign or juvenile convictions that do not count. In such a case, a guideline policy statement suggests that an "upward departure" may be appropriate.

### §8:13.9    Step Nine: The Guideline Range

Once the court has arrived at the applicable offense level and criminal history category, it is a simple matter to determine the guideline range. The court just turns to the Sentencing Table at the beginning of Chapter Five of the Guidelines Manual and goes to the intersection of the appropriate offense level line with the criminal history category column. The range is given in months of imprisonment. For example, if the offense level is 24 and the criminal history category is III, the range is 63-78 months. A 0-6 month range means that the sentencing guidelines recommend a sentence somewhere between probation and six months' imprisonment.

Now that the guidelines are no longer mandatory, there is no significant difference between a guideline and a guideline policy statement. A sentencing court must "consider" guidelines as well as guideline policy statements prior to imposing sentence.

There are two exceptions to this method of arriving at the guideline range. The first is where the guideline range would come out higher than the statutory maximum. For example, if a defendant is convicted on one count of money laundering, a 20-year statutory maximum applies. If the defendant's offense level was 34 and his criminal history category was VI, the range would normally be 262-327 months. However, because the statutory maximum is 20 years (240 months), the 262-327-month range does not apply. Instead, 240 months becomes the recommended guideline sentence.

If the same defendant is being sentenced on one money laundering count *and* one drug count, the court would be able to impose a sentence within the guideline range if it wanted to. The court could construct a sentence within this range by running part of the sentences consecutively. For example, if the drug count had a statutory maximum of 20 years, then the court could impose a 20-year sentence on each count. The Court could run part of one sentence consecutively to achieve a sentence within the 262-327-month guideline range.

The second exception is where the range is lower than a mandatory minimum sentence. For example, if the offense level is 22 and the criminal history category is I, the guideline range would normally be 41-51 months. However, if the defendant was subject to a five-year mandatory minimum sentence, the recommended guideline sentence becomes 60 months (five years). Mandatory life sentences also trump any lower sentence suggested by the guidelines. Mandatory life is required by certain murder and drug statutes and under the "three strikes" law. There is no parole for defendants sentenced for crimes committed on or after November 1, 1987, which is when the Sentencing Reform Act, the law that established the Guidelines, went into effect. A person receiving a life sentence will die in prison unless the sentence is later changed for some reason.

### §8:13.10    Special Situations—Career Offenders, ACCA, Repeat and Dangerous Sex Offenders, Three Strikes, and Mandatory Minimums

The guidelines generally determine the sentencing range by calculating the offense level and the criminal history category in the ways we have already discussed. This method usually produces a sentence that any reasonable person would consider punitive enough. Sometimes, though, Congress wants to make sure that the guideline range is even harsher. Congress has mandated extremely high guideline ranges for four types of defendants. The Sentencing Commission has adjusted the guidelines to comply. The first type of defendant is the "career offender." To be a "career offender," a defendant must meet three conditions. He must have been at least 18 years old when he committed his current offense. His current offense must be a crime of violence or a "controlled substance" offense. Finally, he must have two prior convictions for crimes of violence or controlled substance offenses. The Career Offender guideline sets offense levels based on statutory maximums. It also places all "career offenders" in Criminal History Category VI.

"Armed career criminals" must receive sentences of at least 15 years' imprisonment. They may be sentenced up to life in prison. An "armed career criminal" is someone who violates 18 U.S.C. §922(g) and meets other conditions set by §924(e) (the Armed Career Criminal Act, also known as "ACCA"). Section 922(g) mainly applies to gun possession by previously-convicted felons. Explaining these offenses is beyond the scope of this section. The guideline offense level for ACCA defendants is determined by USSG §4B1.4. This guideline requires the court to calculate a defendant's offense level using the one of several methods that produces the greatest offense level. The first method is to determine the defendant's normal guideline level. The second uses the "career offender" guideline, if that is applicable. The third imposes an offense level of 33 or 34. The ACCA guideline also controls a defendant's criminal history category. It requires a criminal history category of at least IV. In some cases it requires a court to use Category VI.

Repeat sexual offenders are subject to statutory maximums that are twice as long as first offenders. The guidelines take this into account through USSG §4B1.5. This is the guideline for "repeat and dangerous sex offenders against minors." This guideline sets the offense level based on the statutory maximum. It requires a criminal history category of at least Category V.

Some laws require courts to impose a sentence that is no less than a certain number of years. Mandatory minimum sentences are the most common way that Congress makes sure that some defendants receive harsher sentences than their guidelines would otherwise require. For example, a defendant convicted of growing 100 or more marijuana plants must be sentenced to at least five years in prison, no matter how much the plants weigh. If a defendant grew 100 marijuana plants that each produced 100 grams of usable marijuana, he would have grown 10 kilograms of marijuana. This normally results in a base offense level 16. If this defendant received no other levels and was in Criminal History Category I, his guideline range would normally be 21-27 months. However, because of the mandatory minimum, the court would have to impose a five-year (60 month) sentence on that count.

### §8:13.11 §3553(a) Factors

After the sentencing court calculates the guideline range, it must "consider" it along with the other factors listed in 18 U.S.C. §3553(a). Those factors are the "nature and circumstances of the offense and the history and characteristics of the defendant," the purposes of sentencing, "the kinds of sentences available," the policy statements issued by the Sentencing Commission, such as those related to departures, "the need to avoid unwarranted sentence disparities among defendants with similar records who have been found guilty of similar conduct," and "the need to provide restitution to any victims of the offense."

### §8:13.12 Departures and Variances

Another one of the seven 3553(a) factors a sentencing court must "consider" is the Sentencing Commission's policy statements. The sections of the Sentencing Guidelines Manual that deal with "departures" are all "policy statements." When the guidelines were mandatory, a "departure" was the way that they dealt with situations that were either not covered by the guidelines at all, or that were not adequately covered by them. The guidelines themselves recognize that it may be appropriate for a court to impose a sentence that is lower or higher than the otherwise recommended range. When a court lowers the offense level or criminal history category for this reason, it is called a "downward departure." When it raises one of them for this reason, it is called an "upward departure." When a court "departs," it does not have to say that it is departing up or down any particular number of offense levels or criminal history categories. It can simply depart to a sentence that is higher or lower than the guideline range. When the guidelines were still mandatory, "departures" were the only way a court could impose a sentence outside the guideline range.

Now that the guidelines are advisory, it is less important whether a particular mitigating or aggravating factor would justify a "departure." That is because courts may now sentence below or above the guideline range if they think that is necessary to achieve a sentence that is "sufficient, but not greater than necessary" to achieve the goals of sentencing—regardless of whether there are grounds for a "departure" under the guidelines. A sentence above or below the guideline range that is not supported by a "departure" is called a "variance."

Although a court may now impose a below-guideline sentence even with guideline policy statements provide no basis to 'depart,' policy statements are still important. If a mitigating factor would have justified a downward departure under the mandatory guideline system, it may be easier to justify a lower sentence to a court.

There are several factors that sentencing guideline policy statements provide may never support departures. They include: race, sex, religion, lack of youthful guidance, drug or alcohol dependence, and post-sentencing rehabilitation. But now that the guidelines are no longer mandatory, courts may, in appropriate cases, rely on these formerly excluded factors to impose a sentence that is outside the guideline range.

There are three situations in which guideline policy statements state that departures may be appropriate. The first is where the case involves a factor that is not mentioned by the guidelines at all. Such factors are likely to be unique to the case in question. The second situation is where a case involves a factor for which a policy statement "encourages" departures. Encouraged downward departures are listed in USSG §§5K2.1—5K2.18 and §5K2.20. Some of the circumstances for which the guidelines encourage downward departures are:

- The victim's wrongful conduct provoked the offense.
- The defendant committed the offense to avoid a greater harm. The guidelines give "mercy killing" as an example of this.
- The defendant was forced to commit the offense. This departure is helpful when there was coercion, but not enough to warrant an acquittal.
- The offense was out of character for the defendant. The guidelines call this "aberrant behavior."
- The defendant's diminished mental capacity contributed to the offense. "Diminished mental capacity" refers to psychological problems. It also covers very low intelligence. The guidelines recognize two kinds of diminished capacity. One kind of diminished capacity makes it difficult for a defendant to control his behavior. The other kind makes it difficult for a defendant to understand that what he did was wrong. This

departure is encouraged only for non-violent offenses and for offenses that were not caused by voluntary drug or other intoxicant use. It is also not generally available to sex offenses.
- The defendant voluntarily disclosed the offense.

The guidelines encourage *upward* departures for things such as extreme conduct, abduction or unlawful restraint, extreme psychological injury, and significantly endangering the public welfare. Some of the guidelines in Chapter Two also mention "encouraged departures" for specific types of offenses. Most of these point upward, but some encourage downward departures.

The third situation in which guideline policy statements recognize that departures may be appropriate is where a case involves a "discouraged factor" to an extraordinary degree. The guidelines say that these factors are "not ordinarily relevant" to whether a court should depart. Departures based on such factors are recommended only if they are present to an extraordinary extent. Factors for which departures are "discouraged" include:
- A defendant's age;
- A defendant's education;
- A defendant's skills;
- A defendant's physical, mental or emotional condition;
- A defendant's civic and charitable contributions;
- A defendant's employment record;
- A defendant's family ties and responsibilities.

These factors are "discouraged" as reasons for departure because they are more common. For example, it is not unusual for a defendant facing sentencing to have emotional problems. Children and spouses often suffer when one of their family members is sent to prison. Policy statements recommend that courts not depart for these reasons unless the emotional problem or the suffering of the spouse or children is extraordinary.

Sometimes policy statements recommend that courts consider departures based on a factor that the guidelines have considered. This can happen when the factor is present to a degree that the guidelines did not consider. For example, the guidelines provide for a downward adjustment for acceptance of responsibility. Some courts have departed downward for extraordinary acceptance of responsibility. When a court "departs" for this reason, it means that it lowers the offense level even more than the two or three levels provided by the guidelines. Courts have found extraordinary acceptance of responsibility is several situations. Defendants who have begun to pay restitution before they have been charged with an offense have gotten this departure. So have defendants who have taken steps to rehabilitate themselves before being charged. Now that the guidelines are no longer mandatory, courts may choose to impose sentences below the recommended range for reasons that the Sentencing Commission took into account, so long as they "consider" the guidelines, policy statements, and other factors required by 18 U.S.C. §3553(a), and so long as they explain why the lower sentence is "sufficient, but not greater than necessary" to achieve the goals of sentencing.

A defendant also may receive a downward "departure" if he helps the government prosecute or investigate someone else. A guideline policy statement recommends that a court not depart for this reason unless the prosecution files a motion that states that the defendant provided "substantial assistance." Normally, a defendant cannot force the government to file a "substantial assistance" motion. There are two, and in some Circuits, three exceptions to this rule. The first is when the government refuses to file a motion for a unconstitutional reason, such as a defendant's race. The second is when the government has agreed in a plea agreement to file the motion, and then does not. It is unusual for the government to promise in advance to file a "substantial assistance motion." Plea agreements often mention conditions under which the government will file "substantial assistance" motions, but usually give the government sole discretion to determine whether those conditions have been met.

In some Circuits, there is a third exception to the general rule. This exception can help defendants with cooperation agreements which provide that the government will file the motion if it believes the defendant's cooperation amounts to "substantial assistance." Agreements like these, however, are hard to enforce. The government can always say that it did not believe that the defendant's cooperation amounted to "substantial assistance." In some Circuits a defendant can force the prosecution to file a departure motion if he can demonstrate that the prosecution's refusal to file the motion was made in "bad faith." The defendant must prove that his cooperation met the prosecution's standards for "substantial assistance," but the prosecution refused to file the motion anyway.

Unless one of these conditions apply, a defendant cannot force the government to file a departure motion. This is not to suggest that substantial assistance motions are rare. They are not. The latest figures available (the ones for 2006), reflect that a government substantial assistance motion is the most common reason for departure. Courts departed in 14.4 percent of the sentences imposed that year, in response to "substantial assistance" motions.

Now that the guidelines are no longer mandatory, courts have the authority to impose lower sentences to reward cooperation—even where the prosecution has refused to file a departure motion. The one exception to this rule is where a mandatory minimum sentence applies. In that situation, a government motion is *required* before a court can impose sentence below that minimum.

## §8:14    "SUBSTANTIAL ASSISTANCE" MOTIONS, COOPERATION AGREEMENTS, AND THE "SAFETY VALVE"

There are two exceptions to laws that require mandatory minimum sentences. One applies when the prosecutor makes a "substantial assistance" motion. This exception applies to all mandatory minimum cases. The other applies only to drug cases. It is known as the "safety valve."

### §8:14.1    "Substantial Assistance" Motions

"Substantial assistance" motions reward defendants who "cooperate" with the government. There are two kinds of "substantial assistance" motions. One kind permits courts to go below mandatory minimums. That kind of motion is authorized by 18 U.S.C. §3553(e). The other kind asks courts to depart below the guideline range—but not below a mandatory minimum. That kind of motion is authorized by USSG §5K1.1.

Prosecutors do not file departure motions for all cooperators. A prosecutor will file a motion only if the cooperation was "substantial." What is "substantial" in one prosecutor's office may not be "substantial" in another office. All prosecutors think that testifying against another person is "substantial." Some prosecutors think that talking about another person is not "substantial" if it does not lead to an arrest or conviction.

In a case involving a mandatory minimum sentence, a substantial assistance departure motion can give a court the power to impose a sentence as low as probation. A court can impose a lower sentence without a substantial assistance motion in a case that does not involve a mandatory minimum sentence. But it is more likely that a court will impose a lower sentence if the government files a motion. A court will usually impose a lower sentence when the government files a departure motion, but not always. Departure motions do not *require* courts to impose lower sentences. Sometimes prosecutors make recommendations in their motions. A court also does not have to go along with a prosecutor's recommendation. It is up to the court how low to go. In some cases defense counsel can pursuade the court to go even lower than recommended by the prosecutor.

### §8:14.2    Cooperation Agreements

Plea agreements sometimes require defendants to cooperate with the government. These are called "cooperation agreements." Cooperation agreements provide different kinds of benefits to defendants. Sometimes the prosecution promises to file a substantial assistance departure motion. If the government makes the promise without any conditions, it *must* file the motion. More often, a promise by the prosecution comes with conditions attached. The usual condition is that the defendant's cooperation must be "substantial." Usually it is entirely up to the prosecutor to decide what counts as being "substantial." Sometimes the government promises only to "consider" filing a motion. These kinds of agreements often lead to departure motions, but they are not guarantees.

### §8:14.3    The "Safety Valve"

There are no mandatory minimums in drug cases for defendants who quality for the "safety valve." If a defendant qualifies for the safety valve, the court may sentence him below the mandatory minimum. Most defendants who qualify for the safety valve also qualify for a two-level decrease in their offense levels. There is one exception to this rule. A safety valve decrease cannot take a defendant's offense level below Level 17.

A safety valve reduction is not the same thing as a departure. A defendant who qualifies for the safety valve will usually receive a lower sentence because his guideline range will usually be lower. It will usually be lower because no mandatory minimum will make it higher, and because he will receive a two-level decrease.

The prosecution does not have to file any motion to qualify a defendant for the "safety valve." A defendant must meet five conditions:

1.  Not more than one criminal history point;
2.  Defendant did not use or threaten violence; defendant did not possess a dangerous weapon in connection with the offense;
3.  No one was killed or seriously injured by the offense;
4.  Defendant not an organizer, leader, manager or supervisor of other people involved in the offense; and
5.  Prior to sentencing, defendant tells the prosecution everything he knows about his offense and "relevant conduct."

The requirement that a defendant talk to the prosecution about his own offense and "relevant conduct" does not mean that he must give the government new information. It does mean, however, that sometimes a defendant must tell the prosecution about the criminal conduct of other people. A defendant does not have to testify against any one to qualify for the safety valve.

## §8:15    PROBATION, SPLIT SENTENCES, AND COMMUNITY OR HOME CONFINEMENT

Now that the guidelines are advisory, the restrictions they used to impose on probation, split sentences, and community or home confinement, no longer limit courts in the same way. Courts now have the authority to impose these kinds of sentences in almost any case—even if there is no reason to "depart." The exception is where a statute prohibits a certain kind of sentence. Because a court must still "consider" the guidelines, it is important to understand how these restrictions work.

The guidelines recommend probation only if the range is in "Zone A" or "Zone B" of the Sentencing Table (8:42). "Zone A" means the guideline range is between zero and six months. A sentence of probation would be within the guideline range because a sentence of zero months is a sentence within the range. A sentence within this range also does not have to have home or community confinement as a term of probation. "Community confinement" means a halfway house.

Defendants in "Zone B" also may receive sentences of probation that are within the guideline range. "Zone B" ranges have low ends between four and eight months, and high ends of 14 months or less. For defendants in "Zone B," for a probation sentence to be within the guideline range, it must include some kind of confinement as a term of probation. That confinement can be in a halfway house or home confinement. "Zone B" sentences may allow work release from the confinement without being outside the guideline range.

Defendants in "Zone C" may receive what is sometimes called a "split sentence," and still be within the guideline range. "Zone C" ranges have low ends greater than 10 months, but less than 18 months. Defendants in Zone C may receive sentences within the guideline range that require them to serve at least half of the minimum term in prison, and the other half in community confinement or home detention, as a condition of supervised release. For example, if a defendant has a guideline range of 10-16 months, putting him in "Zone C," the judge could give a sentence within the guideline range that includes five months' imprisonment and supervised release that included a condition that the defendant serve five months in a halfway house or in home detention.

The guidelines recommend that defendants in Zone D not be sentenced to terms of probation. Zone D ranges have low ends of at least 12 months. After *Booker,* some creative lawyers have successfully urged judges to place their clients on probation or impose split sentences for people whose guidelines fall within Zone D. For example, judges have imposed sentences of a year and a day of incarceration followed by supervised release, with a year's home confinement as a condition of supervised release, rather than two-year advisory guideline prison sentences.

## §8:16 WHEN THE DEFENDANT IS ALREADY SERVING A SENTENCE

Some defendants are already serving sentences for other crimes when they are sentenced. Sometimes the guidelines recommend a sentence that runs consecutively to the first sentence. If the court accepts that recommendation, the new sentence will not even start until the defendant completes the first sentence. In other cases, the guidelines recommend concurrent sentences. That means that if the court accepts the recommendation, the defendant will serve both sentences at the same time, at least starting from when the second sentence is imposed. In other cases, the guidelines make no specific recommendation, other than that courts use their discretion to impose concurrent or consecutive sentences, or sentences that are a little of both.

The guidelines recommend consecutive sentences for crimes committed while the person was already in prison, or on work release, furlough, or escape status. The guidelines recommend concurrent sentences if two conditions are met. First, the defendant must not have committed the offense in prison, or on work release, furlough, or escape status. Second, the guidelines for the current offense must take the earlier offense conduct into account. This can happen when a defendant is prosecuted for a federal offense after he was prosecuted for a state offense that punishes some or all of the same conduct.

Sometimes a defendant is serving a sentence for an unrelated crime that he did not commit in prison, etc. For these cases, the guidelines make no recommendation, other than that courts use their discretion to run the sentence consecutively or concurrently, or a combination of the two. The guidelines recommend that judges decide what result is most fair in such cases.

## §8:17 SUPERVISED RELEASE

There is no parole for defendants sentenced for cimes committed on or after November 1, 1987. That does not mean that after a defendant is released from prison he is no longer under any supervision. The guidelines recommend that a court impose a term of "supervised release" whenever it sentences a defendant to more than a year in prison. Terms of supervised release range from one to five years, and sometimes even life, depending on the offense and the maximum punishment.

Defendants on supervised release are under the supervision of probation officers. They must report to their probation officers on a regular basis. They also need permission from their probation officers to travel outside of their district. Defendants on supervised release must follow numerous conditions, many of which are listed in USSG §5D1.3. For example, defendants on supervised release must work unless their probation officers excuse them. They are also not allowed to be in touch with the people they met in prison, unless their probation officers allow it. Federal law allows a court to terminate a term of supervised release after a defendant has successfully completed one year of supervised release.

A defendant who violates one of the conditions of supervised release can be sent to prison for up to the full term of supervised release. Before a court can send someone to prison for violating a term of supervised release, it must "consider" many of the same factors that it had to consider before imposing sentence in the first place. Those factors include the sentencing guidelines and policy statements. Chapter Seven of the Guidelines Manual includes policy statements relevant to the revocation of supervised release. Whether a defendant who violates the conditions of supervised release will be sent to prison, and if so, for how long, depends on the seriousness of the violation. Defendants who violate supervised release are not usually sent to prison for the full term of the supervised release. How long a violator must serve depends on the seriousness of the violation and the violator's criminal history category. Chapter 7, part B of the guidelines deals with violations of probation and supervised release.

## §8:18 FINES, RESTITUTION, FORFEITURES, SPECIAL ASSESSMENTS, AND COSTS OF INCARCERATION

Every federal sentence includes a $100 special assessment for each felony count of conviction. For example, if a defendant is convicted on 10 felony counts, he will receive a $1,000 special assessment. Sentences often include other financial penalties as well, such as restitution, fines, and forfeitures.

Restitution is an order to pay money that goes to the victims of the offense. Courts are often required to order defendants to pay the full amount of victims' loss as restitution. A court must order full restitution in most cases, even if the defendant does not and never will have the money to pay it. If a defendant does not have resources to pay the restitution, the guidelines recommend that the court order him to make small monthly payments that he can afford. A court can require a defendant to make payments on a restitution order as a condition of supervised release.

The guidelines recommend that a court impose a fine unless the defendant is unable to pay one and is unlikely to become able to pay one. Courts do not impose fines in most cases, because most defendants are unable to pay them. The guidelines recommend a range for fines based on a defendant's offense level. A defendant's criminal history does not affect the fine range. For example the fine range for offense levels 16-17 is $5,000 to $50,000. The fine table is found at USSG §5E1.2(c)(3). A court must consider this range, just as it must consider the guideline imprisonment range. But it is no more required to impose a fine within the range than it is to sentence within a range. If a court orders a defendant to pay restitution and a fine, any money the defendant pays will be used to pay the restitution first.

A few statutes require defendants to pay the cost of their prosecution. These include several tax offenses, as well as larceny or embezzlement in connection with commodity exchanges. These statutes are listed in the commentary that follows USSG §5E1.5.

Finally, some statutes require a court to impose an order of forfeiture as part of the sentence. When property is forfeited, it is turned over to the government. Racketeering and drug laws, for example, require defendants to forfeit to the government certain property used in the offense or purchased with money gained from the offense.

## §8:19 APPEALS FROM SENTENCING DECISIONS

Prior to the guidelines, it was nearly impossible to appeal a sentence. That changed with the guidelines system. When the guidelines were mandatory, it was possible to appeal a sentence if it was imposed as a result of an incorrect application of the guidelines or if the court departed upwards. The government could also appeal sentences it believed were imposed as a result of an incorrect application of the guidelines or if the court departed downwards. After *Booker,* it is still possible for defendants and the government to appeal sentences. Now Courts of Appeals review sentences for "reasonableness."

There are two types of "reasonableness" that courts of appeals review. The first thing a court of appeals does is to review a sentence for procedural reasonableness. There are several factors an appeals court looks to to determine procedural reasonableness. First, it looks to whether the district court correctly calculated the guideline range. If the district court did not calculate the guideline range correctly, then it did not consider the correct range as required by §3553(a). That makes the sentence procedurally "unreasonable." Appellate courts review guideline issues *de novo.*

The appeals court will also determine procedural reasonableness by looking at whether the district court considered the other §3553(a) factors and the arguments of the parties for a sentence outside the guideline range. District courts must adequately articulate their reasons for imposing a particular sentence. If a court rejects an argument for a sentence outside the guideline range, it must adequately explain its reasoning. If it does not, the sentence is procedurally unreasonable.

Appeallate courts also review sentences for substantive reasonableness. Although *Booker* promised that district court judges would finally be freed from the constraints of the guidelines and allowed to exercise their discretion to do justice at sentencing, appellate courts soon rejected numerous below-guideline sentences as "unreasonable" simply because they did not believe that the mitigating circumstances on which the district courts relied were significant enough to support large "variances" from the bottom of the guideline ranges. After the Supreme Court held that appellate courts (but not district courts) may presume that sentences within the advisory guideline range are "reasonable," the message seemed to be that while the guidelines were "advisory," district courts that didn't want to be reversed should not stray too far from the "advisory" range. All that changed in December 2007, when the Supreme Court announced its decisions in *Gall v. United States,* and *Kimbrough v. United States*, opening up a new era in federal sentencing in which judges will once more be allowed to be judges.

*Gall* involved a conspiracy to distribute the illegal drug "ecstasy." Although the guidelines recommended a sentence of 30-37 months' imprisonment, the district court sentenced Gall to 36 months' probation. The court cited several unusual mitigating factors to supports its sentence. First, Brian Gall committed his offense when he was an immature 21-year-old college sophomore, and an ecstasy user himself. Second, several months after joining the conspiracy, Gall voluntarily stopped using illegal drugs and formally notified other members of the conspiracy that he was withdrawing from it. After that, Gall not only never used or distributed any illegal drugs, he finished his education and went to work in the construction industry. After four years of leading an exemplary life, the government rewarded his rehabilitation with an indictment. Gall pled guilty. At sentencing, the court explained that a probationary sentence was sufficient, but not greater than necessary, to meet the goals of sentencing, because Gall had in essence rehabilitated himself some four years before he had even been indicted. The government appealed and the Eighth Circuit reversed, holding that the district court's "100%" variance from the guideline range was not supported by sufficiently extraordinary reasons. The Supreme Court reversed the Court of Appeals.

Although *Gall* noted that it is "uncontroversial that a major departure should be supported by a more significant justification than a minor one," the Court explicitly "reject[ed] an appellate rule that requires 'extraordinary' circumstances to justify a sentence outside the Guidelines range." It also "reject[ed] the use of a rigid mathematical formula that uses the percentage of a departure as the standard for determining the strength of the justifications required for a specific sentence." The Court noted that these approaches come perilously close to establishing a presumption that sentences outside the guideline range are "unreasonable"—a presumption the Court previously rejected in *Rita.* The Court was particularly critical of what it termed the "mathematical approach." Viewing variances as percentages of the bottom of the guideline range tend to make sentences of probation seem "extreme," since "a sentence of probation will always be a 100% departure regardless of whether the Guidelines range is 1 month or 100 years." The Court was also critical of the fact that this approach also "gives no weight" to what the Court characterized as the "substantial restriction of freedom involved in a term of supervised release or probation,"—a subtle invitation to courts to impose sentences of probation more often.

But *Gall* did more that invalidate particular approaches to reviewing variances from the guidelines. It reminded the Courts of Appeals that *Booker* invalidated the statutory provision that made the Guidelines mandatory (18 U.S.C. §3553(b)(1)). It also invalidated 18 U.S.C. §3742(e), which directed appellate courts to review departures from the Guidelines *de novo.* Prior to *Gall,* the Courts of Appeals seemed to ignore the significance of *Booker's* invalidation of §3742(e). While the Supreme Court thought *Booker* had "made it . . . clear that the familiar abuse-of-discretion standard of review now applies to appellate review of sentencing decisions," the Court found that the decisions of the Courts of Appeals that required "extraordinary" reasons for significant deviations from the guidelines "more closely resembled *de novo* review."

*Gall* makes it clear that the Supreme Court meant what it said in *Booker*: While sentencing courts must consider the guideline range as a "starting point," the "Guidelines are not the only consideration." District courts must also consider *all* of the other factors listed in 18 U.S.C. §3553(a). Once a Court of Appeals is satisfied that a district court has properly considered all of the factors listed in 18 U.S.C. §3553(a), its review of a sentence is under the deferential abuse of discretion standard. While a Court of Appeals "may consider the extent of the deviation, [it] must give due deference to the district court's decision that the §3553(a) factors, on a whole, justify the extent of the variance. The fact that the appellate court might reasonably have concluded that a different sentence was appropriate is insufficient to justify reversal of the district court." *Gall* does not mean that a district court's non-guideline sentence cannot be reversed for substantive unreasonableness. But reversal is unlikely in a case in which the district court has provided a detailed written explanation of why the §3553(a) factors support the variance.

While *Gall* held that a district court does not abuse its discretion by basing a below-guideline sentence on offender characteristics, *Kimbrough* held that a district court does not abuse that discretion when it bases a below-guideline sentence on disparities in sentencing caused by the guidelines themselves. In *Kimbrough,* the district court imposed a below-guideline sentence in a crack cocaine case because it disagreed with the Sentencing Commission's and Congress's judgment that the distribution of any quantity of crack cocaine should be punished as severely as the distribution of one hundred times as much powder cocaine—the infamous "100 to 1 ratio."

The essence of the holding in *Kimbrough* is that a district court's judgment that a particular sentence is "sufficient, but not greater than necessary" (the overarching command of 18 U.S.C. §3553(a)) is entitled to great weight, even if the district court's judgment is based in part on its disagreement with the policies behind the applicable guideline. *Kimbrough* gave defense attorneys license to think creatively about how guideline sentences themselves create "unwarranted disparities." It may now be entirely possible to obtain a lower non-guideline sentence by arguing, among other reasons, that a particular guideline sentence would create unwarranted disparities with sentences imposed in similar state cases.

Although the promise of *Kimbrough* is great, it is important to remember that in many ways the history of the crack guideline makes it unique. While the majority observed that in the "ordinary" case, "the Commission's recommendation of a sentencing range will 'reflect a rough approximation of sentences that might achieve §3553(a)'s objectives,'" it seemed to place special significance on the fact that the Sentencing Commission long ago concluded that the 100-to-1 ratio was unjust. It remains to be seen whether the broadest reading of *Kimbrough* will enable future challenges to overly harsh guidelines.

The pendulum has finally swung to the point that judges now have more discretion than they have ever had since pre-guideline days to fashion an appropriate sentence in a particular case. Now it's up to defense attorneys to present sentencing courts with the evidence and arguments they need to exercise that discretion to produce just sentences.

## §8:20    AFTER SENTENCING—TAKING ADVANTAGE OF FAVORABLE GUIDELINE CHANGES

The guidelines that a court uses at sentencing can change. Some amendments make the guidelines harsher. Once a defendant is sentenced, he is protected from that kind of change. Amendments can also reduce offense levels. Defendants who have already been sentenced can sometimes take advantage of these reductions. Before a defendant who has already been sentenced can take advantage of an amendment, the amendment must be listed in USSG §1B1.10.

If an amendment is listed in §1B1.10, the sentencing court has the *discretion* to modify a defendant's sentence. The sentencing court does not have to reduce a defendant's sentence based on a retroactive amendment. Once the guidelines make an amendment retroactive, the defendant may make a motion to modify the sentence. The sentencing court could also modify the sentence on its own, without a motion.

One of the most recent significant changes to the guidelines (which was shortly thereafter made retroactive) involved the "crack" cocaine guidelines.

On November 1, 2007, a new guideline amendment (Amendments 706 and 711) became effective that results in somewhat lower offense levels in many crack cocaine cases. Generally speaking, after November 1, offense levels in cases involving crack cocaine will be two levels lower than they would have been. The amendments make changes to the drug quantity table in USSG §2D1.1(c), as well to Application Note 10 of that guideline.

On November 1, 2014, another new guideline amendment (Amendment 782) became effective that results in lowering the drug quantity table by two levels across the board, and further, made the amendment retroactive to apply to those previously sentenced (although implementing the retroactive portion will not become effective until November 1, 2015). The Commission estimates that this amendment, which applies to all drug offenses (with some narrow exceptions), will lower sentences for drug offenders by 25 months on average.

These amendments are the culmination of a more than ten years' effort by the Sentencing Commission and sentencing reform groups to correct a serious pattern of unfairness in the sentencing of drug offenders. The problem began when Congress passed the Anti-Drug Abuse Act of 1986.

The Sentencing Commission's decision to make a new guideline retroactive is a good thing, but it does not guarantee a lower sentence. When the Sentencing Commission makes a guideline retroactive, it gives the court the *power* to lower a sentence—but it does not *require* the court to lower it. Before deciding to lower a particular defendant's sentence, someone has to make a motion asking for the sentence to be modified. Then the court first has to consider the factors listed in 18 U.S.C. §3553(a). These are the same factors a court must consider before imposing sentence in the first place, although in some pre-Booker cases the factors will have been given only limited consideration because the Guidelines were thought to be mandatory prior to *Booker*. If after considering those factors, the Court believes that a lower sentence would be "sufficient, but not greater than necessary" to achieve the goals of sentencing, it may lower the defendant's sentence—but only "if such a reduction is consistent with applicable policy statements issued by the Sentencing Commission." 18 U.S.C. §3582(c)(2). A defendant's post-sentencing conduct may also be considered. U.S.S.G.§ (B)(iii).

This last requirement used to be satisfied simply by showing that the amendment is listed in USSG §1B1.10(c) (p.s.). However, beginning March 3, 2008, the Sentencing Commission has added new requirements designed to reduce a court's discretion. This amended policy statement says that courts may not lower a sentence in cases where the amended guideline does not result in a lower guideline range. Even if the new range is lower, the policy statement attempts to prevent courts from imposing sentences lower than the bottom of the new range. The policy statement makes an exception for cases in which the court had previously departed downward. In such cases, the new sentence may be proportionally less than the new guideline range. The new policy statement also attempts to prevent courts from lowering sentences where defendants already received lower non-guideline sentences pursuant to *United States v. Booker*, 543 U.S. 220 (2005).

## §8:30   ARTICLES

### §8:30.1   At a Loss For Justice : Federal Sentencing for Economic Crimes

According to the United States Sentencing Commission data, economic offenses—which include larceny, fraud, and nonfraud white-collar offenses—now constitute the third largest portion of the federal criminal docket, with drug offenses holding second place and immigration first. (*See* US Sentencing Comm'n, *Sourcebook of Federal Sentencing Statistics* tbl. A (2009).) Such offenses can "rang[e] from large-scale corporate malfeasance, to small-scale embezzlements, to simple thefts." (*See* US Sentencing Comm'n, *Fifteen Years of Guidelines Sentencing: An Assessment of How Well the Federal Criminal Justice System Is Achieving the Goals of Sentencing Reform*, 55 (Nov. 2004).)

Such a wide array of disparate economic offenses both in kind and degree primarily are sentenced under USSG §2B1.1, which arguably (and perhaps necessarily) is the most complex of all the sentencing guidelines with more than 16 specific offense characteristics and cross-references, 19 application notes, and more amendments than any other guideline—40 to date, with more on the way. Currently, more than 300 federal criminal statutes are covered by this single guideline, far more than any other guideline.

This article argues that the lengthily named guideline "Theft, Embezzlement, Receipt of Stolen Property, Property Destruction, and Offenses Involving Fraud or Deceit" at USSG §2B1.1, which, for purposes of brevity, we shall refer to simply as the "fraud guideline," frequently relies too heavily on the ambiguous concept of "loss" (or "gain" in some cases). Although the calculation of "loss" is a "critical determinant" of a defendant's sentence, *see United States v. Rutkoske*, 506 F.3d 170, 179 (2d Cir. 2007), and is often "the single most important factor in the application of the Sentencing Guidelines," according to Peter J. Henning, in *White Collar Crime Sentences After Booker: Was the Sentencing of Bernie Ebbers Too Harsh?* (37 MCGEORGE L. REV. 757, 767 (2006)), loss, as measured by the guideline, nevertheless, does not adequately account for extrinsic factors such as market conditions, inflation, credits from insurance payments, or the scienter of the offender. As applied by federal judges around the country, the fraud guideline often results in widely unwarranted sentencing disparity and a lack of certainty in sentencing, and produces sentences grossly disproportional to the actual seriousness of the offense. (*See United States v. Parris*, 573 F. Supp. 2d 744, 754 (E.D.N.Y. 2008) (noting that "the Sentencing Guidelines for white-collar crimes [can produce] a black stain on common sense"); *United States v. Adelson*, 441 F. Supp. 2d 506, 512 (S.D.N.Y 2006) (lamenting "the utter travesty of justice that sometimes results from the guidelines' fetish with absolute arithmetic, as well as the harm that guideline calculations can visit on human beings if not cabined by common sense").)

"Loss" simply needs to be given less weight under the fraud guideline relative to other factors germane to economic offenses, particularly in large-loss cases. Furthermore, in order to bring loss back to reality, the intrinsically speculative concept of "intended loss" should be substantially discounted if used as an alternative to "actual loss."

In short, the increasingly complex fraud guideline is rapidly becoming a mess. While the Sentencing Commission valiantly attempted to make the economic crime guidelines more coherent a decade ago, those efforts have all but disappeared among the avalanche of congressional directives. Commission efforts to reform section 2B1.1 to incorporate new offenses add to the overall complexity of the guideline, and the now-advisory status of the guidelines necessarily has led to an increasing number of departures and variances.

As the commission continues several ongoing studies regarding the effects of *Booker* (543 U.S. 220 (2005)) and its progeny on federal sentencing law, policy, and practice, a substantive reevaluation of the role of loss in calculating guideline sentences for economic offenses, and, indeed, section 2B1.1 overall, needs to be incorporated into these studies.

### A Brief History of the Fraud Guideline

The fraud guideline originally was located at USSG §2F1.1 and the theft guideline at USSG §2B1.1. As with the guidelines generally, the commission was tasked by Congress to collect data on past sentencing practices. Based on Sentencing Reform Act directives, the commission's reading of legislative history, and its overall policy objectives, the commission modified past practices to roughly equalize sentences for "white collar" fraud and embezzlement offenses and "blue collar" theft offenses (in contrast to past practices in which theft offenders generally received more severe sentences). The commission also made all sentences for economic offenses somewhat more severe than what a review of past practice data had revealed in order to better achieve deterrence and just punishment sentencing goals.

Nevertheless, initial sentences for even the most severe fraud offenses were far less severe than the guideline sentences for economic offenses today. For example, the loss table topped out at a mere $5 million, and the fraud guideline had only two specific offense characteristics.

The commission took steps to ensure that fraud sentences were proportionally less onerous than for other offenses considered more serious (e.g., bribery, serious drug trafficking, and offenses involving violence).

Between November 1, 1987, when the initial guidelines took effect, and today, there have been three significant amendments that increased the severity of the loss table itself and extended the loss brackets to larger dollar amounts.

**The Savings and Loan Scandal Prompts Change.** First, the 1989 amendments increased the severity for moderate- and large-loss offenses, as they were defined at the time (offenses greater than $140,000 in loss received an increase), and the amendments extended the loss table by four loss bracket increments from losses greater than $5 million to losses greater than $80 million. This early reconsideration by the commission in part responded to external developments, principally the savings and loan fraud crisis of the late 1980s.

Concurrent with these changes, the commission began adding additional specific offense characteristics (SOCs) that sought to address particular factors sometimes present in particular types of fraud offenses. Nearly all of these SOCs were of an aggravating nature. This practice began a trend that, over the years, has added some 16 SOCs, several of which are multipronged, to the fraud guideline. (One SOC for more than minimal planning was deleted by incorporating it into the loss tables in 2001.)

Many, if not most, of these new SOCs responded to congressional directives of a general or sometimes very specific nature. Approximately 21, or half the total number of amendments, were of this nature. For example, the savings and loan financial crisis of the late 1980s led to legislation that increased maximum penalties for financial fraud offenses and concurrently directed the Sentencing Commission to add specific aggravating factors to the fraud guideline.

As a result, the commission added major, four-level increases equating to an average 50 percent penalty increase for conduct that "substantially jeopardized the safety and soundness" of a financial institution, and for so-called "fat cats" who derived more than $1 million from the offense. (This SOC was later reduced two levels because of overlap/"double-counting" concerns.)

**The Economic Crimes Package Overhauls Sentencing for Economic Offenses.** The second major severity increase in the fraud guideline loss table occurred in 2001 as part of the commission's "Economic Crimes Package." This comprehensive amendment merged three guidelines, 2Fl.l-fraud, 2B1.1-theft/embezzlement, and 2B3.1-property destruction, into one guideline, 2B1.1, with a new and more severe loss table, and combined specific offense characteristics.

This new loss table used two-offense level increments instead of the former one-level increment. It assumed the applicability of and incorporated the previously separate enhancement for more than minimal planning by gradually phasing it into the loss table. The amendment additionally provided severity increases ranging from two levels for losses greater than $5 million, to four levels (approximately a 50 percent increase) for losses greater than $200 million.

The amendment also provided a comprehensive and far more sophisticated new definition of "loss," changing it from a theft-based definition to one of legal causation more akin to how financial losses are understood in the civil context. The new definition of "reasonably foreseeable pecuniary harm" had the effect of increasing the countable loss in many cases, because it included some previously excluded consequential and other harms.

Finally, the amendment also introduced a new, multi-pronged enhancement for multiple victims that henceforth would frequently interact with the loss table enhancement.

**Attack of the Sarbanes-Oxley Act.** A third severity increase for many fraud offenses occurred a little more than a year later in response to the Sarbanes-Oxley Act and legislative directives in it. The commission increased the base offense level from level 6 to level 7 for fraud offenses carrying a statutory maximum penalty of 20 years or more, which now covered the frequently prosecuted wire and mail fraud offenses. And the loss table was again extended by two additional brackets such that the highest loss amounts went from offenses greater than $100 million to offenses greater than $400 million.

Additional enhancements were added for circumstances in which: (i) the offender was an officer or director of an organization (+4 levels or a 50 percent increase in the sentence), (ii) company insolvency resulted from the offense, and (iii) more than 250 victims were involved.

These multiple amendments to the loss table in and of themselves have dramatically increased sentencing severity for fraud offenses having substantial monetary losses. For example, without considering any other guideline enhancements, the adjusted total offense level for an offense causing just over $20 million in loss has been increased from level 19, which equated to a guideline sentencing range of 30-37 months, to level 29, or 87-108 months. In other words, the three amendments to the loss table in 1989, 2001, and 2003 effectively *tripled* sentences for large-scale fraud offenses.

At the same time, the commission has added a host of SOCs to the fraud guideline, most in response to congressional legislation creating new offenses, increasing statutory penalties, and frequent directives to the commission for higher penalties. Although these enhancements do not apply in all cases, their cumulative effect has been to further increase severity in some types of fraud cases, sometimes dramatically.

### Structural Criticisms of the Fraud Guideline

For the reasons stated above, the loss table often overstates the actual harm suffered by the victim. Multiple, overlapping enhancements also have the effect of "double counting" in some cases. Furthermore, the guidelines fail to take into account important mitigating offense and offender characteristics.

With respect to the loss table specifically, while the commission has made multiple aggravating amendments over the years, it has failed to make any adjustments for the effects of inflation, which itself has effectively increased penalties.

The commission also has arbitrarily selected the loss brackets in the table rather than using a uniform multiplier. A lower multiplier at the high-dollar end of the loss table effectively escalates penalties more rapidly, especially when used in conjunction with the sentencing table, where every increase in offense level causes a progressively greater increase in nominal months of imprisonment. The net effect of this steadily escalating mathematical structure contrasts with an arguably more reasonable and rational approach exhibited in the multiple count guidelines (in chapter 3, part D). The latter structure increases guideline penalties as additional offenses occur, but it does so at a "progressively decreasing rate."

Furthermore, in response to legislative directives, the commission has added a host of SOCs and some additional chapter three enhancements. The net effect has been to heighten penalty severity, sometimes dramatically. For example, an executive officer of a publicly traded company who causes a large fraud loss can face a high guideline penalty derived from the loss table, further accentuated by a +6 level increase for 250 or more victims, +2 levels for receiving more than $1 million from the offense, +4 levels for being a corporate officer, up to +4 levels for an aggravating role in the offense, and possibly +2 levels for abuse of trust. The net guideline score can easily equate to a life sentence, which generally under the guidelines has been reserved for dangerous and/or violent offenses such as murder, terrorism, or high-level drug traffickers.

In early versions of the guidelines, penalty levels and enhancements were derived primarily from empirical analyses of past sentencing practices. The commission was careful to maintain proportionality among offenses, and it had a good sense of the effects of adding enhancements within a guideline. However, as legislatively directed enhancements have proliferated, particularly within the fraud guideline, the objective of proportionality among offenses has gone by the wayside. Guideline sentences for large-dollar fraud offenses can easily equal those of violent crimes such as murder, and far exceed those of other white-collar offenses such as bribery, which the commission initially considered more serious.

While the fraud guideline focuses primarily on aggregate monetary loss and victimization, it fails to measure a host of other factors that may be important, and may be a basis for mitigating punishment, in a particular case. Among these considerations are:

1. the scope and duration of the offense;
2. the extent to which the offender did or did not personally profit from the offense;
3. the motivation for the offense;
4. the extent to which the offense was exacerbated by factors beyond the offender's control.

Historically, the guidelines also have failed to measure offender character-istics other than criminal history. In large scale fraud offenses, the likelihood of important mitigating offender characteristics is greater than in many other types of offenses. Among these are:

1. age;
2. physical and/or emotional health;
3. positive contributions to the community, public service, charitable contributions; and,
4. family and community responsibilities.

## Continued Criticism from the Judiciary

As discussed in detail below, especially as loss amount grows, the correlation between loss and the sentence imposed becomes increasingly arbitrary. Loss simply is not always an appropriate proxy for the seriousness of the offense, as even the guidelines themselves concede. (*See* USSG §2B1.1, cmt. n.19(C) (noting a downward departure may be warranted in cases where the guideline sentence "substantially overstates the seriousness of the offense").)

> [S]ince Booker, virtually every judge faced with a top-level corporate fraud defendant in a very large fraud has concluded that sentences called for by the Guidelines were too high. This near unanimity suggests that the judiciary sees a consistent disjunction between the sentences prescribed by the Guidelines [in economic offense cases] and the fundamental requirement of Section 3553(a) that judges impose sentences "sufficient, but not greater than necessary" to comply with its objectives.

(Frank O. Bowman, III, *Sentencing High-Loss Corporate Insider Frauds After Booker*, 20 Fed. Sent'g Rep. 167, 169 (Feb. 2008).)

In fact, in a recent letter to the US District Court for the Northern District of Iowa regarding a high-profile sentencing case before that court (in which the authors of this article were part of the legal team), Brett Tolman, former US attorney for the District of Utah, and Paul G. Cassell, former US district court judge for the District of Utah, wrote that "[r]ather than resting on evidence of past, national sentencing practices, the white collar Guidelines are a product of the political environment in which they were promulgated, the Commission's desire that the Guidelines reflect perceived congressional policy, and the Commission's own independent policy determinations concerning the severity of a particular class of conduct." (Letter to Chief US District Judge Linda Reade at 5 (Apr. 19, 2010) in *United States v. Comparison of Loss to Sentence ($20M+) Rubashkin*, ___ F. Supp. 2d ___, 2010 WL 2471877 (N.D. Iowa 2010).) In this letter, the authors concluded that "[i]mposing massively lengthy sentences in white collar cases is not only wasteful of taxpayer dollars, but it is insulting to the victims of violent crimes. It is hard for victims of truly violent crimes to understand why defendants who have violently harmed them should receive a far shorter prison sentence than" a white-collar offender. (*Id.* at 7.)

### A Review of Sentencing Data for Economic Offenses

In fiscal year (FY) 2009, 7,951 individuals were sentenced under the fraud guideline constituting 10.5 percent of all 81,732 guidelines cases. Only those sentenced under the drug guideline at USSG §2D1.1 (24,901 or 32.9 percent) and the unlawful entry guidelines at USSG §2L1.2 (17,310 or 23.6 percent) constituted larger groups of offenders.

The total loss amount aggregated over all 7,951 cases totaled nearly $9 billion (and that is assuming the loss was at the low end of the guideline range). (*See* US Sent'g Comm'n, Use Of Guidelines And Specific Offender Characteristics (2009).)

Again, using commission data (see Table 1), of the 7,951 fraud sentences in FY 2009, 7,879 or 99.11 percent involved loss amounts of less than $20 million. Adding these losses together (using the lowest loss level in the guideline range), these frauds resulted in a combined loss of just over $2.2 billion or 25.79 percent of the total overall loss amount. The average loss amount, however, was just over $287,000. In fact, over three-quarters of the frauds (76.34 percent) in the sub-$20 million loss class involved losses of less than $20,000.

| [Table 1] | $20 Million + Frauds | Sub $20 Million Frauds |
|---|---|---|
| Number | 71 | 7,879 |
| % of All Frauds | 0.89% | 99.11% |
| Total Loss | $6,530,000,000 | $2,268,970,000 |
| % of Total Loss | 74.21% | 25.79% |
| Average Loss | $91,971,831 | $287,977 |

So, in sum, more than 99 percent of frauds involve amounts far less than $20 million and total only a quarter of total fraud losses. However, the 1 percent (71 cases) of large frauds constitutes three-quarters of the aggregate fraud loss, and therefore as a group provide an excellent model for testing the correlation between loss and the resultant sentence.

| [Table 2]<br>Offender | Loss | Sentence | $ per mo. |
|---|---|---|---|
| Richard Harkless | $39,000,000 | 1,200 (mos.) | 32,500 |
| James R. Nichols | $21,123,830 | 292 | 72,342 |
| Sholom Rubashkin | $27,000,000 | 324 | 83,333 |
| John Miller | $21,000,000 | 159 | 132,075 |
| Gary Vanwaeyenberghe | $25,521,966 | 168 | 151,916 |
| Calude LeFebrve | $64,850,000 | 240 | 270,208 |
| Jeff Skilling | $80,000,000 | 288 | 277,778 |
| Joseph Nacchio | $28,000,000 | 72 | 388,889 |
| Kevin S. Jackson | $20,000,000 | 51 | 392,157 |
| Morad Abu Sliman | $26,000,000 | 57 | 456,140 |
| John Rigas | $102,708,142 | 144 | 713,251 |
| Louis Pearlman | $300,000,000 | 300 | 1,000,000 |
| Mark Turckan | $25,000,000 | 12 | 2,083,333 |
| Marc Dreier | $700,000,000 | 240 | 2,916,667 |
| Lance Poulsen | $2,000,000,000 | 360 | 5,555,556 |
| Tom Peters | $3,670,000,000 | 600 | 6,116,667 |
| Ronald Ferguson | $500,000,000 | 24 | 20,833,333 |
| Bernard Madoff | $65,000,000,000 | 1,800 | 36,111,111 |
| Bernard Ebbers | $11,000,000,000 | 300 | 36,666,667 |

Given the complexity of these cases, a straight comparison of loss amount to the sentence received is not very telling. Accordingly, we have made the comparison between loss amount and ultimate sentence received in these cases by dividing the amount of loss attributed to the defendant to the sentence received by the defendant in months. In short, we wanted to know how much a month in prison is worth under the fraud guideline, which is intended to promote greater uniformity and certainty in sentencing. One would expect, therefore, that a month in prison is worth approximately the same amount regardless of the amount of total loss attributed to the offender.

We found some startling, counterintuitive results as Table 2 illustrates from noteworthy, published cases.

Perhaps the most infamous white-collar criminal over the past decade, Bernard Madoff, received one of the longest sentences ever—150 years or

1,800 months—for a white-collar offender. However, when compared to the incomprehensible magnitude of the loss—$65 billion—Madoff's sentence may not have been as incredible as it may seem at first blush. As Table 2 illustrates, Madoff received one month's imprisonment for every $36.1 million of fraud he committed. Under this methodology, Marc Dreier should have received a sentence of approximately 19 months instead of 240 months.

Or, taking Marc Dreier as an example, Jeff Skilling should have only received 2.21 months, given the ratio of loss to months' imprisonment for Dreier. Mark Turkcan, president of First Bank Mortgage based in St. Louis, who misapplied $35 million in loans that resulted in a loss of approximately $25 million, received a sentence of only a year and a day. But Gary Vanwaeyenberghe, with a loss amount approximately the same as Turkcan, received a sentence of 168 months or 14 times Turkcan's sentence.

And to take examples from the opposing ends of Table 2, if Richard Harkless had been sentenced according to the same loss/months ratio as Bernard Ebbers, he should have only received just over one month in prison as opposed to 100 years.

Upon reviewing the data sample, there simply is no consistent correlation between loss and offense seriousness with respect to the ultimate sentence imposed. While the list of offenders in this table obviously is neither exhaustive nor a scientific sampling, it nevertheless strongly suggests that loss is a poor proxy for offense seriousness, at least as seen by federal judges under the now advisory guideline system. Table 3 makes a graphic comparison of the data in Table 2.

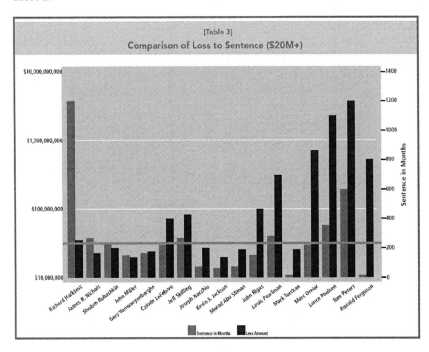

**Conclusion**

As the Supreme Court explicitly recognized, "in the ordinary case, the Commission's recommendation of a sentencing range will reflect a rough approximation of sentences that might achieve §3553(a)'s objectives." (*Kimbrough v. United States*, 552 U.S. 85, 89 (2007) (emphasis added).) But the sentences resulting from the use of loss under the fraud guideline can hardly be considered even a "rough" approximation in light of the data reviewed, especially in large dollar-loss cases.

As it stands, the fraud guideline constitutes a series of ad hoc amendments covering a vast array of distinctly dissimilar conduct applying to offenders from the Gordon Gecko variety to the well-intentioned but desperate business owners. There simply is no way the sentences that result from them can be considered principled or even reasonable, especially because loss plays such a central role in determining the ultimate sentence.

It is time that the fraud guideline is revisited by the commission. First, the commission should conduct a serious, scholarly analysis of how well the guideline achieves the purposes of sentences and the goals of the Sentencing Reform Act. Second, the commission needs to conduct a comprehensive proportionality comparison of sentences in relation to offense seriousness within the fraud guideline, in comparison to other white-collar offenses, and then in comparison to other offenses generally. These analyses should inform a thorough revision of the fraud guideline. One would hope that revision would result in (i) less reliance on loss and the use of a loss table with fewer brackets and a progressively decreasing scale; (ii) less overlap between loss and other SOCs; and (iii) more weight given to the nature of the offense and the offender.

Until such a comprehensive review and revision is undertaken by the commission, defense counsel will have to challenge and work around the fraud guideline on a case-by-case basis, and judges will have to do the commission's work by fashioning sentences as best they can per the mandates of 18 U.S.C. §3553(a) to achieve justice.

## §8:30.2   Litigating in a Post-*Booker* World

On January 12, 2005, the Supreme Court announced its much-anticipated opinion in *United States v. Booker,* 543 U.S. 220, 125 S. Ct. 738 (Jan. 12, 2005). This section explains the case, its probable effect on federal sentencing practice, and suggests potential areas for litigation in a post-*Booker* sentencing environment.

*Booker* is the latest in a series of cases that began with *Apprendi v. New Jersey*, 530 U.S. 466 (2000). The *Apprendi* decision held that any fact (other than the fact of a prior conviction) that affects the statutory maximum sentence must be charged in the indictment and then proven to a jury beyond a reasonable doubt. The Court grounded this ruling on the Fifth Amendment's Due Process Clause, which requires that every element in a criminal offense be proven beyond a reasonable doubt, and the Sixth Amendment, which gives defendants the right to have juries make that determination.

*Apprendi* decided whether a judge could increase a defendant's sentence above the statutory maximum, based on supplemental facts found by the judge at sentencing—not that the tops of correctly calculated guideline ranges were also "statutory maximums." (530 U.S. at 484-89.) After the Court's 2000 decision, every one of the federal courts of appeals held that *Apprendi* did not apply to determinations made under the U.S. Federal Sentencing Guidelines. (*See, e.g., United States v. Casas*, 356 F.3d 104, 128 (1st Cir. 2004); *United States v. Parmelee*, 319 F.3d 583, 592 (3d Cir. 2003); *United States v. Ochoa*, 311 F.3d 1133, 1134-35 (9th Cir. 2002)).

The correctness of these circuit opinions came into question when the Supreme Court decided *Ring v. Arizona*, 536 U. S. 584 (2002). *Ring* involved an Arizona death penalty statute that in some ways worked like the federal sentencing guidelines. In *Ring*, the Supreme Court held that the Arizona death penalty statute violated the principle it had established in *Apprendi*. Arizona law precluded a judge from imposing the death penalty in a capital case unless he or she found certain aggravating factors, over and above the facts found by the jury. That procedure violated the Sixth Amendment, even though the judge had to make his or her finding using a standard of beyond a reasonable doubt. The Court ruled that to be constitutional, the aggravating factors used to increase the penalty from a maximum of life imprisonment to death had to be charged in the indictment and proved to the jury beyond a reasonable doubt. Despite the *Ring* ruling, no federal circuit revisited its conclusion that the federal sentencing guidelines were exempt from the principle established in *Apprendi*.

On June 24, 2004, the Supreme Court issued its decision in *Blakely v. Washington*, 542 U. S. 296, 124 S. Ct. 2531 (2004). *Blakely* arose out of a Washington State sentencing appeal in which the defendant had pleaded guilty to kidnapping. The Washington state legislature, much like the U.S. Congress, had enacted a Sentencing Reform Act that provided determinate sentencing guideline ranges for each offense. Although one Washington statute provided for a 10-year maximum for kidnapping, the Sentencing Reform Act provided for a sentence of from 49 to 53 months based solely on the facts that Blakely had admitted as part of his guilty plea.

The *Blakely* decision clarified the definition of what constitutes a statutory maximum sentence for purposes of applying the *Apprendi* principle. The Supreme Court ruled that the statutory maximum was not the 10 years designated generally for second-degree felonies. Rather, it was ". . . the maximum (the judge) may impose without any additional findings. When a judge inflicts punishments that the jury's verdict alone does not allow, the jury has not found all the facts . . . and the judge exceeds his proper authority." (124 S. Ct. at 2537.) Thus, the statutory maximum was the 53 months established in the sentencing guideline presumptively applicable based upon the defendant's guilty plea.

The *Blakely* decision resulted in a flood of litigation over the federal sentencing guidelines. The circuits split over whether *Blakely* rendered the sentencing guidelines, or the Sentencing Reform Act, unconstitutional in whole or in part. (*Compare United States v. Ameline*, 376 F.3d 967 (9th Cir. 2004), *with United States v. Pineiro*, 377 F.3d 464 (5th Cir. 2004).)

The government separately petitioned the Supreme Court for certiorari in two cases that held that the *Blakely* decision rendered the implementation of the federal sentencing guidelines unconstitutional. (*See United States v. Booker*, 375 F.3d 508 (7th Cir. 2004), cert. granted, 04-104, and *United States v. Fanfan*, cert. granted while pending in the 1st Circuit, 04-105.)

## The *Booker* Decision

In *United States v. Booker*, 543 U.S. 220, 125 S. Ct. 738 (2005), five Supreme Court Justices concluded that the Sentencing Reform Act was unconstitutional to the extent that it mandated that a judge increase a defendant's sentence above the statutory maximum, which was either inherent in the jury's verdict, the defendant's plea of guilty, or in admissions made by the defendant. The five Justices reiterated that a defendant's sentence was limited by the Fifth and Sixth Amendments to facts "reflected in the jury verdict or admitted by the defendant." (*Booker, supra*, 125 S. Ct. at 749 (*quoting Blakely*, 124 S. Ct. at 2537)). The Court acknowledged that if the federal sentencing guidelines could be read merely as advisory provisions, their use would not implicate the Sixth Amendment. However, the guidelines were by law not merely advisory, but mandatory and binding, despite the availability of departures in specified circumstances. (*Id.* at 750-52.)

The Justices parted company, however, on the remedy for the constitutional violation that occurred in the *Booker* case. Justice Breyer wrote Part II of the Court's opinion, which set forth the remedy for the constitutional flaw identified in the first part of the opinion. (*See* 125 S. Ct. at 756.) Justice Ginsburg joined the four Justices who dissented as to Part I of the Court's opinion. The Court concluded that to apply the jury trial requirement to the sentencing decisions previously governed by the guidelines would thoroughly contradict Congress's intent in enacting the Sentencing Reform Act and the guidelines, and would be too difficult to administer. (125 S. Ct. at 761-64.) Instead, the Court adopted a remedy that it believed to be closer to its view of congressional intent by employing a severability analysis. (*Id.* at 764-68.) On this basis, the Court excised two provisions of the Sentencing Reform Act that the Court deemed incompatible with the constitutional holding. These provisions, 18 U.S.C. §3553(b)(1) and 18 U.S.C. §3742(e), mandated a sentence within the federal sentencing guidelines, and set forth the standards of review on appeal, including a de novo standard of review for any departures. (*Id.* at 764-66.)

The end result of the *Booker* decision is that the federal sentencing process is governed by 18 U.S.C. §3553(a). Under that law, the sentencing guidelines have only an advisory function. Because the guidelines are advisory, a district judge must consider the guidelines, along with all other relevant information, in imposing an individualized sentence, *see* 18 U.S.C. §3553(a) (listing the factors to be considered in imposing sentence), but need not impose a sentence within the guideline range, even if there are no grounds to depart. The Court did not preclude district courts from imposing sentences based on facts that were neither inherent in the jury's verdict nor admitted by the defendant. Instead, because the guidelines are now advisory, they no longer create a "statutory maximum' under

*Apprendi* and *Blakely*. Instead, the statutory maximum is the term set forth in the United States Code section that either establishes the offense of conviction or establishes the penalty for a particular offense. There is no constitutional impediment to a sentence anywhere within the statutory maximum.

### The Impact of *Booker* Prior to Sentencing

The immediate effect of *Booker* is profound. Although the Supreme Court expressly directed district courts to consider the guidelines in imposing sentence, the courts are not bound by the guidelines. Rather, the courts are bound by 18 U.S.C. §3553(a). Under 18 U.S.C. §3553(a), the key requirement is that the sentence in each case must be "sufficient, but not greater than necessary" to:

- (A) Reflect the seriousness of the offense, to promote respect for the law, and to provide just punishment for the offense;
- (B) Afford adequate deterrence to criminal conduct;
- (C) Protect the public from further crimes of the defendant; and
- (D) Provide the defendant with needed educational or vocational training, medical care, or other correctional treatment in the most effective manner.

(18 U.S.C. §3553(a)(2).)

Further, the court must consider the kinds of sentences available, 18 U.S.C. §3553(a)(3); the need to avoid unwarranted sentence disparities among defendants with similar records who have been found guilty of similar conduct, 18 U.S.C. §3553(a)(6); and the need to provide restitution to any victims of the offense, 18 U.S.C. §(a)(7).

Section 3553 (a)(1) also bears on the sentence to be imposed; that section directs the court to consider the nature and circumstances of the offense and the history and characteristics of the defendant. The history and characteristics of the offender include matters beyond a defendant's criminal history, and encompass matters excluded from the court's consideration by the sentencing guidelines. For example, guideline policy statements largely precluded consideration of a defendant's history of childhood abuse, lack of youthful guidance, or drug addiction. (See, *e.g.*, U.S.S.G. §5H1.1 (discouraging consideration of age); §5H1.2 (discouraging consideration of education and vocational skills); §5H1.3 (discouraging consideration of mental and emotional condition); §5H1.4 (discouraging consideration of physical condition, including drug or alcohol dependence); §5HL5 (discouraging consideration of employment record); §5H1.6 (discouraging consideration of family ties and responsibilities); §5H1.11 (discouraging consideration of civic and military contributions); and §5H1.12 (discouraging consideration of lack of guidance as a youth).) Those policy statements are no longer binding on district courts. Rather, 18 U.S.C. §3662 provides that "no limitation shall be placed on the information concerning the background, character, and conduct of a person convicted of an offense which a court . . . may receive and consider for the purpose of imposing an appropriate sentence." This directive might conflict with the guidelines, which in most cases offer only prison. For example, in some cases, a defendant's education, treatment, or medical needs may be better served by a sentence that permits the offender to remain in the community. Thus, a court may impose a sentence outside the guideline range based on factors precluded from consideration by the guidelines. (*See United States v. Ranum*, 353 F. Supp. 2d 984 (E.D. Wis. 2005).)

In cases in which a defendant's history and character are positive, or where the defendant's history contains significant mitigating factors, such as a chaotic and neglectful childhood, an appropriate sentence may be one outside the guideline range.

Another immediate effect of the *Booker* decision is that it is no longer appropriate to speak of the judge granting only a "departure" from the guidelines. (*But see United States v. Wilson*, 355 F. Supp. 2d 1269 (D. Utah. 2005) (ruling that judges must calculate the traditional guideline range, decide whether to depart from that range, and then, decide whether a variance from the guidelines is appropriate).) The departure methodology was based on the notion that the district courts retained a limited amount of discretion to sentence outside of the guidelines, provided that either the defendant or the government could establish that the case fell "outside the heartland" of the guidelines. (*Koon v. United States*, 518 U.S. 81, 95-96 (1996).) Departures either were based on a ground that had not been taken into account by the Sentencing Commission, or had been identified as a basis for departure by the commission. Since the guidelines themselves are advisory, it is no longer appropriate to refer only to departures. Rather, the advocate should seek a sentence outside the established guideline range using also the vernacular of "variances." Unlike departures, variances are not constrained to the framework of the Guidelines, and can be exercised rather liberally through the inherent decision the judiciary emjoys at sentencing.

As the Court of the Appeals for the Ninth Circuit has noted, a "'departure' is typically a change from the final sentencing range computed by examining the provisions of the Guidelines themselves. It is frequently triggered by . . . factors that take the case 'outside the heartland' contemplated by the Sentencing Commission when it drafted the Guidelines for a typical offense. A 'variance,' by contrast, occurs when a judge imposes a sentence above or below the otherwise properly calculated final sentencing range based on application of the other statutory factors in 18 U.S.C. §3553(a)." *United States v. Cruz-Perez*, 567 F.3d 1142, 1146 (9th Cir. 2009).

Courts are likely to continue to calculate a defendant's guideline range the way they did before *Booker*. Judges will determine the offense level using the application principles established by the federal sentencing guidelines. As before, they will select the offense guideline based on the offense of conviction and will make other guideline decisions using the relevant conduct principles. While there are good arguments on due process grounds for applying a higher standard, *see United States v. Zolp*, 479 F.3d 715, 718 (9th Cir. 2007), courts might still make factual determinations using the preponderance of the evidence standard. Still, because the guidelines are now advisory, there are fewer impediments to a sentence outside the established guideline range. As in pre-guideline sentencing, other factors may be more important than the guidelines.

The possibilities for creative sentencing practice abound through the use of variances. For example, in crack cocaine cases, the recently revised federal guidelines for drug offenses now treat one gram of crack as equivalent to 18 grams of powder cocaine (thanks to the Fair Sentencing Act of 111-220. Before the FSA, the federal guidelines treated one gram of crack as equivalent to 100 grams of powder cocaine). Still, a judge who, upon considering "the nature of the offense," does not think that crack cocaine is 100 times worse than powder may impose a lower sentence than the guidelines recommend, even though such a disagreement would not have supported a "downward departure" under the guidelines—at least so long as the judge does not go below a statutory mandatory minimum sentence. (*See United States v. Smith*, CR 02-163 (E.D. Wis. March 2, 2005) (reducing sentence for substantial assistance and for disparity between crack and powder cocaine).)

The *Ranum* decision, recently authored by Judge Lynn Adelman, is a fine example of the type of result that can be obtained after *Booker*. There, the judge concluded that a sentence below the sentencing guidelines was justified, because the defendant did not commit the offense for personal gain. In sentencing the defendant to one year and a day in custody instead of the 37 to 46 months called for by the guidelines, the court also considered his positive history and character, his health, and his family circumstances, which included an elderly father suffering from Alzheimer's disease. (*Id.*) Another judge recently imposed a sentence outside the guidelines in a case involving a defendant with a lengthy history of mental illness, whose need for treatment was best addressed by a split sentence in Zone C. (*United States v. Jones*, 2005 WL 12730 (D. Me. Jan. 21, 2005).) *See also United States v. Nellum*, 2005 WL 300073 (N.D. Ind. Feb. 3, 2005); *United States v. Galvez-Barrios*, 355 F. Supp. 2d 958 (E. D. Wis. 2005); *United States v. Kelley*, 355 F. Supp. 2d 1031 (D. Neb. 2005).)

A third judge has explained why *Booker* is not an invitation to "unmoored decision making, but to the type of careful analysis of the evidence that should be considered when depriving a person of his or her liberty." (*United States v. Myers*, 2005 WL 165314 (S.D. Iowa, Jan. 26, 2005).) In imposing the sentence, Judge Pratt considered the defendant's history and character, including his moral standards, his service as a role model for his children, the severe negative impact that the felony conviction alone would have on the defendant, the fact that he presented no danger to the community, and his undergoing significant alcohol evaluation and treatment. After considering all of these factors, the judge sentenced the defendant to probation, rather that the term of imprisonment called for by the guidelines.

### *Booker* and Plea Agreements

How *Booker* affects defendants who have pled guilty under a pre-*Booker* plea agreement, but who have not yet been sentenced, depends on the particular language of each plea agreement. To the extent that a defendant admitted the existence of certain facts, those facts may be used to determine the defendant's sentence. (*See United States v. Parsons*, 2005 WL 180495 (8th Cir. Jan. 26,

2005).) However, at least in non-binding agreements under Rule 11(e)(1)(B), stipulations to guideline ranges are not binding on the judge, and would likely not preclude the defendant from seeking a sentence outside the guidelines. On the other hand, the fact of the *Booker* decision does not provide a basis to withdraw a guilty plea on the ground that it was involuntary. (*United States v. Sahlin,* 399 F.3d 27 (1st Cir. 2005).)

### Imposition of Longer Sentences

Theoretically, the *Booker* decision, to the extent that it permits imposition of "reasonable sentences" outside the guideline range, may sometimes permit district judges to impose even longer sentences on criminal defendants. After all, the rules restraining the court from imposing upward departures have been removed, just as have the restraints on downward departures. This is certainly a risk for defendants who committed their crimes after the date the *Booker* decision was issued. Still, it is a small risk to be sure. The rate of above-guideline sentences has remained consistently quite low, generally between 1% and 2% per year.

There also is a risk of a longer sentence for a defendant who appeals, seeking resentencing. The Due Process Clause may protect against this result for those defendants who committed their crimes before January 12, 2005. Because *Booker* in effect rewrote an important aspect of the Sentencing Reform Act, defendants may be protected from a longer sentence, either initially or on remand, by the due process principle precluding retroactive application of a new, adverse judicial interpretation of a statute. (*See Marks v. United States,* 430 U.S. 188 (1977).) This due process principle operates similarly to the Constitution's *Ex Post Facto* Clause that protects against adverse retroactive legislation. (*See Garner v. Jones,* 529 U.S. 244 (2000); *Miller v. Florida,* 482 U.S. 423 (1987).)

Defendants who are being resentenced on remand also may be protected by *North Carolina v. Pearce,* 395 U.S. 711 (1969), and cases interpreting *Pearce,* which prevent courts from imposing higher sentences at resentencing after a successful appeal, unless the appearance of vindictiveness is eliminated.

### Plea Negotiation After *Booker*

*Booker* has affected plea negotiations. Since locking in offense levels will no longer guarantee a sentence within a particular range, counsel will want to think about whether it is better to be free to argue for a much lower sentence or to ensure a particular sentence with a Rule 11(c)(1)(C) plea. Locking in a sentence may be particularly attractive where there is a greater than average possibility that a court will exercise its discretion to impose a sentence higher than the guideline range.

It also is likely that counsel for the government may begin seeking additional defense waivers. For example, government counsel may seek a plea agreement under which the defense agrees not to seek a sentence below the guideline range based on a list of factors. Whether the rules of an open plea warrant entering into such agreements will have to be carefully considered in each case.

### *Booker* and Second or Successive §2255 Motions

Defendants cannot file second or successive (§2255) motions without first getting permission from the court of appeals. There are two bases on which the court of appeals can give permission to file a second (§2255) motion. The first is that there is new evidence that the defendant is innocent (evidence that would not have allowed any reasonable jury to have found him or her guilty). The second is a new rule of constitutional law that the Supreme Court itself has made retroactively applicable to cases on collateral review. (*See Tyler v. Cain*, 533 U.S. 656, 667 (2001).) Although the rule announced in *Apprendi/Ring/ Blakely/ Booker* is arguably a new rule of constitutional law, so far the Supreme Court has not made it retroactively applicable to cases on collateral review (such as §2255 motions.) Until and unless it does so, defendants will not be able to get permission to file a second or successive §2255 motion to raise a *Booker* issue. (*See In re Dean*, 375 F.3d 1287, 1290-91 (11th Cir. 2004).)

## §8:30.3    The Federal Presentence Investigation Report

The federal presentence investigation report (PSR) is crucial for two purposes:

1.  It is the document most heavily relied on by the judge in imposing sentence—particularly in those cases where a guilty plea has been entered and the court knows little about the defendant. Had the defendant gone to trial, the court would have more information about the individual—or at least his or her offense conduct.
2.  Equally important, it is the document that the Federal Bureau of Prisons relies on in making designations and placements and many other decisions throughout an inmate's period of incarceration, including, but not limited to, whether to grant early release through halfway house and, if so, for how much time.

After a guilty verdict by trial or a guilty plea, the court will order the preparation of a PSR. In most US district courts, the procedures are as follows:

First, there is a meeting with the US Probation Office shortly after sentencing, during which counsel and the defendant will be scheduled for an interview with a US probation officer (USPO) who will prepare the report. Typically, in most probation offices there are two divisions: PSR preparers and those officers who supervise people on probation or supervised release. Often, to facilitate the USPO's task, counsel will be provided with a worksheet to be filled out and given to the USPO at or before the meeting. It is strongly advised that counsel meet with the client, fill out the report, and have it neatly typed and ready to present to the USPO along with the documents identified in the instructions on the worksheet (birth certificate, financial statements, income tax returns, etc.). This makes the USPO's job easier.

**Practice Tip.** By the time of the interview, the assistant US attorney or federal prosecutor assigned to the case will have provided to the USPO a prosecutorial memo outlining the government's version of the offense. In most cases, this memo is neither flattering nor helpful to the client. Accordingly, our office prepares our own memo for the USPO that we submit along with the completed worksheet and the required documents. In addition to the memo, we provide the USPO with any favorable mental health reports and character letters. We also advise interested individuals how to prepare letters that reflect favorably on a defendant's character.

The PSR worksheet will also have a section called "Acceptance of Responsibility" or "Defendant's Version of the Offense." It is our practice to leave that blank and submit our written version to the USPO at the interview or shortly thereafter.

In many cases, in order to qualify for a downward adjustment for acceptance of responsibility under the US Sentencing Guidelines (USSG), all that is required is an acknowledgement of guilt. The USPO is best able to advise during the interview what will be needed to satisfy this requirement. Often, the memo we submit along with the worksheet will provide our client's acceptance of responsibility/version of the offense.

During the course of the interview, the defendant will be asked little other than to confirm or clarify what is on the worksheet. In short, the interview is mostly a demographic interview as opposed to interrogating the defendant as to the offense.

Federal Rule of Criminal Procedure 32(e)(2) states that the probation officer "must give the presentence report to the defendant, the defendant's attorney, and an attorney for the government at least 35 days before sentencing unless the defendant waives this minimum period." In some districts, the draft report will contain a sentencing recommendation by the USPO to the court. In some jurisdictions, the sentencing recommendation is left for the final PSR that is presented to the court and the parties. Please note that the draft report is not submitted to the court. In other districts, probation officers either do not make sentencing recommendations or, if they do, they are not made available to the parties.

## Contents of Report

The PSR will start with the face sheet identifying the sentencing judge, prosecutor, defense counsel, sentencing date, offense counts in the indictment/information, arrest date, release status (identifying how much time, if any, the defendant has spent in custody), detainers, codefendants, any related cases, and date the draft report was prepared.

It will also contain the defendant's identifying data such as his or her name, date of birth, age, race, national origin, sex, Social Security number, FBI number, and US Marshal number (this will become the Bureau of Prisons' register number assigned to the defendant should he or she be incarcerated). It will also list any education, dependents, and citizenship (important because only a US citizen can be designated to a minimum security federal prison camp). If the defendant is a naturalized US citizen, that fact must be noted as verified along with, if possible, the date of the naturalization. Without this information, an otherwise eligible offender may not be designated by the Bureau of Prisons to a minimum security federal prison camp. The face sheet will also contain the defendant's country of birth, place of birth, and, very important, legal address and residence address. This is crucial information because the Bureau of Prisons will attempt to designate a defendant to a facility as close to the individual's residence as possible—generally within 500 miles—should he or she be sentenced to a term of incarceration.

The body of the report will contain information regarding the offense, starting with the actual charges and convictions and then the actual offense conduct (generally as reported by the prosecution). Where there are multiple defendants, the defendant named on the PSR will often be identified in terms of relative culpability.

The PSR will next address a victim impact statement indicating to whom and how much restitution is owed, which is not necessarily the same as the total loss attributable to any economic crime scheme. This loss is governed by USSG § 2B1.1 and often includes intended loss rather than actual loss listed in the victim impact section.

The report will then move on to a section indicating whether the defendant has obstructed justice. Next, the PSR will outline the defendant's acceptance of responsibility—if the defendant indeed has accepted responsibility—which he or she must do in all cases in which a guilty plea was entered in order to obtain a downward adjustment under USSG § 3E1.1.

The offense conduct will then calculate preliminary advisory federal sentencing guidelines for the total offense level.

The next part of the PSR will be the defendant's criminal history. Here the defendant's prior criminal record will be discussed, including arrests not leading to convictions. The PSR often lists details regarding the offense. Based on these convictions, the defendant will receive a criminal history score that is used to calculate where the defendant will fall within the federal sentencing guidelines.

**Practice Tip.** The Bureau of Prisons will look closely at the prior record section of the PSR. If there are any pending charges, the bureau may very well treat these as detainers or unresolved charges that may preclude placement in a minimum security federal prison camp. Prior convictions indicating violence or flight risk may have the same impact.

The offense characteristics part of the PSR will list personal and family data, physical condition, mental and emotional health, and substance abuse. Physical and mental health can be mitigating factors at sentencing, and substance abuse will be viewed by the Bureau of Prisons to determine eligibility for its Residential Drug and Alcohol Program (RDAP). Generally speaking, if the PSR reflects substance abuse that includes illicit and/or prescription drugs and/or alcohol use within one year prior to the offender's arrest, it will make the individual eligible for the program. Successful completion of the RDAP can lead to up to one year off the defendant's sentence and generally a six-month halfway house placement at the end of the sentence for transitional care in the community.

The offender part will then list educational, vocational, and special skills; employment record; financial condition; and ability to pay restitution. This financial condition section will be considered by the court in determining whether the defendant is able to pay a fine and, if so, how much and under what terms and conditions.

Finally, the report will indicate the calculated guideline range.

**Objections to the PSR**

Generally, within 14 days of the issuance of the draft PSR—which only goes to the concerned parties and not to the court—objections can be filed. Within seven days before sentencing, the final report will be issued and made available to the court. Generally, those objections not made during the 14-day window before the PSR is presented to the court cannot be raised for the first time at sentencing, so it is critical that all objections be raised when the report is in its draft version.

### §8:30.4    Trends for Representing Child Pornography Offenders at Sentencing

**A Quiet Revolution in Federal Sentencing Grows Loud: Trends and Practice Tips for Representing Child Pornography Offenders**

By Alan Ellis, Tess Lopez and Mark Allenbaugh

Among all types of federal offenses, child pornography inherently draws the most visceral reaction. As the internet and other technologies have allowed increased access to videos and photographs of child pornography, the detection and prosecution of the same also has increased, with states and the federal government devoting substantial resources toward the investigation and prosecution of such offenses. Simultaneously, the number of referrals, prosecutions, and convictions for child pornography also has been increasing as the graph below illustrates.

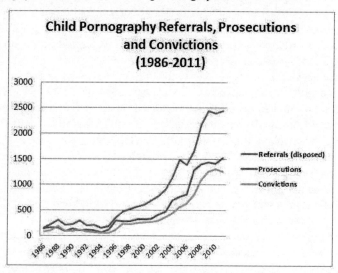

Source: Transactional Records Clearinghouse, Syracuse University. Data search performed June 2012. Search was limited to referrals, prosecutions and convictions where violations of 18 U.S.C. § 2552 was recorded as the lead offense. Referrals are limited only to those referrals that were disposed of, meaning acted upon. According to TRAC, the Department of Justice since 1999 has not released complete data on referrals and declinations.

Since the mid-90s, referrals, prosecutions and convictions for child pornography have increased dramatically, with referrals increasing at a far greater rate than either prosecutions or convictions. Accordingly, the increasing trend of prosecutions and convictions necessarily will continue for the foreseeable future.

It is not surprising, therefore, that penalties for such offenses also have been steadily increasing during the same period. *See generally United States v. Henderson*, 649 F.3d 955, 960-62 (9th Cir. 2011) (reviewing in detail the history of the child pornography guidelines). As a result,

> In recent year[s], the [U.S. Sentencing] Commission has received feedback from judges, the Department of Justice, defense attorneys, and organizations such as the National Center for Missing and Exploited Children, a leading advocate for victims of these offenses, all indicating that a review of the penalties for child pornography offenses is appropriate at this time because of the evolving nature of how these offenses are committed. In light of this feedback, the Commission is undertaking a thorough examination of these offenses and the offenders who commit them, including the technological and psychological issues associated with child pornography offenses. The Commission anticipates issuing a comprehensive report later this year.

Judge Patti B. Saris, Chairwoman, Introductory Comments at U.S. Sentencing Commission Hearing on Child Pornography Offenses (Feb. 15, 2012), available at http://www.ussc.gov/Legislative_and_Public_Affairs/Public_Hearings_ and_Meetings/20120215-16/Hearing_Transcript_20120215.pdf.

The law and practice regarding child pornography offenses likewise has evolved considerably, especially since *United States v. Booker*. At its core, the history of the Child Pornography Guidelines continues a trend that first arose during the evolution of the Drug Guidelines, namely, a critical assessment by the judiciary of the empirical support and rationality of the particular guideline. As with the Drug Guidelines, the critique from the bench has grown to critical mass such that the Child Pornography Guidelines now, too, in all likelihood will be revised downward by Commission amendment if not Congressional directive. This article reviews some of the more pertinent developments for the practitioner, and provides tips on how best to advocate for your client in the current, fast-changing legal climate.

## I. A Brief Review of Child Pornography Offenders
### and the History of the Guidelines

According to the U.S. Sentencing Commission's 2010 Sourcebook of Federal Sentencing Statistics, Appendix A, "Child Pornography includes the sale distribution, transportation, shipment, receipt, or possession of materials involving the sexual exploitation of minors." The typical child pornography defendant is a first-time offender with no history of harming or touching children. The best empirical research shows that the vast majority of these offenders do not go on to molest children, according to Richard Wollert, Ph.D., who testified before the U.S. Sentencing Commission at a public hearing on February 15, 2012, about a study regarding the lack of correlation between passive child pornography viewers, and active child molesters. See Richard Wollert, Ph.D., Written Testimony to the U.S. Sentencing Commission, *The Implication of Recidivism Research and Clinical Experience for Assessing and Treating Federal Child Pornography Offenders* 12 (Feb. 15, 2012) available at http://www.ussc.gov/Legislative_and_Public_Affairs/ Public_Hearings_and_Meetings/20120215-16/Testimony_15_Wollert_2.pdf. The study followed 72 individuals referred to federally-funded outpatient treatment programs after being charged with or convicted of a child pornography offense for four years found that none were rearrested for a contact offense. Dr. Wollert cited a recent study that followed 231 child pornography offenders without prior contact offenses for six years after their initial offense. Only two of those people (0.8%) committed a contact offense. *See* Jerome Endrass *et al, The consumption of Internet Child Pornography and Violent Sex offending*, 9 BMC Psychiatry 43 (2009).

It is widely known that the Child Pornography Guidelines have been amended dramatically since the inception of USSG §2G2.2 in 1991. In 2003, Congress passed the Prosecutorial Remedies and Other Tools to End the Exploitation of Children Today Act (PROTECT ACT ), Pub. L. 108-21, which resulted in significant changes to the statute and Child Pornography Guidelines, and paved the way for Congress to enact mandatory minimum sentences for Child Pornography offenses. The Sentencing Commission responded by adding enhancements and increasing the penalties for possession. Consequently, in response to directives from Congress, there have been numerous increases in the guidelines for these offenses. As a result, the average sentence length for first time child pornography offenders is now over three times what it was for both first time *and recidivist offenders* in 1994. The average guideline sentence for possession currently is 119 months, or nearly 10 years. *See United States Sentencing Comm'n*, Sourcebook of Federal Sentencing Statistics 2011, tbl. 13.

## II. Challenging the Reasonableness of the
### Child Pornography Guidelines

Much like the Drug Guidelines, which were also formulated and regulated by directives from Congress rather than in response to empirical data, practitioners, academics and sentencing courts also are questioning the reasonableness of the

Child Pornography Guidelines. For example, the child pornography guidelines do not distinguish offenders with differing levels of culpability, and nearly all of the enhancements apply to all child pornography offenders. Nearly all use a computer, nearly all have at least one image of a pre-pubescent minor under the age of 12, and most images reflect violence (intercourse with a minor) and due to file sharing programs, most possess more than 600 images, intentionally or unintentionally. *See generally*, U.S. Sentencing Comm'n, *The History of the Child Pornography Guidelines* (Oct. 2009). The enhancements combine to reflect an effective base offense level of 31 with a range of 108 to 135 months.

It would be reasonable to assume that a case involving attempts to lure a minor into sexual activity is more serious conduct than possession of child pornography. Surprisingly, however, the child pornography guidelines often result in <u>higher</u> sentences for possessing child pornography than for actually attempting to abuse a child. *See United States v. Dorvee*, 616, F.3d 174, 187 (2nd Cir. 2010). The problem with the Child Pornography Guidelines, therefore, is not so much unwarranted disparity as it is unwarranted similarity such that dissimilarly situated offenders are treated similarly. That, as well as the overly onerous sentence imposed under these Guidelines as a result of Congressional intervention, squarely places the reasonableness of any sentence imposed within the range questionable.

And in those instances where a downward departure or variance is given by a court, the matter is not necessarily settled. The resulting sentence, of course, still could be far too onerous and otherwise inconsistent with the principle of parsimony set forth at 18 U.S.C. § 3553(a). In short, even a sentence that was the result of a downward variance still could be infected by the irrationality of the Child Pornography Guidelines. As we discuss in more detail below, it is the *degree* of the variance and not the variance *per se* that is relevant for purposes of 18 U.S.C. § 3553(a).

### III. Use Data Recovery Specialists and Know the Technology

The Guidelines focus solely on the number and type of images possessed, rather than the offender's level of culpability. Indeed, there is no evidence to suggest that the volume of images possessed increases the risk to the community. The number of images simply is not an accurate reflection of the seriousness of the conduct. Given the online climate of file sharing programs such as Gigatribe or Limewire, an offender may receive far more images than he requested or intended to receive. In fact, other programs offer unlimited access to another user's files. Not surprisingly, many offenders end up with material that is too voluminous for any individual to review or with images they did not intend to possess.

Often after data recovery investigation, some images, or entire files, have never been opened while others were viewed quickly and deleted. Such investigation also reveals a majority or "type" of image an offender is interested in with very few containing sadomasochistic images or pre-pubescent minors. The current Specific Offender Characteristics ("SOCs") add points if even one of these images is present among thousands of images. Therefore, it is important to use the result of such investigations to ensure your client is not hit with SOCs that should be reserved for the most egregious or violent content that knowingly and intentionally was possessed, not simply accidentally so.

For example, a data recovery specialist conducting forensic review of the images often discovers very important information such as hard drives containing numerous images/files that were downloaded but never reviewed or opened, a large amount of duplicate images, multiple videos that are clipped into mini parts of one video but are counted separately, the amount of time the offender spent viewing the image, and many other relevant factors. If an offender spends one second viewing any image and then deletes it, it is reasonable to assume that type of image was not the focus of his search. In other words, the offender was not specifically looking for images of pre-pubescent minors and possessed a small amount of these images as a result of looking for other images. Many offenders' collection of child pornography is part of an even larger collection of adult pornography. The Child Pornography Guidelines do not account for these differences and for an offender's true conduct and actual risk for harming a child.

## IV. Cite Statistics and Trends in Sentencing

It is no surprise, then, that federal judges are not following the guidelines in child pornography cases. A survey of U.S. District Judges conducted by the USSC from January 2010 to March 2010 revealed that 70% of the judges opined that the guidelines for possession of child pornography were too high. Their sentences imposed reflect their displeasure with the guidelines. The latest USSC Annual Report indicates that judges imposed sentences below the child pornography guidelines 45% of the time in 2016

The graph below shows the dramatic increase in non-government-sponsored below guidelines sentences for child pornography offenses. A little over a quarter (29.1%)of child pornography offenders are now sentenced within the guidelines. When compared to other major offense categories, it is clear that the judiciary practices what it has been preaching, i.e., that these guidelines are far too onerous.

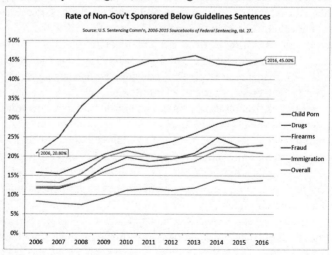

166

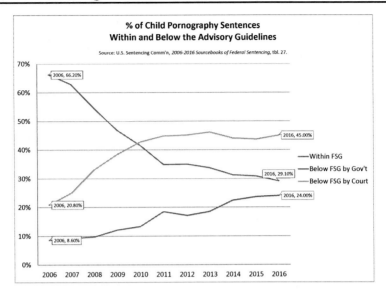

Source: *U.S. Sentencing Comm'n, Sourcebook on Federal Sentencing Statistics* 2006-2016, tbl. 27.

And looking at the last 11 years' data, it is telling not only that non-government-sponsored below-Guidelines sentences imposed for Child Pornography Offenses consistently had the highest degree of variance (in terms of months) from the bottom of the otherwise applicable guidelines range, but that such a *degree* of variance (like the number of variances per se) also is increasing faster than any other major offense category. The graph below illustrates these comparisons and trends quite dramatically.

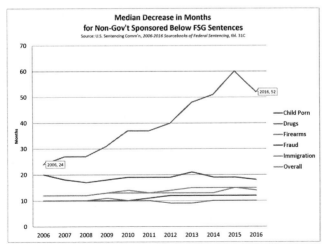

Source: *U.S. Sentencing Comm'n, Sourcebook on Federal Sentencing Statistics* 2006-2011, tbl. 31C.

Finally, a review of state sentencing practices can be extremely enlightening, especially when comparing sentences not just for child pornography but for actual contact offenses such as child molestation. While historically reference to state sentencing practices was not considered appropriate, the tide slowly is changing in this regard. *See, e.g., United States v. Ringgold*, 571 F.3d 948, 952 (9th Cir. 2009)(courts not precluded from considering state sentencing practices); *United States v. Clark*, 434 F.3d 684, 688-89 (4th Cir. 2007) (in separate concurrences, majority of panel holding that "some cases in which consideration of state sentences will not conflict with § 3553(a)(6)'s mandate to avoid unwarranted sentence disparities . . . may in fact help courts to apply correctly the other factors set forth in § 3553(a)")(Motz, J., concurring). Such data can illustrate the substantive unreasonableness of a defendant's sentence regardless of whether it was the result of a downward departure or variance.

For example, on January 1, 2007, California's new child pornography statute went into effect. *See* Calif. Penal Code § 311.11. Section 311.11 provides for a felony sentence of up to one year for a first offense, and up to six years on a subsequent offense. Since its implementation, 241 male offenders have been sentenced with an overall median sentence of 44 months. *See* Calif. Dep't of Corr. and Rehab., Datafile P311_11_11_2001_2010_MALE.xls (on file with authors). The median federal sentence for child pornography offenses in 2011 was 84 months, or nearly 91% greater than California's median sentence.

California's child molestation statute is located at Penal Code § 288(A). In the 10-year period covering January 1, 2001 to December 31, 2010, 14,111 male offenders were sentenced for violating this statute. See Calif. Dep't of Corr. and Rehab., Datafile P288(AB)_2001_2010_MALE.xls (on file with authors). The overall median sentence was 72 months. Thus, the median sentence for federal child *pornography* offenders still is nearly 17% greater than the median state sentence for child molesters.

## V. Propose Less Incarceration and a Longer Term of Supervision

Child pornography offenders are very closely monitored and their freedom greatly restricted. To address the concern of public protection, the U.S. Probation Office utilizes a myriad of tools to protect the community such as search and seizure of offenders' residences; search and seizure of computers and phones; computer restrictions such as use only for employment; electronic monitoring and surveillance; and compliance with treatment. Additionally, child pornography offenders are required to register as sex offenders, alerting local law enforcement to also monitor their actions closely. Sentences for those who possess child pornography should focus more on counseling, treatment, prevention, monitoring and supervision and less on imprisonment. This can be accomplished cost-effectively through sentences of supervised release as opposed to long terms of imprisonment.

Still, counsel should be cognizant that the Guidelines default position that sex offenders should receive a lifetime of supervised release, *see* USSG §5D1.2(b), p.s., is *not* required by law. And as with terms of imprisonment generally, the length of supervised release should be tailored to the characteristics of the client; where recidivism is unlikely, lengthy supervised release is unnecessary.

## VI. Restitution

While this issue does not come up all that frequently, it still is important for the practitioner to be aware that orders of mandatory restitution are not automatic. A relatively new area of litigation has arisen out of the so-called *Amy* and *Vicky* series of child pornography. These victims and others actively seek restitution in child pornography cases where pictures or videos of them have been identified. The plurality of circuits, however, has held that in order for a victim of child pornography to obtain restitution, there must be a showing that the offender's conduct was a "proximate cause" of the victim's harm. *See United States v. Monzel*, 641 F.3d 528, 535 (D.C. Cir. 2011)(citing *United States v. McDaniel*, 631 F.3d 1204, 1208-09 (11th Cir. 2011); *United States v. Laney*, 189 F.3d 954, 965 (9th Cir. 1999); *United States v. Crandon*, 173 F.3d 122, 125 (3d Cir. 1999)); *United States v. Evers*, 669 F.3d 645 (6th Cir. 2012). The Fifth Circuit, however, recently ruled that only "but for" causation need be established. *See In re Amy Unknown*, 636 F.3d 190 (5th Cir. 2011). Yet, as of this writing, it appears the Fifth Circuit may reverse itself and join the plurality. *See In re Amy Unknown*, 668 F.3d 776, 2012 U.S. App. LEXIS 1514 (5th Cir. Jan. 25, 2012)(granting *en banc* review).

In those cases where your client may have assets, it is important that counsel be cognizant of these recent developments. The plurality of circuits rightly have held that common-law principles of causation still apply with respect to restitution awards in child pornography cases. Without a showing of proximate cause, therefore, an order of restitution should not be imposed.

## VII. Recent Commission Activity regarding Child Pornography

In February 2012, the USSC conducted a public hearing with invited guests who provided testimony regarding the federal penalties for child pornography offenses. After a three-year review of this issue, the USSC plans to release a report by the end of the year which may propose changes to the Child Pornography Guidelines. Proposed changes could include less focus on number of images and more focus on actual conduct. The Guidelines also should be modified to reflect a lower base offense level for "child pornography" offenses with fewer specific offense characteristics (SOCs). Rather than SOCs adding levels for the number of images or types of images, they should focus on actual risk to children. For example, there should be a distinction between an offender who possesses, views, receives pornography and an offender who attempts to arrange a meeting with a child in an online "community". Everyone shares the outrage regarding conduct that harms and abuses children. However, there needs to be different levels of accountability for various crimes involving child pornography.

The Protect Act propelled into action numerous SOCs with the idea that possessors of child pornography present a direct risk to children. They are essentially being punished for things they "might" do in the future. Since there is no direct link to possessing pornography and actual risk of harm to children, a sentence of probation or a short prison sentence is more than sufficient to address punishment. Child pornography offenders are punished far beyond incarceration. They suffer more collateral consequences than other offenders. They must suffer the stigma of being a sex offender and are restricted to where they can live, work and even whether they can visit family for the rest of their lives.

On July 3, 2012, for the first time the Commission began publishing its prison and sentencing impact assessments on its new "Research and Statistics" page. The Commission is required to perform these assessments by statute. *See* 18 U.S.C. § 4047, 28 U.S.C. § 994(g). Furthermore, pursuant to Rule 4.2 of the Commission's Rules of Practice and Procedure, "the Commission *shall* consider the impact of any amendment on available penal and correctional resources, and on other facilities and services and shall make such information available to the public." In the future, it is presumed that any amendments to the Child Pornography Guidelines will also have published prison and sentencing impact assessments. Such assessments, especially those showing a decrease in prison beds and otherwise lowering the costs of incarceration, could be used by counsel to support the application of a downward adjustment, departure or variance in appropriate circumstances. While past assessments have not been published, it is hoped the Commission will do so soon. In all events, this is an extremely helpful and positive development that counsel must be aware of.

Finally, since one of the Commission priorities for the upcoming amendment cycle is to undertake a comprehensive multi-year study of recidivism and make recommendations for using information obtained from the study to reduce costs of incarceration and overcapacity of prisons and whether any amendments to the guidelines may be appropriate, defense practitioners should be utilizing the studies already available regarding low rates of recidivism and low risk of actual harm to children. According to the Justice Department, federal prosecutors obtained at least 2,713 indictments for sexual exploitation of minors in 2011, up from 1,901 in 2006. Since the average sentence for possession of child pornography is nearly 10 years, in 2011, 2,713 viewers of child pornography entered our prisons to serve 10 year sentences.

Defense practitioners should challenge these guidelines, provide current sentencing statistics and offer alternative sentences that reflect the client's true conduct, rather than sentences that respond to public outcry and punish offenders for the erroneous assumption of "what they might do in the future."

## Conclusion

The quiet revolution against Guidelines without reason began shortly after the promulgation of the Drug Guidelines. The revolution has since grown in volume to encompass the Child Pornography Guidelines (and perhaps others). A chorus of critics uniformly has condemned these Guidelines for lacking empirical support, being a product of Congress rather than the Commission, and otherwise being far, far too punitive. Courts have acted. Fewer now follow the Guidelines advisory range, while more impose sentences at ever greater degrees of variance below the bottom of the range.

Practitioners are therefore well-advised to bring the issues outlined in this article front-and-center to the sentencing judge as well as to the government's counsel, who may not be aware of some of the trends in sentencing child pornography offenders. While such offenses create visceral reactions, sentencing such offenders still must comport with reasoned and dispassionate applications of the law, and take into account the nature of the offender as much as the offense. The Guidelines for Child Pornography offenses, nearly all now agree, simply do not achieve a parsimonious, let alone just, result.

### §8:30.5 Child Pornography Guidelines are Ripe for Challenge

In the current version of the U.S. Sentencing Guidelines, U.S.S.G. §2G2.2 governs possession of child pornography. (In 2004, §2G2.4, which strictly covered possession, was eliminated and §2G2.2 revised to cover both possession and trafficking offenses.) In 1987, when the guidelines were first enacted, possession of child pornography was not a federal crime, and the guidelines covered only trafficking in child pornography. When the U.S. Sentencing Commission first enacted a guideline for possession of child pornography in 1990, the base offense level was 10. The guideline had available one upward adjustment: two levels for images of minors under age 12, resulting in a total exposure based on an offense level of 12, and the defendant's criminal history. (U.S.S.G. §2G2.4 (1990).)

Since its enactment, however, the guideline governing possession and trafficking of child pornography has undergone 11 amendments. These amendments are relatively unique: They largely resulted from Congressional directives that are fairly described as legislative fiats requiring an upward modification to the guidelines. While such Congressional directives are legally permissible, guidelines adopted thereunder do not carry the weight given to guidelines developed by the commission as an expert sentencing agency working in consultation with penological and sociological experts.

The amendments also are notable for their consistent increase in both the base offense level applicable to offenses involving child pornography, and the creation of new and additional specific offense characteristics. All of the specific offense characteristics have the effect of dramatically increasing the guideline range applicable to an offender. The increases in the mean guideline sentence between 2002 and 2007 were particularly noteworthy. Each calendar year, the mean-imposed sentence on an offender convicted of a child pornography-related offense increased by 11.9 months. (Troy Stabenow, *Deconstructing the Myth of Careful Study: A Primer on the Flawed Progression of the Child Pornography Guidelines*, at 2,) available at http://www.fd.org/pdf_lib/ Deconstructing%20the%20Child%20Pornography%20Guidelines%206.1.08. pdf). Thus, from 1994 to 1995, child pornography offenders received a mean sentence of 36 months, and the 24 offenders convicted only of possessing illegal images received a mean sentence of 15 months' confinement. (*Id.*) By 2007, the mean sentence for a child pornography offender had grown to 109.6 months. (*Id.*) This represents more than a 300 percent increase "in the *typical* imposed sentence." (*Id.*)

Practitioners should consider a number of relevant historical facts in seeking a below-guideline sentence in child pornography offenses.

The changes to the child pornography guidelines did not result from an empirical need for consistently harsher sentencing.

> [T]hese changes [were] largely the consequence of numerous morality earmarks, slipped into larger bills over the last fifteen years, often without notice, debate, or study of any kind. Congressionally mandated changes were even enacted to prevent the Commission from implementing carefully considered modifications which would have lowered applicable offense levels.

(*Id.* at 3.)

As a result, numerous district courts have concluded that the current version of U.S.S.G. §2G2.2 "diverges significantly from the Sentencing Commission's typical, empirical approach," frequently producing a sentence "greater than necessary to provide just punishment." (*United States v. Hanson*, 561 F. Supp.2d 1004, 1008 (E.D.Wis. 2008); *United States v. Stern*, 2008 U.S. Dist. LEXIS 102802 (N.D. Ohio Dec. 19, 2008).) Several district courts have expressed concern:

> The Court is particularly troubled that the Guidelines for sentencing those who possess child pornography 'have been repeatedly raised despite evidence and recommendations by the [U.S. Sentencing] Commission to the contrary.'

(*Hanson*, 561 F. Supp.2d at 1009.) A recent study shows that "[o]ver the last six years, the mean imposed sentence on [child pornography] offenders has increased an average of 11.9 months per calendar year." (Stabenow, *supra*, at 2.)

In addition to dramatically increasing the applicable base offense level, the changes in the guidelines have made almost every enhancement apply to almost every case. These guideline changes, in turn, cause most guideline sentences for defendants convicted of possession of child pornography to approach the statutory maximum. (*See United States v. Grober*, 595 F. Supp.2d 382, 384-85 (D.N.J. 2008).) As a result, probation officers frequently recommend sentences of 97 months or more for defendants whose statutory maximum is 10 years, who fall into Criminal History Category I, and who have never sexually exploited a child.

The U.S. Supreme Court recently emphasized that guidelines not supported by empirical data are entitled to less deference than are guidelines that exhibit the Sentencing Commission's "exercise of its characteristic institutional role" as an expert agency tasked with promulgating empirically-based guidelines. (*See* 28 U.S.C. §§991(b)(1)(C), 994 (describing empirical starting point for promulgation of guidelines and independent development of same); *Spears v. United States,* 555 U.S. 261 (2009) (internal quotation marks omitted; explaining *Kimbrough v. United States,* 552 U.S. 85, 109 (2007)).) The child pornography guidelines, like those for crack cocaine, are not based on empirical research and should receive little deference. Several district courts have so held. (*Grober,* 595 F. Supp.2d at 392-93; *United States v. Phinney,* 2009 U.S. Dist. LEXIS 13277 at *23-24 (E.D. Wis. Feb. 20, 2009); *United States v. Gellatly,* 2009 U.S. Dist. LEXIS 2693 (D. Neb. Jan. 5, 2009).)

The guidelines achieve unreasonable sentences in several ways. First, over time, the base offense level for possession of child pornography has been increased from 10 to 18 months, or even 22 months if the defendant is convicted of "receipt." Second, the child pornography guidelines achieve unreasonable sentences by imposing multiple enhancements that are applicable to almost every case involving the possession or receipt of child pornography, not merely those that are most aggravated. For example, the guidelines exponentially increase the number of images attributed to video files, counting a single video file as having 75 images. Thus, a defendant with only six video files is treated as possessing more than 600 images of child pornography and is subject to the maximum upward adjustment for the number of images. (U.S.S.G. §2G2.2, App. Note 4(B)(ii).) Third, the upward adjustments for use of a computer, an image of a child under 12 years of age, and sadistic images are applicable to almost every case. (*E.g., Gellatly,* 2009 U.S. Dist. 2693 LEXIS at *32-34; *Grober,* 595 F. Supp. 2d at 393-94.) The upward adjustment for use of a computer is applicable generally, and not only to cases where the use of a computer makes the offense more serious, such as when a defendant uses a computer to promote or widely distribute child pornography. (*Gellatly,* 2009 U.S. 2693 Dist. LEXIS at *32-34.) Similarly, almost every case involves at least one image of a child under 12 and one image that falls into the category of sadistic. (*Id.*) These adjustments are applicable whether or not the defendant specifically intended to possess such material. (*Id.*) The widespread applicability of these adjustments pushes most sentences toward the statutory maximum. (*Id.; United States v. Hanson,* 561 F. Supp.2d 1004, 1010-11 (E.D.Wis. 2008).)

Ultimately, the lack of empirical support for the child pornography guidelines and the general applicability of the enhancements result in sentences that are not fairly individualized. The history of legislative enactments reflects Congressional concerns with the use of computers to lure minors into sex acts, the use of materials to desensitize and entice victims, and the production of such materials. (*Gellatly,* 2009 U.S. 2693 Dist. LEXIS at *24.) However, the upward adjustments apply to all defendants who possess child pornography, regardless of whether they have ever attempted to exploit a minor and whether they simply downloaded and possessed child pornography.

Defendants who possess and receive child pornography are a particularly despised group of individuals. Their lack of popularity makes them especially vulnerable to receiving unduly harsh sentences and increases their need of effective advocacy at sentencing.

In light of the lack of empirical support for and facial arbitrariness of U.S.S.G. §2G2.2, a number of recent Circuit Court of Appeals opinions have made clear the federal judiciary's concern about the sentences imposed under this Guideline. In *United States v. Henderson*, 649 F.3d 955 (9th Cir. 2011), the Ninth Circuit held that "similar to the crack cocaine Guidelines, district courts may vary from the child pornography Guidelines, §2G2.2, based on policy disagreement with them, and not simply based on an individualized determination that they yield an excessive sentence in a particular case." *Id.* at 963. In so holding, the Ninth Circuit joined both the Second and Third Circuits in finding these particular Guidelines worthy of little to no weight at sentencing. *See, e.g., United States v. Dorvee*, 616 F.3d 174 (2d Cir. 2010); *United States v. Grober*, 624 F.3d 592 (3d Cir. 2010); *but see United States v. Pugh*, 515 F.3d 1179, 1201 n.5 (11th Cir. 2008) (child pornography Guidelines "do not exhibit the deficiencies the Supreme Court identified in *Kimbrough*").

Indeed the U.S. Sentencing Commission's own data clearly indicate the judiciary's increasing refusal to impose sentencing with the ranges produced by U.S.S.G. §2G2.2. In 2006, over 20% of child pornography sentences were imposed below the sentencing range set by U.S.S.G. §2G2.2 not as a result of a government motion in the case of substantial assistance, but rather by the sentencing judge. This rate of non-government-sponsored below guidelines sentences increased to to 45% in 2016. In contrast, non-government-sponsored below guidelines sentences for all offenses overall were imposed a mere 20.8% of the time.

The graph below illustrates the dramatic increase in the percentage of non-government sponsored below guidelines sentences relative to other major offense categories.

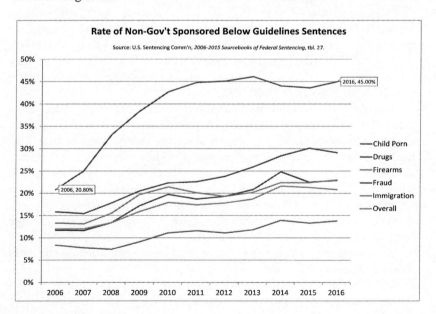

Additionally, the graph below illustrates the declining number of child pornography sentences imposed within the advisory guidelines range, and the corresponding rise in the number of child pornography sentences imposed below the guidelines as the result of a judge departing or varying below the advisory range.

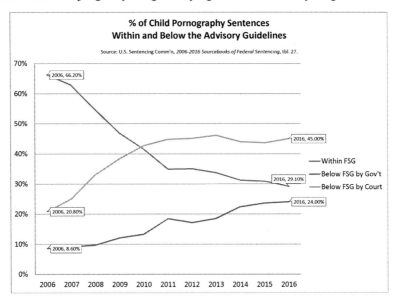

**% of Child Pornography Sentences
Within and Below the Advisory Guidelines**

Source: U.S. Sentencing Comm'n, *2006-2016 Sourcebooks of Federal Sentencing*, tbl. 27.

In 2012, the Commission issued a ground-breaking report to Congress entitled *Federal Child Pornography Offenses*, which continued its research into child pornography sentencing, and further corroborated earlier findings regarding the excessively harsh nature of the child pornography sentencing guidelines. In addition to reviewing sentencing trends, the Report also canvassed a wide array of literature, which questions many common assumptions about child pornography offenders, i.e., that they are necessarily pedophiles or have a propensity to engage in actual contact offenses with children. The report in its entirety is available at http://www.ussc.gov/news/congressional-testimony-and-reports/sex-offense-topics/report-congress-federal-child-pornography-offenses.

### §8:30.6    Inside Baseball: Interview With Former Federal Probation Officer

Author Alan Ellis interviewed Tess Lopez, a former U.S. probation officer for the Northern District of California in San Francisco. For 13 years, she specialized in presentence investigations. In 2005, she took her expertise in the area of sentencing to the private sector and is now a mitigation specialist with a national practice. Contact her at sentencinghelp@gmail.com.

**Ellis:** *As a former probation officer, how do you think probation officers (POs) have responded to the* Booker *decision?*

**Lopez:** Well, unfortunately, I am not seeing that the presentence reports (PSR) have changed significantly, even though the sentencing guidelines are only one of seven factors the court is now required to consider in imposing a sentence. In order for POs to determine which 18 U.S.C. §3553(a) factors apply, they need to conduct four-hour interviews with offenders and another four to six hours of interviews with family members and close friends to gain this insight. Obviously, that is not going to happen in the current environment of insufficient staff and high case loads.

**Ellis:** *How would the probation officers obtain this information?*
**Lopez:** The defense community, as a whole, needs to change its approach to sentencing. When probation officers receive a case, they are bombarded with information from the government, including graphic photos of child pornography, pictures of bank robbers, automatic weapons, drugs, and victim impact statements detailing how the offender has robbed good ol' granny of her life savings. The victim may add that your client should rot in jail in the worst of conditions. Such information is presented by the government to the PO in a nice little package complete with a letter outlining its version of the case, its guideline calculations, and an invitation to meet with the FBI agent or case agent to further "enlighten" the PO. Defense counsel usually calls the PO to schedule the presentence interview and mails the probation form completed by the client providing basic background information.

**Ellis:** *What can the defense community do differently?*
**Lopez:** They cannot simply act like "business as usual." The court is not going to receive the information needed to consider sentences outside the guideline range or "variances" from the probation officer, and certainly not from the government. Defense counsel needs to either spend sufficient time with the client and his (or her) family or friends, getting to know him or her so that the attorney can identify which §3553(a) factors may support a sentence outside the guideline range, or hire a sentencing mitigation specialist to obtain and analyze this information. The lawyer should obtain this information as early in the process as possible so that it is immediately available for presentation to the probation officer when he or she receives the case and prior to the probation interview. This would provide the probation officer with a more balanced view of the case and presents a preview of the §3553(a) factors that you have identified for consideration.

**Ellis:** *What else can defense lawyers do to assist the PO in understanding clients?*
**Lopez:** Provide verification of everything. If your client has an alcohol problem, if not documented by prior arrests, document it, get him or her evaluated, and have family members or friends comment about it. Could the client be abusing alcohol to "self-medicate" and relieve an underlying mental health problem? If your client has significant medical issues, document them and provide a list of medications as well as your client's limitations. If there is a mental health issue, or even if you suspect it's possible, obtain a psychological evaluation. Gather as much information as possible to help the PO, and ultimately the judge, understand who your client is and what led him or her to commit the offense.

**Ellis:** *Can you provide an example of how such detailed information can support a sentence outside the guideline range?*

**Lopez:** I'll give you two. First, historically, lack of guidance as a youth and unfortunate childhood experiences were not relevant in determining whether a sentence outside the guideline range was appropriate. It was called a "prohibited factor." I could never understand this "logic." Repeated studies have shown that a disadvantaged youth is a root cause of crime in this country. At last, post-*Booker*, this information must be considered by the court as it relates to the personal history or characteristics of the defendant. Second, as you often say, Alan, "If you think your client is crazy, guess what? He may be crazy. Have him or her evaluated by a mental health professional." I second the motion. If your client has suffered significant abuse or trauma, these experiences may have contributed to his or her pattern of making poor decisions or engaging in risky, unacceptable behavior. Defense counsel may be able to show that the childhood experiences were extreme and contributed to the client's participation in the offense. Perhaps the client recently commenced counseling and can demonstrate new insight about wrongful conduct. These unfortunate childhood circumstances and the client's motivation to address his or her behavior may convince the court that a lower sentence is warranted.

**Ellis:** *In your experience, do many clients have mental health issues?*

**Lopez:** To illustrate an example: In a white collar case, the client is an exceptionally bright, high-functioning and very successful individual. By all appearances, he is very skilled, highly motivated, and works 18-20-hour days, landing promotions and executive privileges. Where is the mental health issue here? A little digging and a psychological evaluation reveals that the client is an obsessive-compulsive perfectionist who suffers from depression and anxiety. The overwhelming desire to be successful personally and financially may cause an ordinarily law-abiding person to "cross the line" into inappropriate or illegal behavior. The exceptionally bright, successful client is later diagnosed with bipolar disorder. Studies have shown that many people silently and unknowingly suffer from mental illness. The Justice Department estimates that half of America's prison and jail inmates have symptoms of mental health problems. However, the latest statistics by the U.S. Sentencing Commission (2002) reflect that only 2.6 percent of inmates received downward departures for diminished capacity (U.S.S.G. §5K2.13). If half of the inmates have symptoms of mental health problems, yet only 2.6 percent are receiving departures, are the judges simply insensitive? Or, does the problem lie at the feet of defense counsel who are not taking the time to conduct a thorough investigation into the client's social and psychological history? Unfortunately, I believe it is the latter.

**Ellis:** *How can defense lawyers make sure the court gets the detailed information?*

**Lopez:** Unfortunately, it is often too late to wait and simply respond to the draft presentence report (PSR). When the lawyer first makes contact with the probation officer, ask for the "dictation deadline" or date that the draft PSR is due to the supervisor. Make sure all information regarding the client's background is provided by that date. As experienced federal practitioners well know, it is often difficult to convince a PO to make significant changes to the report once it is disclosed. However, if the information is simply not available until after the draft report is disclosed, the lawyer who responds to the draft PSR should request that the PO include the more detailed information into each section of the PSR. Defense counsel may even e-mail a detailed report to the probation officer so he or she can cut and paste the information into the report. Finally, outline each factor that you want the PO to consider under parts E (factors that may warrant a departure) and F (factors that may warrant a sentence below the guideline range under 18 U.S.C. §3553(a)) of the PSR and make strong arguments to support these requests.

**Ellis:** *Why not skip the process and just put everything in the sentencing memo to the court?*

**Lopez:** Two reasons: First, judges continue to rely on probation officers during sentencing and some judges are significantly influenced by the probation officer's opinion. If the PO is receptive to a variance, it may be key to convincing the court to consider a sentence below the guideline range.

Second, in the event that your client receives a prison sentence, the only documentation received by the BOP about your client is the PSR. This information (or lack of information) will dictate whether the client is sent to a dormitory-style camp or, at the very worst, a maximum security prison. For example, if your client has a pending state case and no disposition is noted, the BOP may treat the open case as a detainer. As a result, clients may be scored higher, be precluded from participation in programs that could benefit them and reduce their sentences, and affect whether or not they are sent to a more secure facility with fewer privileges.

**Ellis:** *How can lawyers address a pending state matter that may result in a detainer?*

**Lopez:** Defense counsel should schedule a court date to have the previous matter disposed and then alert the judge that the matter is pending disposition. Request that the sentencing go forward, and notify the judge that you will provide a certified copy of the disposition. Request that the judge order the probation officer to modify the PSR to include the disposition (before sending the PSR to the BOP) once the PO receives this documentation. Also, request that the judge's clerk wait to release the judgment and commitment order (J&C) until this happens since the issuance of the judgment triggers the BOP designation process. Having the client sentenced on the prior offense *after* sentencing prevents the client from having another scorable conviction. Requesting that the PO be directed to change the previously pending matter to one that has been disposed of eliminates the issue of having a pending matter or "detainer" for BOP designation purposes.

**Ellis:** *Is there anything else defense counsel can do to get their point across to the probation officer?*

**Lopez:** Yes, in cases in which the client is convicted by a jury or enters a plea without a written plea agreement, the parties have not agreed on guideline calculations or departures. Often, the parties have opposing views on loss figures, guideline calculations, *ex post facto* issues, criminal history and departures. I recommend that defense counsel present their entire view of the case in a straightforward letter to the PO as soon as possible. More importantly, I strongly recommend that defense counsel request to meet with the probation officer to discuss their position on these issues. This is particularly important in a complex case involving numerous counts, various ways to calculate the guidelines, which guideline is appropriate, and which guideline book is appropriate, etc. Personal contact with the probation officer builds rapport and offers an opportunity to explain your position. Sometimes a case is so complex that the PO would welcome the opportunity for defense counsel to explain their version of the case. Remember, the PO wasn't present at trial. A personal meeting also assures the lawyer that the PO understands the case and his or her position. Generally speaking, when working with the probation officer, a little extra effort goes a long way.

**Ellis:** *Is it your impression that the judges are responding to the* Booker *decision and the* Booker *remedy by treating the guidelines as just one of seven factors and are sentencing outside the guideline range?*

**Lopez:** Unfortunately, the data indicate that federal sentences are not lower post-*Booker*. Once again, it is up to the defense bar to bring about change through creative advocacy. As noted by Karen L. Landau, whom I know is "of counsel" to your firm, in an article she co-authored with you and your senior associate, James H. Feldman, Jr., "Litigating in a Post-*Booker* World" (CRIM. JUST., Spring 2005, at 24.)

> [F]ederal criminal defense lawyers may need to take a lesson from their comrades in the realm of capital litigation: These attorneys have repeatedly demonstrated how to save clients' lives through conducting a thorough investigation into the client's social and psychological history and producing evidence that mitigates the crimes committed.

I think it is easier for a judge who was on the bench in the preguideline days to welcome the wiggle room and lack of structure than it is for those judges whose only experience has been with guideline sentencing. It will take time for the defense community to appreciate the importance of operating differently and more thoroughly, and it's going to take time for some judges who like the structure of the guidelines to adapt to the change, as it "goes against their grain." But you and your colleagues can help them do so.

## §8.40    CHARACTER LETTER INSTRUCTIONS

Clients, family and friends often ask us if character letters will help, and if so, how they should be written. We have drafted a character instructional letter which gives people ideas how to write a character letter. It contains enough suggestions that the letters don't come out looking like they have been drafted by a law firm. We take the best of the letters and quote from them in our sentencing memo. Sometimes, a letter may be so helpful that we will contact the writer to learn more, and occasionally, if the court will permit, call the writer as a character witness at the sentencing hearing. Some letters are good but need work. We will get back to the writer and offer suggestions for improvement. Those that are not salvageable, get tossed. The following is a template that can be tailored to a particular client.

Client
Address

Dear :

I understand that there are a number of individuals, including friends, family members and business associates, who know you and wish to write letters to the Court about you, but who believe they could use some guidance about how to convey their messages. Character letter writers often could use some guidance about how to convey their messages. I told you I would attempt to provide some guidance, and am doing so in this letter for their use.

The letters should be addressed to the Judge:

Honorable _____ , Judge
United States District Court
[Address]

**but should be sent to me** so that I may review them to make copies for the prosecutor and the Probation Officer before sending them on to the Judge. The letters should be in the words of the letter writer, should be concise, and should be genuine. There should be no orchestrated letter-writing campaign; instead, individuals who strongly feel they have relevant information for the Judge should be given a copy of this letter to assist in expressing those views. Please refrain from including your address and telephone number on the letter as it will need to be redacted.

What follows are some suggestions which these letter writers may wish to incorporate:

1. State their present or former position, *e.g.*, "I am/was the Pastor of the XYZ church."
2. Describe their relationship with you, including the nature and the length of the relationship, and how you met.

3. Describe the good that you have done in charitable, educational, civic or business activities.

4. Particular experiences which the writer has had with you and which demonstrate your human virtues would be helpful. An anecdote—an act of charity, or a particular kindness—briefly stated may be worth far more than merely describing you in abstract terms as "decent."

5. Express belief in your honesty and how your conduct was out-of-character with everything else you've done in your life.

6. Tell the Judge, in the strongest possible terms, why imprisonment would be tragic to you, your family, and the community.

7. Plead for consideration as a human being based on what you have been during your entire life.

8. Plead for mercy or compassion based on your service to others (without your having expected anything in return), not as a special favor.

9. Use their own thoughts and language as they see fit.

Of course, the suggestions above are not all inclusive, and some letter writers may not be in a position to make statements based on their experience about all areas described above. What is important is that the letters be genuine and reflect the deeply-held beliefs of the letter writer.

Additionally, I strongly suggest that letter writers NOT:

1. Question the guilty verdict or finding of guilt;
2. Comment on the evidence in the case;
3. Suggest a particular sentence;
4. Express personal views on the criminal justice system;
5. Use the words "lenient" or "leniency" in requesting sentencing by the judge.

I would be happy to discuss these suggestions further with you, or with any person interested in writing to help you.

Finally, even though your sentencing date is not until __/__, it would be useful for me to receive the letters no later than __/__.

Sincerely yours,

[Attorney signature]

## §8.41   THE IMPORTANCE OF SENTENCING STATISTICS

As several of the above sections discussed, the post-Booker era of the Federal Sentencing Guidelines has ushered in significant changes to sentencing law, policy and practice. Among the most important is the increasing use of statistics at sentencing. How other judges sentence often can be a useful tool when advocating on behalf of your client. While every case is different in many aspects, there are just as many similarities. Accordingly, the average sentence for an offense in a particular district, circuit or even nationwide can be quite powerful to present to a judge at a sentencing hearing. Statistics can be useful not only to demonstrate possible issues regarding unwarranted disparity among similarly situated defendants, but also unwarranted similarity among offenders who have engaged in dissimilar conduct.

Likewise, statistics can be used to urge a different sanction. For example, statistics may demonstrate how costly incarcerating your client may be versus sentencing him to home confinement.

Below is an annotated list of some useful websites, but it is by no means comprehensive:

**http://www.ussc.gov**
> The U.S. Sentencing Commission's website contains an enormous amount of data for the practitioner to review in both graph and table forms as well as various reports written by Commission staff.

**http://www.bop.gov/locations/weekly_report.jsp**
> The Bureau of Prisons website contains information on inmate populations, updated weekly.

**http://www.fjc.gov/**
> The website for the Federal Judicial Center, the "think tank" for the federal judiciary. Several good reports on the operation of the federal judiciary generally, as well as biographical information about all federal judges, past and present.

**http://bjs.ojp.usdoj.gov/**
> The Bureau of Justice Statistics' website contains reports and data on state and federal criminal arrests, prosecutions, and sentencings, among other matters.

**http://trac.syr.edu/**
> The Transactional Records Access Clearinghouse is run by Syracuse University. The most useful data requires a subscription, but allows the user to drill down to prosecution trends by district or by agency, and sentencing trends by individual judges.

**https://www.ncjrs.gov/index.html**
> The National Criminal Justice Reference Service, operated by the U.S. Department of Justice, provides an enormous variety of reports on many aspects of state and federal criminal justice and policy issues.

**https://sentencingstats.com**
> Sentencing Stats, LLC is a premier data analytical firm providing federal sentencing data, tables, charts and analyses to attorneys and their clients.

## §8:42    SENTENCING TABLE

### SENTENCING TABLE
### (in months of imprisonment)

| Offense Level | Criminal History Category (Criminal History Points) | | | | | |
|---|---|---|---|---|---|---|
| | I (0 or 1) | II (2 or 3) | III (4, 5, 6) | IV (7, 8, 9) | V (10, 11, 12) | VI (13 or more) |
| 1 | 0–6 | 0–6 | 0–6 | 0–6 | 0–6 | 0–6 |
| 2 | 0–6 | 0–6 | 0–6 | 0–6 | 0–6 | 1–7 |
| 3 | 0–6 | 0–6 | 0–6 | 0–6 | 2–8 | 3–9 |
| 4 | 0–6 | 0–6 | 0–6 | 2–8 | 4–10 | 6–12 |
| 5 | 0–6 | 0–6 | 1–7 | 4–10 | 6–12 | 9–15 |
| 6 | 0–6 | 1–7 | 2–8 | 6–12 | 9–15 | 12–18 |
| 7 | 0–6 | 2–8 | 4–10 | 8–14 | 12–18 | 15–21 |
| 8 | 0–6 | 4–10 | 6–12 | 10–16 | 15–21 | 18–24 |
| 9 | 4–10 | 6–12 | 8–14 | 12–18 | 18–24 | 21–27 |
| 10 | 6–12 | 8–14 | 10–16 | 15–21 | 21–27 | 24–30 |
| 11 | 8–14 | 10–16 | 12–18 | 18–24 | 24–30 | 27–33 |
| 12 | 10–16 | 12–18 | 15–21 | 21–27 | 27–33 | 30–37 |
| 13 | 12–18 | 15–21 | 18–24 | 24–30 | 30–37 | 33–41 |
| 14 | 15–21 | 18–24 | 21–27 | 27–33 | 33–41 | 37–46 |
| 15 | 18–24 | 21–27 | 24–30 | 30–37 | 37–46 | 41–51 |
| 16 | 21–27 | 24–30 | 27–33 | 33–41 | 41–51 | 46–57 |
| 17 | 24–30 | 27–33 | 30–37 | 37–46 | 46–57 | 51–63 |
| 18 | 27–33 | 30–37 | 33–41 | 41–51 | 51–63 | 57–71 |
| 19 | 30–37 | 33–41 | 37–46 | 46–57 | 57–71 | 63–78 |
| 20 | 33–41 | 37–46 | 41–51 | 51–63 | 63–78 | 70–87 |
| 21 | 37–46 | 41–51 | 46–57 | 57–71 | 70–87 | 77–96 |
| 22 | 41–51 | 46–57 | 51–63 | 63–78 | 77–96 | 84–105 |
| 23 | 46–57 | 51–63 | 57–71 | 70–87 | 84–105 | 92–115 |
| 24 | 51–63 | 57–71 | 63–78 | 77–96 | 92–115 | 100–125 |
| 25 | 57–71 | 63–78 | 70–87 | 84–105 | 100–125 | 110–137 |
| 26 | 63–78 | 70–87 | 78–97 | 92–115 | 110–137 | 120–150 |
| 27 | 70–87 | 78–97 | 87–108 | 100–125 | 120–150 | 130–162 |
| 28 | 78–97 | 87–108 | 97–121 | 110–137 | 130–162 | 140–175 |
| 29 | 87–108 | 97–121 | 108–135 | 121–151 | 140–175 | 151–188 |
| 30 | 97–121 | 108–135 | 121–151 | 135–168 | 151–188 | 168–210 |
| 31 | 108–135 | 121–151 | 135–168 | 151–188 | 168–210 | 188–235 |
| 32 | 121–151 | 135–168 | 151–188 | 168–210 | 188–235 | 210–262 |
| 33 | 135–168 | 151–188 | 168–210 | 188–235 | 210–262 | 235–293 |
| 34 | 151–188 | 168–210 | 188–235 | 210–262 | 235–293 | 262–327 |
| 35 | 168–210 | 188–235 | 210–262 | 235–293 | 262–327 | 292–365 |
| 36 | 188–235 | 210–262 | 235–293 | 262–327 | 292–365 | 324–405 |
| 37 | 210–262 | 235–293 | 262–327 | 292–365 | 324–405 | 360–life |
| 38 | 235–293 | 262–327 | 292–365 | 324–405 | 360–life | 360–life |
| 39 | 262–327 | 292–365 | 324–405 | 360–life | 360–life | 360–life |
| 40 | 292–365 | 324–405 | 360–life | 360–life | 360–life | 360–life |
| 41 | 324–405 | 360–life | 360–life | 360–life | 360–life | 360–life |
| 42 | 360–life | 360–life | 360–life | 360–life | 360–life | 360–life |
| 43 | life | life | life | life | life | life |

Zone A: Offense Levels 1–8
Zone B: Offense Levels 9–11
Zone C: Offense Levels 12–13
Zone D: Offense Levels 14–43

November 1, 2016

## §8:50    ADVICE FROM THE BENCH

### §8:50.1    What Judges Want to Know

Over the past two years, I interviewed almost two dozen federal judges, discussing with them their philosophies on and advice for lawyers representing clients at federal sentencing. As I analyzed the information shared during the interviews, a disturbing fact became apparent. The judges feel that we criminal defense lawyers are falling down on the job when it comes to sentencing. Simply stated, judges said they are not getting the information they need during the sentencing phase of a case. Below I have summarized some of the themes and advice that emerged from those interviews.

### Allocution and Internalization

Judge Mark W. Bennett wrote about the importance of allocution in his article "Heartstrings or Heartburn: A Federal Judge's Musing on Defendants' Right and Rite of Allocution," which appeared in the March 2011 issue of *The Champion*—NACDL's monthly magazine. He followed this article with a survey of fellow judges that showed the high value most place on allocution ("A Survey and Analysis of Federal Judge's Views on Allocution in Sentencing," 65 Ala. L. Rev. 735 (2013)). None of the 21 judges I interviewed told me that allocution is not important to them. On the contrary, they would often rather hear from your client than you, the lawyer, during the sentencing hearing, unless you have new information not contained in your sentencing memorandum and other submissions.

Judge John R. Adams of the U.S. District Court for the Northern District of Ohio, who sits in Akron and is widely considered to be a tough sentencer, said, "Sentencing is very personal. The more I see a defendant, the more I get to know him. A defendant's allocution is generally more important than what a lawyer says at sentencing. I don't want to have the defendant making excuses for his conduct." Judge Otis D. Wright, II, of the Central District of California in Los Angeles, who like Judge Adams, has the reputation of being a tough sentencer, concurs, "I want the unvarnished truth. It can really help if I believe that they are sincere. I can tell whether a defendant is being sincere by what he says in court."

Judge Walter H. Rice, who sits in the Southern District of Ohio in Dayton, and who is considered by many observers to be at the opposite end of the spectrum, says, "I can often determine a defendant's sincerity during a colloquy at sentencing. I often engage the defendant in conversation so I can learn more about him." He points out that he does not want to hear a canned speech, stating that "I come out on the bench with a tentative range of sentence in mind, but a good allocution can cause me to impose a lower sentence. I may ask the defendant if he has harmed others and I may ask him what he plans to do about it." Judge Rice says he will often ask a defendant what he is going to do upon release from prison in order to determine whether he is likely to reoffend.

If this is your first time before a particular judge, find out from other lawyers how he or she views allocution and what questions, if any, the judge is likely to ask your client if he allocutes. Sit in on another of the judge's sentencings to see how he treats allocution. Prep your client for allocution just as if you would prep him for testifying on his own behalf in trial. Judge Robert N. Scola, Jr., of the Southern District of Florida in Miami, a past president of the Miami Chapter of the Florida Association of Criminal Defense Lawyers, even suggests that you have a colleague listen to your client's proposed allocution and ask him the questions that the judge may ask. He also recommends that if co-defendants are being sentenced on a date earlier than your client, sit in and listen to their allocutions and any questions put to them.

When asked which of the cases coming before them they find most challenging, there was agreement - predatory child sexual offenders where children have been harmed and white-collar criminals where vulnerable people have been harmed. Judge Patrick Schiltz of the District of Minnesota in Minneapolis, a former Scalia law clerk, shared that among his hardest cases are those involving white collar "con men who prey on vulnerable victims." He commented, "you need to show me your client is not a con artist at heart, that he is not a psychopath or a sociopath. If there is a mental illness that contributed to the commission of the crime, let me know about it."

## Restitution

Judge Neil V. Wake of the District of Arizona in Phoenix says that what is important is that the defendant has internalized his crime and taken ownership of his mistake. "The payment of restitution is a good example of internalizing and owning the offense. Even as little as $25 a month demonstrates to me that the defendant is committed to rehabilitation."

Judge Adams doesn't want to see a defendant wallow in self-pity, instead preferring the defendant to begin by apologizing to the victims. Judge Adams followed with, "I also want to see what a defendant has done in an attempt to make the victims whole, particularly in white collar fraud cases. If I see a Presentence Report that says the defendant has spent a lot of money on luxuries and has nothing left to pay back restitution, I get very annoyed." Similarly, Judge Wright will hold it against a defendant if he feels that your client has not done what he could have to make things right with his victims and says it is important for the defendant to make restitution prior to sentencing, particularly where there are vulnerable victims.

Judge Wright expects a defendant to make restitution, or, in other words, to "put his money where his mouth is. I want heartbroken, vulnerable victims to know that I take what happens to them very seriously. My sentences will reflect this, particularly where I believe a defendant has not done what he could have to make things right with his victims," he says.

Judge Scola commented that if a defendant is ordered to pay a "large" amount of restitution, he doesn't expect that the defendant is going to be able to pay the full amount. "If the loss in the case is $1 million, but the defendant only received $10,000 for his participation, he should pay that amount back or offer to do so with arrangements." Judge Scola gave examples of what he considers real efforts for restitution, saying "If he has equity in a home, he should get a home equity loan. If his family and friends truly love him, they should help him." In other words, do what you can. "I'd rather have 50 character witnesses pay $100 each toward the defendant's restitution than to provide 50 character letters. Making reasonable efforts to pay restitution is one indication of sincere remorse." He added, "If your client is leasing a car for $900 a month while on bond and pays no restitution, that's not going to help him."

## Pet Peeves

Every single one of the judges, in responding to my question about their pet peeves with defense lawyers, has told me how much they dislike boilerplate citations to *Booker* and its progeny. Judge Bennett told me "I get annoyed when lawyers cite *Booker* and the 18 U.S.C. §3553(a) factors, as if I didn't know the law." Judge Rice adds "If I don't know it by now, the republic is in danger."

Of course, if there are disputed guideline or other legal issues, cite cases in support of your position.

## Sentencing Videos

More and more of the judges I've interviewed have seen and commented on the value of sentencing videos. Chief Judge Lawrence J. O'Neill, Jr. of the Eastern District of California in Fresno says the videos are an excellent way of getting character witnesses, often far better than letters. He tells the story of a father of a boating accident victim who described how the defendant had saved his daughter's life. No way can a letter have this kind of impact. See "Use of Video," by Alan Ellis and Tess Lopez, *Criminal Justice*, Vol. 26, No. 2 (Summer 2011) and "Using Moving Pictures to Build the Bridge of Empathy at Sentencing, by Doug Passon, *The Champion* (June 2014).

## Disparity

Judge Justin L. Quackenbush of the Western District of Washington in Spokane recommends that lawyers provide statistics in their sentencing memorandum: "Sentencing statistics from the United States Sentencing Commission should be consulted as those statistics show other judges have often departed from 'draconian' guideline ranges; for example, child pornography possession cases."

Use statistics of other sentences to show unwarranted disparity in the district, the districts within a particular state, the circuit, and nationwide. We used to append charts. Now we are embedding the charts into the sentencing memorandum itself.

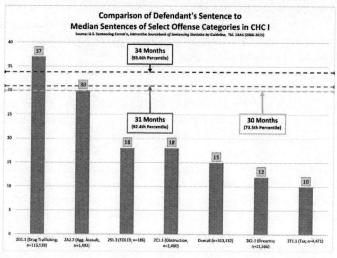

**Conclusion**

What struck me most during these interviews is how the judges feel that we lawyers frequently do not give them the information they need at sentencing. Judge Patrick J. Schiltz says it this way: "It's surprising how many otherwise competent attorneys 'punt' at the sentencing hearing." Judge Robert Scola suggests that we lawyers take a page out of the book from our death penalty colleagues and advises, "Don't wait to think about sentencing advocacy." In other words, since 99% of one's federal criminal clients will be facing sentencing, start preparing the case for sentencing early on.

More than one judge has told me don't minimize the seriousness of what the client did. Don't sugarcoat your client. You gain credibility if you show his strengths and weaknesses. In other words, if you can show that you are on the same page with the court as to the seriousness of the offense, the chances of having your other statements accepted increase.

## §8:50.2 Judges Think We Can Do Better

In my interviews with the more than two dozen federal judges, I have asked them to share some do's and don't's for lawyers who appear before them at sentencing. Below are some interesting quotes from my interviews:

"Many lawyers don't submit sentencing memoranda and those who do, submit it on the eve of sentencing or submit poor ones. Get me everything well in advance of the hearing. If you've got five or six good character letters, put them in the sentencing memorandum, quote from them, and attach them as Exhibit A. Put the rest in a later exhibit."

"Tell me something I don't know about your client. Don't regurgitate what's in the Presentence Report." "I welcome sentencing recommendations from defense counsel unless they are ridiculously low. When this happens, the lawyer loses his credibility with me."

"Psychological reports are particularly helpful if I know and respect the expert. If however, the report is based on erroneous information provided by the client, it will carry little if any weight with me."

"I appreciate community service, particularly if a defendant performed it prior to sentencing and there is a good letter from the agency asking that he be allowed to perform community service. It is even more important to me if your client has performed community service even before he knew he was under investigation or charged."

"If you have a case on point that is factually and legally close to your case wherein another judge in my district has imposed a relatively low sentence, it carries some weight with me, assuming, of course, that I respect that judge."

"With character letters, I am looking for good deeds that are unknown to others. For example, a defendant who has done something for an elderly disabled neighbor such as shoveling ice from her sidewalk without any thought of obtaining anything in return."

"I'd rather have 50 character witnesses pay $100 each toward a defendant's restitution rather than provide 50 character letters."

"I put a lot of stock in collateral civil consequences of your client's conviction particularly if he is in a small community and will be shunned by his neighbors. This has a big impact on me."

"In child pornography cases, I am interested in risk assessments."

"I don't know a single judge who doesn't recognize that he has a human being in front of him being sentenced."

### §8:50.3    White-Collar Clients

I've been practicing law for nearly 50 years. During that time, I have had a great deal of experience with judges who have been willing to share all manner of suggestions. Here is some of their best advice for white-collar criminal defense attorneys whose clients are facing sentencing.

**Be Credible**

Not surprisingly, the judges stressed the importance of the credibility of the lawyers appearing before them. What might be surprising are some of the recommendations the judges provided as to how that creditability is established. While they appreciate a lawyer's vigorous defense of their client, they caution lawyers to remember their audience: the court. The judges do not want a white washed version of the defendant's crimes. They want candor, otherwise, they can feel the lawyer is being manipulative. In a particularly reprehensible case, the judges recommended that the lawyer acknowledge that the offense is, indeed, a heinous one. As Judge Otis D. Wright II of the Central District of California put it, "Once we are both in agreement as to what the client did and how the victims have been impacted by it, that lawyer has a lot of credibility going forward."

While most judges welcome a lawyer's sentencing recommendation, they all agree that a critical mistake they see lawyers make is to ask for too low of a sentence. Recommending a ridiculously low sentence to please your clients damages the creditability of the other aspects of the information presented in the judges' eyes. Judge Wright says "Don't take yourself out of the conversation." It was recommended that a lawyer should not worry about asking for a higher sentence than is ultimately imposed. After all, it is not likely that your client is going to be unhappy if they get a low sentence. Judge Schiltz readily welcomes a lawyer's recommendation of a sentence, saying that some attorneys have a real "knack" for making well-reasoned, principled and appropriate recommendations.

Judges also find it off putting and useless when lawyers regurgitate information the judge already knows. A common comment was: Tell me something I don't already know about your client.

I frequently heard the words "trust" and "credibility" from the judges. Attorneys would be wise to keep this in mind, especially with respect to the information presented, arguments made and sentences recommended.

Another aspect of establishing credibility with the judge is the presentencing memorandum. Judges dislike when lawyers do not submit them, submit them on the eve of sentencing, and submit a poorly prepared memorandum.

### Your Clients Need to Sell Themselves

The judges take the view that sentencing is personal, and they want the victims and their families to know that they care about them. To that end, judges want to see that your client has internalized what he has done, why he did it, what he has learned from it and why he is not going to do it again, and in a white collar crime case, how he is going to make the victim whole.

Virtually all want to see that the defendant has internalized what he has done so that they can determine whether he has seriously taken responsibility and is truly remorseful. Allocution can play a big part in humanizing the defendant. They want to hear from the defendant, personally, but caution that they typically can spot insincerity or an attorney-authored script.

A lawyer needs to carefully prepare his or her client for this. Your overall purpose needs to be humanizing your client. Tell and help your client to tell a compelling story.

Judge Jon Levy of the District of Maine in Portland is interested in what the defendant has done since being apprehended. For example, if detained, has defendant taken advantage of any rehabilitation programming or performed a useful service like teaching other inmates a new job skill at the jail? On the other hand he says:

> "If the defendant was on presentence release, I want to know what she or he has done during that period, whether the defendant has made amends or paid restitution; was the defendant working and how did it go; has the defendant received mental health or substance abuse treatment and what do the providers have to say about the defendant's progress; and generally anything that bears on whether the defendant has taken meaningful steps to turn his or her life around."

Similarly, Judge Paul L. Friedman of the U.S. District Court for the District of Columbia says, "It is helpful when a defendant who is intelligent and educated tutors other inmates in prison or helps them with letters, legal research and writing."

If the presentence report says that defendant is the sole supporter of his family, the lawyer should document and give examples of this. For example, Judge Quackenbush recommends that, "[i]f there is an elderly family member who will suffer as a result of his incarceration, I want to know precisely how. The lawyer needs to bring this to life."

However, none of the judges are comfortable with the defendant bringing young children to the sentencing.

## Psych Evaluations Can Make a Difference

Many judges feel that mental illness is rampant among criminal defendants, and most of them welcome psychological reports to better understand your client. However, they caution that they are only going to give these reports weight if they are credible. The judges say they want to know whether mental illness was a contributing factor to the defendant's crime and they find influential evaluations that were done prior to the defendant being caught as opposed to a professional who spent more than an hour with the client awaiting sentencing.

Judge Amy St. Eve of the Northern District of Illinois in Chicago finds it more helpful if the expert is someone who has treated the defendant for a significant period of time rather than someone who has just met the defendant at the jail and interviewed him or her for two hours.

Judge Quackenbush says that if a defendant has a substance and/or a mental health problem, he looks favorably on defendants who seek rehabilitation and treatment prior to sentencing. Better yet, prior to being caught. Serious medical issues also are of importance to Judge Quackenbush. He notes that general deterrence is not a major factor, but says that positive family connections are an important consideration. "A supportive family plays an important role in the sentencing decision," he says.

More judges than you would think welcome live testimony by the expert. They just don't want the expert to parrot what's in his report. They want to engage the expert in questioning. Judge John R. Adams of the Northern District of Ohio in Akron finds it useful when the parties agree on an independent expert to be appointed or if not appointed, a mutual choice of the parties.

Along these lines, I often ask the prosecutor in the case who he likes to use. I find their experts only too happy to work for the defense occasionally and, of course, their opinions are virtually unassailable.

## Restitution

All the judges want any victims to be made whole particularly if they are vulnerable individuals. Most of the judges welcome even a step in the right direction in making restitution. Judge Scola says it is better for the 50 character letter writers to contribute $50 each to the restitution fund. Starting to make payments throughout sentencing can also go a long way.

Judge Neal Wake of the District of Arizona in Phoenix repeated that what is important is that the defendant has internalized his crime and takes ownership of his mistake.

> "The payment of restitution is a good example of internalizing and owning the offense. Even as little as $25 a month demonstrates to me that the defendant is committed to rehabilitation."

Judge Wright expects a defendant to make restitution, or, in other words, to: "put his money where his mouth is. I want heartbroken, vulnerable victims to know that I take what happens to them very seriously. My sentences will reflect this, particularly where I believe a defendant has not done what he could have to make things right with his victims," he says.

Similarly, Judge Adams says, "If I see a presentence report that says that the defendant spent a lot of money on luxuries, but has nothing left to pay back on restitution, I get very annoyed. A defendant needs to acknowledge what he has done and do his very best to make the victims whole."

### Letters

Character letters can be important to the judges, unless they are form letters. All agree that, to be credible, the writer should acknowledge that he/she is aware of what the defendant has done. The judges agree that it is the quality that counts, not the quantity. Through character letters, judges are looking for additional insight into who the defendant really is and they would like to see information not otherwise shared by the lawyer.

Judge Schiltz recommends that lawyers carefully screen character letters before submitting them. He said that he appreciates learning about a good deed that is not otherwise known about the defendant. He gave an example of "a defendant who, during a heavy snowstorm, shovels the sidewalk of an elderly disabled neighbor."

Judge Schiltz feels that inarticulate character letters that give examples of a defendant's kindness often come across as more genuine.

Judge Jed Rakoff of the Southern District of New York says, "the number of character letters is not that important, it's the quality that counts. What I am looking for is good deeds that are unknown to others. For example, a defendant who has done something for a neighbor without any thoughts of obtaining anything in return." He also notes that one thing a character letter should not state is that the writer "can't believe that the defendant did what he was convicted of."

A letter from an employer stating that he knows what your client has done but would rehire him upon his release, can be particularly helpful.

### Collateral Civil Consequences

In appropriate circumstances many judges have told me that they are interested. For example, explain what a loss of a professional license means to your client. Point out that it is unlikely that he or she will be able to pursue a lifelong dream.

### Community Service

In cases where probation or a short sentence are in play, have your client secure a community service option. The defendant's community service carries weight with Judge Bennett.

"If I am considering probation, it can tip the scales."

Have the defendant start doing the work, get a letter from the organization confirming that he or she is doing the work, and then urge the judge to make it a condition of probation or supervised release that your client be required to continue to perform a significant number of hours of this service to the sponsoring agency. Judge Bennett appreciates community service, particularly if a defendant has performed it prior to sentencing, and there is a good letter from the agency asking that the defendant be allowed to return to the community performing community service.

**And lastly:**

**Minimize citations in your sentencing memorandum.** For example, don't cite or quote Booker, Kimbrough, Gall, or the § 3553 factors. Judges tell me they do not need to be reminded of boilerplate-type information presented in lengthy memoranda. Like most in the legal profession, judges are very busy and often in the midst of a trial. One suggestion for sparing the judge—and you—the time and effort that goes into preparing and reviewing such a memorandum is to create a sentencing video. In addition to saving time, a sentencing video can portray the defendant's remorse and the struggles of those who would be adversely affected by the incarceration, as well as provide the benefit of a personal connection with well-spoken character witnesses. (See Alan Ellis & Tess Lopez, Use of Video, 26 Crim. Just., no. 2, Summer 2011, at 60.)

**Point out instances of disparity.** Show what sentences other judges in the same district are imposing on similarly situated offenders in similar cases. Use data from the Sentencing Commission from the same and other districts within the state, as well as data for all such cases within the circuit. Finally, include national data and statistics. Judges admit to being more inclined to follow what their fellow judges in their district have done and, to a certain degree, those within the same state and circuit. It is not particularly helpful to talk about a case in a distant geographic area unless it is right smack on point. Make sure any cases you cite are close to yours in offense, facts, prior record, and offender characteristics. Otherwise, you may be comparing apples to oranges—and the judge will know it.

**Address collateral civil consequences..** In appropriate circumstances, explain what a loss of a professional license means to your client. For example, point out that it is unlikely that he or she will be able to pursue a lifelong dream.

## §8:50.4    Recommendations Judge-by Judge

### §8:50.4.1    Judges Jed Rakoff and Mark Bennett

Senior Judge Jed Rakoff of the Southern District of New York emphasizes how important it is to "know your judge." If you are not familiar with him or her, ask other lawyers, particularly the federal defender in the district. A judge's former law clerks are another good source of information. One of the things that you may want to ask them is whether the judge reads sentencing memos and character letters, and how long those letters should be.

"The number of character letters is not that important, it's quality that counts," says Judge Rakoff. "What I am looking for is good deeds that are unknown to others. For example, a defendant who has done something for a neighbor without any thoughts of obtaining anything in return." He also notes that one thing a character letter should not state is that the writer "can't believe that the defendant did what he was convicted of."

Data and statistics from the court, the other federal courts in the state, the circuit and nationwide, mean "zilch" to Judge Rakoff. "However, if you have a case on point that is factually and legally close to your case, wherein another judge in the district has imposed a relatively low sentence, it carries some weight with me — assuming, of course, that I know and respect that judge," he says.

Judges want to hear from your client at sentencing, Judge Rakoff asserts. He suggests that if your client can make a good allocution, "don't save him until the end of the sentencing after hours' worth of legal argument." It is acceptable for a defendant to read his allocution, provided it sounds like the client's own words rather than something scripted by his or her lawyer.

On the other hand, Judge Rakoff is wary of victim impact statements that urge a particular sentence. "What do they know about the federal criminal justice system?"

Nor is he a big fan of the sentencing guidelines. He advises lawyers to avoid wasting a judge's time addressing guideline issues unless they are absolutely crucial to the case. He especially disfavors boilerplate citations to Booker and the 18 U.S.C. §3553(e) factors.

On the other hand, Judge Rakoff welcomes a reasonable, well-principled sentence suggestion. However, he warns that a lawyer can lose credibility by requesting an unreasonably low sentence. "Also, it is a mistake to vouch for your client unless you are sure of what you are saying," he adds. "A lawyer's reputation for veracity is very important. We judges talk among ourselves about lawyers and their credibility."

Asked what a lawyer can do when he/she has a client who has been convicted of a exceptionally heinous offense, Judge Rakoff contends that there generally is something good to be said about everyone. "I don't know a single judge who doesn't recognize that he has a human being in front of him being sentenced," he says.

Senior Judge Mark Bennett of the Northern District of Iowa agrees that lawyers should minimize citations in their sentencing memoranda. "I get annoyed when lawyers cite Booker and the 18 U.S.C. §3553(a) factors, as if I didn't know the law," he says. He also recommends that sentencing memoranda ideally should be between 10 and 20 pages and cautions, "Don't repeat what is in the pre-sentence investigation report."

As for sentencing recommendations, Judge Bennett often will give a lower sentence than recommended by the attorney. He admits that while this might embarrass a lawyer who is supposed to be zealously advocating for a low sentence, he never holds the defendant to the lawyer's recommended sentence, especially if he thinks the client deserves less.

Judge Bennett reminds us that if a ridiculously and unreasonably low sentence is recommended, the lawyer loses credibility. "If a lawyer every once in a while vouches for a client who he knows, that's OK with me," he explains. "If a lawyer does it repeatedly, on the other hand, it is worthless. It is particularly useful if I trust the lawyer's judgment."

Judge Bennett believes that allocution also is very important. In fact, he has published on allocution and is a noted authority on the subject. "I like to have a conversation with the defendant," he says. "That's one reason allocution is very important to me. I read every character letter, but I don't like it when the writer tells me what the sentence should be."

The defendant's community service carries weight with Judge Bennett. "If I am considering probation, it can tip the scales," he notes. Restitution is important, too, although he cautions that a defendant will not be able to buy his way out of prison. Restitution may, however, result in a shorter sentence.

Asked about difficult cases, Judge Bennett says that he finds egregious white collar cases that have innocent victims and a defendant who has acted out of greed. "I am not going to be very sympathetic unless there is a strong mitigation factor like addiction, mental illness or good deeds in the client's past," he says. "I find it very helpful if the defendant has done good deeds," especially if a character letter describes a defendant's good deeds. By way of example, he points to "those cases where a defendant has mowed the lawn of an elderly neighbor or something else that few others would have known about. I appreciate community service, particularly if a defendant has performed it prior to sentencing, and there is a good letter from the agency asking that the defendant be allowed to return to the community performing community service."

He adds that he appreciates "defendants who attempt treatment for substance abuse. Even if they have relapsed, I understand relapse is a part of addiction and I won't hold it against the defendant."

In child pornography cases, risk assessments are important to Judge Bennett, who emphasizes that "whenever you are going to use an expert, I put a lot of stock in an expert who I know and respect."

Judge Bennett describes sexual contact offenses as "troubling." "In child pornography cases, if the defendant did not believe what he was doing was a crime, I will consider that as a mitigation factor," he says.

As for psychological reports, Judge Bennett finds it is sometimes better for a lawyer to present a solid report rather than bring in an expert witness and subject him to cross-examination. Again, the report is more likely to be influential if the judge knows and respects the expert who made it.

Judge Bennett puts a lot of stock in collateral civil consequences, particularly if an individual in a small community is shunned by the neighbors. "This has a big impact on me," he says.

As for data and statistics, Judge Bennett agrees with Judge Rakoff and puts little stock in them, but notes that "it is important, since I sentence so many people, if a defense lawyer reminds me of a particular sentence that I imposed in a particular case that is similar."

Also like Judge Rakoff, if Judge Bennett knows and respects a fellow judge, it is often helpful to point out that, in a very similar case, the other judge imposed a sentence that the lawyer is advocating for his own client. Otherwise, Judge Bennett says that data and statistics have virtually no impact on his sentencing decision.

Asked about sentencing videos, Judge Bennett says that he's not yet seen one, but he has seen "day in the life" videos in civil cases, and finds them often to be impactful. He advises that even pictures could be helpful.

When asked if they are willing to entertain requests for a judicial recommendation to the Bureau of Prisons for designation and placement, Judge Bennett said he would never recommend a facility that he was not familiar with without discussing it with the defendant and counsel.

Judge Rakoff shared that he almost always recommends the facility requested by defense counsel.

As for voluntary surrendering, Judge Bennett says that except for those defendants who are mandatorily detained at plea or verdict, he makes "an individual assessment of the statutory factors." He adds that, "if the government agrees, I always allow self-reporting and sometimes allow it over the objection of the government, especially if the defendant is not a current drug addict." Judge Rakoff says he always agrees to a self-surrender, saying, "I've never had a defendant fail to appear when he is supposed to."

### §8:50.4.2    Judges Patrick J. Schiltz and Robert N. Scola, Jr.

Judge Patrick J. Schiltz and Judge Robert N. Scola, Jr. could not have two more dissimilar backgrounds.

Judge Schiltz was editor of the Harvard Law Review and clerked for the late U.S. Supreme Court Justice Antonin Scalia. He helped found the University of St. Thomas School of Law. Judge Schiltz was a George W. Bush appointee in 2006.

President Obama appointed Judge Scola to the district court in 2011. Prior to that, he was a state court judge in Miami. Before that, he was an active criminal defense practitioner serving for one year as the Miami chapter president of the Florida Association of Criminal Defense Lawyers.

Both judges were asked how they determine whether a defendant feels remorseful about his crime. Both answered with their version of "actions speak louder than words." Judge Scola said, "I'd rather have 50 character witnesses pay $100 each toward the defendant's restitution than to provide 50 character letters. Making reasonable efforts to pay restitution is one indication of sincere remorse." He added, "If your client is leasing a car for $900 a month while on bond and pays no restitution, that's not going to help him."

Judge Scola further commented that if a defendant is ordered to pay a large amount of restitution, he doesn't expect that the defendant is going to be able to pay the full amount. "If the loss in the case $1 million, but the defendant only received $10,000 for his participation, he should pay that amount back or offer to do so with arrangements." Judge Scola gave examples of what he considers real efforts for restitution, saying "If he has equity in a home, he should get a home equity loan. If his family and friends truly love him, they should help him." In other words, do what Alan Ellis U.S. District Judge Robert N. Scola Jr. you can. On the other hand, he added, "I don't want to have a defendant offer to pay restitution only if he stays out of jail. No quid pro quo."

Judge Schiltz shared his thoughts on how a defendant can demonstrate that he is sincere about turning his life around. He recommends your client "[g]o get a job. Work at McDonald's. Go back to school or get your GED. Do something."

When asked his opinion about the best thing a lawyer can do when representing a defendant who has committed a particularly reprehensible crime, Judge Schiltz first shared that the hardest cases are those involving white collar "con men." He then commented, "You need to show me your client is not a con artist at heart; that he is not a psychopath or a sociopath. If there is a mental illness that contributed to the commission of the crime, let me know about it."

Both judges also shared their pet peeves. For Judge Scola, these include (1) lawyers who do not submit presentence memorandums, those who submit them on the eve of sentencing and those who submit poorly prepared ones; (2) lawyers who give him boilerplate Booker and its progeny citations in a presentence memorandum; (3) lawyers who ask for ridiculously low sentences; (4) lawyers who don't prep the defendant or character witnesses prior to the hearing; (5) lawyers who don't interrupt their clients who, during allocution, start digging a hole for themselves; and (6) lawyers who forget that the court is the audience and put on a useless show for their client, family and friends.

So, what makes a positive impression on Judge Scola? "I am very impressed with lawyers who show good legal advocacy in their presentence memorandum, particularly as to disputed guideline issues," he said. He appreciates lawyers who get him everything he needs well in advance of the hearing, suggesting that if you have five or six good character letters, you should "put them in the sentencing memorandum, quote from them, and attach them as Exhibit. A. Put the rest in another exhibit."

Judge Schiltz bemoans the quality of lawyering he frequently sees at sentencing. "Practicing criminal law in federal court is largely federal sentencing," he said, and correctly points out that 97 percent of defendants plead guilty and appear before for sentencing. In 10 years of trying criminal cases, he says the conviction rate before him has been close to 100 percent. With these types of statistics, Judge Schiltz says, "It's surprising how many otherwise competent attorneys 'punt' at the sentencing hearing." Simply stated, "I don't get the help I'd like."

Judge Schiltz says that he picks a range of months before he comes into court with a written explanation in support so the written submission of counsel is very important. "I don't want 40 pages of regurgitated Booker and 3,553 factors but rather a handful of heart felt letters," he says. "Six to eight pages would be ideal, but no more than 20." He strongly added, "Tell me something I don't know about your client."

Judge Schiltz recommends that lawyers carefully screen character letters before submitting them. He said that he appreciates learning about a good deed that is not otherwise known about the defendant. He gave an example of "a defendant who, during a heavy snowstorm, shovels the sidewalk of an elderly disabled neighbor." Judge Schiltz feels that inarticulate character letters that give examples of a defendant's kindness often come across as more genuine.

The bottom line for both judges is that it is essential to humanize your client as much as possible.

Judge Scola says that live witnesses should speak for two minutes at most and share why the defendant is a good husband, brother or son. They should not read what they are saying. "I am looking for the human element," he comments. He feels that character letters and character witnesses are helpful if they can be truly incisive to whom the person is, why they did what they did and why they are unlikely to do it again. Like Judge Schiltz, Judge Scola is "touched by genuineness."

Allocution generally makes no difference in Judge Scola's sentencings. In 5 percent of cases, it might actually hurt a defendant. "On the other hand, I once had a defendant appear in front of me thank me for appointing his CJA lawyer and explained why he felt he was treated fairly by the system. I was impressed by his insight and his appreciation and I gave him a lower sentence than intended."

In part 1 of this article series, Judge Jed Rakoff said that he doesn't know any judge who doesn't appreciate the fact that he has a human being appearing in front of him. Judge Schiltz agrees. "Help me appreciate that the defendant is a human being who will spend years in a cage." Judge Scola echoed the same sentiment.

Judge Schiltz readily welcomes a lawyer's recommendation of a sentence, saying that some attorneys have a real "knack" for making well-reasoned, principled and appropriate recommendations. However, he also warned that he will dismiss recommendations that are unreasonably low. He conceded, however, that "in fact, if I go down in court from my written number, it's not that much." He further comments that "going from 48 to 44-46 months is typical, and I do this only if I learn something in court that I didn't know before."

Interestingly, Judge Scola views his discretion more narrowly than Judge Schiltz, pointing out that he wants to give the lowest possible sentence in accord with the sentencing guidelines, 18 USC §3553 and Eleventh Circuit precedent. "I am very mindful that the Eleventh Circuit requires a valid reason for a variance and also a justifiable reason for the amount of the variance," he says. "I try to impose a sentence that will not be overturned on appeal."

Indeed, Judge Scola has never had a sentence overturned on appeal in his four and a half years on the bench. "The first job of a lawyer is to provide me with law on the disputed legal issues that will be upheld by the Eleventh Circuit," he says.

Both judges welcome evidence of the defendant's community service, but less so when performed while awaiting sentencing. A promise of future community service has no impact on sentencing. Those, however, who have a history of community service before their arrest, and, better yet, before they knew they were under investigation, receive very favorable consideration.

Judge Schiltz doesn't like canned psychological/psychiatric reports by professional "hired gun" experts. Also, if he sees that the report is based on inaccuracies about the offense, he says, "I am going to give it little weight." He says he is less concerned with appeals because, in the Eighth Circuit, it is hard to get reversed, as long as no procedural mistakes are made and the basis for the sentence is adequately explained.

Both judges are very concerned with disparity in sentencing, and want to avoid imposing disparate sentences on defendants who have committed a similar offense with a similar criminal background. Judge Schiltz says that if a lawyer wants to argue that another judge on the bench in the District of Minnesota imposed a particular sentence, it won't impact him unless the cases are "apples to apples" adding, "the lawyer needs to be as specific as possible in showing me this." Judge Scola says that while he is not interested in what judges in California and New York do, he is interested in what judges in the Southern District of Florida have done. Again, like Judge Schiltz, he said that he finds it helpful if a lawyer can identify the particular case and state why it is similar to his or her case and why the particular judge did what he did. Both judges indicated that they would welcome statistics on sentences imposed on similar defendants who have committed similar offenses with similar prior records in their district and their circuit and nationwide.

Both judges offered excellent suggestions. They want to know what a defendant will do once they get out of prison. Having a support system is very important, said Judge Schiltz. "A defendant who has support, in my opinion, is at a lower risk of reoffending. I might give a defendant who has good support a shorter term of supervised release than a defendant who doesn't have much support and may very well reoffend."

Judge Scola suggests that, in a multidefendant case, if co-defendants have been sentenced earlier than your client, attend that sentencing. "See what I have determined to be their guidelines. Learn how I feel about the case. At times your client's name will come up. Listen to what I say about him."

Finally, both judges (and every judge I have interviewed so far) have a problem with child pornography offenders. Judge Schiltz says, "I am post-Booker judge. The guidelines are a benchmark for me. A starting point." However, he added, "In child pornography cases, they are utterly useless." In child pornography cases, both Judge Scola and Judge Schiltz make a big distinction between offenders who have merely looked at child pornography versus those who are trolling the Internet for potential victims, offenders who actively distribute or produce it, or who have had contact or tried to have contact with a child. Both judges say that they treat the former far more leniently than the latter, especially on first offenses.

### §8:50.4.3    Judges Cynthia A. Bashant and Jon D. Levy

Judge Cynthia A. Bashant of the Southern District of California in San Diego and Judge Jon D. Levy of the District of Maine in Portland were both appointed by President Obama in 2014 and confirmed at the same time. They preside literally on opposite sides of the country, but have kept in touch exchanging ideas on judging, including sentencing. Judge Bashant was formerly a state court judge who handled both juvenile and criminal matters, and Judge Levy was formerly a state trial judge and an associate justice on the Supreme Court of Maine. Lawyers consistently describe both as "right down the middle" at sentencing. Like many judges, these two jurists come out on bench with tentative guideline rulings and sentences in mind.

### Before the Proceedings Begin

In Maine, the judges convene a presentence conference in chambers several weeks before the sentencing, which Judge Levy finds extremely helpful. At the meeting, the lawyers are expected to discuss any objections to the presentence report that they intend to raise at the sentencing, any remaining documents or information that should be exchanged prior to the sentencing, the nature of any testimony or other evidence that will be required to resolve objections to the presentence report, and whether there are any questions regarding the Guidelines or the applicable law that deserve briefing. A schedule for the submission of sentencing memos and exhibits is established, as are the time, date and length of the sentencing hearing. This allows the lawyers to schedule the sentencing around the availability of the witnesses, victims, and family members who will attend.

The presentence conference is a critical first step, says Judge Levy, because it provides him insight as to the issues that the lawyers feel are most consequential. This, in turn, influences how he prepares for the sentencing. "Effective defense presentation at this stage can be very important to the ultimate outcome of the case. It is an opportunity for the lawyer to direct my attention to the key sentencing issues. The information I receive at the conference should be solid."

Judge Bashant comes out on the bench and begins by announcing her tentative sentence, including how she intends to rule on disputed guideline issues. Therefore, it is very important that counsel provide her with a sentencing memorandum at least one week in advance of the sentencing hearing. Judge Bashant says, "A lawyer should get me a sentencing memorandum at least one week in advance because that is when I am going to start reading the presentence report, any addendum and the parties' sentencing memoranda. This is when I will first start developing my tentative sentence. If the prosecution already has submitted a sentencing memorandum, a late filing by defense counsel puts the defendant 'behind the eight ball.'"

### Credible Sentencing Recommendations Welcomed

Like all judges I have interviewed so far, Judges Bashant and Levy don't like boilerplate citations to Booker, its progeny or 18 U.S.C. §3553 factors in sentencing memoranda. Judge Bashant also doesn't like cut-and-paste jobs, offering the advice to "tailor your sentencing memorandum to this particular defendant." While she doesn't need to be reminded of pertinent case law, of course, she states, "If there is good authority on a disputed guideline issue, I want to see it."

Judge Levy gives great weight to the lawyers' sentencing recommendations. "It is important that the lawyers be clear on what they are asking for and the rationale for it. This is where focused advocacy is critical because if they want me to adopt their recommendation, they have to link that recommendation to facts that are in the record and sound reasons that support the sentence. There are occasions when lawyers are not clear as to what sentence they would like me to consider imposing and the facts and reasoning that support it."

Judge Bashant also welcomes lawyers' sentence recommendations, if they are well reasoned. "If the recommendation is particularly low, it often causes me to question the lawyer's credibility, not just on the recommendation, but in other arguments he's making." In court, Judge Bashant wants counsel to listen to her concerns and respond to them. She advises, "If I've given a tentative indication about how I am going to rule on a particular guideline issue, and it is in the defendant's favor, don't argue it. On the other hand, if I am going to go with the presentence report or the government's position, then I want to hear it argued."

Lawyers often do their clients a disservice when they simply adopt what is in the presentence report (PSR), according to Judge Bashant. "What I typically see in our district is for the 'Defendant's Statement of the Offense' section of the PSR to read 'Upon the advice of counsel, Defendant refused to answer any questions, but adopted the facts outlined in the factual basis of the plea agreement as his statement of offense.'" Judge Bashant says that while she understands that lawyers likely take this approach because they fear their client may further incriminate themselves, it is her opinion that this is a missed opportunity.

"This is a chance for the defendant to give his version of what he did, why he did it, why he is not going to do it again and why this was aberrant behavior." She thinks lawyers who do not allow their clients to answer the probation officer's questions sometimes do their clients a disservice, adding, however, that she realizes that "it requires that a defense attorney spend time with a client preparing him for the presentence interview beforehand. "Where a lawyer can play a large role is when there are facts that U.S. District Judge Cynthia A. Bashant are missing from the records — facts about the client's background, motivation and future plans. That's where the lawyer's role can become quite important," says Judge Bashant.

When assured the defendant will not reoffend, Judge Bashant is looking for concrete examples. "For example, in an unlawful immigration case, show me that your client has a job waiting for him back in Mexico." Employer letters stating that they know the defendant and would rehire him upon his release from prison carry a lot of weight with Judge Bashant.

The same is true for Judge Levy. Also important to Judge Levy is what the defendant has done since being apprehended. For example, if detained, has the defendant taken advantage of any rehabilitation programming or performed a useful service like teaching other inmates a new job skill at the jail? "If the defendant was on presentence release, I want to know what she or he has done during that period, whether the defendant has made amends or paid restitution; was the defendant working and how did it go; has the defendant received mental health or substance abuse treatment and what do the providers have to say about the defendant's progress; and generally anything that bears on whether the defendant has taken meaningful steps to turn his or her life around."

Judge Levy goes on to emphasize the importance of defense counsel establishing trust with him, as well. "Don't minimize the seriousness of what your client did." In other words, if a lawyer can show that he/she is on the same page with their client as to the seriousness of the offense, the chances of having your other statements accepted by Judge Levy increase. In a difficult case, Judge Levy, like Judge Bashant, feels strongly that the lawyer needs to "humanize" his or her client in explaining why the client did what he did, why he won't do it again, and why he is deserving of a light sentence. If there are any aggravating factors, be sure to address them.

Judge Bashant is particularly interested in knowing why the offense was committed. "Was it done because the defendant was in financial straits? If so, I want to know the defendant's plans for the future so that this doesn't happen again," she says. "I am very interested in why the defendant will be able to make a go of it, particularly if his crime was committed for economic reasons."

**Allocution Is Serious Business**

Like most judges I've interviewed, these two judges both take allocution very seriously. "Allocution matters," says Judge Levy. "I will never hold poor communication skills against a defendant," he emphasizes. What's important is whether he is persuaded that the defendant is sincere and demonstrates insight about the crime and the actual changes the defendant must make in order to live a positive and successful life. He observed, "I am mindful that a highly educated sociopath may deliver an eloquent allocution. If I conclude that a defendant is not sincere, that will work against him."

Judge Bashant doesn't want the defendant to apologize to her. "I want him to apologize to the victim and his or her family, particularly if they are in the courtroom. Just like a parent with a child who has done wrong, I am looking for 'insight' from the defendant," she says. She wants lawyers to know that she will dialogue with their client.

**Do Psych Evaluations and Character Letters Make Any Difference?**

Asked for her views on mental health reports, Judge Bashant responded that they could be helpful only if the evaluator has spent a considerable amount of time with the defendant. "A report where the expert has spent 50 minutes with the defendant and has concluded that he or she is not a risk to reoffend is not particularly helpful," she shared. A lawyer, therefore, should not hesitate to submit a report by a mental health professional who has treated the defendant for a significant period of time rather than one from a professional forensic expert. "I recognize that clinicians who have spent a lot of time with their patient may come across as advocates," says Judge Bashant, but, so, too, forensic experts also often seem to be advocates. She is particularly interested in knowing whether the offender has a diagnosable mental health disorder that may have contributed to the commission of the offense and which is treatable.

Judge Levy finds psych evaluations to be helpful in determining why the defendant did what he did and the likelihood of recidivism. He is familiar with many of the experts who testify in Maine, and he will give serious consideration to any assessment that credibly demonstrates that the expert has exercised independent professional judgment. Like Judge Bashant, Judge Levy welcomes a report from a treating professional, though he has concern that the expert may be acting as an advocate as opposed to an evaluator. "In any event, I want to know the risk of the defendant reoffending." Judge Levy commented. He is of a mixed mind when it comes to the expert testifying in court. On one hand, it makes the expert subject to cross-examination and allows Judge Levy to question the expert. On the other hand, he doesn't want the expert to simply "parrot" what he says in his report.

Character letters are important to Judge Bashant, and she finds them very helpful if they demonstrate that the writer knows what the defendant has done and then explains why this is aberrant behavior unlikely to recur if the defendant is a first offender. She is "interested in the protection of the public."

Both judges welcome community service recommendations as alternatives to incarceration. Judge Bashant is impressed if the community service is related to the offense, for example, a talk to school groups about the problems of drugs. If the defendant has previously or is currently performing community service, Judge Levy finds it helpful to receive a detailed letter from the director of the agency that discusses the defendant's work ethic, attitude, relationships with coworkers and actual contributions to the agency's mission. "I will consider whether the continued service the offender wishes to perform is a needed service to the community and measure that against the need for incarceration. It all goes to just punishment," he says.

Judge Levy is interested to receive comparative sentencing information that describes the sentences imposed by other judges in comparable cases.

Collateral civil consequences are important to Judge Bashant, who said that, with San Diego being so close to the Mexico border, "if a long-term, legal, permanent resident with an American family is going to be deported, I will take this into consideration when deciding the appropriate punishment."

In short, both judges want lawyers to "humanize" their clients. Judge Levy is equally concerned about collateral civil consequences and believes it is incumbent on defense counsel to identify and explain those consequences in a sentencing memorandum or at sentencing.

### Conclusion

Judge Bashant and Judge Levy, like most of the judges I've interviewed, want counsel to address the four "why" questions: (1) Why did the defendant do what he did? (2) Why was the behavior out of character with an otherwise law-abiding life? (3) Why is he unlikely to reoffend? (4) Why should they cut him a break?

Virtually all want to see that the defendant has internalized what he has done so that they can determine whether he has seriously taken responsibility and is truly remorseful. Allocution can play a big part in humanizing the defendant. A lawyer needs to carefully prepare his or her client for this. Your overall purpose needs to be humanizing your client. Tell a compelling story. Tell the judge something new, something she or he doesn't already know. I keep hearing the words "trust" and "credibility" from the judges. Attorneys would be wise to keep this in mind, especially with respect to the information presented, arguments made and sentences recommended.

### §8:50.4.4      Judges John R. Adams, Otis D. Wright II, Justin L. Quackenbush, and Walter H. Rice

Criminal defense lawyers consider Judges John R. Adams and Otis D. Wright II tough sentencers. Judges Justin L. Quackenbush and Walter H. Rice are viewed as being at the opposite end of the spectrum. With their reputations, it was interesting to learn how similar they were on what constitutes good defense sentencing advocacy. Judge Quackenbush sits in the Eastern District of Washington in Spokane and Judge Rice sits in the Southern District of Ohio in Dayton. Both were appointed in 1980. Judge Adams, of the Northern District of Ohio in Cleveland, was appointed in 2003. Judge Wright sits in the Central District of California in Los Angeles and took the federal bench in 2007. All but Judge Quackenbush were former state court judges.

**Allocution**

Judge Mark W. Bennett of the Northern District of Iowa, whom I interviewed in part 1 of this series, has written on the importance of allocution in the article "Heartstrings or Heartburn: A Federal Judge's Musing on Defendants' Right and Rite of Allocution," which was published in March 2011 issue of The Champion. He followed this article with a survey of fellow judges which showed the high value most place on allocution ("A Survey and Analysis of Federal Judge's Views on Allocution in Sentencing," 65 Ala. L. Rev. 735 (2013)).

All of the judges here agree on its importance. Judge Quackenbush, a 37-year jurist, likes to hear a defendant allocute at sentencing, even if he is reading from written notes, unless, of course, the lawyer drafted those notes.

Judge Rice agrees, saying, "I can oft determine a defendant's sincerity during a colloquy at sentencing. I often engage the defendant in conversation so I can learn more about him." He also commented that he does not want to hear a canned speech. "I come out on the bench with a tentative range of sentence in mind, but a good allocution can cause me to impose a lower sentence. I may ask the defendant if he has harmed others and I may ask him what he plans to do about it."

Judge Adams says, "Sentencing is very personal. The more I see a defendant, the more I get to know him." Judge Wright notes, "I want the unvarnished truth. It can really help if I believe that they are sincere. I can tell whether a defendant is being sincere by what he says in court." Judge Adams comments, "A defendant's allocution is generally more important than what a lawyer says at sentencing. I don't want to have the defendant making excuses for his conduct."

Judge Adams doesn't want to see a defendant wallow in self-pity. "He should start his allocution by apologizing to the victims. I also want to see what a defendant has done in an attempt to make the victims whole, particularly in white collar fraud cases. If I see a presentence report that says the defendant has spent a lot of money on luxuries and has nothing left to pay back restitution, I get very annoyed."

Similarly, Judge Wright will hold it against a defendant if he feels that your client has not done what he could have to make things right with his victims and says it is important for the defendant to make restitution prior to sentencing, particularly where there are vulnerable victims. "I will communicate to these victims that the defendant will not hurt you again. I want victims to know that I care about them. It is important to me that a defendant tries to make things right."

One of the key points made by the majority of the judges that I've interviewed is the notion of whether a defendant has "internalized" what he has done, why he did it, what he has learned from it and why he is not going to do it again. Judge Rice will often ask a defendant what he is going to do upon release from prison in order to determine whether the offender is likely to re-offend. "I often engage a defendant in allocution so I can hear more about him."

This is not to say that a lawyer need be a potted plant during the sentencing. Judge Quackenbush suggests it is important for lawyers to present any favorable information to the U.S. probation officer prior to the preparation of the presentence report. "Get it to the probation officer early. It is extremely helpful if provided even prior to the PSR interview itself," he recommends.

Judge Adams stresses how important it is that the defendant be honest with his probation officer. He likes to meet with the probation officer prior to sentencing to get an idea of how honest and forthright the defendant has been.

## The Lawyer's Credibility

All four of these judges stress the importance of the lawyer's credibility. Judge Rice says, "Lawyers need to be candid with me. They should not whitewash their client's crimes. I don't want a lawyer to sugarcoat his client or the offense." For example, if the defendant has a bad record, say so, but explain what you want me to understand about this record and about the likelihood of rehabilitation.

Judge Rice also wants help in fashioning the best sentence. For example, he appreciates it when a lawyer poses a well-reasoned alternative to incarceration.

Judge Wright doesn't want to feel that he's being manipulated. "The best thing a lawyer can do is to start out by making sure that he and I are on the same page." For example, in a particularly reprehensible case, he wants the lawyer to acknowledge that the offense is, indeed, a heinous one if it is. "Once we are both in agreement as to what the client did and how victims have been impacted by it, that lawyer has a lot of credibility going forward. When I see that the lawyer and I are talking about the same defendant and the impact their actions had on the victims, I oftentimes will give the defendant a lower sentence than the attorney even asked for," he shared.

Lawyers who make frivolous arguments turn off Judge Adams. "It is important that a lawyer put together a good sentencing memorandum and make a good presentation in court," he shared. Judge Quackenbush expects a lawyer to cite cases involving important guidelines issues. Mindful that the presentence report always contains the government's version, Judge Rice says, "It's incredibly important for the defense lawyer to object to erroneous statements, even if they don't impact the guidelines because they will follow the defendant throughout his time in the Bureau of Prisons." He also says that he wants a picture of the defendant that is different from what is in the presentence report. "A good lawyer knows how to humanize his client. If the lawyer is going to make claims about a defendant being in poor health or family members suffering, he or she should give me evidence to support that claim," he says.

While three of the judges welcome a lawyer's sentencing recommendation, they all agree that a critical mistake they see lawyers make is to ask for too low of a sentence. Attorney sentencing recommendations are less important to Judge Adams; however, he notes that, "if a lawyer suggests a sentence within the realm of reasonable, I'll take it into consideration." Judge Wright went on to say that while a lawyer should not "take himself out of the conversation by asking for too low a sentence, he should never worry about asking me for a higher sentence than ultimately imposed. After all, a client who gets a relatively low sentence is not going to be unhappy with what his lawyer did."

All judges find that the earlier a lawyer can get his sentencing memoranda filed the better. None of them like boilerplate citations to Booker and the 3553 factors. As Judge Rice said, "If I don't know it by now, the republic is in danger." All of these judges expect the lawyer in a sentencing memorandum to tell them something they don't already know.

Positive family connections are very important to Judge Quackenbush, who says, "A very supportive family plays an important role in my sentencing." Asked whether he would recommend bringing a supportive spouse to the presentence interview, he says that this might be a very good idea.

If a defendant has a substance abuse and/or mental health issue, Judge Quackenbush looks favorably on getting treatment prior to sentencing.

All of the judges are concerned with unwarranted disparity. Judge Quackenbush is interested in nationwide sentencing statistics and recommends that lawyers provide them at sentencing. "Sentencing statistics from the United States Sentencing Commission should be consulted as those statistics show other judges have often departed from 'draconian' guideline ranges; for example, child pornography possession cases."

## Psych Reports and Letters from Family, Friends and Employers

The judges differ about psych reports. They are not especially important to Judge Wright, who feels many of them come from "hired guns." On the other hand, he says that if he appoints the expert or the report comes from the Bureau of Prisons, they may carry substantial weight. "The timing of the exam is important," he says. "The earlier in the process, the better. Not just after the verdict or plea and before sentencing. In fact, if the report was done prior to the defendant being caught having been aware that he was under investigation, it will receive even more credit."

Judge Adams finds it useful when the parties agree that an independent expert should be appointed, commenting that, "it is very important that a defendant make full disclosure to the examiner as to what brought him into court." If a defendant has a substance or a mental health problem, Judge Quackenbush looks favorably on his getting treatment prior to sentencing.

Judge Rice notes that he likes to see a psych evaluation and even orders them in child pornography and child sexual exploitation cases, adding that if the defendant has committed a particularly heinous offense, he wants to know whether or not there is a mental disorder which contributed to its commission and, if so, whether the defendant is amenable to treatment and, if so, what his prognosis of the success of treatment. He also is impressed with a defendant who has, on his own, gotten treatment for a substance abuse or mental health problem.

Judge Adams notes, "A solid psych report followed by live in-court testimony can be very, very helpful." By and large, the judges find it useful to engage the examiner in the court in questioning. Judge Adams looks for consistency from the defendant. "Oftentimes he will tell his pretrial services officers that he has no drug and alcohol problem and then tell the psych examiner that he does."

Character letters can be important to the judges, unless they are form letters. All agree that, to be credible, the writer should acknowledge that he/she is aware of what the defendant has done.

Judge Quackenbush suggests that counsel submit no more than four or five character letters. All the judges agree that it is the quality that counts, not the quantity.

Letters from employers who indicate that they know what the defendant has done but nevertheless are willing to offer his job back when he gets released from prison particularly impresses Judge Wright.

Offenders who perform community service by "using their acumen in keeping a not-for-profit alive when it otherwise would go out of business can have a considerable impact." A defendant who, on his own and prior to sentencing, has demonstrated an intention to pay his debt to society by performing community service impresses Judge Rice. He recalls one notable case where the director of the agency lauded the defendant's service and urged him to allow him to perform community service rather than be incarcerated, saying how important the defendant's help was to keeping the agency afloat.

If the presentence report says that defendant is the sole supporter of his family, the lawyer should give examples of this. For example, Judge Quackenbush recommends that, "if there is an elderly family member who will suffer as a result of his incarceration, I want to know precisely how. The lawyer needs to bring this to life." However, none of the judges is comfortable with the defendant bringing young children to the sentencing.

Judge Adams allows character witnesses to testify at sentencing, and says he will ask character witnesses if they understand what the defendant did.

## Restitution

The judges agree that restitution can demonstrate sincerity. Judge Wright says that, in a case where there are vulnerable victims and the money can't be found, if he believes that a defendant is secreting the money with the hope of spending it when he gets out, "I will do whatever I can to make sure that he doesn't get out to spend the ill-gotten gains." Judge Wright expects a defendant to make restitution, or, in other words, to: "Put his money where his mouth is. I want heartbroken, vulnerable victims to know that I take what happens to them very seriously. My sentences will reflect this, particularly where I believe a defendant has not done what he could have to make things right with his victims," he says.

Similarly, Judge Adams says, "If I see a presentence report that says the defendant spent a lot of money on luxuries, but has nothing left to pay back on restitution, I get very annoyed. A defendant needs to acknowledge what he has done and do his very best to make the victims whole."

It is very important to Judge Adams that a defendant disclose all of his assets. "If I learn that the defendant has been hiding or transferred assets to avoid paying restitution, it will be very harmful to the defendant," he says. Like Judges Adams and Wright, Judge Quackenbush has a problem with defendants who he perceives are hiding assets, particularly where restitution is in order.

### Conclusion

One of the best things a lawyer can do is to make sure he/she and the judge are on the same page at the outset of the sentencing process. The more judges I've interviewed, the more I've come to appreciate how important allocution is. Clients can often sell themselves at the sentencing hearing. It is essential that we prepare them for allocution and the fact that judge may engage them in conversation.

The judges are looking for "internalization." While it is helpful for us to explain why a client did what he did, what he has learned from it and why he's not going to do it again, it's better when it comes from the defendant.

### §8:50.4.5      Judges James S. Gwin, Amy J. St. Eve, and Paul L. Friedman

Among other nontraditional federal sentencing factors, Judge Gwin considers what a state sentence would be in a similar case with a similar defendant with a similar background, noting that 18 U.S.C. §3553(a) says that courts should avoid unwarranted disparity for offenders who engage in "similar conduct." He notes that this reference to "similar conduct as opposed to similar offenses, allows me to look at state sentences. To the extent that cases say that a judge should not consider state cases for similar conduct for a defendant with similar backgrounds, I think they are wrong."

Judge Gwin often views a defendant who has been dealt a seemingly bad hand as often being less blameworthy than an individual born to advantaged circumstances.

On the other hand, Judge Amy J. St. Eve of the U.S. District Court for the Northern District of Illinois in Chicago will automatically not hold the fact that the defendant comes from a privileged background against him. In white collar cases, she is most concerned where there are victims. Judge St. Eve, who has been on the bench for 14 years, was one of the youngest judges ever appointed to the federal bench at age 36. She believes in the importance of mental health reports and wants to see the psych report in advance of sentencing. It may surprise readers to learn that, as with many judges I've interviewed, she also prefers to hear from the expert at sentencing, commenting, "I find it most helpful if the expert is somebody who has treated the defendant for a significant period of time rather than somebody who has just gone over to the jail and interviewed him for two hours." Judge St. Eve likes to question these experts. "The more information I have; the more informed decision I can make," she added.

Judge Paul L. Friedman of the U.S. District Court for the District of Columbia in Washington, D.C., who has been described by lawyers as one of "the smartest and best judges"[1] on that court says, "Explain to me why, after I had to sentence a low-level drug offender to a mandatory minimum of 10 years, I should give probation to your white collar crime client, who has led a previous life of luxury and didn't need to commit his crime, so that he can get back to his country club." Judge Friedman advises attorneys to not routinely ask for probation and he recalls a case where defense counsel said, "Judge, we are not asking for probation in this case. We don't believe that it is appropriate in this case; however, we believe that the guidelines are too high and what the prosecutor is asking for is also too high and would recommend that you impose the following sentence and this is why." In that case, as well as in a fair number of others, he was persuaded to go below the tentative sentence that he came into court with.

Like Judge St. Eve, Judge Friedman welcomes live witnesses at sentencing. "For one thing, I want to engage people in conversation," he says. He also recalls, as an example, a case involving a former law enforcement officer where the lawyer called a host of lawyers, government and law enforcement officials who simply came up to the podium, told him their name, who they were, what they did, how they knew the defendant, and simply that "they were there to support him." Judge Friedman also particularly likes when an employer says that knowing everything he knows about the defendant and what he has done, he will welcome back his employee when he gets released from prison.

### Allocution

All three judges address the importance of allocution. A defendant does himself no good by apologizing to Judge Gwin. Judge Gwin has, however, been moved when the defendant credibly apologizes to his family for what he's put them through and the pain that he has caused them. Defendants who apologize to the victim also impact him. He recalls one case in which the victim, himself, asked that the defendant not be sentenced to jail. He imposed a lower sentence than he had anticipated he viewed the lower sentence as "just punishment" for what the defendant had done.

Judge St. Eve says, "I like allocution. I like to engage the defendant during allocution. Remorse is important. Restitution is also important because actions speak louder than words. Recidivism is an important concern to me. I want to hear from a defendant what he intends to do so that he won't reoffend. Does he have family support? Is there a job waiting for him? What are his plans upon release?"

Judge Friedman is interested in knowing why the defendant did what he did, saying, "I want him to give me an answer." He also comments that if a defendant is on pretrial release, "he should in addition to abiding by all the conditions of release, particularly staying free from drugs while on release if that is the defendant's problem, make efforts to find a job if he doesn't have a job, perform community service, and get treatment, if that's what his mental health professional recommends."

If a defendant tells Judge Friedman that he recognizes that he needs help and explains what he intends to do once released from prison, it can be very impactful for a reduced sentence.

### The Role of the Lawyer

Judge St. Eve says that the best thing a lawyer can do for her is give her a full picture as to who their client is. She says, "I am trying to figure out who this person is. For example, character letters can be very meaningful. It's important for lawyers to review these character letters before they are submitted. I oftentimes listen to live testimony; but often the character letters suffice." Another key thing is to identify a case of hers where she imposed a sentence that was lower than the sentence that she might otherwise impose in your case.

All three judges want quality pre-sentence memoranda and none of them want boilerplate arguments or boilerplate citations to Booker and the 3553(a) factors. However, they do understand that arguments on disputed guideline matters are important. What these judges say is equally if not more important is helping them understand who the client is, why he did what he did, and what can be done to insure that he won't do it again.

In a few cases, particularly egregious ones with challenging clients, Judge Friedman believes that the lawyer should have the client evaluated by a mental health professional to determine whether there is any type of mental disability that contributed to the commission of the offense. He recommends, "If it turns out there is, come up with a treatment plan."

With respect to sentencing memorandum, Judge Gwin says counsel should begin with a two or three paragraph executive summary of the case, saying, "Get to the point. Make it easy to read and understandable."

"Try to tell me something good about your client," says Judge St. Eve. "I am looking for the good in everyone that I sentence. I also expect the defendant to make restitution and to right the wrong that he has done."

Judge Gwin suggests that a lawyer develop a theory of the sentence just like a theory of the defense for trials. Take a theme, such as the defendant's terrible childhood, and support it with proof. He also welcomes data and statistics showing what sentences have been imposed across the country for similar offenses for people who have similar issues and backgrounds. He is interested to learn, if a defendant has been detained, that he has completed any programs that were available to him.

Similarly, Judge Friedman says that it is helpful when a defendant who is intelligent and educated tutors other inmates in prison or helps them with letters, legal research and writing. "Reports and statements by correctional officers are very helpful," he adds.

One of Judge Gwin's pet peeves is a lawyer who doesn't listen to the questions that he poses, commenting, "When arguing to me, they need to be straight with me." Judge Gwin feels that lawyers can do a better job at sentencing.

All three judges welcome sentencing recommendations, but all also stress that if a lawyer makes an unreasonably low one, he or she is going to lose credibility. They also recommend that lawyers help their clients develop a plan for paying restitution, particularly to vulnerable victims who have been harmed.

## Conclusion

The importance of allocution is very clear. It's crucial that you prepare your client for what to say and how to respond to questions put to them by the judge. Similarly, live witnesses at sentencing are often welcome, particularly mental health experts. Many lawyers feel that judges don't want to hear a witness whose report they already have. This is so if the expert is simply going to parrot what is in his or her report. However, if you preface your notice to the court that you are going to be calling the expert so as to make him or her available for questioning by the court and the prosecutor, it will often be well received.

Letters from employers stating that knowing everything they know now about the defendant and his offense, they would nonetheless hire him now or upon his release from prison can also go a long way.

Finally, restitution plans are very helpful. Even if your client is only able to pay $25 a month, starting early in paying restitution and in putting together a plan for continued payment cannot be underestimated. The best thing a lawyer sometimes can say in court is: "Your Honor, I hereby tender a check in the amount of X in full payment of restitution."

### §8:50.4.6          Judges James C. Mahan, Mark L. Wolf, Jerome B. Simandle

What can you do if faced with the government argument that a lesser sentence for your client would depreciate the seriousness of the offense and promote disrespect for the law? As one judge once told me, "Tell me something that your client did when no one was keeping score."

In my recent interviews with Judge James C. Mahan of the U.S. District Court for the District of Nevada, Judge Mark L. Wolf of the U.S. District Court for the District of Massachusetts in Boston and Chief Judge Jerome B. Simandle of the U.S. District Court for the District of New Jersey in Camden, they all agreed: Demonstrate that your client is essentially a good person and rehabilitatable.

Judge Mahan is not particularly interested in this general deterrence argument. "I'm focused on this guy in front of me," he says. "What do we do with him?"

Judge Simandle points out that the lawyer should remember that "I am sentencing the individual."

Judge Wolf cautions that a defendant's good deeds do not include giving money to charities that he would not have been able to assist generally except for the crime he committed.

### Sentencing Memorandum

A lawyer's sentencing memorandum is very important to Judge Simandle. It's a lawyer's first opportunity to make a good impression with him. "Don't waste your time with the first five pages using boilerplate citations," he advises. "Put the important stuff in these first five pages. Don't make it too long. I read every word. Don't submit a sentencing memorandum late or out of time. Don't submit character letters that lack credibility." Judge Simandle says that it's a good idea to quote from the better letters and attach them as Exhibit A, with the rest of the letters as Exhibit B, leaving out the ones that are worthless or counterproductive. While he allows a few live witnesses, he says, "Less is more." He may ask the witness, "Have you spoken to the defendant about his crime?"

Judge Simandle recommends that lawyers develop a theme, a theory of the sentencing: why the defendant did what he did, why he's a good human Alan Ellis Chief Judge Jerome B. Simandle being at heart, why he's rehabilitatable, why he's unlikely to do it again, and why he has earned a break.

Judge Mahan comes to the bench, as do most judges, with an inclination as to what sentence he is going to impose. He has already discussed the case with his "brain trust" — his law clerks, who have reviewed the presentence report and any sentencing memoranda. Thus, it is important that a lawyer present all of his arguments, including a well-crafted sentencing recommendation, in the sentencing memorandum.

Judge Wolf requires a sentencing memorandum to be filed two weeks prior to sentencing and replies one week thereafter. "The best lawyers take advantage of this opportunity to educate me in advance about the case," he declares.

He does not want boilerplate citations, but does welcome legal arguments on disputed guideline issues. Judge Wolf, like so many of the judges I've interviewed, says, "Tell me something I don't already know about your client."

Judge Wolf is interested in character letters that demonstrate the defendant's good deeds and other qualities that are not apparent in the presentence report. He appreciates letters that use common language and are not based on a lawyer's template about what to say. Like Judge Simandle, Judge Wolf finds it helpful if the sentencing memorandum quotes from the best letters, and prefers lawyers to attach those letters as Exhibit A and the remainder as Exhibit B.

All three judges emphasized credibility, reminding lawyers not to sugarcoat their clients and to tell the judges the client's strengths and weaknesses.

Lawyers Can't Do All That Much at the Sentencing Hearing

Asked what a lawyer can do in court if she or he has presented a good sentencing memorandum, Judge Simandle responded, "Hit the high points and reemphasize them. Begin with the guidelines, which are the starting point. Be prepared to respond to the government's argument."

Judge Mahan notes that "a lawyer can't do much at the sentencing hearing to add to what they have already presented." While he wants to hear what steps the defendant has taken to show that he is unlikely to reoffend, this information should also be in the sentencing memorandum.

## Allocution

Although the lawyer can't add much at the hearing, the defendant can. Allocution is important to Judge Mahan who wants to hear what the defendant has done to clean up his act.

Allocution is equally important to Judge Wolf, who says, "I sometimes give a lower sentence based on allocution. I am sentencing the defendant, not the lawyer. I want to understand the person that I am sentencing. From the lawyers, I am particularly interested in information that is not in the presentence report."

Judge Simandle says that he won't hold it against an individual who is inarticulate or so nervous that he can't allocute well. "On the other hand," he cautions, "a sociopath can give a very good speech that is often insincere. I am looking for sincerity."

## Judges Welcome Sentencing Recommendations

All three judges welcome sentencing recommendations if they are well crafted, present a program for rehabilitation and are not unreasonably low. Judge Mahan asks, "What do we do with this guy? Does he need drug and alcohol and/or mental health treatment? Give me a plan. Tailor it to this defendant."

## Unwarranted Disparity

State court sentences can be important to Judge Wolf, who also was once a state court judge. He gives as an example a low-level drug case involving a relatively small amount of drugs and a case involving large amounts but in which the defendant had a relatively minor role. If the case normally could have been prosecuted in state court, an argument as to what the state sentence would be can be useful.

Judge Wolf says he's not often swayed by a sentence imposed by other U.S. district court judges in Massachusetts, because he doesn't have that defendant's presentence report in front of him to know what unique characteristics that individual may possess. Likewise, Judge Mahan doesn't want a lawyer to argue that another judge has sentenced a similar defendant to Y months because "I don't know the facts of that case."

By contrast, Judge Simandle welcomes Sentencing Commission data as to what sentences have generally been imposed in New Jersey, the Third Circuit and nationwide. The sentencing situations of co-defendants in the same case should also be mentioned when known.

## Mental Health and Substance Abuse Professionals

Judge Simandle shared that he thinks highly of mental health professionals who have evaluated the defendant, particularly those professionals who are used by both sides. If such an expert is supportive of the defendant, it can carry considerable weight with him. "I respect psychology and criminology," he says. His opinion is that an expert who has been used by the government and who has credibility is often better than one who solely aids the defense.

**Other Considerations**

Judge Mahan takes a broader view of aberrant behavior than what the guidelines might define. If a defendant has committed a one-time offense in a marked departure from an otherwise law-abiding life, Judge Mahan wants to know about it. "Show me a compelling reason why the defendant did what he did," he says. He is interested in a defendant who has a low likelihood of recidivism.

What can a lawyer do when he represents the "challenging defendant" — a client who has committed a heinous offense and who has a serious prior record? Judge Wolf finds it advantageous in such a case if the defendant promptly admits the offense and makes restitution to the victims. He says that ordinarily he does not find family needs to be persuasive, because such adverse impacts are common when someone commits a crime. An exception would be considered in unusual circumstance, such as the defendant is a sole provider and caretaker for a special needs child.

Judge Simandle gives civil collateral consequences importance unless they are related to the commission of the offense. For example, a lawyer who embezzles funds from his client trust account and is going to lose his license as a result, doesn't carry much weight with him. On the other hand, a lawyer who has committed a crime unrelated to the practice of law and will lose his license may receive some consideration.

Such collateral civil consequences do not carry much weight with Judge Wolf, who maintains that "oftentimes these are self-inflicted wounds, which generally impact privileged defendants who had a choice in doing what they did." Judge Wolf emphasizes that he is concerned with "rich man's justice versus poor man's justice" when he sentences highly disadvantaged individuals as opposed to those who come from a privileged background.

Nor is restitution of great importance to Judge Wolf, particularly if a wealthy family is paying it. "It doesn't tell me anything about the defendant," he says. However, serious mental health issues can be important to Judge Wolf. Despite the the Bureau of Prisons' protestations to the contrary, he is concerned that they cannot always adequately care for a defendant who has a unique serious medical problem. "This is something that I wrestle with," he says candidly.

A defendant who has been detained and who helps other inmates is someone who makes a good impression on Judge Simandle, particularly if the activities are documented by certificates or comments from jail staff. "Defendants who make the best of a bad situation are important to me," he avows, adding that he takes very seriously what a defendant has done while on pretrial release if he or she is not detained. For instance, if a defendant has made serious efforts at rehabilitation, such as dealing with a mental health or substance abuse problem, this is important. "If Pretrial Services has required a defendant to take certain steps towards rehabilitation, I want to know if he has followed through on this. I believe in redemption and reward extraordinary efforts at rehabilitation."

**Conclusion**

The key message that I hear over and over from judges is, "Don't sugarcoat your client. Tell me his strengths and the weaknesses. Tell me his story. Humanize your client."

Also, virtually every judge I've interviewed welcomes well-crafted sentencing recommendations provided sound reasons for them are given. For example, recommending a carefully planned treatment program for a defendant who suffers from a mental disorder or substance abuse can help the judge to structure a sentence that includes supervised release with specific proposed programming for rehabilitation. Judges care about what a defendant has done to clean up his act. An effective lawyer recognizes a judge's preferences and acts in concert with them.

## §8:60    PRISON AND SENTENCING PRACTICE TIPS

### Presentence Reports – Citizenship

Your client's presentence report (PSR) is critical when it comes to Bureau of Prisons (BOP) placement and programming. Therefore, the PSR must be accurate. For instance, be candid about your client's drug or alcohol history, don't oversell medical and health issues, and verify the defendant's education level. Also try to get judicial recommendations concerning placement and programming, but be specific. A recommendation supported by a well-crafted rationale can influence redesignation. Because many defendants face both federal and state charges and sentences, and because confinement in federal prison is generally more desirable than state imprisonment, work to get your client transferred to primary federal custody. If your client is a naturalized U.S. citizen, make sure that the PSR indicates that this is verified. To accomplish this, provide the U.S. Probation Officer with your client's naturalization certificate. And, while non-US citizens are generally ineligible for minimum-security placement (federal prison camp), there are exceptions if deportation is found to be unwarranted and necessary documentation is provided to the BOP.

### Presentence Reports – Criminal History Score

It is important for counsel to make sure that the PSR's Criminal History Score (CHS) is accurate. The addition of one criminal history point may not change a defendant's CHS, but can negatively impact prison designation. Since the BOP uses criminal history points to calculate an individual's security level, CHS can affect the type of facility to which the offender may be assigned, even if the judge sentences below the guideline range.

### Presentence Reports – Errors

If the sentencing judge is reluctant to direct the probation officer to make corrections to the final PSR, you can accomplish the same thing (sometimes even better) by asking him or her to issue a Statement of Reasons with the findings. This will be transmitted to the BOP along with the Judgment and the PSR. The Bureau rarely sees Statements of Reasons and when they do, they pay close attention to them. The Statement of Reasons trumps the PSR in the eyes of the BOP. For example, if the PSR states that your client has "an occasional glass of wine with dinner," it will not make him eligible for the RDAP program. A

Statement of Reasons indicating that he was drinking heavily within 12 months prior to his arrest will make him eligible, all other things being equal.

## RDAP

The following categories of inmates are not eligible for the RDAP Program: (1) Immigration and Customs Enforcement detainees; (2) Pretrial inmates; (3) Contractual boarders (for example, State or military inmates) and; (4) Inmates with detainers that preclude halfway house placement.

- In terms of assessing a prisoner's substance abuse history, the BOP places primary reliance on a prisoner's self-reporting to the PSR writer. Whatever is written in the PSR is presumptively valid, and any claim of a disorder that the PSR does not plainly substantiate is treated as suspect.
- The BOP has implemented a sliding scale for the amount of a sentence reduction: those serving 30 months or less are ineligible for more than a six-month reduction; those serving 31-36 months are ineligible for more than a nine-month reduction; and those serving 37 months or longer are eligible for the full 12 months.
- A judicial recommendation by the sentencing judge to the BOP that defendant be placed in or considered for the BOP 500-hours Comprehensive Drug and Alcohol Treatment program (RDAP) is worthless insofar as actually getting the inmate into the program. The only thing it does is to help get him or her designated to a facility that has the RDAP program.

## BOP Judicial Recommendations

When I would like a judge to recommend a particular facility, I draft the language that I would like to be used in the Judgment. I file a Motion for Judicial Recommendation containing the requested language prior to sentencing. I don't include it in my sentencing memorandum, as it may get overlooked. Of course, the first thing I do is run it by the prosecutor, so I can caption the motion as "unopposed." If the court agrees to make the requested recommendation, make sure the Judgment accurately contains the language. For example, if you've asked the court to recommend the Federal Prison Camp (FPC) at Bastrop, Texas and the court recommends FCI Bastrop in the Judgment, this may result in the BOP rejecting the recommendation because the defendant may not qualify for FCI Bastrop where he might qualify for FPC Bastrop.

## Voluntary Surrender

If your client has been permitted to self-surrender and has not received within a reasonable time a notice of where to report, contact Pre-Trial Services and/or the U.S. Marshal in the district to find out where the client is to report.

## Sex Offenders

Sex offenders are assigned a "Sex Offender" Public Safety Factor by the BOP. This means that they rarely, if ever, will be allowed to serve their sentences in a minimum-security federal prison camp.

## Pending Charges

In scoring for designation and placement, the BOP counts detainers. The type of detainer can increase an inmate's security level. The BOP treats unresolved charges as a detainer, even when none has been lodged. This results in additional security points and possibly placement at a more secure institution, particularly for individuals who otherwise qualify for minimum-security placement. Accordingly, where a client is sentenced and has a case that may resolve soon thereafter with a sentence to run concurrent with and to be absorbed within the instant sentence or no additional term of imprisonment, counsel should ask the court to (1) hold the judgment in abeyance until after the pending case's disposition and (2) direct U.S. Probation to amend the PSR to reflect the resolution before it sends the report to the BOP. If the Court refuses such a request, counsel should obtain a certified copy of the disposition (if State), and forward it to the U.S. Marshal and Designation and Sentence Computation Center (DSCC) of the BOP before the client's designation package is processed. If Federal, there is no need to have it certified, as DSCC can confirm on PACER, if the case information and document number are included.

## Do These Four Things to Help Ensure Your Client Serves Time in the Best Facility

Once a defense attorney understands how the system works, there are four things he or she can do to ensure that a client serves time in the best possible facility.

1.  Ensure the accuracy of the information on which the BOP will rely to make its designation decision.
2.  Score the client and search for Public Safety Factors (PSFs) to determine the appropriate security level. PSFs such as "sex offender," "deportable alien," or "greatest severity," for instance, can preclude camp placement for otherwise-qualified defendants.
3.  Consult with the client to determine which facility at the appropriately calculated security level the client prefers and then ask the sentencing judge to recommend that facility to the BOP, as well as to provide reasons in support of that recommendation.
4.  If the defendant is not already in custody, counsel should always request voluntary self-surrender.

## Interplay Between Federal and State Sentences

Many clients face both federal and state charges and/or sentences. This is a very complex area fraught with landmines. Issues concerning time credits in such situations are typically highly fact-dependent. Because federal sentences are usually longer and because confinement within the BOP is often seen as more desirable than state imprisonment, the presumptive preference for most clients is that the federal case control. In such instances, counsel should confirm what jurisdiction exercises primary custody over the client and, if it is the state, work to effect the client's transfer to primary federal custody (*e.g.*, bonding out on the state case; persuading state prosecutors to drop their case). Guideline Section

5G1.3 dictates when and how courts are to adjust sentences to account for undischarged terms of imprisonment, though, as with the entire Manual, provisions are merely advisory, meaning courts are free to deviate from the Commission's approach to these complicated issues. Furthermore, *Sester v. United States,* 132 S.Ct. 1463 (2012), which recognizes a federal court's ability to order a federal sentence run concurrently with a not-yet imposed state sentence (a scenario that would present where the state has primary custody and the state case does not resolve before the federal case), expands the opportunity for a federal sentence to capture time served in state custody. *See* 18 U.S.C. §§ 3584, 3585. *Sester* resolved a split in the circuits concerning the authority of a federal judge to impose a sentence consecutive to or concurrently with a state sentence yet to be imposed. The court held that a federal sentencing court has inherent authority to order a federal sentence to be served either concurrently or consecutive to a state sentence yet to be imposed. A federal sentence, however, may not be ordered to run concurrently with a state sentence that has already been served. *United States v. Kerlin,* 701 F.3d 177 (5th Cir. 2012). For an excellent discussion of the interplay between federal and state sentences, see, Henry Sadowski's "Federal Sentence Computation Applied to the Interaction of Federal and State Sentences," *The Champion* (April 2014).

### Home Confinement

A judge cannot sentence a defendant to home confinement nor can he sentence a defendant to time in a halfway house. The best he can do is to place the defendant on probation or time served followed by supervised release with a *special condition* that he or she serve x months of home confinement and/or reside in a halfway house for x months. You may want to point out to the court that a sentence of probation with time served with supervised release conditioned upon a defendant serving for example, a year and a day in a halfway house and/or home confinement, will result in the defendant actually serving that full time whereas if a similar sentence of imprisonment is imposed, defendant will receive good conduct time if the sentence is a year and a day or longer. You may also want to emphasize you are only seeking a change in the conditions of confinement rather than length of confinement.

### Variances*

Below-guideline variance sentences are on the rise while sentences within the guidelines continue to decrease. According to the statistics compiled by the U.S. Sentencing Commission since *Booker,* non-government-sponsored (e.g., non-§5K1.1 departures) below guideline sentences have increased from 12% of all sentences imposed in 2006 to 21.3% in 2015. Conversely, within guideline sentences have decreased from 61.7% of all sentences imposed in 2006 to 47.3% in 2015. The increase in below guideline sentences is even more dramatic when looking at particular offense categories. For example, non-government-sponsored below-guideline sentences for child pornography offenses—perhaps the most controversial of all types of guideline sentences—have more than doubled from only 20.8% of all such sentences imposed in 2006 to 43.9% in 2015. The chart below shows the trends for non-government-sponsored below-guideline sentences in the top five offense categories as well as the trend for sentences overall.

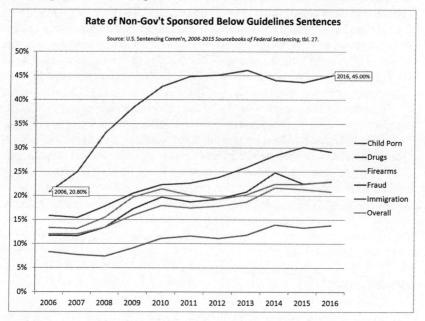

* Mark H. Allenbaugh, Of Counsel to the Law Offices of Alan Ellis, is a former staff attorney with the U.S. Sentencing Commission. In private practice since 2000, he is one of only a handful of attorneys nationwide with an expertise in assessing the U.S. Sentencing Commission's complex data files, which contain data on every individual sentenced under the Guidelines since 2002. He also serves as a principal for SentencingStats.com, which provides robust data and statistical analyses and charts to attorneys and their clients that can assist in mitigation.

## ACKNOWLEDGMENTS

**James H. Feldman, Jr.**, is a practicing attorney in the Philadelphia, Pennsylvania area specializing in the post-conviction representation of federal criminal defendants. In addition to having his own practice, he is Of Counsel to the Law Offices of Alan Ellis. The information contained in the article has been subsequently edited by Mark H. Allenbaugh.

**Mark H. Allenbaugh** is a former staff attorney to the U.S. Sentencing Commission, and is currently an executive with Sentencing Stats, LLC (www.sentencingstats.com), a premier data analytical firm providing federal sentencing data and analyses to attorneys and their clients. He is a nationally recognized expert on federal sentencing law, policy, and practice.

## ARTICLE REPRINTS

§§8:10-8:20 are adapted from a two-part article series entitled "Federal Sentencing Under the Advisory Guidelines: A Primer for the Occasional Federal Practitioner—Parts 1 and 2," *The Champion*, July 2008, November-December 2008, co-authored by Alan Ellis and James H. Feldman, Jr.

§8:30.1 is reprinted from an article entitled "At a 'Loss' for Justice: Federal Sentencing for Economic Offenses," *Criminal Justice* magazine, Volume 25, Number 4, Winter 2011, by Alan Ellis, John R. Steer, and Mark H. Allenbaugh.

§8:30.4 is reprinted from an article entitled "Trends and Practice Tips for Representing Child Pornography Offenders," *Criminal Justice* magazine, Volume 27, No. 3, Fall 2012, by Tess Lopez, Mark H. Allenbaugh and Alan Ellis.

§8:30.5 is adapted from an article entitled "Child Pornography Guidelines are Ripe for Challenge," *Criminal Justice* magazine, Volume 24, Number 2, Summer 2009, by Alan Ellis and Karen L. Landau.

§8:30.6 is reprinted from an article entitled "Inside Baseball: Interview With Former Federal Probabtion Officer," *Criminal Justice* magazine, Volume 24, Number 2, Summer 2009, by Alan Ellis and Tess Lopez.

The Views from the Bench articles series was originally published by Law360, White Collar Expert Analysis. It is reprinted with permission.

(This page intentionally left blank.)

# CHAPTER 9

# DIRECT APPEALS

(This page intentionally left blank.)

## §9:10 INTRODUCTION

A direct appeal is a creature of statute. *See* 18 U.S.C. §§3732, 3742. The appeal is the first way in which a federal criminal defendant who has been convicted of a crime, either after a guilty plea or a trial, may challenge a conviction or sentence. A defendant's conviction is not final until it has been affirmed on direct appeal. An appeal is a review by a court of appeals of the trial court proceedings to see that the proceedings were carried out according to law. The review by the court is based entirely upon written records of the trial court proceedings (including the reporter's transcripts, which are the verbatim transcript of oral proceedings). The appellate court does not hold a new trial or accept new evidence. The attorneys present most of their arguments in writing, and the defendant, who is known as the "appellant," does not appear before the court. The attorneys appear briefly and orally argue the case in many appeals, but not all.

Every defendant convicted after a trial or guilty plea is entitled to a direct appeal. If a defendant is indigent, he is entitled to appeal without the payment of a filing fee (in forma pauperis), to a free copy of the reporter's transcript (the verbatim account of in-court proceedings), and is entitled to the appointment of counsel to represent him on appeal. *See* 18 U.S.C. §3006A, 28 U.S.C. §753(g).

## §9:20 ISSUES THAT CAN BE RAISED IN AN APPEAL

The appellate court does not decide whether a defendant is guilty or innocent. Rather, the question before the court of appeals is whether there are one or more legal errors that affected the verdict. If these legal mistakes are important enough, then the case is sent back to the trial court, usually for a retrial. On fewer occasions, where the law prohibits further prosecution, a case will be reversed with directions to dismiss it. If the legal mistakes only concerned a sentence, then the defendant may be entitled to resentencing.

Many issues may be raised on direct appeal. Examples of issues raised in criminal appeals are arguments that the defendant should not have been convicted because the evidence does not support the verdict, or because evidence was improperly admitted or excluded. A judge's pretrial and trial rulings also can be raised on appeal. Other issues for appeal include problems with jury voir dire, such as when a prosecutor exercises peremptory challenges based on race, or when the district court improperly refuses to excuse a biased juror. Issues regarding the correctness of a defendant's sentence also may be raised on direct appeal.

Because the Court of Appeal does not consider evidence not presented to the district court, claims that require outside record support cannot be presented on direct appeal. *United States v. Quintero-Barraza,* 78 F.3d 1344, 1347 (9th Cir. 1995), *cert. denied,* 519 U.S. 848 (1996). The best example of such a claim is ineffective assistance of counsel which in most cases cannot be presented on direct appeal. *See United States v. Hanoum,* 33 F.3d 1128, 1131 (9th Cir. 1994). However, other claims, such as those involving the discovery of new evidence, prosecutorial misconduct involving the withholding of exculpatory evidence, or juror misconduct, also may need to be presented outside of a direct appeal, when the facts supporting those claims are not contained within the trial and pretrial record or require additional investigation and discovery.

Unfortunately, even if a defendant can establish that the district court committed legal error, he or she may not have his conviction reversed unless the error was prejudicial. If the error is harmless, *i.e.* one that does not affect the outcome of the case, the error will not result in reversal of the conviction or the sentence. Constitutional errors usually result in reversal unless the government can prove beyond a reasonable doubt that the error was harmless. Nonconstitutional errors only result in reversal if it is reasonably probable that the error affected the verdict. In short, "no harm, no foul."

### §9:20.1    Sentencing Appeal vs. Appeal
### From the Underlying Conviction

Federal sentencing appeals have changed dramatically during the past few years. Prior to 2005, the Sentencing Guidelines were mandatory in Federal criminal cases, and sentencing appeals in the great majority of cases hinged on whether the district court properly applied the guidelines. Since the Supreme Court decided *United States v. Booker*, 543 U.S. 220 (2005), however, the guidelines have been "advisory" rather than mandatory. The guidelines still carry great weight, and they are the starting point for any Federal sentence, but the district court need not impose a sentence within the guideline range.

Post-*Booker* sentencing appeals now focus on the "reasonableness" of the sentence. There are two types of reasonableness that can be appealed: procedural reasonableness and substantive reasonableness. A sentence is procedurally reasonable if the district judge: (a) correctly calculates the guidelines; (b) does not violate the defendant's due process rights, such as the right to speak at sentencing and/or the right to present evidence regarding disputed issues; (c) does not sentence the defendant for some impermissible reason such as his race or nationality; (d) takes into account all the relevant sentencing factors, including the arguments made by the parties and the factors set forth in 18 U.S.C. §3553(a); and (e) sufficiently explains, on the record, his reasons for imposing sentence. If the district judge fails to do these things, then a procedural reasonableness issue may exist on appeal. Notably, although the guidelines are no longer mandatory, it is still necessary that the judge correctly calculate them because they are the starting point of the sentence; thus, guideline errors may still lead to reversal of a sentence on appeal.

Substantive reasonableness contrasts with procedural reasonableness in that its focus is not on the procedures used in reaching the sentence but on whether "the punishment fits the crime." A sentence is substantively reasonable if it is sufficient *but not greater than necessary* to accomplish the goals of sentencing listed in §3553(a). The "not greater than necessary" language is known as the "parsimony clause," and binds a district judge to impose the lowest sentence that is sufficient to meet those goals.

A defendant, or the Government, may contend that a sentence above, within or even below the guideline range is substantively unreasonable. This is a departure from pre-*Booker* practice, in which a defendant could not appeal a district court's refusal to impose a below-guideline sentence. However, in many (although not all) circuit courts, a sentence within the guideline range enjoys a presumption of reasonableness, placing the burden on the appealing party to show why it was not reasonable under the facts of the case. Moreover, the Supreme Court has issued a series of decisions highlighting the broad discretion that district courts have to either vary from or comply with the guidelines so long as their reasons for doing so are sufficiently explained. Thus, reversals for substantive reasonableness are rare, although in exceptional cases, appellate courts have indeed vacated sentences for this reason.

### §9:20.2    Obstacle: Waiver of Particular Issues

Appellate courts must address the question of whether an argument presented on appeal was properly raised in the district court. The defendant's attorney must give the district court the opportunity to rule on the issue first, usually by making a timely objection. Frequently, if a timely objection was not made, the appeals court will conclude that the issue has been waived. If an issue was waived in the lower court, an appeals court will grant relief on the issue only if it finds "plain error." Plain error is defined as an error which is "clear" or "obvious," and that affects the defendant's substantial rights. *Olano v. United States,* 507 U.S. 725 (1993). An error affecting a defendant's substantial rights is one that affects the outcome of the proceedings. The effect of the plain error rule is that even if a defendant raises a valid legal issue on appeal, the court will rarely grant relief if the issue was not first raised in the district court in compliance with the applicable rules.

### §9:20.3    Obstacle: Standard of Review

Appellate courts give varying degrees of deference to the decision of the district court, depending on the type of legal argument presented. If the issue is purely legal, for example, whether the District Court correctly instructed the jury, or presents a mixed question of law and fact, such as whether a police officer had reasonable suspicion to stop an individual, the appellate court will review the argument independently. *See United States v. Jimenez-Medina,* 173 F.3d 752, 754 (9th Cir. 1999). In other words, the Court of Appeals will not defer to the district court's ruling. *See Lake Mohave Boat Owners Ass'n v. National Park Serv.,* 138 F.3d 759, 762 (9th Cir. 1998).

If the legal argument challenges a finding of fact made by the district court, such as whether the defendant held a managerial role in the offense or whether a police officer testified truthfully, the Court of Appeals will review the finding of fact for clear error. Clear error means a definite and firm conviction that a mistake has been committed. *United States v. Murdoch,* 98 F.3d 472, 475 (9th Cir. 1996). This is a significantly deferential standard. *Sawyer v. Whitley,* 505 U.S. 333, 346 n.14 (1992).

Finally, some legal arguments are reviewed for abuse of discretion. An abuse of discretion is found only when a lower court's ruling is not within the range of decisions a reasonable judge could have made under the circumstances. *Cooter & Gell v. Hartmarx Corp.*, 496 U.S. 384, 400 (1990). An example of a ruling reviewed for abuse of discretion is the trial court's denial of a continuance.

### §9:20.4    Direct Appeal vs. §2255 Motion

One of the most significant differences between a direct appeal and a motion to vacate conviction and/or sentence (28 U.S.C. 2255, a so-called "2255" motion) is that direct appeals are decided based on the district court record as it exists as of the time the notice of appeal is filed. Section 2255 motions offer defendants the opportunity to present the court with new evidence. However, unlike in a direct appeal, not all issues may be raised in a §2255 motion. Section 2255 motions may only be used to raise jurisdictional, constitutional, or other funda-mental errors. Because a §2255 motion cannot be used for all legal challenges, even if a defendant has a claim that requires extra-record support, it is generally not a good idea to forego a direct appeal and proceed directly to a §2255 motion. For more information, see Chapter 10, "Habeus Corpus: §2255 Motions."

## §9:30    HOW AND WHERE TO FILE

An appeal is started by the filing of a notice of appeal with the clerk of the court in which the case was tried within ten days after the district court enters the judgment of conviction, *or* within ten days after the government files a notice of appeal. Fed. R. App. P. 4(b)(1)(A). A notice of appeal may be filed immediately after sentencing, even if the judgment has not yet issued. Fed. R. App. P. 4(b)(2), 4(b)(3)(B).

The ten-day time limit is mandatory and jurisdictional. *Browder v. Director,* 434 U.S. 257 (1978). However, within the thirty days after the ten-day period has expired, a defendant may move for leave to file a late notice of appeal based on excusable neglect. Fed. R. App. P. 4(b)(4). Such a motion is filed with the district court. The denial of a motion for leave to file a late appeal is itself a final appealable order.

After filing the notice of appeal, the record must be prepared. The record on appeal consists of the reporter's transcripts (the word-for-word record of all proceedings before, during, and after trial), and the clerk's records (composed of written pleadings such as motions, court orders and jury instructions).

The Federal Rules of Appellate Procedure apply to all appeals. Rule 4(b) addresses the procedure for filing a notice of appeal. Rule 3 addresses what information must be contained in the notice of appeal. The appendix to the rules contains a sample form for the notice of appeal.

### §9:30.1    Schedule for Appeals

A briefing schedule for the appeal is set shortly after the notice of appeal is filed. This includes a date by which the appellant must order the reporter's transcripts, and a due date for the opening brief. Frequently, the reporter's transcripts are not prepared on time, and briefing schedules are continued because of court reporter delays. In addition, sometimes attorneys find it necessary to obtain an extension of time.

Most appeals take 12 to 18 months from the filing of the notice of appeal to the issuance of a decision. However, in certain complicated cases, appeals have been known to take several years to resolve.

### §9:30.2    The Appellant's Brief

The appellant's brief is a written argument stating the reasons why the trial court's decision should be reversed. Again, the brief is limited to the record and cannot contain arguments which are based on statements, documents, or events which are not included in the record or the sentencing. The brief contains the defendant's reasons why the conviction should be reversed, or the sentence lower, together with the factual and legal authorities in support. The law requires that an appellate court view the facts in the light most favorable toward the party which prevailed. Thus, except in limited circumstances, the evidence will be viewed most favorably to the prosecution.

Following the filing of the opening brief, the prosecution prepares its answering brief. The Assistant United States Attorney assigned to the case has 30 days to prepare and file his brief. In many cases he will ask for and be given extra time to file his brief. The prosecution's brief also must be based solely on the record, but its arguments support the trial court's actions.

### §9:30.3    Oral Argument

Once all the briefs in the case are filed, the appellate court may set a date for oral argument. On that date, the Assistant United States Attorney and defense counsel appear before the judges of the court of appeals and argue the case. The defendant will not be brought to court for the oral argument. The court does not hear from any witnesses nor any new evidence. Not all cases are set for oral argument. Some are decided by the court of appeals only on the written briefs. These are usually cases in which the case presents simple issues which involve clearly established law.

### §9:30.4    Judges' Ultimate Decision

After the judges of the Court of Appeals have read the briefs and heard oral argument (if there was oral argument), they decide whether the case should be affirmed, reversed, or the judgment modified in some way. Once their decision is reached, a judge is assigned the case to write an opinion stating the court's decision and the reasons for it. An opinion may be expected anywhere from 30 days to six months after oral argument. Usually, however, a decision is issued between 30 days and three months.

### §9:30.5     Giving Up the Right to Appeal

While every criminal defendant has a right to an appeal, the right to appeal may be waived. Many government attorneys insist upon a waiver of the right to appeal pursuant to a plea agreement under which the defendant pleads guilty in exchange for some promises or concessions from the government. Waivers of the right to appeal are enforceable if they are voluntary and knowing. The Federal Rules of Criminal Procedure require a court to specifically advise the defendant that he is waiving his right to appeal at the time he pleads guilty. *See* Fed. R. Crim. P. 11(c)(6).

A waiver of the right to appeal does not waive everything. Generally, if the government breaches a plea agreement, the defendant may still appeal. *See United States v. Bowe,* 257 F.3d 336 (4th Cir. 2001). Additionally, many courts have held that a waiver of the right to appeal contained in a plea agreement does not waive claims of ineffective assistance of counsel. *E.g., United States v. Henderson,* 72 F.3d 463, 465 (5th Cir. 1995). Sometimes waivers of the right to appeal permit appeals in limited circumstances, such as when the district court departs upward from the sentencing guidelines. In order to determine whether a waiver of the right to appeal is enforceable, your attorney must carefully examine the plea agreement and the circumstances surrounding the guilty plea and the sentencing.

### §9:30.6     Prevailing on Appeal

When a defendant prevails on appeal, it does not usually mean that a judgment of "not guilty" will replace the guilty verdict and the person will be set free, although this is possible, and does occasionally happen. More often, the defendant obtains more modest, although significant relief, such as a new trial or resentencing.

Even if the defendant "wins" on appeal, the government can and may file a petition for rehearing with the three-judge panel of the court of appeals that decided the case or, alternatively, with the entire Court of Appeals *en banc. See* Fed. R. App. P. 35, 40. A petition for rehearing must be filed within 14 days after entry of judgment, but an extension of time may be requested. Fed. R. App. P. 40(a)(1). Generally, a petition for panel re-hearing seeks to persuade the panel that its decision was wrong, because the decision overlooked a significant point of law or fact. Fed. R. App. P. 40(a)(2). Rehearing *en banc* is reserved for significant legal issues, involving situations where *en banc* consideration is "necessary to secure or maintain the uniformity of the court's decisions," or where the proceeding involves a "question of exceptional importance." Fed. R. App. P. 35(a)(1) & (2). If the petition for rehearing or rehearing *en banc* is denied, the government may file a petition for review (Petition for Certiorari) in the Supreme Court. S.Ct. R. 10, 12, 13.

### §9:30.7     Losing to Appeal

If the appellant loses the appeal or does not prevail on one or more issues, he may file a petition for rehearing with the three-judge panel of the Court of

Appeals that decided the case or, with the entire Court *en banc. See supra,* at 7; Fed. R. App. P. 35, 40. If this petition is denied, the appellant may file a petition for review (Petition for Certiorari) in the Supreme Court; however, the Supreme Court rarely grants such a petition. S.Ct. R. 10.

Unfortunately, the chances of obtaining relief in a criminal appeal are low. Appellants in criminal cases received some measure of success in only 5.6% of cases decided on the merits by all 12 federal Circuit Court of Appeals for the 12-month period ending September 30, 2011. The Seventh Circuit had the highest rate of reversal (12.3%) with the Tenth Circuit having the lowest rate of reversal (3.0%).

When looking at appeals involving sentencing issues only, the chances for obtaining relief improve significantly. In fiscal year 2011, 12.6% of defendant sentencing appeals decided on the merits resulted in a reversal or remand. Excluding the Circuit Court of Appeals for the District of Columbia, which only had 34 sentencing appeals, the Second Circuit had the highest rate of reversal or remand (27.0%) with the Eleventh Circuit having the lowest rate of reversal or remand (7.7%).

These statistics were compiled by the Administrative Office of the United States Courts and the United States Sentencing Commission.

### §9:30.8    Legal Assistance

A defendant is entitled to legal assistance on appeal. If he cannot afford to retain counsel, he is entitled to have counsel appointed to represent him. 18 U.S.C. §3006A. Usually, indigent defendants are either represented by an Assistant Federal Public Defender, or by an attorney from the Criminal Justice Act panel. Because the chances of obtaining success on appeal are relatively small, a criminal defendant can often significantly improve his chances by retaining an appellate specialist to handle his or her appeal.

### ACKNOWLEDGMENTS

**Mark H. Allenbaugh** is a former staff attorney to the U.S. Sentencing Commission, and is currently an executive with Sentencing Stats, LLC (www.sentencingstats.com), a premier data analytical firm providing federal sentencing data and analyses to attorneys and their clients. He is a nationally recognized expert on federal sentencing law, policy, and practice.

**Jonathan Edelstein** also contributed to the information in this chapter. He is a practicing attorney with a practice focusing on criminal appeals and Federal and State post-conviction remedies. In addition to having his own practice, he is Of Counsel to the Law Offices of Alan Ellis.

**Karen L. Landau** also contributed to the information in this chapter. She is a practicing attorney in Oakland, California, specializing in appellate representation in criminal and civil matters.

**ARTICLE REPRINTS**

Chapter 9 "Direct Appeals" is adapted from the article entitled "A Federal Criminal Appeal Primer: A Guide for Clients and Their Family and Friends," *Criminal Justice* magazine, Spring 2002, co-authored by Alan Ellis and Karen L. Landau.

# CHAPTER 10

# HABEAS CORPUS: §2255 MOTIONS

(This page intentionally left blank.)

# §10:10   §2255 MOTIONS

The motion to vacate, set aside or correct a sentence provided by 28 U.S.C. §2255 is a modern descendant of the common law petition for a writ of habeas corpus. It is available only to people convicted in federal courts who are in custody. (The corresponding federal postconviction tool for state prisoners is the habeas petition governed by 28 U.S.C. §2254.) The §2255 motion is the postconviction tool most federal prisoners turn to after they have exhausted their appeals. When it is used effectively, it can be a powerful tool to right injustices that were not or could not have been raised on direct appeal. This is because it gives courts broad discretion in fashioning appropriate relief, including dismissal of all charges and release of the prisoner, retrial, or resentencing.

Occasionally, the remedy provided by §2255 will be "inadequate or ineffective to test the legality of [a prisoner's] detention." 28 U.S.C. §2255. In those rare instances, federal prisoners may petition for traditional writs of habeas corpus pursuant to 28 U.S.C. §2241.

## §10:10.1   Who Can File?

Only "prisoners" who are "*in custody* under sentence of a court established by Act of Congress" may file motions pursuant to 28 U.S.C. §2255 to vacate their convictions or sentences. 28 U.S.C. §2255 (emphasis added). To satisfy this "custody" requirement, a defendant must either be in prison or jail, or else have his or her liberty under some other form of restraint as part of a federal sentence. In other words, the "in custody" requirement is important, while the limitation of the remedy to "prisoners" is not literally enforced. Examples of restraints short of imprisonment which qualify as "custody," include probation, parole, supervised release, and being released on bail or one's own recognizance. A defendant need only satisfy the "custody" requirement at the time he or she files a §2255 motion. A defendant's being released from custody during the pendency of a §2255 motion does not make the case moot or divest a court of jurisdiction to hear the case.

A defendant who has completely finished his or her sentence, or who has been sentenced only to a fine, may not obtain relief through §2255. Similarly, because corporate defendants never have restraints placed on their physical liberty as a result of a federal criminal conviction (corporations receive only fines as criminal punishments), they can never meet the "custody" requirement. Defendants who can not meet the custody requirement may still be able to obtain relief under the All Writs Act, 28 U.S.C. §1651, by petitioning for a writ in the nature of Coram Nobis, which has no custody requirement.

## §10:10.2   What Issues Can Be Raised?

Section 2255 provides that "prisoners" may move for relief "on the ground that the sentence was imposed in violation of the Constitution or laws of the United States, or that the court was without jurisdiction to impose such sentence, or that the sentence was in excess of the maximum authorized by law, or is otherwise subject to collateral attack." Most Circuits of the Court of Appeals have interpreted this language to mean that defendants who meet §2255's custody requirement may not raise issues which challenge aspects of their sentence which are unrelated to their custody. Most §2255 motions allege violations of the defendant's Sixth Amendment right to the effective assistance of counsel.

### §10:10.3   Differences From Direct Appeals

One of the most significant differences between a direct appeal and a §2255 motion is that direct appeals are decided based on the district court record as it exists as of the time the notice of appeal is filed. In contrast, §2255 motions offer defendants the opportunity to present the court with new evidence. While issues which may be raised in a §2255 motion are not limited by the record as it exists at the time the motion is filed, unlike in a direct appeal, not all issues may be raised in a §2255 motion. Section 2255 motions may only be used to raise jurisdictional, constitutional, or other fundamental errors. For example, some circuits hold that guideline calculation errors that escaped notice on direct appeal cannot be raised under §2255. Others have not questioned the appropriateness of raising guideline issues in a §2255 motion. A §2255 motion is, however, always the proper vehicle to question whether an attorney's failure to raise a guideline issue deprived a defendant of his or her Sixth Amendment right to effective assistance of counsel, either at sentencing, or on direct appeal.

### §10:10.4   Encountering Obstacles in Litigating

Identifying an appropriate §2255 issue is no guarantee of success. Even prisoners who have good issues must often overcome numerous obstacles before a court will even address them. For example, if an issue could have been raised on direct appeal, but was not, a district court will not consider the issue in a §2255 proceeding unless the defendant can demonstrate "cause" (such as ineffective assistance of counsel) for not raising the issue earlier and "prejudice" (that is, that the error likely made a difference in the outcome). For this reason, it is generally not a good idea to forego a direct appeal and proceed directly to a §2255 motion. Conversely, if an issue was raised and decided on appeal, a defendant is procedurally barred from raising it again in a §2255 motion, absent extraordinary circumstances, such as an intervening change in the law or newly discovered evidence.

Section 2255 motions may not be used as vehicles to create or apply new rules of constitutional law. While new interpretations of substantive law may be applied retroactively in a §2255 motion, with rare exceptions, new rules of constitutional law may not.

### §10:10.5   Prisoners' Rights

Prisoners who cannot afford to hire private counsel have no right to appointed counsel to assist them in filing §2255 proceedings. Indigent litigants may, however, petition the court for appointment of counsel. A court has discretion to appoint counsel "at any stage of the proceeding if the interest of justice so requires." 18 U.S.C. §3006A(a)(2)(B); Fed.R.Gov. §2255 Proc. 8(c). Appointment of counsel is mandated only if the court grants an evidentiary hearing, Rule 8(c), or if the court permits discovery and deems counsel "necessary for effective utilization of discovery procedures." Rule 6(a).

### §10:10.6   Time Limits

Prior to Congress' enacting the Antiterrorism and Effective Death Penalty Act ("AEDPA") in 1996, there was no specific limit on the time within which a prisoner was required to file a §2255 motion. The AEDPA's amendment of 28 U.S.C. §2255 imposed a one-year statute of limitations which is triggered by the latest of four events:

(1)  the date on which the judgment of conviction becomes final;

(2)  the date on which the impediment to making a motion created by governmental action in violation of the Constitution or laws of the United States is removed, if the movant was prevented from making a motion by such governmental action;

(3)  the date on which the right asserted was initially recognized by the Supreme Court, if that right has been newly recognized by the Supreme Court and made retroactively applicable to cases on collateral review; or

(4)  the date on which the facts supporting the claim or claims presented could have been discovered through the exercise of due diligence.

All defendants thus have one year from the date on which their judgments of conviction become final within which to file §2255 motions. Occasionally a particular defendant will be able to file a §2255 motion beyond that date when a new year-long limitation period is triggered by one of the other events listed above.

Unfortunately, there is no consensus among the Courts of Appeals as to when a judgment of conviction becomes "final," thus triggering the one-year statute of limitations. Prior to the AEDPA, the Supreme Court held, in the context of deciding when a "new rule" could be applied on collateral attack, that a conviction becomes final when "the judgment of conviction was rendered, the availability of appeal exhausted, and the time for petition for certiorari ha[s] elapsed ...." Although a "new rule" may not be applied retroactively on collateral attack, it may be applied in a particular case if it was announced prior to the judgment of conviction becoming "final" in that case. Although it may seem intuitive that the same rule should trigger the statute of limitations in §2255 cases, not all Courts of Appeals have seen it that way.

It is clear that when a defendant petitions the Supreme Court for a writ of certiorari as part of the direct appeal, the judgment of conviction becomes final on the date the Supreme Court denies the writ. If the Supreme Court grants the writ, then the judgment of conviction becomes final either on the date the Supreme Court rules (if there is no remand), or on the date that the conviction and sentence are ultimately affirmed on remand. What is not so clear is when a conviction becomes final when a defendant fails to appeal, or when he or she appeals, but fails to petition for writ of certiorari. Two Courts of Appeals have held that where a defendant appeals, but fails to petition for writ of certiorari, the conviction becomes final, triggering the statute of limitations, when the Court of Appeals issues its mandate. Other Courts of Appeals have held that the judgment of conviction becomes final, triggering the statute of limitations, on the last day a defendant has to petition the Supreme Court for certiorari.

If a defendant does not appeal, it is clear that in the Third, Fifth, Ninth, and Tenth Circuits, the judgment of conviction becomes final on the last day the defendant could file a notice of appeal—*i.e.,* on the tenth day following the entry of the judgment of sentence. It is not clear yet when the judgment would become final in the Fourth or Seventh Circuits, or in the circuits which have not yet addressed the question of when a judgment of conviction becomes "final" under the AEDPA. If you are in a jurisdiction which has not decided the issue, the prudent course may be to assume that the year runs from the date the judgment of conviction is entered on the docket (if no notice of appeal is filed), or on the date the court of appeals decides the case or denies a timely-filed petition for rehearing.

If a defendant wins a new trial or a resentencing on appeal (or even as a result of a §2255 motion), then the new judgment of conviction and sentence which is entered after the new trial or resentencing would begin a new year-long statute of limitations.

### §10:10.7    The AEDPA's One Year Rule

The AEDPA's one year rule is not hard and fast. Every Circuit to have considered the issue has ruled that the AEDPA's one-year statute of limitations is not jurisdictional in nature, and is therefore subject to equitable tolling. Equitable tolling excuses a movant's untimely filing "because of extraordinary circumstances that are both beyond his control and unavoidable even with diligence." Courts, however, have rarely found that movants meet the requirements of equitable tolling. For example, "mere excusable neglect is not sufficient." Nor is delay by the Postal Service,19 or the unclarity of a deadline. A *pro se* movant's being misled by a court, however, *has* supported equitable tolling.

### §10:10.8    How and Where to File

Section 2255 motions must be filed with the district court which sentenced the defendant. The local rules of most district courts require *pro se* prisoners to use forms supplied by the Clerk. Some local rules even require attorneys to use the forms. There is no filing fee.

### §10:10.9    After the Motion Is Filed

Section 2255 motions are first presented to the judge who presided over the defendant's trial and sentencing if that judge is available. The judge examines the motion and attached exhibits, as well as the rest of the case record (including transcripts and correspondence in the file). The court then either dismisses the motion or orders the government to file an answer. Dismissal is required where the court concludes that the claims raised in the motion, even if true, would not provide a ground for §2255 relief, or where the claims are conclusively refuted by the files and records of the case.

After the government files its answer, the defendant may want to refute the government's arguments. This can be done by filing a memorandum in reply. Sometimes the right to file a reply memorandum exists under local court rules or court order. Sometimes a defendant must file a motion for leave to file a reply.

At this point, the court will either grant or deny relief, or will hold a hearing. While the language of 28 U.S.C. §2255 seems to require a hearing whenever the court orders the government to file an answer, the rules governing §2255 motions leave the necessity of a hearing to the court's discretion. Fed.R. Gov. §2255 Proc. 8(a). In practice, courts grant hearings only where there are critical facts in dispute. Whenever a court holds an evidentiary hearing, Rule 8(c) requires it to appoint counsel for *pro se* defendants who cannot afford to hire counsel. The prisoner can be brought to court for the hearing if his or her testimony is required, or for any other reason approved by the judge.

### §10:10.10 Length of the Process

Once a defendant files a §2255 motion, it can take anywhere from several weeks (in the event of a summary dismissal) to over a year (if the government is ordered to respond, and a hearing is held) for a court either to grant or dismiss a §2255 motion.

### §10:10.11 Special Rules

There are special rules that apply to §2255 motions—"Rules Governing Section 2255 Proceedings For the United States District Courts." The rules address the following issues: scope of the rules (Rule 1), form of the motion (Rule 2), filing of the motion (Rule 3), preliminary consideration by the judge (Rule 4), answer of the government (Rule 5), discovery (Rule 6), expansion of the record (submitting evidence) (Rule 7), evidentiary hearing (Rule 8), delayed or successive motions (Rule 9; this rule has been largely, if not entirely, superseded by the AEDPA's more stringent restriction on successive motions), the powers of U.S. Magistrate Judges to carry out the duties imposed on the court by the rules (Rule 10), and the time for appeal (Rule 11). If no Rule specifically applies, Rule 12 provides that "the district court may proceed in any lawful manner not inconsistent with these rules, or any applicable statute, and may apply the Federal Rules of Criminal Procedure or the Federal Rules of Civil Procedure, whichever it deems most appropriate ..."

Rule 22 of the Federal Rules of Appellate Procedure addresses the procedure for applying for a certificate of appealability (permission to appeal). Local district court and appellate rules often have special sections devoted to §2255 motions and prisoner petitions.

### §10:10.12  Rules of Discovery

Rule 6 of the Rules Governing §2255 Proceedings allows defendants as well as the government to conduct discovery pursuant to the Federal Rules of Civil Procedure—but only with permission from the court. The rule gives the district court discretion to grant discovery requests "for good cause shown, but not otherwise."

### §10:10.13  Appealing the Denial of §2255 Motions

The denial of a §2255 motion can be appealed only if "a circuit justice or judge issues a certificate of appealability." 28 U.S.C. §2253(c)(1). A circuit justice or judge "may issue a certificate of appealability ... only if the applicant has made a substantial showing of the denial of a constitutional right." *Id.* §2253(c)(2). (Under this language, even if the §2255 motion properly raised a non-constitutional issue, the denial of that ground for relief cannot be appealed at all.) If a certificate is issued, it must "indicate which specific issue or issues satisfy" the required showing of the denial of a constitutional right. *Id.* §2253(c)(3). Only defendants need certificates of appealability to appeal the denial of §2255 motions; the government needs no certificate to appeal the granting of a motion to vacate. Fed.R.App.P. 22(b)(3).

Although the appeal of the court's denial of a §2255 motion may not proceed without a certificate of appealability, a notice of appeal must nevertheless be filed within 60 days from the date judgment is entered. Fed.R.Gov. §2255 Proc. 11 (time to appeal is as provided in Fed.R.App.P. 4(a), governing civil appeals). Since there is no time limit within which a court must rule on an application for a certificate of appealability (some courts have been taking a year or more to rule on such requests), the rules of appellate procedure provide that the notice of appeal itself "constitutes a request [for a certificate of appealability] addressed to the judges of the court of appeals." Fed.R.App.P. 22(b)(3). The filing of a notice of appeal also triggers a requirement that the "district judge who rendered the judgment must either issue a certificate of appealability or state why a certificate should not issue." Rule 22(b)(1). If the district court denies the certificate, the defendant "may request a circuit court judge to issue the certificate." *Id.* Rule 22(b)(2) provides that "A request addressed to the court of appeals may be considered by a circuit judge or judges, as the court prescribes." Some Courts of Appeals assign this task to a single judge. Others refer such requests to panels of the Court. Even when consideration of a request for a certificate of appeal-ability is referred to a panel, the support of only one judge is required for the certificate to issue.

### §10:10.14  Making a "Substantial Showing of the Denial of a Constitutional Right"

The standard for appealability under 28 U.S.C. §2253(c)(2) is somewhat different depending upon whether the district court has rejected the issue sought to be appealed on its merits or on procedural grounds. With respect to constitutional claims rejected on their merits, the Supreme Court has applied to certificates of appealability the standard for granting certificates of probable cause set forth in *Barefoot v. Estelle,* and followed in the AEDPA. Under this standard, the appellant must make a showing that each issue he or she seeks to appeal is at least "debatable among jurists of reason; that a court could resolve the issues [in a different manner]; or that the questions are adequate to deserve encouragement to proceed further." The "substantial showing" standard "does not compel a petitioner to demonstrate that he or she would prevail on the merits." As to claims denied on procedural grounds (that is, where the district court has not reached the merits), the Court in *Slack* clarified that the certificate of appealability standard is somewhat different and easier to meet: (1) "whether jurists of reason would find it debatable whether the petition *states* a valid claim of the denial of a constitutional right" (in other words, does the petition at least allege a valid claim, even though it hasn't been proven yet), and (2) whether "jurists of reason would find it debatable whether the district court was correct in its procedural ruling."

### §10:10.15  Filing More Than One §2255 Motion

As provided in 28 U.S.C. §2255, before a prisoner may file a second §2255 to challenge a particular judgment, a "*panel* of the appropriate court of appeals" must "certif[y]" that the motion "contain[s]" either:

(1)  newly discovered evidence that, if proven and viewed in the light of the evidence as a whole, would be sufficient to establish by clear and convincing evidence that no reasonable factfinder would have found the movant guilty of the offense; or

(2)  a new rule of constitutional law, made retroactive to cases on collateral review by the Supreme Court, that was previously unavailable.

This harsh rule is tempered slightly by the fact that it applies only to motions which attack the a judgment that a defendant has previously moved pursuant to §2255 to vacate. Defendants may file one §2255 motion as of right for each judgment of conviction and sentence. For example, if a defendant's conviction is vacated as a result of a §2255 motion, he receives a new trial and is convicted and sentenced again (or simply resentenced), he may file a §2255 motion to challenge that new judgment without receiving permission from the Court of Appeals.

If a defendant wants to file a second §2255 motion attacking the same judgment, his or her options are severely limited. The newly discovered evidence ground, for example, applies only to newly discovered evidence which establishes a defendant's factual innocence. It does not, for example, apply to evidence which, had it been known prior to sentencing, would have resulted in a shorter term of imprisonment. Nor would it apply to newly discovered evidence which, if it had been introduced at trial, might have engendered a reasonable doubt. The evidence must be such that had it be introduced, "no reasonable factfinder would have found the movant guilty of the offense."

The second ground is also quite narrow. It applies only to "new rule[s] of constitutional law"—not to changes in substantive law. The "new rule" must also have been "previously unavailable" *and* have been "made retroactive to cases on collateral review by the Supreme Court." A "new rule" has been "made retroactive to cases on collateral review by the Supreme Court" only if the Supreme Court itself has previously declared it to be retroactive—something which ordinarily can happen only on appeal of someone else's timely *first* §2255 or habeas petition.

Not only must a second §2255 motion meet one of these criteria before it may be filed, it must also be filed within an applicable clause of the statute of limitations. For most defendants, that will mean within one year of the discovery of the new evidence, or "the date on which the right asserted was initially recognized by the Supreme Court, if the right has been newly recognized by the Supreme Court and made retroactively applicable to cases on collateral review." §2255 (¶ (3)).

## §10:20   HABEAS CORPUS (§2241) PETITIONS

A §2241 action, also known as a petition for a writ of habeas corpus, is essentially a civil law-suit filed by a federal prisoner to challenge the legality of his or her custody in situations where the §2255 motion would be inadequate or ineffective. There are two types of habeas petitions—those that challenge the validity of the underlying convictions or sentences, and those that do not. Because §2255 motions are, except in rare instances, "adequate" (even if not successful) to challenge the validity of underlying convictions and sentences, habeas petitions are generally limited challenges to federal custody which do not challenge the underlying convictions or sentences.

### Challenges to Underlying Convictions and Sentences

The §2255 remedy is not "inadequate or ineffective" simply because a defendant has filed a §2255 motion and failed to obtain relief, or because a defendant is barred by the statute of limitations, or by the statutory limitations on second and successive motions, from filing a §2255 motion. Circumstances under which courts have permitted criminal defendants to employ the habeas petition to challenge their convictions and sentences include abolition of the sentencing court, refusal of the sentencing court even to consider the §2255 motion, and inordinate delay in disposing of a §2255 motion.

The limitations imposed by the AEDPA on second or successive petitions have created a new (although still rare) circumstance under which the remedy afforded by §2255 is "inadequate or ineffective." After a defendant has already filed a §2255 motion challenging his underlying conviction and sentence, and lost, he may receive permission from the Court of Appeals to file a second §2255 only in the two limited circumstances discussed previously. A second or successive §2255 is not permitted when the Supreme Court reinterprets the meaning of the statute under which the defendant had been convicted so as to render him innocent on the facts. While substantive criminal law rulings by the Supreme Court, such as this, are retroactively applicable on collateral attack (and therefore could support *first* §2255 motions, so long as the motions are timely-filed), they do not come within the two narrow grounds for receiving permission to file a second motion. Under these circumstances, courts have held that §2255 is inadequate or ineffective and have permitted defendants to challenge their underlying convictions through habeas petitions.

The section 2241 petition is the proper vehicle for challenging the duration of a prisoner's confinement without challenging the underlying conviction. The Supreme Court has suggested in dictum that §2241 petitions may also be used to challenge a prisoner's conditions of confinement. Some courts have permitted federal prisoners to use §2241 petitions to challenge prison conditions. Other courts have ruled that such challenges must be made through civil rights actions, such as those brought under the authority of *Bivens v. Six Unknown Named Agents of the Federal Bureau of Investigation.* A court's mandamus jurisdiction may also sometimes be invoked to seek redress of prison conditions.

### §10:20.1   Who May File

Federal habeas corpus relief under 28 U.S.C. §2241(c)(3) is available to anyone held "in custody in violation of the Constitution, laws or treaties of the United States." However, by law, the §2241 remedy is limited to situations which are not covered by either 28 U.S.C. §§2254 (state prisoner challenging state conviction) or 2255 (federal prisoner challenging conviction or sentence). In addition to incarceration, being on parole or bail count as being "in custody." Section 2241 is also used to obtain review of forms of official custody not resulting from convictions, such as detained aliens and military members seeking discharge.

### §10:20.2   When to File

A prisoner must first exhaust (use all of) his or her administrative remedies, if any, before filing a §2241 action. For instance, if the Bureau of Prisons has sanctioned a prisoner with the loss of good time credits, the prisoner must exhaust BOP administrative remedy procedures, if any, before he or she files a §2241 action. Courts generally recognize an exception to the "exhaustion" requirement where no timely and potentially effective administrative remedy exists.

### §10:20.3   How and Where to File

A §2241 action is a new civil law-suit which should be filed in the district court having territorial jurisdiction over the prison or other person or agency having custody of the petitioner. Habeas petitions differ in many ways from normal civil lawsuits, however. For example, the filing fee is only $5. Also, a few, but not most, districts, require the use of a form petition. Neither the Federal Rules of Civil Procedure nor the rules applicable to §2254 cases necessarily applies to §2241 habeas petitions. The question of which rules do apply is complex, and unfortunately beyond the scope of this article.

Once the court reviews the petition, it will do one of four things: dismiss it (but only if the petitioner would lose even if the court accepted its allegations as true), order the petitioner to amend it (for instance, where there is some technical defect), order the respondent to show cause why the petition should not be granted—*i.e.,* to answer the petition by a certain date, or summarily grant the writ (extremely rare). After the respondent answers the petition (assuming it is ordered to do so), the petitioner may file a "traverse" (*i.e.,* a written reply to the reasons the respondent gave for why the court should not grant the petition). If an evidentiary hearing is held, the prisoner has a right to be present. Once a hearing is held (if one is necessary) and all the briefing is complete, the court will decide the case, "as law and justice require." 28 U.S.C. §2243.

### §10:20.4   Appealing a Denial of §2241 Relief

Notice of appeal must be filed within 60 days of the entry of final judgment. Rule 4(a) of the Federal Rules of Appellate Procedure. No certificate of appealability is required.

### §10:20.5   Filing More Than One §2241 Habeas Petition

No permission from the Court of Appeals is required to file more than one §2241 habeas petition. A second petition which raises an issue which could have been raised in the first petition must show cause why it was not raised in the first, or be dismissed under the "abuse of the writ" doctrine. Similarly, a second petition which raises an issue which was decided in a prior petition will also be dismissed as an "abuse of the writ."

### §10:20.6   Legal Assistance

Prisoners need not hire an attorney to file a §2241 petition for a writ of habeas corpus. In fact, most §2241 petitions are filed by prisoners without the assistance of attorneys. Unfortunately, due in part to the legal minefield that any federal habeas litigant must cross, most of these are summarily denied without a hearing. To maximize his or her chances of success, a prisoner should retain the services of competent counsel. Prisoners who are unable to afford private counsel may ask the court to appoint an attorney under the Criminal Justice Act to represent them. 18 U.S.C. §3006A(a)(2)(B). Prisoners filing for habeas corpus are not entitled to appointed counsel as a matter of right.

## §10:30   STEMMING THE TIDE OF
##          POST-CONVICTION WAIVERS

Over the past several years, waiver of a defendant's appellate and post-conviction rights had become a standard feature of plea agreements in federal cases. An example of the type of appeal and post-conviction waiver language commonly found in federal plea agreements was:

> The Defendant waives any and all rights, including those conferred by 18 U.S.C. 3724 and/or 28 U.S.C. 2255, to appeal or collaterally attack his conviction and any sentence of imprisonment of XX months or less, including any related issues with respect to the establishment of the Sentencing guidelines range.

Courts generally found that if the waiver was knowingly, intelligently and voluntarily made, they would enforce it. In response to the efforts by the National Association of Criminal Defense Lawyers (NACDL) and various state bars, on October 14, 2014 the Department of Justice issued a new policy on Waivers of Claims of Ineffective Assistance of Counsel. The memo issued by Deputy Attorney General James M. Cole provides that:

> Prosecutors should no longer seek in plea agreements to have a defendant waive claims of ineffective assistance of counsel whether those claims are made on collateral attack i.e., a 2255 motion or when permitted by circuit law, made on direct appeal. For those cases in which a defendant files an ineffective assistance claim would be barred by a previously executed waiver prosecutors have been directed to decline to enforce the waiver when defense counsel rendered ineffective assistance resulting in prejudice or when the defendant's ineffective assistance claim raises a serious debatable issue that a court should resolve.

This section suggests areas that defense counsel should be aware of in order to afford clients the greatest opportunity for post-conviction relief. In particular, we explore ethical constraints on defense counsel's ability to advise clients and to shield themselves from ineffective assistance claims, as well as constraints on prosecutors' ability to demand such waivers or to shield themselves from prosecutorial misconduct claims.

## §10:30.1    The Department of Justice Cole Memorandum

U. S. Department of Justice

Office of the Deputy Attorney General

---

The Deputy Attorney General                     *Washington, D.C. 20530*

October 14, 2014

MEMORANDUM FOR ALL FEDERAL PROSECUTORS

FROM:              James M. Cole
                   Deputy Attorney General

SUBJECT:           Department Policy on Waivers of Claims of Ineffective Assistance of
                   Counsel

    As we all recognize, the right to effective assistance of counsel is a core value of our Constitution. The Department of Justice has a strong interest in ensuring that individuals facing criminal charges receive effective assistance of counsel so that our adversarial system can function fairly, efficiently, and responsibly. Accordingly, in recent years, the Department has made support of indigent defense a priority. We have worked to ensure that all jurisdictions — federal, state, and local – fulfill their obligations under the Constitution to provide effective assistance of counsel, especially to those who cannot afford an attorney.

    When negotiating a plea agreement, the majority of United States Attorney's offices do not seek a waiver of claims of ineffective assistance of counsel. This is true even though the federal courts have uniformly held a defendant may generally waive ineffective assistance claims pertaining to matters other than entry of the plea itself, such as claims related to sentencing. While the Department is confident that a waiver of a claim of ineffective assistance of counsel is both legal and ethical, in order to bring consistency to this practice, and in support of the underlying Sixth Amendment right, we now set forth uniform Department of Justice policies relating to waivers of claims of ineffective assistance of counsel.

    Federal prosecutors should no longer seek in plea agreements to have a defendant waive claims of ineffective assistance of counsel whether those claims are made on collateral attack or, when permitted by circuit law, made on direct appeal. For cases in which a defendant's ineffective assistance claim would be barred by a previously executed waiver, prosecutors should decline to enforce the waiver when defense counsel rendered ineffective assistance resulting in prejudice or when the defendant's ineffective assistance claim raises a serious debatable issue that a court should resolve.

    As long as prosecutors exempt ineffective-assistance claims from their waiver provisions, they are free to request waivers of appeal and of post-conviction remedies to the full extent permitted by law as a component of plea discussions and agreements.

## ACKNOWLEDGMENT

**James H. Feldman, Jr.** contributed to the information in §§10:10-10:20.6. He is an associate in the Ellis firm's Pennsylvania office. Since joining the firm in 1989, he has handled numerous sentencings, appeals, and §2255 motions in federal courts throughout the United States. Mr. Feldman is the editor of Federal Presentence and Postconviction News and has co-authored a number of articles on federal sentencing and post-conviction remedies with Alan Ellis. He is a 1976 graduate of the University of Cincinnati Law School.

## ARTICLE REPRINTS

§§10:10-10:20.6 is reprinted from the article entitled "A 2255 and 2241 Primer: A Guide for Clients and Their Family and Friends," *The Champion*, April 2002.

# CHAPTER 11

# PRACTICE TIPS

(This page intentionally left blank.)

## §11:10   TIPS ON GETTING YOUR CLIENT THE LOWEST POSSIBLE SENTENCE

Approximately 97 percent of all federal criminal defendants plead guilty. Seventy-five percent of the remaining individuals who proceed to trial are convicted. There is, therefore, almost a 99 percent chance that a person charged with a federal crime will ultimately face a judge for purposes of sentencing. Over 87 percent will be sentenced to prison. Thus, for most offenders "How much time am I going to do?" and "Where am I going to do it?" are key concerns. We offer the following tips to help attorneys and their clients obtain the lowest possible sentence.

- Studies suggest that 80 percent of the time, a judge has a "tentative sentence" in mind, even before the sentencing hearing begins. Accordingly, the best way to influence the judge's selection of "tentative sentence" is to file a sentencing memorandum, which fully sets forth the facts and arguments supporting the requested disposition, approximately seven days before sentencing (unless otherwise required by local rule). If you present the judge a solid memorandum that uses the §3553(a) factors to demonstrate why a sentence below the guideline range is "sufficient, but not greater than necessary" to achieve the goals of sentencing, including character letters from people willing to offer insight into a client's true nature notwithstanding their awareness of the offense(s) of conviction, you will go a long way toward achieving the sentence you want. Waiting until the actual hearing to make your sentencing case, as has been a historic practice in state courts, makes it far less likely that the court will give appropriate weight to your position.

- Document, document, document. Don't just assert the existence of mitigating factors; provide as much supporting evidence as possible. For instance, if your client has a physical or mental impairment, or drug or alcohol dependency issues, corroborate the issue with a doctor's letter and/or report and with medical/treatment records (under seal, preferably via the Probation Office so that the information is appended to the PSR and given to the BOP). Similarly, if your client has a military service record or a history of good works, provide appropriate documents or testimonials. Remember that judges won't necessarily take your client's word on anything—he is, after all, a convicted felon—and that even if the court *does* accept his word, evidentiary documents will flesh out and add weight to the sentencing presentation.

- There is a prevailing feeling in the defense community since *Booker* that applications for a sentence below the guideline range should be couched as requests for variances or for non-Guidelines sentences; that the days of motioning for a "downward departure" have passed. While this position has strong facial appeal, the fact remains that even after *Booker,* a court must "consider" guideline policy statements prior to imposing sentence. Not to mention many judges still prefer to engage in departure analysis. It is therefore important to show, if you can, how the policy statements

in Parts 5H and 5K call for a lower sentence. Even though a single mitigating factor may not warrant a downward departure, a combination
of factors might (*see* USSG §5K2.0 Commentary). Present the court
with every credible mitigating factor that the case presents, both in
terms of "departure" and in terms of "variance" and/or "non-Guidelines
sentence." Even if you don't get a sentence below the guideline range,
mitigating factors can often help in getting a sentence at the low end of
the range, which is especially important when the offense level and/or
the criminal history score render high guidelines.

• The U.S. Sentencing Commission revised the policy statement to Guideline Section 5H1.3 to provide that "[m]ental and emotional conditions
may be relevant in determining whether a departure is warranted,"
especially "[i]n certain cases … to accomplish a specific treatment purpose" (emphasis added). Prior to the amendment (Amend. 739), mental
and emotional conditions were not considered "ordinarily relevant."
Counsel should argue in appropriate cases, that an inmate's mental
and emotional condition cannot be adequately treated by the Bureau
of Prisons. Since 18 U.S.C. §3553(a)(2)(D) requires a sentencing court
to consider the need for the sentence imposed to provide the defendant
with needed medical care, significant incarceration will not meet this
purpose. Additionally, the expense of treating a client's condition may
support a cost-related mitigation argument (see above), particularly in
light of the BOP budgetary problems and overcrowding.

• If your client is a cooperating witness, accompany him or her to any
debriefings. Not only will you be able to clear up any future dispute as
to what was said, your presence will often facilitate the discussions,
particularly if you have debriefed and prepped your client in advance.

• Many of us have been in the situation where even though our client
has cooperated, the government has refused to file a 5K1.1 motion for
downward departure based on substantial assistance. If you are ever
faced with this unpleasant situation, either seek a downward departure
based on "super/extraordinary acceptance of responsibility" or, since
the "government motion requirement" of §5K1.1 is now only a guideline policy to be considered, argue that even without a 5K motion, the
cooperation would make a lower sentence "sufficient," and a higher
one "greater than necessary" to meet the goals of sentencing. Every
Circuit to have considered the issue has ruled that a sentencing court
may consider a defendant's cooperation as part of its §3553(a) analysis,
and grant a variance on that basis, even in the absence of a Government
motion. For more information on maximizing the benefits of cooperation, take a look at the lead article in the Summer 2007 issues of *Federal
Sentencing and Postconviction News,* our firm's quarterly newsletter,
which can be found on the publications page of our website, http://
www.alanellis.com/CM/Publications/newsletter-2007-summer.pdf.
Finally, even where the government files a substantial assistance motion,

unless otherwise precluded by the plea agreement, you are permitted to argue for a more generous reduction, and the court will be free to grant a greater reduction. While a substantial assistance reduction cannot be based on non-cooperation grounds, experience shows that judges unwilling to grant a relief for non 5K1.1 reasons oftentimes grant a more generous 5K1.1 reduction than recommended by the government when presented a compelling mitigation case, especially since such an approach insulates them from appellate review.

- Seek a "lateral" departure or "variance" that requires your client to serve the same amount of time the Guidelines call for but under more favorable conditions. For example, if the Guidelines call for a 21-month sentence, ask the judge to impose a sentence of seven months of incarceration, followed by supervised release with a special condition that the client serve seven months in Residential Corrections Center (RCC or halfway house), and then followed by seven months of supervised release with home confinement and an appropriate amount of community service. This adds up to the same 21 months for which the Guidelines call. However, it actually requires more time served, since the client will not get good conduct time credit for any portion of the sentence. While your client will serve the entire 21 months, the conditions of confinement will be better, and the opportunities for your client to work and support a family will be greater.

- Accompany your client to probation officer meetings that are part of the Presentence Investigation Report (PSR) process. Since probation officers are overburdened, obtain in advance the forms and documents they need, and have your client complete and bring them to the initial interview (subject to your prior review). If you have case law or other materials supporting your sentencing position, bring copies with you, highlighting the relevant portions. Probation officers, most of whom are not lawyers, often prefer highlighted cases to memoranda of law, which they find off-putting.

- When you meet with the probation officer, find out the "dictation date" (the date by which the first draft of the PSR must be dictated). When possible, it is extremely helpful to have the probation officer and the Assistant U.S. Attorney (AUSA) buy into your client's position regarding offense behavior, role in the offense, and any grounds for relief from the Guidelines before the dictation date. "Buying in" does not mean paying anybody off. It means getting them to agree that your position is not unreasonable. Remember that probation officers often have a psychological investment in their original draft PSR, which can make getting them to change a PSR difficult. By putting your effort into trying to get a good initial draft, you will not have to file that many objections.

- While the Federal Bureau of Prisons (BOP) will not credit an inmate's sentence for time served on pretrial release under home confinement or in a halfway house if that placement was as a condition of bond, as opposed to an alternative custody arrangement (*see Reno v. Koray*, 515 U.S. 50 (1995)), courts are nonetheless free to account for such time as a basis for variance. *Gall* provides useful language concerning the punitive nature of home detention, depending on the nature and scope of court-ordered conditions.

• Read "Inside Baseball: An Interview with Former Federal Probation Officer" by Alan Ellis and Tess Lopez, which is reprinted in §9:30.6. It is valuable advice by a former U.S. Probation Officer who is now a mitigation specialist on how to best approach a probation officer. In short, it encourages educating the probation officer about your clients before the prosecutor has had an opportunity to poison the well. One way to do so is by providing the probation officer with favorable character letters. (*See* §9:80 for an example of a character instructional letter that we send to clients.) The article contains an easy-to-understand explanation of the Presentence Investigation Report. Give it to your client so s/he better understands the process in preparation for the interview with the U.S. Probation Office.

• Below guideline variance sentences are on the rise, while sentences within the guidelines continue to decrease. According to the statistics compiled by the U.S. Sentencing Commission since *Booker*, non-government-sponsored (*e.g.*, non-§5K1.1 departures) below guideline sentences have increased from 12% of all sentences imposed in 2006 to 20.8% in 2014. Within guideline sentences have decreased from 61.7% of all sentences imposed in 2006 to 47.2% in 2014. The increase in below guideline sentences is even more dramatic when looking at particular offense categories. For example, non-government-sponsored below guideline sentences for child pornography offenses—perhaps the most controversial of all types of guideline sentences—have more than doubled from only 20.8% of all such sentences imposed in 2006 to 43.8% in 2014. The chart below shows the trends for non-government-sponsored below guidelines sentences in the top five offense categories, as well as the trend for sentences overall (y-axis reflects percentages, and x-axis indicates years

• The foregoing trend reinforces the importance of using a sentencing specialist able to help humanize your client, preferably someone familiar with the federal system's many nuances. If your client cannot afford this service, ask for funds under the Criminal Justice Act, noting that such providers typically bill at below the CJA rate—meaning that the court receives information pertinent to the disposition process that attorneys are not typically trained to elicit at a cost savings. Sentencing advocates, who are akin to capital mitigation specialists (though their case work-ups are not as intensive), are often social workers, former U.S. probation officers, or criminologists. Their training makes their interviewing techniques more effective than that of most lawyers, and often allows them to obtain information a lawyer cannot. For example, a forensic social worker with a background in psychiatric social work is better able to recognize when a client has a mental illness, which may provide a ground for diminished capacity-type relief. These advocates are also better able to identify and develop information concerning unique family circumstances. The National Alliance of Sentencing Advocates & Mitigation Specialists (NASAMS, www.nlada. org/Defender/Defender_NASAMS) has listings for advocates around the country. Judges always want to know why the defendants engaged in criminal activity, not only the instant offense, but also prior criminal convictions. A sentencing presentation that can help you and the court answer the "why" question contributes significantly toward securing the lowest possible sentence.

- *Booker* altered the ground rules for justifying lower sentences. Be creative. Don't limit yourself to factors that would have supported downward departures under the Guidelines. Think of unique aspects about your client and/or the offense that make a sentence below the guideline range "sufficient" to meet the goals of sentencing, that is, why a sentence within the range is "greater than necessary" to meet those goals. As a recent example, there has been a growing trend, given recent economic realities, to argue that the cost of incarceration should be factored into whether a sentence is "greater than necessary." Such an argument carries greater force when the court understands what the client would be doing if not incarcerated (*i.e.*, working, supporting a family, paying taxes).

- For older clients or those facing significant sentences, make the court aware of the client's life expectancy. Data on life expectancy is readily available online through the Centers for Disease Control and Prevention, among many other places. http://www.cdc.gov/nchs/fastats/lifexpec.htm. In the absence of studies measuring the impact of incarceration on life expectancy significant anecdotal evidence supports the contention that extended incarceration significantly reduces life expectancy. Data from any life expectancy charts should be augmented by arguments specific to your client and/or where your client will serve time. Some facilities are more onerous than others and hard time doesn't help life expectancy. This argument meshes well with arguments regarding susceptibility to abuse in prison depending on the characteristics of the offender and/or the nature of the offense and/or the likely designated prison.

- Traditionally, federal courts did not consider any disparity between the punishments meted out by state courts vis-à-vis federal courts for the same or similar conduct. After *Booker*, that has changed. *See, e.g., United States v. Clark*, 434 F.3d 684, 687 (4th Cir. 2007) ("the consideration of state sentencing practices is not necessarily impermissible per se"). Depending on your jurisdiction, the statutory maximum penalties for certain state law offenses often can be dramatically less than their federal counterparts. Likewise, good-time credits and other opportunities for early release (*e.g.*, parole) can be far more generous at state levels than at the federal level, meaning that a state offender will not only receive a far less onerous sentence for the same or similar conduct as his federal counterpart, but he may also serve far less time, as an overall percentage, of sentence imposed. Such comparisons both go to arguments regarding unwarranted disparity and, more importantly, serve as a measure of the disproportionate effect that the federalization of crime and the guidelines have on the particular offense.

- Sentencing judges and appellate courts are often concerned with unwarranted disparity with other defendants and cases. To bolster any predilection the court may have to exercise leniency in your case—both when considering how the disposition might be received in the Court of Appeals or the court of public opinion—emphasize what sentences other judges have imposed in similar cases, in the sentencing district, in neighboring jurisdictions, in other districts in the circuit, and around the country.

- The addition of one criminal history point may not change a defendant's Criminal History Category (CHC). But it can still be important to object to these seemingly harmless additions, and then to appeal if the district court denies the objection. Normally, a criminal history point that does not affect the sentencing range is "harmless error." But not always. In *United States v. Vargas,* 230 F.3d 328 (7th Cir. 2000), the Seventh Circuit remanded for resentencing based on a seemingly inconsequential criminal history point. The Court reasoned that the error was not "harmless," because it "might have affected" the district court's denial of the defendant's motion for downward departure based on the defendant's contention that his criminal history category significantly overrepresented the seriousness of his criminal history (*see* USSG §4A1.3 (p.s.)). As discussed in the Prison Tips section below, criminal history points can also impact prison placement.

- Do not forget to remind the Court of the continuing crisis in over-crowding the Bureau of Prisons is experiencing, which necessarily makes access to rehabilitation and medical care all the more difficult, and further can accentuate any vulnerability to abuse that a client may face. The latest statistics indicate the current population is at 138% of capacity. As of 2014, the Inspector General for the Department of Justice has listed for the past two years reform of the federal prison system as the top challenge facing the Department; higher than even terrorism.

- Don't overlook the importance of allocution. For an excellent discussion, see U.S. District Judge Mark W. Bennett's article entitled, "Heartstrings or Heartburn: A Federal Judge's Musings on Defendants' Right and Rite of allocution, *The NACDL Champion*, March 2011.

- Finally, if the facts are against you, argue the law. If both the law and the facts are against you, take the U.S. Probation Officer out to lunch!

## §11:20   TIPS ON GETTING YOUR CLIENT INTO THE BEST PRISON AND RELEASED AT THE EARLIEST POSSIBLE OPPORTUNITY

- Once a defense attorney understands how the system works, there are four things he or she can do to ensure that a client serves time in the best possible facility. First, counsel should ensure the accuracy of the information on which the Bureau will rely to make its designation decision. Second, counsel should score the client and search for Public Safety Factors (PSF) to determine the appropriate security level. PSFs (such as "deportable alien") can preclude camp placement for otherwise qualified defendants. Third, counsel should consult with the client to determine which facility at the appropriately-calculated security level the client prefers and then ask the sentencing judge to recommend that facility to the BOP, as well as to provide reasons in support of that recommendation. Counsel should, of course, suggest reasons as part of his or her request. Finally, counsel should, in appropriate cases, request self-surrender.

- The most important thing defense counsel can do to ensure designation to the lowest security prison possible is to make sure that any inaccurate information in the Presentence Investigation Report (PSR) is corrected. The BOP relies almost exclusively on the information contained in the PSR to decide where a defendant will do time, as well as to make other important correctional decisions (such as whether a defendant is eligible for the Bureau's Residential Drug Abuse Program—"RDAP").1 It is for good reason that the PSR is known as the "bible" by prisoners and BOP staff alike. If defense counsel objects to inaccurate information at the time of sentencing and the judge sustains those objections, defense counsel must make sure that the PSR is corrected before it is sent to the BOP or, at a minimum, that formal findings are made by the judge pursuant to Fed.R.Crim.P. 32(c)(1) and attached to the PSR before it is forwarded to the Bureau. A finding made in the judgment in a criminal case (preferably in the "statement of reasons" portion) will also suffice.

- It is important for counsel to make sure that the PSR's criminal history score is accurate. The addition of one criminal history point may not change a defendant's Criminal History Score (CHS); but it can negatively impact prison designation. Since the BOP now uses Criminal History Points to calculate an individual's security level (see Program Statement 5100.08). Criminal History Points can affect the type of facility to which the offender may be assigned, even if the judge sentences below the guideline range.

- It is important for defense counsel to make sure that the PSR adequately documents any drug (illegal as well as prescription) abuse or alcoholism. Many defense lawyers and defendants tend to downplay substance abuse problems, under the mistaken belief that revealing such problems can harm the client. Unless a client's substance abuse problem is adequately documented in the PSR, he or she may not qualify for the Bureau's Residential Drug Abuse Program (RDAP) and will not get the chance to earn up to a one-year reduction in sentence pursuant to 18 U.S.C. §3621(c)(2), which permits such a reduction for nonviolent inmates who successfully complete a residential drug treatment program in a BOP facility.

- It is important to ensure that the PSR lists the correct client address. Since "release residence" is defined by the BOP as the defendant's legal address that's listed on the PSR, the BOP will attempt to house your client near that address. If that address is not only far from family and friends who want to visit your client, but also far from the area to which your client intends to relocate upon release, you should consider requesting that another address be used.

- It is important to ensure that if your client is a United States citizen, the citizenship is verified by the U.S. Probation Officer and duly noted as <u>verified</u> in the PSR. This is not generally a problem for persons born in the United States, but can be especially important for naturalized citizens, because if such citizenship is not <u>verified</u> in the PSR at the time of initial designation by the BOP, an individual who might otherwise be eligible for placement in a Minimum security camp will be designated instead to a low-security prison, the next higher security level. Provide the U.S. Probation Officer with the client's naturalization certificate.

- A defendant's Presentence Report (PSR) is the Bible in terms of BOP placement and programming. It is thus imperative that counsel ensure the document's accuracy, even where a particular issue may not affect the court's sentencing decision. When scoring a prisoner's security points, the BOP considers, among other things, the individual's criminal history score, as calculated (the BOP does not account for findings that the score tends to overstate the offense history); *verified* education level, meaning a diploma or GED must be documented; and substance abuse history. To the extent a client may qualify for the BOP's RDAP (*see* Chapter 3), it is important that he candidly discuss his drug and/or alcohol history with Probation during the PSR interview.

- Do not "oversell" medical and mental health issues to the Probation Office. Because the BOP operates on a Care Level system (*see* Chapter 8) inaccurate clinical information may result in a disfavored placement (*e.g.*, farther from home) in the BOP's attempt to accommodate issues identified in the PSR. On the other hand, make every effort to substantiate a client's medical and/or mental health problems, including medication, and have that information reflected in and/or appended to the PSR. Whatever valid criticism of correctional health care may exist, the BOP cannot be faulted for failing to predict those problems from which a prisoner suffers if the information was available to but withheld from the Court.

- The BOP generally gives due consideration to judicial recommendations concerning placement and also programming. In order for such recommendations to carry the weight sought, however, they must be specific (*i.e.*, not just "close to home) and consistent with policy. A recommendation supported by a well-crafted rationale in support has far more weight than a generic recommendation of a particular facility. Specific, reasoned recommendations are especially important in these days of prison overcrowding. We have even found that where an offender is designated to a particular unfavorable facility, the designation can be changed with an amended Judgment or other court issuance with a well-founded statement in support of a redesigation.

- A judicial recommendation is *required* for the BOP to consider directly committing an otherwise qualified defendant to a halfway house, as it did historically. However, in keeping with the BOP changing the name of halfway houses from Community Corrections Centers to Residential Reentry Centers (RRCs) the mission of these intermittent confinement facilities has also changed. Placement priority for RRCs' limited bed space is given to prisoners with identified transitional need, usually meaning individuals needing halfway house services to help facilitate reintegration into the community at the conclusion of a sentence. Accordingly, while technically available, direct RRC placement is not a realistic option in most jurisdictions given the dearth of available beds. An alternate approach is to ask the court to forego a term of imprisonment (at a Federal Prison Camp) and instead sentence a defendant to probation or supervised release conditioned on halfway house placement. In this way, the BOP is removed from the process.

- A year and a day sentence results in an inmate serving approximately 47 days less than he would serve on a 12-month sentence, because the 12-month sentence does not provide for good conduct time (*see* 18 U.S.C. §3624(b)(1)).

- Generally, non-United States citizens are ineligible for Minimum-security (federal prison camp) placement and, in fact, are housed in contract facilities operated by private companies. However, if U.S. Immigration and Customs Enforcement (ICE) or the Executive Office for Immigration Review (EOIR) determine that deportation proceedings are unwarranted, or there is a finding not to deport at the completion of deportation proceedings, an otherwise qualified individual may be eligible for camp placement if otherwise qualified and assuming necessary documentation is timely provided to the BOP.

- Many clients face both federal and state charges and/or sentences. This is a very complex area fraught with landmines. Issues concerning time credits in such situations are typically highly fact-dependent. Because federal sentences are usually longer and confinement within the BOP is often seen as more desirable than state imprisonment, the presumptive preference for most clients is that the federal case control. In such instances, counsel should confirm what jurisdiction exercises primary custody over the client and, if it is the state, work to affect the client's transfer to primary federal custody (*e.g.*, bonding out on the state case; persuading state prosecutors to drop their case). Furthermore, *Sester v. United States*, 132 S.Ct. 1463 (2012), which recognizes a federal court's ability to order a federal sentence run concurrent with a yet-to-be-imposed state sentence (a scenario that would present where the state has primary custody and the state case does not resolve before the federal case), expands the opportunity for a federal sentence to capture time served in state custody. *See* 18 U.S.C. §§3584, 3585; Chapter 1.10.22. An excellent article discussing the interaction between federal and state sentences by former Bureau of Prisons' Northeast Regional Counsel Hank Sadowski is contained in the Bureau's Legal Resources Guide, www.bop.gov.

• The BOP treats unresolved charges as carrying a detainer, even when none has been lodged. This results in additional security points and possibly placement at a more secure institution, particularly for individuals who otherwise qualify for minimum-security placement. Accordingly, where a client is sentenced while in primary federal custody and has a state case that may resolve soon thereafter with a sentence of time served or better (*i.e.*, no additional term of imprisonment), counsel should ask the federal court to (1) hold the judgment in abeyance until after the state sentencing and (2) direct Probation to amend the PSR to reflect the state resolution before it sends the report electronically to the BOP via eDesignate. If the Court refuses such a request, counsel should obtain a certified copy of the state disposition and forward to the BOP, preferably via Probation and eDesignate, before the client's designation package is processed.

• Feedback the authors have received indicates that most judges, and the probation officers who advise them, are unaware that defendants sentenced to less than 27 months' imprisonment do not qualify for RDAP, regardless of the severity of their addictions. Courts cannot increase a defendant's sentence to facilitate RDAP participation. *See Tapia v. United States*, 131 S. Ct. 2382 (2011) (under 18 U.S.C. §3582(a), rehabilitation is not to be considered in terms of the need for or length of a term of imprisonment). They can, however, consider this conundrum relative to the propriety of imposing a non-guidelines sentence. Support for such an approach, at least by analogy, is found in the 2010 amendments to the *Guidelines Manual*, specifically Application Note 6 to Guideline §5C1.2. If anything, the unavailability of RDAP in this circumstance speaks to judges' need to structure sentences consistent with their statutory authority, for instance, through the imposition of a mitigated term of imprisonment (*e.g.*, one year and a day) followed by a term of supervised release conditioned on the completion of an inpatient treatment program. Another option in those districts with reentry/support courts is a mitigated term of imprisonment followed by admission into that community-based, court-supervised program. Such an approach has the added effect of shifting the cost burden to the offender.

• Inmates often say that 99% of lawyers don't know the first thing about the Bureau of Prisons and the 1% who do, are all doing time themselves. Understanding these practice tips will decrease the 99 percent number!

## ACKNOWLEDGMENTS

**Mark H. Allenbaugh** is a former staff attorney to the U.S. Sentencing Commission, and is currently an executive with Sentencing Stats, LLC (www.sentencingstats.com), a premier data analytical firm providing federal sentencing data and analyses to attorneys and their clients. He is a nationally recognized expert on federal sentencing law, policy, and practice.

(This page intentionally left blank.)

# CHAPTER 12

---

# THE MID-ATLANTIC REGION

(This page intentionally left blank.)

**Central Office**
Federal Bureau of Prisons
320 First St., NW
Washington, DC 20534
Phone: 202-307-3198

**Mid-Atlantic Regional Office**
Federal Bureau of Prisons
302 Sentinel Drive, Suite 200
Annapolis Junction, MD 20701
Phone: 301-317-3100

# §12:10  FPC ALDERSON

FPC Alderson
Federal Prison Camp
Glen Ray Rd., Box A
Alderson, WV 24910
ALD/ExecAssistant@bop.gov
304-445-3300
Fax: 304-445-3320

**Location:** The Town of Alderson is located in the foothills of the Allegheny Mountains in West Virginia, on both sides of the Greenbrier River. There are four other towns within commuting distance: Hinton, Lewisburg, Ronceverte, and White Sulphur Springs. Alderson is 270 miles southwest of Washington, D.C., 12 miles south of Interstate 64, off State Highway 3. The area is served by the Greenbrier Valley Airport in Lewisburg, West Virginia; Amtrak; and commercial bus lines.

**History:** Opened in 1927 as the Federal Reformatory for women, FPC Alderson was the first institution for female federal offenders. The inmate population represents all states and several foreign countries.

**Judicial District:** Southern West Virginia.

**Security Level:** Minimum-security facility housing female offenders.

**Population:** As of 6/07/2017, the FPC inmate population is 973. Weekly population figures are available on the BOP website (www.bp.gov) https://www.bop.gov/locations/institutions/ald/.

**Education:** GED, ESL, post-secondary (correspondence), continuing education, and college. Special classes are offered in high-interest areas and on an as-needed basis.

**Vocational/Apprenticeship:** FPC Alderson offers advanced apprenticeship education in air conditioning and refrigeration, cooking, electrical, plumbing, teaching assistance, cosmetology, and dog training. To be enrolled in the apprenticeship program, an inmate should have at least one year left in the institution, possess a high school diploma or GED certificate and have worked at least 60 days in the program for which the inmate is applying.

Employment opportunities include the following: food service, facilities department, business/office, health services unit, education, clothing room/laundry, unit(s).

The Federal Fire Department is the only all-female unit of its kind in the country. Select volunteers receive training and certification by the state.

**Library:** The electronic law library is open Sunday through Friday 9am-8:45pm, and Saturdays 12:45pm-8:45pm, except during count times. The law library is maintained by Central Office staff and updated accordingly. It is located on the second floor of the Recreation Center, along with the leisure library. Typewriters are available for legal use, and a copier is available at the cost of 10 cents per page, charged to an inmate's debit card. The leisure library is open 9am-3:30pm and 6pm-8:45pm Tuesday through Friday, and Sunday, and 12:45pm-3:35pm after and 4:15pm count to 8:45pm Saturday and holidays. The leisure library participates in an inter-library loan program with the local community library. Video and audio cassette players are also available in the leisure library. Magazines, newspapers, basic reference books, and video cassettes cannot be checked out or removed from the library.

**Counseling/Rehab Services:** The camp offers a 500-hour Residential Drug Abuse Program (RDAP). The RDAP program is voluntary, nine months long, and could result in a reduced sentence. In addition, the camp offers a non-residential drug treatment program and Alcoholics Anonymous, Narcotics Anonymous, Gamblers Anonymous, and numerous self-improvement groups. A trauma program for survivors of physical or sexual abuse is offered. Psychologists offer counseling services as needed and groups are offered periodically on topics such as depression and anxiety management. A contract psychiatrist is also available by appointment.

**Health Services:** Routine medical care and sick call sign-up is 6:45am-7am Mondays, Tuesdays, Thursdays and Fridays, excluding holidays. Physical examinations are provided upon arrival. For those under the age of 50, a physical exam will be provided every two years; however, inmates are eligible for a breast exam and a pap smear every year. For inmates 50 or older, a physical exam is provided annually. Anyone serving 18 months or less can submit a request for one dental cleaning. For those serving more than 18 months, a dental cleaning will be provided every 12 months. An eye care specialist is available for visual problems, but you must first submit an Inmate Request to Staff form for an evaluation. Pill times are posted outside of the Health Services Unit.

**Fitness/Recreation:** The recreation center is open Sunday through Friday 6:30am-8:45pm and Saturday 12:45pm-8:45pm. Hours are subject to change during staff vacations. Activities include arts and crafts, aerobics, Pilates, Sweating to the Oldies, fusion, low impact spinning, indoor and outdoor volleyball, pool, basketball, ping pong, jogging, brisk walking, softball, roller skating, table games, bingo, bocce ball, game shows, progressive relaxation, talent shows, and the Yarn Project. Intramural team sports include basketball, softball, and volleyball.

**Religious Services:** The camp has one full-time chaplain and an on-site religious library. Religious programming includes worship, prayer, and study of various religions, as well as counseling and spiritual guidance. The Chapel is located on the first floor of the recreation center. The Outside Worship Grounds are located in the yard behind the recreation center.

**Housing:** The housing units consist of dormitories. Inmates may be housed either individually or in two-person rooms. There is one television room per unit, open Sunday through Thursday 6am-11pm, and Friday and Saturday 6am-2am. Inmates decide programming.

**Telephone Policy:** Inmates can talk on the telephone for up to 300 minutes per month using the have the Inmate Telephone System (ITS). Telephones are located in each housing unit for inmate use. Calls are limited to 15 minutes, with a one hour waiting period until the next call can be made. This system allows inmates to call up to thirty approved numbers. Phone time is purchased from the commissary by transfer of funds to the inmate's individual telephone account.

**Inmate Mail:** The institution accepts mail from the U.S. Postal Service via First Class, U.S. Priority, and Express mail. For those interested in sending overnight mail via a private carrier (FedEx or UPS Overnight), it is recommended that you first contact the institution to find out whether the receipt of such mail is permitted. Inmates may receive publications without prior approval, although the warden will reject publications that are determined to be detrimental to the security, good order or discipline of the institution, or if it might facilitate criminal activity. Inmates may accumulate up to five magazines, five books, and two newspapers. All hardcover books and newspapers must come directly from the publisher.

**Inmate Mail to FPC:**
        INMATE NAME & REGISTER NUMBER
        FPC Alderson
        Federal Prison Camp
        Glen Ray Rd., Box A
        Alderson, WV 24910

**Visiting Hours:** Visiting hours are 8:15am-3:15pm on Mondays, Saturdays, Sundays and holidays. Visiting hours on Fridays are 11:15am-6:30pm. All inmates will be allowed a minimum of four hours visiting time per month. The warden may limit the length or frequency of visits to avoid overcrowding.

There will be a limit of four visitors per inmate at one time (not including children) in the visiting room unless prior approval is received from the unit manager for regular visiting days, and from the associate warden on holidays.

Visits by attorneys are not subject to auditory supervision. Normally, attorney-client visits will be conducted in the visiting room. Additional visiting information can be found at https://www.bop.gov/locations/institutions/ald/.

**Lodging/Accommodations:** Should visitors be spending the night, the following is a short list of accommodations that are available in the Alderson area:

| | |
|---|---|
| Country Inn & Suites | 304-252-5100 |
| Hampton Inn Lewisburg | 304-645-7300 |
| Quality Inn Lewisburg | 304-645-7722 |

**Directions to Facility:** From the East (New York, Washington, D.C., etc.): Follow I-64 to Alta Exchange seven miles West of Lewisburg, WV. Exit #161, turn South (left) onto Route 12 to Alderson, West Virginia.

## §12:11   FCI ASHLAND

FCI Ashland
Federal Correctional Institution
St. Route 716
Ashland, KY 41105
ASH/ExecAssistant@bop.gov
606-928-6414
Fax: 606-929-4395

**Location:** The facility is located in the highlands of northeastern Kentucky, 125 miles east of Lexington and five miles southwest of Ashland.

**History:** Opened in 1940, FCI Ashland houses male prisoners with sentences ranging from six months to life. The camp opened in 1990, and employs camp inmates in maintenance positions in support of the main institution.

**Judicial District:** Eastern Kentucky.

**Security Level:** The Federal Correctional Institution (FCI) Ashland is a low-security institution housing male inmates with a satellite camp that houses minimum-security inmates.

**Population:** As of 6/07/2017, the FCI inmate population is 1,017, and the camp population is 229. Weekly population figures are available on the BOP website at https://www.bop.gov/locations/institutions/ash/www.bop.gov.

**Education:** The FCI and the camp offer GED, ESL, adult continuing education course, and post-secondary through correspondence courses, including college level classes through Ashland Community College.

**Vocational/Apprenticeship:** FCI Ashland offers advanced occupational education in business technology, and computer applications. It offers vocational training in autobody helper, autobody man, autobody painter, and welding. Apprenticeship programs are available for baker, cook, electrician and combination welder. Work assignments include plumbing, painting, masonry, cooking, baking and other food service related jobs.

**Library:** Legal materials and books are available in the law library. The FCI law library is open during school hours and during the evenings Monday through Thursday 4:30pm-8pm, and Saturday 7am-3:30pm. A copy machine is available to reproduce materials needed for research. Inmates are afforded access to legal materials and an opportunity to prepare legal documents in the Electronic Law Library. A wide variety of paperbacks, magazines, newspapers, and reference books are available in the leisure library. The camp's leisure and legal library is open 7am-9pm, seven days a week, with typewriters available for legal use during that time. An inter-library loan program is available with the Boyd County Public Library.

**UNICOR:** FCI and camp inmates and staff employees manufacture office furniture for sale to United States government agencies. Factory sections include Quality Assurance, Business Office, and Warehouse, providing skills in accounting, clerical positions, and quality control. The camp provides clerks and laborers for the warehouse.

**Counseling/Rehab Services:** Ashland offers non-residential drug treatment and programming to inmates. This consists of a 40-hour drug education class as well as groups on Relapse Prevention, Breaking Barriers, 12-Step Study Group, Narcotics Anonymous, Alcoholics Anonymous, and Criminal Thinking. The Psychology Services Department has three full-time psychologists and one drug abuse treatment specialist providing numerous services for inmates at the FCI and camp, including evaluations, crisis intervention, educational groups, individual therapy and chronic care clinics. Crisis counseling, coping skills, suicide prevention, mental health counseling, and spiritual counseling are all available from a psychologist or chaplain.

**Health Services:** Routine medical care and non-emergency sick call is conducted Monday through Friday, excluding holidays. A sick call request form is obtained from the unit officer, and must be completed and brought to the Health Services Unit before 6:30am, Monday through Friday. The Pill Line schedule for the FCI is daily at 6:45am, 9:05am for designated inmates, and 7:05pm. The Pill Line schedule for the camp is Monday through Friday, 7am and 6pm, and Saturday, Sunday, and holidays 8:30am and 6pm.

**Fitness/Recreation:** Schedules for athletic and competitive activities at the FCI are widely posted and are included in the monthly activities calendar. The recreation building at the camp contains three pool tables, cable television, and exercise equipment. The camp's recreation building is open seven days per week 6am-9pm.

**Religious Services:** There are usually three full-time chaplains, including one for the camp. All faiths are represented in the chapel and the schedule of activities is widely posted. Inmates may confirm and coordinate religious dietary accommodations with a chaplain.

**Housing:** The FCI houses inmates in two-person cells, two-person dorms, and two-person cubicles. The FCI also has one unit of single-person rooms available. Some of the units are wheelchair accessible. There is one television room per unit. A television committee of inmates decides television programming on a majority-vote basis. The camp consists of two-person dormitory-style cubicles.

**Commissary:** The FCI commissary schedule is posted on inmate bulletin boards. The camp commissary is only open Tuesdays and Wednesdays, 6:15am-3:30pm. An inmate's purchase is based on his unit, i.e. "Appy Unit" inmates shop one day and "Blue Unit" inmates shop the other day. Each inmate is allowed to shop once a week. Bureau of Prisons policy currently sets a monthly commissary spending limit of $360.

**Telephone Policy:** Phone calls must be paid for by the inmate or they may call collect. Telephones are available at the FCI daily from 6am-11:30am, except for the following periods Monday through Friday, excluding holidays: 7am-after 10:30am; and 12:30pm-after 4pm count. The telephone room at the camp is located in Building 300 and is open daily 6:30am-11pm. Phone calls are limited to 15 minutes and are monitored by staff.

**Inmate Mail:** The institution accepts mail from the U.S. Postal Service via First Class, U.S. Priority, and Express mail. For those interested in sending overnight mail via a private carrier (FedEx or UPS Overnight), it is recommended that you first contact the institution to find out whether the receipt of such mail is permitted. Inmates may receive publications without prior approval, although the warden will reject publications that are determined to be detrimental to the security, good order or discipline of the institution or that promote criminal activity. Magazines and paperback books may come from any source, but all hardcover books and newspapers must come directly from the publisher.

**Inmate Mail to FCI:**
    INMATE NAME & REGISTER NUMBER
    FCI Ashland
    Federal Correctional Institution
    P.O. Box 6001
    Ashland, KY 41105

**Inmate Mail to Camp:**
    INMATE NAME & REGISTER NUMBER
    FCI Ashland
    Satellite Camp
    P.O. Box 6000
    Ashland, KY 41105

**Visiting Hours: Notice:** *as of june 2017, visitation on Thursdays has been suspended indefinitely. This policy may have changed by the time you read this entry.* Social visits at the Federal Correctional Institution are permitted 8am-3pm, Friday through Monday, including all federal holidays, with no visiting on Tuesday and Wednesday. Social visits at the camp are permitted 8am-3pm, Saturday, Sunday, and all federal holidays. The maximum number of persons who may visit an inmate at any one time is six, with a limit of four adult visitors. A point system will be utilized at the FCI, with each inmate receiving ten points per month. A weekday visit will count as one point and weekend or holiday visits will count as three points. A point system will also be utilized at the camp, with each inmate receiving ten points per month. The first visit of the month will count as five points and any visit thereafter, including federal holidays, will count as one point. Attorney visits will be scheduled through the respective unit manager. Unit teams will be responsible for the supervision of these visits. All attorneys will be required to complete ATTACHMENT A, Attorney-Client Visit, prior to the visit. Additional visiting information can be found at https://www.bop.gov/locations/institutions/ash/.

**Lodging/Accommodations:** Should visitors be spending the night, the following is a short list of accommodations available in the Ashland, Kentucky area:

| | |
|---|---|
| Ashland Plaza Hotel | 606-329-0055 |
| Fairfield Inn and Suites | 606-928-1222 |
| Hampton Inn | 606-928-2888 |
| Days Inn | 606-928-3600 |
| Knights Inn | 606-928-9501 |

**Directions to Facility:** From Ohio: After crossing the bridge into Ashland, you will be on 12th Street. Follow 12th Street for six blocks until it merges with 13th Street, which is U.S. 60 West. Continue west on U.S. 60 (13th Street) until you leave the city. Approximately three miles out of town you will see the Kentucky State Police Barracks on the right and at the intersection of U.S. 60 and KY 716. Other landmarks include a SuperAmerica Station and a McDonald's Restaurant. Turn right on KY 716 and go about 3/4 mile to a four-way stop. Turn right. You will see the institution. Make the first left into the parking lot.

From West Virginia: Follow I-64 West to Exit 185 (Canonsburg, KY 180). Turn left at the end of the exit and proceed approximately 5.5 miles (seven traffic lights from the interstate). At the seventh traffic light, turn left at the intersection of U.S. 60 and KY 716. Landmarks at that intersection include the Kentucky State Police Barracks, a SuperAmerica Station and a McDonald's Restaurant. Turn left on KY 716 and go about 3/4 mile to a four-way stop. Turn right. You will see the institution. Make the first left into the parking lot.

## §12:12   FCI BECKLEY

FCI Beckley
Federal Correctional Institution
1600 Industrial Road
Beaver, WV 25813
BEC/ExecAssistant@bop.gov
304-252-9758
Fax: 304-256-4956

**Location:** FCI Beckley is located in Raleigh County, West Virginia, approximately 51 miles southeast of Charleston, and 136 miles northwest of Roanoke, Virginia.

**History:** The FCI and the satellite camp opened in 1995.

**Judicial District:** Southern West Virginia.

**Security Level:** FCI Beckley is a medium-security facility housing male inmates. An adjacent satellite camp houses minimum-security inmates.

**Population:** As of 6/08/2017, the FCI inmate population is 1,492, and the camp population is 292. Weekly population figures are available on the BOP website at https://www.bop.gov/locations/institutions/bec/.

**Education:** Both the FCI and the camp offer GED, ESL, Vocational, Adult Continuing Education (ACE) and Post-Secondary activities. ACE classes offered are inmate-taught and last ten weeks. Parenting classes include child development, child health, child safety, and abusive relationships. Inmates may also take correspondence courses, provided by New River Community and Technical College, with the approval of the education supervisor. Inmates may also enroll in correspondence courses from other colleges at their own expense.

**Vocational/Apprenticeship:** FCI Beckley offers a one-year certificate in business. Vocational/occupational training is offered in a number of fields, including blueprints, carpentry, computer applications, electrical work, and masonry. Apprenticeship programs are offered in carpentry and electrical and work. Computers and small engine repair are also offered at the camp.

**Library:** The law library is located in the Education Department, and contains a variety of legal reference materials for use in preparing legal papers. Reference materials include the United States Code Annotated, Federal Reporter, Supreme Court Reporter, Bureau of Prisons Program Statements, Institution Supplements, Indexes, and other legal materials; the law library is open during non-working hours, including weekends. An inmate law library clerk is available for assistance in legal research. The video library, located in the Recreation Department, has educational videos, magazines, literature, and other wellness and leisure reading materials available for inmates to check out. An Inter-Library Loan program is available to request books which are not available in the institution library.

**UNICOR:** An ergonomic chair factory employs approximately 200 inmates. Inmates must sign up on the waiting list if employment is desired.

**Counseling/Rehab Services:** There are many alternatives for inmates who have personal problems and would like to correct them. These options include informal counseling sessions, formal group counseling, Alcoholic Anonymous, self-image groups, and other voluntary groups. Inmate participation in these activities will be encouraged upon the staff's assessment of inmate needs, but participation in such activities is voluntary. Psychology Services includes psychologists, treatment specialists, and a psychology technician under the direction of the chief psychologist. Each unit has a psychologist assigned or available to it to provide counseling and other mental health services to unit inmates. Psychology Services offers a wide range of group educational programs including stress management, anger management and smoking cessation, as well as other such programs. In addition to these programs, a variety of services are available with respect to drug treatment, such as drug education, non-residential treatment and a 500-hour Residential Drug Abuse Program (RDAP).

Psychology Services provides services in two other significant areas. The BRAVE Program is a 6-month residential self-improvement program for young offenders serving lengthy terms of incarceration. Inmates 32 years of age or younger with sentences of 60 months or more may volunteer for program participation. A contract psychiatrist is available for regular consultation for those needing medications or medication monitoring. Access to these services occurs either by consulting Health Services or Psychology Services staff.

**Health Services:** Inmates who wish to be seen for routine evaluation of medical problems are required to report to the Health Services Department during the morning sick-call move on Monday, Tuesday, Thursday, and Friday (except for holidays) to request an appointment. A medical staff member also tours each housing unit at least once a day. Inmates are eligible for a complete physical every three years if under 50 years of age, and a complete physical and EKG every year for inmates over 50 years of age. Medical staff is available 24 hours a day, seven days a week. The pill line schedule for the FCI is 7am-7:15am every day, including holidays, 3pm-3:30pm for daily medications, refills, and prescriptions, after 4pm count for insulin only, and at Institution Recall for restricted medications only. The camp sick call is from 6:30-6:45am (Monday, Tuesday, Thursday, and Friday) at Camp Health Services.

**Housing:** The FCI houses inmates in two-man cells. There are approximately four television rooms per unit. Limited cable television is available. Unit televisions may be viewed during established off-duty hours. Only the Unit Officer can change the channel on the televisions. The camp houses inmates in "open bay" dormitories, which consist of two-man cubicles.

**Fitness/Recreation:** Leisure activities and recreation programs are supervised by the Education Department. These programs include indoor and outdoor activities, and range from individualized arts and crafts programs to intramural team sports such as softball, basketball, soccer, volleyball and football. Fitness and wellness programs (including Yoga, Calisthenics, and Aerobics) are also available. Musical instruments are available in the recreation area and must remain there.

**Religious Services:** Religious Services provides pastoral care, counseling, and a variety of religious programs to assist in one's spiritual formation. There are regularly scheduled services, special programs, high holy days, and periodic guest speakers who speak on a variety of faith issues. The Religious Meal program is available for inmates after the chaplain verifies the need.

**Commissary:** The commissary is open Monday through Thursday 4pm-7pm. Shopping days are rotated according to an inmate's unit. Inmates are allowed to spend up to $340 each month for purchases. The commissary access time for inmates in each unit is scheduled on a rotating basis, and the schedule is posted in the unit and on the commissary item sheet.

**Telephone Policy:** FCI/FPC Beckley has the Inmate Telephone System (ITS). It allows inmates to call up to thirty approved numbers. In order to use the system, inmates must to transfer funds from their commissary account to their individual telephone account. There are telephones located in each housing unit for use. Collect calls can also be made to approved telephone numbers. Forms for updating telephone numbers may be obtained from the unit counselor. All calls are automatically terminated after 15 minutes, and there is a one-hour waiting period between calls. Each inmate is allowed 300 telephone minutes per month. Changes to a phone list may be made up to three times each month by submitting a request through the unit counselor at any time.

**Inmate Mail:** The institution accepts mail from the U.S. Postal Service via First Class, U.S. Priority, and Express mail. For those interested in sending overnight mail via a private carrier (FedEx or UPS Overnight), it is recommended that you first contact the institution to find out whether the receipt of such mail is permitted. Inmates may receive publications without prior approval, although the warden will reject publications that are determined to be detrimental to the security, good order or discipline of the institution. Inmates may accumulate up to five magazines and two newspapers. All publications must come directly from the publisher, bookstore or book club.

**Inmate Mail to FCI:**
INMATE NAME & REGISTER NUMBER
FCI Beckley
Federal Correctional Institution
P.O. Box 350
Beaver, WV 25813

**Inmate Mail to Camp:**
INMATE NAME & REGISTER NUMBER
FCI Beckley
Federal Correctional Institution
Satellite Camp
P.O. Box 350
Beaver, WV 25813

**Visiting Hours:** Social visits to the FCI and camp are 8am-3pm on Saturday, Sunday, Monday, and federal holidays. Inmates will be allowed a maximum of five visitors at one time (including children). Exceptions will be requested through the unit manager. Staff will maintain a record of all inmate visits through the use of a point system. Each inmate is allotted eight visiting points per month. One point will be assessed for each visit during the weekdays. Two points will be assessed for each visit on the weekends and federal holidays. At the Camp, the point system will not be used unless the visiting volume dictates that it be implemented. Legal visits at the FCI and camp can be scheduled during normal social visiting hours. Additional visiting information can be found on the BOP website, https://www.bop.gov/locations/institutions/bec/.

**Lodging/Accommodations:** Should visitors be spending the night, the following is a short list of accommodations in the Beckley area:

| | |
|---|---|
| Fairfield Inn by Marriott | 304-252-8661 |
| Hampton Inn | 304-252-2121 |
| Best Western Hotel | 304-252-0671 |
| Comfort Inn | 304-255-5291 |
| Sleep Inn | 304-255-4222 |
| Super 8 Motel Beckley | 304-250-4371 |

## §12:13   USP BIG SANDY

USP Big Sandy
U.S. Penitentiary
1197 Airport Road
Inez, KY 41224
BSY/ExecAssistant@bop.gov
606-433-2400
Fax: 606-433-2577

**Location:** USP Big Sandy is located in eastern Kentucky approximately 133 miles from Frankfort, 140 miles from Lexington, and 321 miles from Washington, D.C.

**Judicial District:** Eastern Kentucky.

**Security Level:** The United States Penitentiary (USP) Big Sandy, located in Inez, Kentucky, is a high-security facility housing male inmates. An adjacent minimum-security satellite prison camp houses male inmates.

**Population:** As of 6/08/2017, the USP inmate population is 1,242, and the camp population is 79. Weekly population figures are available on the BOP website at https://www.bop.gov/locations/institutions/bsy/.

**Education:** The institution offers GED, adult continuing education, some college courses, vocational training and parenting classes.

**Vocational/Apprenticeship:** USP main facility trains and employs inmates in maintenance projects as needed by the Facilities Department. Areas include plumbing, construction, and electrical work. No apprenticeship programs are offered.

**UNICOR:** A textile factory at the USP employs inmates in three departments. Inmates may work in production, business, or quality assurance.

**Counseling/Rehab Services:** Crisis intervention services are available for inmates on an as-needed basis. Psychiatric treatment is available for inmates who need psychotropic medication for the management of psychotic problems. The USP houses a self-help library with books and tapes relating to mental health concerns. Drug abuse treatment services includes drug education, non-residential substance abuse treatment, and residential substance abuse treatment. The Challenge Program is a voluntary, residential program that offers motivated inmates the opportunity and resources to adopt pro-social values and a pro-social lifestyle. All Challenge inmates will reside on the Challenge Unit and will attend classes in anger management, criminal thinking, stress management, impact of crime on victims, values and more.

**Health Services:** Both the USP and camp provide full primary health care including diagnosis, education, treatment, and counseling. Sick call hours Monday, Tuesday, Thursday, and Friday, at the time dedicated for an inmate's particular unit to move. Sick call for the camp is held on the same mornings as the USP. In case of emergency, an inmate must first contact their supervising officer. Pill line hours are: beginning at 6am. (running until the last unit is called for the morning meal) and 8pm. All inmates under the age of 50 are allowed, upon written request to the Health Services department, to have a physical examination every three years. All inmates over the age of 50 are permitted, upon written request to the Health Services Department, to have a physical examination once a year.

**Fitness/Recreation:** Physical exercise is allowed in activity rooms at specified times and in the inmate's own assigned cell. Table games or other forms of passive recreation may be conducted in the activity rooms or designated area. All activity ceases at 9:45pm. Recreation times, gym hours, hobby crafts available, and all other matters concerning recreation in the facility's the Education and Recreation Handbook.

**Religious Services:** There is a wide range of religious programs for inmates. Chaplains of various faiths are available for pastoral care, counseling, or other professional services. Volunteers are also available. A current copy of the Religious Services schedule will be posted in the Chapel area, as well as in the housing units. A large number of religious books, audiotapes, and videotapes are available for group or personal use.

**Telephone Policy:** All telephone calls will be made at the inmate's expense through the use of his commissary account in order to utilize the Inmate Telephone System (ITS II). A collect call system is available and still will require the use of the inmate's personal PAC number. Third-party and credit card calls are not permitted at any time. All calls are limited to 15 minutes with a 30minute waiting period in-between calls. Telephones may be used from 6am-9:15pm daily.

**Inmate Mail:** The institution accepts mail from the U.S. Postal Service via First Class, U.S. Priority, and Express mail. For those interested in sending overnight mail via a private carrier (FedEx or UPS Overnight), it is recommended that you first contact the institution to find out whether the receipt of such mail is permitted. Inmates are permitted only five books, five magazines, and five newspapers in their possession at any given time. All books, magazines and newspapers must come directly from the publisher or the bookstore.

**Inmate Mail to USP:**
INMATE NAME & REGISTER NUMBER
USP Big Sandy
U.S. Penitentiary
P.O. Box 2068
Inez, KY 41224

**Inmate Mail to Satellite Camp:**
INMATE NAME & REGISTER NUMBER
USP Big Sandy
U.S. Penitentiary
Satellite Camp
P.O. Box 2068
Inez, KY 41224

**Visiting Hours:** For general population inmates: Saturday, Sunday, and holidays 8:30am-3pm. At both the USP and camp, visiting is open to inmates on a point system, with each inmate being afforded 10 points per month. Each visit during the month will count as one point. If an inmate leaves the visiting room after a visit is completed and returns later in the day for another visit, the inmate will be charged two points for the day. Attorneys, paralegals, legal assistants, and mental health professionals performing court-ordered examinations will contact the executive assistant, who will notify the appropriate unit team. These visitors will receive priority when processing. Every effort should be made to schedule the visit during normal visiting hours. Additional visiting information can be found on the BOP website, https://www.bop.gov/locations/institutions/bsy/.

**Lodging/Accommodations:** Should visitors be spending the night, the following is a short list of accommodations near Inez, Kentucky:

| | |
|---|---|
| Best Western Village Inn | 606-638-9417 |
| Brookshire Inn | 606-298-7800 |
| Days Inn Paintsville | 606-789-3551 |
| Ramada Inn Paintsville | 606-789-4242 |
| Super 8 Motel Louisa | 606-638-7888 |

## §12:14   FCI BUTNER—LOW

FCI Butner Low
Federal Correctional Institution
Old NC Hwy 75
Butner, NC 27509
BUF/ExecAssistant@bop.gov
919-575-5000
Fax: 919-575-5023

**Location:** FCI Butner Low is located near the Research Triangle area of Durham, Raleigh, and Chapel Hill, five miles off I85 on Old Highway 75. The area is served by Raleigh-Durham International Airport, Amtrak, and commercial bus lines.

**History:** Opened in 1995.

**Judicial District:** Eastern North Carolina.

**Security Level:** FCI Low is part of the Butner Federal Correctional Complex and houses low-security male inmates. It includes a satellite camp.

**Population:** As of 6/08/2017, the FCI Low inmate population is 1,314. Weekly population figures are available on the BOP website at https://www.bop.gov/locations/institutions/buf/.

**Education:** The institution offers GED, ESL, adult education (commercial driver's license, math, history, science, personal development, and general interest), basic skills enhancement, special needs learning, life skills, parenting skills classes, and college correspondence courses.

**Vocational/Apprenticeship:** FCI Butner has the Meineke Vocational Trades program and a 3-4 month HVAC certificate program. UNICOR sponsors an industrial sewing class for inmates who wish to work in the UNICOR textile factory.

**Library:** The law library is open 7:30am-10:30am, 12:30pm-3:30pm, and 5:30-8:30pm Monday through Thursday; 7:30am-10:30am and 12:30pm-2:30pm on Friday; 7:30am-3:30pm on Saturday; closed Sundays and holidays. Several electric typewriters are available, and inmates must purchase their own typewriter ribbon at the Commissary. The law library was converted to the electronic version in TRULINICS in 2011. An inmate law clerk is available for assistance in obtaining needed resource material. Reference and legal materials cannot be checked out and must be used in the law library only. Copier services are available by purchasing a copy card in the Commissary for $5.20, with 50 copies per card. The leisure library has an inter-library loan program. The leisure library offers a wide selection of recreational reading, magazines, periodicals, and reference books.

**UNICOR:** The UNICOR at FCI Butner Low consists of a textile factory, which manufactures utility shirts and dress shirts for the U.S. military, and a CAPS (Combined Accounts Payable) data-entry section. The UNICOR factory has a priority and regular waiting list.

**Counseling/Rehab Services:** The institution offers a non-residential drug treatment program, a drug education program, Alcoholics Anonymous and Narcotics Anonymous groups, self-image groups, and other voluntary groups. Psychologists are available for individual and/or group psychotherapy. The psychology department is staffed by three full-time psychologists. The facility also has a fully staffed Mental Health Hospital with full time psychiatrists.

**Health Services:** The institution provides outpatient care. The pill line is open to the general population on weekdays from 6:30am-6:45am (insulin line only), 6:45am-7:15am, 11:30am-12noon, 4:30pm-4:45pm (insulin line only), and 7:30pm-8pm. On weekends and holidays, pill line is available from 7am-7:15am (insulin line only), and 7:45am-8am. Routine medical or dental sick call is available from 6:45am-7:15am, Monday, Tuesday, Thursday and Friday. At least one physician's assistant is on duty or on call 24 hours per day. A medical staff member is on duty seven days a week from 6am-10pm.

**Housing:** The institution is comprised of four housing units (named Durham, Granville, Vance, and Wake). There are two sides to each housing unit (an "A side" and a "B side"), each of which house up to 170 inmates. Most of the inmates are placed in three-man cubicles, with a few placed in two-man cubicles. Each side has two TV rooms: a larger TV room with five televisions for general/sports programming, and a smaller TV room for Spanish-language shows.

**Fitness/Recreation:** The recreation department is open every day from 6am-8:30pm. The recreation department offers intramural team sports, aerobics, exercise bicycles, five racquetball courts, musical instruments, pool tables, piano rooms, card/table games, bingo, ping-pong tables and a music listening room with CDs. The hobby craft center offers dedicated rooms for painting and ceramics, and materials for knitting and drawing, which can be done in inmates' units or the recreation area. Musical Instruments are also available in the recreation area.

**Religious Services:** The FCI and camp offer a wide range of religious programs to inmates. Staff chaplains of specific faiths are available, as well as contract and volunteer representatives of other faiths. The institution is staffed by two full-time chaplains. Contract rabbi and imam religious services are available. A sweat lodge is provided for Native-American services. A community of contract volunteers provides services for most faiths.

**Commissary:** The commissary is open Monday through Thursday, 12:45pm-2:30pm and 4:45pm-7:30pm. Inmates are allowed to shop once per week. All sales are final. The commissary access time for inmates is scheduled on a rotating basis. Bureau of Prisons policy currently sets a monthly commissary spending limit of $360.

**Telephone:** Inmates may either call collect or dial direct using the Inmate Telephone System (ITS). The telephones are in operation from 6am-11:55pm each day, except Fridays and Saturdays when they are open until 2am. Telephones are available in each unit for inmate use. Each inmate is allowed 30 telephone numbers to call through the approval of his Unit Counselor. Additions or deletions to the list may be submitted 3 times per month. Inmate Telephone Request Forms (to add or change numbers) are normally processed within five days.

**Inmate Mail:** The institution accepts mail from the U.S. Postal Service via First Class, U.S. Priority, and Express mail. For those interested in sending overnight mail via a private carrier (FedEx or UPS Overnight), it is recommended you contact the institution to find out whether the receipt of such mail is permitted.

**Inmate Mail to FCI:**
INMATE NAME & REGISTER NUMBER
FCI Butner Low
Federal Correctional Institution
P.O. Box 999
Butner, NC 27509

**Inmate Mail to Satellite Camp:**
INMATE NAME & REGISTER NUMBER
FCI Butner Low
Federal Correctional Institution
Satellite Camp
P.O. Box 1000
Butner, NC 27509

**Visiting Hours:** Thursday and Friday, 2:30pm-8pm; Saturday, Sunday, and all federal holidays, 8:30am-3pm, Monday, 11am-3pm. Inmates are allotted 12 visiting points per calendar month. The points used shall be dependent upon which day the visit occurs. Visits that occur on weekdays are counted as one point, and visits that occur on weekends and holidays will count as two points. Five adults are allowed to visit an inmate at one time (an adult is considered 16 years of age and above). No limit is set for children less than 16 years of age.

Inmates may submit requests for special visits to their unit team. Additional visiting information can be found at https://www.bop.gov/locations/institutions/buf/.

**Lodging/Accommodations:** The following is a short list of accommodations near Butner, North Carolina:

| | |
|---|---|
| Carolina Inn Chapel Hill | 919-933-2001 |
| Comfort Inn Research Triangle Park | 919-361-2656 |
| Radisson Research Triangle Park | 919-549-8631 |
| Sheraton Chapel Hill | 919-968-4900 |
| Econo Lodge Creedmoor | 919-575-6451 |

**Directions to Facility:** <u>From Raleigh:</u> U.S. 70 West to U.S. 70 bypass. Take the bypass for 2.1 miles to Geer Street exit 185 North sign. Turn right on Geer Street and proceed 1.7 miles to Club Boulevard. Turn left on Club Boulevard and proceed .3 miles to the I-85 ramp. Take I-85 North nine miles to exit 189. Turn left on Central Avenue. Proceed straight on Central Avenue to Veazey Street. Turn right onto Veazey Street. Proceed to stop sign and turn left onto Old Highway 75. Continue one mile. FCI Butner is on right.

<u>From Durham:</u> Take I-85 north to exit 189. Turn left onto Central Avenue. Proceed straight on Central Avenue to Veazey Street. Proceed to stop sign and turn left onto Old Highway 75. Continue one mile. FCI Butner is on right.

## §12:15   FCI BUTNER—MEDIUM I

FCI Butner Medium I
Federal Correctional Institution
Old NC Hwy 75
Butner, NC 27509

BUF/ExecAssistant@bop.gov
919-575-4541
Fax: 919-575-5023

**Location:** FCI Butner Medium I is located near the Research Triangle of Durham, Raleigh, and Chapel Hill, five miles off I-85 on Old Highway 75. The area is served by Raleigh-Durham International Airport. Amtrak, and commercial bus lines.

**History:** Opened in 1976, FCI Butner Medium functions as an inpatient psychiatric hospital and medium-security facility for inmates serving varied and complex sentences. Inmates are primarily from the southeast with ages ranging from 18-71 years.

**Judicial District:** Eastern North Carolina.

**Security Level:** FCI Medium I is part of the Butner Federal Correctional Complex. FCI houses medium-security male inmates and also has an adjacent satellite camp that houses minimum-security male inmates.

**Population:** As of 6/08/2017, the FCI Medium inmate population is 699 and the camp population is 321. Weekly population figures are available on the BOP website at https://www.bop.gov/locations/institutions/but/.

**Education:** The institution offers GED, ESL, adult education, and college-level courses using contract teachers from nearby colleges.

**Library:** The law library is located in the Education department and open during convenient hours, including weekends and holidays. An inmate law library clerk is available for assistance in locating material. Electric typewriters are available to inmates for the preparation of legal documents. Inmates must purchase their own typewriter ribbon. A copier is available. The leisure library does not have an inter-library loan program.

**UNICOR:** A textile factory, which manufactures utility shirts and dress shirts for the U.S. military, employs approximately 431 inmates. An industrial products factory employs 64 inmates. Both have a "priority and a regular" waiting list averages around 20-40 inmates, while the "regular" waiting list.

**Counseling/Rehab Services:** The institution offers a Sex Offender Treatment Program and a 500-hour Residential Drug Abuse Program (RDAP). The Residential Drug Abuse Program is nine months in length. In addition, the institution offers a non-residential drug treatment program, a drug education program, Alcoholics Anonymous, self-image groups and other voluntary groups. Each newly committed inmate whose offense is directly attributable to drugs or alcohol abuse will be required to attend the 40-hour Drug Education Program. The psychology and psychiatric program units each have an assigned psychologist. The institution also has a fully staffed mental health hospital with full time psychiatrists who are medical doctors and can be seen by appointment after referral by a psychologist. Psychologists are available for individual and/or group psychotherapy.

The sex offender program, which began in 1990 and houses low-, medium-, and high-security inmates, consists of group therapy sessions and individual counseling. It is an intensive 24-bed residential program for male sexual offenders.

**Health Services:** The institution provides outpatient care. Sick call sign up for the FCI is from 6:30am-7am on Monday, Tuesday, Thursday, and Friday. The inpatient pill line is open to the general population weekdays from 7am-7:30am, 11:30am-last meal call, and 7:30pm-8pm, and on weekends and holidays from 7am-7:30am, 12noon-12:30pm, and 7:30pm-8pm. At least one physician assistant is available 24 hours per day. Sick call line for the camp is 7:15am-7:45am. The camp pill line is open weekdays from 6:45am-7:15am, 11:45am-noon, and 7:30pm-8pm, and on weekends and holidays from 7:15am-7:45am, 11:00am-11:30am and 7pm-7:30pm. Physical examinations are available for inmates under the age of 50 every three years, and every year for those over 50. Medical staff members are on duty or on call 24 hours a day.

**Housing:** The institution is comprised of eight housing units. Three of the units are reserved for mental health inmates. The units house inmates in two-man dorms. The units are wheelchair accessible. There are approximately six television rooms per unit (or three TV rooms each per sides A and B). Spanish, sports, and general viewing television rooms are available. Videos are rented on the weekends.

**Fitness/Recreation:** The recreation department offers team sports, exercise bicycles, stairmasters, physical fitness, weight reduction, stress reduction, pool tables, and ping-pong tables. The hobby craft center offers painting, leather craft, and art; completed projects may be mailed home. Musical instruments are available in the recreation area.

**Religious Services:** The institution is staffed by three full-time chaplains. Contract rabbi services are available. A community of volunteers provides services for most faiths. Special religious diets, holiday observances, and other worship activities are coordinated through the Chaplain's Office.

**Commissary:** The commissary access time is scheduled on a rotating basis; the schedule is posted in the units. Bureau of Prisons policy currently sets a monthly commissary spending limit of $360.

**Telephone Policy:** Inmates dial direct using the Inmate Telephone System (ITS). It allows you to call up to thirty approved Inmate Telephone Services (ITS) credits can be transferred from your commissary account after 4:30pm daily. Inmates can have 30 telephone numbers on their phone list and can update their lists once per month. Each inmate gets 300 calling minutes per month. Hours of telephone operation are normally 6am-11:30pm.

**Inmate Mail:** The institution accepts mail from the U.S. Postal Service via first Class, U.S. Priority, and Express mail. For those interested in sending overnight mail via a private carrier (FedEx or UPS Overnight), it is recommended that you first contact the institution to find out whether the receipt of such mail is permitted.

**Inmate Mail to FCI:**
INMATE NAME & REGISTER NUMBER
FCI Butner—Medium I
Federal Correctional Institution
P.O. Box 1000
Butner, NC 27509

**Inmate Mail to Camp:**
INMATE NAME & REGISTER NUMBER
FCI Butner—Medium I
Federal Correctional Institution
Satellite Camp
P.O. Box 1000
Butner, NC 27509

**Visiting Hours:** FCI and Monday, Thursday, and Friday 2:30pm-8pm. Saturday, Sunday and all federal holidays 8:30am-3pm. Inmates will be allotted 16 visiting points per calendar month. The points used will be dependent upon which day the visit occurs. Visits that occur on weekdays are counted as one point, and visits that occur on weekends and holidays will count as four points. Three adults are allowed to visit an inmate at one time (an adult is considered 16 years of age and above). No limit is set for children less than 16 years of age. Additionally, visitors are prohibited from bringing animals on institution grounds unless the animal is a dog that assists disabled persons.

**Lodging/Accommodations:** See §12:14 for FCI Butner—Low.

**Directions to Facility:** See §12:14 for FCI Butner—Low.

## §12:16   FCI BUTNER—MEDIUM II

FCI Butner Medium II
Federal Correctional Institution
Old NC Hwy 75
Butner, NC 27509
BTF/ExecAssistant@bop.gov
919-575-8000
Fax: 919-575-8020

**Location:** Located near the Research Triangle area of Durham, Raleigh, and Chapel Hill.

**Judicial District:** Eastern North Carolina.

**Security Level:** FCI Medium II is part of the Butner Federal Correctional Complex. FCI II houses medium-security male inmates.

**Population:** As of 6/09/2017, the FCI Medium II inmate population is 1,398. Weekly population figures are available on the BOP website at www.bop.gov, https://www.bop.gov/locations/institutions/btf/.

**Inmate Mail to FCI:**
    INMATE NAME & REGISTER NUMBER
    FCI Butner Medium II
    Federal Correctional Institution
    P.O. Box 1500
    Butner, NC 27509

**Visiting Hours:** See §12:15 for FCI Butner—Medium I.

**Lodging/Accommodations:** See §12:14 for FCI Butner—Low.

**Directions to Facility:** <u>From Raleigh to FCC Butner:</u> U.S. 70 West to I-85 North on ramp. Take I-85 North nine miles to exit 189. Turn left on Central Avenue. Proceed straight on Central Avenue to Veazey Street. Turn right onto Veazey Street. Proceed to stop sign. Turn left onto Old Highway 75. Proceed approximately one mile. LSCI and FCI Butner is located on the first right. FPC Butner will be located on the second right and FMC Butner will be located at the third right.
    <u>From Durham to FCC Butner:</u> Take I-85 North nine miles to exit 189. Turn left on Central Avenue. Proceed straight on Central Avenue to Veazey Street. Turn right onto Veazey Street. Proceed to stop sign. Turn left onto Old Highway 75. Proceed approximately one mile. LSCI and FCI Butner is located on the first right. FPC Butner will be located on the second right and FMC Butner will be located at the third right.

## §12:17  FMC BUTNER

FMC Butner
Federal Medical Center
Old NC Hwy 75
Butner, NC 27509
BUH/ExecAssistant@bop.gov
919-575-3900
Fax: 919-575-4801

**Location:** FMC Butner is located near the Research Triangle area of Durham, Raleigh, and Chapel Hill., five miles off I-85 on Old Highway 75. The area is served by Raleigh-Durham International Airport, Amtrak, and commercial bus lines.

**Judicial District:** Eastern North Carolina.

**Security Level:** FMC is part of the Butner Federal Correctional Complex and is an administrative facility that houses male inmates of all security levels. An adjacent satellite prison camp houses minimum-security male inmate.

**Population:** As of 6/09/2016, the FMC inmate population is 926. Weekly population figures are available at on the BOP website at www.bop.gov, at https://www.bop.gov/locations/institutions/buh/.

**Education:** The programs provided for FMC inmates include GED, English as a Second Language, college/post-secondary education, Adult Continuing Education, parenting, and employment preparation. Accredited curriculum and certification classes are offered through Vance-Granville Community College and Durham Technical Community College. Courses vary from semester to semester. Inmates may also take college correspondence courses at their own expense.

**Library:** The Leisure and Legal Library is open Monday through Saturday during the day and Monday through Thursday during evenings. The Leisure Library has various publications including newspapers, magazines, fiction and non-fiction books, and educational materials. Inmates may create an account in order to use the Electronic Law Library, which uses the Lexis/Nexis database to access materials digitally. Typewriters and a copier are available.

**Counseling/Rehab Services:** FMC Butner offers individual and group counseling on an as-needed, voluntary basis and coordinates treatment with psychiatry services. The Psychology Services Department is staffed by a complex chief psychologist, a deputy chief psychologist, eight staff psychologists, psychology interns, a drug treatment specialist, and a psychology technician. While this institution does not offer a resident drug abuse program, they do offer three different drug programs, including a 40-hour drug education class, transitional drug treatment and non-residential drug treatment.

**Health Services:** Sick call is available on Monday, Tuesday, Thursday, and Friday from 6:45am to 7:15am. Insulin and pill lines are announced by the staff. Chronic care and consultant clinics are available at the FMC for inmates who need consistent or specialized care. Preventative health screens are routinely provided, as well as physical examinations (every three years for inmates under the age of 50, and every year for inmates 50 years of age and older).

**Fitness/Recreation:** The Recreation Department include activities including intramural sports, leisure activities, passive and non-competitive activities, unit-based activities, a CD music program, a movie program, a wellness program, and other activities. There are also biannual Health Fairs where inmates can learn and participate in diet and exercise programs.

**Religious Services:** Staff chaplains have an open-door policy. The are available six nights a week until 9pm. Counseling is available through the chaplains or religious volunteers. Group and religious meetings are held in the Chapel area.

**Inmate Mail:** The facility accepts mail from the U.S. Postal Service via First-Class, U.S. Priority, and Express Mail. For those interested in sending overnight mail via private carrier (FedEx or UPS Overnight), it is recommended you first contact the institution to find out whether the receipt of such mail is permitted. Inmates may receive publications without prior approval, although the warden will reject publications that are determined to be detrimental to the security, good order or discipline of the institution. Inmates may accumulate up to five magazines, five books, and three newspapers (in two newspaper subscriptions). All publications must come directly from the publisher, bookstore or book club.

**Inmate Mail to FMC:**
INMATE NAME & REGISTER NUMBER
FMC Butner
Federal Medical Center
P.O. Box 1600
Butner, NC 27509

**Visiting Hours:** Friday 2:30pm-8:00pm Saturday, Sunday, and all federal holidays 8:30am-3pm. Inmates will be allotted 16 visiting points per calendar month. The points used shall be dependent upon which day the visit occurs. Visits that occur on weekdays (Friday), are counted as one (1) point. Visits that occur on weekends (Saturday and Sunday), will count as four (4) points. No points will be deducted on Federal holidays. It is the inmate's responsibility to budget the allowable 16 points during each month. All visits will have a limit of three (3) adult visitors. Adult visitors are deemed as persons sixteen (16) years or older. There are no limits to the number of child visitors, under the age of sixteen (16). Additional visiting information can be found on the BOP website, at https://www.bop.gov/locations/institutions/buh/.

**Lodging/Accommodations:** See §12:14 for FCI Butner—Low.

**Directions to Facility:** See §12:16 for FCI Butner Medium II.

# §12:18   FCI CUMBERLAND

FCI Cumberland
Federal Correctional Institution
14601 Burbridge Rd
SE Cumberland, MD 21502
CUM/ExecAssistant@bop.gov
301-784-1000
Fax: 301-784-1008

**Location:** In western Maryland, 130 miles northwest of Washington, D.C., six miles south of interstate 68, off State Route 51 South. The area is served by the Cumberland Area Regional Airport, Amtrak, and commercial bus lines.

**History:** Opened in 1994.

**Judicial District:** District of Maryland.

**Security Level:** FCI Cumberland houses medium-security male offenders. The FCI has an adjacent minimum-security satellite camp that houses male offenders.

**Population:** As of 6/09/2014, the FCI inmate population is 1,016, and the camp population is 243. Weekly population figures are available on the BOP website at https://www.bop.gov/locations/institutions/cum/.

**Education:** The FCI and the camp offer GED, ESL, adult continuing education, parenting classes, Correctional Learning Network classes, and the Hope House Book Reading program. The FCI allows college correspondence classes at the inmate's expense. The camp also offers the Tail of Freedom Dog Training Program and a Job Readiness class.

**Vocational/Apprenticeship:** The FCI offers vocational training and an apprenticeship programs.

**Library:** The law libraries in both the FCI and the camp contains a variety of legal reference materials for use in preparing legal papers. Reference materials include the United States Code Annotated, Federal Reporter, Supreme Court Reporter, Bureau of Prisons Program Statements, Institution Supplements, Indexes, and other legal materials. The law libraries are open Monday through Saturday, 7:30am-8:30pm, excluding count and meal times. The law library is closed on Sundays and federal holidays. An inmate law library clerk is available for assistance in legal research. Inmates wishing to use typewriters in the law library for legal work must purchase print wheels, typing ribbon and correction ribbon from the commissary for this purpose. In the FCI, inmates are afforded access to legal materials and an opportunity to prepare legal documents in the

Electronic Law Library (ELL). Legal materials are also available in the Special Housing Unit ordinarily via a delivery system or satellite collection. Leisure libraries offer inmates a variety of reading materials, including but not limited to: periodicals, newspapers, fiction, non-fictions, and reference books. The leisure library also contains a multimedia section.

**UNICOR:** Federal Prison Industries (FPI) employs and trains approximately 95 inmates through the operation of, and earnings from, factories producing high-quality products and services for the federal government. The factory at FCI Cumberland produces signs and license plates for various government agencies.

**Counseling/Rehab Services:** Psychology services are available at the FCI and the camp Monday through Friday 7:30am-3:30pm, on an appointment basis only, and on an open house basis on Tuesday and Thursday from 11:30a.m. until the afternoon work call. An on-call psychologist is available after hours to deal with emergency situations. Various services provided include individual counseling, crisis intervention, drug and alcohol treatment and special group programs.

FCI Cumberland offers an intensive nine-month residential drug abuse treatment program. Non-residential drug abuse treatment is also available for inmates who wish to receive treatment for substance abuse problems, but who do not qualify for residential drug treatment or lack sufficient time remaining on their sentence for participation in this program. Anger Management and Stress Management programs are offered throughout the year. Psychology Services staff also work closely with a consulting Psychiatrist and Health Services staff in order to provide treatment to inmates who require medication for their psychological symptoms.

**Health Services:** Sick call and dental sick call sign up for emergency sick call is held Monday, through Friday from 6:30am-7am. For routine sick call sign up, inmates must obtain a sick call sign-up sheet from their housing unit officer or sign up electronically using TRULINCS. Sick call sign-up sheets must be completed and turned into the collection box inside the front entrance of the Health Services Department. Pill line hours for the FCI: 6am-7am, 3:30pm-3:45pm, 4:45pm-5pm, 7pm-7:30pm. Weekend and holiday hours: 7am-7:30am, 10:30 (insulin only), 4:45pm-5pm (insulin only), 7pm-7:30pm. Pill Line hours for the camp: 6am-6:30am, 11:30am-12:15pm (insulin, new prescriptions, refills), 3:30pm-3:45pm, 4:45pm-5pm (insulin and restricted pills), 7pm-7:30pm. Weekend and holiday hours: 7am-7:15am, 11:30am-12:15pm, 4:45pm-5pm, 7pm-3:30am. Periodic health examinations including age-specific preventative health examinations for the inmate population will be provided at the clinical director's discretion.

**Housing:** Inmates are housed in two-man and three-man cells. The units are wheelchair accessible. There are approximately eight television rooms per unit (or four TV rooms per sides A and B). Basic cable is provided. The television rooms are open Sunday through Thursday from 5:30 am-12am (midnight) and Friday and Saturday 5:30am-2am.

**Fitness/Recreation:** The recreation department offers a variety of activities on the recreation yard, in the gymnasium, and in the leisure center for "off-duty" inmates, including team sports, exercise bicycles, stair steppers, Nautilus equipment, music room, musical instruments, pool tables, and ping-pong tables. The hobby craft center offers leather craft and ceramics, painting, drawing, crocheting, and knitting. Physical fitness and weight reduction programs are also offered, and contribute to mental health, good personal relations, and stress reduction. Special events, including unit or institution-wide tournaments, are held on all major holidays and on weekends.

**Religious Services:** The camp provides staff chaplains as well as contract and volunteer representatives of various faiths. Special dietary restrictions, holiday observances, and other worship activities are accommodated by the Chaplain's office.

**Commissary:** The FCI commissary is open Monday through Thursday from after the 4pm count until 8:30pm, and on Wednesday afternoon 1:30pm-3pm for inmates who work evenings. The commissary conducts sales according to the inmate's housing unit. Commissary shopping lists are accepted from 11am to until work call is announced. Inmates are permitted to shop once per week. Only those inmates who are on the approved shopping list are permitted to shop. Evening shift inmates must have their names submitted by their work detail supervisor no later than 4pm on Tuesday of the same week. The shopping day sequence for the FCI Cumberland is rotated on a quarterly basis, and the schedule is posted on the commissary bulletin board along with a current shopping list. The commissary at the camp is open Monday and Tuesday 4pm-8:30pm, and on Monday afternoon 1:30pm-3pm for inmates who work evenings. Commissary shopping lists are accepted from 11am to until work call is announced. Evening shift inmates must have their names submitted by their work detail supervisor no later than 4pm on Friday of the prior week. The BOP policy currently sets a monthly commissary spending limit of $360.

**Telephone Policy:** The institution utilizes the ITS Inmate Telephone System. There are telephones in each housing unit for inmate use. Inmates may only use the telephone in their assigned housing units. All calls are limited to 15 minutes, and each inmate is limited to 300 minutes per month. Inmates are allowed a total of 30 approved telephone numbers on their telephone list. This includes numbers for collect calls. Changes to telephone lists must be made electronically using TRULINCS. The telephones will normally be operated during the following hours; Monday through Friday 6am-8am; 10:30am-12:30pm; 3pm-11:30pm; Saturday, Sunday and holidays 6:30am-11:30pm.

**Inmate Mail:** The FCI and the camp accept mail from the U.S. Postal Service via First Class, U.S. Priority, and Express mail. For those interested in sending overnight mail via private carrier (FedEx or UPS Overnight), it is recommended that you first contact the institution to find out whether the receipt of such mail is permitted. Inmates may receive publications without prior approval, although the warden will reject publications that are determined to be detrimental to the security, good order or discipline of the institution. All incoming publications, newspapers, soft and hard cover books, magazines, and calendars must come directly from the publisher, book club, or bookstore.

**Inmate Mail to FCI:**
Inmate Name & Register Number
FCI Cumberland
Federal Correctional Institution
P.O. Box 1000
Cumberland, MD 21501

**Inmate Mail to Camp:**
INMATE NAME & REGISTER NUMBER
FCI Cumberland
Federal Correctional Institution
Satellite Camp
P.O. Box 1000
Cumberland, MD 21501

**Visiting Hours:** Visiting hours for the FCI are Fridays 4:30pm-8:30pm, and 8:45am-3pm on weekends and holidays. Visiting hours at the camp are Monday and Friday 4:30pm-8:30pm, and 8:45am-3pm on weekends and holidays. Inmates will be allowed no more than six weekend and holiday visiting days per month. There is no limitation on weekday, non-holiday visits. Any visit, regardless of the length of visit, will constitute one day of visiting. Federal holidays, unless stated, will count as a weekend visit. Attorney visits do not count as part of the six days of authorized weekend and holiday visits. Attorneys should ordinarily make advance appointments for each visit, and attorneys are encouraged to visit during the regular visiting hours. However, visits from an attorney can be arranged at other times. Additional visiting information can be found on the Bureau of Prisons website, www.bop.gov, at https://www.bop.gov/locations/institutions/cum/.

**Lodging/Accommodations:** Should visitors be spending the night, the following is a short list of accommodations that are available near Cumberland, Maryland:
| | |
|---|---|
| Fairfield Inn & Suites | 301-722-0340 |
| Ramada Cumberland Downtown | 301-724-8800 |
| Diplomat Hotel | 301-729-2311 |
| Rodeway Inn | 301-729-6700 |
| Super 8 Motel | 301-729-6265 |

**Directions to Facility:** Take Interstate Route I-68 to the Industrial Boulevard exit (Route 51 South) in Cumberland, Maryland. Westbound, this is Exit 43B.

Eastbound from Morgantown, this is also Exit 43B. Take State Route 51 (Industrial Boulevard) south for 5.6 miles. Turn right into Allegany County Industrial Park at PPG Road. Follow PPG Road for 1.6 miles. Turn left into main gate of the Federal Correctional Institution (FCI). The entrance to the Federal Prison Camp is the second left turn. To get to the FCI, follow the main road for .4 miles, ending at the FCI parking lot on the right.

## §12:19   FCI GILMER

FCI Gilmer
Federal Correctional Institution
201 FCI Lane
Glenville, WV 26351
GIL/ExecAssistant@bop.gov
304-626-2500
Fax: 304-626-2593

**Location:** FCI Gilmer is located in central West Virginia, 85 miles northeast of Charleston and 150 miles from Pittsburgh, Pennsylvania.

**History:** A medium-security FCI with a minimum-security satellite camp.

**Judicial District:** Northern West Virginia.

**Security Level:** FCI Gilmer is a medium-security facility housing male offenders. An adjacent satellite prison camp houses minimum-security male inmates.

**Population:** As of 6/10/2017, the FCI inmate population is 1,333, and the camp population is 115. Weekly population figures are available on the BOP website at https://www.bop.gov/locations/institutions/gil/.

**Education:** Education opportunities include a literacy program, ESL, adult continuing education, post-secondary education, a wide range of occupational training programs, correspondence courses, and parenting classes. Depending upon interest, the FCI may also offer college-level courses, using contract instructors from nearby colleges.

**Library:** The law library is located in the Education Department, and contains a variety of legal reference materials for use in preparing legal papers. Reference materials include the United States Code Annotated, Federal Reporter, Supreme Court Reporter, Bureau of Prisons Program Statements, Institutional Supplements, Indexes, and other legal materials. The law library is open during convenient non-working hours, including Saturdays. An inmate law library clerk is available for assistance in legal research. Legal materials are also available to inmates in the Special Housing Unit. Inmates have access to legal materials and an opportunity to prepare legal documents in the Electronic Law Library (ELL). The leisure library has a variety of books in both English and Spanish. Several typewriters and a copy machine are available in the leisure library.

**UNICOR:** The FCI offers a range of jobs in an automotive repair shop and in the factory operated by UNICOR. The factory manufactures high-quality goods for the Federal Government. Inmates who wish to work in the factory are placed on a waiting list for employment.

**Counseling/Rehab Services:** The Psychology Services Department offers a wide range of group educational programs including stress management, anger management, and smoking cessation, self-image groups, and other voluntary groups. Participation in such activities is voluntary. The Psychology Services Department consists of one psychologist, one drug treatment specialist, and a psychology secretary under the direction of the chief psychologist. In addition to the mentioned programs, a variety of services are available with respect to drug treatment, including drug abuse education and non-residential drug treatment.

**Health Services:** Medical care is available from 6am-10pm on weekdays and daily. All inmates' health care will be provided by the appropriate primary care team. Sick call is held Mondays, Tuesdays, Thursdays and Fridays at 10:30am. Dental sick call is on the same days at 6:45am. The Pill Line occurs during specified time periods that are posted for reference. Physical examinations are available every two years for inmates under the age of 50, and every year for inmates over the age of 50.

**Fitness/Recreation:** Programs include indoor and outdoor activities and range from individualized arts and crafts programs to intramural team sports such as softball, basketball, soccer, and volleyball. All sporting activities will be held in the recreation area. The band/music program, hobby craft programs, music listening, wellness & fitness research and walking or running may be offered by the Recreation Department. Leisure time activities include board games, cards, dominoes, television viewing, and bingo. Inmates may participate in some of these leisure activities in their unit.

**Religious Services:** The Religious Services Department provides pastoral care, counseling, and a variety of religious programs. There are regularly scheduled services, studies, special programs, holy days, and periodic guest speakers who speak on a variety of faith issues. The staff chaplains are also assisted by contract staff and volunteers.

**Commissary:** Inmates can shop at the commissary Monday through Thursday, with the specific day of the week according to the inmate's registration number. The commissary access time in each unit is scheduled on a rotating basis. The total value of an inmate's accumulated commissary items (including special purchases) will be limited to the Bureau of Prison's monthly spending limit, which increased in January 2012 to $360. Special purchases such as watches and radios require approval of the Unit Manager.

**Telephone Policy:** Telephone hours begin at 6:00am and end no later than 11:30pm. Inmate access to telephones will normally be limited during the following times, Monday through Friday, not including holidays: 7:30am until 10:30am, and 12:30pm until after 4:00pm count. There is no specific limit on the number of phone calls an inmate may make. Calls are limited to 15 minutes in duration. Inmates, unless on telephone restriction, are allowed 300 minutes of phone time per month. FCI/SCP Gilmer has the Inmate Telephone System (ITS). Inmates are allowed to have 30 approved numbers on their phone list. In order to use the system, inmates will have to transfer funds from their commissary account to their individual telephone account. Collect calls can also be made to approved telephone numbers. There are telephones located in each housing unit for inmate use.

**Inmate Mail:** The FCI and the camp accept mail from the U.S. Postal Service via First-Class, U.S. Priority, and Express mail. For those interested in sending overnight mail via a private carrier (FedEx or UPS Overnight), it is recommended that you first contact the institution to find out whether the receipt of such mail is permitted. All inmate packages received at the institution must have prior authorization. Inmates may receive publications without prior approval, although the warden will reject publications that are determined to be detrimental to the security, good order or discipline of the institution. All publications must come directly from the publisher, bookstore or book club. Inmates are limited to five magazines (no more than three months old) and to the amount that can be stored neatly in their lockers.

**Inmate Mail to FCI:**
> INMATE NAME & REGISTER NUMBER
> FCI Gilmer
> Federal Correctional Institution
> P.O. Box 6000
> Glenville, WV 26351

**Inmate Mail to Camp:**
> INMATE NAME & REGISTER NUMBER
> FCI Gilmer
> Federal Correctional Institution
> Satellite Camp
> P.O. Box 7000
> Glenville, WV 26351

**Visiting Hours:** FCI and camp visiting hours: Friday, Saturday, Sunday, & federal holidays 8am-3pm. There is no limit on the amount of visits an inmate may have. A maximum of six visitors (including children) will be allowed at one time. Attorneys are encouraged to visit during regular visiting hours, and must make arrangement through the unit team for visitation. Additional visiting information can be found on the BOP website, www.bop.gov, at https://www. bop.gov/locations/institutions/gil/.

**Lodging/Accommodations:** Should visitors be spending the night, the following is a short list of accommodations that are available in the Glenville, West Virginia area:

| | |
|---|---|
| Glenville Inn | 304-462-5511 |
| Quality Inn | 304-269-7000 |
| Conrad Inn | 304-462-7316 |
| Super 8 Motel | 304-269-1086 |

**Directions to Facility:** FCI Gilmer is located about one mile from Glenville. The area is serviced by bus transportation and by Harrison Marion Regional Airport (approximately 50 miles away) and Yeager Airport (90 miles away).

## §12:20   USP HAZELTON

USP Hazelton
United States Penitentiary
1640 Sky View Drive
Bruceton Mills, WV 26525
HAZ/ExecAssistant@bop.gov
304-379-5000
Fax: 304-379-5039

**Location:** Located in the mountains of Preston County, West Virginia, approximately 35 minutes from Morgantown; 45 minutes from Uniontown, PA; and 45 minutes from Cumberland, MD.

**Judicial District:** Northern West Virginia.

**Security Level:** Hazelton is a high-security institution housing male inmates, with a satellite camp that houses minimum-security male inmates.

**Population:** As of 6/10/2017, the USP inmate population is 1,342; the camp population is 105. Weekly population figures are available at https://www.bop. gov/locations/institutions/haz/.

**Education:** Individualized competency-based instruction is available to each inmate, progressing at their own pace, while completing behavioral objectives. In addition, GED, ESL, adult continuing education, post-secondary education, parenting classes, career counseling, and vocational training are offered.

**Vocational/Apprenticeship:** USP Hazleton and the camp offers vocational training is offered in administrative assistant, start-up business, and culinary arts. Apprenticeship programs are offered in HVAC, plumbing, and Microsoft Office. At the camp, apprenticeship programs are offered in electrical, power plant mechanic, and Microsoft Office.

**UNICOR:** The UNICOR factory at USP Hazelton has three product lines including Army Combat Uniforms Trousers, GSA Tarps and Diplomatic Bags. Inmates interested in UNICOR must submit the required form to be placed on the waiting list.

**Library:** The law library offers a variety of legal resources, as well as typewriters and clerical supplies for preparing legal work only. Typing ribbon, correction tape, and print wheels are available for purchase in the commissary. A copier is also available for inmate use and costs $.13 per copy. The leisure library is located in the Education Department and offers a selection of periodicals and books. Though periodicals may never leave the library, books may be checked out to the general population for two-week terms. The library is open every day and engages in an inter-library loan program through a local library.

**Recreation:** The Recreation Department offers a hobby craft program and classes in introductory drawing, painting, crocheting, art appreciation, and comic book development. Inmates wishing to enroll must submit the required form to the designated Recreation staff member.

**Counseling/Rehab Services:** USP Hazelton offers services in smoking cessation, Alcoholics Anonymous, self-image groups, and other voluntary groups for interested inmates. Inmate participation is encouraged but voluntary, and counseling staff are available in each unit for informal counseling sessions. Mental health services are offered in the areas of drug and alcohol abuse, as well as other behavioral or emotional problems. Referral for a psychiatric (medication) evaluation may be made at the direction of a psychologist or other Health Services provider.

**Health Services:** For routine care, inmates who wish to be seen for an evaluation must submit a request in the designated drop box in the Green Corridor. The requests will be triaged and scheduled appropriately. A staff member from Medical Services tours the detention and segregation units regularly. Controlled medications are dispensed at a prescribed location pill line during specified time periods. Inmates in detention or segregation are provided their medication by medical staff in their cells. The USP has a preventative health care program that emphasizes specific preventative services rather than routine annual physical examinations.

**Religious Services:** The USP has chaplains on staff as well as volunteers of various faith traditions. Consistent with Bureau policy, USP Hazelton offers a certified religious diet for qualified inmates. Religious holidays and other worship activities are coordinated through the chaplain's office.

**Housing:** Single and double occupancy cells in the USP, and dormitory housing in the minimum-security camp.

**Commissary:** Currently, the Bureau of Prisons sets a spending limit of $360 per month on commissary visits. Special purchase items such as tennis shoes, gym clothes, and radios require a form completed by the inmate and routed to commissary.

**Telephone Policy:** Telephones at USP Hazelton are located in each housing unit and are available for inmate use. Inmates are allowed to talk on the telephone for up to 300 minutes per validation cycle. Calls will be limited to 15 minutes. After the call is completed, there will be a 30-minute waiting period until the next call can be made. Telephone procedures are posted in each side of the units. USP Hazelton and the camp have the Inmate Telephone System (ITS) and collect call capabilities. This system uses a Personal Access Code (PAC). It allows you to call up to thirty approved Inmate Telephone Services (ITS) credits can be transferred from your commissary account after 4:30pm daily. Inmates can have 30 telephone numbers on their phone list and can update their lists once per month.

**Inmate Mail to USP:** The USP and camp accept mail from the U.S. Postal Service via First-Class, U.S. Priority, and Express mail. For those interested in sending overnight mail via a private carrier (FedEx or UPS Overnight), it is recommended that you first contact the institution to find out whether the receipt of such mail is permitted. Inmates may receive publications without prior approval, although the warden will reject publications that are determined to be detrimental to the security, good order or discipline of the institution. All publications must come directly from the publisher, bookstore or book club. Inmates are limited to five magazines (not to be more than three months old).

**Inmate Mail to USP:**
> INMATE NAME & REGISTER NUMBER
> USP Hazelton
> United States Penitentiary
> P.O. Box 2000
> Bruceton Mills, WV 26525

**Inmate Mail to SCP:**
> INMATE NAME & REGISTER NUMBER
> USP Hazelton
> United States Penitentiary
> Satellite Camp
> P.O. Box 2000
> Bruceton Mills, WV 26525

**Visiting Hours:** Visiting schedule for the USP and camp 8am-3pm on Saturday, Sunday, Monday and federal holidays. The maximum number of visitors an inmate may have at one time is six, including children. A maximum of four adult visitors will be allowed in at one time. Attorneys are encouraged to visit during regular visiting hours. All attorney visits will be scheduled through the appropriate unit team and monitored by unit staff. Additional visiting information can be found on the BOP website, www.bop.gov, at https://www.bop.gov/locations/institutions/haz/.

**Lodging/Accommodations:** Should visitors be spending the night, the following is a short list of accommodations that are available near USP Hazelton:

| | |
|---|---|
| Clarion Hotel Morgan | 304-292-8200 |
| Waterfront Place Hotel | 304-296-1700 |
| Maple Leaf Motel | 304-379-4075 |
| Microtel Inns and Suites | 304-379-7900 |

## §12:21  FCI HAZELTON

FCI Hazelton
Federal Correctional Institution
1640 Sky View Drive
Bruceton Mills, WV 26525
HAX/ExecAssistant@bop.gov
304-379-1500
Fax: 304-379-1531

**Location:** Located in the mountains of Preston County, West Virginia, approximately 35 minutes from Morgantown; 45 minutes from Uniontown, PA; and 45 minutes from Cumberland, MD.

**Judicial District:** Northern West Virginia.

**Security Level:** Hazelton FCI, which opened in 2015, is a high-security institution housing male inmates, a secure unit (SFF) that houses female inmates.

**Population:** As of 6/13/2017, the USP inmate population is 1,342; the camp population is 583. Weekly population figures are available at https://www.bop.gov/locations/institutions/haf/.

**Education:** Individualized competency-based instruction is available to each inmate, progressing at their own pace, while completing behavioral objectives. In addition, GED, ESL, adult continuing education, post-secondary education, parenting classes, career counseling, and vocational training are offered.

**Vocational/Apprenticeship:** FCI Hazelton offers vocational training in building trades, culinary arts, graphic arts, and Microsoft Office. The SFF offers vocational training in administrative assistant, start-up business, basic/advanced horticulture, culinary arts and Microsoft Office. App-renticeship programs are offered in offered in electrical, HVAC, plumbing, industrial maintenance repair, and welding.

**Library:** The law library offers a variety of legal resources, including Electronic Law Libraries (ELL). A copy machine is available. The leisure library offers inmates a variety of reading materials, including but not limited to: periodicals, newspapers, fiction, non-fiction, and reference books.

**Recreation:** The Recreation Department offers a hobby craft program including drawing, painting, ceramics, leatherworks, models, clay, mosaics, crocheting, sculpture, woodworking, and lapidary. Inmates are encouraged to participate in unit-based hobby craft. Other leisure activities include organized and informal games, sports, physical fitness, table games, hobby crafts, music programs, intramural activities, social and cultural organizations, and movies.

**Counseling/Rehab Services:** FCI Hazelton offers psychiatric counseling in mental health and suicide prevention. The FCI and SFF have drug abuse programs, and non-residential Drug Abuse Treatment. Early Release and Community Transitional Drug Treatment programs are also available. The Resolve Program, a non-residential program for female inmates who have a history of physical or sexual abuse, and a 500-hour Residential Drug Abuse Program (RDAP) is available at the SFF only.

**Health Services:** For routine care, inmates who wish to be seen for an evaluation must submit a request in the designated drop box in the Green Corridor. The requests will be triaged and scheduled appropriately. A staff member from Medical Services tours the detention and segregation units regularly. Controlled medications are dispensed at a prescribed location pill line during specified time periods. Inmates in detention or segregation are provided their medication by medical staff in their cells. The FCI has a preventative health care program that emphasizes specific preventative services rather than routine annual physical examinations. Emergency health care workers are available 24 hours a day.

**Religious Services:** The FCI has chaplains on staff as well as volunteers of various faith traditions. Religious holidays and other worship activities are coordinated through the chaplain's office. The Chaplains offer religious worship, education, counseling, spiritual direction, support and crisis intervention to meet the diverse religious needs of inmates. Consistent with Bureau policy, FCI Hazelton maintains religious books, pamphlets, audio tapes, video tapes and DVDs for group or personal use. Audio and video viewing will only take place at times scheduled for such viewing. Only inmates who are on the Call-Out will be allowed in the chapel during regularly scheduled working hours (Monday-Friday 7:30am-4pm).

**Commissary:** Commissary and validation schedules are posted on the inmate bulletin boards. Currently, the Bureau of Prisons sets a spending limit of $360 per month on commissary visits. Special purchase items such as tennis shoes, gym clothes, and radios require a form completed by the inmate and routed to commissary.

**Telephone Policy:** Telephones at FCI Hazelton and the SFF are located in each housing unit and are available for inmate use. Inmates are allowed to talk on the telephone for up to 300 minutes per validation cycle. Ordinarily, inmates will be allowed an extra 100 minutes per month in November and December. Calls will be limited to 15 minutes. After the call is completed, there will be a 30-minute waiting period until the next call can be made. Telephone procedures are posted in each side of the units. Both FCI Hazelton and the SFF have the Inmate Telephone System (ITS) and collect call capabilities. This system uses a Personal Access Code (PAC). It allows you to call up to thirty approved Inmate Telephone Services (ITS) credits can be transferred from your commissary account after 4:30pm daily. Inmates can have 30 telephone numbers on their phone list and can update their lists once per month. Hours of telephone operation are normally 6am-11:30pm. Inmate access to telephones will normally be limited during the following times, Monday through Friday, not including holidays: 7:30am until 10:30am; and 12:30pm until after 4:00 pm count.

**Inmate Mail to USP:** The FCI and camp accept mail from the U.S. Postal Service via First-Class, U.S. Priority, and Express mail. For those interested in sending overnight mail via a private carrier (FedEx or UPS Overnight), it is recommended that you first contact the institution to find out whether the receipt of such mail is permitted. Inmates may receive publications without prior approval, although the warden will reject publications that are determined to be detrimental to the security, good order or discipline of the institution. At the FCI, softcover publications may come from any source, though hardback publications must come directly from the publisher, bookstore or book club. At the SFF, all publications must come directly from the publisher, bookstore or book club.

**Inmate Mail to USP:**
    INMATE NAME & REGISTER NUMBER
    FCI Hazelton
    Federal Correctional Institution
    P.O. Box 2000
    Bruceton Mills, WV 26525

**Inmate Mail to SCP:**
    INMATE NAME & REGISTER NUMBER
    FCI Hazelton
    Federal Correctional Institution
    Satellite Camp
    Secure Female Facility
    P.O. Box 2000
    Bruceton Mills, WV 26525

**Visiting Hours:** As of June 2017, all visiting at this facility has been suspended until further notice. This policy may have changed by the time you read this entry. See https://www.bop.gov/locations/institutions/haf/.

Normally, the visiting schedule for the USP and camp 8am-3pm on Saturday, Sunday, Monday and federal holidays. The maximum number of visitors an inmate may have at one time is six, including children. At the FCI, a maximum of two adult visitors will be allowed in at one time. At the SFF, maximum of four visitors is allowed at one time. Attorneys are encouraged to visit during regular visiting hours. All attorney visits will be scheduled through the appropriate unit team and monitored by unit staff. Additional visiting information can be found on the BOP website, www.bop.gov, at https://www.bop.gov/locations/institutions/hax/.

**Lodging/Accommodations:** See the entry for §12:20 USP Hazelton.

## §12:22 USP LEE

USP Lee
United States Penitentiary
Lee County Industrial Park
Hickory Flats Rd.
Pennington Gap, VA 24277
LEE/ExecAssistant@bop.gov
276-546-0150
Fax: 276-546-9115

**Location:** Located in southwest Virginia in Lee County, eight miles east of Jonesville, off U.S. 58 at the intersection of State Route 638. There are no taxi, bus or airline services in the immediate area of the institution. However, taxi and airline service are available in Kingsport, Tennessee, which is approximately 50 miles from USP Lee County.

**Judicial District:** Western Virginia.

**Security Level:** USP Lee houses high-security male offenders. An adjacent minimum-security satellite prison camp houses male offenders.

**Population:** As of 6/10/2017, the USP inmate population is 1,165, and the camp population is 112. Weekly population figures are available on the BOP website at www.bop.gov.

**Education:** USP Lee and the camp offer GED, ESL, adult continuing education, parenting and vocational training classes.

**Vocational/Apprenticeship:** USP Lee offers no advanced occupational education. Vocational training is offered in computer applications, HVAC, and building trades. Apprenticeship programs are offered in quality assurance inspector, and administrative assistant. At the camp, a vocational training program in horticulture/landscape is offered.

**Library:** USP Lee and SCP inmates have access to the Electronic Law Library (ELL) in the Education Department and in SHU. A limited number of books may still be available, but they are being phased out over time. Reference materials include the United States Code Annotated, Federal Reporter, Supreme Court Reporter, Bureau of Prisons Program Statements, Institution Supplements, Indexes, and other legal materials. The Law Library is open during convenient non-working hours, including weekends and holidays. An inmate Law Library Clerk is available for assistance in legal research. The Education Department also maintains a legal Library.

**UNICOR:** UNICOR employs and trains inmates through the operation of and earnings from factories producing high-quality products and services for the federal government. The UNICOR factory at USP Lee County manufactures textile products.

**Counseling/Rehab Services:** Alcoholic Anonymous, Narcotics Anonymous, self-image groups, and other voluntary groups are available for interested inmates. Institutions have staff members, who are trained in the social science fields. Inmate participation in these activities will be encouraged upon the staff's assessment of inmate needs, but participation in such activities is voluntary. Staff members in each unit are available for informal counseling sessions.
　　Psychologists are available for individuals and/or group psychotherapy. Mental health services are offered in the areas of Drug Education and Non-Residential Drug Abuse Programming, as well as other behavioral or emotional problems.

**Health Services:** Medical triage (sick call) is on Monday, Tuesday, Thursday and Friday at 8am. Urgent situations and injuries will be given priority treatment. Controlled medications are dispensed at the Pill Line during specified time periods. Inmates in detention or segregation are provided their medication by medical staff members in their staff. All inmates can request preventative health visits to review needed health services: every two years for inmates under the age of 50, and every year for inmates over the age of 50.

**Fitness/Recreation:** Recreation programs include indoor and outdoor activities, individualized arts and crafts program, and intramural team sports. Physical fitness and weight reduction programs are also available. Hobby craft programs include activities such as painting, leather, art, and drawing. Sports and recreation equipment will be available for inmate use in the Recreation Department.

**Religious Services:** Staff chaplains of specific faiths are available, as well as contract and volunteer representatives of other faiths. Special religious diets, holiday observances, and other worship activities are coordinated through the chaplain's office.

**Commissary:** Inmates are permitted to spend up to $145 bi-weekly for regular purchases, and an additional amount for special items (such as kosher meals, stamps, over-the-counter medications, and copy cards). Inmates will be advised of the current spending limit during Admission and Orientation.

**Telephone Policy:** Inmates can talk on the telephone for up to 300 minutes per month. Telephones are located in each housing unit for inmate use. Calls are limited to 15 minutes, with a one hour waiting period until the next call can be made. Both USP and the camp have the Inmate Telephone System (ITS). This system allows inmates to call up to thirty approved numbers. Phone time is purchased from the commissary by transfer of funds to the inmate's individual telephone account. Collect calls can also be made to approved numbers.

**Inmate Mail:** The USP and SCP accept mail from the U.S. Postal Service via First-Class, U.S. Priority, and Express Mail. For those interested in sending over-night mail via a private carrier (FedEx or UPS Overnight), it is recommended that you first contact the institution to find out whether the receipt of such mail is permitted. Inmates may receive publications without prior approval, although the warden will reject publications that are determined to be detrimental to the security, good order or discipline of the institution. Softcover publications can come from any source. Hardcover books and newspapers must come directly from the publisher or book club. Inmates are limited to ten magazines (no more than three months old) and to the amount that can be stored neatly in their lockers.

**Inmate Mail to USP:**
> INMATE NAME & REGISTER NUMBER
> USP Lee
> U.S. Penitentiary
> P.O. Box 305
> Jonesville, VA 24263

**Inmate Mail to Camp:**
> INMATE NAME & REGISTER NUMBER
> USP Lee
> U.S. Penitentiary
> Satellite Camp
> P.O. Box 644
> Jonesville, VA 24263

**Visiting Hours:** As of June 2017, all visiting at this facility has been suspended until further notice. This policy may have changed by the time you read this entry. See https://www.bop.gov/locations/institutions/lee/.

Normal visiting hours are Saturday, Sunday and federal holidays 8am-3pm; and Friday 5pm-8:30pm. No more than three adult visitors, not including dependent children, will be permitted for each inmate at any given time. Inmates are required to submit a visiting list of acceptable visitors, and attorneys should be placed on the inmate's approved visiting list. Additional visiting information can be at https://www.bop.gov/locations/institutions/lee.

**Lodging/Accommodations:** Should visitors be spending the night, the following is a short list of accommodations that are available near Pennington Gap, Virginia:

| | |
|---|---|
| Comfort Inn Big Stone Gap | 276-523-5911 |
| Convenient Inn | 276-546-5350 |
| Travel Inn-Duffield | 276-431-4300 |
| Super 8 Norton | 276-679-0893 |

**Directions to Facility:** From Interstate 75: Take exit 29 in Corbin, Kentucky and proceed east on Highway 25E (approximately 50 miles). After driving through the Cumberland Gap Tunnel, turn north on Highway 58. Follow Highway 58 into Jonesville, Virginia (34 miles). Turn right on Highway 58 in downtown Jonesville. USP Lee County is nine miles beyond Jonesville, on the left side of the road, State Route 638.

From Interstate 81: Take Interstate 81 Northwest to Weber City, Virginia. Turn west on Highway 23 toward Duffield, Virginia (16 miles), then turn left onto Highway 58 in Duffield and drive 13 miles to USP Lee County. The prison is on the right side of the road, State Route 638.

## §12:23 FMC LEXINGTON

FMC Lexington
Federal Medical Center
3301 Leestown Road
Lexington, KY 40511
LEX/ExecAssistant@bop.gov
859-255-6812
Fax: 859-253-8821

**Location:** FMC Lexington is located seven miles north of Lexington on U.S. Highway 421. Lexington is served by Bluegrass Field Airport, commercial bus lines, and taxis.

**History:** Opened in 1974, FMC Lexington was formerly a U.S. Public Health Service facility. It houses offenders whose average length of stay is 2.5 years. A 100-bed hospital accepts inmate referrals from throughout the United States.

**Judicial District:** Eastern Kentucky.

**Security Level:** FMC Lexington is an administrative security medical center for male inmates. There is an adjacent minimum-security satellite camp.

**Population:** As of 6/11/2017, the FMC inmate population is 1,353, and the camp population is 302. Weekly population figures are available on the BOP website at https://www.bop.gov/locations/institutions/lex/.

**Education:** The FMC and camp offer GED, ESL, adult education, and a parenting program. Inmates do not have to pay for tuition and books. The Career Resource Center offers counseling and referral sources to assist in the development of realistic educational and employment goals.

**Vocational/Apprenticeship:** The FMC offers vocational training in Braille transcription, building trades, computer applications, and horticulture. The FMC also offers apprenticeship training programs. These programs combine classroom and live work experience. The camp does not offer vocational or apprenticeship training programs. Inmates are only permitted to participate in vocational or apprenticeship if they have completed a GED equivalent.

**Library:** The main institution's law and leisure libraries are open Monday through Friday 7:45-10am, 10:30am-3:15pm, and 5pm-7:30pm. On Saturdays, Sundays, and holidays, the libraries are open from 11am-3:50pm. Electric typewriters are available for the preparation of legal documents. Inmates must purchase their own typewriter ribbon. A coin-operated copy machine is available at the camp. Copies are 20 cents per page, and are charged to the inmate's debit card. The camp's law and leisure libraries are open from Monday Through Friday at 8:30am to 7:30pm, and Saturdays and Sundays from 12:30pm-7:30pm. Inmates can obtain books from the McNaughton Book Company. Both leisure libraries contain numerous books available for circ-ulation and reference, as well as a multimedia section.

**UNICOR:** An electronic cable factory, quality control department, business office, warehouse, customer service center, and accounts receivable operation all employ up to 350 inmates who are qualified for UNICOR. Factory products include radio frequency cables, junction boxes for communications, wiring harnesses and telephone cabling. A small metal/cardboard recycling operation employs inmates from the camp.

**Counseling/Rehab Services:** The Residential Drug Abuse Program is nine months in length. The FMC and the camp also offer a non-residential drug treatment program, a drug education program, Alcoholics Anonymous, and Narcotics Anonymous groups, and transitional drug treatment. Weight control, anger management, stress management, and chronic pain management programs are also offered. Several housing units have particular missions, such as residential drug treatment, forensic studies, or behavioral medicine. The Dual Diagnosis program provides specialized treatment for participants who have been diagnosed with both substance and mental health disorders. A psychologist is available to inmates at the camp on an as-needed basis.

**Health Services:** The FMC has an ambulatory care facility with a 21-bed infirmary. The medical center and camp are served by several hospitals in the immediate area (all within 5-10 miles of the prison). Pill line is seven days per week at 7am, 11am, 1:50pm, and 2:50pm. Sick call for the FMC is 6:30am-7am, four days per week (Monday, Tuesday, Wednesday and Friday) except for holidays. The adjacent camp offers both a dental clinic and infirmary for sick call and minor medical problems. Sick call is Monday, Tuesday, Thursday, and Friday, 6:30am-6:45am. Outpatient care is available for those cases beyond the scope of the camp's health services. Pill line is seven days per week. Medical staff at the FMC and camp are on duty or on call 24 hours a day, seven days a week. Physical examinations may be requested every two years for inmates under 50, and every year for inmates over the age of 50.

**Housing:** There are several housing units at the FMC. The Antaeus Unit is on three floors and is comprised of three dormitories and rooms. The Bluegrass Unit has three floors comprised of three dormitories and rooms. The Commonwealth Unit and the Health Care Units provide specialized services to inmates who have acute or chronic health problems. The Mary Todd unit is on one floor, comprised of six-man rooms. Inmates who are classified under "general population" are housed in 36-man dorms, two-man cubicles, and single-man rooms. The units are wheelchair accessible. Inmates who are classified under "medical population" are double-bunked in two-man rooms. The FMC has approximately three television rooms per unit (or one television per floor). The camp houses inmates in two-person or three-person dormitory cubicles. Camp residents must sign up a day in advance to select television programs.

**Fitness/Recreation:** The recreation department is open 6:30am-8:15pm and offers exercise bicycles, stair-steppers, some nautilus equipment, music room, pool tables, and ping-pong tables. Intramural team sports are available. Structured fitness classes such as aerobics, yoga, spinning, and jump rope are also offered. The hobby craft center offers leather craft and ceramics, painting, drawing, and copper works. The camp offers intramural team sports, physical fitness and weight reduction programs, and arts and crafts.

**Religious Services:** The FMC and camp share three full-time chaplains. A contract rabbi and imam provide religious services. Pastoral counseling and consultation is available according to need. Religious items are sold through the commissary.

**Commissary:** The FMC's commissary is open Tuesday, Wednesday, and Thursday 4pm-7pm, and Monday and Friday 2pm-3pm. The camp's commissary is open Tuesday and Thursday 1:30-9pm. Inmates at the camp are permitted to shop once per week, with the day determined by a weekly cycle. Bureau of Prisons policy currently sets a monthly commissary spending limit of $360.

**Telephone Policy:** The Inmate Telephone System (ITS) is used at the FMC. Inmates may have up to 30 phone numbers entered via TRULINCS on their phone list. Inmates may use the phones from 5am-11:30pm seven days a week. Inmates are limited to 300 call minutes per week, and calls are not to exceed 15 minutes in length.

**Inmate Mail:** The FMC and camp accept United States Postal Service First Class, U.S. Priority, and Express Mail. Inmates may receive publications without prior approval, although the warden will reject publications that are determined to be detrimental to the security, good order or discipline of the institution. All publications must come directly from the publisher or bookstore. Accumulation of publications is limited to five magazines and five books.

**Inmate Mail to FMC:**
    INMATE NAME & REGISTER NUMBER
    FMC Lexington
    Federal Medical Center
    3301 Leestown Road
    Lexington, KY 40511

**Inmate Mail to Camp:**
    INMATE NAME & REGISTER NUMBER
    FMC Lexington
    Federal Medical Center
    Satellite Camp
    3301 Leestown Road
    Lexington, KY 40511

**Visiting Hours:** Visiting hours for the FMC are Monday, Thursday, and Friday 2:25pm-8:40pm, and Saturday, Sunday, and federal holidays, 8:30am-3pm. Camp visiting hours are Friday 5pm-8:30pm, Saturday and Sunday, 8:30am-3pm. There are no camp visiting hours on federal holidays. Inmates are grant-ed 12 visiting points per month. Weekday visits cost two points and weekends (including Friday) cost four. However, only one point is deducted for Friday visits at the camp. Attorney visits must be made by advance arrangement. Additional visiting information can be found on the BOP website, www.bop.gov, at https://www.bop.gov/locations/institutions/lex/.

**Lodging/Accommodations:** Should visitors be spending the night, the following is a short list of accommodations that are available in Lexington, Kentucky:
    Hilton Garden Inn                          859-543-8300
    Baymont Inn & Suites                       859-293-0047
    La Quinta Inn                              800-231-7551
    Quality Inn Northwest                      859-233-0561

**Directions to Facility:** FMC Lexington is located approximately seven miles north of Lexington, Kentucky, on U.S. Highway 421 (Leestown Pike). To drive from Interstate 64 or 75, take exit 115 to Kentucky Highway 922 and proceed to Highway 4 (New Circle Road). Drive west on New Circle Road to exit 7, and take Highway 421 North for approximately four miles. The institution is on the right.

## §12:24  FCI MANCHESTER

FCI Manchester
805 Fox Hollow Road
Manchester, KY 40962
MAN/ExecAssistant@bop.gov
606-598-1900
Fax: 606-598-4115

**Location:** FCI Manchester is located in Clay County in eastern Kentucky, 75 miles south of Lexington off Interstate 75, and 28 miles east of London off Hal Rogers Parkway (formerly known as Daniel Boone Parkway). Go three miles north on State Highway 421, then 1.4 miles off Highway 421 on Fox Hollow Road. The area is served by Bluegrass Field Airport in Lexington, and McGee Tyson Airport in Knoxville.

**History:** Opened in 1992.

**Judicial District:** Eastern Kentucky.

**Security Level:** FCI Manchester is a medium-security facility housing male inmates. An adjacent satellite prison camp houses minimum-security male offenders.

**Population:** As of 6/11/2017, the FCI inmate population is 871, and the camp population is 208. Weekly population figures are available on the BOP website at https://www.bop.gov/locations/institutions/man/.

**Education:** The FCI and camp offer GED, ESL, parenting classes, and adult education. Inmates may also take courses from any accredited college or university, pending approval from the Education Department and acceptance from the university. The cost for correspondence courses must be paid by the inmate.

**Vocational/Apprenticeship:** The FCI offers vocational training in both marketable and exploratory skills. Inmates must be enrolled in GED or have a high school diploma to qualify. Several apprenticeships are offered. At the FCI, inmates can take part in a Building Trades VT program, to include Carp-entry, Electrical, and Masonry; or an Apprenticeship VT for Baker, Cabinet Maker, Carpentry, Cook, Drafting, Electrician, HVAC, Landscape Management Technician, Machine Operator I, Painter, and Plumber. At the camp, inmates can take part in

VT programs in Horticulture or, Hydroponics, or in an Apprenticeship VT program for Baker, Boiler Operator, Carpentry, Cook, Dental, HVAC, Horticulture, Landscape Management Technician, and Weld-ing. Each program is accredited through the U.S. Department of Labor and takes two to four years to complete.

**Library:** The main institution's law library is open Monday through Thursday 8:30am-8:30pm, and Friday and Saturday 8:30am-4pm. It is closed on Sunday. Manual typewriters and a copier are available. Inmates are afforded access to legal materials and an opportunity to prepare legal documents in the Electronic Law Library (ELL). A copying machine is available to reproduce materials for research. Leisure libraries offer inmates a variety of reading materials, including but not limited to: periodicals, newspapers, fiction, non-fiction, and reference books. The leisure library has an inter-library loan program.

**UNICOR:** A textile factory at the FCI makes tarps and shirts for the U.S. Army. The factory employs approximately 300 inmates. Typical work hours are 7:15am-3pm, Monday through Friday.

**Counseling/Rehab Services:** The FCI and camp offer a non-residential drug treatment program, a drug education program, Alcoholics and Narcotics Anonymous, and a suicide prevention program. Available group counseling focuses on issues to encourage personal growth and change in areas such as stress management, anger management, and abstinence from alcohol and drugs. Counselors conduct individual and group counseling sessions. Psychological Services also offers self-help programs that can be completed at the inmate's own pace.

**Health Services:** The health services facility employs a physician, health services administration staff, mid-level practitioner(s), health information staff, nursing staff, an X-ray technician, pharmacist, dentists, a phlebotomist, and a dental hygienist. Consultants, physicians of various specialties, and optometrists are also available on a contract basis. The FCI and camp provide outpatient care, and are served by several hospitals in the area, approximately five to ten miles away. Pill line for the FCI is seven days a week at 7am-7:30am, and after the pm count clears. Pill line for the camp is 7am-7:35am, and after the pm count clears. At the FCI, sick call sign-up is at 7am-7:30am Monday, Tuesday, Thursday, and Friday. At the camp, sick call is 7am-7:15am on the same days. Medical staff is on duty or on call 24 hours a day.

**Housing:** The FCI houses inmates in two-man cells. There are eight housing units: Clay A&B, Knox A&B, Laurel A&B, and Whitley A&B. One of the units houses handicapped inmates. The units are wheelchair accessible. The camp has four housing units: Manchester A&B and Oneida A&B. There are approximately four to six televisions per housing unit. Basic cable television is available. Sports, movies, and miscellaneous television rooms are available. In the FCI, televisions may be viewed during established off-duty hours. During normal working hours, unit televisions may be viewed at the discretion of staff. In the camp, televisions may be viewed by inmates during their estab-lished off-duty hours. The televisions are turned off at 11:00 p.m., Sunday through Thursday, and 11:30 p.m., on Friday and Saturday, or at the discretion of the Unit Officer. They remain turned off until 6:00 a.m.

**Fitness/Recreation:** Scheduled recreation activities include sports, athletics, arts, crafts, organized and informal games, table games, physical fitness, social and cultural organizations, music, and entertainment. The FCI offers an intramural sports program to provide an organized, safe, and enjoyable form of recreation.

**Religious Services:** Chaplains are available upon request to provide pastoral care, counseling, religious education, spiritual direction, support, crisis intervention, and to conduct religious services. There is a religious library from which inmates may obtain devotional and reference material.

**Commissary:** Commissary and validation schedules are posted on the inmate bulletin boards. The National Spending Limit is $360.00 but may be further restricted at the local level. Each inmate account is revalidated on a monthly, bi-weekly, or weekly cycle. FCI Manchester has a current spending limit of $320 per month. Stamps and OTC medication are exempt from the spending limit.

**Telephone Policy:** Inmates at the FCI and camp dial direct using the Inmate Telephone System (ITS). The following are standard features of ITS: (1) inmate calls will automatically terminate after 15 minutes; (2) an inmate's calling list is limited to 30 callers; (3) calls are charged to an inmate's commissary account; and (4) calls are limited to 300 minutes per month. Ordinarily, inmates are allowed an extra 100 minutes per month in November and December. Inmates are permitted to change their telephone list no more than three times per month. Telephones are available daily 6am-11:30pm, with limitations from 7:30am-10:30am, and 12pm until after 4pm count.

**Inmate Mail:** The FCI and camp accept mail from the U.S. Postal Service via First-Class, U.S. Priority, and Express mail. For those interested in sending over-night mail via a private carrier (FedEx or UPS Overnight), it is recommended that you first contact the institution to find out whether the receipt of such mail is permitted. Inmates are only allowed to receive publications directly from the publisher, a book club, or a bookstore.

**Inmate Mail to Both FCI and Camp:**
INMATE NAME & REGISTER NUMBER
Federal Correctional Institution
FCI Manchester
P.O. Box 4000
Manchester, KY 40962

**Visiting Hours:** Approved visiting hours at both the FCI and camp are Friday, Saturday, Sunday, and federal holidays 8am-3pm. Visits are not allowed Monday through Thursday unless they are attorney-client visits. Attorney visits can be arranged by contacting either the inmate's case manager or counselor. Inmates are allowed eight visiting points per month. One point is deducted for each weekday visit, and two points are deducted for each weekend visit. However, no points are deducted for federal holiday visits. Additional visiting information can be found on the BOP website, www.bop.gov, at https://www.bop.gov/locations/institutions/man/.

**Lodging/Accommodations:** Should visitors be spending the night, the fol- lowing is a short list of accommodations that are available near Manchester, Kentucky:

| | |
|---|---|
| Hampton Inn London | 606-864-0011 |
| Holiday Inn Express | 606-862-0077 |
| Budget Hotel Westgate Inn | 606-878-7330 |
| Sleep Inn | 606-576-7829 |
| Super 8 Motel | 606-878-9800 |

**Directions to Facility:** The Federal Correctional Institution is located north of Manchester, Kentucky, off Highway 421 on Fox Hollow Road. Manchester is located approximately 26 miles east of Interstate 75, Exit 41 in London, Kentucky. Take the Daniel Boone Parkway (toll road, $.40 per vehicle) to the Manchester exit, turn north onto Kentucky Highway 421 (left). Continue on Kentucky Highway 421 through the town of Manchester (approximately four miles) to Fox Hollow Road, which is immediately past the Kentucky Department of Transportation buildings (on left). Turn left onto Fox Hollow Road and proceed to the main entrance of the institution (approximately one mile).

## §12:25  USP MCCREARY

USP McCreary
United States Penitentiary
330 Federal Way
Pine Knot, KY 42635
MCR/ExecAssistant@bop.gov
606-354-7000
Fax: 606-354-7190

**Location:** USP McCreary is located approximately 88 miles north of Knox-ville, Tennessee, 125 miles south of Lexington, Kentucky, and 208 miles south of Cincinnati, Ohio. The area is served by Williamsburg Airport, Amtrak, and major bus lines.

**History:** USP McCreary was activated in 2003.

**Judicial District:** Western Virginia.

**Security Level:** USP McCreary is a high-security facility that houses male offenders, with an adjacent minimum-security satellite camp that houses male offenders.

**Population:** As of 6/11/2017, the USP inmate population is 1,310, and the camp population is 157. Weekly population figures are available on the BOP website at https://www.bop.gov/locations/institutions/mcr/.

**Education:** The education department offers a wide variety of academic and vocational programs ranging from adult literacy to post-secondary studies through correspondence. All programs are voluntary with the exception of general education development (GED) and English as a second language (ESL).

**Vocational/Apprenticeship:** USP McCreary does not offer advanced occupational education. Vocational training is offered in computer-based programs. The main facility and the camp offer Introduction of Office. The camp offers apprenticeship programs in automotive mechanics, powerhouse mechanics, cooking, welding and landscaping. The main facility offers apprenticeship programs in painting, draftsman, electrician, cook, HVAC, and plumber.

**Library:** The law library is located in the Education Department and contains a variety of legal reference materials and a CD-ROM law library for use in preparing legal papers. The law library is open Monday through Thursday, 8am-10am, 12:30pm-3:30pm, and 4:45pm-8pm; Friday 8am-10am and 12:30-3:30pm; Saturday, Sunday, and federal holidays, 7:30am-9:30am and 12noon-3pm. An inmate law library clerk is available for assistance in legal research. Inmates may copy materials necessary for their research or legal matters via a debit/commissary card-operated machine. A leisure library is also available in the Education Department. An inter-library loan service is offered. The leisure library is open Monday through Thursday, 7:50am-10:10am, 12:50pm-3:10pm, and 5:10pm-8pm; Friday, 7:50am-10:10am, 12:50pm-3:10pm; and Saturday, Sunday, and federal holidays, 7:50am-9:30am and 10:55am-3:10pm.

**UNICOR:** UNICOR at McCreary employs inmates in Automated Data Processing (ADP). USP McCreary processes patents for the U.S. Patent Office and employs approximately 180 inmates.

**Counseling/Rehab Services:** Psychologists are available to provide counseling and other mental health services. USP McCreary provides programs to assist inmates in overcoming problems with substance abuse, including drug education, Alcoholics Anonymous and Narcotics Anonymous. Living Free, Anger Management, Stress Management, Breaking Barriers, and the Challenge Program, for inmates who want to make positive lifestyle changes, are also offered. USP McCreary and the camp do not have a Residential Drug Abuse Program, but can refer inmates who meet the eligibility requirements.

**Health Services:** Medical staff are available seven days a week, 6am-10pm. Medical and dental sick call for the USP is 6:30am-7:15am Monday, Tuesday, Thursday, and Friday. The camp sick call is Monday, Wednesday, Thursday, and Friday 6:30am-7:15am or 10am. The pill line is Monday through Friday 6am until completion, 2:30pm (insulin line and self-carry meds), and 5:30pm until completion, and 7am and 2:30pm promptly for insulin only; weekends and holidays, 8am-2:30am, 2:30pm (insulin line and self-carry meds), and 5:30pm until completion. Inmates under 50 years of age are eligible for a complete physical examination every two years, while inmates 50 years of age and older are eligible for an annual physical.

**Housing:** Inmates at the USP are generally housed in two-man cells in twelve housing units: Unit 1 A&B, Unit 2 A&B, Unit 3 A&B, Unit 4 A&B, Unit 5 A&B, and Unit 6 A&B. Unit televisions may be viewed during established off duty-hours providing appropriate noise levels are maintained.

**Fitness/Recreation:** Recreation and leisure programs include intramural team sports such as softball, basketball, soccer, and volleyball. Indoor activities include individual arts and crafts programs. Wellness programs are also offered. Recreation hours are as follows: weekdays, 8:30am-9:45am, 10:30am-1:20pm, 1:50pm-3pm, and 5:20pm-7:10pm; weekends and holidays, 8:25am-9:30am, 10:50am-12:55pm, 1:15pm-3:20pm, and 5:15pm-7:55pm.

**Religious Services:** The facility offers a wide range of religious programs to inmates. Staff chaplains are available, as well as contract and volunteer representatives of other faiths. Religious diets, holiday observances, and worship activities are coordinated through the chaplain's office.

**Commissary:** The USP commissary schedule is Monday through Thursday from the time the 4pm count clears until the last call is given. Shopping days are determined by the last two digits of the first five of an inmate's register number. Inmate shopping days at the camp commissary are Tuesday and Thursday, 10:45am-12pm, by register number. Inmates whose last two numbers of the first five digits of their register number are 00-50 shop on Tuesdays. Those whose numbers are 51-99 shop on Thursdays. Inmates may shop once per week. Federal Bureau of Prisons policy currently sets a monthly spending limit of $360.

**Telephone Policy:** USP McCreary uses the Inmate Telephone System (ITS). Calls are limited to 15 minutes, and inmates may use up to 300 minutes per month. These minutes can be used as either debit or collect calls, or any combination of the two. Inmates may have up to 30 telephone numbers on their call lists. Telephones are placed in each housing unit. The USP and camp telephones are available from 6am until lockdown.

**Inmate Mail:** The USP and camp accept mail from the U.S. Postal Service via First-Class, U.S. Priority, and Express mail. For those interested in sending overnight mail via a private carrier (FedEx or UPS Overnight), it is recommended that you first contact the institution to find out whether the receipt of such mail is permitted. Inmates may subscribe to and receive publications without prior approval, though the warden will reject a publication if it is determined to be detrimental to the security, good order, or discipline of the institution, or if it might facilitate criminal activity. A camp inmate may receive soft-covered publications (paperback books and magazines) from any source; however, the packaging or envelope must indicate on the outside "authorized reading material". USP and camp inmates may receive hard-covered publications only from a publisher, book store, or a book club. In addition, soft-covered publications for USP inmates must also be received from the publisher, book store, or book club. Accumulation of publications will be limited to five (5) magazines (not to be more than three months old) and to the amount that can be neatly stored in the locker provided in each room because of sanitation and fire safety reasons.

**Inmate Mail to USP:**
    INMATE NAME & REGISTER NUMBER
    USP McCreary
    U.S. Penitentiary
    P.O. Box 3000
    Pine Knot, KY 42635

**Inmate Mail to Satellite Camp:**
    INMATE NAME & REGISTER NUMBER
    USP McCreary
    U.S. Penitentiary
    Satellite Camp
    P.O. Box 3000
    Pine Knot, KY 42635

**Visiting Hours:** As of June 11, 2017, all visiting at this facility has been suspended until further notice. This policy may have changed by the time you read this entry. See https://www.bop.gov/locations/institutions/mcr/.

Normally, visiting is conducted Saturdays, Sundays, and federal holidays 8:30am-3pm. No more than four adult visitors can visit an inmate at any one time. Normally, all immediate family members (wife, children, parents, brothers and sisters) are approved. Non-relatives may be approved to visit. However, inmates may not have more than 10 friends/associates on their visiting list. Attorneys of record can be placed on an inmate's approved visiting list. Attorneys should try to visit during normal visiting hours. Attorneys are required to make prior arrangements with the inmate's unit team for a legal visit during non-visiting hours. Additional visiting information can be found on the BOP website at https://www.bop.gov/locations/institutions/mcr/.

**Lodging/Accommodations:** Should visitors be spending the night, the following is a short list of accommodations that are available near Williamsburg, Kentucky:

| | |
|---|---|
| Cumberland Falls State Resort | 606-528-4121 |
| Cumberland Inn | 606-539-4100 |
| Hampton Inn | 606-549-3775 |
| Super 8 Motel | 606-620-0189 |

**Directions to Facility:** From I-75: take Exit 11 in Williamsburg, Kentucky, and travel west on KY-92. Travel approximately 17 miles (drive carefully as this road has numerous sharp turns). Turn right on the second turn for KY-1044. There will be a green road sign stating "United States Penitentiary" just prior to this turn. Drive approximately one mile on KY-1044. USP McCreary is on the right. Once on the institution property, the United States Penitentiary parking area is on the second right. The camp parking area is straight past the Penitentiary on the left.

From Us Hwy 27: turn onto KY 92 and travel east. Turn left on KY-1044. There will be a green road sign stating "United States Penitentiary" just prior to this turn. Drive approximately one mile on KY-1044. USP McCreary is on the left. Once on the institution property, the United States Penitentiary parking area is the second right. The camp parking area is straight past the Penitentiary on the left.

## §12:26   FCI MCDOWELL

FCI McDowell
Federal Correctional Institution
101 Federal Drive
Welch, WV 24801
MCD/ExecAssistant@bop.gov
304-436-7300
Fax: 304-436-7318

**Location:** FCI McDowell is located in southern West Virginia, approximately four miles north of the City of Welch and about 48 miles Southwest of Beckley, West Virginia. No local transportation is available.

**History:** This is one of the newest federal correctional institutions. Construction finished in January of 2010.

**Judicial District:** Southern West Virginia.

**Security Level:** FCI McDowell is a medium security facility housing male offenders. This institution also includes an adjacent satellite prison camp housing minimum security male offenders.

**Population:** As of 6/11/2017, the USP inmate population is 1,112, and the camp population is 76. Weekly population figures are available on the BOP website at https://www.bop.gov/locations/institutions/mcd/.

**Education:** The Education Department at FCI McDowell offers ESL, GED, adult continuing education, post-secondary education, and parenting classes.

**Vocational/Apprenticeship:** There are occupational training programs at FCI McDowell. The programs offered are not set in stone yet, and may vary.

**Library:** The law library is located in the Educational Department and contains a variety of legal reference materials for use in preparing legal papers. The law library is open during convenient non-working hours, including weekends.

**Counseling/Rehab Services:** Psychologists are available to provide individual counseling and other mental health services. The staff of each unit is available for informal counseling sessions and formal group counseling activities. Self-image groups and other voluntary groups are conducted by correctional counselors. The FCI has a self-help library program, including books, audio, and video materials. Drug treatment programs are also provided, including the 12-15 hour drug education course, the 12-14 week non-residential drug treatment program, and the 500-hour Residential Drug Abuse Program (RDAP).

**Health Services:** Sick call appointments may be made during the morning sick-call move, Monday, Tuesday, Thursday, and Friday (except holidays). Camp sick call appointments may be made 6:30am-6:45am on the same days. Inmates under the age of 50 are entitled to physical examinations every two years, and health care prevention visits every three years. Inmates over the age of 50 are entitled to both physical exams and prevention visits every year, as well as yearly EKG. The Health Services Department includes a dental department and a consultant eye doctor.

**Fitness/Recreation:** Indoor and outdoor activities are available, with a variety of arts and crafts programs and intramural team sports. Physical fitness and weight reduction programs are also offered.

**Religious Services:** Religious services consist of pastoral care, counseling, and a variety of religious programs, with regularly scheduled services, studies, special programs, holy days and periodic guest speakers.

**Commissary:** The Commissary access time for inmates in each unit is scheduled on a daily basis. The schedule is posted in the unit and on the Commissary item sheet. Federal Bureau of Prisons policy currently sets a monthly spending limit of $360.

**Telephone Policy:** FCI McDowell uses the Inmate Telephone System (ITS). Calls are limited to 15 minutes, and inmates may use up to 300 minutes per month. Each inmate is allowed up to 30 approved telephone numbers.

**Inmate Mail:** The FCI and camp accept mail from the U.S. Postal Service via First-Class, U.S. Priority, and Express mail. For those interested in sending overnight mail via a private carrier (FedEx or UPS Overnight), it is recommended that you first contact the institution to find out whether the receipt of such mail is permitted. Inmates may receive publications without prior approval, although the warden will reject publications that are determined to be detrimental to the security, good order, and discipline of the institution. Publications may only be received directly from the publisher, bookstore or book club. Each inmate is allowed to retain up to five magazines no older than three months old.

**Inmate Mail to FCI:**
INMATE NAME & REGISTER NUMBER
FCI McDowell
Federal Correctional Institution
P.O. Box 1009
Welch, WV 24801

**Inmate Mail to Satellite Camp:**
INMATE NAME & REGISTER NUMBER
FCI McDowell
Federal Correctional Institution
Satellite Camp
P.O. Box 1009
Welch, WV 24801

**Visiting Hours:** Visiting at the FCI is conducted Saturday, Sunday, Monday and federal holidays, 8am-3pm. Visiting at the camp is Saturday, Sunday and federal holidays from 8am-3pm. Each inmate has six visiting points per month. One point will be assessed for weekday visits, and two points will be assessed for weekends and federal holidays. Additional visiting points may be granted under unusual circumstances, such as visitors traveling long distances or to meet other special needs, with advance approval. There is no point system at the camp; visiting privileges are unlimited. There may be a maximum of five visitors, including children, for each visit. Inmates may have up to 20 visitors on their pre-approved visiting lists. Attorneys are encouraged to visit during normal visiting hours, but special arrangements can be made for a legal visit during non-visiting hours. Additional visiting information can be found on the BOP website https://www.bop.gov/locations/institutions/mcd/.

**Lodging/Accommodations:** Should visitors be spending the night, the following is a short list of accommodations that are available near Welch, West Virginia:

| | |
|---|---|
| Elkhorn Inn & Theater | 304-862-2031 |
| Count Gilu Motel | 304-436-3041 |
| Pocahontas Motel | 304-436-2250 |
| Big Four Motel | 304-585-7313 |

**Directions to Facility:** <u>From Beckley</u>: turn left on WV-16 , stay straight on WV-121 South, turn right onto Slab Fork RD/CR-34, continue on CR-34 then turn Right onto WV-97, then take a left onto WV-10, and then turn right onto WV-16 continue South until you enter McDowell County, take the first Right onto 101 Federal Drive. There will be a Federal Institution sign marking the location.

<u>From Bluefield</u>: Take US-52 North and then make right onto WV-16N continue on WV-16 North for approximately 7 miles there will be a Federal Institution sign marking location.

## §12:27   FCI MEMPHIS

FCI Memphis
1101 John Denie Road
Memphis TN 38134
MEM/ExecAssistant@bop.gov
901-372-2269
Fax: 901-380-5462

**Location:** FCI Memphis is located in the northeast section of Memphis, Tennessee, at the intersection of Interstate 40 and Sycamore View Road. Memphis is served by Memphis International Airport, Amtrak, and commercial bus lines.

**History:** Opened in 1977, FCI Memphis houses male offenders primarily from the southeastern United States. There is also a detention unit for pre-trial and pre-sentence federal detainees.

**Judicial District:** Western Tennessee.

**Security Level:** FCI Memphis is a medium-security facility housing male inmates. A satellite prison camp houses minimum-security male offenders.

**Population:** As of 6/12/2017, FCI inmate population is 1,027, and the camp population is 253. Weekly population figures are available at the BOP website at https://www.bop.gov/locations/institutions/mem/.

**Education:** Both the FCI and the camp offer GED, ESL, adult education, and correspondence courses. A two-year college degree program in business commerce and technology (73 credit hours) is offered by State Technical Institute. In order to enroll in the college degree program inmates must have a high school diploma/GED and one year remaining on their sentence.

**Vocational/Apprenticeship:** FCI Memphis offers advanced occupational education in quality & productivity basic/advanced and computerized business education. Most areas of study take approximately four years to complete; however, accumulated hours can be transferred to apprenticeship programs in the community upon release. Currently, apprenticeships are available in the following trades or skill areas: Dental Assistant, Quality Control, Carpentry, Electrician, Plumber, Landscape Gardener, Refrigeration and Air-Conditioning, Welding, Architectural Drafting, Quality Assurance and Supervision, Food Service, Painter, Electronics Tester, Electrical Maintenance, Printer Press Operator and Purchasing Agent.

**Library:** The FCI's leisure and law libraries are open Monday through Friday 7:35am-11:30am, and 12:30-3:45pm; Saturday 7:30am-3:30pm; closed on Sunday. A law clerk is available to help inmates with researching and preparing legal material. Electric typewriters and a copier are available. Copies are 10 cents per page and are charged to an inmate's debit card. The camp's library is open daily from 8am-8pm. Inmates will be allowed use of the Electronic Law Library (ELL) by submitting an Inmate Request to Staff. The leisure libraries have an inter-library loan program with the Memphis/Shelby County Library. Fiction and non-fiction literature is available in Spanish as well as English. A professional librarian is available several hours each week to provide assistance.

**UNICOR:** FCI Memphis' UNICOR employs approximately 256 inmates and operates electronic cable assemblies and a printing operation. There is a waiting list for employment

**Counseling/Rehab Services:** The FCI and the camp offer a non-residential drug treatment program, a drug education program, and Alcoholics Anonymous and Narcotics Anonymous groups. Each unit has a psychologist available to provide counseling and other mental health services. FCI Memphis also has a staff or contract psychiatrist, who is a medical doctor and who is available by appointment for individual problem solving. Unit staff are available for informal counseling sessions and conducting formal counseling activities.

**Health Services:** The Health Services Unit is staffed by physicians, physician assistants, dentists and dental staff, and a pharmacist. Specialists visit the institution on an as-needed basis to see inmates. These specialists include an optometrist, orthopedist, dietician, podiatrist, psychiatrist, urologist, and audiologist. The FCI and camp provide outpatient care, and are served by several hospitals in the area approximately 15 miles away. At the FCI, sick call sign-up is available Monday, Tuesday, Thursday and Friday 6:30am-7am. At the camp, sick call sign-up is 6am-6:30am Monday and Wednesday. The pill line at the FCI runs on weekdays at 6am, 11am, 5pm and 8pm. On weekends and holidays the morning pill line is at 8am. Pill line at the camp is 6am, 3:30pm, and 8:30pm. At least one physician's assistant is on duty or on call 24 hours a day. Age-specific periodic health examinations are available.

**Housing:** The FCI houses inmates in two-man cells. There are a total of five housing units, one of which is wheelchair accessible. The camp houses inmates in four dormitories in two-man or four-man cubicles. Unit televisions may be viewed during established off-duty hours. Ordinarily, the televisions will be turned off while unit inmates are completing sanitation requirements.

**Fitness/Recreation:** Inmates are given the opportunity for a minimum of five hours of recreation per week. The recreation department offers team sports, bicycles, stair-steppers, rowing machines, a music room (musical instruments and amplifiers are provided), pool tables, and ping-pong tables. The hobby craft center offers leather craft, woodworking, crocheting, knitting, painting, and beading. Inmates may also choose from a wide selection of organized sports. Feature films are shown in each housing unit Wednesday through Friday. Feature films in Spanish are shown once each quarter and on Spanish holidays. The camp offers team sports, billiards, bocce ball, hobby crafts, music, and ping-pong. The Recreation Department also offers a wellness program that encourages physical and mental health such as weight management, AIDS awareness, nutrition, smoking cessation and stress management.

**Religious Services:** FCI Memphis offers a wide range of religious programs to inmates. Staff chaplains are available to all inmates and certain contract and volunteer representatives of specific faiths are also available. Religious holidays and special diets are coordinated through the chaplain's office.

**Commissary:** Inmates are allowed to shop once per week. The FCI commissary is open for sales four days per week (Monday-Thursday) during mainline from 11am-2:30p.m. and reasonably after the 4pm count until the last inmate is served, (no later than 7pm). The camp's commissary is open Tuesday and Wednesday, 11am-12:30pm and after the 4pm count until the last inmate is served (no later than 7pm). Shopping days are assigned according to an inmate's register number. Bureau of Prisons policy currently sets a monthly commissary spending limit of $360.

**Telephone Policy:** At the FCI there are three telephones for long distance, international, and collect calls available in each housing unit. The telephones are available to the inmate population daily 6am-9:30pm. The telephone room at the camp closes at 9:45pm. Inmates at the camp dial direct using the Inmate Telephone System (ITS). Each call is limited to 15 minutes, and an inmate may have 300 telephone minutes per month.

**Inmate Mail:** The FCI and camp accept mail from the U.S. Postal Service via First Class, U.S. Priority, and Express mail. Inmates may receive publications without prior approval, although the warden will reject publications that are determined to be detrimental to the security, good order or discipline of the institution. All publications must come directly from the publisher, bookstore or book club. Inmate may retain up to 11 magazines, books and newspapers.

**Inmate Mail to FCI:**
INMATE NAME & REGISTER NUMBER
Federal Correctional Institution
FCI Memphis
P.O. Box 34550
Memphis, TN 38134

**Inmate Mail to Camp:**
INMATE NAME & REGISTER NUMBER
FCI Memphis
Federal Correctional Institution
Satellite Camp
P.O. Box 2000
Millington, TN 38083

**Visiting Hours:** Approved visitors may visit the FCI and camp on Saturdays, Sundays, and Mondays (excluding federal holidays) 8am-3pm. Each inmate is allowed 30 visiting points per month. Each visiting point is equal to one hour of visiting on weekdays. On weekends, inmates are charged two points per hour. Visiting lists are limited to no more than ten friends and associates, and a total of 25 visitors (including family). A small children's room is available at the FCI. At the camp, a children's playground is located in the outer visiting area. Attorney visits can be made by special arrangement by contacting either the inmate's case manager or counselor. Additional information can be found on the BOP website, https://www.bop.gov/locations/institutions/mem/.

**Lodging/Accommodations:** Should visitors be spending the night, the following is a short list of accommodations that are available in Memphis, Tennessee:

| | |
|---|---|
| Comfort Inn Downtown | 901-526-0583 |
| Comfort Inn & Suites | 901-373-8200 |
| La Quinta Inn | 901-381-0044 |
| Memphis Inn | 901-373-9898 |
| Motel 6 | 901-382-8572 |
| Super 8 Motel | 901-373-4888 |

**Directions to Facility:** <u>From Downtown Memphis:</u> take I-240 east toward Nashville approximately 11.4 miles. Merge onto the I-40 east via Exit 12C toward Nashville and drive for 1.4 miles. Take Exit 12, drive .2 miles. Keep right at the fork and go on Sycamore View Rd. Take Sycamore View Rd. approximately .5 miles, then turn right onto Longline Rd. In .2 miles Longline Rd. becomes John A. Denie Dr. Drive 1.1 miles farther to FCI Memphis.

# §12:28  FCI MORGANTOWN

FCI Morgantown
446 Greenbag Road, Route 857
P.O. Box 1000
Morgantown, WV 26501
MRG/ExecAssistant@bop.gov
304-296-4416
Fax: 304-284-3600

**Location:** FCI Morgantown is located in the mountainous region of north central West Virginia, on the southern edge of the city of Morgantown, off State Highway 857 (Greenbag Road). The area is served by the Hartsfield Municipal Airport and Greyhound.

**History:** Opened in 1969, FCI Morgantown houses male offenders with substantial program needs (chemical abuse treatment, vocational training, education, or counseling).

**Judicial District:** Northern West Virginia.

**Security Level:** FCI Morgantown houses minimum-security male inmates.

**Population:** As of 6/12/2017, FCI inmate population is 814. Weekly population figures are available on the BOP website at www.bop.gov, https://www.bop.gov/locations/institutions/mrg/.

**Education:** FCI Morgantown offers GED and ESL classes.

**Vocational/Apprenticeship:** FCI Morgantown offers advanced occupational education in administrative assistant and AutoCAD. Vocational training is offered in computer literacy, and welding. Apprenticeship programs are offered for those who have sentences of three years or longer. The FCI also offers a class in job searching and mock job fairs to develop interview skills.

**Library:** The law library is open Monday through Sunday from 7:30am-8:30pm. The camp is recognized as having one of the largest libraries in the Bureau of Prisons. Electric typewriters are available to inmates for the preparation of legal documents. A copier is also available. An inmate law library clerk is available for assistance in legal research. Inmates may also reference the Law Library material via the Electronic Law Library(ELL). The leisure library does not have an inter-library loan program. Books may be checked out one at a time for up to 10 days. Video recorders and audio-cassette players are available to inmates in the leisure library.

**UNICOR:** FCI Morgantown employs approximately 101 inmates in call center/ help desk services in partnership with a private industry customer. UNICOR offers awards, training and scholarships for inmates as well.

**Counseling/Rehab Services:** The camp offers a 500-hour Residential Drug Abuse Program (RDAP). The program is nine months in length. In addition, the camp offers a non-residential drug treatment program, a drug education program, Alcoholics Anonymous, Narcotics Anonymous and Gambler's Anonymous groups, and individual and group counseling. The psychology department is staffed by psychologists and drug treatment specialists. The non-residential treatment program lasts six months.

**Health Services:** The camp is staffed by one physician, six physician's assistants, one dentist, and one pharmacist. Inmates are provided with outpatient care. The institution is served by the University of West Virginia Medical Center (approximately 15 minutes away). Sick call is 6:45am-7am. The pill line is available during weekdays at 6:30am, 11am, and 8:30pm. On weekends, pill line is available at 7:30am, 12:30pm, and 8:30pm. At least one physician's assistant is on duty or on call 24 hours a day.

**Housing:** The facility is comprised of seven housing units. The units have dormitory-style areas, cubicles, and double room housing. New admissions usually live in the dormitory and cubicle areas until rooms become available.

**Fitness/Recreation:** The recreation department offers a weight room, exercise bicycles, aerobic exercise/nutrition (wellness program), pool tables, ping-pong tables, foosball, and bumper-pool tables. The hobby craft center offers painting, leather craft, beading, art, and wood carving. Completed projects must be mailed home. The Recreation Department includes an auditorium, multi-purpose room, gymnasium. Inmates are limited to crochet and small drawing projects in their housing unit.

**Religious Services:** FCI Morgantown provides inmates of all faith groups with reasonable and equitable opportunities to pursue religious beliefs and practices. All issues of religious concern are to be coordinated through religious services. Programs and activities are held weekly in the chapel or in the outdoor worship area. Religious Services is aided by a large cadre of volunteers and contractors in the endeavor to provide representative of each faith group.

**Commissary:** The commissary is open Monday through Thursday 6:30am-8am, 9am-10am, and 10:45am-12:30pm. Inmates are permitted to visit the commissary only once each shopping day, and are only permitted to shop once per week on their regularly scheduled shopping day. Inmates are permitted to spend up to $300 per month. Stamps, over-the counter medications, and telephone credits do not come off this spending limit.

**Telephone Policy:** Inmates at the camp dial direct using the Inmate Telephone system (ITS). The following are standard features of ITS: (1) inmate calls automatically terminate after 15 minutes; (2) an inmate's calling list is limited to 30 callers; and (3) calls are charged to the inmate's debit card. Each housing unit is equipped with telephones. Telephones are operational during non-programming and non-work hours. One telephone (red phone) is operational 24 hours a day. Inmates are allowed a total of 300 minutes per month and their telephone lists may be updated up to three times per month or up to a maximum of nine times per quarter.

**Inmate Mail:** The camp accepts mail from the U.S. Postal Service via First-Class, U.S. Priority, and Express mail. For those interested in sending overnight mail via a private carrier (FedEx or UPS Overnight), it is recommended that you first contact the institution to find out whether the receipt of such mail is permitted. Inmates may receive publications without prior approval, although the warden will reject publications that are determined to be detrimental to the security, good order or discipline of the institution. Softcover publications may come from any sources. Hardcover publications must come directly from the publisher, book club, or bookstore. Inmates are limited to 12 publications each (or 12 inches, stacked together) which can be neatly stored in their lockers.

**Inmate Mail to FCI:**
>INMATE NAME & REGISTER NUMBER
>FCI Morgantown
>Federal Correction Institution
>P.O. Box 1000
>Morgantown, WV 26507

**Visiting Hours:** Approved visitors may visit on Friday 5pm-9pm, and on Saturday, Sunday, and federal holidays 8am-3pm. The maximum number of visitors an inmate may receive at one time is limited to three adults. A children's room is available. Attorneys are encouraged to visit during regular visiting hours. However, visits from an attorney can be arranged at other times based on the circumstances of each case and available staff. Additional visiting information can be found https://www.bop.gov/locations/institutions/mrg/.

**Lodging/Accommodations:** Should visitors be spending the night, the following is a short list of accommodations that are available in Morgantown, West Virginia:

| | |
|---|---|
| Hampton Inn | 304-599-1200 |
| Holiday Inn Express | 304-291-2600 |
| Quality Inn | 304-296-9364 |
| Econo Lodge | 304-296-8774 |
| Super 8 Motel | 304-296-4000 |

**Directions to Facility:** <u>From the North:</u> take I-79 south to I-68, Exit 148. Once on I-68 take Exit 1, University Avenue. At the end of the off ramp turn left, go through one traffic light, and at the second traffic light at the bottom of the hill turn right. This is Greenbag Road. The institution is approximately one mile on the right.

From the South: take I-79 north to Exit 148 (I-68). Once on I-68, take Exit 1, University Avenue. At the end of the off ramp turn left, go through one traffic light, and at the second traffic light at the bottom of the hill turn right. This is Greenbag Road. The institution is approximately one mile on the right.

From the East (MD, DC, VA): take I-68 to Exit 1, University Avenue. At the end of the off ramp turn left, go through one traffic light, and at the second traffic light at the bottom of the hill turn right. This is Greenbag Road. The institution is approximately one mile on the right.

## §12:29   FCI PETERSBURG—LOW

FCI Petersburg Low
Federal Correctional Institution
1100 River Road
Hopewell, VA 23860
PET/ExecAssistant@bop.gov
804-733-7881
Fax: 804-863-1510

**Location:** FCI Petersburg Low is located 25 miles southwest of Richmond, Virginia. The area is served by Petersburg Municipal Airport and Richmond International Airport, Amtrak, and commercial bus lines.

**History:** Opened in 1932, FCI Petersburg houses male offenders primarily from the eastern United States. Opened in 1978, the satellite camp is a minimum-security facility for male offenders, most of who will be released to the mid-Atlantic region of the United States.

**Judicial District:** Eastern Virginia.

**Security Level:** FCI Petersburg is a low-security facility housing male offenders. It is part of the Petersburg Federal Correctional Complex. A satellite prison camp adjacent to the FCI Low houses minimum-security male offenders.

**Population:** As of 6/12/2016, FCI Low inmate population is 1,108, and the camp population is 295. Weekly population figures are available on the BOP website at https://www.bop.gov/locations/institutions/pet/.

**Education:** The FCI and the camp offer GED, ESL, adult continuing education (foreign languages, typing, resume writing), parenting courses, and college correspondence courses. Inmates must pay for their own tuition, books, and materials for all post-secondary courses.

**Vocational/Apprenticeship:** Vocational training offered in basic carpentry, cabinet making, computer aided drafting, and machine shop work. Various apprenticeship programs are also offered.

**Library:** The institution's general library includes a variety of magazines, newspapers, reference materials, and fictional and nonfictional books necessary for meeting inmates' educational, cultural, and leisure needs. An interlibrary loan program available through the Appomattox Regional Library. Inmates also have the opportunity to prepare legal documents and reasonable access to legal materials via the Electronic Law Library (LexisNexis). The law libraries contain required legal publications, general legal reference materials, and a selection of Bureau of Prisons policies so inmates can conduct legal research.

**UNICOR:** FCI Petersburg employs approximately 212 inmates in a print plant.

**Counseling/Rehab Services:** FCC Petersburg offers a 500-hour residential drug abuse treatment program (RDAP). It also includes the voluntary Sex Offenders Management Program. Unit staff and a psychologist are available for both informal counseling and traditional group counseling programs.

**Health Services:** FCC Petersburg provides outpatient care. The FCC is served by nearby hospitals in Petersburg and Richmond (approximately ten to 20 minutes away). Sick requests are collected daily between 7am-7:30am. On weekdays, the pill line at the FCI is open at 6am-6:30am (insulin only), 7am-7:30 am, 11:30am-12:30pm, TBA after the 4pm count (insulin only), and 7pm-7:30pm. Weekend pill line is 7am-7:30am (insulin only) and 11:30am. An earlier or later pill line hour may be implemented as deemed necessary. The pill line at the camp is open daily at 6am-6:15am (insulin only), 6:15-6:30am, and 5pm-5:15pm. Physical examinations are available every three years for inmates under the age of 50, and every year for those over the age of 50.

**Housing:** FCI Petersburg-Low is comprised of six housing units. Inmates are housed in two-man rooms or cubicle dormitories (bunk beds). Some single-man rooms are available for handicapped inmates. Limited cable television is available. Sports, news, and movie television rooms are available.

**Fitness/Recreation:** The recreation department offers team sports, weights, various courts, and a walking track area, and offers organized intramural leagues throughout the calendar year to include following sports: Soccer, Volleyball, Softball, Basketball, and Flag Football. The hobby craft center also offers drawing, acrylics, watercolor, and leather craft. All completed projects must be mailed home and are not allowed in the housing units.

**Religious Services:** Staff chaplains, contract employees, and volunteers are available to represent various inmate faith communities. A total of 22 different religious Communities/Programs are available. Information concerning religious issues, programs, or activities is discussed during orientation by the chaplains. A weekly schedule of activities is posted in all units and departments throughout the institution.

**Commissary:** The commissary is open Monday through Thursday. Inmates are assigned one shopping day per week. Hobby craft sales are conducted Thursday after the census. Bureau of Prisons policy currently sets a monthly commissary spending limit of $360.

**Telephone Policy:** Inmates at the FCI-Low and the camp dial direct using the Inmate Telephone System (ITS). The following are standard features of ITS: (1) inmate calls automatically terminate after 15 minutes; (2) an inmate's calling list is limited to 30 callers; and (3) calls are charged to the inmate's debit card. The initial telephone list is activated within five working days of the inmate's arrival at the facility. Unit phones will be available from 4:30pm to 11:30pm each evening (except during count time). Phones will also be available from 6:00 a.m. to 4:00 p.m. on weekends and holidays (except during count time).

**Inmate Mail:** The FCI and the camp accept mail from the U.S. Postal Service via First-Class, U.S. Priority, and Express mail. For those interested in sending overnight mail via private carrier (FedEx or UPS Overnight), it is recommended that you first contact the institution to find out whether the receipt of such mail is permitted. Inmates may receive publications without prior approval, although the warden will reject publications that are determined to be detrimental to the security, good order or discipline of the institution. At FCI Petersburg Low and the camp, hardcover publications and newspapers must be received directly from the publisher, bookstore or book club; softcover publications can come from any source. The Unit Manager may allow more space for legal publications upon request.

**Inmate Mail to FCI:**
    INMATE NAME & REGISTER NUMBER
    FCI Petersburg Low
    Federal Correctional Institution
    P.O. Box 1000
    Petersburg, VA 23804

**Inmate Mail to Camp:**
    INMATE NAME & REGISTER NUMBER
    FCI Petersburg Low
    Federal Correctional Institution
    Satellite Camp
    P.O. Box 1000
    Petersburg, VA 23804

**Visiting Hours:** Approved visitors may visit the FCI-Low and camp on Monday, Thursday, and Friday 5pm-9pm, and on Saturday, Sunday, and federal holidays 8am-3pm. The camp has visitation on Friday, Saturday, Sunday and federal holidays. Inmates receive 10 points per month. One point is deducted for weekday visits; two points are deducted for weekends and holidays. No more than four visitors are permitted to visit an inmate at one time. Attorney visits can be made by special arrangement. A small television room is available for children. Additional visiting information can be found on the BOP website, at https://www.bop.gov/locations/institutions/pet/.

**Lodging/Accommodations:** Should visitors be spending the night, the following is a short list of accommodations that are available in Petersburg, Virginia:

| | |
|---|---|
| Comfort Inn | 804-732-2000 |
| Holiday Inn Express | 804-404-9948 |
| Days Inn | 804-733-4400 |
| Rodeway Inn | 804-733-0600 |
| Super 8 Motel | 804-861-0793 |

**Directions to Facility:** Take Temple Avenue (Exit 54) off Interstate 95 in Colonial Heights. Follow Temple Avenue (Route 144 East) for three miles. Turn left onto River Road (Route 725). River Road leads to the main entrance of the institution.

# §12:30  FCI PETERSBURG—MEDIUM

FCI Petersburg Medium
Federal Correctional Institution Petersburg Medium
1060 River Road
Hopewell, VA 23860
PEM/ExecAssistant@bop.gov
804-504-7200
Fax: 804-504-7204

**Location:** FCI Petersburg Medium is located 25 miles southeast of Richmond, Virginia, off Interstate 95. The area is served by Petersburg Municipal Airport and Richmond International Airport, Amtrak, and commercial bus lines.

**History:** FCI Petersburg Medium was opened in 2002.

**Judicial District:** Eastern Virginia.

**Security Level:** FCI Petersburg Medium houses medium-security male offenders. It is part of the Petersburg Federal Correctional Complex.

**Population:** As of 6/12/2017, FCI Petersburg Medium inmate population is 1,564. Weekly population figures are available on the BOP website at https://www.bop.gov/locations/institutions/pem/.

**Education:** The FCI offers GED, ESL, adult continuing education (foreign languages, typing, resume writing), parenting courses, and college correspondence courses. Inmates must pay for their own tuition, books, and materials for all post-secondary courses.

**Vocational/Apprenticeship:** Vocational training offered in basic carpentry, cabinet making, computer aided drafting, and machine shop work. Various apprenticeship programs are also offered.

**Library:** The institution's general library includes a variety of magazines, newspapers, reference materials, and fictional and nonfictional books necessary for meeting inmates' educational, cultural, and leisure needs. An interlibrary loan program available through the Appomattox Regional Library. Inmates also have the opportunity to prepare legal documents, and reasonable access to legal materials via the Electronic Law Library (LexusNexus). The law libraries contain required legal publications, general legal reference materials, and a selection of Bureau of Prisons policies so inmates can conduct legal research.

**UNICOR:** The FCI houses the UNICOR Distribution Center, which became operational in January 2004, and Pro-Mail which began early March 2004. Pro-Mail is an Internet program used between the Distribution Center and the Federal Retirement Thrift Investment Board. The system communicates the status of TSP inventory, tracks the status of production orders and allows TSP to monitor when material has been shipped from our location and the mode of transportation of the shipment. The Distribution Center ships orders to various Federal agencies, ships UNICOR catalogs to various government and private vendors that are in partnership with the Federal Prison Industries, and handles bulk mailings for our Corporate Marketing Group in Washington, DC. The Distribution Center also receives, sorts, and repackages at least 48 different styles of clothing hangers for a private vendor. In addition, the Distribution Center assembles toiletry kits (administrative kits), for inmates as well as for other government agencies. The factory is also responsible for the Inmate Boot Program.

**Counseling/Rehab Services:** FCC Petersburg offers a 500-hour residential drug abuse treatment program (RDAP). It also includes the voluntary Sex Offenders Management Program. Unit staff and a psychologist are available for both informal counseling and traditional group counseling programs.

**Health Services:** FCI Petersburg Medium provides outpatient care. The FCI is served by nearby hospitals in Petersburg and Richmond (approximately ten to 20 minutes away). Sick requests are collected daily between 7am-7:30am. On weekdays, the pill line at the FCI is open at 6am-7am or as announced in the compound (insulin only), 7am-7:30 am, 11:30am-12:30pm, TBA after the 4pm count (insulin only), and 7pm-7:30pm. Weekend and holiday pill line is 7:30am (insulin only) and 11:30am. An earlier or later pill line hour may be implemented as deemed necessary. Physical examinations are available every three years for inmates under the age of 50, and every year for those over the age of 50.

**Housing:** FCI inmates are generally housed in two-man cells.

**Fitness/Recreation:** The Recreation Department offers team sports, weights, various courts, and a walking track area, and offers organized intramural leagues throughout the calendar year to include following sports: Soccer, Volleyball, Softball, Basketball, and Flag Football. The hobby craft center also offers drawing, acrylics, watercolor, and leather craft. All completed projects must be mailed home and are not allowed in the housing units.

**Religious Services:** Staff chaplains, contract employees, and volunteers are available to represent various inmate faith communities. A total of 22 different religious Communities/Programs are available. Information concerning relig-ious issues, programs, or activities is discussed during orientation by the chaplains. A weekly schedule of activities is posted in all units and depart- ments throughout the institution.

**Commissary:** The commissary is open Monday through Thursday. Inmates are assigned one shopping day per week. Hobby craft sales are conducted Thursday after the census. Bureau of Prisons policy currently sets a monthly commissary spending limit of $360.

**Telephone Policy:** Inmates at the FCI-Low and the camp dial direct using the Inmate Telephone System (ITS). The following are standard features of ITS: (1) inmate calls automatically terminate after 15 minutes; (2) an inmate's call- ing list is limited to 30 callers; and (3) calls are charged to the inmate's debit card. The initial telephone list is activated within five working days of the inmate's arrival at the facility. Unit phones will be available from 4:30pm to 11:30pm each evening (except during count time). Phones will also be available from 6:00 a.m. to 4:00 p.m. on weekends and holidays (except during count time).

**Inmate Mail:** The FCI and the camp accept mail from the U.S. Postal Service via First-Class, U.S. Priority, and Express mail. For those interested in sending overnight mail via private carrier (FedEx or UPS Overnight), it is recommend- ed that you first contact the institution to find out whether the receipt of such mail is permitted. Inmates may receive publications without prior approval, although the warden will reject publications that are determined to be detrimen- tal to the security, good order or discipline of the institution. At FCI Petersburg Low and the camp, hardcover publications and newspapers must be received directly from the publisher, bookstore or book club; softcover publications can come from any source. The Unit Manager may allow more space for legal publications upon request.

**Inmate Mail to FCI:**
INMATE NAME & REGISTER NUMBER
FCI Petersburg Medium
Federal Correctional Institution
P.O. Box 1000
Petersburg, VA 23804

**Visiting Hours:** Approved visitors may visit the FCI on Thursday and Friday 5pm-8pm, and on Saturday, Sunday, and federal holidays 8am-3pm. Inmates are allotted 10 points per month. One point is deducted for weekday visits; two points are deducted for weekends and holidays. No more than four visitors are permitted to visit an inmate at one time. Attorney visits can be made by special arrangement. Additional visiting information can be found on the BOP website, at https://www.bop.gov/locations/institutions/pem/.

**Lodging/Accommodations:** Should visitors be spending the night, the following is a short list of accommodations that are available in Petersburg, Virginia:
| | |
|---|---|
| Comfort Inn | 804-732-2000 |
| Holiday Inn Express | 804-404-9948 |
| Days Inn | 804-733-4400 |
| Rodeway Inn | 804-733-0600 |
| Super 8 Motel | 804-861-0793 |

**Directions to Facility:** From Interstate 95, take exit 34 (Temple Ave/Highway 144), proceed east approximately three miles, then turn left onto River Road. Turn left onto River Road (Route 725). River Road leads to the main entrance of the institution.

# CHAPTER 13

---

# THE NORTH CENTRAL REGION

(This page intentionally left blank.)

**Central Office**
Central Office
Federal Bureau of Prisons
320 First St., NW
Washington, DC 20534
Phone: 202-307-3198

**North Central Regional Office**
North Central Regional Office
Federal Bureau of Prisons
400 State Avenue, Suite 800
Kansas City, KS 66101
Phone: 913-621-3939

# §13:10   MCC CHICAGO

MCC Chicago
Metropolitan Correctional Center
71 West Van Buren Street
Chicago, IL 60605
CCC/ExecAssistant@bop.gov
312-322-0567
Fax: 312-347-4012

**Location:** The institution is located near the U.S. District Court in downtown Chicago, at the intersection of Clark and Van Buren Streets. Chicago is served by Midway and O'Hare Airports (Midway is closest to the MCC), Amtrak, and Greyhound.

**History:** Opened in 1975, MCC Chicago is a 26-story triangular structure housing pre-trial detainees, inmates awaiting sentencing and designation, sentenced holdovers on writ, convicted inmates who comprise a work cadre, and INS detainees.

**Judicial District:** Northern District of Illinois.

**Security Level:** The Metropolitan Correctional Center (MCC) in Chicago, Illinois, is an administrative facility designed to house federal prisoners of all security levels, including both male and female offenders appearing before federal courts in the Northern District of Illinois.

**Population:** As of 6/13/2017, the MCC inmate population is 656. Weekly population figures are available on the BOP website at www.bop.gov, https://www.bop.gov/locations/institutions/ccc/.

**Education:** The institution offers GED, ESL, parenting programs and entrepreneurial programs.

**Vocational/Apprenticeship:** No advanced occupational education, vocational training or apprenticeship programs are offered.

**Library:** The Electronic Law Library located in the Education Department is available for use for a minimum of 3 hours per week/per unit. Requests for additional law library time may be made to the Attorney Advisor. These requests will be individually evaluated and arrangements for additional time made when deemed appropriate. A copy machine is available in the Education Department.

**UNICOR:** None.

**Counseling/Rehab Services:** The Psychology Services Department offers the following services: intake screening for designated inmates, evaluations, requested by staff or the court, group and/or individual treatment, and crisis intervention. The institution is staffed by several psychologists.

**Health Services:** The institution has physicians, physician assistants, dentists, and pharmacists on staff. Inmates are provided with outpatient care. The institution also has X-ray and laboratory testing facilities. Sick call is Monday, Tuesday, Thursday, and Friday 6am-730am. The pill line is available three times a day (early morning, noon, and early evenings), seven days a week. Sick call sign-up is available four times a week.

**Fitness/Recreation:** The Recreation Department offers aerobics, stationary bicycles, tread mills, various board games, and ping-pong tables. The hobby craft center is limited.

**Religious Services:** The institution is staffed by one full-time chaplain. Contract rabbi services are available on a bi-monthly basis. Religious services and counseling are available upon request.

**Housing:** There are five types of units: Female (B-12), Pretrial (A-6, C-13, D-15, E-17, & F-19), Holdover (G-21 & H-23), Cadre Unit (I-25) and the Special Housing Unit (Z-11). All female inmates are housed in Unit B-12. Male inmates not currently serving a sentence, but going through the court process, will ordinarily be housed in a Pretrial Unit. Sentenced male inmates, parole violators, and writ cases not designated to MCC Chicago will ordinarily be assigned to the Holdover Unit. Male inmates designated to MCC Chicago for the service of their sentence will ordinarily be housed in the Cadre Unit. It should also be noted, male inmates may be housed in SHU or female inmates may be secured in their rooms, when staff deem necessary, based on security concerns or other reasons documented in the Program Statement on Inmate Discipline and Special Housing Units.

**Commissary:** The commissary is open weekdays. Inmates are assigned one shopping day a week. Assignments are made by floor. Bureau of Prisons policy currently sets a monthly commissary spending limit of $360.

**Telephone Policy:** Telephones are placed in each unit for inmate use. Inmates call using TRUFONE credits from their commissary accounts. Inmates are limited to 300 minutes per month. An inmate is allowed 30 telephone contacts. There are two types of telephones in the MCC: monitored and unmonitored. All social calls are monitored, while attorney-client (pre-trial inmate) conversations are unmonitored.

**Inmate Mail:** The institution accepts mail from the U.S. Postal Service via First-Class, U.S. Priority, and Express mail. For those interested in sending overnight mail via a private carrier (FedEx or UPS Overnight), it is recommended that you first contact the institution to find out whether the receipt of such mail is permitted.

**Inmate Mail to MCC:**
INMATE NAME & REGISTER NUMBER
MCC Chicago
Metropolitan Correctional Center
71 West Van Buren
Chicago, IL 60605

**Visiting Hours:** Approved visitors may visit the MCC Monday through Friday from 12noon-3pm and 5pm-8pm; and Saturday, Sunday, and federal holidays from 8am-11am and 12noon-3pm. Pretrial and holdover inmates will be permitted to visit with a maximum of six immediate family members and/or the father/mother of the inmate's children. Male pretrial and holdover inmates may only visit with a maximum of three visitors (including children/infants) during each visit. Designated inmates will be permitted to visit with immediate family, other relatives, friends and associates. They may have up to 10 individuals on their approved visiting lists; however, they may only visit with a maximum of five visitors (including children/infants) during each visit. The same holds true for all female inmates. All visitors will have to go through an ion spectrometer, which detects traces of drugs. Additional visiting information can be found on the BOP website, www.bop.gov, at https://www.bop.gov/locations/institutions/ccc/.

**Lodging/Accommodations:** Should visitors be spending the night, the following is a short list of accommodations that are available in Chicago, Illinois:

| | |
|---|---|
| Courtyard by Marriott—Downtown | 312-329-2500 |
| Fairfield Inn—Downtown | 312-787-3777 |
| Red Roof Inn—Downtown | 312-787-3580 |
| Residence Inn by Marriott—Downtown | 312-943-9800 |

## §13:11   FPC DULUTH

FPC Duluth
Federal Prison Camp
4464 Ralston Drive
Duluth, MN 55811
DTH/ExecutiveAssistant@bop.gov
218-722-8634
Fax: 218-733-4701

**Location:** The camp is located on the former Duluth Air Force Base near the southwestern tip of Lake Superior, halfway between Minneapolis-St. Paul and the U.S.-Canadian border, and seven miles north of Duluth, off Highway 53 at Stebner Road. The area is served by Duluth International Airport and Greyhound.

**History:** Opened in 1983, FPC Duluth was formerly Duluth Air Force Base. Inmates are primarily from the north central United States.

**Judicial District:** District of Minnesota.

**Security Level:** The Federal Prison Camp (FPC) in Duluth, Minnesota, houses minimum-security male offenders.

**Population:** As of 6/13/2017, the FPC inmate population is 512. Weekly population figures are available on the BOP website at www.bop.gov, https://www. bop.gov/locations/institutions/dth/.

**Education:** The camp offers GED, ESL, and adult continuing education (ACE) (foreign languages, business, math, real estate, etc.).

**Vocational/Apprenticeship:** The camp offers advanced occupational education in construction technology and sales and marketing. Vocational training is offered in Braille. Apprenticeship programs are offered in HVAC, and painting. Instruction for the vocational training course is offered by Lake Superior College.

**Library:** The leisure library is open daily (see posting in library for hours). A wide range of daily newspapers, magazines periodicals, and reference books are available inmate use. The law library is open Monday through Thursday from 6am-9pm; Friday from 6:am-3:30pm; and Saturday from 7am-3:30pm. Electric typewriters are available for the preparation of legal documents. Inmates must purchase their own typewriter ribbon and correction tape from the commissary. A copier is also available. Copies are 15 cents and charged to an inmate's debit card. The Arrowhead Bookmobile visits the institution every three weeks.

**UNICOR:** None.

**Counseling/Rehab Services:** The camp offers a 9-month Residential Drug Abuse Program (RDAP) with 10-15 hour courses; it takes both voluntary participants and mandatory referrals. The camp also provides a non-residential drug treatment program, a drug education program, and Alcoholics Anonymous and Narcotics Anonymous groups, individual and group counseling or psychotherapy and psychological testing. The camp is staffed by two psychologists and five drug treatment specialists. Psychology Services are available Monday through Friday from 730am-4pm.

**Health Services:** The camp is staffed by a physician, physician assistants or nurse practitioners, dentist, dental assistant, pharmacist, EMT paramedic, and health information technician. The clinic is open from 6am-6:30pm on weekdays, and 6:30am-6:30pm on weekends and holidays. Some services available to inmates are: sick call, x-rays, lab, dental, pharmacy, etc. The pill line schedule is available outside the pharmacy window. Medical sick call is available four times a week (M-W, F) from 6:30am-6:50am. Dental sick call is available 7:10am-7:30am on weekdays. A physician's assistant is on duty from 6am-10pm. At least one physician's assistant is on call 24 hours a day.

**Fitness/Recreation:** The camp offers a gymnasium, theater, activity center (including pool tables, ping-pong and a card room), music room, hobby craft area and outdoor areas. Card games and all other games can only be played in the television rooms. All television rooms are open Sunday through Thursday, and close each night at 12midnight.

**Religious Services:** The camp is staffed by one full-time chaplain. Numerous meeting rooms provide a place for bible study, audio and video programs, discussion groups, and a variety of self-help programs. A weekly schedule of religious activities is published and posted in the chapel and the dorms. It includes Jewish, Catholic, Christian, Native American, and Muslim services and programs. A community of volunteers provides services for all faiths.

**Housing:** Inmates are housed in one of five dormitories. The dormitories contain two-man, three-man, and four-man rooms.

**Commissary:** The commissary is open daily from 6:15am-7:15am, 10:30am-11:45am, and 1:30pm-3pm. Price and hours of operation are subject to change and are normally posted on the bulletin board located in the commissary. The monthly commissary spending limit is currently $360.

**Telephone Policy:** Inmates dial direct using the Inmate Telephone System (ITS). The following are standard features of ITS: (1) inmate calls will automatically terminate after 15 minutes; (2) an inmate's calling list is limited to 30 callers; and (3) calls are charged to an inmate's debit card. Inmates are limited to 300 minutes a month, and must wait at least 30 minutes between calls. All telephone request forms to change an inmate's calling list will be processed ordinarily within five working days, excluding the date the inmate submitted the form to unit staff. Inmates are permitted to make a maximum of three changes to the telephone list each month. The telephones provide local, long distance, and international direct dial service. Telephones are available in the Inmate Telephone Room: Monday through Friday, 6am-7:30am, 10:30am-12pm, and 4:30pm-9pm; weekends and federal holidays, 6am-10am, 10:30am-3:30pm, and 4:30pm-9pm. Unmonitored calls may be requested for legal reasons.

**Inmate Mail:** The camp accepts mail from the U.S. Postal Service via First-Class, U.S. Priority, and Express mail. For those interested in sending overnight mail via a private carrier (FedEx or UPS Overnight), it is recommended that you first contact the institution to find out whether the receipt of such mail is permitted. An inmate may receive hardcover publications and newspapers from the publisher, bookstore or book club. Inmates who wish to order a publication should first speak to the Mail Room Officer during open house (Tuesday and Thursday, 10:30am-11:45am) to ascertain that their publication will be approved. Inmates are authorized to keep up to 10 magazines.

**Inmate Mail to FPC:**
INMATE NAME & REGISTER NUMBER
FPC Duluth
Federal Prison Camp
P.O. Box 1000
Duluth, MN 55814

**Visiting Hours:** Approved visitors may visit the camp Saturday, Sunday, Monday, and all federal holidays from 8:15am-3:15pm. An inmate's visiting list is limited to 24 visitors. No more than a maximum of six persons may visit an inmate at any one time, and inmates are limited to eight visits a month. Attorney visits can be made by special arrangement. Additional visiting information can be found at https://www.bop.gov/locations/institutions/dth/.

**Lodging/Accommodations:** Should visitors be spending the night, the following is a short list of accommodations that are available in Duluth:

| | |
|---|---|
| Radisson Hotel Duluth | 218-727-8981 |
| The Inn on Lake Superior | 218-726-1111 |
| The Olcott House Bed & Breakfast Inn | 218-728-1339 |
| Edgewater Hotel | 218-728-3601 |

**Directions to Facility:** The Federal Prison Camp is located north of Duluth, next to the airport. Travelers coming from the northeast will travel south down U.S. 61 to I-35 south. From I-35 south, they will turn north on U.S. 53. Follow U.S. 53 past Miller Hill Mall to Stebner Road. Go right on Stebner Road, which will bring you to the Visiting Center entrance road. Once you get to the entrance road, go left and follow the road to the Visiting Center. Travelers coming from Superior, Wisconsin, will follow U.S. 53 across the Blatnik Bridge and remain on Highway 53 past Miller Hill Mall to Stebner Road. Go right on Stebner Road, which will bring you to the Visiting Center entrance road. Travelers coming from the north will follow U.S. 53 south to Stebner Road and go left, which will bring you to the Visiting Center entrance road. Travelers coming from the south will follow I-35 north to U.S. 53 north. Follow U.S. 53 past the Miller Hill Mall to Stebner Road. Go right on Stebner Road, which will bring you to the Visiting Center entrance road.

## §13:12   FCI ENGLEWOOD

FCI Englewood
Federal Correctional Institution
9595 West Quincy Avenue
Littleton, CO 80123
ENG/ExecAssistant@bop.gov
303-763-4300
Fax: 303-763-2553

**Location:** The institution is located 15 miles southwest of Denver, off U.S. Highway 285 and South Kipling Street. The area is served by the Denver Airport.

**History:** Opened in 1940, FCI Englewood houses both sentenced and unsentenced male inmates. A detention center that is separate from the correctional institution primarily houses Cuban detainees and unsentenced inmates. The camp opened in 1990 and serves as a satellite facility to the main institution. It houses minimum-security male offenders primarily from the western United States.

**Judicial District:** District of Colorado.

**Security Level:** FCI Englewood is a low-security facility housing male offenders. The institution also has an administrative detention center and an adjacent satellite prison camp for minimum-security male offenders.

**Population:** As of 6/13/2017, the FCI inmate population is 929, and the camp population is 167. Weekly population figures are available on the BOP website at www.bop.gov.

**Education:** FCI Englewood and the camp offer GED, ESL, adult continuing education, satellite distance learning program, parenting classes, college correspondence courses, and pre-release and career counseling.

**Vocational/Apprenticeship:** No advanced occupational education programs offered. Vocational training is offered in business education, drafting, and horticulture. Apprenticeship programs offered in HVAC, and electrician. Apprenticeship programs are not offered at the camp.

**Library:** The main institution's leisure and law libraries are open Monday through Friday, 7am-10am, 12noon to 3pm, and 6pm-8pm; Saturdays, 7am-3pm. Electric typewriters are available for the preparation of legal documents. Inmates may purchase typewriter ribbons from the commissary. A copier is also available. Inmates have access to the Electronic Law Library. The leisure library participates in an inter-library loan program with the Jefferson Public Library System, which allows inmates the opportunity to obtain leisure library materials not otherwise available at FCI Englewood. Inmates also have access to video cassette players, a video library, and several audio cassette players.

**Counseling/Rehab Services:** The main institution is staffed by full-time psychologists and drug treatment specialists. The camp offers a nine-month, 500-hour Residential Drug Abuse Program (RDAP). In addition, the FCI and the camp offer a non-residential drug treatment program, a drug education program, and Alcoholics Anonymous and Narcotics Anonymous groups. A psychologist at the camp conducts individual and group counseling with inmates who have emotional concerns. A psychologist is available at all times to address any suicide concerns or other mental health crisis situations.

**Health Services:** The main institution is staffed by physicians, physician assistants, dentists, and pharmacists. The FCI and the camp provide outpatient care. The pill line is available 6:30am-7am and 3pm-3:30pm on weekdays, 7:30am-8am and 3pm-3:30pm on weekends and holidays. Sick call sign-up is available from 6am-6:30am on weekdays, except Wednesday. Camp medical care is at the FDC. Inmates under the age of 50 may request a physical once every two years, and once a year if over the age of 50. At least one physician's assistant is on duty or on call 24 hours a day.

**Fitness/Recreation:** The institution has a recreation yard, gymnasium, weight room, hobby shop, music room, and wellness center. Recreational activities are available seven days per week Monday through Friday 6:30am-8pm; weekends and holidays 7am-8pm. The gymnasium is closed during spring and summer, except on days with inclement weather. The hours, when open, are imm-ediately following the 4:15pm count until 8pm and on the weekends and holidays after the brunch meal until 3:30pm and again following the 4:15pm count until 8pm. During good weather, the Big Yard will be open from 6:30am to 10am and 10:30am to 3:30pm and after the 4:15 p.m. count clears until dusk. A six-month schedule is published for all leagues and recreational activities. Special events, tournaments, and entertainment are sponsored by the Recreation Department on each holiday. An Arts and Crafts Program is open seven days a week on leather, fine arts, pottery, painting, beading and ceramics. The Hobby Shop is opened weekdays from 6:30am to 8pm, and is open weekends and holidays from 7:00am to 8pm. The camp has a walking track with fitness trail, softball field, soccer field, volleyball and basketball courts, a bocce ball area, weight room, and hobby shop/.

**Religious Services:** Staff chaplains coordinate resources to meet inmates' spiritual needs at the FCI. Camp, and FDC. Protestant and Catholic services are held on a regular basis. Community clergy and over 50 volunteers provide services for all faiths.

**Housing:** Inmates at the FCI are housed in 4-man "open" cubicles and two-man rooms. Inmates at the camp are housed in dormitories in four-man rooms in two living units. Inmates at the FDC are housed in two-man cells.

**Commissary:** Commissary sales hours and procedures are posted in each unit. Inmates are assigned one shopping day per week. Bureau of Prisons policy currently sets a monthly commissary spending limit of $360

**Telephone Policy:** Telephones are located in each housing unit. Inmates at the FCI and the camp may place either collect calls or dial direct using the Inmate Telephone System (ITS). The following are standard features of ITS: (1) inmate calls automatically terminate after 15 minutes; (2) an inmate's calling list is limited to 30 callers; and (3) calls are charged to an inmate's debit card. Inmates may submit up to 30 telephone numbers of people for their call list. Telephone calling hours and instructions for use of ITS are posted on bulletin boards located in the housing units. No calls are allowed during counts.

**Inmate Mail:** The FCI and the camp accept mail from the U.S. Postal Service via First-Class, U.S. Priority, and Express mail. For those interested in sending overnight mail via a private carrier (FedEx or UPS Overnight), it is recommended that you first contact the institution to find out whether the receipt of such mail is permitted. Magazine and newspaper subscriptions received at other institutions are permitted here. Magazines and newspapers are not allowed after 60 days.

**Inmate Mail to FCI:**
> INMATE NAME & REGISTER NUMBER
> FCI Englewood
> Federal Correctional Institution
> 9595 West Quincy Avenue
> Littleton, CO 80123

**Inmate Mail to Camp:**
> INMATE NAME & REGISTER NUMBER
> FCI Englewood
> Federal Correctional Institution
> Satellite Camp
> 9595 West Quincy Avenue
> Littleton, CO 80123

**Visiting Hours:** Approved visitors may visit the FCI on Friday and Monday from 5pm-9pm; and Saturday, Sunday, and federal holidays from 8:30am-3:30pm. The camp is open for social visits on Monday and Friday from 5:30pm-9:30pm; and Saturday, Sunday, and federal holidays from 8:30am-9:45am and 11:30am-3:30pm. FDC visiting hours are Friday, 5pm-9pm, Saturday, Sunday, and federal holidays from 8:30am- 3:30pm. Inmates will be allowed a total of 40 points per month at the FCI and the camp; 30 points will be allowed at the FDC. One point will be charged for each hour on Mondays and Fridays and two points will be charged for each hour on weekend and holiday visits. Any visit exceeding 15 minutes is considered a full hour. Legal visits will not be counted towards the point total.

For additional visiting privileges, an FCI inmate must submit an "Inmate Request to Staff" form to the unit manager, stating the visitor's name and the reason for the visit. Inmates arriving at the FCI will be afforded the opportunity to submit an initial request for visitors at any time. Thereafter inmates will be permitted to change their visiting list once each quarter: January, April, July, and October. Attorney visits can be made by special arrangement. Inmates are allowed three people per visit. Additional visiting information can be found on the BOP website, www.bop.gov, at https://www.bop.gov/locations/institutions/eng/.

**Lodging/Accommodations:** Should visitors be spending the night, the following is a short list of accommodations that are available in Littleton, Colorado:

| | |
|---|---|
| American Motel | 303-422-7200 |
| Hyatt Place Denver/Park Meadows | 303-662-8500 |
| Fairfield Inn | 303-290-6700 |
| Hampton Inn | 303-973-2400 |

**Directions to FCI Englewood:** The institution is located south of Hampden Avenue (also known as route #285) approximately one mile. Exit south off Hampden onto Wadsworth Avenue or Kipling Avenue to get to the institution. At the intersection of Wadsworth Avenue and Quincy Avenue, turn west (towards the mountains) and drive approximately 1 ½ miles. The institution will be on the north side of Quincy. At the Kipling and Quincy Avenue intersection, the institution can be seen just east of the mountains. Denver International Airport is located on the northeast side of Denver and FCI Englewood is approximately 50 miles from the airport. Directions from the airport: Take Pena (airport) Boulevard south, to I-70 west, to Wadsworth south, to Quincy west or Kipling south, to Quincy east. An alternate route from the airport: Take Pena Boulevard south, to I-70 west, to C-470 south, to Quincy east.

## §13:13   USP FLORENCE—ADMINISTRATIVE MAXIMUM FACILITY

USP Florence Administrative Maximum Facility/
United States Penitentiary Florence ADMAX
5880 Hwy 67 South
FLM/ExecAssistant@bop.gov
Florence, CO 81226
719-784-9464
Fax: 719-784-5290

**Location:** The institution is located on State Highway 67, from State Highway 115, 90 miles south of Denver, 45 miles south of Colorado Springs, and 40 miles west of Pueblo. The area is served by airports in Denver, Colorado Springs, and Pueblo; Amtrak in Denver and Colorado Springs; and commercial bus lines.

**History:** Opened in 1994.

**Judicial District:** District of Colorado.

**Security Level:** The Administrative Maximum (ADMAX) facility in Florence houses offenders requiring the tightest controls. The ADMAX supervises a minimum-security satellite prison camp that houses male offenders.

**Population:** As of 6/13/2017, the FCI inmate population is 426. Weekly population figures are available on the BOP website at www.bop.gov, at https://www.bop.gov/locations/institutions/flm/.

**Education:** The institution offers GED, ESL, adult continuing education, post-secondary education, adult basic education, and correspondence courses. All education programming is done within the inmate's cell.

**Vocational/Apprenticeship:** The institution does not offer advanced occupational education, vocational training or apprenticeship programs at this time.

**Library:** The law library is open daily from 8am-8:30pm. Electric typewriters are not available to inmates. A copier is available. Inmates must fill out a "copout" to request photocopies.

**UNICOR:** A chair factory employs approximately 10 to 15 inmates.

**Counseling/Rehab Services:** The institution offers a variety of programs through closed-circuit television in conjunction with an inmate's unit team in place of group counseling. These programs include stress management, the drug education program, anger management, and various other topics. The institution also offers a 500-hour Residential Drug Abuse Program (RDAP). Psychology staff members regularly visit the housing unit to talk to inmates, and emergency visits can be requested by inmates from their unit teams. Psychiatric care is available via teleconference twice a month with a staff psychiatrist from USMFCP Springfield.

**Health Services:** The institution provides outpatient care. A small infirmary is also available. The pharmacy follows a limited formulary. There are up to four restricted medication deliveries for every 24-hour period. Non-prescription drugstore items are delivered Monday, Thursday, or Friday. Days and hours are determined by housing unit. Sick call is available four days a week by filling out a sick call sign-up form. Sick call is Monday, Tuesday, Thursday and Friday mornings, excluding holidays. Physicals are available once every three years for inmates under 50, and yearly for inmates over 50. Eye exams are available yearly. At least one physician's assistant is on call or on duty 24 hours a day.

**Fitness/Recreation:** The Recreation Department offers pull-up bars, dip bars, individual and team sports (indoor or outdoor). The hobby craft center offers crocheting and drawing.

**Religious Services:** The institution is staffed by one chaplain, one religious services coordinator, and one religious services secretary. The chaplain regularly visits inmates in each unit. The closed-circuit television also broadcasts religious videos, psychology service videos, education programs, institutional information, and entertainment. A large variety of religious books are available.

**Housing:** Inmates are housed in single-man cells. There is a total of 10 housing units at the USP. The different units, in order from the most secure and restrictive to the least secure and restrictive, are: Control Unit, High Security Unit, Special Housing Unit, General Population Units, Intermediate Unit/Transitional Unit, and the Pre-Transfer Unit. With the exception of the Special Housing Unit and Disciplinary Segregation in the Control Unit, all cells are equipped with a closed-circuit television. Operations, privileges and procedures vary depending upon unit. The purpose of the television system is to provide inmates with information and entertainment. New inmates are required to view the admission and/ or orientation program on the Institutional Channel.

**Commissary:** The commissary delivery dates are Monday (Units D & Z), Tuesday (Units F & H), Wednesday (Units J-A, J-B & K), Thursday (Unit G), and Friday (Units B & E). Bureau of Prisons policy currently sets a monthly commissary spending limit of $360.

**Telephone Policy:** Inmates may either call collect or dial direct using the Inmate Telephone System (ITS). The following are standard features of ITS: (1) inmate calls automatically terminate after 15 minutes; (2) an inmate's calling list is limited to 30 callers; and (3) calls are charged to an inmate's debit card. You may request approval of up to 30 numbers. It takes one to two weeks for inmates to add phone numbers to their caller-approved list.

**Inmate Mail:** The institution accepts mail from the U.S. Postal Service via First-Class, U.S. Priority, and Express mail. For those interested in sending overnight mail via a private carrier (FedEx or UPS Overnight), it is recommended that you first contact the institution to find out whether the receipt of such mail is permitted. Inmates are permitted to subscribe to publications only if they come directly from the publisher, bookstore, or book club. Hardcover books are only allowed if they are not available in softcover, and must be approved in advance by the department head.

**Inmate Mail to USP:**
INMATE NAME & REGISTER NUMBER
USP Florence ADMAX
U.S. Penitentiary
P.O. Box 8500
Florence, CO 81226

**Visiting Hours:** Approved social visitors may visit on Thursday, Friday, Saturday, Sunday, and federal holidays from 8am-3pm. Each inmate will be allowed to receive a total of five visits per month with a maximum of seven hours per visit. Any portion of a visit will be charged as one visit. Attorney visits must be conducted on the same days and during the same hours as social visits. Additional visiting information can be found on the BOP website, https://www.bop.gov/locations/institutions/flm/.

**Lodging/Accommodations:** Should visitors be spending the night, the following is a short list of accommodations that are available near Florence, Colorado:

| | |
|---|---|
| Abriendo Inn | 719-544-2703 |
| Quality Inn & Suites | 719-275-8676 |
| Riviera Motel | 719-784-6716 |
| Super 8 Motel | 719-784-4800 |

**Directions to Facility:** From Colorado Springs, take Highway 115 south to Florence, turn south on State Highway 67, then proceed approximately two miles to the main entrance of the Federal Correctional Complex. From Pueblo, take State Highway 50 west approximately 30 miles to State Highway 115, turn south on 115 and proceed five miles to State Highway 67, turn south on 67 for two miles to the main entrance of the Federal Correctional Complex.

# §13:14   FCI FLORENCE

FCI Florence
Federal Correctional Institution
5880 Highway 67 South
Florence, CO 81226
FLF/ExecAssistant@bop.gov
719-784-9100
Fax: 719-784-9504

**Location:** The institution is located on State Highway 67, from State Highway 115, 90 miles south of Denver, 45 miles south of Colorado Springs, and 40 miles west of Pueblo. The area is served by airports in Denver, Colorado Springs, and Pueblo; Amtrak in Denver and Colorado Springs; and commercial bus lines.

**History:** Opened in 1993.

**Judicial District:** District of Colorado.

**Security Level:** The Federal Correctional Institution (FCI) in Florence, Colorado, is a medium-security facility housing male offenders with an adjacent minimum security satellite camp. It is part of the Florence Federal Correctional Complex (FCC).

**Population:** As of 6/14/2017, the FCI inmate population is 1,010, and the camp population is 456. Weekly population figures are available on the BOP website at www.bop.gov, https://www.bop.gov/locations/institutions/flf/.

**Education:** The FCI and the camp offer GED, ESL, post-secondary education, advanced occupational training, vocational education, social education (life skills), career counseling or release preparation, adult continuing education (foreign language, math, and economics), and correspondence courses. Pueblo Community College also offers instruction in culinary arts and business technology (see Vocational/Apprenticeship). The camp also provides a parenting course. The FCI Florence Education Department is state-accredited by the North Central Association of Schools and Colleges.

**Vocational/Apprenticeship:** FCI offers advanced occupational education programs in fundamentals of business. Vocational training is offered cabinet-making, building maintenance, and restaurant management. The camp offers advanced occupational education in fundamentals of business through Pueblo Community College, and an apprenticeship program in food services.

**Library:** The leisure and law libraries are open daily. The leisure library offers a wide variety of book selections for check out. Reference books, magazines, and newspapers are available for reading in the library only. The leisure library also contains a wide selection of literature and videotapes on how to seek, prepare, and maintain employment as well as a wide selection of popular movies and audio cassette players. An inter-library loan program is available. The law library is open daily. Electric typewriters are available for legal use only on a first-come, first-serve basis. Typewriter ribbons and correction tape are sold through the commissary. A copier is also available.

**UNICOR:** An upholstery furniture factory that employs approximately 154 inmates. Applications are open to all inmates, but priority is given to inmates with previous UNICOR experience.

**Counseling/Rehab Services:** The FCI offers a 500-hour Residential Drug Abuse Program (RDAP). The program is nine months in length and available in Spanish. In addition, the FCI and the camp offer a non-residential drug treatment program, a drug education program, Alcoholics Anonymous and Narcotics Anonymous groups, and People in Prison Entering Sobriety Program. It also offers anger and stress management classes, and sexual abuse or assault prevention and intervention classes. The main institution has a staff of psychologists and drug treatment specialists. Inmates may request psychologist appointments.

**Health Services:** Inmates that need medical attention should report to Health Services at 6:45am-7:15am, Monday, Tuesday, Thursday, or Friday. Medical or dental needs will be evaluated and an appointment time to return for further evaluation will be given if necessary. All other visits to the Health Services Unit, except emergencies, will be by appointment only. No inmate is permitted in the Health Services Unit without a sick call slip, an appointment, or being listed on the call-out roster. Inmates may request an eye examination from the contract optometrist to receive prescription eyeglasses. Certain medications are dispensed one dose at a time. The times for the medication line or pill line are offered Monday through Friday 6am-6:30am, 11am-12noon, and 4:30pm-5pm; Saturday, Sunday, and holidays 8am-8:15am and 4:30pm-5pm.

**Fitness/Recreation:** The Recreation Department offers a weight room, treadmills, exercise bicycles, music rooms, pool tables, foosball, and ping-pong tables. The hobby craft center offers etching, leather craft, and art. The recreation yard is open every day, but closes during inclement weather.

**Religious Services:** Chaplains are available during scheduled and non-scheduled times to assist with an inmate's spiritual needs, as well as to provide counseling on an individual basis. Participation in religious programs is voluntary. A community of volunteers provides services for most faiths. A schedule of regular religious activities is posted on bulletin boards in the chapel and housing units.

**Housing:** Inmates at the FCI are housed in two-man cells. There is a total of eight housing units at the FCI. One of the housing units is wheel-chair accessible. The FCI contains eight television rooms per housing unit. Inmates are not permitted to possess a television in their cell. Inmates at the camp are housed in dormitories in two-man cubicles. There are a total of two housing units at the camp. The television room is open Monday through Thursday from 5:30am- 9:45pm; and Friday, Saturday, Sunday and holidays from 5:30am-11:45pm.

**Smoking Areas:** Inmates at the FCI and camp are permitted to smoke outdoors in designated areas only.

**Commissary:** The FCI commissary is open for sales Monday through Thursday evenings. At the camp, inmates can shop once per week, Monday, Tuesday or Wednesday, 4pm-8pm. An inmate's shopping day is determined by housing unit assignment. The monthly commissary spending limit is currently $360.

**Telephone Policy:** Inmates at the FCI and the camp dial direct using the Inmate Telephone System (ITS). The following are standard features of ITS: (1) inmate calls automatically terminate after 15 minutes; (2) an inmate's calling list is limited to 30 callers; and (3) calls are charged to an inmate's debit card. There are four telephones located on the bottom tier near the inmate showers on each unit wing at the FCI. Norwood Alpha Unit has one handicapped telephone on the bottom tier. Telephone hours at the FCI are Monday through Friday, 6am-7:30am, 10:30am-12:30pm, and 4:30pm until lockdown for the night; Saturday and Sunday from 6am until lockdown for the night. At the camp, telephone use on weekdays is from 6am-7:30am, 10:30am-11:30am, 5:30pm-9pm, and weekend hours are 6am-9pm.

**Inmate Mail:** The FCI and the camp accept mail from the U.S. Postal Service via First-Class, U.S. Priority, and Express mail. For those interested in sending overnight mail via a private carrier (FedEx or UPS Overnight), it is recommended that you first contact the institution to find out whether the receipt of such mail is permitted. Inmates may receive publications without prior approval, although the warden will reject those that are determined to be detrimental to the security, good order or discipline of the institution. Newspapers may be received through direct subscriptions only, and hardcover books may only come from the publisher, bookstore, or book club.

**Inmate Mail to FCI:**
> INMATE NAME & REGISTER NUMBER
> FCI Florence
> Federal Correctional Institution
> P.O. Box 6000
> Florence, CO 81226

**Inmate Mail to Camp:**
> INMATE NAME & REGISTER NUMBER
> FCI Florence
> Federal Correctional Institution
> Satellite Camp
> P.O. Box 5000
> Florence, CO 81226

**Visiting Hours:** Approved visitors may visit the FCI and the camp on Friday from 5pm-8pm, and Saturday, Sunday, and federal holidays from 8am-3pm. The number of persons allowed while visiting one inmate is limited to five. Inmates are limited to a maximum of 20 visitors on their approved visitor list, which does not include inmate's attorney or minister of record. There are no restrictions on the number of monthly social visits. Attorneys are encouraged to visit during regular visiting hours. However, attorney visits can be arranged at other times based on the circumstances of each case. An indoor children's room is also available. Additional visiting information can be found on the BOP website at https://www.bop.gov/locations/institutions/flf/.

**Lodging/Accommodations:** Should visitors be spending the night, the following is a short list of accommodations that are available near Florence, Colorado:

| | |
|---|---|
| Abriendo Inn | 719-544-2703 |
| Quality Inn & Suites | 719-275-8676 |
| Riviera Motel | 719-784-6716 |
| Super 8 Motel | 719-784-4800 |

**Directions to Facility:** When traveling from Colorado Springs, take Highway 115 South to Florence. Take Highway 67 South to the Correctional Complex. When traveling from Pueblo, take Highway 50 West toward Canon City, Highway 115 South can be accessed in Penrose, leading toward Florence. Continue on Highway 115 South to Highway 67 South in Florence. There are two routes from Cañon City that would provide you access to the Complex. One route is Highway 50 East to Highway 67 South. Continue to Highway 67 South through Florence until you arrive at the Complex. A second route would be Highway 115 South in Canon City to Highway 67 South in Florence.

## §13:15   USP FLORENCE

USP Florence—High
United States Penitentiary
5880 Hwy 67 South
Florence, CO 81226
FLP/ExecAssistant@bop.gov
719-784-9454
Fax: 719-784-5157

**Location:** The institution is located on State Highway 67, from State Highway 115, 90 miles south of Denver, 45 miles south of Colorado Springs, and 40 miles west of Pueblo. The area is served by airports in Denver, Colorado Springs, and Pueblo; Amtrak in Denver and Colorado Springs; and commercial bus lines.

**History:** Opened in 1994.

**Judicial District:** District of Colorado.

**Security Level:** The United States Penitentiary (USP) in Florence, Colorado, is a high-security facility housing male offenders. It is part of the Florence Federal Correctional Complex (FCC).

**Population:** As of 6/14/2017, the USP inmate population is 825. Weekly population figures are available on the BOP website at www.bop.gov, at https://www.bop.gov/locations/institutions/flp/.

**Education:** The penitentiary offers GED, ESL, adult continuing education, and college correspondence courses through Pueblo Community College.

**Vocational/Apprenticeship:** USP offers advanced occupational education in business foundations and vocational training in basic computer concepts. Inmates must have one and one-half to three years remaining to serve on their sentence to be eligible for these programs.

**Library:** The leisure library is open Monday through Saturday, 7am-8pm. Reference books, magazines and newspapers are located in the library for use in education. An interlibrary loan program is available through Pike's Peak and Arkansas Valley Public Libraries. Typewriters, cassette players (for language or music programs), video monitors and computer-assisted programs are also available. The law library is open daily. Inmates are afforded access to legal materials and an opportunity to prepare legal documents in the Electronic Law Libraries (ELL). Electric typewriters and a copier are available. Copies are 10 cents and charged to an inmate's debit card.

**UNICOR:** None

**Counseling/Rehab Services:** The penitentiary has a full-time staff of psychologists who are always available to assist inmates' problems. The penitentiary offers a non-residential drug treatment program, a drug education program, Alcoholics Anonymous and Narcotics Anonymous groups, Anger Management, Stress Management, Commitment to Life, and Transitional Analysis. In addition, the Psychology Services Group coordinates a five-month unit-based Residential Values Program.

**Health Services:** The penitentiary is staffed by full-time physicians and their assistants, one dentist and other health services staff. For medical or dental sick call, inmates report to the Health Services Unit at 6:30am Monday, Saturday. For medical or dental concerns that do not need to be addressed on sick call, a member of the Health Services Staff is available Monday through Friday, during the noon meal, to address those concerns. For emergency care, a medical staff member is on call 24 hours a day. Inmates are provided with outpatient care. Local hospitals are approximately 10 minutes away. The medication line is available four times daily, seven days a week.

**Fitness/Recreation:** The Recreation Department offers seasonal sports, a weight room, music room, and ping-pong tables. The hobby craft center offers leather craft, ceramics, and music programs. Recreational activities and program times are posted on inmate bulletin boards in each housing unit and in the Recreation Department.

**Religious Services:** The penitentiary is staffed by one full-time chaplain. Rabbi services are available on a monthly basis. Religious services are provided for all existing faith groups, along with a study time period throughout the week. A variety of religious or spiritual video and audiotapes, along with theological reference books and periodicals, are also available. A community of volunteers provides services for most faiths. Pastoral and grief counseling is also available when inmates are notified of family deaths, hospitalization or illness.

**Housing:** Inmates are housed in single-man and two-man cells. Unit televisions may be turned on when rooms are unlocked in the morning. Television rooms may remain open daily until 9pm. Televisions on the flats will remain on until 10pm.

**Commissary:** The commissary is open Monday-Thursday from 6am-12:30pm. The commissary is closed for stocking on Friday, and on weekends and holidays. Inmates are assigned one shopping day per week. The monthly commissary spending limit is $360

**Telephone Policy:** Inmates may either call collect or dial direct using the Inmate Telephone System (ITS). The following are standard features of ITS: (1) inmate calls automatically terminate after 15 minutes; (2) an inmate's calling list is limited to 30 callers; and (3) calls are charged to an inmate's debit card. Telephone use times are 6am-7:30am, 10:30am-12:30pm, and 4pm-10pm, with the exception of one phone in each unit that remains on from 6am-10pm. Telephone use is limited to 300 minutes per month.

**Inmate Mail:** The institution accepts mail from the U.S. Postal Service via First-Class, U.S. Priority, and Express mail. For those interested in sending overnight mail via a private carrier (FedEx or UPS Overnight), it is recommended that you first contact the institution to find out whether the receipt of such mail is permitted. An inmate may only receive publications from the publisher, a book club, or a bookstore.

**Inmate Mail to USP:**
INMATE NAME & REGISTER NUMBER
USP Florence—High
United States Penitentiary
P.O. Box 7000
Florence, CO 81226

**Visiting Hours:** Approved visitors may visit the penitentiary on Saturday, Sunday, and federal holidays, from 8am-3pm. The number of persons allowed to visit one inmate is limited to 10, a limit of four adults and six children. Inmates are limited to a maximum of 10 visitors on their approved visitor list. Attorney visits can be made by special arrangement. A children's room is also available. Additional visiting information can be found on the BOP website, www.bop.gov, at https://www.bop.gov/locations/institutions/flp/.

**Lodging/Accommodations:** Should visitors be spending the night, the following is a short list of accommodations that are available near Florence, Colorado:

| | |
|---|---|
| Abriendo Inn | 719-544-2703 |
| Quality Inn & Suites | 719-275-8676 |
| Riviera Motel | 719-784-6716 |
| Super 8 Motel | 719-784-4800 |

**Directions to Facility:** From Colorado Springs, take Highway 115 south to Florence. Turn south on State Highway 67. Go approximately two miles to the main entrance of the Correctional Complex. From Pueblo, take US Highway 50 West approximately 30 miles to State Highway 115. Turn south on Highway

115. Go approximately five miles to State Highway 67. Turn south on Highway 67, and go two miles to the main entrance of the FCC.

## §13:16  FCI GREENVILLE

FCI Greenville
Federal Correctional Institution
100 U.S. Hwy 40
Greenville, IL 62246
GRE/ExecAssistant@bop.gov
618-664-6200
Fax: 618-664-6372

**Location:** The institution is located 43 miles east of St. Louis, Missouri, and 63 miles from Springfield, Illinois. The area is served by airports in St. Louis, Greenville, and Vandalia, IL; Amtrak passenger rail service in Alton, IL, and St. Louis, MO; and commercial bus service in Vandalia.

**History:** Opened in 1994.

**Judicial District:** Southern District of Illinois.

**Security Level:** The Federal Correctional Institution (FCI) in Greenville, Illinois, is a medium-security facility housing male offenders. An adjacent satellite prison camp houses minimum-security female offenders.

**Population:** As of 6/14/2017, the FCI inmate population is 1,033, and the camp population is 330. Weekly population figures are available on the BOP website at https://www.bop.gov/locations/institutions/gre/.

**Education:** The FCI and the camp offer GED, ESL, adult continuing education (ACE), parenting classes, offender placement, and correspondence courses. ACE course offerings change quarterly based on inmate interests and availability of instructors. Current classes are posted on the bulletin board in the Education Department. It also offers certificate programs in business concepts and commercial food. Instruction is taught by Kaskaskia College.

**Vocational/Apprenticeship:** FCI Greenville offers advanced occupational education in Microsoft Office. Vocational training is offered in cabinetmaking. Apprenticeship programs are offered in culinary arts, electrical maintenance, HVAC, landscaping, machinist, and teacher's aide. The camp offers advanced occupational education in animal husbandry, and PAWS (Prisoners Assisting With Support Dogs). The camp offers apprenticeship programs in animal trainer, baker, cook, landscape technician, welding and teacher's aide. Enrollment prerequisites to vocational or apprenticeship training programs: high school diploma or GED.

**Library:** The main institution's library is open Monday through Thursday, 8:30am-10:30am, 1:30pm-3:30pm, and 5pm-8:30pm; Friday, 8:30am-10:30am and 1:30pm-3:30pm; Saturday and Sunday, 7:30am-9:30am and 10:30am-3:30pm; closed on federal holidays. There are electric typewriters available to inmates for legal work only on a first-come, first-serve basis. A copier is available. Copies are 10 cents per page and charged to an inmate's debit card. An inter-library loan program is available through the Lewis and Clark Public Library System (includes 15-20 public libraries). Resources include videotapes, audiotapes, listening laboratory media or study kits, reference materials and a computer laboratory. The law library is open daily during non-working hours, but closed on Sundays and holidays. The camp library is open Monday through Friday, 7:30am-10:30am, 12:30pm-3:30pm, and 5pm-8:30pm); Saturday and Sunday, 6:30am-9:30am and 10:30am-3:30pm; closed on federal holidays.

**UNICOR:** An Army Combat Uniform (ACU) factory employs approximately 200 inmates from the FCI, and 10 inmates from the camp. The following positions are available for inmates: production workers, quality assurance inspectors, office accounting, and contracting clerks. Inmates may apply for the waiting list through their corrections counselor.

**Counseling/Rehab Services:** The FCI and the camp offer a non-residential drug treatment program, a drug abuse education program, Alcoholics Anonymous and Narcotics Anonymous groups, and a 6-month Values Program. The main institution is staffed by full-time psychologists. Individual and group therapy sessions are available.

**Health Services:** The main institution is staffed by full-time physicians, physician assistants, dentists, one pharmacist, and other health services staff. Health care services include medical sick call, dental sick call, and all support services. The FCI and the camp provide outpatient care, and the medication line is twice daily. Open pill lines at the FCI are conducted Monday through Friday, 6:20pm, 11:15am, 5:30pm, and 8:40pm (on weekends and holidays, the early pill line is at 8:30am). Pill lines at the camp are Monday through Friday, 6:30am-7am and 5:15am-5:45pm; weekends and holidays, 9am-9:30am and 4:30pm-5:30pm. Sick call sign-up is on Monday, Tuesday, Thursday and Fridays, 6:45-7am at the FCI and 6:30am-7am at the camp. Wednesdays are reserved for physical exams. Inmates under the age of 50 may request a physical examination every three years, while those over the age of 50 may request one annually. Routine dental and optometry services can be requested via cop-out. Medical staff is available 24 hours a day.

**Fitness/Recreation:** The Recreation Department offers team sports, a weight room, a gymnasium, music rooms, aerobic conditioning, and yoga. The hobby craft center offers activities such as: leather, art, yarn and crochet, beads, music, billiards, foosball, and a variety of card and board games. Movies are shown weekly via television in all units. The recreation center is open every day, 10:30am-8:30pm. The gym, weight room and recreation yard are open weekdays, 6:20am-8:30pm; weekends and holidays, 7:30am-8:30pm (yard closed at dusk, depending on the season).

**Religious Services:** The Religious Services Department has a department head, a staff chaplain, and a programs assistant. Emergency, grief, and spiritual counseling are available on a walk-in basis or call-out. Staff chaplains of specific faiths are available, as well as a community of volunteers of other faiths. The following is a partial list of religious activities that are available: Rastafarian services, Catholic mass, Christian services, Moorish Science Temple, Nation of Islam, Promise Keepers, Hispanic Christians, Sunni Taleem, Jehovah Witness, Hindu, Sunni Shiite Jumah, Buddhist, Seventh Day Adventist, and Universal Church of God.

**Housing:** Inmates at the FCI are housed in single-man, two-man, and three-man cells. There are four housing units at the FCI. Inmates at the camp are housed in dormitories in two-man cubicles.

**Commissary:** The commissary is open Monday through Friday. Shopping days and hours are determined by fifth digit of an inmate's register number (odd or even). The standard Bureau of Prisons monthly commissary spending limit is $360.

**Telephone Policy:** Inmates at the FCI and the camp may either call collect or dial direct using the Inmate Telephone System (ITS). The following are standard features of ITS: (1) inmate calls automatically terminate after 15 minutes; (2) an inmate's calling list is limited to 30 callers; and (3) calls are charged to an inmate's debit card. Inmates may use a total of 300 telephone minutes per month; during the months of November and December, the monthly limit is increased to 400 telephone minutes. Telephones can be used weekdays from 6am-7:30am, 10:30am-12:30pm, and 4:30pm-10pm. On weekends and federal holidays, telephones may be used from 6am-10pm.

**Inmate Mail:** The FCI and the camp accept mail from the U.S. Postal Service via First-Class, U.S. Priority, and Express mail. For those interested in sending overnight mail via a private carrier (FedEx or UPS Overnight), please use FCI Greenville (or FCI Greenville, Satellite Camp), 100 U.S. Highway 40, Greenville, IL 62246. Inmates may receive publications without prior approval, although the warden will reject those that are determined to be detrimental to the security, good order or discipline of the institution. At the FCI, all publications must come directly from the publisher, book club or bookstore. At the camp, the same rules apply, but softcover publications may be received from any source. Altered materials will be confiscated.

**Inmate Mail to FCI:**
INMATE NAME & REGISTER NUMBER
FCI Greenville
Federal Correctional Institution
P.O. Box 5000
Greenville, IL 62246

**Inmate Mail to Camp:**
INMATE NAME & REGISTER NUMBER
FCI Greenville
Federal Correctional Institution
Satellite Camp
P.O. Box 6000
Greenville, IL 62246

**Visiting Hours:** Approved visitors may visit the FCI on Saturday, Sunday, Monday and federal holidays from 8:00am-3pm. Visits on the weekends will be scheduled on an odd or even rotation. Inmates will be limited to four adult visitors at one time and five children under the age of 16. An inmate's visiting list will not contain more than 10 friends and associates, other than immediate family members. At the FCI, each inmate will be given forty (40) points every month. One point will represent one hour of visiting time on weekdays. Two points will represent one hour of visiting time on weekends and federal holidays. The camp is open for visitation on Saturday, Sunday, and federal holidays, 8am-3pm; and Monday, 9:30am-3pm. There are no limitations on the number of monthly social visits at the camp, but inmates are allotted a limited number of visitation hours. Attorney visits must be scheduled at least 24 hours in advance of the requested visit. A children's television room is available. Additional visiting information can be found on the BOP website, www.bop.gov, at https://www. bop.gov/locations/institutions/gre/.

**Lodging/Accommodations:** Should visitors be spending the night, the following is a short list of accommodations that are available near Greenville, Illinois:
Econo Lodge                                  618-664-3030
Budget Host Inn                              618-664-1950
Super 8 Motel                                618-664-0800

**Directions to Facility:** From Lambert International Airport, exit the airport on Interstate 70 east. Take Interstate 170 North approximately three miles to I-270 East, and I-270 connects to I-70 East in Illinois. Take the first Greenville exit, turn left at the stop sign, and make the first right-hand turn. Follow Illinois Rt. 40 for approximately two miles, make a right turn at the stop light at the intersection of 4th Street and Rt. 40, and the prison is on your left.

# §13:17   USP LEAVENWORTH

USP Leavenworth
United States Penitentiary
1300 Metropolitan
Leavenworth, KS 66048
LVN/ExecAssistant.bop.gov
913-682-8700
Fax: 913-578-1010

**Location:** The institution is located 25 miles north of Kansas City on Highway 73. The area is served by Kansas City International Airport (15 miles from the facility). There is no metropolitan mass transit available throughout the metropolitan area; however, taxis and rental cars are available. Google Maps coordinates for USP Leavenworth are available on the www.bop.gov website at https://www.bop.gov/locations/institutions/lvn/.

**History:** Opened in 1906, USP Leavenworth was the site of the first federal prison. In 1895, congress transferred the military prison at Fort Leavenworth to the Department of Justice. When the War Department objected, Congress authorized 1,000 acres adjacent to the prison for a new penitentiary to confine 1,200 inmates. USP Leavenworth houses adult male offenders primarily from mid-western and western states, and Cuban detainees.

**Judicial District:** District of Kansas.

**Security Level:** The United States Penitentiary (USP) in Leavenworth, Kansas, is a medium-security facility housing male inmates. An adjacent satellite prison camp houses minimum-security male offenders.

Population: As of 6/05/2017, the USP inmate population is 1,483, and the camp population is 426. Weekly population figures are available on the BOP website at https://www.bop.gov/locations/institutions/lvn/.

**Education:** The USP and the camp offer GED, ESL, adult continuing education, a literacy program, a parenting program, and correspondence courses.

**Vocational Training:** At this time, the USP offers vocational training in graphic arts and custodial maintenance.

**Library:** The main institution's law library is open to inmates when they are off duty or with special permission. Electric typewriters are available for legal matters only. Inmates must purchase their own typewriter print wheels, ribbons, or correctional ribbons from the commissary. A copy machine is available. Copies are charged to an inmate's debit card. Law Library hours are charged to an inmate's debit card. Law Library hours are Monday through Thursday, 8am to 10am and 4:45pm to 8pm, Friday 8am to 11am, and Saturday from 7:30am to 10am, and 12pm to 3pm The library is closed on Sundays and Federal holidays. Library hours are posted on inmate bulletin boards in the Education building and in the library area. The leisure library provides books, magazines, and newspapers for educational reading. Cassette players for language programs and audio books on cassette, and video monitors for the video library program are available for use. Personal headphones are required for use with video monitors. A limited inter-library loan program is available for inmates who want to borrow books and materials from outside libraries.

**UNICOR:** The UNICOR at USP Leavenworth has a print shop, a textile factory, a distribution factory, and an electronics waste recycling program.

**Counseling/Rehab Services:** The USP and the camp offer a non-residential drug treatment program, Alcoholics Anonymous and Narcotics Anonymous groups, self-image groups, and other voluntary groups. The main institution is staffed by several full-time psychologists. Psychology services are available Monday through Friday from 7:30am-4pm, by appointment only.

**Health Services:** The main institution is staffed by several full-time physicians, physician assistants, dentists, dental assistants, pharmacists, and other health services staff. The USP and the camp provide outpatient care. Several local hospitals are located approximately 10-35 minutes away. The pill line at the USP is available Monday through Friday 7:15am-7:45am and 3:20pm-3:50pm; Saturday, Sunday and holidays, 7:30am-8am and 3:20pm-3:45pm. The pill line at the camp is available Monday through Friday 6am-6:30am and 3pm-4pm; Saturday, Sunday and holidays, 6:30am-7am and 3pm-4pm. Sign-up for Sick Call at the USP is held Monday, Tuesday, Thursday and Friday, 7am-7:30am; sign-up at the camp is on the same days from 6:30am-7am. At least one physician's assistant is on duty or on call 24 hours a day. Requested age specific health screenings are done by call-out. Urgent care needs may be evaluated or treated at any time. Emergency dental care requests are handled at Sick Call only. Routine dental care is handled via a waiting list and call-out. The Health Services Unit, Recreation and/or Psychology Services offer Health Promotion and Disease Prevention Activity in the areas of stress management, nutrition counseling, dental hygiene/personal hygiene, infectious disease, low back pain, cardiopulmonary health/stroke, cancer/effects of smoking, substance abuse, hyperlipidemia, and exercise/weight loss.

**Fitness/Recreation:** The Recreation Department offers intramural sports, individualized arts and crafts programs, physical fitness and weight reduction programs, and other activities. There is a photography program, which allows inmates to take photographs, a music program, which allows inmates to play instruments and listen to music, and a movie program, which allows inmates to watch movies in the auditorium.

**Religious Services:** Staff chaplains, as well as contract and volunteer representatives of other faiths, are available to assist inmates. There is a residential 18-month Life Connections Program to help inmates with their moral and spiritual growth; this is an extensive program involving one-on-one mentors and community service.

**Housing:** Inmates at the USP are housed in single-man and two-man cells grouped into units, containing both housing sections and offices for the unit staff. There are approximately three to four television rooms per unit. The television rooms operate from 6:30am until 9:45pm. Inmates at the camp are housed in open dormitories (50 inmates to every dorm).

**Commissary:** The commissary is open for general sales Monday through Thursday from 4pm-8:30pm. General Population inmates are permitted to shop once per week. Bureau of Prisons policy currently sets a monthly commissary spending limit of $290. Postage stamps do not affect the monthly spending limitation.

**Telephone Policy:** Inmates at the USP or the camp dial direct using the Inmate Telephone System (ITS). The following are standard features of ITS: (1) inmate calls automatically terminate after 15 minutes; (2) an inmate's calling list is limited to 30 callers; and (3) calls are charged to an inmate's debit card. Inmates are authorized 300 minutes per month. There is a 30-minute wait between calls. It takes approximately one week for inmates to add phone numbers to their caller-approved list. Three changes are allowed to an inmate's call list per month. Inmate telephones are located in each living unit and are available from 6:30am until 10pm daily. Inmates may purchase phone credits from 4:30pm to 10pm on weekdays and any time on weekends.

**Inmate Mail:** The USP and the camp accept mail from the U.S. Postal Service via First-Class, U.S. Priority, and Express mail. For those interested in sending overnight mail via a private carrier (FedEx or UPS Overnight), it is recommended that you first contact the institution to find out whether the receipt of such mail is permitted. Inmates may subscribe to and receive publications without prior approval, although the warden will reject those that are determined to be detrimental to the security, good order, and discipline of the institution. All publications must come directly from the publisher, bookstore or book club. Each inmate is allowed up to six magazines and six books (excluding books for current coursework). Inmates desiring to use certified, registered, or insured mail may do so, subject to procedures established at the institution. Inmates are not provided services such as express mail, private carrier services, COD, or stamp collecting while confined. Legal mail, Monday thru Friday only, 11: a.m. to 12:00 noon.

**Inmate Mail to USP:**
INMATE NAME & REGISTER NUMBER
USP Leavenworth
U.S. Penitentiary
P.O. Box 1000
Leavenworth, KS 66048

**Inmate Mail to Camp:**
INMATE NAME & REGISTER NUMBER
USP Leavenworth
U.S. Penitentiary
Satellite Camp
P.O. Box 1000
Leavenworth, KS 66048

**Visiting Hours:** As of June 5, 2017, all visiting at this facility has been suspended until further notice. This policy may have changed by the time you read this entry. See https://www.bop.gov/locations/institutions/lvn/.

Under normal circumstances, approved visitors may visit the USP Friday through Monday from 8am-3pm. The camp is open for visitation Saturday through Monday, 8:30am-3:30pm. The visiting point system at USP Leavenworth allows an inmate 24 points of visiting time per month. One hour of weekday visiting time equals one point, and one hour of visiting time on the weekends equals two points. Attorney or clergy visits can be made by special arrangement.

There is a maximum of five visitors with a limit of three adults or children at any time, and the maximum number of individuals allowed on the inmate's approved visiting list is 20. Visitors are required to adhere to specific guidelines and dress codes. More visiting information can be found at https://www.bop.gov/locations/institutions/lvn/LVN_visit_hours.pdf.

Lodging/Accommodations: Should visitors be spending the night, the following is a short list of accommodations that are available near Leavenworth, Kansas:

| | |
|---|---|
| Days Inn | 913-651-6000 |
| Hampton Inn | 913-680-1500 |
| Commander's Inn | 913-651-5000 |
| Terrace Court Motel | 913-682-0499 |

**Directions to Facility:** Both USP and FPC Leavenworth are easily accessible from the metropolitan Kansas City area. Visitors may take I-29 north to the Platte City exit. After taking the exit, turn left and follow the road all the way through Platte City. After crossing the Platte River bridge, a sign will direct the visitor to the Leavenworth turn-off, which is HWY 92. USP and FPC Leavenworth are approximately 12 miles west of Platte City on HWY 92. Signs will be posted near both institutions regarding visitor parking.

## §13:18 USP MARION

USP Marion
United States Penitentiary
4500 Prison Road
Marion, IL 62959
Email: MAR/ExecAssistant@bop.gov
618-964-1441
Fax: 618-964-2058

**Location:** USP Marion is located approximately nine miles south of the city of Marion, 300 miles from Chicago, and 120 miles from St. Louis, Missouri. Google Maps coordinates for USP Marion are available on the www.bop.gov website at https://www.bop.gov/locations/institutions/mar/.

**History:** Opened in 1963 to replace the former USP at Alcatraz, USP Marion houses male offenders from all parts of the country who have demonstrated a need for high-security confinement. Typically, offenders have serious records of institutional misconduct, have been involved in violent or escape-related behavior, or have lengthy and complex sentences that indicate they require an unusually high level of security. The average age of inmates is 38, with an average period of incarceration of 41.1 years. Over 56 percent of the inmates have been involved in murder, and 91.3 percent have a history of some type of violent behavior. Opened in 1971, the satellite camp houses minimum-security offenders serving short-term sentences or nearing the completion of their sentences. Inmates comprise a work force for the support and maintenance of the penitentiary and camp area.

**Judicial District:** Southern District of Illinois.

**Security Level:** The United States Penitentiary (USP) in Marion, Illinois, is a medium-security facility housing male inmates. The facility also has an adja- cent satellite prison camp that houses minimum-security male offenders.

**Population:** As of 6/05/2017, the USP inmate population is 1,119, and the camp population is 202. Weekly population figures are available on the BOP website at https://www.bop.gov/locations/institutions/mar/.

**Education:** The USP and the camp offer GED, ESL, ABLE (Adult Basic Learning Examination), ACE (Adult Continuing Education), and college correspondence courses.

**Vocational/Apprenticeship:** Vocational programs are offered at the USP in building trades, information processing, and certified production technician. Apprenticeship programs are offered at the USP in electrical, plumbing, paint- ing, and HVAC. Apprenticeship programs are offered at the camp in water treatment and waste water treatment. During operating hours. Typewriters for legal work and materials for preparing legal documents are available. The camp has a law library in the Education Department, which is open during convenient non-working hours every day. Staff members bring books and resources to inmates upon request. An inter-library loan program is not available.

USP Marion has a limited leisure reading library containing a good selection of educational books and leisure reading materials. The Library is open during general population's open-movement hours.

**UNICOR:** An electronics cable factory produces cables and cable assemblies ranging from simple to complex. The work day is from 7:00am until 2:30pm Monday through Friday.

**Counseling/Rehab Services:** The USP offers a nine-month, 500-hour Res-iden-tial Drug Abuse Program (RDAP). In addition, the USP and the camp offer a non-residential drug treatment program, a drug education program, and other voluntary individual and/or group psychotherapy. The USP is staffed by full-time psychologists. The camp is staffed by one full-time psychologist, as well as one contract psychiatrist. The USP also offers anger management, communication skills, criminal thinking, rational behavior therapy, values clarification, and various other life skills programs, as well as individual therapy for mentally ill inmates. Inmates with a history of sexual offenses may be designated to the Sex Offender Management Program (SOMP). Sex Offender Treatment Program (SOTP-NR) offers inmates individualized non-residential treatment six to eight hours a week for six months. All participation in non-residential treatment ser-vices is voluntary.

**Health Services:** The main institution is staffed by physicians, health services administration staff, mid-level practitioner(s), health information staff, nursing staff, a contract X-ray technician, a pharmacist, a dentist, and a dental hygien- ist. The USP and the camp provide outpatient care. Sick call sign-up at the USP is Monday, Tuesday, Thursday, and Friday, 7am-7:30am. Dental sick call is held at the USP at 7:30am, Monday, Tuesday, Thursday and Friday. Pill line hours at the USP are 6:15am-6:45am, 11am-12noon, 4:40pm-5:30pm (insulin only), and 8pm-8:30pm. Sick call sign-up at the camp is Monday, Tuesday, Wednesday, and Friday, 7am-7:15am, with on-site medical care available from 6am-2:30pm weekdays. Dental sick call at the camp is Wednesday, 7:30am. Pill line hours at the camp are 6am-6:15am and 2:30pm-3pm. At least one physician's assistant is on duty or on call 24 hours a day. Inmates under the age of 50 may request a physical examination every two years, while those over the age of 50 may request one annually.

**Fitness/Recreation:** The Recreation Department offers a music room, table games, billiards, cultural events, movies, a talent and stage show, a wellness program, athletic equipment, and indoor/outdoor team sports. Radios and MP3 players are allowed in the recreation yard and individual cells, but not in the corridors or on work details. Recreation programs include indoor and outdoor activities, and intramural team sports such as softball, basketball, and volleyball. There are Gatorade awards for sports leagues and holiday events. Physical fitness programs are also important activities for inmates. The hobby craft center offers artwork, leather craft, crocheting, knitting, drawing, bead work and card-making. The camp offers indoor or outdoor team sports, and arts and crafts. Sports offered at the camp include tennis, racquetball, bocce ball, softball, basketball and volleyball. The facility hosts a variety of entertainment, including inmate concerts and inspirational and motivational speakers. Inmates may own harmonicas; the facility provides all other approved musical instruments on request.

**Religious Services:** There are regular organized religious services in most major faiths. The schedule of regular religious activities and chaplains' duty hours is posted on bulletin boards in the chapel and the units. A variety of faiths are represented in the chapel program, such as Protestant, Catholic, Jewish, Muslim, Nation of Islam, Moorish Science Temple, Jehovah's Wit- nesses and Native American. If an inmate's religion is not represented on the schedule, the chaplain can provide the appropriate accommodation. The camp is staffed by two full-time chaplains and one religious services assistant.

**Housing:** Inmates at the USP are housed in East Corridor and North Corridor blocks. The East Corridor consists of Units B, C, D, E, F, and G, where inmates are housed in single-man cells. The North Corridor has L, N, and X units, where inmates are housed in two-man or three-man cells. Y Unit is designated as the Residential Drug Abuse Program unit. Housing units vary in restrictions and availability of work assignments. Inmates at the camp are housed in open dormitories and in two-man cubicles. Television viewing hours are 6am-12am (midnight).

**Commissary:** At the USP, commissary sales are conducted Monday-Thursday after count clear, until 8:30 p.m. or last call. Sales are limited to one sale weekly per inmate. The inmate must have an approved commissary list for items when entering the sales unit. Shopping day will be determined by the in-mate's current housing unit. A rotating schedule is posted on the TRULINCS Electronic Bulletin Board. The camp's commissary is open at 10:30am until the last call is announced, Tuesday and Thursday. The schedule for inmates is a rotating one, and includes extra shopping time on Monday during certain months. The current spending limit is $320 per month.

**Telephone Policy:** Inmates at the USP and the camp may either call collect or dial direct using the Inmate Telephone System (ITS). The following are standard features of ITS: (1) inmate calls automatically terminate after 15 minutes; (2) an inmate's calling list is limited to 30 callers; and (3) calls are charged to an inmate's debit card. Telephones are available in each housing unit. Inmates are limited to 300 minutes allocated to a certain number of calls per month, depending on their housing unit. Inmates must utilize TRULINCS for processing additions or deletion to approved telephone lists via the contact form. At the camp, there are three telephones located in the West Dorm and eight telephones in the New Dorm. Camp telephones are available Monday through Friday 6am-7:30am, 10:30am-12:30pm, and after the 4pm count until midnight (except for the 10pm count). Inmates may request unmonitored legal calls.

**Inmate Mail:** The USP and the camp accept mail from the U.S. Postal Service via First-Class, U.S. Priority, and Express mail. All incoming packages require an Authorization to Receive Package or Property form. Inmates may subscribe to and receive publications without prior approval, although the warden will reject material that is determined to be detrimental to the security, good order, or discipline of the institution. An inmate may only receive books, magazines, and newspapers from the publisher, bookstore or book club. Inmates may not receive more than five books in a parcel. At the camp, an inmate may receive hardcover publications only from the publisher or bookstore. Accumulation of publications is limited to six magazines and 10 books.

**Inmate Mail to USP:**
> INMATE NAME & REGISTER NUMBER
> USP Marion
> U.S. Penitentiary
> P.O. Box 1000
> Marion, IL 62959

**Inmate Mail to Camp:**
> INMATE NAME & REGISTER NUMBER
> USP Marion
> U.S. Penitentiary
> Satellite Camp
> P.O. Box 1000
> Marion, IL 62959

**Visiting Hours:** Approved social visitors may visit the USP or the camp from 8:30am-3pm on weekends and federal holidays only. Inmates at the USP have an unlimited amount of visiting time, but are limited to five adult visitors at one time. Inmates at the camp may receive a total of 10 visits per month. Each inmate at the USP will receive 12 points per month for visiting; each inmate will be charged one (1) point per weekday visit and two (2) points per weekend day or holiday visit. Attorney visits can be made by special arrangement. They are encouraged to visit during regular visiting hours and must make appointments 24 hours in advance. Additional visiting information can be found at https://www.bop.gov/locations/institutions/mar/.

**Lodging/Accommodations:** Should visitors be spending the night, the following is a short list of accommodations that are available near Marion, Illinois:

| | |
|---|---|
| America's Best Inn & Suites | 618-997-9421 |
| Comfort Inn | 618-993-0183 |
| Comfort Suites | 618-997-9133 |
| Drury Inn | 618-997-9600 |
| Hampton Inn | 618-998-9900 |
| Super 8 | 618-993-5577 |

**Directions:** From Interstate 57, take Illinois 148 to Grange Hall Road. Turn left onto Grassy Road, then right onto Prison Road.

## §13:19  FCI MILAN

FCI Milan
Federal Correctional Institution
4004 East Arkona Road
Milan, MI 48160
MIL/ExecAssistant@bop.gov
734-439-1511
Fax: 734-439-5534

**Location:** FCI Milan is located in southeastern Michigan, 45 miles south of Detroit, 15 miles south of Ann Arbor, and 30 miles north of Toledo, Ohio. The area is served by Detroit Metro and Toledo Express Airports, Amtrak, and commercial bus lines.

**History:** Opened in 1933, FCI Milan houses male offenders whose ages range from 20-71 years and whose average length of incarceration is 10.7 years. There is also a jail unit for pre-trial detainees from the Detroit area.

**Judicial District:** Eastern District of Michigan.

**Security Level:** The Federal Correctional Institution (FCI) in Milan is a low-security facility housing male inmates with a detention center for pre-trial and holdover male inmates.

**Population:** As of 6/15/2017, the FCI inmate population is 1,404. Weekly population figures are available on the BOP website at www.bop.gov, https://www.bop.gov/locations/institutions/mil/.

**Education:** The institution offers GED, ESL, adult continuing education, and correspondence courses. Milan High School is the only high school diploma program within the Bureau of Prisons. A 500 hour-program in business sales is offered by Washtenaw Community College. Washtenaw Community College is accredited by the North Central Association of Colleges. Telecourses are also available through Colorado State University.

**Vocational/Apprenticeship:** FCI Milan offers advanced occupational education in custodial technician. Vocational training available in Microsoft Office and automotive. Apprenticeship programs are offered in mason, millwright, plumber, stationary engineer, tool and die maker, tool machinist, dental assistant, industrial electrician, carpenter, auto mechanic, and A/C mechanic. Inmates must have either a high school diploma, GED, or be GED enrolled in order to be eligible for the vocational or apprenticeship training programs.

**Library:** The leisure or law library is open seven days a week from 8:30am-10:30am, 12:30pm-3:30pm, and 5:30pm-8:30pm. Electric typewriters are available to inmates on a first-come, first-served basis. Inmates must purchase their own typewriter ribbon from the commissary. A copier is available. An inter-library loan program is available.

**UNICOR:** A metal specialty plant employs approximately 411 inmates. There is a pre-industrial training program for inmates who are waiting to be hired.

**Counseling/Rehab Services:** The institution offers a nine-month, 500-hour Residential Drug Abuse Program (RDAP). In addition, the institution offers a non-residential drug treatment program, a drug education program, Alcoholics Anonymous and Narcotics Anonymous groups, and other volunteer groups. The Psychology Department is staffed by one RDAP coordinator and several doctoral-level psychologists.

**Health Services:** The institution is staffed by several physicians, physician assistants, dentists, one dental assistant, pharmacists, and one pharmacist's technician. An optometrist makes regular visits to the clinic. Inmates who wish to attend sick call may do so by reporting to the Health Service Department on Monday, Wednesday, Thursday and Friday between 6:30am-7am (routine call is not held on Tuesdays, weekends or holidays). Inmates are provided with outpatient care. The pill line is available at 6am, 3pm, and 8pm. Physical examinations are offered every two years for inmates under the age of 50, and every year for inmates over the age of 50. Medical staff is on duty or on call 24 hours a day.

**Fitness/Recreation:** The Recreation Department offers weights, a music room, pool tables, foosball, and ping-pong tables. The hobby craft center offers leather craft and ceramics. The recreation yard are open seven days a week all year.

**Religious Services:** The FCI is staffed by two full-time chaplains. A contract rabbi provides religious services on a bi-monthly basis. A sweat lodge is provided for Native American services. A community of volunteers provides services for most faiths. FCI Milan is the pilot site for the Life Connections Program, an 18-month program to help reduce recidivism by helping offenders pursue their faith, with increased opportunity for study and worship. The program offers one full-time chaplain, contractors for specific faith groups, and individual mentors.

**Housing:** Inmates are housed in dormitories in two-man cubicles. Each unit is equipped with cable television.

**Commissary:** The commissary is open Monday through Thursday from 6am-10am, 10:30am-11:30am (UNICOR only), 11:30am-2pm, and 2pm-3:30pm (outside details and UNICOR). Bureau of Prisons policy currently sets a monthly commissary spending limit of $360.

**Telephone Policy:** Inmates dial direct using the Inmate Telephone System (ITS). The following are standard features of ITS: (1) inmate calls will automatically terminate after 15 minutes; (2) an inmate's calling list is limited to 30 callers; and (3) calls are charged to an inmate's debit card. Each housing unit is equipped with telephones. Telephone credits may be purchased via the inmate telephone after 4pm on weekdays and all day on weekends.

**Inmate Mail:** The institution accepts mail from the U.S. Postal Service via First-Class, U.S. Priority, and Express mail. For those interested in sending overnight mail via a private carrier (FedEx or UPS Overnight), call the institution for more information. Inmates may receive hardcover publications and softcover books from the publisher, bookstore, or book club (with the contents marked on the package), and newspapers directly from the publisher.

**Inmate Mail to FCI:**
>   INMATE NAME & REGISTER NUMBER
>   FCI Milan
>   Federal Correctional Institution
>   P.O. Box 1000
>   Milan, MI 48160

**Visiting Hours:** Approved visitors may visit the institution on Thursday, 4:30pm-8pm; Friday, 12:45pm-8pm; and Saturday, Sunday, and federal holidays, 8:15am-3pm. Attorney visits can be made by special arrangement. A small television room for children is available. Additional visiting information can be found on the BOP website, www.bop.gov, https://www.bop.gov/locations/institutions/mil/.

**Lodging/Accommodations:** Should visitors be spending the night, the following is a short list of accommodations that are available near Milan, Michigan:

| | |
|---|---|
| Bell Tower Hotel | 734-769-3010 |
| Kensington Court-Ann Arbor | 734-761-7800 |
| Red Roof Inn | 734-665-3500 |
| Sleep Inn & Suites | 734-439-1400 |
| Extended Stay America | 734-997-7623 |

**Directions to Facility:** Take U.S. 23 north from Toledo or south from Ann Arbor to Milan, exit at Carpenter Road, Exit 27; turn onto Arkona Road; follow the signs to the detention center parking area.

## §13:20   FCI OXFORD

FCI Oxford
Federal Correctional Institution
County Road G & Elk Avenue
Oxford, WI 53952
OXF/ExecAssistant@bop.gov
608-584-5511
Fax: 608-584-6371

**Location:** FCI Oxford is located in central Wisconsin, 60 miles north of Madison & I-39; approximately eight miles west of Westfield; 13 miles east of Adams near junction E & G, at the intersection of County Road G and Elk Avenue. Area is served by Dane County Regional Airport, and commercial bus service in Portage and Wisconsin Dells.

**History:** Opened in 1973, FCI Oxford houses male offenders serving long-term sentences. Inmates are primarily from the north central United States.

**Judicial District:** Western District of Wisconsin.

**Security Level:** The Federal Correctional Institution (FCI) in Oxford is a medium-security institution for male offenders. An adjacent satellite prison camp houses minimum-security male offenders.

**Population:** As of 6/15/2017, the FCI inmate population is 927, and the camp population is 104. Weekly population figures are available on the BOP website at https://www.bop.gov/locations/institutions/oxf/.

**Education:** The FCI and the camp offer GED (under the literacy program), ESL, adult continuing education, and correspondence courses. The FCI offers professional studies in advanced occupational studies, and a certificate program in business or computer science, as well as other courses that lead to an associate of arts or science degree.

**Vocational/Apprenticeship:** FCI offers advanced occupational education in computer science technology, business administration, janitorial, soldering, and electrical cable wiring. Vocational training is offered in culinary arts, with the possibility for certification from the American Culinary Federation of America. Apprenticeship programs are offered in bricklayer, carpenter, cook (hotel/restaurant), dental assistant, HVAC, welder, mechanic, machinist, painter, waste water treatment, plumber, stationary engineer, and tool and die maker. The camp does not offer vocational or apprenticeship training programs.

**Library:** The law and resource/leisure libraries are located in the Education Department. Hours for both libraries: Monday through Friday, 8:30am-10:30am, 12:30pm-3:30pm (with extra hours Monday through Thursday, 5:30pm-8:30pm); Saturday, 7:30am-3:30pm. A law librarian is available to provide supplies and assist inmates. Electric typewriters are available to inmates on a first-come, first-serve basis. A copier is available. Copies are 15 cents per page and charged to an inmate's debit card. An inter-library loan program is available. Inmates have limited access to video cassette recorders and audio cassette players.

**UNICOR:** None.

**Counseling/Rehab Services:** The FCI offers a 500-hour Residential Drug Abuse Program (RDAP). The program is nine months in length. The FCI and the camp also offer a non-residential drug treatment program, a drug abuse education program, Alcoholics Anonymous groups, self-image and Positive Mental Attitude (PMA) programs. The main institution is staffed by three full-time psychologists and 5-6 drug treatment specialists. A contract psychiatrist visits the institution on a regular basis.

**Health Services:** The main institution is staffed by several full-time physicians, physician assistants, dentists, one pharmacist, and other health services staff. The FCI and the camp have an outpatient clinic. The nearest hospital is approximately 30 minutes away. The Health Unit offers the following programs: Drug Education, Wellness Program, Chronic Disease Education, and Preventative Health Care Program. The medication line is at 6:15am-12:30, and 8pm, seven days per week. There are two pill line times at the camp: 7:15am, 12:30, and 4:30. Sick call at the camp is Monday, Tuesday, Thursday and Friday, starting at 6:15am. A clinician is on duty 6am-9pm every day, and at least one physician's assistant is on duty or on call 24 hours per day. Inmates under the age of 50 are eligible for a physical examination every three years, while those over the age of 50 are eligible for a physical examination every year.

**Fitness/Recreation:** The FCI offers a well-equipped gymnasium, outside recreation yard, hobby craft center, and art program. The FCI's Recreation Department offers aerobics, a nutrition class, a stress reduction class, a weight room (limited), musical instruments, pool tables, and ping-pong tables. Some of the sports available include basketball, handball, racquetball, volleyball, soccer, softball, tennis, bocce ball, horseshoes and running. The hobby craft center offers knitting and crocheting. The camp offers indoor or outdoor team sports and hobby crafts.

**Religious Services:** The main institution is staffed by one full-time chaplain. The chaplains are available for individual pastoral counseling. A community of volunteers provides services for most faiths.

**Housing:** There are four housing units at FCI: Portage House, Waupaca House, Sauk House, and Waushara House. Inmates are housed in single-man and two-man cells. The housing units are wheel-chair accessible. Inmates at the camp are housed in dormitories in 4-man cubicles.

**Commissary:** Shopping days and times for inmates in each unit are scheduled on a rotating basis, and will be posted in each housing unit. Bureau of Prisons policy currently sets a monthly commissary spending limit of $360.

**Telephone Policy:** Inmates at the FCI and the camp dial direct using the Inmate Telephone System (ITS). The following are standard features of ITS: (1) inmate calls automatically terminate after 15 minutes; (2) an inmate's calling list is limited to 30 callers; and (3) calls are charged to an inmate's debit card. Inmates are limited to 300 minutes per month, which increases to 400 minutes during November and December. There is a 15-minute waiting period between calls. Inmates may request unmonitored legal calls.

**Inmate Mail:** The FCI and the camp accept mail from the U.S. Postal Service via First-Class, U.S. Priority, and Express mail. For those interested in sending overnight mail via a private carrier (FedEx or UPS Overnight), it is recommended that you first contact the institution to find out whether the receipt of such mail is permitted. Inmates are permitted to subscribe to and receive publications without prior approval, although the warden will reject material that is determined to be detrimental to the security, good order, or discipline of the institution. All publications must come directly from the publisher, bookstore or book club and to the amount that can be neatly stored in the space provided in the inmate's room.

**Inmate Mail to FCI:**
INMATE NAME & REGISTER NUMBER
FCI Oxford
Federal Correctional Institution
P.O. Box 1000
Oxford, WI 53952

**Inmate Mail to Camp:**
INMATE NAME & REGISTER NUMBER
FCI Oxford
Federal Correctional Institution
Satellite Camp
P.O. Box 1085
Oxford, WI 53952

**Visiting Hours:** Approved visits are permitted at the FCI on Saturday, Sunday and federal holidays, 8am-3pm. Visiting hours for the camp are Friday, 4:30pm-8:30pm, and Saturday, Sunday and federal holidays, 8am-3pm. Visiting lists can have up to 15 approved visitors/ For the FCI, the maximum number of visitors at any given time is six. For the camp, the maximum number of visitors at any given time is four. Attorneys should ordinarily make advance appointments for each visit. Additional visiting information can be found on the BOP website, at https://www.bop.gov/locations/institutions/oxf/.

**Lodging/Accommodations:** Should visitors be spending the night, the following is a short list of accommodations that are available in the Oxford, Wisconsin area:

| | |
|---|---|
| Best Western Resort & Conference Center | 608-742-2200 |
| Crossroads Motel | 608-589-5151 |
| Indian Trail Motel | 608-253-2641 |
| Westfield Pioneer Motor Inn | 608-296-2135 |

**Directions to Facility:** <u>From Westfield to FCI Oxford</u>: Take County Road E west approximately eight miles to County Road G. Turn left. Go less than one mile, then turn right at Elk.

<u>From Wisconsin Dells to FCI Oxford</u>: Take Hwy. 13 through WI Dells. At the stoplight on the north edge of town, go straight onto Hwy. 23. Follow Hwy. 23 approximately three miles. Turn left on County Road B. Follow County Road B to Hwy. 82. Cross Hwy 82 and continue on County Road B approximately eight more miles. Turn right onto Elk Avenue. The FCI is about three miles ahead on the left.

## §13:21   FCI PEKIN

FCI Pekin
Federal Correctional Institution
2600 South Second Street
Pekin, IL 61554
PEK/ExecAssistant@bop.gov
309-346-8588
Fax: 309-477-4670

**Location:** Located on the south edge of Pekin on Illinois Route 29, approximately 10 miles south of Peoria, 180 miles southwest of Chicago, and 180 miles northeast of St. Louis, Missouri. The area is served by the Greater Peoria Regional Airport, Amtrak, and bus service to Peoria.

**History:** Opened in late 1994.

**Judicial District:** Central District of Illinois.

**Security Level:** The Federal Correctional Institution (FCI) in Pekin, Illinois, is a medium-security facility housing male inmates. An adjacent minimum-security satellite prison camp houses female offenders.

**Population:** As of 6/15/2017, the FCI inmate population is 996, and the camp population is 326. Weekly population figures are available on the BOP website at https://www.bop.gov/locations/institutions/pek/.

**Education:** The FCI and the camp offer GED, ESL, adult continuing education parenting classes, literacy, and correspondence courses.

**Vocational/Apprenticeship:** FCI offers the following advanced occupational education programs: Small Business Management, certified by Illinois Central College; Certified Associate Addictions Professional (CAAP) Program, which trains inmates in drug and alcohol addiction recovery; Computer Applications; Machinist Program; and AutoCAD (computer-assisted drafting). The FCI offers apprenticeship programs in cook, machinist, and electrician. The camp offers vocational training in, computer applications, and horticulture.

**Library:** The main institution law library is open Monday through Thursday, 7:30am-10:30am, 12:30pm-3:30pm and 5pm-8:30pm; Friday, 7:30am-10:30am and 12:30pm-3:30pm; and Saturday and holidays, 7:30am-3:30pm. An inmate law clerk is available. Interlibrary loan services are provided through the Alliance Library System. Both the FCI and the camp provide electric typewriters and copy machines; however, inmates must buy a typing ribbon in the commissary. Electric typewriters are available to inmates for legal matters only. A copier is available. A videotape library, video cassette recorders, and audio cassette players are available.

**UNICOR:** An industrial products factory employs approximately 400 inmates.

**Counseling/Rehab Services:** The FCI and the camp offer a non-residential drug treatment program, a drug education program, Residential Drug Abuse Program (RDAP), and Alcoholics Anonymous and Narcotics Anonymous groups. The main institution is staffed by several full-time psychologists.

**Health Services:** The main institution is staffed by several full-time physicians, physician assistants, one dentist, one pharmacist, an optometrist, and other health services staff. The FCI and the camp provide outpatient care. The nearest hospital is approximately five to seven miles away. The pill line at the FCI is at 11am-12:45pm and 8:30pm-9pm, with insulin-only lines at 6:15am-7am and 4:30pm-5pm. Sick call sign-up is Monday, Tuesday, Thursday and Friday, 6:30am-7am. The pill line at the camp is at 6am-6:15am and 2:45pm-3pm. At least one physician's assistant is on duty or on call 24 hours a day.

**Fitness/Recreation:** The Recreation Department offers scheduled activities that include sports, athletics, arts, crafts, music and entertainment. Table games are available for check-out and must be returned no later than 9:15pm nightly. Other recreational facilities: recreation yards with basketball, handball, and volleyball courts; softball fields and a soccer or flag football field; billiard tables, bumper pool tables, table tennis; and weight training equipment. The camp offers similar recreational activities and hobby crafts.

**Religious Services:** The main institution is staffed by full-time chaplains. The schedule of regular religious activities is posted on bulletin boards in the chapel and housing units.

**Housing:** FCI is organized into four housing units (A, B, C, and D units). All housing units contain two-, three-, eight-, and 10-man cells. Unit televisions may be used 5:30am-9:30pm. Television rooms are open until 11:30pm on weekdays and 2am on weekends. Inmates may choose from programming available in four television rooms. Inmates at the camp are housed in dormitories in two-man cubicles.

**Commissary:** The commissary is open Monday through Thursday from 6:40am-7:30am and 11am-12:30pm, with extra hours for medically-assigned inmates and inmates with work detail. Early sales for controlled items are held on Fridays from 11am-12:30pm. The commissary is closed on Friday, Saturday, Sunday and federal holidays. Sales are limited to one sale per night per inmate. The monthly commissary spending limit is currently $360.

**Telephone Policy:** Inmates at the FCI and the camp may either call collect or dial direct using the Inmate Telephone System (ITS). The following are standard features of ITS: (1) inmate calls automatically terminate after 15 minutes; (2) an inmate's calling list is limited to 30 callers; and (3) calls are charged to an inmate's debit card. Inmates are allowed 300 minutes per month. Telephones at the FCI and the camp are available daily from 6am-9:30pm. Changes to an established telephone list may be submitted three times per month.

**Inmate Mail:** The FCI and the camp accept mail from the U.S. Postal Service via First-Class, U.S. Priority, and Express mail. For those interested in sending overnight mail via a private carrier (FedEx or UPS Overnight), send mail to: INMATE NAME & REGISTER NUMBER, FCI Pekin, 2600 South Second Street, Pekin, IL 61555. Inmates may receive publications only from the publisher, bookstore or book club. The packages must be labeled clearly as authorized reading material or they will be refused at the post office.

**Inmate Mail to FCI:**
    INMATE NAME & REGISTER NUMBER
    FCI Pekin
    Federal Correctional Institution
    P.O. Box 5000
    Pekin, IL 61555

**Inmate Mail to Camp:**
INMATE NAME & REGISTER NUMBER
FCI Pekin
Satellite Camp
P.O. Box 5000
Pekin, IL 61555

**Visiting Hours:** Approved visitors may visit the FCI on Saturday, Sunday and federal holidays, 8:15 am-3pm and Monday, 1pm-8pm. Inmates at the FCI are limited to a point system, with one point per hour of visiting during weekdays and two points per hour of visiting during weekends and holidays, for a total of 40 points allowed. The camp is open for visitation on Friday evenings from 5pm-8pm; and Saturday, Sunday and federal holidays from 8:30am-3pm. A maximum of seven visitors and an unlimited number of children (under the age of three) are allowed to visit one inmate. Attorney visits can be made by special arrangement 24 hours in advance. A children's room is available. Additional visiting information can be found on the BOP website, www.bop.gov, at https://www.bop.gov/locations/institutions/pek/.

**Lodging/Accommodations:** Should visitors be spending the night, the following is a short list of accommodations that are available in Pekin, Illinois:

| | |
|---|---|
| Econo Lodge | 309-353-4047 |
| Holiday Inn Express-Pekin | 309-353-3305 |
| Mineral Springs Motel | 309-346-2147 |
| Super 8 Motel | 309-760-0696 |

**Directions to Facility:** The institution is located on Route 29 South, approximately five miles south of Peoria, IL, two and a half hours southwest of Chicago, IL and three hours northeast of St. Louis, MO. The Institution is 70 miles north of Springfield, IL, which is the state capital. FCI Pekin is located five miles from interstate 74. The Pekin area is easily accessible by car via U.S. 9 or U.S. 29, which are the primary access roads to the area.

## §13:22  FMC ROCHESTER

FMC Rochester
Federal Medical Center
2110 East Center Street
Rochester, MN 55904
RCH/ExecAssistant@bop.gov
507-287-0674
Fax: 507-424-7600

**Location:** In southeastern Minnesota, two miles east of downtown Rochester, off State Highway 296 (Fourth Street). The area is served by the Rochester Airport and commercial bus lines.

**History:** Opened in 1985, FMC Rochester was formerly a state mental hospital. It serves as a major psychiatric and medical referral center for the Federal Prison System. There is also a work cadre who serves as a manpower resource. The average offender age is 39 years, with a median sentence length of 60 months. A national population is served by the medical staff, although non-patients are primarily from the upper mid-western United States.

**Judicial District:** District of Minnesota.

**Security Level:** The Federal Medical Center (FMC) in Rochester is an administrative facility providing specialized medical and mental health services to male offenders.

**Population:** As of 6/15/2017, the FMC inmate population is 666. Weekly population figures are available on the BOP website at www.bop.gov.

**Education:** The institution offers GED, ESL, adult continuing education, parenting classes, and college correspondence courses.

**Vocational/Apprenticeship:** FMC offers a Landscape Management Vocational Training Program certified by Rochester Community and Technical College (RCTC). Apprenticeship programs are offered in biomedical equipment repair, electrician, HVAC, painter, and plumber.

**Library:** The law library is open Monday through Sunday in the afternoons and evenings. Inmates also have access to the Electronic Law Libraries (ELL)/ Electric typewriters are available. A copier is also available. Copies are 15 cents per page and charged to an inmate's debit card. The leisure library offers inmates a variety of reading materials, including but not limited to: periodicals, newspapers, fiction, non-fiction, and reference books. An interlibrary loan program is not available.

**UNICOR:** None.

**Counseling/Rehab Services:** The institution offers a non-residential drug treatment program, a drug education program, an Alcoholics Anonymous group, stress management, outpatient chemical dependency, and Native American Alcoholics Anonymous. The Mental Health Services Department also offers individual therapy and intensive diagnosis or assessment, inpatient treatment, and outpatient substance abuse treatment.

**Health Services:** The Federal Medical Center offers a complete range of care from primary to advanced specialty and inpatient hospitalization. The institution is staffed by physicians, physician assistants, nurses, a dentist, dental assistants, pharmacists, a radiological technicians, physical therapists, laboratory technologists and a respiratory therapist. The medical center consists of 800 medical/chronic care beds. There is no in-house surgery or dialysis. The medical center works closely with the nearby Mayo Clinic. Sick call is held Monday through Thursday, except holidays, at different times (7am-7:30am for behavioral health and work cadre inmates, 6am-7am for ambulatory care inmates, etc.). Pill line hours: weekdays, 6:30am-7am, 10:30am-11am, 3pm-3:30pm, 7pm-7:30pm; weekends, 7:15am-7:45am, 11am-11:30am, 3pm-3:30pm, 7pm-7:30pm. Extra times for insulin are 6am-6:30am on weekdays and 6:45-7:15am on weekends. Medical staff members are on duty 24 hours a day. Health education classes are offered, including wellness, cardiac education, diet counseling, foot care clinic, disease and medical education, diabetes education, stress management, smoking cessation, spiritual wellness, and injury prevention. Inmates under the age of 50 may request a physical examination every two years, while inmates over the age of 50 may request one annually.

**Religious Services:** FMC Rochester provides a wide variety of religious services. The current monthly schedule will be on unit bulletin boards or at the Religious Activity Center for the specific time and day for a particular religious service or meeting. Chaplains are available for counseling. Inmates should feel free to speak to a chaplain as they make their rounds, or to seek them out at the Religious Activity Center.

**Housing:** Inmates are housed in individual rooms, double rooms, or multiple occupancy wards, and open dormitories. Housing units consist of mental health, forensic, diagnostic and observation units, chemical dependency units, and a general population unit. No patients are housed in dormitories or multiple occupancy rooms. There are television rooms available in the units. Hours of viewing are Sunday through Thursday from 6am-12am, with an extension to 2am on Friday, Saturday, and the evening preceding a holiday.

**Commissary:** The commissary is open for sales on Tuesday, Wednesday and Thursday from 11am-12:30pm. Shopping days are determined by the inmates' register numbers. Mental Health Unit inmates will be escorted to shop after the AM census is completed on Wednesdays. Other inmates with the first five digits of their register number ending 34 through 66 may shop from 11:00am–12:30pm on Wednesdays. Inmates assigned to outside work details only shop at 7:30am on Thursdays. Other inmates with the first five digits of their register number ending in 67 through 99 may shop from 11:00am–12:30pm on Thursdays. Special purpose order sales are conducted on Thursdays from 11:15am-12:15pm. A variety of over-the-counter medications are available for purchase at the commissary and in the vending machines located in the housing units. The current monthly Bureau of Prisons commissary spending limit is $360.

**Telephone Policy:** Inmates dial direct using the Inmate Telephone System (ITS). The following are standard features of ITS: (1) inmate calls automatically terminate after 15 minutes; (2) an inmate's calling list is limited to 30 callers; and (3) calls are charged to an inmate's debit card. Telephones are available for inmate use Monday through Friday, 6am-7:30am, 10:30am-12:30pm, and 4pm-11:30pm; weekends and federal holidays, 6am-11:30pm, except during count times.

**Inmate Mail:** The institution accepts mail from the U.S. Postal Service via First-Class, U.S. Priority, and Express mail. For those interested in sending overnight mail via a private carrier (FedEx or UPS Overnight), it is recommended that you first contact the institution to find out whether the receipt of such mail is permitted.

**Inmate Mail to FMC:**
INMATE NAME & REGISTER NUMBER
FMC Rochester
Federal Medical Center
P.O. Box 4000
Rochester, MN 55903

**Visiting Hours:** Approved visitors may visit the institution on Friday, Saturday, Sunday, Monday and federal holidays from 8:15am-2:30pm. Visiting lists are limited to a maximum of 20 persons. Inmates are limited to 16 visiting points per month. Two points are deducted for weekend and holiday visits, and one point is deducted for weekday visits. No more than five visitors are allowed per visit. A children's room is available (inmates are not allowed inside the play area, although they may request to be placed close to it). Attorney visits can be made by special arrangement; if attorneys are not able to visit during regular visiting hours, they must make an appointment with the unit team. Additional visiting information can be found on the BOP website, at https://www.bop.gov/locations/institutions/rch/.

**Lodging/Accommodations:** Should visitors be spending the night, the following is a short list of accommodations that are available in Rochester, Minnesota:
| | |
|---|---|
| Best Western Soldier's Field Tower & Suites | 507-288-2677 |
| Kahler Grand Hotel | 507-280-6200 |
| Spring Hill Suites by Marriott | 507-281-5455 |
| Travelers Hotel | 507-289-4095 |

**Directions to Facility:** The Federal Medical Center is located approximately two miles east of downtown Rochester. Taking 4th Street southeast, you will pass Olmsted Community Hospital. The Federal Medical Center is located slightly to your left. Turn left on Center Street and right into the parking lot. You may park in the lot identified as "Visitor Parking." Handicap parking is available in the lot nearest the institution's front entrance. Persons waiting for visitors will not be allowed to remain in the parking lot while visiting is in progress.

## §13:23   FCI SANDSTONE

FCI Sandstone
Federal Correctional Institution
2300 County Rd 29
Sandstone, MN 55072
SST/ExecAssistant@bop.gov
320-245-2262
Fax: 320-245-0385

**Location:** FCI Sandstone is located 100 miles northeast of Minneapolis-St. Paul and 70 miles southwest of Duluth, off Interstate 35 (Sandstone exit, follow Highway 23 to Route 123 east). The area is served by Greyhound.

**History:** Opened in 1939, FCI Sandstone houses male offenders with an average age of 35.5 years and serving an average sentence of 7.3 years.

**Judicial District:** District of Minnesota.

**Security Level:** The Federal Correctional Institution (FCI) in Sandstone, Minnesota, is a low-security facility for male offenders.

**Population:** As of 6/15/2017, the FCI inmate population is 1,206. Weekly population figures are available on the BOP website www.bop.gov, at https://www.bop.gov/locations/institutions/sst/.

**Education:** The institution offers GED, ESL, adult continuing education, parenting classes, and college correspondence courses. Monthly Education calendars are posted throughout the institution, listing the current classes and programs.

**Vocational/Apprenticeship:** FCI offers advanced occupational education in general business computer applications. Vocational training in auto mechanics, and welding. Apprenticeship programs are offered in baker, bindery worker, cook, dental assistant, offset press operator, quality control inspector, pre-press operator, sewing machine repair and welder. Inmates must have a high school diploma or GED in order to enroll in the vocational training programs. Inmates must meet the following requirements in order to enroll in the apprenticeship training programs: high school diploma or GED, at least one year remaining on their sentence, and must be working in the area of the apprenticeship before being accepted into the program.

**Library:** The law library is open Monday through Thursday, 6am-9:30pm; Friday, 6am-3:30pm; Saturday 7am-3:30pm; closed during counts, holidays, and Sundays. Inmates also have access to the Electronic Law Libraries (ELL). An inmate law library clerk is available for assistance in legal research. Electric typewriters and a copier machine are available. Inmates must purchase some legal supplies at the commissary. An interlibrary loan program is available in the leisure library. Video cassette recorders and audio cassette players are available to inmates on a limited basis.

**UNICOR:** A graphics factory employs approximately 124 inmates and a services factory employs approximately 88 inmates. Work hours are Monday through Friday, 7:45am-3:30pm.

**Counseling/Rehab Services:** The FCI offers a non-residential drug treatment program, a nine-month, 500-hour education Residential Drug Abuse Program (RDAP), Alcoholics Anonymous and Narcotics Anonymous groups, Values Training, and other voluntary groups. In addition, consultations, crisis intervention-type counseling sessions, relaxation training sessions, self-study, and meditative techniques are also available. Psychiatric medication needs are arranged on a consultation basis through the Health Services Department.

**Health Services:** Each inmate is assigned a primary care provider or mid-level practitioner upon arrival based on health status. Health services include an optical laboratory and dental department. The local hospital is three miles away. The pill line is 6:15am-6:45am and 4:45pm on weekdays, 7am-7:15am and 4:45pm on weekends and holidays. Inmates can be seen for sick call by turning in request forms to Health Services Monday through Friday, 6:15am-6:45am. Periodic age-specific preventative health examinations are available to inmates. Clinical staff are on duty daily from 6am-10pm, and are on call between 10pm-6am. Emergency care is provided 24 hours a day.

**Fitness/Recreation:** The Recreation Department offers intramural or extramural sports, a music room, a weight room, pool tables, and ping-pong tables. The hobby craft center offers leather craft, painting, and stained glass. The gymnasium, recreation yard, and hobby craft are open daily.

**Religious Services:** The institution is staffed by two full-time chaplains who serve as pastors and counselors. A community of outside clergy and volunteers provides services for most faiths. Services are regularly conducted by a Catholic priest (English and Spanish), rabbis, a Muslim imam, a traditional American-Indian spiritual leader, Jehovah's Witnesses elders, Mormon elders, Buddhist teachers, Prison Fellowship Programs, Minneapolis Bible Fellowship Volunteers, and many others. The prison chapel is open seven days a week, including three evenings. A wide variety of religious literature of all faiths is free and available. The chaplaincy offers two long-term religious programs: Life Connections, an 18-month program for developing faith, and Threshold, a 24-month program for examining life patterns and making positive changes.

Televisions are available in each of the housing units. Unit televisions may be viewed during established off-duty hours. During normal working hours, unit televisions may be viewed at the discretion of staff.

**Commissary:** The commissary is open Monday through Sales Hours: Monday thru Thursday, 11:00 a.m. till Close of Main Line or 12:00 p.m., express sales (15 items or less, not including OTC item or stamps), 4:45 p.m. till 8:00 p.m. General shopping list must be placed in drop box outside of staff dining area by 10:30 a.m. on inmate's scheduled shopping day. Inmates are assigned one shopping day per week for regular shopping. Shopping days are assigned by unit based on Unit Sanitation results from the most recent inspection day. Bureau of Prisons policy currently sets a monthly commissary spending limit of $360.

**Telephone Policy:** Inmates dial direct using the Inmate Telephone System (ITS). The following are standard features of ITS: (1) inmate calls automatically terminate after 15 minutes; (2) an inmate's calling list is limited to 10 callers; and (3) calls are charged to an inmate's debit card. The telephone room is open Monday through Friday, 6am to no later than 11:30pm. The hours of telephone operation are normally limited from 6am-7:30am, 10:30am-12noon, and 4:30pm-9:30pm; weekends and holidays, 7am-9:30am, 10:30am-3:30pm, and 4:30pm-9:30pm. Unmonitored legal calls must be requested in advance.

**Inmate Mail:** The institution accepts mail from the U.S. Postal Service via First-Class, U.S. Priority, and Express mail. For those interested in sending overnight mail via a private carrier (FedEx or UPS Overnight), it is recommended that you first contact the institution to find out whether the receipt of such mail is permitted. The BOP permits inmates to subscribe to and receive publications without prior approval, subject to appropriate content matter. An inmate may only receive hard cover publications and newspapers from the publisher, a book club, or a bookstore, but can receive softcover publications (other than newspapers) from any source.

**Inmate Mail to FCI:**
INMATE NAME & REGISTER NUMBER
FCI Sandstone
Federal Correctional Institution
P.O. Box 1000
Sandstone, MN 55072

**Visiting Hours:** Approved visitors may visit inmates on Friday, Saturday, Sunday, Monday and federal holidays from 8:30am-3:30pm. Visiting is on an odd/even basis for Saturday and Sunday, every other weekend, based on the inmate's register number. Social visits are limited to a maximum of six visits per month, with no more than six visitors at any one time (including children), unless special authorization for more has been given by staff. An inmate may have a maximum of 20 visitors on the visiting list. A separate room is available for children. Attorneys should ordinarily make advance appointments for each visit and are encouraged to visit during the regular visiting hours. Attorney visits will be subject to visual monitoring, but not audio monitoring. Additional

visiting information can be found on the BOP website, https://www.bop.gov/
locations/institutions/sst/.

| | |
|---|---|
| America's Best Value Inn | 320-384-6112 |
| Grand Casino Hinckley Hotel | 320-384-7101 |
| Grand Hinckley Inn | 320-384-7622 |
| Grand Northern Inn | 320-384-7171 |

## §13:24  MCFP SPRINGFIELD

MCFP Springfield
Medical Center for Federal Prisoners
1900 West Sunshine Street
Springfield, MO 65807
SPG/ExecAssistant@bop.gov
417-862-7041
Fax: 417-837-1717

**Location:** MCFP Springfield is located at the corner of Sunshine Street and
the Kansas Expressway, off Interstate 44. The area is served by the Springfield
Municipal Airport and commercial bus lines.

**History:** Opened in 1933, MCFP Springfield serves as a major medical, surgical
and psychiatric referral center for the Federal Prison System and the United States
Courts. The average age of the inmate is 36 years old. A work cadre serves as a
man-power resource.

**Judicial District:** Western District of Missouri.

**Security Level:** The U.S. Medical Center for Federal Prisoners (MCFP) in
Springfield, Missouri, is an administrative facility that provides medical, mental
health and dental services to male offenders.

**Population:** As of 6/15/2017, the MCFP inmate population is 1,022. Weekly
population figures are available on the BOP website, www.bop.gov, at https://
www.bop.gov/locations/institutions/spg/.

**Education:** The institution offers GED, ESL, adult continuing education, parenting, and college correspondence courses.

**Vocational/Apprenticeship:** Vocational training is offered in landscaping, introduction to small engine repair, introduction to home maintenance and repair,
automotive engines and advanced small engine repair. Apprenticeship programs
are offered in biomedical equipment technician, carpenter, dental, electrician,
machinist, orthotic technician, painter, plumber, prosthetic technician, refrigeration, steamfitter and sheet metal. Prerequisites to enrollment in the apprenticeship
programs: high school diploma, GED, or enrolled in GED program.

**Library:** The law library is open during convenient non-working hours, including weekends and holidays. An inmate law library clerk is available for assistance in legal research. There are approximately eight electric typewriters available to inmates. A copier is also available. An interlibrary loan program is available through the local library. The leisure library provides a variety of fiction, non-fiction, and reference books, as well as daily newspapers and monthly magazines. A listening library, with videotapes, audio cassettes, DVDs and CDS, is also available.

**UNICOR:** None.

**Counseling/Rehab Services:** The institution offers a 500-hour Residential Drug Abuse Program (RDAP). The institution also offers a non-residential drug treatment program, a drug education program, Alcoholics/Narcotics Anonymous groups, self-image groups and other voluntary groups. Each unit has a psychologist assigned or available to it to provide counseling and other mental health services to unit inmates. The normal hours of operation for the Psych-ology and Psychiatry Programs are 7:30 am till 4:00 pm, Monday through Friday.

**Health Services:** The medical center is staffed by physicians, two dentists, dental assistants, nurse practitioners, physician assistants, nurses, pharmacists, medical laboratory scientists, radiology technologists, physical therapists, an occupational therapist, recreational therapists, pharmacy technicians, a prosthetist/orthotist, certified nurse assistants, and a respiratory therapist. The FMC consists of several hundred medical and chronic care beds. Sick call is in the 1-2 clinic Monday, Tuesday, Thursday and Friday, 7am-7:30am. Pill line times are posted. The dental clinic has a dental sick call/open house on weekdays, 12noon-12:30pm. Inmates may request a physical examination every two years; inmates over 50 can request a physical examination annually. Medical staff is on duty 24 hours a day.

**Fitness/Recreation:** The Recreation Department offers a recreation center, gymnasium, and main recreational yard. There is a weight room, music room, pool tables, ping-pong tables and games. Musical instruments are available for check out from the gym office. The hobby craft center offers crafts including painting, leather craft, ceramics, and stick art. The recreation yard has areas for softball, horseshoes, bocce ball, volleyball, basketball, soccer, handball, and flag football, as well as a walking track, pavilion and tables. There are limited intramural activities. Movies are shown over a closed circuit TV channel.

**Religious Services:** The institution has full-time chaplains on staff. A community of volunteers provide services for most faiths.

**Housing:** Inmates are housed in single-man, two-man and three-man rooms, open dorms, and 20-man rooms. Housing consists of a medical unit, surgical unit, mental health treatment/evaluation units, administrative detention/segregation unit, chronic medical unit, acute medical care unit, and a work cadre unit.

**Commissary:** Inmates are assigned one shopping day per week. Days and hours are assigned by housing unit. It takes approximately three weeks for funds to arrive here from another institution. Bureau of Prisons policy currently sets a monthly commissary spending limit of $360.

**Telephone Policy:** Inmates dial direct using the Inmate Telephone System (ITS). The following are standard features of ITS: (1) inmate calls automatically terminate after 15 minutes; (2) an inmate's calling list is limited to 30 callers; and (3) calls are charged to an inmate's debit card. Inmates have 300 minutes per month, which increases to 400 minutes per month during November and December. Inmates may use the telephones daily from 6am-11:30pm. All inmate telephones, with the exception of one per housing unit, will not be operational 7:30am-10:30am, and 12:30pm-4pm (excluding weekends and holidays). All inmate calls are monitored, with the exception of properly placed legal calls.

**Inmate Mail:** The institution accepts mail from the U.S. Postal Service via First-Class, U.S. Priority, and Express mail. For those interested in sending overnight mail via a private carrier (FedEx or UPS Overnight), it is recommended that you first contact the institution to find out whether the receipt of such mail is permitted. Inmates may receive publications without prior approval, although the warden will reject those that are detrimental to the security, good order, or discipline of the institution. An inmate may receive soft-cover or hard-cover publications only from the publisher, from a book club, or from a book-store. Each inmate is limited to five magazines (no more than three months old) that can be stored in his locker or shelf.

**Inmate Mail to MCFP:**
        INMATE NAME & REGISTER NUMBER
        MCFP Springfield
        Federal Medical Center
        P.O. Box 4000
        Springfield, MO 65801

**Visiting Hours:** Regular visiting hours are 8:15am-3pm, Saturday through Monday, and national holidays. Each inmate has eight points per month; a weekday visit (excluding holidays) is counted as one point, and a weekend or holiday visit is counted as two points, excluding the Thanksgiving, Christmas, and New Year's holidays. There will be no charged points for these three holidays. Clergy and legal visits do not detract from an inmate's visiting points. Inmates are permitted no more than three adults and three children at a time (never exceeding six visitors total). Ordinarily, a maximum of 20 visitors, with no more than 10 friends, will be authorized on an approved visiting list. Children under 16 will not be included as part of the visiting limit for the list. Attorneys should be on the inmate's visiting list; however, this does not preclude other attorneys from visiting if the inmate requests such visits. Camp visiting hours are Saturday, Sunday and federal holidays, 9am-3:30pm. Visitors wishing to visit camp inmates must first report to the front entrance officer (lobby) at the main institution. Additional visiting information can be found at https://www. bop.gov/locations/institutions/spg/.

**Lodging/Accommodations:** Should visitors be spending the night, the following is a short list of accommodations that are available in Springfield, Missouri:

| | |
|---|---|
| Clarion Inn & Suites | 417-520-6200 |
| Microtel Inn & Suites | 417-833-1500 |
| Doubletree Hawthorne Park | 417-831-3131 |
| University Plaza Hotel | 417-864-7333 |

## §13:25   FCI TERRE HAUTE

FCI Terre Haute
Federal Correctional Institution
4200 Bureau Road North
Terre Haute, IN 47808
THA/ExecAssistant@bop.gov
812-238-1531
Fax: 812-238-3301

**Location:** FCI Terre Haute is located on Highway 63, two miles south of the City of Terre Haute, which is 70 miles west of Indianapolis on Interstate 70.

**Judicial District:** Southern District of Indiana.

**Security Level:** The Federal Correctional Institution (FCI) in Terre Haute, Indiana, is a medium-security facility housing male inmates with an adjacent satellite prison camp that houses minimum-security male offenders. It is part of the Terre Haute Federal Correctional Complex (FCC).

**Population:** As of 6/16/2017, the FCI inmate population is 1,047, and the camp population is 323. Weekly population figures are available on the BOP website at https://www.bop.gov/locations/institutions/tha/.

**Education:** FCI offers GED, ESL, adult continuing education, and correspondence courses.

**Vocational/Apprenticeship:** FCI offers advanced occupational education in basic diesel engine repair. The camp offers vocational training in small engine repair, electronics, and computer applications. FCI offers vocational training in computer applications, diesel mechanics and building trades.

**UNICOR:** Terre Haute employs inmates at two textile factories.

**Library:** The law library is open at various times depending on the availability of educational staff. Inmates should consult the bulletin boards for the schedule. The law library contains a variety of legal reference materials for use in preparing legal papers. The law library is open during convenient non-working hours, including weekends and holidays. Fiction books, Nonfiction materials and reference books are provided in the Reference Library.

**Counseling/Rehab Services:** The Psychology Services Department consists of Psychologists, Drug Abuse Treatment Specialists, and CODE Treatment Specialists. FCI offers a 500-hour Residential Drug Abuse Program (RDAP). The institution also offers a non-residential drug treatment program, a drug education program, self-image groups, and Alcoholics Anonymous and Narcotics Anonymous groups.

**Health Services:** The medical staff consists of full-time staff providing 24-hour coverage, including consultants from the Terre Haute community. Regular sick call at the FCI is at 6:30am-7am on Monday, Tuesday, Thursday, and Friday. Medical staff members are on duty or on call 24 hours a day. The medication line is open daily, 6am-6:15am (diabetic/insulin line), 6:15am-7am, 11am-11:15am (diabetic/insulin line), and 8:30pm-9pm. Inmates under the age of 50 may request a physical examination every two years, while inmates over the age of 50 may request one annually.

**Fitness/Recreation:** The FCI Recreation Department offers indoor and outdoor activities that range from individualized arts and crafts programs to intramural team sports such as softball, basketball, and volleyball. Physical fitness and weight reduction programs are also available.

**Religious Services:** A wide variety of religious programs are available to inmates. Chaplains are available for pastoral care, as well as contract and volunteer representatives of various faiths.

**Commissary:** The commissary access time for inmates is scheduled on a rotating basis. The schedule is posted in the housing units, on the commissary information board in the institution's main corridor, and on the electronic sign located in the commissary. The Bureau of Prisons spending limit is currently $360.

**Telephone Policy:** Inmates at the FCI dial direct using the Inmate Telephone System (ITS). The following are standard features of ITS: (1) inmate calls will automatically terminate after 15 minutes; (2) an inmate's calling list is limited to 30 callers; and (3) calls are charged to an inmate's debit card. Inmates are limited to 300 calling minutes per month. The telephones are located in each general housing unit. The telephones at the FCI are available from 6am until lockdown each day.

**Inmate Mail:** The FCI accepts mail from the U.S. Postal Service via First-Class, Priority, and Express mail. For those interested in sending overnight mail via a private carrier (FedEx or UPS Overnight), it is recommended that you first contact the institution to find out whether the receipt of such mail is permitted. Inmates can subscribe to and receive publications without prior approval, though the Warden will reject a publication if it is determined to be detrimental to the security, good order, or discipline of the institution. Inmates may receive books (hard or soft cover) only from a publisher, bookstore, or a book club. Accumulation of publications will be limited to five magazines (not to be more than three months old) and to the amount that can be neatly stored in the locker provided in each room, because of sanitation, and fire safety reasons.

**Inmate Mail to FCI:**
INMATE NAME & REGISTER NUMBER
FCI Terre Haute
Federal Correctional Institution
P.O. Box 33
Terre Haute, IN 47808

**Inmate Mail to Camp:**
INMATE NAME & REGISTER NUMBER
FCI Terre Haute
Federal Correctional Institution
Satellite Camp
P.O. Box 33
Terre Haute, IN 47808

**Visiting Hours:** Approved visitors may visit the FCI Saturday through Monday and federal holidays from 8am-3pm. Approved visitors may visit the camp Friday 2pm-8:30pm, and Saturday through Sunday and federal holidays from 8am-3pm. Inmates will not be able to visit during counts. No more than five visitors are allowed per visit, and a maximum of 10 friends and associates (other than immediate family members) can be on an inmate's approved visiting list. Attorneys should ordinarily make advance appointments for each visit and are encouraged to visit during the regular visiting hours. Additional visiting information can be found on the BOP website, www.bop.gov, at https://www.bop.gov/locations/institutions/tha/.

**Lodging/Accommodations:** Should visitors be spending the night, the following is a short list of accommodations that are available in Terre Haute, Indiana:
| | |
|---|---|
| Quality Inn | 812-235-3333 |
| Pear Tree Inn by Drury | 812-234-4268 |
| Travelodge | 812-232-7075 |

# §13:26 USP TERRE HAUTE

USP Terre Haute
United States Penitentiary
4700 Bureau Road South
Terre Haute, IN 47802
THA/ExecAssistant@bop.gov
812-244-4400
Fax: 812-244-4791

**Location:** USP Terre Haute is located on Highway 63, two miles south of the City of Terre Haute, which is 70 miles west of Indianapolis on Interstate 70. Terre Haute is served by the Hulman Regional Airport and Greyhound.

**History:** Opened in 1940 as the first penitentiary for adult felons to be constructed without a wall, USP Terre Haute houses male offenders with extensive criminal records who are considered to be sophisticated offenders requiring close supervision. The average inmate is in his 30s and serving a sentence of more than 10 years, for either drug law violations or bank robbery. The adjacent camp was opened in 1960 and serves as a satellite facility to the main institution.

**Judicial District:** Southern District of Indiana.

**Security Level:** The United States Penitentiary (USP) in Terre Haute, Indiana, is a high-security facility housing male inmates. It is part of the Terre Haute Federal Correctional Complex (FCC). The USP contains the Special Confinement Unit for inmates serving federal death sentences.

**Population:** As of 6/16/2017, the USP inmate population is 1,387. Weekly population figures are available on the BOP website at www.bop.gov, at https://www.bop.gov/locations/institutions/thp/.

**Education:** The USP and the camp offer GED, ESL, adult continuing education, and correspondence courses.

**Vocational/Apprenticeship:** USP offers no advanced occupational education programs or apprenticeship programs.

**Library:** The library provides non-fiction, fiction, and reference books to inmates who are interested in expanding their knowledge. The library also has an inter-library loan program with the downtown library. A copy machine is available in the camp's reading library for inmate use. Typewriters are also available in the law or leisure library.

**UNICOR:** A textile factory employs approximately 383 inmates.

**Counseling/Rehab Services:** The USP and the camp offer a non-residential drug treatment program, a drug education program, self-image groups, and Alcoholics Anonymous and Narcotics Anonymous groups. The penitentiary is staffed by full-time psychologists, drug abuse treatment specialists, and a psychology technician. The camp is staffed by one full-time psychologist.

**Health Services:** The medical staff consists of full-time staff providing 24-hour coverage, including consultants from the Terre Haute community. Regular sick call at the USP is at 6:30am-7am on Monday, Tuesday, Thursday, and Friday. Medical staff members are on duty or on call 24 hours a day. The medication line is open daily, 6am-6:15am (diabetic/insulin line), 6:15am-7am, 11am-11:15am (diabetic/insulin line), and 8:30pm-9pm. Inmates under the age of 50 may request a physical examination every two years, while inmates over the age of 50 may request one annually.

**Fitness/Recreation:** The USP Recreation Department offers indoor and outdoor activities that range from individualized arts and crafts programs to intramural team sports such as softball, soccer, basketball, and volleyball. Physical fitness and weight reduction programs are also available. The hobby craft center offers painting, leather, and art (inmates are allowed to have one completed project in their room; the rest are to be mailed home). Authorization of musical instruments is required. The camp Recreation Department offers organized sports, miniature golf, pool tables, ping-pong, cards, and television. The camp's hobby craft center offers leatherworking and glass shop areas.

**Religious Services:** The USP is staffed by full-time chaplains. Contract and volunteer representatives of other faiths are available. Contract rabbi services are not offered; a contract imam is available; a sweat lodge is available for Native American services.

**Housing:** The USP is comprised of four general housing units and two administrative units. Inmates are housed in two-man cells and two-man dormitory-style cubicles. The camp houses inmates in eight units of two-man, eight-man, and 12-man rooms.

**Commissary:** The commissary access time for inmates is scheduled on a rotating basis. The schedule is posted in the housing units, on the commissary information board in the institution's main corridor, and on the electronic sign located in the commissary. The monthly commissary spending limit is currently $360.

**Telephone Policy:** Inmates at the USP and the camp dial direct using the Inmate Telephone System (ITS). The following are standard features of ITS: (1) inmate calls will automatically terminate after 15 minutes; (2) an inmate's calling list is limited to 30 callers; and (3) calls are charged to an inmate's debit card. Inmates are limited to 300 calling minutes per month. The telephones are located in each general housing unit. The telephones at the USP are available for inmate use 6am-9pm daily. The telephones at the camp are open 6am-11pm daily.

**Inmate Mail:** The USP and the camp accept mail from the U.S. Postal Service via First-Class, U.S. Priority, and Express mail. For those interested in sending overnight mail via a private carrier (FedEx or UPS Overnight), it is recommended that you first contact the institution to find out whether the receipt of such mail is permitted.

**Inmate Mail to USP:**
> INMATE NAME & REGISTER NUMBER
> USP Terre Haute
> U.S. Penitentiary
> P.O. Box 33
> Terre Haute, IN 47808

**Inmate Mail to Camp:**
> INMATE NAME & REGISTER NUMBER
> USP Terre Haute
> U.S. Penitentiary
> Satellite Camp
> P.O. Box 12014
> Terre Haute, IN 47801

**Visiting Hours:** Approved visitors may visit the USP Saturday through Monday and federal holidays, 8am-3pm. The number of visitors in the visiting room cannot exceed five (groups of more than five may be allowed with prior approval), and an inmate can have no more than 10 people on the approved visitors list. Attorney visits will be held during normal visiting hours, except under emergency circumstances, and will be made by special arrangement. A small child's room is available. Additional visiting information can be found on the BOP website, at https://www.bop.gov/locations/institutions/thp/.

**Lodging/Accommodations:** Should visitors be spending the night, the following is a short list of accommodations that are available in Terre Haute, IN:

| | |
|---|---|
| Quality Inn | 812-235-3333 |
| Pear Tree Inn by Drury | 812-234-4268 |
| Travelodge | 812-232-7075 |

# §13:27  AUSP THOMSON

AUSP Thomson
Administrative United States Penitentiary
1000 University Drive
S.W. Waseca, MN 56093
TOM/ExecAssistant@bop.gov
815-259-1000
Fax: 815-259-0186

**Location:** AUSP Thomson is located less than mile north of Thomson, Illinois, about a mile east of the Mississippi River.

**Judicial District:** Northern District of Illinois.

**Security Level:** The ASUP Thomson Satellite Camp is a minimum security facility housing male inmates. The facility was opened in early 2017.

**Population:** As of 6/16/2017, the camp inmate population is 107. Weekly population figures are available on the BOP website, www.bop.gov, at https://www.bop.gov/locations/institutions/tom/.

**Education:** The institution offers GED, ESL, adult continuing education, parenting, and college correspondence courses.

**Vocational/Apprenticeship:** None at this time.

**Library:** The library is open daily during convenient non-working hours (afternoons and evenings), including weekends and holidays. A law library clerk is available for assistance in legal research. Inmates have access to the Electronic Law Libraries (ELL). Electric typewriters are available. A copier is available. Copies are 10 cents per page and charged to an inmate's debit card. The leisure library offers inmates a variety of reading materials, including but not limited to: periodicals, newspapers, fiction, non-fiction, and reference books.

**UNICOR:** None.

**Counseling/Rehab Services:** Counseling/Rehab Services: The USP and the camp offer a non-residential drug treatment program, a drug education program, self-image groups, a suicide prevention program, sex offender programs, and specialized mental health programs. The penitentiary is staffed by The Psychology Services Department is staffed by a Chief Psychologist and Drug Abuse Program Coordinator.

**Health Services:** The Health Services Unit at SCP Thomson functions as an ambulatory outpatient clinic. The Medical Staff consists of physicians, dentists, mid-level practitioners and medical and administrative ancillary support staff. Health Services staff are available seven days per week. Regular hours of operation are 6:00 a.m. to 6:00 p.m. The institution provides outpatient care. Sick call sign-up is held Mondays, Tuesdays, Thursdays and Fridays from 7am-7:20am. Pill line times may vary depending upon staffing and delayed count, but typically are Monday through Friday, 6:15am-6:30am (insulin only), 6:30am-7am; 11am-12:30pm, 4:30-5pm (insulin only), and 5pm-5:40pm. Saturday, Sunday and holidays, the pill line times are 7:15am-7:30am (insulin only), 7:30am-8am, 4:30pm-5pm (insulin only), and 5pm-5:30pm. Age- specific preventative health examinations will be available to inmates. Inmates under the age of 50 may request a physical examination every two years, while those over 50 may request one every year.

**Fitness/Recreation:** The Recreation Department offers indoor and outdoor activities that range from individualized arts and crafts programs to music programs and intramural team sports such as softball, basketball, and volleyball.

**Religious Services:** The Religious Services Department provides pastoral care and religious accommodation to individual and group religious beliefs and practices. Chaplains also offer pastoral counseling, spiritual direction, support and crisis intervention, and oversee the religious diet program, ceremonial religious meals, and religious holiday observances. New programs are offered year-round as volunteers are recruited.

**Housing:** The main facility is not yet fully activated as of 6/22/17. Inmates as the satellite camp are housed in open bay dormitories.

**Commissary:** Inmates are assigned shopping times and days according to their work schedule and register number. Commissary and validation schedules are posted on the inmate bulletin boards. Inmates are permitted to shop once per week, on Tuesday. Inmates must deposit a completed Commissary list and wait until their name is called to proceed to the sale window. The sales unit will be closed for a pre-determined week in March and again in September to conduct inventory. Bureau of Prisons policy currently sets a monthly commissary spending limit of $360.

**Telephone Policy:** Inmates dial direct using the Inmate Telephone System (ITS). The following are standard features of ITS: (1) inmate calls automatically terminate after 15 minutes; (2) an inmate's calling list is limited to 30 phone numbers; and (3) calls are charged to an inmate's debit card. There is a 15-minute waiting period between calls. Each inmate has 300 minutes per month, with re-validation days for these minutes based on their register numbers. The hours of telephone operation begin at 6:00 a.m. and end no later than 11:30 p.m., excluding count times.

**Inmate Mail:** The institution accepts mail from the U.S. Postal Service via First-Class, U.S. Priority, and Express mail. For those interested in sending overnight mail via a private carrier (FedEx or UPS Overnight), it is recom- mended that you first contact the institution to find out whether the receipt of such mail is permitted. Inmates may subscribe to and receive publications without prior approval, though packages that are not clearly marked and publications with material detrimental to the security, good order and discipline of the institution will be rejected. Inmates may only receive hard cover publications and newspapers from the publisher, a book club, or a bookstore, but may receive softcover publications (other than newspapers) from any source.

**Inmate Mail to FCI:**
INMATE NAME & REGISTER NUMBER
AUSP Thomson
U.S. Penitentiary
P.O. Box 1002 Thomson, IL 61285

**Visiting Hours:** Approved visitors may visit the camp on Fridays from 5pm-8:30pm, and Saturday, Sunday and federal holidays from 8am-3pm. Each inmate is allotted 12 points per month. Each visit, regardless of length, is equal to one point on Friday, and two points for weekend and holiday visits. Inmates are allowed two adults plus children) at any given time. Attorneys are encouraged to visit during regular visiting hours, and to make advance appointments with a member of the unit team for such visits. However, attorney visits can be arranged at other times, depending on the cir- cumstances of each case. Additional visiting information can be found on the BOP website, at https://www.bop.gov/locations/institutions/tom/.

**Lodging/Accommodations:** Should visitors be spending the night, the following is a short list of accommodations that are available in Thomson, Illinois:
| | |
|---|---|
| Sandburr Run and Resort | 815-902-6063 |
| Executive Inn | 815-258-7378 |
| AmericInn Hotel and Suites Fulton | 815-589-3333 |

# §13:28   FCI WASECA

FCI Waseca
Federal Correctional Institution
1000 University Drive, S.W.
Waseca, MN 56093
WAS/ExecAssistant@bop.gov
507-835-8972
Fax: 507-837-4547

**Location:** FCI Waseca is located in southern Minnesota, 75 miles south of Minneapolis on Interstate 35, 13 miles west of Owatonna, on State Highway 57. The area is served by airports in Minnesota (75 miles from the facility) and Rochester (70 miles away).

**History:** Opened in June 1996.

**Judicial District:** District of Minnesota.

**Security Level:** The Federal Correctional Institution (FCI) in Waseca is a low-security facility housing female inmates.

**Population:** As of 6/16/2017, the FCI inmate population is 740. Weekly population figures are available on the BOP website at www.bop.gov, https://www.bop.gov/locations/institutions/was/.

**Education:** The institution offers GED, ESL, adult continuing education, and correspondence courses.

**Vocational/Apprenticeship:** The FCI offers an adult occupational education course in office administration through Riverland Community College an AOE funded Cosmetology program, and Prisoners Assisting With Service dogs (PAWS) program through Can Do Canines, as well as two Vocational Train-ing programs: Cabinetry/Framing, Horticulture (Landscape Technician App-renticeship, Grounds & Turf Management, and Greenhouse Specialist). Enrollment in AOE, PAWS, or VT programs requires a GED or high school diploma and applicants ordinarily must have clear conduct for one year prior to application.

**Library:** The law library is open daily during convenient non-working hours (afternoons and evenings), including weekends and holidays.The Law Library contains a variety of legal reference materials for use in preparing legal papers. Reference materials include the United States Code Annotated, Federal Reporter, Supreme Court Reporter, Bureau of Prison's Program Statements, Institution Supplements, Indexes, and other legal materials. An Inmate Law Library Clerk is available for assistance in legal research. A copier is available in the Law Library for inmate use. Legal materials are also available to inmates in detention or segregation status, ordinarily via a delivery system or satellite collection. The leisure library offers inmates a variety of reading materials, including but not limited to: periodicals, newspapers, fiction, non-fiction, and reference books.

**UNICOR:** A textile sewing factory produces military shorts and employs approximately 200 inmates. Other positions within UNICOR include maintenance, packaging, quality assurance, business office, and warehouse.

**Counseling/Rehab Services:** The institution offers a nine-month, 500-hour residential drug abuse treatment program. The institution also offers a non-residential drug treatment program, a drug education program. Trauma and Life Workshop, Resolve (Trauma and Recovery), Basic Cognitive Skills, Criminal Thinking, and Emotional Self-Regulation. Additionally, Illness Management and Recovery is offered to inmates who are identified as needing additional assistance in self-care due to a mental illness.The institution is staffed by full-time psychologists.

**Health Services:** Each inmate is assigned a primary care provider, which is a physician's assistant working directly under the supervision of a physician. The institution provides outpatient care. The nearest hospital is five minutes away. Sick call sign-up is held Mondays, Tuesdays, Thursdays and Fridays from 6:30am-7am. Dental sick call sign-up is Mondays, Tuesdays, Thursdays and Fridays in the Health Services Department. One weekdays, the pill line is 6:15am-7am,(insulin only), 6:30am, 7pm (insulin only) and 7:15pm. On weekends and holidays, the pill line is 8:45am (insulin only), 9am, 6:15pm (insulin only), and 6:30pm. Age-specific preventative health examinations will be available to inmates. Inmates under the age of 50 may request a physical exam every three years, while those over 50 may request one every year.

**Fitness/Recreation:** In addition to a full sized gymnasium, there are other indoor workout areas for aerobics, exercise machines, spin bikes, stretching and yoga. There is a large DVD library for workout and fitness videos available for check out, as well as DVD's on basic nutrition. Outdoor recreation areas offer a variety of activities, including racquetball, volleyball, bocce ball, tennis, frisbee golf, basketball, horseshoes, and a multi-purpose field, and a large walking track, which is open year-round. A variety of wellness classes are offered in the Recreation to address general wellness, nutrition, and fitness, etc.

In season, the Recreation Department offers an opportunity to participate in a Community Flower Garden. Inmates may choose and purchase six varieties of seeds to plant and care for during the summer months. Basic gardening tools are provided and rainwater is collected and recycled for watering purposes. Hobby craft lockers are available in the Recreation area for inmates enrolled in the hobby craft program. Additionally, hobby craft totes are available through Recreation for inmates enrolled in unit-based hobby craft. The totes are stored in the housing unit, and certain hobby craft projects may be worked on in the housing unit. The totes may also be brought to Recreation as needed to work on hobby craft projects. Inmates may also own harmonicas, but all other musical instruments must be borrowed from the Recreation Department.

**Cosmetology Services:** Because FCI Waseca has a Cosmetology Adult Occupational Education program, certain services are offered to the inmate population as a learning tool. Haircuts, styling, chemical applications, manicures, pedicures, and facials may be scheduled by any inmate in the general population. Scheduling is held during lunch mainline in the Center Hall area.

**Religious Services:** The institution is staffed by full-time chaplains (one Catholic, one Protestant). Services are also conducted regularly by a Catholic priest, rabbi, Muslim imam, Native American spiritual leader and many others. A community of volunteers provides services for most faiths. The Mentor Coordinator establishes partnerships with faith-based organizations for mentoring opportunities locally and nationwide to assist inmates in meeting their reentry needs. This person assists the Chaplain in Religious Services programming and other Reentry Programs at this facility. This person oversees Celebrate Recovery, a faith-based recovery program for all addictions. The Threshold Program is a non-residential faith-based program which focuses on: managing mental and emotional health, decision-making, personal relationships, accepting personal responsibility, daily living, wellness, continued educational growth, positive use of leisure time, and spirituality/spiritual growth. The program is approximately six to nine months in length.

**Housing:** Inmates are housed in "open bay" dormitories, two-man and four-man cubicle dormitories, and four-man rooms. Two units are characterized as general population units. Unit televisions may be viewed during established hours.

**Commissary:** Inmates are assigned shopping times and days according to their work schedule and register number. Sales are conducted Monday through Thursday, 6:15am-7:30am, 8:30am-9:30am and 11am-1pm. Bureau of Prisons policy currently sets a monthly commissary spending limit of $360.

**Telephone Policy:** Inmates dial direct using the Inmate Telephone System (ITS). The following are standard features of ITS: (1) inmate calls automatically terminate after 15 minutes; (2) an inmate's calling list is limited to 30 phone numbers; and (3) calls are charged to an inmate's debit card. There is a 15-minute waiting period between calls. Each inmate has 300 minutes per month.

**Inmate Mail:** The institution accepts mail from the U.S. Postal Service via First-Class, U.S. Priority, and Express mail. For those interested in sending overnight mail via a private carrier (FedEx or UPS Overnight), it is recommended that you first contact the institution to find out whether the receipt of such mail is permitted. Inmates may subscribe to and receive publications without prior approval, though packages that are not clearly marked and publications with material detrimental to the security, good order and discipline of the institution will be rejected. Inmates may only receive hard cover publications and newspapers from the publisher, a book club, or a bookstore, but may receive softcover publications (other than newspapers) from any source.

**Inmate Mail to FCI:**
INMATE NAME & REGISTER NUMBER
FCI Waseca
Federal Correctional Institution
P.O. Box 1731
Waseca, MN 56093

**Visiting Hours:** Approved visitors may visit the institution on Fridays from 4:30pm-8:30pm, and Saturday, Sunday and federal holidays from 8:30am-3pm. Inmates are allowed 10 visitors (five adults and five children) per visit. A small children's room is available. Attorneys are encouraged to visit during regular visiting hours, and to make advance appointments with a member of the unit team for such visits. However, attorney visits can be arranged at other times, depending on the circumstances of each case. Additional visiting information at https://www.bop.gov/locations/institutions/was/.

**Lodging/Accommodations:** Should visitors be spending the night, the following is a short list of accommodations that are available in Waseca, Minnesota:

| | |
|---|---|
| American Motel | 507-835-4300 |
| Lodging at Lake Aire | 507-835-2121 |
| Crossings by GrandStay, Waseca | 507-835-0022 |

**Directions to Facility:** From Minneapolis: I-35 South to Highway 14 West, turn left on Highway 13 South, follow signs to the Federal Correctional Institution, Waseca, Minnesota.

From Iowa: I-35 North to Highway 14 West, turn left on Highway 13 South, follow signs to the Federal Correctional Institution, Waseca, Minnesota.

From Chicago: 94W to 90W to I-35 North to Highway 14 West, turn left on Highway 13 South and follow signs to the Federal Correctional Institution, Waseca, Minnesota.

## §13:29   FPC YANKTON

FPC Yankton
Federal Prison Camp
1016 Douglas Avenue
Yankton, SD 57078
YAN/ExecAssistant@bop.gov
605-665-3262
Fax: 605-668-1113

**Location:** FPC Yankton is located in southeastern South Dakota, 60 miles north-west of Sioux City, Iowa, and 85 miles southwest of Sioux Falls, South Dakota, off U.S. Hwy. 81. The area is served by airports in Sioux City and Sioux Falls, as well as Yankton municipal airport.

**History:** Opened in 1988, FPC Yankton, a former college, houses male offenders primarily from the Midwestern United States who do not have records of escape, violence, sexual offenses, or major medical or psychiatric problems. The average sentence is 53 months for a drug-related offense.

**Judicial District:** District of South Dakota.

**Security Level:** The Federal Prison Camp (FPC) in Yankton is a minimum-security facility housing male inmates.

**Population:** As of 6/16/2017, the FPC inmate population is 485. Weekly population figures are available on the BOP website at www.bop.gov, at https://www.bop.gov/locations/institutions/yan/.

**Education:** The camp offers GED, ESL, literacy, and adult continuing education. College courses are also available, for which inmates must have a high school diploma or GED.

**Vocational/Apprenticeship:** The FPC offers advanced occupational education in accounting, business administration, and business management. Vocational training is offered in horticulture. Apprenticeship programs are offered in baker, boiler operator/mechanic, building maintenance repair, carpenter, cook, dental assistant, electrician, electrician maintenance, HVAC, human services direct support professional, industrial housekeeper, landscape management, landscape technician, painter, refrigeration mechanic and plumber. Enrollment prerequisites to the vocational programs: high school diploma or GED. Prerequisites to enrollment in the apprenticeship programs: high school diploma, GED, or GED enrolled and at least 12 months is remaining on an inmate's sentence.

**Library:** The law library is open Monday through Friday from 8am-11am, 12:15pm-3:45pm and 5pm-8:50pm; and weekends and holidays 8am-9:45am and 11:30am-3:45pm. An inmate law library clerk is available for assistance in legal research. There are electric typewriters available to inmates. A copier is available. Electronic Law Library (ELL): Law Library materials are available. Printing costs 15 cents per page. A Life Skills Library is available where inmates can study, do assignments and work on specialized tasks. DVD's and books are available for check out which are designed to enhance your skills upon release. Normal operating hours for the library are 9am-4pm, Monday thru Thursday. The leisure library participates in an excellent inter-library loan program. Inmates have access to hundreds of books and a 24-hour turnaround time. Inmates have limited access to video cassette recorders. Audio cassette players are available to inmates in the language lab. There is also a "Life Skills Library" provided by the Psychology Department, a reserved quiet area where inmates can study, do assignments and work on specialized tasks to improve their life skills. DVDs and books for life skills are available for check out. Normal hours of operation for this library is Monday through Thursday, 9am-4pm.

**UNICOR:** None.

**Counseling/Rehab Services:** The camp offers a nine-month, 500-hour Residential Drug Abuse Program (RDAP). It also offers a non-residential drug treat- ment program, community transition drug abuse treatment, a parenting program, Alcoholics Anonymous, Narcotics Anonymous, Healthy Lifestyles, Smoking Cessation, Pain Management and other voluntary groups. Drug Education Program (DEP), and Drug Abuse Program (DAP), an intensive 29-week treatment program. The camp is staffed by one full-time psychologist, one DAP coordinator, and eight drug treatment specialists. Psychologist services are available via cop-out.

**Health Services:** Health staff is on-duty 6am-4pm daily on weekdays. Local hospitals are located approximately five minutes away from the institution. All inmates are assigned a specific primary healthcare provider who will handle all sick call requests, as well as monitor any chronic health problems. A con- tract optometrist comes to the institution for eye exams. The medication line is open weekdays, 6:30am-7am, 2:45pm (insulin only), and 3pm-3:30pm; weekends, 8am-8:30am, 2:45pm insulin only), and 3pm-3:30pm. Sick call is available Monday through Friday (except holidays) 6:30am-7am; dental call sign-up is available at the same time. Emergency medical care is available 24 hours a day. Age-specific preventative health examinations are available.

**Fitness/Recreation:** The Recreation Department offers intramural team sports, weight areas, hobby craft center, musical instruments, pool tables, shuffleboard, and ping-pong tables. No gambling card games are allowed. Physical fitness and weight reduction programs are also offered. The hobby craft center offers leather craft, painting, art, and beadwork. Music lessons are also available.

**Religious Services:** The camp is staffed by one full-time chaplain (non- denomi- national). A community of volunteers provides services for most faiths, including an imam, rabbi, priest, Native-American spiritual leaders, Protestant groups, and Seventh Day Adventists. Religious holidays, activities, materials or clothing items must be coordinated through the chaplain.

**Housing:** The housing units at the camp consist of Durand and Kingbury Halls and the upper floor of the Lloyd Building. The Durand Unit is specifically designed to house participants in the residential drug treatment program. The inmates are housed in dormitories containing 4-man to twelve-man rooms. The housing units are wheel-chair accessible. There are three television rooms per unit; viewing hours are Monday through Thursday, 4:30pm-10pm; Friday, 4:30pm-12am; Saturday, 6am-2:45am; and Sunday, 6am-10pm.

**Commissary:** The commissary is open Tuesday and Wednesday evenings after the 4pm count clears until 8pm (or until all inmates in line are processed). There is an express sales line 11am-12noon on Monday and Tuesday. Special Purchase items are available for sale 11am-12noon on Thursdays. Bureau of Prisons policy currently sets a monthly commissary spending limit of $360.

**Telephones:** Each inmate must prepare a contact list. A maximum of 100 contacts may be placed on the list. There are approximately eight phones per housing unit. There is no specific limit on the number of phone calls an inmate may make, but inmates are limited to 300 minutes per month. There is a 30-minute waiting peri- od between calls. Telephones are available Monday through Friday 6am-7:30am, 10:30am-12:30pm, 5pm-10pm and 10:30pm-11:30pm; Saturdays, Sundays and federal holidays 6am-10am, 11am-4pm, 5pm-10pm and 10:30pm-11:30pm.

**Inmate Mail:** The camp accepts mail from the U.S. Postal Service via First-Class, U.S. Priority, and Express mail. For those interested in sending overnight mail via a private carrier (FedEx or UPS Overnight), it is recommended that you first con- tact the institution to find out whether the receipt of such mail is permitted. Inmates are permitted to receive publications without prior approval, although the warden will reject material that is determined to be detrimental to the security, good order or discipline of the institution. Packages must be clearly marked as authorized publications. Hardcover publications and newspapers must come directly from the publisher, bookstore or book club, while softcover materials (paperback books, newspaper clippings, magazines) may come from any source.

**Inmate Mail to FPC:**
INMATE NAME & REGISTER NUMBER
FPC Yankton
Federal Prison Camp
P.O. Box 700
Yankton, SD 57078

**Visiting Hours:** Approved visitors may visit on Fridays from 4:30pm-9:15pm, and Saturdays, Sundays, and federal holidays from 8:15am-3pm. Each inmate is assigned a week during which family and friends may visit. No more than 10 individuals may be placed on an inmate's approved-visitor list. Inmates are limited to a maximum of six visitors at any one time. Attorney visits can be made by special arrangement. A children's play area is available. Inmate visitors are encouraged to park on 12th Street between Douglas and Pine Streets in front of the football field. Additional visiting information can be found on the BOP website, at https://www.bop.gov/locations/institutions/yan/.

**Lodging/Accommodations:** Should visitors be spending the night, the following is a short list of accommodations that are available in Yankton, South Dakota:
| | |
|---|---|
| Best Western Kelly Inn—Yankton | 605-665-2906 |
| Days Inn | 605-665-8717 |
| Lewis & Clark Resort | 605-665-2680 |
| Travelodge Yankton | 605-665-6510 |

**Direction to Facility:** <u>From Sioux Falls</u>: take I-29 South to State Road 46 West. Take State Road 46 West to State Road 81 South into Yankton.

<u>From Sioux City</u>: take I-29 North to State Road 50 into Yankton.

(This page intentionally left blank.)

# CHAPTER 14

# THE NORTHEAST REGION

(This page intentionally left blank.)

**Central Office**

Central Office
Federal Bureau of Prisons
320 First St., NW
Washington, DC 20534
Phone: 202-307-3198

**Northeast Regional Office**

Northeast Regional Office
Federal Bureau of Prisons
2nd & Chestnut St., 7th Flr.
Philadelphia, PA 19106
Phone: 215-521-7301

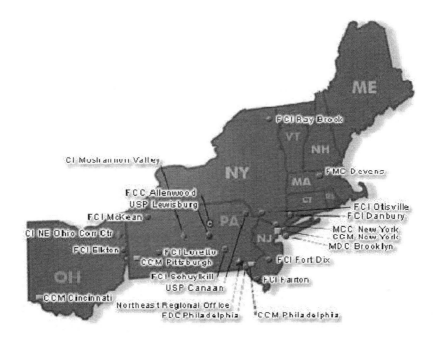

## §14:10   FCI ALLENWOOD—LOW

FCI Allenwood—Low
Federal Correctional Institution
P.O. Box 1000
White Deer, PA 17887
ALX/execassistant@bop.gov
570-547-1990
Fax: 570-547-0343

**Location:** 197 miles north of Washington, D.C., and 11 miles south of Williamsport, Pennsylvania, two miles north of Interstate 80, off Highway 15. The area is served by the Williamsport Lycoming County Airport and commercial bus lines.

**History:** Opened in 1993.

**Judicial District:** Middle District of Pennsylvania.

**Security Level:** FCI Low is part of the Allenwood Federal Correctional Complex. The FCI houses male inmates and its adjacent minimum-security satellite prison camp also houses male offenders.

**Population:** As of 6/17/2015, the FCI Low inmate population is 1,229. Weekly population figures are available on the BOP website, www.bop.gov, at https://www.bop.gov/locations/institutions/alf/.

**Education:** The institution offers GED, ESL, adult education, and college courses.

**Vocational/Apprenticeship:** FCI Allenwood Low offers advanced occupational education in business accounting. Vocational training is offered in culinary arts, and office automation. Apprenticeship is offered in housekeeping and cooking.

**Library:** The law/leisure library is open Monday through Friday 7:30am-10:30am, 11:30am-3:30pm and 4:30pm-8:30pm; Saturday 7:30am-3:30pm; closed on Sundays and holidays. Electric typewriters are available to inmates, as is a copy machine for duplication of legal materials. The leisure library participates in an inter-library loan program.

**UNICOR:** A dimensional mill employs approximately 786 inmates in USP, FCI (Low/Medium).

**Counseling/Rehab Services:** The institution offers a 500-hour Residential Drug Abuse Program (RDAP). The institution also offers a non-residential drug treatment program, a drug education program, Alcoholics and Narcotics Anonymous groups, self-image groups, individual counseling, group psychotherapy, and other voluntary groups.

**Health Services:** The institution provides outpatient care. The pill line is available several times daily Monday through Friday: 6am-6:15am (diabetics only), 7am-7:15am (passes only), 11:30am-12noon (no pass required/open pill line), 3:30pm-3:45pm (no pass required), 5pm-5:15pm (diabetics only), and 8:30pm-8:45pm (passes only). Sick call sign-up is available Monday, Tuesday, Thursday, and Friday 6:15am-6:45am. At least one physician assistant is on duty or on call 24 hours a day. All inmates under the age of 50 are entitled to a routine physical examination every two years, while inmates over the age of 50 are entitled to an exam annually.

**Fitness/Recreation:** The recreation department offers team sports (softball, soccer, volleyball, basketball, etc.), indoor/outdoor weights, a track, pool tables, and handball/racquetball courts. The recreation yard/gymnasium is usually open Monday through Friday, 6am-8:15pm. Inmates may use the recreation yard/gym during convenient non-working hours and after official count times. The leisure room contains a band room, a listening room, two art rooms and outdoor card tables. The leisure center is open daily from 12:30pm-8pm. The hobby craft center offers a wide variety of arts and crafts.

**Religious Services:** Chaplains of various faiths are available for pastoral care, counseling, or other professional services. In addition to the chaplains on staff, volunteers offer a variety of programs and services. Special religious diets, holiday observances, and other worship activities are coordinated through the chaplain's office.

**Housing:** Inmates are housed in dormitories. The dormitories consist of two-man and three-man cubicles. All of the housing units are wheel-chair accessible.

**Commissary:** The commissary is open Monday through Thursday, 6:15am-12:40pm. Inmates are assigned one shopping day per week, determined by housing units (shopping rotation changes quarterly). The Bureau of Prisons currently sets a monthly spending limit of $360.

**Telephone Policy:** Inmates may place either collect calls or dial direct using the Inmate Telephone System (ITS). The following are standard features of ITS: (1) inmate calls automatically terminate after 15 minutes; (2) an inmate's calling list is limited to 30 callers; and (3) calls are charged to an inmate's debit card. There is a 30-minute wait between phone calls and each inmate is limited to 300 minutes per month. There are four telephones on each side of the housing units for inmate use.

**Inmate Mail:** The institution accepts mail from the U.S. Postal Service via First-Class, U.S. Priority, and Express mail. For those interested in sending overnight mail via a private carrier (FedEx or UPS Overnight), it is recommended that you first contact the institution to find out whether the receipt of such mail is permitted. Subscriptions to publications are allowed without prior approval, although the warden may reject publications if they are detrimental to the security, good order, or discipline of the institution.

**Inmate Mail to FCI:**
INMATE NAME & REGISTER NUMBER
FCI Allenwood Low
Federal Correctional Institution
P.O. Box 1000
White Deer, PA 17887

**Visiting Hours:** Approved visitors may visit inmates Friday through Sunday and federal holidays from 8am-3pm. Inmates get a total of twelve points each month. Two points are deducted for visits on weekends and holidays, and one point is deducted for weekday visits. Inmates may place up to 25 members of their immediate family on their visiting list. Friends, associates and relatives not listed will be limited to a total of 10 persons and must be approved four weeks in advance. Inmates may receive up to five authorized visitors at a time, with the possibility for more visitors pending approval. Children under the age of two will not be included in the total number of visitors. A children's play area is available. Attorneys are encouraged to visit during regular visiting hours. However, visits from attorneys can be arranged at other times based on the circumstances of each case and available staff. Additional visiting information can be found on the BOP website, https://www.bop.gov/locations/institutions/alf/.

**Lodging/Accommodations:** The following is a partial list of accommodations near the vicinity of FCI Allenwood:

| | |
|---|---|
| Quality Inn & Suites Danville | 570-275-5100 |
| Hampton Inn Danville | 570-271-2500 |
| Red Roof Inn Danville | 570-275-7600 |
| Best Western Danville | 570-275-5750 |

**Directions to Facility:**
From New York City: From the George Washington Bridge, take Interstate 80 to exit 210B (Route 15) in Pennsylvania and take Route 15 North to the complex.

From Philadelphia: Take the turnpike West to Route 15, and take Route 15 North to the complex.

From Washington, D.C.: Take Interstate 70 West out of D.C. to Route 15 North to the complex.

From Points West: From Interstate 80 East, take exit 210B (Route 15) North to the complex.

## §14:11   FCI ALLENWOOD—MEDIUM

FCI Allenwood—Medium
Federal Correctional Institution
Route 15, two miles north of Allenwood
White Deer, PA 17810
ALX/execassistant@bop.gov
570-547-7950
Fax: 570-547-7751

**Location:** Two miles north of Allenwood on U.S. Route 15; 11 miles south of Williamsport, Pennsylvania; and 197 miles north of Washington, D.C. The area is served by the Williamsport-Lycoming County Airport and commercial bus lines.

**History:** Opened in 1993.

**Judicial District:** Middle District of Pennsylvania.

**Security Level:** FCI Medium is part of the Allenwood Federal Correctional Complex. The FCI houses medium-security male offenders.

**Population:** As of 6/17/2017, the FCI Medium inmate population is 1,268. Weekly population figures are available on the BOP website, www.bop.gov, at https://www.bop.gov/locations/institutions/alm/.

**Education:** The institution offers GED, ESL, adult education, parenting, and correspondence courses.

**Vocational/Apprenticeship:** FCI Allenwood Medium offers advanced occupational education in carpentry, computers, aquaculture, and HVAC. No apprenticeship programs are offered. Prerequisites to enrollment in vocational training programs: high school diploma or GED certificate.

**Library:** The library is open Monday through Thursday 7:30am-8:30pm, and Friday, Saturday, Sunday, and holidays 7am-3:30pm. An inmate law library clerk is available for assistance in legal research. Electric typewriters are available for the preparation of legal documents, and a copy machine is available for the duplication of legal material. The camp has a limited, but very good, hardbound book library. In addition, the leisure library has an inter-library loan program. Inmates also have access to VCRs and audio cassette players in the leisure library.

**UNICOR:** An upholstery factory employs approximately 786 inmates in USP, FCI (Low/Medium). There will be a waiting list for factory employment.

**Counseling/Rehab Services:** The institution offers a 500-hour Residential Drug Abuse Program (RDAP). The institution also offers a non-residential drug treatment program, a drug education program, Alcoholics Anonymous and Narcotics Anonymous groups, self-image groups, individual/group psychotherapy, individualized relaxation training and a video library. The psychology department is staffed by psychologists, treatment specialists, and administrative staff. A self-help library is also available.

**Health Services:** The institution is staffed by one physician, five to six physician assistants, one dentist, and one pharmacist. Outpatient care is provided. Local hospitals are fifteen minutes away. The pill line is open four times daily. Sick call and pill line hours are posted in the Health Services department. At least one physician assistant is on duty or on call 24 hours a day. All inmates under the age of 50 are entitled to a routine physical examination every two years, while inmates over the age of 50 are entitled to an exam annually.

**Fitness/Recreation:** The recreation department offers intramural team sports (softball, basketball, soccer, volleyball, etc.), stair-steppers, treadmills, a universal machine, various musical instruments, pool tables, foosball, and ping-pong tables. The hobby craft center offers ceramics, painting, drawing, leather craft, and knitting.

**Religious Services:** A staff chaplain is available, as well as contract and volunteer representatives of other faiths, for counseling and consultation. A religious diet is available upon permission from the chaplain.

**Housing:** Inmates are housed in two-man cells. Inmates are permitted to watch TV from 6am-11:30pm on weekdays, and 6am-2am on weekends and holidays.

**Commissary:** The commissary is open Monday through Thursday during the noon meal and after the 4pm count clears. Inmates are assigned one shopping day per week, with the day determined by an inmate's unit number. The shopping rotation is changed quarterly. The Bureau of Prisons currently sets a monthly spending limit of $360.

**Telephone Policy:** Inmates dial direct using the Inmate Telephone System (ITS). The following are standard features of ITS: (1) inmate calls automatically terminate after 15 minutes; (2) an inmate's calling list is limited to 30 callers; and (3) calls are charged to an inmate's debit card. Telephones are located in all of the housing units. Telephones are accessible daily from 4:30pm-10:30pm, with extra time 6am-4:30pm on weekends and holidays (except during count times).

**Inmate Mail:** The institution accepts mail from the U.S. Postal Service via First-Class, U.S. Priority, and Express mail. For those interested in sending overnight mail via a private carrier (FedEx or UPS Overnight), it is recommended that you first contact the institution to find out whether the receipt of such mail is permitted. Inmates may subscribe to publications without prior approval, limited to three magazines, three newspapers, and five books. The warden will reject publications if they are determined to be detrimental to the security, good order, or discipline of the institution.

**Inmate Mail to FCI:**
    INMATE NAME & REGISTER NUMBER
    FCI Allenwood Medium
    Federal Correctional Facility
    P.O. Box 2000
    White Deer, PA 17887

**Visiting Hours:** Approved visitors may visit the FCI Friday, Saturday, Sunday, and federal holidays from 8am-3pm. Each inmate is allotted five visiting days per month to avoid overcrowding in the visiting room. Inmates are limited to five visitors at one time, although children under the age of two are not included in the total. Each visit, regardless of length, is equal to one day of visiting, either on weekends, weekdays, or holidays. Attorneys are encouraged to visit during regular visiting hours. Attorney visits can be arranged at other times based on the circumstances of each case. A children's room is available. Additional visiting information can be found on the BOP website, www.bop.gov, at https://www.bop.gov/locations/institutions/alm/.

**Lodging/Accommodations:** See §14:10, FCI Allenwood—Low.

**Directions to Facility:** See §14:10, FCI Allenwood—Low.

## §14:12  USP ALLENWOOD

USP Allenwood
U.S. Penitentiary
Route 15, two miles north of Allenwood
White Deer, PA 17810
570-547-0963
Fax: 570-547-9201

**Location:** 197 miles north of Washington, D.C., and 11 miles south of Williamsport, Pennsylvania, two miles north of Allenwood, off Highway 15. The area is served by the Williamsport-Lycoming County Airport and commercial bus lines.

**History:** Opened in 1993.

**Judicial District:** Middle District of Pennsylvania.

**Security Level:** The USP is part of the Allenwood Federal Correctional Complex. The USP is a high-security facility housing male offenders.

**Population:** As of 6/21/2014, the USP inmate population is 812. Weekly population figures are available on the BOP website www.bop.gov, at https://www.bop.gov/locations/institutions/alp/.

**Education:** The penitentiary offers GED, ESL, adult education, and an evening college degree program.

**Vocational/Apprenticeship:** USP Allenwood offers advanced occupational education in computer word processing and computer assisted drafting, with certification. USP offers vocational training in business and information processing, and AutoCAD. Apprenticeship programs offered in culinary arts, building maintenance, furniture repair/cabinet making, quality control and upholstery. A high school diploma or GED is required.

**Library:** The law library is open Monday through Saturday 7:45am-8:45pm; closed on Sunday and holidays. Manual and electric typewriters are available in the Learning Resource Center for inmate legal work. Inmates must provide the material to utilize the electric typewriters. An inter-library loan program is available through the Lewisburg Public Library and the Philadelphia Free Library. VCRs and audio cassette players are available to inmates in the leisure library.

**UNICOR:** An upholstery factory employs approximately 786 inmates in USP, FCI (Low/Medium).

**Counseling/Rehab Services:** The penitentiary offers a non-residential drug treatment program, a drug education program, Alcoholics Anonymous and Narcotics Anonymous groups, anger management, parenting, and other voluntary and self-help groups. The psychology department is staffed by two full-time psychologists.

**Health Services:** The penitentiary provides outpatient care. Sick call and pill line hours are posted in the Health Services department. Health care programs are offered in smoking cessation, physical fitness, and stress management. Medical staff is on duty 24 hours a day, seven days a week. All inmates under the age of 50 are entitled to a routine physical examination every two years, while inmates over the age of 50 are entitled to an exam annually.

**Fitness/Recreation:** The recreation department offers aerobic exercises, musical instruments, stationary bicycles, and intramural sports such as basketball, softball, and volleyball. The hobby craft center offers painting, leather craft, art and ceramics.

**Religious Services:** The camp chaplains and a community of volunteers provides services for most faiths. Religious holiday observances, worship activities and common fare diet programs are coordinated through the Religious Services Department.

**Housing:** Inmates are primarily housed in two-man cells.

**Commissary:** The commissary is open Monday through Friday in the evenings. Inmates are assigned one shopping day per week. Access time for each housing unit is scheduled on a rotating basis according to inmate register numbers. The Bureau of Prisons currently sets a monthly spending limit of $360.

**Telephone Policy:** Inmates may either call collect or dial direct using the Inmate Telephone System (ITS). The following are standard features of ITS: (1) inmate calls automatically terminate after 15 minutes; (2) an inmate's calling list is limited to 30 callers; and (3) calls are charged to an inmate's debit card. Inmates get 300 minutes of call time per month. Telephones are accessible daily from 6am-10pm.

**Inmate Mail:** The penitentiary accepts mail from the U.S. Postal Service via First-Class, U.S. Priority, and Express mail. For those interested in sending overnight mail via a private carrier (FedEx or UPS Overnight), it is recommended that you first contact the institution to find out whether the receipt of such mail is permitted. Inmates may subscribe to up to five publications without prior approval. The warden will reject publications if they are determined to be detrimental to the security, good order, or discipline of the institution.

**Inmate Mail to USP:**
INMATE NAME & REGISTER NUMBER
USP Allenwood
U.S. Penitentiary
P.O. Box 3000
White Deer, PA 17887

**Visiting Hours:** Approved visitors may visit the penitentiary Friday through Sunday from 8am-3pm. An inmate's list may have an unlimited number of immediate family members, but only ten additional friends or associates. Requests for additional visitors must be approved three weeks in advance. Inmates are limited to nine visiting points per month. One point is deducted for weekday visits, and two points are deducted for weekend and federal holiday visits. An inmate may have up to five visitors at any one time, although children under the age of two are not included in the total. Attorneys should make advance appointments for each visit. Attorneys are encouraged to visit during the regular visiting hours. Additional visiting information can be found on the BOP website, https://www. bop.gov/locations/institutions/alp/.

**Lodging/Accommodations:** See §14:10, FCI Allenwood—Low.

**Directions to Facility:** See §14:10, FCI Allenwood—Low.

## §14:13  FCI BERLIN

FCI Berlin
Federal Correctional Institution
1 Success Loop Road
Berlin, NH 03570
BER/Execassistant@bop.gov
603-342-4000
Fax: 603-342-4250

**Location:** Located 5 miles north of Berlin, New Hampshire off Highway 16.

**History:** The FCI opened in 2012.

**Judicial District:** Eastern District of New York.

**Security Level:** The FCI is a medium-security federal correctional institution for male offenders, with an adjacent minimum-security satellite camp.

**Population:** As of 6/17/2017, the FCI inmate population is 895, with an additional 63 inmates at the camp. Weekly population figures are available on the BOP website, https://www.bop.gov/locations/institutions/ber/.

**Education:** The Education Department at the FCI and camp offer GED, ESL, adult continuing education, college correspondence courses, and parenting courses. Hours of operation are Monday through Thursday, 7:45am-10:30am, 12:30pm-3:30pm; and 5:30pm-8:30pm; Friday, 7:45am-10:30am and 12:30pm-3:30pm; and Saturday, 7:45am-3:30pm.

**Vocational/Apprenticeship:** FCI Berlin offers Vocational Training in carpentry, electrical, and flooring.

**Library:** The law library contains a variety of legal reference materials for use in preparing legal papers. Inmates have access to legal materials and an opportunity to prepare legal documents in the Electronic Law Library (ELL). The law library is open during convenient non-working hours, including weekends. An inmate law library clerk is available for assistance in legal research. Electric typewriters are available for preparation of legal documents. A copier is also available. The leisure libraries offer a variety of reading materials, including but not limited to: periodicals, newspapers, fiction, non-fiction, and reference books. Video cassette recorders and audio cassette players are also available in the leisure library.

**UNICOR:** None.

**Counseling/Rehab Services:** The Psychology Services Department consists of a Chief Psychologist, two Staff Psychologists, a Psychology Technician, a Drug Abuse Program Coordinator, and five Drug Abuse Treatment Specialist. The FCI offers a non-residential drug treatment program, a drug education, program, a Community Transition drug abuse treatment, suicide prevention, and a sexual abuse/ assault prevention program. Psychologists are available for individual counseling.

**Health Services:** The institution is staffed by two physicians and several health services staff. Inmates are provided with outpatient care. Sick call sign-up is Monday, Tuesday, Thursday, and Friday, 7am-7:15am at the FCI, and the same days from 6am-6:30am at the camp. The pill line for the FCI is daily 7am-7:15am, 5pm-5:30pm, and at institution recall. The pill line for the camp is 6:15-6:30amMonday through Friday, 6:30am-7am weekends and holidays, and 5pm-5:30pm, Medical care is available 24 hours a day.

**Fitness/Recreation:** The Recreation Department offers organized and informal games, sports, physical fitness, table games, hobby crafts, music programs, intramural activities, social and cultural organizations, and movies. The hobby craft center offers artwork in any of the usual media (e.g., oils, pastels, crayons, pencils, inks, and charcoal), ceramics, mosaics, crochet, knitting, and sculptures, etc. Wellness programs include screening, assessments, goal setting, fitness/ nutrition prescriptions, counseling and classes. The department The department is open Monday through Friday 6am-3:30pm, 4:30pm-8:30pm; and weekends from 7am-9:30am, 10:30am-3:30pm, and 4:30pm-8:30pm.

**Religious Services:** The Religious Services Department provides pastoral care and religious accommodation to individuals and group religious beliefs and practices. The Chaplains offer religious worship, education, counseling, spiritual direction, support, and crisis intervention to meet the diverse religious needs of inmates. The institution offers a wide range of religious programs. Contract volunteers provide services for most faiths. Each religious faith celebrates a major weekly service and may hold a scriptural study or prayer session at another time during the week.

**Housing:** Inmates are housed in open dormitories, and cells in the East and West building. Unit televisions may be viewed during established off-duty hours. During normal working hours, unit televisions may be viewed at the discretion of staff.

**Commissary:** Commissary and validation schedules are posted on the inmate bulletin boards and on the TRULINCS. The Bureau of Prisons currently sets a monthly spending limit of $360.

**Telephone Policy:** Inmates may either call collect or dial direct using the Inmate Telephone System (ITS). The following are standard features of ITS: (1) inmate calls automatically terminate after 15 minutes; (2) an inmate's calling list is limited to 30 callers; and (3) calls are charged to an inmate's debit card. There are telephones in each housing unit for inmate use. The hours of telephone operation begin at 6:00 a.m. and end no later than 11:30 p.m. at the camp and end no later than 9:30 p.m. at the FCI. Inmate access to telephones will normally be limited during the following times, Monday through Friday, not including holidays: 7:30 a.m. until 10:30 a.m.; and, 12:30 p.m. until after 4:00 p.m. count. Inmates are limited to a total of 300 minutes of phone time per month, including collect calls.

**Inmate Mail:** The institution accepts mail from the U.S. Postal Service via First-Class, U.S. Priority, and Express mail. Overnight mail is a privilege not afforded to the inmates at this federal institution, so all incoming overnight mail will be processed as general correspondence. Inmates subscribe to and receive publications without prior approval. Inmates may only receive hard cover publications and newspapers from the publisher, a book club, or a bookstore. At the camp, inmates may receive softcover publications (other than newspapers) from any source. At the FCI, inmates may receive softcover publications only from the publisher, a book club, or a bookstore. The limit for magazines is no more than five (5). Local newspapers are not allowed after they are three (3) days old and non-local newspapers may be retained for a period of ten (10) days.

**Inmate Mail to FCI:**
    INMATE NAME & REGISTER NUMBER
    FCI Brooklyn
    Federal Correctional Institution
    P.O. Box 9000
    Berlin, NH 03570

**Visiting Hours:** Visiting hours for both FCI and camp are Saturdays, Sundays, and holidays, 8:15am-3pm. Inmates are limited to five visitors per visit, not including children. Attorneys are encourage to visit during regular visiting hours. Special legal visits outside of these hours may be requested. Additional visiting information can be found on the BOP website, www. bop.gov, at https://www.bop.gov/locations/institutions/ber/.

**Lodging/Accommodations:** Should visitors be spending the night, the following is a short list of accommodations that are available in Berlin, NH:

| | |
|---|---|
| Mt. Madison Inn and Suites | (603) 466-3622 |
| Top Notch Inn | (800) 228-5496 |
| Town and Country Inn and Resort | (603) 466-3315 |
| Moose Brook Motel | (603) 466-5400 |
| Gorham Motor Inn | (603) 466-3381 |
| Royalty Inn | (603) 466-3312 |

## §14:14  MDC BROOKLYN

MDC Brooklyn
Metropolitan Detention Center
80 29th Street
Brooklyn, NY 11232
BRO/ExecAssistant@bop.gov
718-840-4200
Fax: 718-840-5005

**Location:** Located near the Gowanus Bay, between 2nd and 3rd Avenue on 29th Street. New York is served by La Guardia, Kennedy, and Newark Airports; Amtrak (Pennsylvania Station); and commercial bus lines (42nd Street Port Authority).

**History:** MDC is designed to house pre-trial and unsentenced detainees (both male and female) appearing in federal courts in the Eastern District of New York. The MDC also houses a work cadre, which is comprised of designated low-and/ or minimum-security inmates, required to meet institutional maintenance and operational work needs that can be filled by utilizing inmate labor.

**Judicial District:** Eastern District of New York.

**Security Level:** MDC is an administrative facility that houses male and female inmates.

**Population:** As of 6/17/2017, the MDC inmate population is 1,781. Weekly population figures are available on the BOP website, www.bop.gov, at https://www.bop.gov/locations/institutions/bro/.

**Education:** The institution offers GED, ESL, adult continuing education, and parenting courses.

**Vocational/Apprenticeship:** MDC offers advanced occupational education in Computer Applications. The institution does not offer vocational or apprenticeship training programs.

**Library:** The law/leisure library on the east side of the institution is open Monday through Friday 8am-8:30pm (except during count times and meal times), and closed on Saturday, Sunday, and holidays. The library on the west side has the same hours, including extra hours Sunday from 7:45am to 3:45pm. An inmate law library clerk is available for assistance in legal research. Electric typewriters are available for preparation of legal documents. A copier is also available. Video cassette recorders and audio cassette players are available in the leisure library.

**UNICOR:** None.

**Counseling/Rehab Services:** The institution offers a non-residential drug treatment program, a drug education program, Alcoholics Anonymous and Narcotics Anonymous groups, and a sexual abuse/assault prevention program. Psychologists are available for individual counseling, and an on-call psychologist is available at all times. The institution also has a contract psychiatrist and a library of self-help books and videos.

**Health Services:** The institution is staffed by two physicians and several health services staff. Inmates are provided with outpatient care. Medication is passed out seven days a week: 5am-6:45am, 9am-11am, and 7pm-10:30pm. Sick call sign-up is Monday through Friday, 6:30am-6:45am. At least one physician assistant is on call 24 hours a day. Specialty contract physicians also regularly visit the institution. Dental appointments can be made by filling out a Request to Staff Member form.

**Fitness/Recreation:** The recreation department offers indoor/outdoor team sports, yoga, weight training, a music room, pool tables, ping-pong tables and board games. The hobby craft center offers a variety of individualized arts and crafts.

**Religious Services:** The institution is staffed by one full-time chaplain and one full-time rabbi. MDC Brooklyn is recognized as having one of the largest and most active religious programs for Jewish inmates. The institution offers a wide range of religious programs. Contract volunteers provide services for most faiths. Each religious faith celebrates a major weekly service and may hold a scriptural study or prayer session at another time during the week.

**Housing:** Inmates are housed in open dormitories, and cells in the East and West building. The unit televisions are available for viewing 6am-11pm, excluding the unit counts, every day of the week. Television rooms will be closed for cleaning Monday through Friday 7:30am-9am.

**Commissary:** Inmates may shop on a bi-weekly basis, alternating between the East building units and the West building units (for example, the East building may shop the first week of the month, and during that week, each floor within the building will have a shopping day). Ordered commissary items are delivered to the housing units after the 4pm count. The Bureau of Prisons currently sets a monthly spending limit of $360.

**Telephone Policy:** Inmates may either call collect or dial direct using the Inmate Telephone System (ITS). The following are standard features of ITS: (1) inmate calls automatically terminate after 15 minutes; (2) an inmate's calling list is limited to 30 callers; and (3) calls are charged to an inmate's debit card. There are telephones in each housing unit for inmate use. Inmates are allowed access to telephones in their respective housing units from 6am until 11pm daily, except during count times. Inmates are limited to a total of 300 minutes of phone time per month, including collect calls.

**Inmate Mail:** The institution accepts mail from the U.S. Postal Service via First-Class, U.S. Priority, and Express mail. Overnight mail is a privilege not afforded to the inmates at this federal institution, so all incoming overnight mail will be processed as general correspondence. Inmates are permitted to subscribe to publications only if they come directly from publishers or book stores. Each inmate is limited to five books and 10 magazines. Sexually explicit publications are prohibited.

**Inmate Mail to MDC:**
> INMATE NAME & REGISTER NUMBER
> MDC Brooklyn
> Metropolitan Detention Center
> P.O. Box 329002
> Brooklyn, NY 11232

**Visiting Hours:** Visiting hours are from 12pm-3pm, evenings from 5pm-7:30pm, and weekends from 8am until 3pm. During the even numbered months (February, April, June, October, and December) the "even" numbered inmates will visit in the afternoon, and the "odd" numbered inmates would visit in the evening. During the odd numbered months (January, March, May, July, September, and November), the visiting times reverse: the odd numbered inmates visit in the afternoon, and even numbered inmates visit in the evenings. For designated inmates, approved social visitors may visit cadre inmates for the duration of 8:00 a.m. until 3:00 p.m. on each day designated for cadre unit visiting, space A room is also set up and equipped for the children who are visiting inmates MDC Brooklyn's attorney visiting hours are Monday through Friday 7:30am-12pm. Visit dur-ing these hours do not have to be scheduled in advance. Additional visiting information can be found on the BOP website, at https://www.bop.gov/locations/institutions/bro/.

**Lodging/Accommodations:** Should visitors be spending the night, the follow-ing is a short list of accommodations that are available in Brooklyn, New York:

| | |
|---|---|
| Marriott at the Brooklyn Bridge | 718-246-7000 |
| Comfort Inn Brooklyn Cruise Terminal | 718-222-3200 |
| Best Western Gregory Hotel | 718-238-3737 |
| Days Inn Brooklyn | 718-732-0117 |
| Atlantic Inn Brooklyn | 718-771-7171 |

# §14:15  USP CANAAN

USP Canaan
U.S. Penitentiary
3057 Easton Turnpike
Waymart, PA 18472
CAA/ExecAssistant@bop.gov
570-488-8000
Fax: 570-488-8130

**Location:** Located in the most northeastern county in Pennsylvania, 20 miles east of Scranton, and 134 miles north of Philadelphia.

**History:** USP Canaan opened in March 2005. This institution is designed to house 1,088 male inmates in six housing units, not including its satellite minimum-security camp.

**Judicial District:** Middle District of Pennsylvania.

**Security Level:** USP is a high-security institution housing male inmates, with a satellite camp that houses male minimum-security inmates.

**Population:** As of 6/17/2017, the USP inmate population is 1,245, and the camp population is 117. Weekly population figures are available on the BOP website at, https://www.bop.gov/locations/institutions/caa/.

**Education:** The USP and the camp offer GED, ESL, adult continuing education, parenting, and correspondence courses.

**Vocational/Apprenticeship:** USP offers vocational training in basic construction, electrical principles, electrical wiring, HVAC, and plumbing. Apprenticeship programs are offered in electrical, HVAC, and plumbing. The camp offers apprenticeship in horticulture.

**Library:** The Electronic Law Library (ELL) is located throughout the institution. Typewriters, legal forms, and law clerks are available in the main library, during normal hours of operation, to assist inmates in the preparation of legal documents. The law library is open Monday through Thursday, 7:30am-9:30am, 12:30pm-8:30pm; Friday, 7:30am-9:30am, 12:30pm-3:30pm; and Saturday, 7:30am-9:30am.

**UNICOR:** USP Canaan employs inmates in contracting services. Some of the services include: data services, warehousing, distribution and fulfillment, assistance and help desk, and custom printing. There is a waiting list for UNICOR.

**Counseling/Rehab Services:** The institution offers a 500-hour Residential Drug Abuse Program (RDAP). In addition, it offers a non-residential drug treatment program, a drug education course, and various support groups. Psychology services include intake screenings, treatment of major mental disorders, crisis intervention, and suicide prevention.

**Health Services:** Appointments for routine medical and dental care are issued at the triage window at the Health Services Unit. Inmates must report to this area on Monday, Tuesday, Thursday, and Friday from 6am-6:30am. Preventive healthcare visits are available to all inmates under the age of 50 every three years, and inmates at or over the age of 50 every year. Pill line hours: 6am-6:45am (insulin and AM pill line), 10:45am-11am, 3:20pm-3:40pm, 4:45pm-4:55pm (PM insulin), 6:30pm-6:45pm.

**Fitness/Recreation:** Leisure activities and recreation programs are supervised by the recreation department. Programs include indoor and outdoor activities and range from individualized arts and crafts programs to intramural team sports, such as softball, basketball, and soccer. Various leisure classes and programs are also available.

**Religious Services:** The USP offers a wide range of religious programs to inmates. Staff chaplains are responsible for conducting religious services for their religious community, providing pastoral care, counseling, or other professional services, and for coordinating religious services on an equitable basis for all religious groups which are authorized to meet at the USP. Programs and services are also supported by outside volunteers or contractors.

**Commissary:** The commissary shopping schedule is based on an inmate's housing unit. The shopping days are rotated monthly. Commissary sales are from 9:30am-3:30pm and 4:30pm-6pm. The current monthly spending limit is $360.

**Telephone Policy:** Telephones are located in all of the units. Inmates may make calls using the Inmate Telephone System (ITS). The telephone area will be accessible daily from 6am until the 4pm count. During the hours of 7:30am-10:30am and 12:30pm-4pm, only one phone will be left on for inmates who work morning or evening shifts, or are on a day off. During the evening hours the phone will be available from the completion of the 4pm count until 9:45pm. Telephone calls will be permitted on a first come-first serve basis. Inmates are limited to 300 minutes per calendar month. There will be a 15-minute time limit on all calls. Calls can only be placed at 30-minute intervals. Consecutive calls will not be permitted. All calls are subject to monitoring and recording, with the exception of non-monitored legal calls. To receive a non-monitored legal call, inmates must have made arrangements with Unit Staff. Three-way telephone calls are strictly prohibited.

**Inmate Mail:** The USP and the camp accept mail from the U.S. Postal Service via First-Class, U.S. Priority, and Express mail. For those interested in sending overnight mail via a private carrier (FedEx or UPS Overnight), it is recommended that you first contact the institution to find out whether the receipt of such mail is permitted. Inmates are permitted to subscribe to publications without prior approval, barring those determined to be detrimental to the security, good order, or discipline of the institution. Each inmate is limited to three magazines, one newspaper, and five books.

**Inmate Mail to USP:**
  INMATE NAME & REGISTER NUMBER
  USP Canaan
  U.S. Penitentiary
  P.O. Box 300
  Waymart, PA 18472

**Inmate Mail to Camp:**
  INMATE NAME & REGISTER NUMBER
  USP Canaan
  U.S. Penitentiary
  Satellite Camp
  P.O. Box 200
  Waymart, PA 18472

**Visiting Hours:** Approved visitors may visit the USP and camp on Friday, Saturday, Sunday, and federal holidays from 8am-3pm. Each inmate housed at FPC Canaan will be given eight visiting points on the first day of each month. Two points are incurred for each visit. Each inmate housed at USP Canaan will be given eight visiting points on the first day of each month. Two points are incurred for each visiting day on weekends and one point is incurred for each visiting day on weekdays. No points will be incurred for recognized federal holidays, legal visits, or prisoner visitation service (PVS) visits. Visiting regulations permit a maximum total of 30 visitors authorized on the inmate's visiting list. No more than 10 of the maximum total will consist of friends and associates. Attorneys should make advance arrangements through the unit team for visiting. Additional visiting information can be found on the BOP website, www.bop.gov, for each facility.

**Lodging/Accommodations:** Should visitors be spending the night, the following is a short list of accommodations that are available near Waymart, Pennsylvania:
  | | |
  |---|---|
  | Cove Haven Resort | 800-432-9932 |
  | Days Inn Scranton | 570-383-9979 |
  | Sleep Inn & Suites Scranton | 570-961-1116 |
  | Comfort Inn Clarks Summit | 570-586-9100 |
  | Ramada Clarks Summit Hotel | 570-586-2730 |

## §14:16   FCI DANBURY

FCI Danbury
Federal Correctional Institution
Route 37
Danbury, CT 06811
DAN/ExecAssistant@bop.gov
203-743-6471
Fax: 203-312-5110

**Location:** In southwestern Connecticut, 70 miles from New York City, three miles north of Danbury on State Route 37. The area is served by Westchester County Airport (45 minutes away), New York City Airports (90 minutes away), and commercial bus lines.

**History:** Opened in 1940, FCI Danbury houses offenders who have been convicted of narcotics violations and property crimes. The institution uses a double fence and structural design as the primary physical security. Opened in 1982, the satellite camp houses low-security females from the northeast United States serving short-term sentences.

**Judicial District:** District of Connecticut.

**Security Level:** FCI and an adjacent satellite prison houses low-security female offenders and also have an adjacent satellite camp that houses minimum-security female offenders.

**Population:** As of 6/17/2017, the FCI inmate population is 860, the FSL (federal Satellite Low) population is 67, and the camp population is 182. Weekly population figures are available at the BOP website, www.bop.gov, https://www.bop.gov/locations/institutions/dan/.

**Education:** The FCI, FSL, and camp offer GED, ESL, adult education, literacy, and correspondence courses.

**Vocational/Apprenticeship:** Alteration Tailor, Baker, Carpenter, Career Development Technician, Chaplain Support Services, Cook, Dental Assistant, Education & Training, Electrician, Floor Cover Layer, Horticulturist, Housekeeper, HVAC, Landscape Management Technician, Legal Secretary, Maintenance Repair, Material Coordinator, Meat Cutter, Office Manager, Painter, Peer Specialist, Plumber, Quality Assurance, Recreation Assistant, Stationary Engineer, Teacher's Aide, and Welder. The FPC offers: Alteration Tailor, Animal Trainer, Baker, Carpenter, Career Development Technician, Carpenter, Chaplain Support Services, Cook, Dental Assistant, Education & Training, Electrician, Floor Cover Layer, Horticulturist, Housekeeper, Landscape Management Technician, Legal Secretary, Maintenance Repair, Material Coordinator, Meat Cutter, Office Manager, Painter, Plumber, Quality Assurance, Recreation Assistant, Teacher's Aide, and Undercar Specialist. The FSL offers: Baker, Career Development Technician, Chaplain Support Services, Cook, Education & Training, Housekeeper, Landscape Management Technician, Legal Secretary, Material Coordinator, Meat Cutter, Office Manager, Recreation Assistant and Teacher's Aide. The FCI has two voc-ational training programs: Culinary Arts and Horticulture.

**Library:** The main institution's law library is open 7 days a week from 7:30am-10:30AM, 11:30am-3:30pm and 5:30pm-8:30pm. The law library at the camp is open daily from 6:00am until 11:30 pm. The law library at the FSL is currently open Monday through Friday from 7:30am-11:30am, 12:30pm-3:30pm and Saturday-Sunday from 11:00am-3:30pm. Regular and electronic typewriters are available to inmates for the preparation of legal documents. The leisure library participates in an inter-library loan program. A copy machine is available for reproducing legal material.

**UNICOR:** None.

**Counseling/Rehab Services:** The FCI offers a Skills Program, a 12-month program to improve the institutional adjustment and overall skill-set of inmates who have intellectual and social deficiencies, as well as a 9-month Residential Drug Abuse Program (RDAP). In addition, the FCI and camp offer an outpatient drug program (12-24 weeks, Non-Residential Drug Program), trauma treatment through the Resolve Program, and other cognitive-behavioral treatment groups. Individual therapy, crisis intervention, and psychological testing are offered on an as-needed basis. The entire FSL operates as a modified therapeutic community and offers the Female Integrated Treatment (FIT) program. The program combines aspects of drug treatment, trauma treatment, mental health treatment, and peer support into one program.

**Health Services:** The FCI is staffed by two physicians, three midlevel providers, one dentist, one hygienist, 6 nurses, one health care administrator and one pharmacist. All Danbury facilities provide outpatient care. Danbury Hospital is five to 10 minutes away. The pill line is available two times per day, seven days a week. Sick call is available Monday, Tuesday, Thursday, and Friday with sign up at 7:30am At least one midlevel provider is on duty or on call 24 hours a day. Preventive health visits are available to inmates under the age of 50 every two years, and every year for inmates over the age of 50.

**Fitness/Recreation:** The recreation department offers wellness programs and leagues such as: spinning, nutrition, yoga, health and fitness, handball, basketball, softball and soccer. There are also leisure programs offered such as: piano, guitar, crochet, knitting, cross stitch, painting and movies for viewing.

**Religious Services:** Three full-time chaplains and one Mentor Coordinator share their time between the camp (female), Federal Satellite Low (female) and the main institution (male) to provide religious services and pastoral counseling. A community of volunteers provides services for most faiths.

**Housing:** Inmates at the FCI are housed in open bay dormitories, multiple occupancy rooms and single rooms. The dormitories consist of two person cubicles. Inmates at the Camp are housed in open bay dormitories and eight to ten person rooms. Inmates at the FSL are housed in in an open bay dormitory style setting with two persons per cubicle. There are approximately two television rooms per housing unit.

**Commissary:** The commissary is open Monday through Thursday during open compound which is normally 6:00am to 7:30am. Shopping days for the camp inmates is on Tuesdays from 6:30am to 12:30pm. Inmates are assigned one shopping day per week. The Bureau of Prisons currently sets a monthly spending limit of $360.

**Telephone Policy:** Inmates at all Danbury facilities may call collect or pay for calls using funds from their inmate commissary account. No third-party, three-way or credit card calls are allowed to be made on these lines. A caller-approved list containing no more than 30 telephone numbers is required for each inmate. The hours of telephone operation begin at 6am and end no later than 11:30pm. All calls are limited to 15 minutes. Inmates are limited to 300 minutes per month. All institution telephones are subject to be monitored. Unmonitored attorney calls must be requested in writing to the inmate's Unit Team.

**Inmate Mail:** The FCI and the camp accept mail from the U.S. Postal Service via First-Class, U.S. Priority, and Express mail. For those interested in sending overnight mail via a private carrier (FedEx or UPS Overnight), it is recommended that you first contact the institution to find out whether the receipt of such mail is permitted.

**Inmate Mail to FCI:**
> INMATE NAME & REGISTER NUMBER
> FCI Danbury
> Federal Correctional Institution
> Route 37
> Danbury, CT 06811

**Visiting Hours:** Approved visitors may visit the FCI on Friday, Saturday, Sunday, Monday, and federal holidays from 8:30am-3pm. Visitors to the camp and FSL may visit on Saturday, Sunday, and federal holidays from 8:30am-3pm. At the FCI and FSL, each inmate will receive 9 visiting points each month. At the camp, each inmate will receive 12 visiting points each month. Each weekday visit will deduct 1 point. Each weekend/holiday visit will deduct 2 points. Up to three adult visitors and five children are permitted at any one time, but children are not counted toward that number. Attorney visits should ordinarily take place during regular visiting hours, or by special arrangement. Additional visiting information can be found on the BOP website, https://www.bop.gov/locations/institutions/dan/.

**Lodging/Accommodations:** Should visitors be spending the night, the following is a short list of accommodations that are available in Danbury, Connecticut:

| | |
|---|---|
| Quality Inn & Suites Danbury | 203-743-6701 |
| Holiday Inn Express & Suites Danbury | 203-205-0800 |
| Crowne Plaza Danbury | 203-794-0600 |
| Super 8 Motel Danbury | 203-501-1535 |
| Hampton Inn Danbury Court | 203-748-6677 |

**Directions to Facility:** FCI Danbury is located in southwestern Connecticut, on Route 37, approximately three miles north of the center of Danbury. Traveling east from New York, on I-84, take Exit 5. Traveling west from Hartford, on I-84, take Exit 6.

## §14:17   FMC DEVENS

FMC Devens
Federal Medical Center
42 Patton Road
Ayers, MA 01432
DEV/ExecAssistant@bop.gov
978-796-1000
Fax: 978-796-1118

**Location:** 39 miles west of Boston and 20 miles north of Worcester, on the decommissioned military base of Fort Devens. A variety of transportation methods service the area. Air transportation in the immediate area includes Boston, Worcester, Manchester, New Hampshire, and Providence, Rhode Island. Limousine, bus, rail and taxi service to Devens is available.

**History:** The Federal Medical Center and the camp were activated in 1999.

**Judicial District:** District of Massachusetts.

**Security Level:** FMC is an administrative facility housing male offenders requiring specialized or long-term medical or mental health care. A satellite camp houses minimum-security male inmates.

**Population:** As of 6/17/2017, the FMC inmate population is 970, and the camp population is 119. Weekly population figures are available on the BOP website at https://www.bop.gov/locations/institutions/dev/.

**Education:** The FMC and the camp offer GED, ESL, adult education, and post-secondary education via correspondence courses.

**Vocational/Apprenticeship:** FMC offers no advanced occupational education programs or apprenticeship programs. FMC offers vocational training in computer applications and culinary arts. Inmates with a documented history of computer abuse (such as having used computers to commit a crime) will not be allowed to participate in the computer applications program. Inmates who participate in vocational training programs may be eligible for a variety of incentive awards, certificates and graduation activities.

**Library:** The leisure and law library is open weekdays, 8:30am-10:30am, 12:30pm-3:30pm, and 5:30pm-8:30pm. On weekends and most holidays, the library will be open from 7:30am-3:30pm. Typewriters are available to inmates for the preparing of legal documents. A copier is also available. The leisure library participates in an inter-library loan program. A satellite leisure library in the recreation department is available every night from 5:30pm-8:30pm.

**UNICOR:** None.

**Counseling/Rehab Services:** The FMC and the camp offer a non-residential drug treatment program, a 40-hour drug education program, various ongoing self-help programs (Alcoholics and Narcotics Anonymous, etc.), individual counseling, and the Residential Drug Abuse Treatment Program (RDAP). Group and individual counseling is also available at the camp. FMC Devens also offers a smoking cessation program for all inmates who quality for the program. Inmates at any BOP institution may choose to volunteer for an intensive residential Sex Offender Treatment Program (SOTP-R) offered at FMC Devens. SOTP-R is a therapeutic community, housed in a 112-bed specialized unit. The program employs a wide range of cognitive-behavioral and relapse prevention techniques to help the sex offender manage his sexual deviance both within the institution and in preparation for release. Participants complete the program in 12 to 18 months. Inmates with a history of sexual offenses may be designated to the Sex Offender Management Program (SOMP). Sex Offender Treatment Program (SOTP-NR) offers inmates individualized non-residential treatment: six to eight hours a week for six months. All participation in non-residential treatment services is voluntary.

**Health Services:** The Health Services Department has outpatient and inpatient services. The overall health care delivery system includes local medical facilities and medical referral centers. The FMC also contains a dialysis unit, but not a surgery unit. The FMC is staffed by three full-time physicians, four to five physician assistants, 23 nurses, three pharmacists and one dentist. The camp provides outpatient care. The medication/pill line is available 7:15am-7:30am (open pill line); 3pm-3:15pm (open pill line), and 8pm-8:15pm (restricted pill line). Inmates at the FMC sign up for sick call Monday, Tuesday, Thursday, and Friday. Sick call sign-up at the camp is 6:15am-6:30am. Medical staff is on duty or on call 24 hours a day.

**Fitness/Recreation:** The FMC and camp recreation department offer a variety of indoor and outdoor activities that range from individualized hobby craft programs to intramural team sports. The Inmate Recreation Yard and Activity Center includes a multi-purpose room, outdoor recreation yard and an indoor inmate activity center. The indoor activity center is located on the recreation yard and is intended for activities such as basketball, soccer and floor hockey. A music practice room is also available.

**Religious Services:** The FMC and camp are staffed by full-time chaplains. A community of volunteers provides services for most faiths. The Chapel comprises facilities for worship services, prayer and religious study areas, and a religious library. Religious programming includes worship, prayer and study of various religious expressions, as well as counseling and spiritual guidance. An inmate may request to participate in the Religious Diet Program by submitting an application to the chaplain.

**Housing:** Inmates at the FMC and the camp are housed in two-man or single room living areas. Inmates at the camp are housed in open bay dormitories.

**Commissary:** The commissary access time for inmates is scheduled on a rotating basis. Inmates are permitted to shop once a week. The Bureau of Prisons currently sets a monthly spending limit of $360.

**Telephone Policy:** Inmates at the FCI and the camp dial direct using the Inmate Telephone System (ITS). The following are standard features of ITS: (1) inmate calls automatically terminate after 15 minutes; (2) an inmate's calling list is limited to 30 callers; and (3) calls are charged to an inmate's debit card. Inmate telephones are located in each of the housing units. Telephone calls are limited to 300 minutes per month, except during the months of November and December, when 400 minutes are provided.

**Inmate Mail:** The FCI and the camp accept mail from the U.S. Postal Service via First-Class, U.S. Priority, and Express mail. For those interested in sending overnight mail via a private carrier (FedEx or UPS Overnight), it is recommended that you first contact the institution to find out whether the receipt of such mail is permitted.

**Inmate Mail to FMC:**
> INMATE NAME & REGISTER NUMBER
> FMC Devens
> Federal Medical Center
> P.O. Box 879
> Ayer, MA 01432

**Inmate Mail to Camp:**
> INMATE NAME & REGISTER NUMBER
> FMC Devens
> Federal Medical Center
> Satellite Camp
> P.O. Box 879
> Ayer, MA 01432

**Visiting Hours:** Approved visitors may visit inmates at the FMC and camp Friday, Saturday, Sunday and federal holidays, 8:30am-3pm. Visiting is limited to 12 points per month. Weekday visits count as one point, and weekend and holiday visits count as two points. There is no point system at the camp. Visiting lists may include immediate family, other relatives, and up to 10 friends and associates. Non-immediate family members are considered to be friends and associates. Children under the age of 16 do not have to be on the list. Only five visitors, including children, will be allowed to visit an inmate at any given time (although more can visit given prior approval). Attorneys are encouraged to visit during regular visiting hours; however, visits from an attorney can be arranged at other times based on the circumstances of each case and available staff. A children's room is available to inmates who have enrolled in the parenting program. Additional visiting information can be found at https://www.bop.gov/locations/institutions/dev/.

**Lodging/Accommodations:** Should visitors be spending the night, the following is a short list of accommodations that are available near Ayers, Massachusetts:
SpringHill Suites Devens                                    978-772-3030
Days Inn Leominster/Fitchburg                               978-537-2800
Residence Inn Boston-Westford                               978-392-1407

**Directions to Facility:** The Federal Medical Center, Devens, is located 40 miles northwest of the city of Boston, Massachusetts. Route 2 runs through the area and is the main artery for east/west travel in the north-central Massachusetts area. Visitors should take Exit 37B if traveling on Route 2 and proceed straight onto Jackson Road. After entering the main gate, take your first right off Jackson Road onto Patton Road. The Devens Federal Medical Center is approximately a half-mile down on the right. The Devens Federal Medical Center is located on the grounds of the former Fort Devens Military Base and is adjacent to the towns of Ayer, Harvard and Shirley.

# §14:18  FCI ELKTON

FCI Elkton
Federal Correctional Institution
8730 Scroggs Road
Elkton, OH 44432
ELK/ExecAssistant@bop.gov
330-420-6200
Fax: 330-420-6436

**Location:** In northeast Ohio, three miles east of Lisbon, 30 miles south of Youngstown, and 45 miles northwest of Pittsburgh, Pennsylvania. The area is served by the Pittsburgh area regional airport, Amtrak, and commercial bus lines.

**History:** Opened in 1997.

**Judicial District:** Northern District of Ohio.

**Security Level:** FCI is a low-security facility housing male offenders. It has a satellite camp that houses low- and minimum-security male offenders. FSL for offenders who do not require the full security of the main low-institution but for whom the Bureau of Prisons determined should not be placed in an open minimum-security camp setting).

**Population:** As of 6/18/2017, the FCI inmate population is 1,874, and the FSL population is 448. Weekly population figures are available on the BOP website at www.bop.gov, https://www.bop.gov/locations/institutions/elk/.

**Education:** The FCI and the camp offers GED, ESL and adult continuing education.

**Library:** The main institution's law library is open daily during non-working hours, including weekends. An inmate law library clerk is available for assistance. There are electric typewriters available to inmates for the preparation of legal documents, and a copy machine is available for duplication of legal materials. Inmates must purchase their own typewriter ribbon, envelopes, and stamps. The leisure library contains limited resources.

**UNICOR:** Data services factory that provides proofreading and editing services.

**Counseling/Rehab Services:** The FCI offers a 500-hour Residential Drug Abuse Program (RDAP). The FCI and the camp also offer a non-residential and drug treatment program and a drug education program. Psychologists are available to provide group and/or individual counseling and other mental health services. FCI offers a nine-month Residential Drug Abuse Program (RDAP), a Sex Offender Management Program (SOMP), and a Residential Sex Offender Treatment Program (SOTP-R).

**Health Services:** The FCI and the camp provide outpatient care 16 hours per day. The pill line at FCI is weekdays, 6:15am (insulin only), 7:15am-7:30am, 11am-12pm, 5pm (insulin only), and 7:30pm-7:35pm; and weekends, 7:15am-7:30am (insulin only) and 12:30pm-12:45pm. The pill line for the camp is 6am and 3pm-3:15pm seven days a week. Sick call sign-up is Monday, Tuesday, Thursday, and Friday from 6:30am-6:45am. At least one physician assistant is on duty or on call 16 hours a day. All inmates under the age of 50 are entitled to a physical examination every three years, while those over 50 are entitled to annual exams.

**Fitness/Recreation:** The recreation department offers exercise bicycles, stair-steppers, rowing machines, treadmills, music room, pool tables, ping-pong tables, foosball, and bumper pool tables. The hobby craft center offers leather craft, art ceramics, and painting. Programs are offered in walking, nutrition, smoking cessation, and intramural sports.

**Religious Services:** The main institution is staffed by full-time chaplains of specific faiths. A community of volunteers provides services for most faiths.

**Housing:** The FCI is comprised of six housing units. Inmates are double-bunked in two-man open cubicles. The units are not wheel-chair accessible. The inmates at the camp are housed in dormitories in two-man and four-man cubicles.

**Commissary:** Hours of operation and inmate population rotation schedules are posted on the Unit bulletin boards and in the commissary lobby. The Bureau of Prisons currently sets a monthly spending limit of $360. Stamps, telephone credits, over-the-counter medication and religious items are exempt from the spending limitation.

**Telephone Policy:** Inmates may either place collect calls or dial direct using the pre-payment method by using the Inmate Telephone Systems (ITS). The following are standard features of ITS: (1) inmate calls will automatically terminate after 15 minutes; (2) an inmate's calling list is limited to 30 callers; and (3) calls are charged to an inmate's debit card. It takes approximately one to two days for inmates to add phone numbers to their caller-approved list. Inmates may change their phone list up to one time per month.

**Inmate Mail:** The FCI and camp accept mail from the U.S. Postal Service via First-Class, U.S. Priority, and Express mail. For those interested in sending overnight mail via a private carrier (FedEx or UPS Overnight), it is recommended you first contact the institution to find out whether the receipt of such mail is permitted. Inmates may subscribe to publications without prior approval, although the warden will reject publications that are detrimental to the security, good order or discipline of the institution. Accumulation of magazines will be limited to five magazines (less than three months old) and to the amount that can be safely and neatly stored in the locker.

**Inmate Mail to FCI:**
    INMATE NAME & REGISTER NUMBER
    FCI Elkton
    Federal Correctional Institution
    P.O. Box 10
    Lisbon, OH 44432

**Visiting Hours:** Approved visitors may visit the FCI and FSL on Friday from 5pm-9pm, and Saturday, Sunday, and federal holidays from 8am-3pm. Visits at the FCI are held on a point system. Each inmate is allotted four points per month. Weekend visits are assessed one point per day; weeknight and federal holiday visits are assessed zero points. No more than six visitors are allowed per inmate at any one time. The camp does not use a point system. Visits on weekend days at the camp are determined by the inmates' register numbers (those with an odd fifth digit will visit one weekend, while those with an even fifth digit will visit the next). Attorney visits can be arranged at other times. Additional visiting information can be found on the BOP website, at https://www.bop.gov/locations/institutions/elk/.

**Lodging/Accommodations:** Should visitors be spending the night, the following is a short list of accommodations that are available near Elkton, Ohio:

| | |
|---|---|
| Days Inn Lisbon | 330-420-3111 |
| Country Inn & Suites Youngstown | 330-544-0300 |
| Super 8 Youngstown/Austintown | 330-793-7788 |
| Quality Inn & Suites North | 330-759-3180 |

**Directions to Facility:** Take Interstate-75 toward Toledo, merge onto I-280 S, exit number 208 toward I-80/I-90/Turnpike, merge onto I-80. Toward Cleveland, merge onto OH-11 S, take OH-154 toward US-30, turn onto OH-154 then turn left onto Scroggs Road. From Interstate 80, take the Route 11 South exit, take the Lisbon exit, turn left onto Route 154, turn left onto Scroggs Road.

## §14:19   FCI FAIRTON

FCI Fairton
Federal Correctional Institution
655 Fairton-Millville Road
Fairton, NJ 08320
856-453-1177
Fax: 856-453-4015

**Location:** In south central New Jersey, 50 miles southeast of Philadelphia and 40 miles west of Atlantic City, off Interstate 55. The area is served by airports in Philadelphia, Atlantic City, and Millville; Amtrak in Philadelphia and Atlantic City; and commercial bus service.

**History:** Opened in 1990, FCI Fairton houses male offenders primarily from the northeastern United States. A pre-trial detention center is in operation, with bed space for 124 inmates. Opened in 1992, the satellite camp houses minimum-security inmates who are employed on landscape and institution support details.

**Judicial District:** District of New Jersey.

**Security Level:** FCI is a medium-security facility for male offenders. It also has an adjacent satellite prison camp housing minimum-security male offenders.

**Population:** As of 6/18/2017, the FCI inmate population is 1,102, and the camp population is 119. Weekly population figures are available on the BOP website at https://www.bop.gov/locations/institutions/fai/.

**Education:** The FCI and the camp offer GED, ESL, adult education, literacy, and correspondence courses. The FCI and the camp offer post-secondary education for inmates who have successfully completed a four-year high school or GED program. All post-secondary education courses are offered through correspondence study or the Cumberland Community College in-house program. There is also a career counseling program.

**Vocational/Apprenticeship:** All inmates are required to work in the food service department during their first 90 days. Upon completion of this work, inmates are assigned to a permanent detail, a training program, or both. Jobs at the facility are in food service, facility maintenance, health services, library services, safety and sanitation, etc. FCI offers advanced occupational education in aquaculture and business administration. FCI offers vocational training in baking, barber, building trades, computer assisted engraving, culinary arts, and horticulture. FCI offers apprenticeship in HVAC, baker, carpenter, cook, dental, dog trainer, electrician, experimental assembler, fish hatchery, industrial housekeeper, injection-molding machine operator, injection-mold setter, landscape gardener, landscape technician, maintenance repair building, quality assurance, and plumber. The camp offers vocational training in baking. Vocational and apprenticeship training is subject to change based upon demand and availability of staffing.

**Library:** The main institution's law/leisure library and typing room are open Monday through Friday 8am-3:30pm, 5pm-8:15pm; Saturday from 7am-3:30pm; closed on Sundays. The libraries are closed during official count times. An inmate law library clerk is available for assistance in legal research. Manual typewriters are available to inmates. Inmates must purchase their own typewriter pinwheels from the commissary. The leisure library participates in an inter-library loan program with the Cumberland County Library. Various newspapers are delivered every day. Audiotapes, film strips, videotapes, laboratory medical/study kits, reference materials and a computer laboratory are available to inmates in the leisure library.

**UNICOR:** An electronics cable and battery factory employs approximately 175 inmates. Positions available include: production worker, quality assurance inspector, office accounting contracting clerk, and job quote clerk. There is a waiting list for factory employment.

**Counseling/Rehab Services:** The FCI offers a 500-hour Residential Drug Abuse Program (called CHOICE). The program is nine months in length. In addition, the FCI and the camp offer a non-residential drug treatment program, a drug education program, Alcoholics Anonymous, Narcotics Anonymous, anger management, stress management, HIV/AIDS awareness, thinking skills, parenting, Nicotine Anonymous, and Living Free groups. An inmate may receive crisis intervention, individual therapy and/or group psychotherapy. The main institution is staffed by one full-time psychologist and five drug treatment specialists.

**Health Services:** The main institution is staffed by two physicians, five to eight physician assistants, one dentist, and one pharmacist. The FCI and the camp provide outpatient care. The medication/pill line is available at 6:45am, 3pm and 8pm. Inmates may request a sick call by dropping off a form between 7am-3pm, and an appointment will be scheduled in one day to two weeks, depending on the urgency of the sick call. Urgent or emergency health services can be requested between 6:15am-6:30am for a same-day appointment. All inmates under the age of 50 are entitled to a physical examination every two years, while those over 50 are entitled to annual exams. At least one physician assistant is on call 24 hours a day.

**Fitness/Recreation:** The recreation department offers intramural sports (softball, basketball, volleyball, etc.), bicycles, treadmills, weights, ping-pong tables, and pool tables. The hobby craft center offers leather craft, ceramics, and painting.

**Religious Services:** Staff chaplains of specific faiths are available, as well as contract and volunteer representatives of other faiths. Special religious diets, holiday observances, and other worship activities are coordinated through the chaplain's office.

**Housing:** Inmates at the FCI are housed in two-man cells. Inmates at the camp are housed in open bay dormitories.

**Commissary:** The commissary access time for inmates is scheduled on a rotating basis. Shopping lists must be turned in to the commissary between 11am and 12:30pm on the schedule day of shopping. The Bureau of Prisons currently sets a monthly spending limit of $360.

**Telephone Policy:** Inmates at the FCI and the camp can call collect or dial direct using the Inmate Telephone System (ITS). Inmate calls automatically terminate after 15 minutes; an inmate's calling list is limited to 20 callers; and calls are charged to an inmate's debit card. Phone credits may be purchased at the commissary daily during lunch hours (except weekends and holidays). There are telephones on each side of the housing unit for inmate use. Telephones may be used at the FCI on weekdays from 6am-7am, 10:30am-12noon, and 4pm-10pm, and on weekends and holidays from 6am-10pm. In the camp, telephone hours are the same, with extra telephone usage available 10pm-11:30pm.

**Inmate Mail:** The FCI and the camp accept mail from the U.S. Postal Service via First-Class, U.S. Priority, and Express mail. For those interested in sending overnight mail via a private carrier (FedEx or UPS Overnight), it is recommended that you first contact the institution to find out whether the receipt of such mail is permitted.

**Inmate Mail to FCI:**
INMATE NAME & REGISTER NUMBER
FCI Fairton
Federal Correctional Institution
655 Fairton-Millville Road
Fairton, NJ 08320

**Inmate Mail to Camp:**
INMATE NAME & REGISTER NUMBER
FCI Fairton
Federal Correctional Institution
Satellite Camp
655 Fairton-Millville Road
Fairton, NJ 08320

**Visiting Hours: Notice:** As of June 2017, all visiting has been suspended until further notice. This policy may have changed by the time you read this entry. See https://www.bop.gov/locations/institutions/fai/.

Normally, approved visitors may visit inmates at the FCI on Thursday, Friday, Saturday, Sunday, and Monday from 8:15am-3:15pm. Visitors may not come in after 2:30pm. Visiting is limited to nine points per month. Weekday visits count as one point; weekend and holiday visits count as three points. The camp is open for social visits on Saturday, Sunday, and holidays from 8:15am-3:15pm. The last visit starts at 2:30pm. Each camp visit counts as two points. Each inmate has an approved list of up to 10 social visitors (friends, associates, and extended family); there is no limit to the number of immediate family members on an inmate's approved visiting list. There is a parenting room where inmates who are enrolled in the parenting program can be alone with their children and other family members for up to one hour. Attorneys are encouraged to visit during regular visiting hours; however, visits from an attorney can be arranged at other times based on the circumstances of each case and available staff. Attorneys are required to contact the inmate's case manager a day before the requested visit. Additional visiting information can be found on the BOP website, https://www.bop.gov/locations/institutions/fai/.

**Lodging/Accommodations:** Should visitors be spending the night, the following is a short list of accommodations that are available in the Fairton, New Jersey area:

| | |
|---|---|
| Country Inn Millville | 856-825-3100 |
| Wingate by Wyndham, Vineland | 856-690-9900 |
| Days Inn Vineland | 856-696-5000 |
| Ramada Inn Vineland | 856-696-3800 |
| Holiday Inn Express Hotel Vineland | 856-293-8888 |

**Directions to Facility:** From the Philadelphia Airport: take I-95 North to I-76 and the Walt Whitman Bridge. Cross the Walt Whitman Bridge and take Route

42 South to Route 55 South. Continue going South (on Route 55) until you reach exit 27 (Route 47) toward Millville. Continue South on Route 47 until you reach Route 49. Make a right onto Route 49 and continue to Fairton-Millville Road. Make a left turn, travel approximately five miles to the institution. FCI Fairton is on the left side of Fairton-Millville Road.

From New York City: take the New Jersey Turnpike to Exit 7. At Exit 7, take Route 206 South to Hammonton, New Jersey. At Hammonton, take Route 54 to Buena Vista, New Jersey. In Buena Vista, take County Road 655 (Lincoln Avenue) to Millville. At Millville, take County 555 (Main Road) to Route 49 West. Continue through Millville on Route 49 to Fairton-Millville Road. Turn left on Fairton-Millville Road and proceed approximately five miles to FCI Fairton. The institution is on the left side of the road.

From Washington, D.C./Baltimore/Delaware: take I-95 North to the Delaware Memorial Bridge. Cross the bridge, take Route 49 East through Bridgeton and make a right onto Buckshutem Road. Take Buckshutem Road to Fairton-Millville Road. Go right on Fairton-Millville Road approximately one-half mile to the institution.

## §14:20   FCI FORT DIX

FCI Fort Dix
Federal Correctional Institution
5756 Hartford & Pointville Road
Fort Dix, NJ 08640
FTD/ExecAssistant@bop.gov
609-723-1100
Fax: 609-724-7557

**Location:** In Burlington County, central New Jersey, on the Fort Dix/McGuire Air Force Base military installation, approximately 40 miles from Philadelphia, Pennsylvania, and 30 miles from the New Jersey shore, off Route 68. The area is served by Philadelphia International Airport, Amtrak, and commercial bus service.

**History:** The FCI was opened in 1992. Most of the inmates are from the immediate area; a large number of them are also deportable aliens. The average sentence is 89 months and the average inmate age is 37 years.

**Judicial District:** District of New Jersey.

**Security Level:** FCI is a low-security facility housing male inmates. A satellite camp is located adjacent to the FCI and houses minimum-security male inmates.

**Population:** As of 6/18/2017, the FCI inmate population is 4,015, and the camp population is 347. Weekly population figures are available on the BOP website at www.bop.gov.

**Education:** The institution offers GED, ESL, adult education, parenting, and college correspondence courses. Participating inmates bear the burden of all associated costs for college courses.

**Vocational/Apprenticeship:** Examples of Vocational Training Programs which may be available at the FC and camp include the following: Electrical Theory, Picture Framing, Computer Application, Apprenticeship Training, Wood Working, and Horticulture/Hydroponics operations. The Education staff can identify which programs are available at the Camp and on the West and East Compounds.

**Library:** The leisure/law library is open Monday through Thursday, 7:30am-10:30am, 12:30pm-3:30pm, and 5pm-8pm; Friday, 7:30am-10:30am and 12:30pm-3:30pm; and Saturday and Sunday, 7:30am-10:30am and 11am-3:30pm. The camp library is open seven days a week, 7:30am-9pm, except during meals and counts. A photocopier is available in the law library. The leisure library participates in an inter-library loan program.

**UNICOR:** UNICOR inmates will be hired from the waiting list on a six-to-one ratio (for every six inmates hired off the waiting list, one inmate will be hired off the general list). Textile/graphics employ approximately 341 inmates, and a contract services factory employs approximately 138 inmates.

**Counseling/Rehab Services:** The institution offers a 500-hour Residential Drug Abuse Program (RDAP). The program consists of nine months of residential treatment at the institution and six months of transitional services at the halfway house. In addition, the institution offers a non-residential drug treatment program, a drug education program, Alcoholics Anonymous, Narcotics Anonymous, criminal thinking errors, anger management, and other groups, individual counseling, a psychology library of self-help books and videos, and a variety of other voluntary groups, including a sexual abuse/assault prevention and intervention program. The psychology department is staffed by two full-time psychologists and five drug treatment specialists.

**Health Services:** Inmates are provided with outpatient care. Medication/pill line is 6:00am-6:30am, after the 4pm count daily (insulin first). Sick call sign-up is 6:30am-6:45am on Monday, Tuesday, Thursday, and Friday, except holidays. Appointments are held 8am-3pm. There is 24-hour medical staff coverage, seven days per week. All inmates under 50 years of age are eligible for a physical examination every two years, and inmates over 50 may request an annual physical examination.

**Fitness/Recreation:** The recreation department offers the following indoor facilities: gymnasium (Sunday through Saturday and holidays from 6:30am-8pm), weightlifting rooms, stationary bicycles and exercise area, music rooms and a television room. Outdoor facilities include a softball field, soccer and football field, handball/racquetball courts, horseshoe pits, volleyball courts, and bocce ball lanes. The hobby craft center offers leather craft, and music (including lessons in piano and guitar). The practical segment of the music program is devoted to band or group players. These groups are allowed time in the music room to practice and refine their acts. The outside recreation yard is open all year. The facility offers a fitness program. An intramural sports program offers basketball, soccer, volleyball, and softball.

**Religious Services:** Full-time chaplains coordinate a wide range of religious activities, and a community of volunteers and contract clergy provide services for most faiths. Each religious faith celebrates a major weekly service and may hold a scriptural study or prayer session at another time during the week. Religious clothing, religious diets, and pastoral visits from outside clergy can all be authorized through the chaplains.

**Housing:** There are two housing compounds (East and West). Inmates are housed in dormitories in 12-man rooms. Preferred housing consisting of two-man rooms may be available under certain circumstances to inmates with a good disciplinary history. There are five televisions located on the first floor of each of the living units. Television viewing is permitted Sunday through Thursday from 11am-11:30pm. On Friday, Saturday, and nights preceding a holiday, television viewing is permitted from 11am-2am. Television rooms will be closed for cleaning from 7:30am to 11am Monday through Friday. In the Honors Community Units viewing will be permitted 6:00 am to 2:00 am (excluding institution count times)- Sunday through Thursday. Viewing will be permitted from 6:00 am to 3:00 am on Friday, Saturday and nights preceding a holiday. Television rooms will be closed for cleaning 7:30 am to 10:30 am for cleaning Monday through Friday. In the Enhanced Community Units viewing will be permitted 10:30 am to 12:45 pm. Viewing will continue after the 4:00 pm count until 11:30 pm Monday through Friday. Viewing will be permitted from 11:00 am to 2:00 am on Friday, Saturday and nights preceding a holiday. If scheduled programming is being conducted during the evening hours, there will be no television viewing until programming is complete.

**Commissary:** The commissary is open Monday through Thursday after the 4pm count. Inmates are assigned one shopping day per week based on the last fourth and fifth digits of their register number. The shopping days will rotate on a quarterly basis. Inmates must turn in their shopping list between 11am-1pm on their scheduled shopping days to receive a commissary pass. The Bureau of Prisons currently sets a monthly spending limit of $360.

**Telephone Policy:** Inmates may either call collect or dial direct using the Inmate Telephone System (ITS). The following are standard features of ITS: (1) inmate calls automatically terminate after 15 minutes; (2) an inmate's calling list is limited to 30 callers; and (3) calls are charged to an inmate's debit card.

Inmates receive 300 calling minutes per month. There are telephones located in the housing units. Telephones are operational 6am-11:30pm, except during count times. All phone calls are subject to being monitored and recorded except where approval for unmonitored legal calls has been obtained.

**Inmate Mail:** The institution accepts mail from the U.S. Postal Service via First-Class, U.S. Priority, and Express mail. For those interested in sending overnight mail via a private carrier (FedEx or UPS Overnight), it is recommended that you first contact the institution to find out whether the receipt of such mail is permitted. Inmates may choose to not receive mail during initial processing. Inmates are allowed to subscribe to soft-cover publications (paperback books, magazines) from any source, and hardcover books and newspapers directly from the publishers, bookstore or book club. The warden will reject publications determined to be detrimental to the security, good order, or discipline of the institution. Each inmate can receive up to six magazines and eight books.

**Inmate Mail to FCI:**
>    INMATE NAME, REGISTER NUMBER & UNIT
>    FCI Fort Dix
>    Federal Correctional Institution
>    P.O. Box 2000
>    Joint Base MDL, NJ 08640

**Inmate Mail to Camp:**
>    INMATE NAME, REGISTER NUMBER & UNIT
>    FCI Fort Dix
>    Federal Correctional Institution
>    Satellite Camp
>    P.O. Box 2000
>    Joint Base MDL, NJ 08640

**Visiting Hours:** Regular visiting hours at the FCI are 8:30am-3pm on Sunday, Monday, Thursday, Friday, and Saturday of each week, including federal holidays. Visiting hours at the camp are Saturday through Monday, 8:30am-3pm. Each inmate will be allotted four points at the beginning of each month to be used as follows: (1) Each day or fraction of a day visited on a weekend or holiday will count as one point; and (2) no points will be used for weekdays. No more than three adults and three children are allowed to visit an inmate at any one time. All visitors must be pre-authorized for visiting lists. Attorney visits should be scheduled during regular visiting hours whenever possible, but can be made outside regular visiting hours; however, if made outside regular visiting hours, the visit will be monitored by the unit team staff. All legal visits must be arranged with the unit team in advance. Additional visiting information can be found on the BOP website, www.bop.gov, at https://www.bop.gov/locations/institutions/ftd/.

**Lodging/Accommodations:** Should visitors be spending the night, the following is a short list of accommodations that are available near Fort Dix, New Jersey:

| | |
|---|---|
| Budget Inn Wrightstown | 609-723-4555 |
| Days Inn Wrightstown | 609-723-6900 |
| Passport Inn | 609-723-2323 |
| Quality Inn McGuire AFB | 490-569-4616 |
| Hampton Inn Bordentown | 609-298-4000 |

**Directions to Facility:** <u>From east coast</u>: If coming from any town directly east, take Garden State Parkway to Exit 82 (Route 37 West). Follow 37 West to 70 West (will pass through two circles). Follow Route 70 to Route 530 (it will be a right hand exit, sign says Fort Dix, Browns Mills). Follow Route 530 until you cross a bridge over a lake. At stoplight, go to the right onto Route 545 or Texas Avenue. Turn right on Hartford. Building 5756 (Administration Building) is the first building on your right.

<u>From Philadelphia crossing Ben Franklin Bridge</u>: Cross bridge and follow 30 East to 38 East. Follow 38 East approximately 20 miles and turn left onto Route 616. Go two stoplights and turn right onto Route 630. Route 630 will change to Pointville Road, and continue straight until you reach Hartford Road. Make a left onto Hartford. Building 5756 is the first building on your right.

<u>From Philadelphia crossing Walt Whitman Bridge</u>: Cross bridge into New Jersey and get on 295 North (exit 1B). Follow 295 North to exit 40 (Route 38 East). Follow 38 East approximately 20 miles and turn left onto Route 616 (Pemberton) (see alternate route below if entrance to Fort Dix from Pointville Road is blocked). Go two stoplights and turn right onto Route 630. Route 630 will change to Pointville Road, and continue straight until you reach Hartford Road. Make a left onto Hartford. Building 5756 (Administration Building) is the first building on your right.

<u>From northern New Jersey coming down New Jersey turnpike</u>: Follow New Jersey turnpike to exit 7. Once off exit, follow 206 South and stay in the left lane to get 68 South (there will be a sign that says Fort Dix, McGuire AFB). Follow 68 South to a circle in the road, then go halfway around the circle and take the exit that points to the hospital. Follow to stoplight (hospital should be across the street) and turn right onto New Jersey Avenue. Take this road all the way to the end and make a left onto Pointville Road. Look to make a left onto Hartford Road. Make immediate right into parking lot. Building 5756 is the first building on your right.

<u>From any southern state (Delaware, Virginia, Maryland)</u>: Follow 95 North to 295 North. Follow 295 North to exit 40 (which is 38 East). Follow 38 East approximately 20 miles and turn left onto Route 616 (Pemberton) (see alternate route below if entrance to Fort Dix from Pointville Road is blocked). Go two stoplights and turn right onto Route 630. Route 630 will change to Pointville Road, and continue straight until you reach Hartford Road. Make a left onto Hartford. Building 5756 (Administration Building) is the first building on your right.

<u>From Browns Mills</u>: Get on Texas Avenue (also called Route 545) and go north towards Fort Dix. Follow to a flashing yellow light and turn left onto

Pointville Road (just pass light). First possible right beyond the fence is Hartford Road, make a right there. Building 5756 (Administration Building) is the first building on your right.

From Pemberton: From the main street in Pemberton/Route 616, go two stoplights and turn right onto Route 630. Route 630 will change to Pointville Road (see alternate route below if entrance to Fort Dix from Pointville Road is blocked), and continue straight until you reach Hartford Road. Make a left onto Hartford. Building 5756 (Administration Building) is the first building on your right.

From Wrightstown or Commissary: If coming from Wrightstown, go around circle and take exit that is Texas Avenue. If coming from Commissary, get directly onto Texas Avenue. Follow Texas Avenue to Pointville Road and turn right. First possible right beyond the fence is Hartford Road, make a right. Building 5756 (Administration Building) is the first building on your right.

*Alternate Route:* Follow Route 616 onto Fort Dix to traffic signal, then turn right onto Juliustown Road. Follow to left and onto 17th Street. Follow to second stop sign and make a right on Pennsylvania. Follow to last building and parking lot on the left, Building 5756 (Administration Building).

## §14:21 USP LEWISBURG

USP Lewisburg
U.S. Penitentiary
2400 Robert F. Miller Drive
Lewisburg, PA 17837
LEW/ExecAssistant@bop.gov
570-523-1251
Fax: 570-522-7745

**Location:** In central Pennsylvania, outside the town of Lewisburg, 200 miles north of Washington, D.C., and 170 miles west of Philadelphia. Six miles south of Interstate 80, two miles off U.S. Route 15.

**History:** Opened in 1932, USP Lewisburg is the only high-security federal penitentiary on the East Coast. Inmates are primarily from the New England and Mid-Atlantic States.

**Judicial District:** Middle District of Pennsylvania.

**Security Level:** USP is a high-security facility housing male offenders. An adjacent satellite prison camp houses minimum-security male offenders.

**Population:** As of 8/21/2014, the USP inmate population is 672, and the camp population is 43. Weekly population figures are available on the BOP website at https://www.bop.gov/locations/institutions/lew/.

**Education:** The USP and the camp offer GED, ESL, adult education, literacy program, a parenting program and correspondence courses. Advanced occupational program degree studies are offered in business, leading to an associate arts degree from Newport Institute. Additional correspondence courses are offered through Penn State University and Ohio University.

**Vocational/Apprenticeship:** USP and the camp offer advanced occupational education in business accounting and customer service. USP offers vocational training in graphic arts and printing, and apprenticeships in HVAC, dental technician, quality control inspector, tool and die maker, and commercial housekeeper. Vocational training at the USP is offered in accordance with residential surveys (needs and interests of inmates), and instructor/institutional resources. In addition to the on-the-job training and experience, the apprentice will receive a minimum of 150 hours of related classroom instruction from the trade instructor.

**Library:** Each housing unit is equipped with an electronic law library (ELL). To access the institution's main library, inmates must submit a request. The main institution's law library is open during the daytime and most evenings. The leisure library is open six days a week and contains approximately 4,000 volumes as well as a Hispanic library section. The leisure library participates in an inter-library loan program. Audio cassette players are available to inmates in the leisure library.

**UNICOR:** An industrial products factory employs approximately 257 inmates. There is a waiting list for UNICOR.

**Counseling/Rehab Services:** The USP and the camp offer a non-residential drug treatment program, a drug education program, and Alcoholics Anonymous and Narcotics Anonymous groups. The USP offers the CODE program, which is Challenge, Opportunity, Discipline, and Ethics. The CODE program is a residential self-help program that offers inmates the resources and opportunities to adopt a pro-social lifestyle. CODE is highly structured, teaching ways to cope with life's challenges, both in prison and in the community. The camp offers a 500-hour Residential Drug Abuse Program (RDAP). The program is nine months in length. Group therapy is also offered in such areas as stress management, anger control, and coping skills. The main institution is staffed by five psychologists, five treatment specialists, and one psychology technician.

**Health Services:** The main institution is staffed by two physicians, 10 to 12 physician assistants, two dentists, and one to two pharmacists. The USP and the camp provide a managed care model of health services, which is based on delivery of necessary medical services within the constraints of cost efficiency. The daily pill line hours at the USP are 6:45am-7:15am, 11:15am-12:15pm, 4:30pm-4:45pm, and 8:30pm-9:15pm; the pill line hours at the camp are 6am-6:15am and 3pm-3:30pm, Monday through Friday, and 8am-8:30am on weekends and holidays. Sick call sign-up is available Monday, through Friday, 6:40am-6:45am. Appointments for the next day are posted on the unit bulletin boards by 4pm. At least one physician assistant is on call 24 hours a day. All inmates under the age of 50 are entitled to a physical examination every two years, while inmates over the age of 50 are eligible for an annual physical examination.

**Fitness/Recreation:** The recreation department offers many leisure, wellness and structured programs so that every inmate has the opportunity to participate. The exercise/recreation areas offer table-top games, pool, ping-pong, bocce ball, horseshoes, stationary bicycles and weightlifting rooms; these are available Monday through Thursday, 7am-3pm and 5:30pm-8pm, and Friday through Sunday 8pm-3pm and 5:30pm-9pm. Wellness programs include CORE training, fitness training, spinning and yoga. Courses are offered in acoustic guitar, crocheting and salsa dancing. Structured leagues are available for basketball, bocce ball, horseshoes, volleyball, soccer, softball, flag football, chess, dominoes, ping-pong, pool, etc. The hobby craft center offers leather craft, art (including instruction in drawing and painting) and music (including instruction in piano and guitar). The fieldhouse and camp grounds are available for use for all camp inmates after morning count.

**Religious Services:** The main institution is staffed by full-time chaplains; a community of volunteers help to provide services for most faiths.

**Housing:** Inmates at the USP are housed in one- and two-man cells, open dormitories, and in single to multiple-person rooms. Inmates at the camp are housed in dormitories and cubicles. The camp housing units are climate controlled. There are TV rooms for the housing units available from 6am-11:45pm, except during cleaning at 7:30am. Sunbathing is permitted during regular working hours (Monday through Friday, 7:30am-4pm).

**Commissary:** The commissary is open Monday through Wednesday in the evenings, after the 4pm count. Inmates are assigned one shopping day per week based upon the housing unit in which they live. The shopping schedule is rotated on a quarterly basis. The Bureau of Prisons currently sets a monthly spending limit of $360.

**Telephone Policy:** Inmates at the USP and the camp dial direct using the Inmate Telephone System (ITS). The following are standard features of ITS: (1) inmate calls automatically terminate after 15 minutes; (2) an inmate's calling list is limited to 30 callers; and (3) calls are charged to an inmate's debit card. Each inmate gets 300 calling minutes per month. At the USP, inmate telephones are located in the housing units. The phones are in operation daily during the hours of 6am-7:30am, 11am-12:30pm, and 4pm-11pm; weekend operation is all day, 6am-11pm. An inmate is delayed for 30 minutes after completing a phone call before he can place another call. The phones used by inmates are monitored and taped, as well as visually recorded.

**Inmate Mail:** The USP and the camp accept mail from the U.S. Postal Service via First-Class, U.S. Priority, and Express mail. For those interested in sending overnight mail via a private carrier (FedEx or UPS Overnight), it is recommended that you first contact the institution to find out whether the receipt of such mail is permitted.

**Inmate Mail to USP:**
> INMATE NAME, REGISTER NUMBER & UNIT
> USP Lewisburg
> U.S. Penitentiary
> P.O. Box 1000
> Lewisburg, PA 17837

**Inmate Mail to Camp:**
> INMATE NAME, REGISTER NUMBER & UNIT
> USP Lewisburg
> U.S. Penitentiary
> Satellite Camp
> P.O. Box 2000
> Lewisburg, PA 17837

**Visiting Hours:** Visiting hours for the USP are Saturday and Sunday and federal holidays, 8am-3pm. Visiting hours for the camp/RDAP are Saturday and Sunday, 8am-3pm. Inmates may receive up to five visits per month (not including attorney and parole representative visits). No more than five persons, including children, may visit an inmate at one time. The number of non-relatives on a visiting list may not exceed four persons. Attorney visits can be made by special arrangement. A small children's room is available. Additional visiting information can be found on the BOP website, www.bop.gov, at https://www.bop.gov/locations/institutions/lew/.

**Lodging/Accommodations:** Should visitors be spending the night, the following is a short list of accommodations that are available in the Lewisburg, Pennsylvania area:

| | |
|---|---|
| Days Inn Lewisburg | 570-661-4823 |
| Super 8 Williamsport | 570-368-8111 |
| Hampton Inn Lewisburg | 570-522-8500 |
| Best Western Country Cupboard Inn | 570-524-5500 |
| Country Inn & Suites Carlson Lewisburg | 570-524-6600 |

**Directions to Facility:** The institution is located just north of the city of Lewisburg, PA. The entrance road (William Penn Road) leads West from U.S. Route 15 at J.P.M. Mfg. Co.

# §14:22  FCI LORETTO

FCI Loretto
Federal Correctional Institution
772 St. Joseph Street
Loretto, PA 15940
LOR/ExecAssistant@bop.gov
814-472-4140
Fax: 814-472-6046

**Location:** In southwest Pennsylvania between Altoona and Johnstown, 90 miles east of Pittsburgh, off Route 22, midway between Interstate 80 and the Pennsylvania Turnpike via Route 220. Served by Pittsburgh Airport, Amtrak, and commercial bus lines.

**History:** Opened in 1984, FCI Loretto is a former Catholic seminary built in 1960. It houses inmates primarily from the northeast, most of whom are first offenders serving between five and 14 years, in the 33-39 year age group. The majority of the offenders are serving sentences for violating drug laws. A perimeter fence was constructed in 1990, which increased the security level.

**Judicial District:** Western District of Pennsylvania.

**Security Level:** FCI is a low-security facility housing male inmates. An adjacent minimum-security satellite prison camp houses male inmates.

**Population:** As of 6/18/2017, the FCI inmate population is 885, and the camp population is 96. Weekly population figures are available on the BOP website at www.bop.gov, https://www.bop.gov/locations/institutions/lor/.

**Education:** The FCI and camp offer GED, ESL, Adult Basic Education, and Adult Continuing Education courses, which are inmate-taught and last from eight to 12 weeks. Classes that may be offered include foreign languages, history, legal research, and business, among others. Inmates may also pursue independent study via correspondence courses. A parenting class is provided by the Family Services Foundation.

**Vocational/Apprenticeship:** The FCI and the camp offer vocational training programs in fiber optics retail sales and customer service, automotive repair, and personal fitness trainer. The Facilities Department at FCI offers job placement opportunities to learn trade-related skills in drafting, electric, landscape, garage, communications, powerhouse, plumbing, welding, painting and construction. The FCI does not offer apprenticeship programs. There is an Employment Resource Center (ERC) that helps inmates in career development, job search skills, resume writing, interview skills and job retention.

**Library:** The main institution's leisure/law library is open six days a week, closed on Saturdays. Inmates are permitted to use the library during their off The Law Library is electronic and provides all the required resource material. The leisure library contains a wide variety of newspapers, magazines, listening and videotapes, and books.

**UNICOR:** An electronics (cable) factory employs approximately 500 inmates. Priority placement in UNICOR will be given to inmates with financial obligations over $1,000 (at least 50 percent of UNICOR earnings will be applied toward the balance).

**Counseling/Rehab Services:** The FCI and the camp offer a non-residential drug treatment program, drug education program, residential drug treatment program, smoking cessation program, crisis intervention, individual counseling, suicide prevention, incarcerated veterans, and Alcoholics Anonymous and Narcotics Anonymous groups. The main institution is staffed by full-time psychologists. The facility does not have a staff psychiatrist.

**Health Services:** The FCI and the camp also provide outpatient care, including optometry services. Local hospitals are 20-30 minutes away. All inmates are assigned a personal care provider. Sick call sign-up is from 6:30am-7am, Monday, Tuesday, Thursday, and Friday, and from 6:15am-6:30am at the camp. The pill line is available every day during these times: 7:45am-8am, 11:30-12noon, and 8:30pm-8:45pm at the FCI; the camp pill line runs from 6:15am-6:30am, and 7pm-7:15pm. At least one physician assistant is on duty or on call 24 hours a day.

**Fitness/Recreation:** The recreation department offers intramural and varsity team sports (basketball, softball, and volleyball), stationary bicycles, weights, outdoor track area, a music room, ping-pong tables, pool tables, and card game tables. The hobby craft center offers leather craft, ceramics, and fine art.

**Religious Services:** The main institution is staffed by one full-time chaplain. The chaplain, who will counsel inmates regardless of faith or denominational affiliation, is available every day. The chapel also has areas for worship, prayer, and study, as well as a library consisting of books, CDs, and videos/DVDs. A community of volunteers provides services for most faiths.

**Housing:** Inmates at the FCI are housed in open dormitories, multiple occupancy rooms and cubicles. The dormitories contain 40-man, 10-man, 6-man, and two-man rooms. Housing is assigned based on seniority, adjustment, and program participation. Inmates at the camp are housed in military-style barracks (100 inmates per barrack). At the FCI, televisions are available in each of the housing units (allowed 6am-11:50pm). Viewing of special events that continue later than 11:50pm requires special permission.

**Commissary:** Inmates are permitted to shop one day of the week. Merchandise lists are used to make commissary selections. These lists are completed by the inmate and turned into the sales unit staff on the same day. The Bureau of Prisons currently sets a monthly spending limit of $360.

**Telephone Policy:** Inmates at the FCI and the camp dial direct using the Inmate Telephone System (ITS). The following are standard features of ITS: (1) inmate calls automatically terminate after 15 minutes (calls are limited to 15 minutes every 45 minutes); (2) an inmate's calling list is limited to 30 callers; and (3) calls are charged to an inmate's debit card. Each inmate gets 300 call minutes per month. Telephones are located in the housing units for local, long distance, international, and collect calls, and are available 6am-11:30pm (except during count times).

**Inmate Mail:** The FCI and the camp accept mail from the U.S. Postal Service via First-Class, U.S. Priority, and Express mail. For those interested in sending overnight mail via a private carrier (FedEx or UPS Overnight), it is recommended that you first contact the institution to find out whether the receipt of such mail is permitted. Inmates may subscribe to publications without prior approval (magazines, newspapers, books, etc.), but the warden will reject publications that are determined to be detrimental to the security and orderly running of the institution. Softcover books may be received from any source, but hardcover publications are allowed only through the publisher or bookstore. Publications are limited to 10 magazines (not more than three months old) and must be able to be neatly stored in the locker and/or on the shelf of the inmate's room.

**Inmate Mail to FCI:**
> INMATE NAME & REGISTER NUMBER
> FCI Loretto
> Federal Correctional Institution
> P.O. Box 1000
> Loretto, PA 15940

**Visiting Hours:** Approved visitors may visit the FCI Friday through Sunday and federal holidays, 8:15am-2:15pm. Camp visiting is Saturday, Sunday, and federal holidays, 8:15am-2:15pm. Each inmate is permitted eight visit points per month. Two points will be assessed for all visits. Visiting points will be levied against an inmate on a per visit basis. An inmate's initial visiting list will only include immediate family, but additional friends and relatives may be added by submitting a request to the inmate's assigned counselor. The number of adult visitors is limited to four (4) at any given time. Children under the age of 16 will not be counted, though they must be accompanied by an adult. No more than 10 persons will be on the approved visiting list. Attorney visits can be made by special arrangement and do not count against the monthly visiting limit. Additional visiting information can be found on the BOP website, www.bop.gov, at https://www.bop.gov/locations/institutions/lor/.

**Lodging/Accommodations:** Should visitors be spending the night, the following is a short list of accommodations that are available in Altoona, Pennsylvania:

| | |
|---|---|
| Hampton Inn Altoona | 814-941-3500 |
| Courtyard by Marriott Altoona | 814-312-1800 |
| Super 8 Altoona | 814-942-5350 |
| Holiday Inn Express Hotel Altoona | 814-693-1004 |

**Directions to Facility:** From Johnstown Cambria County airport: Upon leaving the airport, make a right. Proceed to the stop sign (approximately 1/ 12 miles). At stop sign, make a left. After turning left, go only 1/8 mile and make another left, and this will put you on Rt. 219 North. Proceed on Route 219 North for 15 miles. Take the exit that says Route 22 East, Ebensburg. Proceed on Route 22 East for five miles and take the exit that says Route 164, Munster/Portage. At the stop sign after taking the exit, make a left and go 1/8 mile to the stop light. At the light, make a right and go approximately three miles. You will see Mount Aloysius College on your right. Take the road to the left that immediately follows the college. The sign will say "Loretto 4 miles." Follow this road approximately three miles. You will see FCI Loretto sitting up on a hill on your left.

From Altoona Airport: Upon leaving the airport, make a right and proceed on Route 866 North. Continue on 866 North until you see Route 164 in Martinsburg. At Route 164 make a left (164 West) and go towards Roaring Spring. At Roaring Spring, Routes 164 West and 36 North join; make a right and continue on Routes 164/36. Approximately three miles on routes 164/36, you will see a sign saying Route 220 North to Altoona. Go a short distance and make a right onto Route 220 North. Proceed on Route 220 North for approximately five miles. You will see a sign saying Route 22/764 Ebensburg/ Hollidaysburg. Make a right here to get onto Route 22 and proceed on Route 22 West to Ebensburg. Travel approximately nine miles until you see the Cresson Summit Exit. After taking this exit, make a right at the stop sign. Proceed until you reach a stop light. Pass straight through this light. Approximately 1/2 mile you will see a sign that says "Loretto 4 miles." Make a right here. Proceed approximately three miles and you will see FCI Loretto sitting up on a hill to your left.

## §14:23   FCI MCKEAN

FCI McKean
Federal Correctional Facility
6975 Route 59
Lewis Run, PA 16738
MCK/ExecAssistant@bop.gov
814-362-8900
Fax: 814-363-6821

**Location:** In northwest Pennsylvania on the edge of the Allegheny National Forest between Bradford and Kane. 90 miles south of Buffalo, off Route 59,

1/4 mile east of the intersection of State Route 59 and U.S. Route 219. Served by Buffalo Airport and Bradford Airport.

**History:** Opened in 1989, FCI McKean houses male offenders primarily from the northeastern United States. The average sentence length is 98 months. The average age of inmates is 36.1 years. Opened in 1989, the camp houses male offenders with an average sentence of 24 months.

**Judicial District:** Western District of Pennsylvania.

**Security Level:** FCI is a medium-security facility housing male inmates. An adjacent satellite prison camp houses minimum-security male offenders.

**Population:** As of 8/21/2014, the FCI inmate population is 916, and the camp population is 263. Weekly population figures are available on the BOP website at www.bop.gov, https://www.bop.gov/locations/institutions/mck/.

**Education:** The FCI and the camp offer GED, ESL, adult education, parenting, and college correspondence courses. Typical adult education courses offered include typing, computer literacy, foreign languages, and business skills, etc.

**Vocational/Apprenticeship:** The FCI offers vocational training in building trades, culinary arts, and computers. The camp offers vocational training in computers. FCI offers apprenticeship in professional cooking and building maintenance. Apprenticeship programs are certified through the U.S. Department of Labor, Bureau of Apprentice Training.

**Library:** The institution's law library is open Monday through Friday at 7:10am-3:30pm, and 4:30pm-8:30pm. It is open on weekends and federal holidays at 10:30am-3:30pm and 4:30pm-8:30pm. Typewriters and a copier are available. Inmates also have access to Electronic Law Libraries (ELL). VCRs and audio cassette players are available for check out from the leisure library. Reference materials include the United States Code Annotated, Federal Reporter, Supreme Court Reporter, Bureau of Prisons Program Statements, Institution Supplements, and other legal materials. The leisure library offers inmates a variety of reading materials, including but not limited to periodicals, newspapers, fiction, non-fiction, and reference books.

**UNICOR:** FCI McKean does not have a UNICOR factory at this time. FPC McKean employs four inmate clerks in the UNICOR division.

**Counseling/Rehab Services:** The FCI offers a 500-hour Residential Drug Abuse Program (RDAP). The program is nine months in length. The FCI and the camp offer a non-residential drug treatment program, a drug education program, an outpatient program, individual therapy, Anger Management, Emo-tional

Self-Regulation, Criminal Thinking, and Seeking Safety, and other groups. The main institution is staffed by a full-time psychologist, a Drug Abuse Program Coordinator, several Drug Treatment Specialists, and a Psychology Technician. The psychology department's normal hours of operation are Monday through Friday, 7:30am-4pm.

**Health Services:** The main institution is staffed by two physicians, two to four physician assistants, two dentists, one dental assistant, and one pharmacist. The FCI and the camp have an outpatient clinic. Bradford Hospital is located approximately 10 minutes away. There is a Health Services Open House held every Wednesday at the FCI from 11:30am-12noon for inmates with questions or concerns about their healthcare. Medication at the FCI is dispensed Monday through Friday at 7am-7:30am, 11:15am-12noon, 3:15pm, and 7pm-7:15pm; Saturday, Sunday, and federal holidays at 8:30am-8:40am, 11:15am-12noon, and 7pm-7:30pm. Medication at the camp is dispensed Monday through Friday at 6:30am-7am and 5pm-5:30pm; Saturday, Sunday and holidays from 9am-9:15am and 5:15pm-5:30pm. Urgent care evaluation and sick-call application is weekdays 7am-7:30am. At least one physician assistant is on call 24 hours a day. Inmates under the age of 50 may request a physical examination every two years; those over 50 may request one annually.

**Fitness/Recreation:** The recreation department offers a modern gymnasium and weight room, a music center, a large recreation yard and pool tables. The hobby craft center offers leather, ceramics, and painting. The outdoor recreation yard by the camp has a softball diamond, soccer field, basketball courts, handball courts, horseshoe courts, bocce ball courts, outside weight area, and volleyball court.

**Religious Services:** The main institution is staffed by two full-time chaplains. Contract rabbi and imam services are available. A sweat lodge for Native-American services is also available. A community of volunteers provide services for most faiths. Religious diets, holiday observances, and other worship activities are coordinated through the chaplain's office.

**Housing:** Inmates at the FCI are housed in two-man cells. Inmates at the camp are housed in dormitories in two-man cubicles.

**Commissary:** Sales hours for the commissary are posted in the housing unit common areas as well as in the commissary. Inmates are assigned one shopping day per week, determined by the last two digits of the first five-digit number of their register numbers. The Bureau of Prisons currently sets a monthly spending limit of $360.

**Telephone Policy:** Inmates at the FCI and the camp dial direct using the Inmate Telephone System (ITS). The following are standard features of ITS: (1) inmate calls automatically terminate after 15 minutes; (2) an inmate's calling list is limited to 30 callers; and (3) calls are charged to an inmate's debit card. Inmates are limited to a total of 300 minutes of telephone calls per month. It takes approximately five working days for inmates to clear their initial caller-approved list and an additional five working days to modify the list. There are telephones in each general housing unit for inmate use (7am-10pm daily). Camp telephone hours are 10am-11:30pm daily. Inmate access to telephones will normally be limited during the following times, Monday through Friday, not including holidays.

**Inmate Mail:** The FCI and camp accept mail from the U.S. Postal Service via First-Class, U.S. Priority, and Express mail. For those interested in sending overnight mail via a private carrier (FedEx or UPS Overnight), it is recommended that you first contact the institution to find out whether the receipt of such mail is permitted. Inmates may subscribe to publications without prior approval, although the warden will reject publications determined to be detrimental to the security, good order, or discipline of the institution. All publications must come directly from the publishers, bookstores, or book club. The number of magazines, newspapers and books an inmate can keep in his room is limited.

**Inmate Mail to FCI:**
INMATE NAME & REGISTER NUMBER
FCI McKean
Federal Correctional Facility
P.O. Box 8000
Bradford, PA 16701

**Visiting Hours:** Approved visitors may visit the FCI on Monday 1:30pm-8pm and on Saturday, Sunday, and federal holidays from 8am-3pm. At the camp, visitors may visit on Monday from 5:30pm-8pm, and Saturday, Sunday, and federal holidays from 8:30am-3pm. At the FCI and the camp, the number of persons allowed to visit an inmate at one time is limited to three adults and three children. During the months of May, June, July, August, September, and October, inmates are limited to two weekend visits per month. There is no limit on Monday evening visits (except for federal holidays). For attorney visits, appointments should be made in advance. Additional visiting information can be found on the BOP website, www.bop.gov, at https://www.bop.gov/locations/institutions/mck/.

**Lodging/Accommodations:** Should visitors be spending the night, the following is a short list of accommodations that are available in Bradford, Pennsylvania:

| | |
|---|---|
| The Lodge at Glendorn | 814-362-6511 |
| Best Western Bradford Inn | 814-362-4501 |
| Comfort Inn Bradford | 814-368-6772 |
| America's Best Value Inn Bradford | 814-362-3567 |

## §14:24   MCC NEW YORK

MCC New York
Metropolitan Correctional Center
150 Park Row
New York, NY 10007
NYM/ExecAssistant@bop.gov
646-836-6300
Fax: 646-836-7751

**Location:** In downtown Manhattan adjacent to Foley Square and across the street from the Federal Courthouse, two blocks from the Brooklyn Bridge. New York City is served by LaGuardia, Kennedy, and Newark International Airports; Amtrak (Pennsylvania Station 34th Street); and Greyhound (42nd Street Port Authority bus station).

**History:** Opened in 1975, MCC New York is a twelve-story, high-rise detention facility housing male and female holdover inmates who appear in federal courts in the Eastern and Southern Districts of New York and the District of New Jersey. The average length of stay is 90-120 days.

**Judicial District:** Southern District of New York.

**Security Level:** MCC is an administrative facility housing male and female pre-trial and holdover inmates.

**Population:** As of 6/19/2017, the MCC inmate population is 809. Weekly population figures are available on the BOP website, www.bop.gov, at https://www.bop.gov/locations/institutions/nym/.

**Education:** The institution offers GED, ESL, adult education, and correspondence courses.

**Vocational/Apprenticeship:** None.

**Library:** The law/leisure library is open during these times: Monday through Thursday, 8am-11am, 12noon-3pm and 5pm-8pm; Friday through Sunday, 8am-11am and 12noon-3pm. Electric typewriters are available to inmates for use in preparing legal documents. A copier is available. Copies are charged to an inmate's debit card. Video cassette recorders are available in the housing units and audio cassette players are available in the leisure library. The leisure library collection includes fiction, non-fiction, major newspapers, and reference materials.

**UNICOR:** None.

**Counseling/Rehab Services:** The institution offers a non-residential drug treatment program, a drug education program, and Alcoholics Anonymous and Narcotics Anonymous groups. Individual counseling is also available on an as-needed basis. The psychology department is staffed by two to three full-time psychologists.

**Health Services:** The institution is staffed by one physician, one dentist, and five to eight physician assistants. The institution provides outpatient care. Pill line is available three times a day, seven days a week. Sick call is available five days a week. At least one physician assistant is on call 24 hours a day.

**Fitness/Recreation:** The recreation department offers team sports, physical fitness/weight reduction, yoga, weight training, and board games. The hobby craft department also offers various individualized craft programs.

**Religious Services:** The institution is staffed by two full-time chaplains. A community of volunteers provide services for most faiths.

**Housing:** Inmates are housed in two-man cells and open dormitories holding up to twenty inmates.

**Commissary:** The commissary is open weekdays. Inmates are assigned one shopping day per week. The Bureau of Prisons currently sets a monthly spending limit of $360.

**Telephone Policy:** Inmate Telephone System (ITS) or collect calling can be made. Inmates can add up to 30 approved telephone numbers by submitting a Telephone Number Request form. Phone calls automatically terminate after 15 minutes. Inmates get 300 calling minutes per month. Inmates may request an unmonitored legal telephone call, which may be approved upon review.

**Inmate Mail:** The institution accepts mail from the U.S. Postal Service via First-Class, U.S. Priority, and Express mail. For those interested in sending overnight mail via a private carrier (FedEx or UPS Overnight), it is recommended that you first contact the institution to find out whether the receipt of such mail is permitted.

**Inmate Mail to MCC:**
    INMATE NAME & REGISTER NUMBER
    MCC New York
    Metropolitan Correctional Center
    150 Park Row
    New York, NY 10007

**Visiting Hours:** Sentenced inmates who are designated to the MCC New York work cadre may receive visits on Saturday and Sunday. Pre-trial and holdovers inmates may receive only one social visit per week, for no more than one hour.

An inmate is limited to having no more than three adult visitors, and no more than three children, at any one time. Inmate visiting lists are restricted to 10 approved visitors for pre-trial inmates and twelve approved visitors for designated cadre inmates. Immediate family members and one person of "meaning" will be placed on an inmate's visiting list absent strong circumstances that preclude visiting. While attorney visiting can occur 24 hours a day, attorneys are generally expected to visit with their clients in the attorney conference room 6am-8pm daily. Additional visiting information can be found at https://www.bop.gov/locations/institutions/nym/.

**Lodging/Accommodations:** Should visitors be spending the night, the following is a short list of accommodations that are available in New York, New York:

| | |
|---|---|
| Courtyard by Marriot, Manhattan-Chelsea | 212-967-6000 |
| Best Western Seaport Inn Downtown | 212-766-6600 |
| Holiday Inn Wall Street | 212-227-4780 |
| Cosmopolitan Hotel Tribeca | 212-566-1900 |
| Ramada Inn Eastside | 212-545-1800 |

## §14:25   FCI OTISVILLE

FCI Otisville
Federal Correctional Institution
Two Mile Drive
Otisville, NY 10963
OTV/ExecAssistant@bop.gov
845-386-6700
Fax: 845-386-6727

**Location:** In southeast New York, near the Pennsylvania and New Jersey borders, and 70 miles northwest of New York City. The area is served by several airports, the closest of which is in Newburgh, New York. Bus and train services connect Otisville to New York City.

**History:** Opened in 1980, FCI Otisville houses an overflow of pre-trial and holdover inmates from MCC New York.

**Judicial District:** Southern District of New York.

**Security Level:** FCI is a medium-security facility housing male offenders. The satellite prison camp is a minimum-security facility that houses male offenders.

**Population:** As of 6/19/2017, the FCI inmate population is 589, and the camp population is 119. Weekly population figures are available on the BOP website at www.bop.gov, https://www.bop.gov/locations/institutions/otv/.

**Education:** The FCI and the camp offer GED, ESL, adult education, and correspondence courses.

**Vocational/Apprenticeship:** The FCI offers advanced occupational education in Business Leadership. The FCI offers vocational training in horticulture, business computer applications, and textiles and materials. The FCI offers apprenticeship in plumber, plant maintenance, cabinet maker, electrician, cook, and refrigeration and air conditioning mechanic.

**Library:** The main institution's law library is open Monday through Friday, 8:30am-9pm, and on Saturday and Sunday, 1pm-9pm. Typewriters are available. A copier is also available. The leisure library participates as a member of the Ramapo-Catskill inter-library loan system. This system provides for books not found in the institution library to be sent in from other libraries. The leisure library maintains audio-visual stations for individual viewing in the evening of videotapes from its collection.

**UNICOR:** An electronics factory employs approximately 174 inmates.

**Counseling/Rehab Services:** The FCI and the camp offer a non-residential drug treatment program, a 40-hour drug education program, and Alcoholics Anonymous and Narcotics Anonymous groups. The main institution is staffed by one chief psychologist, one staff psychologist, one drug abuse program coordinator, one treatment specialist, and one psychology technician. A psychologist is available on an as-needed basis to assist with mental health issues.

**Health Services:** The main institution is staffed by two physicians, eight to 10 physician assistants, one dentist, dental assistants, one optometrist, and one pharmacist. The FCI and the camp have health care provider teams. The medication/pill line is offered three times daily at the FCI, and twice daily at the camp. Sign up for triage, formerly known as sick call, is 7am-7:15am Monday through Friday (except Wednesdays and federal holidays).

**Fitness/Recreation:** The recreation department offers team sports, musical instruments (guitars), board games, etc. A variety of art and crafts are also available.

**Religious Services:** The main institution is staffed by two full-time chaplains and one full-time rabbi. A community of volunteers provides services for most faiths. Religious Services has reading materials and videos to help inmates develop their spirituality. Religious diets and ceremonial meals are available upon approval from one of the Religious Services staff members.

**Housing:** Inmates are housed in two-man rooms and dormitories.

**Commissary:** The commissary is open Monday through Friday, 7am-6:30pm. Inmates are permitted to shop one day per week in accordance with the schedule posted in the housing units and on the commissary bulletin board. The Bureau of Prisons currently sets a monthly spending limit of $360.

**Telephone Policy:** Inmates at the FCI and the camp call collect or dial direct using the Inmate Telephone System (ITS). The following are standard features of ITS: (1) inmate calls automatically terminate after 15 minutes; (2) an inmate's calling list is limited to 30 callers; and (3) calls are charged to an inmate's debit card. Telephones are available in each housing unit. Inmates are limited to 300 minutes per month, but are allowed 400 minutes during the holiday season (November/December). No third-party, three-way or credit card calls are permitted on these lines.

**Inmate Mail:** The FCI and the camp accept mail from the U.S. Postal Service via First-Class, U.S. Priority, and Express mail. Overnight mail is not permitted for federal inmates, and will be processed as general mail. Inmates may receive up to five magazines or soft-covered books at a time, and possession of publications is limited to five books and three magazines. Packages from family containing legal papers cannot weigh more than one pound.

**Inmate Mail to FCI:**
> INMATE NAME & REGISTER NUMBER
> FCI Otisville
> Federal Correctional Institution
> P.O. Box 1000
> Otisville, NY 10963

**Inmate Mail to Camp:**
> INMATE NAME & REGISTER NUMBER
> FCI Otisville
> Federal Correctional Institution
> Satellite Camp
> P.O. Box 1000
> Otisville, NY 10963

**Visiting Hours:** Visiting hours at the FCI are Friday through Monday and federal holidays, 8am-2:45pm. Camp visiting is Monday, Thursday and Friday, 1pm-8pm; Saturday, Sunday, and federal holidays, 8am-3pm. Inmates are limited to 12 visiting points per month, with one point assessed for each weekday visit, and two points assessed for weekend/holiday visits. A maximum of four adults and four children may visit an inmate at any one time. Authorized visiting lists are limited to immediate family and 25 additional adults. Attorney visits can be permitted at any time. All attorney visits during non-visiting days or non-visiting hours are to be coordinated and supervised by the inmate's unit team. Additional visiting information can be found on the BOP website, www.bop.gov, https://www.bop.gov/locations/institutions/otv/.

**Lodging/Accommodations:** Should visitors be spending the night, the following is a short list of accommodations that are available in the Otisville, New York area:

| | |
|---|---|
| Courtyard by Marriott Middletown | 845-695-0606 |
| Howard Johnson Middletown | 845-342-5822 |
| Days Inn Middletown | 845-374-2411 |
| Hampton Inn Middletown | 845-344-3400 |
| Holiday Inn Middletown | 845-343-1474 |

**Directions to Facility:** The entrance road (Two Mile Drive) to FCI Otisville is located on County Road 90 (Sanitarium Road), 1/4 mile off of New York State Highway 211. The facility is located 2.2 miles up the mountain from the beginning of the entrance.

## §14:26   FDC PHILADELPHIA

FDC Philadelphia
Federal Detention Center
700 Arch Street
Philadelphia, PA 19106
PHL/ExecAssistant@bop.gov
215-521-4000
Fax: 215-521-7220

**Location:** From the Philadelphia airport, take I-95 North to the 676 Exit. Turn Left on 8th Street. Proceed down 8th Street to Arch Street. The facility is located on the corner of 7th Street and Arch.

**History:** Opened in 2000.

**Judicial District:** Eastern District of Pennsylvania.

**Security Level:** FDC is an administrative facility housing male and female pre-trial inmates for the Eastern District of Pennsylvania, all of Delaware, and Southern New Jersey.

**Population:** As of 6/19/2017, the FDC inmate population is 977. Weekly population figures are available on the BOP website at www.bop.gov, https://www.bop.gov/locations/institutions/phl/.

**Education:** The institution offers GED and ESL programs. Adult continuing education (ACE) and parenting classes are offered at different times during the year. Post-secondary education (PSE) classes are offered to the inmates at their own expense.

**Vocational/Apprenticeship:** The institution does not offer advanced occupational education, vocational or apprenticeship training programs.

**Library:** The main law library is maintained by the Education Department and a basic law library is maintained in each unit. Reference materials, reading materials, legal papers and legal forms are available. Typewriters are located in the housing units, and inmates will need to purchase their own ribbons and typing paper. A copier is available. Inmates must submit an Inmate Request (cop-out) to the Education Department in order to reproduce legal material. FDC Philadelphia is equipped with the Electronic Law Library (ELL). Inmates can print items from the ELL on the unit at a rate of $0.15 per page. Leisure books are available in each of the housing unit's library/discovery room and in the Special Housing Unit (SHU). A variety of newspapers are delivered to each housing unit and SHU on a weekly basis. Inmates may check out books from the main library by submitting an electronic request to the education department. Only one book per inmate, for a maximum of up to two weeks is permitted. Cadre inmates have access to interlibrary loan.

**UNICOR:** None.

**Counseling/Rehab Services:** The institution offers a non-residential drug treatment program. Drug abuse treatment at FDC Philadelphia consists primarily of drug education groups for cadre inmates, and transitional services for cadre inmates who have completed the RDAP. There is a Pre-Release Program and the possibility for transfer to a Residential Reentry Center (RRC) to prepare inmates for their release. Other programs available to inmates include crisis intervention and psychiatric consultation. The Psychology Department has several psychologists to assist inmates.

**Health Services:** The institution provides routine health care through triage/sick call and specialty clinics. A full-time dentist and complete dental department are available. Triage/sick call is available Monday, Tuesday, Thursday, and Friday, 6:30am-8am. The morning pill line is 6:45am-8:45am and the evening pill line is 5pm-8pm. Inmates can sign up for triage/sick call in their housing units. Emergencies will be given priority and appropriate treatment will be provided. Routine physicals are performed on Wednesdays. Physicals can be requested every three years by individuals under 50 years of age, and every year by individuals over 50 years of age. The health services department provides 24-hour coverage, and medical emergencies take precedence.

**Fitness/Recreation:** The recreation department offers a variety of indoor and outdoor activities, as well as individualized arts and crafts programs. Recreation equipment and board games are available within each housing unit.

**Religious Services:** The institution is staffed by full-time chaplains who are available to assist inmates in religious practices. A list of available religious activities is posted in each unit. A community of volunteers provide services for most faiths. Pastoral counseling and religious diet programs may be requested through the chaplains.

**Housing:** Inmates are housed in two-person cells and dormitories. Designated and pre-trial female inmates are housed on the third floor. All male inmates are housed from the fourth floor through the seventh floor.

**Commissary:** Inmates can purchase commissary items on a weekly basis by submitting a Commissary Sheet. Commissary Sheets are available from unit staff and must be submitted one day prior to the scheduled commissary day. The spending limit for the Work Cadre is $250 per month, and for pretrial inmates, $200 per month.

**Telephone Policy:** Inmates may either call collect or dial direct using the Inmate Telephone System (ITS-2) for a total of 300 minutes monthly. The following are standard features of ITS: (1) inmate calls automatically terminate after 15 minutes; (2) an inmate's calling list is limited to 30 callers; and (3) calls are charged to an inmate's debit card. Inmates get 300 calling minutes per month. All telephone regulations and telephone usage schedules are posted in each unit. Three-way calls are prohibited. All calls are monitored, although inmates may request an unmonitored legal call.

**Inmate Mail:** The institution accepts mail from the U.S. Postal Service via First-Class, U.S. Priority and Express mail. If you are interested in sending overnight mail via a private carrier (Federal Express or UPS Overnight), it is recommended that you first contact the institution to find out whether the receipt of such mail is permitted. Inmates are not authorized to request merchandise or materials, or anything for which they could be billed, through the mail.

**Inmate Mail to FDC:**
    INMATE NAME & REGISTER NUMBER
    FDC Philadelphia
    Federal Detention Center
    P.O. Box 562
    Philadelphia, PA 19106

**Visiting Hours:** Visiting hours for cadre inmates are Wednesday through Monday, 6:5am-2:30pm. Wednesday through Saturday, visitation is on a scheduled rotation by floor assignment. Female inmates will be permitted to visit during their entire visiting day, up to 64 hours per month. with immediate family, other relatives, friends and associates. Male inmates are allowed three hours per visit once per week, for a total of 12 hours per month. Inmates may have up to 10 non-immediate family members on an approved visiting list, and are allowed up to five visitors at a time. Attorneys are permitted to visit from 6:15am-8pm, seven days a week. If an attorney requires a legal visit at a different time, it is the attorney's responsibility to contact the institution 24 hours in advance. Additional visiting information can be found on the BOP website, www.bop.gov, at https://www.bop.gov/locations/institutions/phl/.

**Lodging/Accommodations:** The following is a short list of motels/hotels in the immediate area:

| | |
|---|---|
| Hilton Garden Inn | 215-923-0100 |
| Franklin Hotel at Independence Park | 215-925-0000 |
| Penn's View Hotel | 215-922-7600 |
| Loews Philadelphia Hotel | 215-627-1200 |
| Courtyard Marriott Philadelphia Downtown | 215-496-3200 |

**Directions to Facility:** <u>From New York City & New Jersey</u>: 295 to 30 West. Follow 30 West across the Ben Franklin Bridge and exit at 8th Street. Left on 8th Street to Arch Street. The institution is located at 7th & Arch Streets.

<u>From Delaware & Points South</u>: 95 North, exit at 676/Callowhill Street. Follow Callowhill Street to 6th Street and make a left onto 6th Street. Follow 6th Street to Arch Street and make a right onto Arch Street. The institution is located on 7th & Arch Streets.

<u>From Points North</u>: 95 South, exit at Callowhill Street. Follow Callowhill street to 6th Street and make a left onto 6th Street. Follow 6th Street to Arch street and make a right onto Arch Street. The institution is located on 7th and Arch Streets.

<u>From Points West</u>: 76 to 676 East. Exit at 8th street and follow to Arch Street. The institution is located on 7th and Arch Streets.

## §14:27   FCI RAY BROOK

FCI Ray Brook
Federal Correctional Institution
128 Ray Brook Road
Ray Brook, NY 12977
RBK/ExecAssistant@bop.gov
518-897-4000
Fax: 518-897-4216

**Location:** In the Adirondack Mountain region of upstate New York, midway between the villages of Lake Placid and Saranac Lake, off Route 86. The area is served by the Adirondack Airport, the Albany Airport, and the Burlington, Vermont, Airport; Amtrak in Albany; and commercial bus lines.

**History:** Opened in September 1980, FCI Ray Brook was formerly the Olympic Village for the 1980 Winter Olympic Games. It houses male offenders from the northeastern United States.

**Judicial District:** Northern District of New York.

**Security Level:** FCI is a medium-security facility for male offenders.

**Population:** As of 6/19/2017, the FCI inmate population is 708. Weekly population figures are available on the BOP website at www.bop.gov, at https://www.bop.gov/locations/institutions/rbk/.

**Education:** The institution offers GED, ESL, adult education, and post-secondary education through correspondence courses. Additionally, ESL Tutoring, Kids at Risk, parenting, literacy, and reading therapy programs are offered with the assistance of FCI Ray Brook's community volunteer program.

**Vocational/Apprenticeship:** The FCI offers advanced occupational education in alcohol substance abuse studies and vocational training in electronics. No apprenticeship programs are offered.

**Library:** The leisure library is open Monday through Thursday from 7:30am-11:30am, 12:30pm-3:30pm, and 4:30pm-8:30pm. It is open on Fridays from 7:30am-11:30am, and 12:30pm-3:30pm. It is open on Saturday from 7:15am-3:15pm (closed on Sunday). Inmates may check out books and read, magazines, reference materials, and a number of newspapers. The law library is open 7:30am-8:30pm Monday through Thursday, 7:30am-6:30pm Friday, and 7:30am-3:30pm Saturday. An inter-library loan service is offered. Typewriters and a copier are available. An inmate law library clerk is available for assistance in legal research.

**UNICOR:** A textile factory employs approximately 200 inmates.

**Counseling/Rehab Services:** The institution offers a non-residential drug treatment program, a drug education program, Alcoholics/Narcotics Anonymous groups, and other voluntary groups, along with referrals to residential drug programs (RDAP). The psychology department is staffed by two full-time psychologists. A contract psychiatrist, who is a medical doctor, is also available by appointment through the psychology department.

**Health Services:** The institution has a full medical staff, including a dental department and consultant optometrist. The pill line is open for all medical patients at 7:30am, 3pm, and 7:30pm Monday through Friday. Weekend pill line hours are the same, except for the morning pill line, which begins at 8am. Sick call sign-up is between 6am-6:30am Monday, Tuesday, Thursday, and Friday. All urgent care medical issues will usually be seen the same day, while others will necessitate a later appointment. Medical coverage on evenings, weekends, and holidays is provided for non-routine medical problems. Inmates under the age of 50 are entitled to one physical examination every two years, and inmates over the age of 50 may request one annually.

**Fitness/Recreation:** The recreation department offers intramural team sports such as softball, volleyball, and basketball. Also available is a weight area (limited), a music room (acoustic instruments), pool tables, stationary bicycles, and stair-steppers. The hobby craft center offers ceramics, leather craft, painting, drawing and a knitting course. Recreation times during weekdays are 6:15am-7:30am, 8:30am-10:15am, 10:30am-3:15pm, and 4:30pm-8:15pm. On weekends, the recreation times are 7:15am-9:15am, 10:30am-3:15pm, and 4:30pm-8:15pm. Outdoor activities are for daylight hours only.

**Religious Services:** The institution is staffed by one chaplain. Services are provided in Bible studies, Catholic catechism, Christian ministry, Islamic studies, Jehovah's Witnesses, and Spanish ministries. Special religious diets, holiday observances and worship activities are coordinated through the chaplain's office.

**Inmate Organizations:** FCI Ray Brook is a recipient of the Point of Light Award for inmate volunteerism in community improvement and help projects. For additional information, please contact the institution's volunteer coordinator.

**Housing:** Inmates are housed in two-man and four-man rooms.

**Commissary:** The commissary is open Monday through Friday. Regular sales are from the clearing of 4pm count until 10 minutes after the Dining Hall is closed. Those already in line at that time will be served. Stamps, copier cards, and vending credit sales are from 10:40am-12:30pm. Inmates are assigned one shopping day per week, determined by the fifth digit of their registration numbers. The Bureau of Prisons currently sets a monthly spending limit of $360, although FCI Ray Brook increases this limit during the month of December.

**Telephone Policy:** Inmates dial direct or collect using the Inmate Telephone System (ITS). The following are standard features of ITS: (1) inmate calls automatically terminate after 15 minutes; (2) an inmate's calling list is limited to 30 callers; and (3) calls are charged to an inmate's debit card. Inmates are limited to 300 minutes per calendar month for all calls placed through ITS. After placing a call of any length, each inmate is subject to a 30-minute waiting period before he may place another call. Telephones are located in the housing units, and are generally available for use daily from 6am-11:30pm. All telephones will be turned off at 3:30pm and turned back on at 4:30pm.

**Inmate Mail:** The institution accepts mail from the U.S. Postal Service via First-Class, U.S. Priority and Express mail. If you are interested in sending overnight mail via a private carrier (FedEx or UPS Overnight), it is recommended that you first contact the institution to find out whether the receipt of such mail is permitted. Inmates may subscribe to and receive publications without prior approval, although the warden will reject a publication if it is determined to be detrimental to the security, good order, or discipline of the institution. Each inmate is limited to 10 magazines (no older than three months), and to the amount that can be neatly stored in his locker and/or on his shelf.

**Inmate Mail to FCI:**
INMATE NAME & REGISTER NUMBER
FCI Ray Brook
Federal Correctional Institution
P.O. Box 300
Ray Brook, NY 12977

**Visiting Hours:** Approved visitors may visit on Saturday, Sunday, and federal holidays, 8:30am-3pm. Inmates may have a maximum of 12 relatives. Up to five adult visitors can visit at any one time (children under age 16 are not limited). Attorney visits may occur during regularly scheduled visiting hours and on weekdays during regular business hours if arranged by prior appointment with unit team staff. Additional visiting information can be found on the BOP website, https://www.bop.gov/locations/institutions/rbk/.

**Lodging/Accommodations:** Should visitors be spending the night, the following is a short list of accommodations that are available near Ray Brook, New York:
| | |
|---|---|
| Adirondack Motel | 518-891-2116 |
| Mirror Lake Inn | 518-523-2544 |
| Best Western Mountain Lake Inn | 518-891-1970 |
| Hotel Saranac | 518-891-6900 |

**Directions to Facility:** <u>From North/South of Ray Brook</u>: Take I-87 to Exit 30 towards Route 73. Turn left onto US-9, then a slight left onto Route 73 N for 26 miles. Take a slight left onto Old Military Rd/CD-35, then left onto Route 86. Follow Route 86 to New York State Troopers Barracks (Troop B), which is located on the route, directly from the left turn onto Old Ray Brook Road.

<u>From West of Ray Brook:</u> Take I-90 E toward I-290. Merge onto I-81 N via Exit 36 toward Syracuse Airport/Watertown. Take the Arsenal St/Route 3 exit, Exit 45, toward Sackets Harbor/Downtown. Turn right onto Route 3 N, and follow it until it turns into River Street. Turn right onto Lake Flower Ave./Route 86 and follow it to the Princess Pine Floral Shop. Take immediate right onto Old Ray Brook Road.

<u>From East of Ray Brook:</u> Take Route 73 N to Old Military Rd/CD-35, then turn left onto Route 86. Follow Route 86 to New York State Troopers Barracks (Troop B), which is located on the route, directly from the left turn onto Old Ray Brook Road.

## §14:28  FCI SCHUYKILL

FCI Schuylkill
Federal Correctional Institution
Interstate 81 & 901 West
Minersville, PA 17954
SHC/ExecAssistant@bop.gov
570-544-7100
Fax: 570-544-7224

**Location:** Located in north-central Schuylkill County, 15 miles northwest of Pottsville, 46 miles north of Harrisburg, and 175 miles north of Washington, D.C. West of Interstate 81, off State Hwy 901. The area is served by the Harrisburg Airport, Amtrak, and commercial bus lines.

**History:** Opened in 1991, FCI Schuylkill houses male offenders primarily from the northeastern United States. A pre-trial detention unit was opened in 1992. Opened in 1991, the satellite camp houses minimum-security male offenders who provide services for the main institution.

**Judicial District:** Middle District of Pennsylvania.

**Security Level:** FCI is a medium-security facility housing male offenders. An adjacent minimum-security satellite prison camp houses male offenders.

**Population:** As of 6/19/2017, the FCI inmate population is 1,143, and the camp population is 235. Weekly population figures are available on the BOP website at www.bop.gov, https://www.bop.gov/locations/institutions/sch/.

**Education:** The FCI and the camp offer GED, ESL, adult education, and correspondence courses. Inmates who have a verified high school diploma or GED can enroll in vocational training in carpentry, horticulture, and culinary arts.

**Vocational/Apprenticeship:** The FCI does not offer advanced occupational education programs. The FCI offers vocational training in horticulture, carpentry, and culinary arts, while the camp offers vocational training in horticulture. The FCI offers a cook apprenticeship program.

**Library:** The main institution's law library hours are: Monday through Thursday, 7:30am-10:15am, 11:30am-3:30pm, and 5:30pm-8:30pm; Friday, 7:30am-10:15am and 11:30am-3:30pm; and weekends and holidays, 7am-3:30pm. The law library is closed on Thanksgiving and Christmas. The camp's law library is open daily, including holidays, 10am-11:30pm. Typewriters and a copier are available. An inmate law library clerk is available for assistance in legal research. Video cassette players are available to inmates in the leisure library. The leisure library is open Monday through Thursday, 7:30am-10:15am, 11:30am-3:30pm, and 5:30pm-8:30pm; Friday, 7:30am-10:15am and 11:30am-3:30pm; and weekends and holidays, 7am-3:30pm (closed Thanksgiving and Christmas Day). The leisure/law library at the camp is open daily.

**UNICOR:** A furniture factory employs approximately 252 inmates. The camp employs about 20-30 inmates. There is a significant waiting list to be employed through UNICOR.

**Counseling/Rehab Services:** The FCI and the camp offer a non-residential drug treatment program, a drug education program, Alcoholics Anonymous,

Narcotics Anonymous, and self-image groups. Referrals are given for the off-site Residential Drug Abuse Program. The main institution is staffed by two full-time psychologists, five drug abuse treatment specialists, and one psychology technician. The psychological services department is open weekdays, 7:30am-4pm. A contract psychiatrist provides psychiatric outpatient care.

**Health Services:** The main institution is staffed by two physicians, six physician assistants, one dentist, one optometrist, and one pharmacist. The FCI and the camp provide outpatient care. Medication line is available four times daily on the weekdays, and three times daily on weekends/holidays. Sick call sign-up is available Monday, Tuesday, Thursday, and Friday, 6:30am-7am. FCI pill line hours: Monday through Friday, 6:30am-7am, 11:30am-12:15pm, and 8pm-8:30pm; weekends and holidays, 7am-7:30am and 8pm-8:30pm. Camp pill line hours: Monday through Friday, 6:30am-7am, 3pm-3:15pm, and 7pm-7:20pm; weekends and holidays, 8:15am-8:30am, 3pm-3:15pm, and 7pm-7:20pm. On-site medical coverage is provided 16 hours a day, 6am-10pm, with medical staff on call during the remaining eight hours per day. Inmates under the age of 50 may request a physical examination every three years (in the camp, every two years), while those over the age of 50 may request one annually.

**Housing:** Inmates at the FCI are housed in two-man cells. Inmates at the camp are housed in open bay dormitories in two-man cubicles. The television rooms at the camp allow viewing 24 hours on the weekends and until 11pm on weekdays.

**Fitness/Recreation:** The FPC recreation area encompasses indoor and outdoor recreational opportunities with a gymnasium, outside recreation yard, and a leisure center. The outdoor recreation area includes a weight pile, basketball, soccer, flag football, volleyball, softball, indoor floor hockey, racquetball, handball, bocce ball, wiffle ball and horseshoes. Physical fitness and health educations are available. The indoor recreation area offers hobby craft, a weight room, a music room and game room with various table games. The hobby craft center offers leather craft and ceramics.

**Religious Services:** The main institution is staffed by full-time chaplains. Contract rabbi and imam services are available. Special religious diets, holiday observances and other worship activities are coordinated through the chaplain's office. A community of volunteers provide services for most faiths. Inmates of all faiths and creeds may apply for participation in the faith-based 6-month Threshold program, or the 18-month Life Connections program (the latter requires transfer to another institution).

**Commissary:** The commissary has regular sale hours Monday through Thursday, 11am-12:30pm and in the evening after the 4pm count. Inmates are assigned to shop one day per week, according to the last two digits of the first five digits of an inmate's registration number. The Bureau of Prisons currently sets a monthly spending limit of $360.

**Telephone Policy:** Inmates at the FCI and the camp dial direct using the Inmate Telephone System (ITS). The following are standard features of ITS: (1) inmate calls automatically terminate after 15 minutes; (2) an inmate's calling list is limited to 30 callers; and (3) calls are charged to an inmate's debit card. It takes approximately two to three days for inmates to add phone numbers to their caller-approved list. Inmates are limited to no more than five calls per day, and a limit of up to 300 minutes per month. There will be a minimum of one hour between calls so all inmates may have an opportunity to use the telephones. Telephones are located in the housing units and are available daily. Two unit telephones will be turned on at 6am and remain on until 10:30pm (11:30pm at the camp). One additional phone in each unit is on from 6am-7:30am, 10:30am-12:30pm and from 4pm-10:30pm.

**Inmate Mail:** The FCI and the camp accept mail from the U.S. Postal Service via First-Class, U.S. Priority, and Express mail. For those interested in sending overnight mail via a private carrier (FedEx or UPS Overnight), it is recommended that you first contact the institution to find out whether the receipt of such mail is permitted. Inmates may subscribe to and receive publications without prior approval, although the warden will reject a publication if it is determined to be detrimental to the security, good order, or discipline of the institution. All publications must be received directly from the publisher, bookstore or book club. Each inmate is limited to 25 letters, five books, 25 loose photographs, six magazines, and three newspapers, which can be stored in the locker provided in each cell.

**Inmate Mail to FCI:**
INMATE NAME & REGISTER NUMBER
FCI Schuylkill
Federal Correctional Institution
P.O. Box 759
Minersville, PA 17954

**Inmate Mail to Camp:**
INMATE NAME & REGISTER NUMBER
FCI Schuylkill
Federal Correctional Institution
Satellite Camp
P.O. Box 670
Minersville, PA 17954

**Visiting Hours:** Approved visitors may visit the FCI and camp Thursday through Sunday and federal holidays from 8:30am-3pm. Inmates at the FCI are given eight visiting points per month, with one point deducted for each weekday visit and two points deducted for weekend and holidays visits. Inmates at the camp have eight visiting points per month and are limited to four social visits per month, since two points are deducted for weekday and weekend visits. No more than six visitors, including children, may visit at any one time, and no more than four visitors may be adults. An inmate may have up to 10 relatives and/or friends on his visiting list, in addition to immediate family members. Attorney visits should be during regular visiting hours and do not take away from visiting points. Additional visiting information can be found on the BOP website, www. bop.gov, https://www.bop.gov/locations/institutions/sch/.

**Lodging/Accommodations:** Should visitors be spending the night, the following is a short list of accommodations that are available in the Minersville, Pennsylvania area:

| | |
|---|---|
| Hampton Inn Pine Grove | 570-345-4505 |
| Econo Lodge Frackville | 570-874-3838 |
| Econo Lodge Pine Grove | 570-345-4099 |
| Ramada Pottsville | 570-622-4600 |

**Directions to Facility:** From New York: Take I-78 W to PA-61 N, then I-81 S. Take I-81 S to Minersville Exit (116). Turn right, then right again onto Institution Road after approximately 1/4 of a mile.

From Philadelphia: Take I-76 towards Valley Forge, then I-476 N via Exit 331B toward Plymouth Meeting (toll road). From I-476 N, merge onto 22 W via Exit 56. From 22 W, take Exit 29B toward Pottsville to PA-61. Take PA-61 N to I-81 S. Take I-81 S to Minersville Exit (116). Turn right, then right again onto Institution Road after approximately 1/4 of a mile.

From Baltimore/Washington D.C.: Take I-83 N towards York to I-81 N. Take I-81 N to Minersville Exit (116). Turn right, then right again onto Institution Road after approximately 1/4 of a mile.

(This page intentionally left blank.)

# CHAPTER 15

# THE SOUTH CENTRAL REGION

(This page intentionally left blank.)

## Central Office

Central Office
Federal Bureau of Prisons
320 First St., NW
Washington, DC 20534
Phone: 202-307-3198

## South Central Regional Office

South Central Regional Office
Federal Bureau of Prisons
4211 Cedar Springs Rd
Dallas, TX 75219
Phone: 214-224-3389

## §15:10   FCI BASTROP

FCI Bastrop
Federal Correctional Institution
1341 Highway 95 North
Bastrop, TX 78602
BAS/ExecAssistant@bop.gov
512-321-3903
Fax: 512-304-0117

**Location:** The institution is located 30 miles Southeast of Austin, eight miles south of Elgin, Highway 95 and eight miles north of Bastrop. Off of Highway 95. The area is served by Austin Municipal Airport (27 miles from the facility).

**History:** Opened in 1979, FCI Bastrop houses male offenders of all ages primarily from the south central United States.

**Judicial District:** Western District of Texas.

**Security Level:** It is a low-security facility and a minimum-security satellite camp.

**Population:** As of 6/19/2017, the FCI inmate population is 1,203, and the camp population is 195. Weekly population figures are available on the BOP website at www.bop.gov, https://www.bop.gov/locations/institutions/bas/.

**Education:** The FCI and the camp offer GED, ESL, SLN, and Mexican Literacy classes. Post-secondary education programs are available through correspondence courses. Adult Continuing Education courses include typing, financial planning, consumer education and refresher training in basic skills.

**Vocational/Apprenticeship:** FCI offers advanced occupational education programs in consumer electronic repair and computer applications. Vocational training: building trades, and landscape management. Apprentice training in building maintenance, baker, cook, carpenter, dental assistant, electrical, heating and air conditioning, painter, plumber, quality control technician, stationary engineer, and welding. The camp does not offer vocational and apprenticeship training programs.

**Library:** The inmate law library is available Monday through Friday from 7:30am-8pm; Saturday 7:30am-3:45pm. For inmates who must meet an imminent court deadline, special allowance can be requested for research and document preparation. Inmates must purchase copy cards in the commissary to use the copier in the library. Inmates who lack funds for the card may request unit staff to have the cost waived. Typewriters and a copier are available to inmates for the preparation of legal documents. Video cassette recorders and audio cassette players are available.

**UNICOR:** The UNICOR Factory at FCI Bastrop retrofits mission-ready vehicles for other government agencies.

**Counseling/Rehab Services:** FCI Bastrop offers a 500-hour residential drug abuse treatment program (RDAP). The program is nine to 11 months in length. In addition, the FCI and the camp offer a non-residential drug treatment program, a drug education program, Alcoholics Anonymous and Narcotics Anonymous groups, and other voluntary self-help groups. Inmates who participate in the residential program are housed together in a separate unit of the prison that is reserved for drug treatment. The residential program provides intensive half-day programming five days a week. Upon RDAP completion, aftercare treatment services are provided to the inmate while he or she is in the general population, and later at the Residential Reentry Center. Inmates have access to a psychologist who provides counseling and other mental health services. Each psychologist has an office inside the institution, and at the satellite camp, where he or she can be easily reached by inmates to help develop ongoing counseling programs, or for personal crisis intervention. Individual and group therapy are available along with a variety of substance abuse programs. There is one contract psychiatrist available by referral from the psychologist.

**Health Services:** The Health Services Department consists of a clinical director, staff physician, a dental staff, several physician assistants, a health services administrator, a pharmacist and other specialty positions, which include contractors. Sick call sign-up at the FCI is 6:30am-7am Monday, Tuesday, Thursday, and Friday (except federal holidays). Inmates at the satellite camp fill out a sick call sign-up sheet the evening before the above mentioned days for sick call. Sick call at the camp begins at 6:30am. Requests for dental appointments may be made at 7:45am-8am on Monday, Tuesday, Thursday and Friday. Pill line is held four times daily, weekdays at 6:15am or weekends at 7am, 11:30am, 3:30pm, and 8pm. Physician assistants provide coverage from 5:30am-10pm during weekdays and 6am-10pm weekends and federal holidays. Medical staff members are on call 24 hours a day. Local hospitals are 20 minutes away.

**Housing:** Inmates at the FCI are housed in dormitories in two-man rooms. There are four general housing units and one DAP housing unit. Inmates at the camp are housed in "open bay" dormitories.

**Fitness/Recreation:** The wellness/fitness program consists of instruction on nutrition, aerobic exercise, fitness training and flexibility exercises, spinning program, fat burn, walking program, and abs program. Team-oriented sports such as soccer, volleyball, softball, basketball, and indoor soccer are provided on a seasonal basis. Additional information will be posted on recreation bulletin boards in each unit. Competitive sports are provided year-round including billiards, bocce ball, ping-pong, handball, horseshoes and racquetball. Non-competitive sports are provided year-round including pinochle, spades, chess, checkers, dominoes, Frisbee, walking, jogging, jump rope, life cycle, stair climber, stair-stepper and cardiovascular stations. The gym is open Monday through

Friday, 11:30am-8:30pm; Saturday, Sunday and holidays, 7:30-8:30pm. The weight area and recreation yard are available 8am-8pm everyday. The camp's fitness area is available 7:30-8:30pm every day. The hobby craft program includes beading, braiding, stick art, pencil art and basic leather. Hobby craft hours: Monday through Friday, 12:30pm-8pm; Saturday, Sunday and holidays, 7:30am-8pm. The camp's hobby craft shop hours are 12:30pm-8pm every day. Music instruments are also available in the recreation area.

**Religious Services:** Institution chaplains provide pastoral care to inmates. Chaplains are available to assist the inmate with any pastoral concern he may have. This is usually thought to be with reference to the beliefs and practices of the inmate's religion. However, beyond scheduling religious activities, chaplains are available for consultation. The chaplains would like inmates to feel free to approach them at any time. All religious activities are open to any inmate in the general population.

The main institution is staffed by two full-time chaplains (one Protestant and one Catholic). Contract rabbi and imam services are available. A sweat lodge for Native-American services is also available. Community volunteers also assist with providing services for most faiths. Religious literature and materials (audiotapes, videotapes, etc.) are available.

**Commissary:** Inmates are assigned two shopping days per week and have a spending limit of $180 bi-weekly.

**Telephone Policy:** Inmates at the FCI and the camp may place either collect calls or dial direct using the Inmate Telephone System (ITS). The following are standard features of ITS: (1) inmate calls automatically terminate after 15 minutes; (2) an inmate's calling list is limited to 30 callers; and (3) calls are charged to an inmate's debit card. There is a 45-minute interval between each completed call. Each inmate gets 300 calling minutes per month.

**Inmate Mail:** First-Class mail is distributed Monday through Friday (except holidays). All inmate packages received at the institution must have prior authorization. The FCI and the camp accept mail from the U.S. Postal Service via First-Class, U.S. Priority, and Express Mail. For those interested in sending overnight mail via a private carrier (FedEx or UPS Overnight), it is recommended that you first contact the institution to find out whether the receipt of such mail is permitted. Inmates may subscribe to and receive publications without prior approval. Softcover publications may come from any source, but hardcover publications may only come from a publisher, bookstore or book club.

**Inmate Mail to FCI:**
    INMATE NAME & REGISTER NUMBER
    FCI Bastrop
    Federal Correctional Institute
    P.O. Box 1010
    Bastrop, TX 78602

**Inmate Mail to Camp:**
INMATE NAME & REGISTER NUMBER
FCI Bastrop
Federal Correctional Institution
Satellite Camp
P.O. Box 629
Bastrop, TX 78602

**Visiting Hours: Notice:** As of June 2017, all visiting at this facility has been suspended indefinitely. This policy may have changed by the time you read this entry.

Normally, approved visitors may visit inmates at the FCI on Friday, Saturday, Sunday, and federal holidays from 8am-3pm. The camp is open for visitation on Saturday, Sunday and federal holidays, 8am-3pm. Inmates at the FCI are given 32 visiting points per month, with one point deducted for each hour of visiting on weekdays, and two points deducted for each hour of visiting on weekends and holidays. The camp does not use a point system. No more than five persons, including children, can visit at any one time. Attorneys should visit during regular visiting hours, and must make special arrangements for visits at other times. Additional visiting information can be found at https://www.bop.gov/locations/institutions/bas/.

**Lodging/Accommodations:** Should visitors be spending the night, the following is a short list of accommodations that are available in Bastrop, Texas:

| | |
|---|---|
| Bastrop Inn Motel | 512-321-3949 |
| Days Inn Bastrop | 512-321-1157 |
| Holiday Inn Express Hotel & Suites Bastrop | 512-321-1900 |
| Quality Inn | 512-321-3303 |
| Super 8 | 512-321-6000 |

## §15:11   USP BEAUMONT

USP Beaumont
U.S. Penitentiary Beaumont
6200 Knauth Road
Beaumont, TX 77705
BMP/ExecAssistant@bop.gov
409-727-8188
Fax: 409-626-3700

**Location:** USP Beaumont is located approximately 35 miles from the Gulf of Mexico; 100 miles east of Houston; and 268 miles west of New Orleans, Louisiana. Take Highway 69 North from Port Arthur (south from Beaumont). Get off on the Florida exit, then five miles to West Port Arthur Road. The area is served by airports in Houston and Beaumont, Amtrak, and commercial bus lines.

**History:** Opened in 1996, the USP is part of a Federal Correctional Complex (FCC) that also includes a low-security FCI with a satellite minimum-security camp, and a medium-security FCI. The FCC involves shared administrative services and staff.

**Judicial District:** Eastern District of Texas.

**Security Level:** High-security facility housing male inmates; also has a satellite camp that houses minimum-security male inmates.

**Population:** As of 6/20/2017, the USP inmate population is 1,526, and the camp population is 586. Weekly population figures are available on the BOP website at www.bop.gov, https://www.bop.gov/locations/institutions/bmp/.

**Education:** The USP and the camp offer GED, ESL, adult continuing education and correspondence courses.

**Vocational/Apprenticeship:** USP offers advanced occupational education in major appliance repair, basic diesel engine repair, advanced diesel mechanics, building trades, micro-computer application, advanced micro-computer applications, industrial sewing, commercial driver's license (CDL), culinary arts, HVAC, business education, and intro to plastic VT. USP offers apprenticeship in carpentry, electrical, painting, teacher's aide, plumbing and HVAC.

**Library:** The law library is open Monday through Friday 8am-9pm, Saturday and Sunday 8am-3:30pm, and closed on holidays. Electric typewriters and a copier are available to inmates for the preparation of legal documents. Inmates must purchase their own typewriter ribbons. A small leisure library is available, and an inter-library loan program is also available. Cassette players, video monitors, and computer assisted programs are also available.

**UNICOR:** A textile factory employs some inmates. There is a waiting list to be employed by UNICOR.

**Counseling/Rehab Services:** Psychology staff is available to provide counseling and other services to inmates. Each newly committed inmate, whose offense is directly attributable to drugs or alcohol abuse or who receives a court recommendation for drug programming, will be required to attend a 40-hour drug education program. Alcoholics Anonymous, self-image groups and other voluntary groups are available. The USP and the camp offer a non-residential drug treatment program, drug education program, and Alcoholics Anonymous and Narcotics Anonymous groups. The camp offers a 500-hour Residential Drug Abuse Program (RDAP). The RDAP is nine months in length.

**Health Services:** FCC Beaumont medical services are provided by League Medical Concepts (LMC). The LMC managed care contract operates like an

HMO in the community. Medical services are provided by LMC physicians, mid-level practitioners, nurses, and other health care ancillary staff. Services that are not covered through LMC are those determined to be medically acceptable, but not medically necessary. Specialty consultations are available as required. FCC Beaumont offers optometry services through LMC, and will furnish glasses every two years if there has been a significant change in visual acuity. Comprehensive dental care is also available. Sick call is available each morning before the morning meal on Monday, Tuesday, Thursday, and Friday (except holidays). Medical care is available 24 hours a day, seven days a week.

**Housing:** The penitentiary consists of six housing units. Inmates are housed in two-man cells. Unit television viewing is permitted 6am-10pm at the USP. At the camp, television is permitted until 12midnight on weekends.

**Fitness/Recreation:** The recreation department offers stationary bicycles, stair-steppers, rowing machines, a music room, pool tables, and ping-pong tables. There are also physical fitness and weight reduction programs, as well as intramural team sports such as softball, basketball, and volleyball. The recreation department is open daily until 8:30pm. The hobby craft center offers leather craft and art.

**Religious Services:** Staff chaplains as well as community volunteers provide assistance by offering services for various faiths. A wide range of religious programs is available. Religious diets, holiday observances, and other worship activities are coordinated through the chaplain's office.

**Commissary:** The commissary at the USP is open Monday through Friday. Inmates are assigned a shopping day based on the 4th and 5th digits of their register number. Inmates may shop in the morning or during the noon sales of their assigned shopping day. The monthly commissary spending limit is $360.

**Telephone Policy:** Inmates dial direct using the Inmate Telephone System (ITS). The following are standard features of ITS: (1) inmate calls automatically terminate after 15 minutes; (2) an inmate's calling list is limited to 30 callers; and (3) calls are charged to an inmate's debit card. Inmates are limited to 300 minutes of telephone calls per month. Each inmate prepares a list of up to 30 telephone numbers during their orientation. It takes approximately two to five days for inmates to add phone numbers to their caller-approved list. Telephones are located in the housing units of both institutions.

**Inmate Mail:** The FCI and the camp accept mail from the U.S. Postal Service via First Class, U.S. Priority, and Express Mail. For those interested in sending overnight mail via a private carrier (FedEx or UPS Overnight), it is recommended that you first contact the institution to find out whether the receipt of such mail is permitted. Inmates are permitted to subscribe to publications without prior approval, although the warden will reject publications if they are determined to be detrimental to the security, good order, or discipline of the institution. All publications must come directly from the publisher, bookstore, or book club.

**Inmate Mail to USP:**
INMATE NAME & REGISTER NUMBER
USP Beaumont
U.S. Penitentiary
P.O. Box 26030
Beaumont, TX 77720

**Inmate Mail to Camp:**
INMATE NAME & REGISTER NUMBER TO USP
USP Beaumont
U.S. Penitentiary
Satellite Camp
P.O. Box 26010
Beaumont, TX 77720

**Visiting Hours:** Approved visitors may visit the USP on Friday, 5pm-8pm, and on Saturday, Sunday and federal holidays, 8:30am-3pm. Visitors may visit the camp on Saturday, Sunday and federal holidays, 8:30am-3pm. Visits on Saturdays and Sundays is based on an odd/even schedule (inmates with odd register numbers will have visits on odd dates, and inmates with even register numbers will have visits on even dates). A limit of five visitors, including children, are permitted to visit inmates at one time. Infants who are carried by an adult visitor are not included in the total count. Inmates are given 12 visiting points per month, with one point deducted for a visit on Friday, and two points deducted for weekend or holiday visits. Attorney visits are during regular visiting hours and do not count towards the inmates' visiting points. Additional visiting information can be found on the BOP website, www.bop.gov, https://www.bop.gov/locations/institutions/bmp/.

**Lodging/Accommodations:** Should visitors be spending the night, the following is a short list of accommodations that are available near Beaumont, Texas:

| | |
|---|---|
| Hampton Inn & Suites Port Arthur | 409-722-6999 |
| Holiday Inn Express Hotel & Suites Port Arthur | 409-853-4114 |
| La Quinta Inn & Suites Port Arthur | 409-722-8383 |
| Baymond Inn and Suites Port Arthur | 409-962-9858 |
| Super 8 Port Arthur/Nederland | 409-722-1012 |

## §15:12 FCI BEAUMONT (MEDIUM AND LOW)

FCI Beaumont—Medium
Federal Correctional Institution
5830 Knauth Road
Beaumont, TX 77705
BML/ExecAssistant@bop.gov
409-727-0101
Fax: 409-720-5000

FCI Beaumont—Low
Federal Correctional Institution Low
5830 Knauth Road
Beaumont, TX 77705
BMM/ExecAssistant@bop.gov
409-727-8172
Fax: 409-626-3500

**Location:** See entry for §15:11 USP Beaumont.

**History:** Opened in 1996, the USP is part of a Federal Correctional Complex (FCC) which also includes a high-security USP. The FCC involves shared administrative services and staff.

**Judicial District:** Eastern District of Texas.

**Security Level:** Medium-security facility housing males; also a low-security facility housing males (adjacent to the minimum/male camp).

**Population:** As of 6/20/2014, the FCI Medium inmate population is 1,492, and the FCI Low inmate population is 1,696. Weekly population figures are available at www.bop.gov.

**Education:** The low- and medium-security institutions offer GED, ESL, adult continuing education, and college correspondence courses.

**Vocational/Apprenticeship:** Medium facility offers advanced occupational education in the following areas: microcomputer applications, building trades, and plastics. Vocational training: major appliance repair. Apprenticeships: carpenter, electrician, painter, teacher aide, plumber. FCC Low offers basic diesel repair, advanced diesel repair, commercial driver's license, and microcomputer applications. Vocational training: major appliance repair, building trades, HVAC. Apprenticeship program offered include electrician, HVAC, landscaper, materials handler coordinator, plumbing, painter, and maintenance carpenter.

**Library:** The low-security institution's law library is open Monday through Friday, 7:30am-8:45pm; Saturday and Sunday, 7:30am-4pm; closed on holidays. Electric typewriters are available. A copier is also available. Copies are 20 cents and charged to an inmate's debit card. The leisure library participates in an inter-library loan program. VCRs and audio cassette players are available to inmates in the leisure library. The medium-security institution's law library contains a variety of legal reference materials for use in preparing legal papers.

**UNICOR:** Engine rebuilding/remanufacturing employs approximately 300 inmates. UNICOR inmates are required to complete the basic diesel engine repair vocational training class prior to UNICOR. If there are no current VT graduates and a need for workers exists, UNICOR will hire from the regular and prior waiting list on a 50/50 basis, and will then place those inmates in the next available class. Inmates who are employed at UNICOR also receive holiday, vacation and longevity benefits. A textile factory employs inmates from both USP and FCI.

**Counseling/Rehab Services:** Alcoholics Anonymous, Narcotics Anonymous and self-image groups are available to inmates. Weekly non-residential drug counseling groups are open to anyone. The low-security institution has a 500-hour Residential Drug Abuse Program (RDAP). Six-week and 12-week courses are available in written communications, goal setting and time management, basic and advanced career counseling, anger management, basic and advanced stress management. transitional services, 40-hour drug education, living free, verbal communications, psychological wellness, victim empathy, non-residential drug program, commitment to change, fathering groups, and breaking barriers. Spanish groups available. Psychology staff is available to provide counseling and other services to inmates. Each newly committed inmate whose offense is directly attributable to drugs or alcohol abuse, or who receives a court recommendation for drug programming, will be required to attend a 40-hour drug education program.

**Health Services:** FCC Beaumont medical services are provided by League Medical Concepts (LMC). The LMC managed care contract operates like an HMO in the community. Medical services are provided by LMC physicians, mid-level practitioners, nurses, and other health care ancillary staff. Services that are not covered through LMC are those determined to be medically acceptable, but not medically necessary. Specialty consultations are available as required. FCC Beaumont offers optometry services through LMC, and will furnish glasses every two years if there has been a significant change in visual acuity. Comprehensive dental care is also available. Sick call is available each morning before the morning meal on Monday, Tuesday, Thursday, and Friday (except holidays). Medical care is available 24 hours a day, seven days a week. Both FCIs and the camp have sick call sign-up four days a week. Any inmate in the general population desiring medical attention will be responsible for making his own sick call appointment. Sick call (triage) opens each morning prior to the morning meal and will remain open for at least one hour on Monday, Tuesday, Thursday, and Friday—except on holidays—at the Health Services Unit (HSU). Inmates with acute dental problems such as severe dental pain and/or swelling should sign up for dental sick call at the same time as regular sick call. The pill line will be open during established guides or as announced, seven days a week, unless specifically directed.

**Housing:** Inmates are housed in dormitories in two-man and three-man cells. There are four televisions located in each living unit of the low-security facility. Inmates at the camp are housed in dormitories. Television viewing is permitted weekdays from 6am-11pm, and until 12midnight on Fridays and Saturdays.

**Fitness/Recreation:** Recreation activities of both facilities include: arts and crafts, intramural team sports such as softball, basketball, and volleyball, physical fitness and weight reduction programs. The passive recreation building has pool tables, ping-pong tables, television viewing areas, musical equipment, hobby craft opportunities (leather work, art, etc.) and various games. Recreation equipment and games can be checked out with a commissary card. Various organized activities and programs are offered by the Recreation Department. Activity schedules will be distributed to the inmate population indicating which activities are available during the various seasons.

**Religious Services:** Staff chaplains of specific faiths are available to inmates, as well as contract and volunteer representatives of other faiths. Special religious diets, holiday observances and other worship activities are coordinated through the chaplain's office. FCC Beaumont (Low) offers a comprehensive Religious Services Program. Full time staff chaplains coordinate a wide range of religious activities for all faith groups among the inmates. Contract clergy and volunteers enrich the services of the different religious groups. Each religious faith celebrates a major weekly service and may hold a scriptural study or prayer session at another time during the week. FCC Beaumont (Medium) offers a wide range of religious programs to inmates. Staff chaplains of specific faiths are available, as well as contract and volunteer representatives of other faiths. Special religious diets, holiday observances, and other worship activities are coordinated through the chaplain's office. Information about these programs is available from the chaplains.

**Commissary:** The commissary at the low-security institution is open Monday through Friday from 4pm until 9pm. An inmate's specific shopping day is determined by his registration number. The commissary access time for medium-security inmates is scheduled on a rotating basis. Hours of operation are posted in the housing units. The monthly commissary spending limit is $360.

**Telephone Policy:** Inmates dial direct using the Inmate Telephone System (ITS). The following are standard features of ITS: (1) inmate calls automatically terminate after 15 minutes; (2) an inmate's calling list is limited to 30 callers;

and (3) calls are charged to an inmate's debit card. Inmates get 300 minutes of calling time per month. Telephones are available in each of the housing units for inmate use. Telephones at the Low FCI are available daily between 6am-10pm Monday-Sunday, except during count times. All inmate telephones are subject to monitoring and recording. Inmates must contact their Case Manager or Counselor to arrange an unmonitored attorney call. Inmates at the camp may use the telephone daily until 12midnight (except during count times).

**Inmate Mail:** Both institutions accept mail from the U.S. Postal Service via First-Class, U.S. Priority, and Express Mail. For those interested in sending overnight mail via a private carrier (FedEx or UPS Overnight), it is recommended that you first contact the institution to find out whether the receipt of such mail is permitted.

**Inmate Mail to Medium:**
INMATE NAME & REGISTER NUMBER
FCI Beaumont (Medium Federal Correctional Institution)
P.O. Box 26040
Beaumont, TX 77720

**Inmate Mail to Low:**
INMATE NAME & REGISTER NUMBER
FCI Beaumont Low
Federal Correctional Institution
P.O. Box 26020
Beaumont, TX 77720

**Visiting Hours:** See entry for §15:11 USP Beaumont.

**Lodging/Accommodations:** See entry for §15:11 USP Beaumont.

## §15:13  FCI BIG SPRING

FCI Big Spring
Federal Correctional Institution
1900 Simler Avenue
Big Spring, TX 79720
BIG/ExecAssistant@bop.gov
432-466-2300
Fax: 432-466-2576

**Location:** Midway between Dallas and El Paso on the southwest edge of Big Spring, at the intersection of Interstate 20 and U.S. Highway 80. The area is served by Midland Odessa Airport (50 miles from Big Spring), a small municipal airport within the Big Spring Industrial Park.

**History:** Opened in 1979 as a prison camp, FCI Big Spring is part of the former Webb Air Force Base. It was converted to a low-security facility in September 1990. It houses male offenders of all ages, primarily from Texas. Opened in 1992, the satellite camp house minimum-security male offenders.

**Judicial District:** Northern District of Texas.

**Security Level:** Low-security male inmates and has a satellite camp housing minimum-security male inmates.

**Population:** As of 6/20/2014, the FCI Low inmate population is 1,068, and the camp population is 203. Weekly population figures are available on the BOP website at https://www.bop.gov/locations/institutions/big/.

**Education:** Educational opportunities include post-secondary education, GED and ESL programs, and a wide range of occupational training programs. To enroll in a correspondence course, approval must be obtained from the supervisor of education via cop-out. Education hours in the library: Monday through Friday, 7:15am-3:30pm and 5:30pm-9:45pm; Saturday 6:30am-9:45am and 11am-3:45pm; closed Sunday.

**Vocational/Apprenticeship:** The FCI and the camp offer vocational training in 14 fields: soldering, commercial housekeeping, plumbing trades, building trades, masonry skills, electrical trades, HVAC, computer-aided drafting/graphics, computer skills (beginning and advanced), desktop publishing, green building technologies, wind technology, commercial food service, and workforce training.

**Library:** The Law Library for both the FCI and the camp is located in the east end of the Education Building. It is open Monday through Friday, 7:15am-3:30pm, and 5:30pm-8:45pm; Saturday, 6:30am-9:45am and 11am-3:45pm; closed Sundays and holidays. Typewriters and a copier are available to inmates for the preparation of legal documents. Legal reference material is available for preparation of legal documents in the law library. Inmates may copy materials necessary for their research or legal matters. A Debitec copy machine is available in the Education Department. The cost per page is 20 cents. A collection of hardcover books, paperback books, magazines, and newspapers are maintained in the leisure library. Reference books are provided for use in the leisure library only. Reserve books are available to students in particular education courses (see instructor). Interlibrary loan books are ordered through the librarian. Spanish books are available in the Spanish Library.

**UNICOR:** None.

**Counseling/Rehab Services:** Substance abuse services include: Alcoholics/ Narcotics Anonymous, drug abuse counseling, and a 40-hour drug education class provided in English and Spanish. The staff of each unit is available for informal counseling sessions, and they conduct formal group counseling activities. Mental health services include: crisis intervention, individual and group counseling, pre-release counseling and evaluation and testing. A variety of special topic groups, such as relationships, "Living Free" values development group, "Commitment to Change: Overcoming Errors in Thinking" group; "Dealing with Anger" group; stress management group, Breaking Barriers, Framework for Recovery, Living Sober, and a victim's impact group are offered by or co-sponsored by the department. The department also offers an inmate resource library of psychology and self-help related books, pamphlets and audiotapes.

**Health Services:** Medical doctors, physician assistants, a medication technician, and a dentist provide medical and dental care. A clinician assistant will issue sick call appointments at the Health Services Unit between 6am and 6:30am, each Monday, Tuesday, Thursday and Friday (except holidays). Satellite camp sick call sign-up is at the camp Health Services Unit 8am-8:30am each Monday, Tuesday, Thursday, and Friday (except holidays). FCI pill line hours: Monday through Friday 7am-7:15am, 4:30pm-4:45pm (insulin only), and 7pm-7:30pm; weekends/holidays 8am-8:15am, 4:30pm-4:45pm (insulin only), and 6:30pm-7pm. Camp pill line hours: Monday through Friday 8:30 am-8:45am, and 6pm-6:30pm; weekends/holidays 9:30am-9:45am and 5:30pm-5:45pm. Inmates under the age of 50 may request a physical examination every two years, while those over the age of 50 may request one annually.

**Housing:** Inmates at the FCI are primarily housed in two-man cells. There are 12 housing units. Inmates at the camp are housed in dormitories in two-man cubicles. There are four television rooms per housing unit. Televisions are turned off at 12 midnight on weekdays and 2am on weekends and holidays.

**Fitness/Recreation:** The recreation department offers a weight area, cardio equipment, pool and ping-pong tables, TV viewing rooms, quiet game room, and music rooms. The gym and weight pile are available on weekdays from 6am-3:30pm and 5pm-9pm; weekends and holidays, 6:30am-9:30am, 11am-3:30pm, and 5pm-9pm. The track area is open at sunrise and closes at sunset every day. The recreation center is open 12noon-3:30pm and 5pm-9pm every day. The music rooms are available by schedule, and sign-ups for individual practice times are in the Recreation Office every Saturday at 1pm. The hobby craft center offers ceramics, leather craft, puritan sticks, painting, sketching, knitting, and beadwork. The hobby craft center is open Monday through Friday, 6am-10:30am, 11am-3:15pm, and 5pm-9pm; weekends and holidays, 6:30am-9:30am, 11am-3:15pm, and 5pm-9pm. Free and machine weights, stationary bicycles, rowing machines, stair-steppers, treadmills and gravity riders are available in the gymnasium. Fitness programs include aerobics, nutrition, and time management; intramural sports offered include basketball, soccer, softball, tennis, volleyball. There are also horseshoe pits, bocce ball courts, washer courts, handball/racquetball courts, and a running track. Two movies per week are shown in the Housing Unit and recreation TV rooms.

**Religious Services:** Worship services, scripture studies, discussion groups and pastoral care are provided by two full-time staff chaplains and a number of volunteer ministers and lay persons from a variety of faith groups. In addition, periodic revivals, concerts, lectures and seminars are presented. Chaplains provide scriptures, general religious books and pamphlets, videos, and other similar literature. A small lending library and a reference library complement the books and confirm periodicals that are free to all inmates. Various kinds of greeting cards are available, as well as religious medals with chains. Religious services are available in Spanish. A community of volunteers provides services for most faiths.

**Commissary:** The commissary is open Monday through Friday, 6am-7:30am; and Monday through Tuesday, 10:30am-12noon. Inmates working in the VT programs and facilities shop on Mondays. All other inmates shop based on the fourth and fifth digits of their registration numbers. There is no special shopping. The monthly spending limit is $360 (which does not include telephone credits, nicotine patches, copy cards, copy paper, stamps, or certain over-the-counter medications).

**Telephone Policy:** Inmates at the FCI and the camp dial direct using the Inmate Telephone System (ITS). The following are standard features of ITS: (1) inmate calls automatically terminate after 15 minutes; (2) an inmate's calling list is limited to 30 callers; and (3) calls are charged to an inmate's debit card. Inmates are limited to 300 minutes per month and must wait 15 minutes between calls. The telephones at the camp are operational on a daily basis from 6am-12midnight.

**Inmate Mail:** The FCI and the camp accept mail from the U.S. Postal Service via First-Class, U.S. Priority, and Express Mail. For those interested in sending overnight mail via a private carrier (FedEx or UPS Overnight), it is recommended that you first contact the institution to find out whether the receipt of such mail is permitted. Inmates may subscribe to publications without prior approval, although the warden will reject a publication if it is determined to be detrimental to the security, good order, or discipline of the institution. Inmates may receive soft cover publications (paperback books, etc.) from any source. Newspapers and hardcover publications may be received only from a publisher, a bookstore or a book club. Each inmate is limited to up to five publications total (books, newspapers, and/or magazines). This limitation does not apply to educational material for courses or legal material for ongoing court cases, and the Unit Manager may allow more space for legal publications upon request.

**Inmate Mail to FCI:**
   INMATE NAME & REGISTER NUMBER
   FCI Big Spring
   Federal Correctional Institution

1900 Simler Avenue
Big Spring, TX 79720

**Visiting Hours:** Approved visitors may visit the FCI and the camp on Saturday, Sunday, and federal holidays from 8am-3pm. No more than five persons can visit an inmate at any one time including children. Each FCI inmate is allotted six points on the first of each month. One point will be deducted each time an inmate has a visit (not including federal holidays). FPC inmates are exempt from the point system. Attorneys should ordinarily make advance appointments for each visit. Attorneys are encouraged to visit during the regular visiting hours. However, visits from an attorney can be arranged at other times based on the circumstances of each case and available staff. Attorney visits will be subject to visual monitoring, but not audio monitoring. For information can be found at https://www.bop.gov/locations/institutions/big/.

**Lodging/Accommodations:** Should visitors be spending the night, the following is a short list of accommodations that are available in near Big Spring, Texas:

| | |
|---|---|
| Camelot Inn | 432-268-9926 |
| Comfort Inn Stanton | 432-756-1100 |
| Days Inn | 432-267-5237 |
| Holiday Inn Express | 432-263-5400 |
| Quality Inn | 432-264-7086 |

## §15:14   FPC BRYAN

FPC Bryan
Federal Prison Camp Bryan
1100 Ursuline Avenue
Bryan, TX 77803
BRY/PublicInformation@bop.gov
979-823-1879
Fax: 979-821-3316

**Location:** The FPC is located 95 miles north of Houston and 165 miles south of Dallas, in the town of Bryan at the intersection of Ursuline Avenue and 23rd Street. The area is served by the Easterwood Airport in College Station, connecting through Houston Intercontinental and Dallas-Fort Worth Airports.

**History:** Opened in 1988, FPC Bryan is a 37-acre compound housing female inmates from Texas and surrounding states.

**Judicial District:** Southern District of Texas.

**Security Level:** FPC Bryan is a minimum-security prison camp that houses female inmates.

**Population:** As of 6/20/2017, the inmate population is 893. Weekly population figures are available at https://www.bop.gov/locations/institutions/bry/.

**Education:** The camp offers ESL, GED and adult continuing education courses. Blinn College, a fully accredited junior college, offers a one-year certificate program in administrative assistant, medical transcription/coding, small business, and accounting technology.

**Vocational/Apprenticeship:** FPC offers advanced occupational education in cosmetology and horticulture, and apprenticeship programs in dental assisting.

**Library:** The leisure library contains a wide variety of reading material, which includes fiction and non-fiction books, bilingual books, magazines, newspapers, encyclopedias, and reference books. The law library contains a collection of legal reference materials mandated by Congress and monitored by the Bureau of Prisons. The law library is open for inmates to prepare legal documents and to do legal research. Inmates also have access to the Electronic Law Library (ELL). Typewriters in the law library are for legal document preparation only. Photocopy machine also available.

**UNICOR:** Currently FPC Bryan operates a federal prison industries (UNICOR) distribution center. UNICOR employs inmates in production, assembly, warehouse, and distribution of various products produced by UNICOR as well as partnership companies. The center employs approximately 283 inmates.

**Counseling/Rehab Services:** An array of therapy and psycho-educational groups are provided by psychology department staff members and contractors. Frequent group offerings deal with the following issues: managing stress, depression and anger, controlling impulses, relationships, self-improvement issues, assertiveness, and problems related to childhood sexual abuse, resolving trauma, and domestic violence. The drug abuse programs section of the psychology department offers drug education classes, Residential Drug Abuse Program (500-hour residential program nine months in length), Non-Residential Drug Abuse Treatment, and follow-up. Parenting classes include: communication skills, building self-esteem, discipline, child abuse, and childhood illness, immunization and nutrition. Normal hours of operation are Monday through Friday, 7:30am-3:30pm. A psychologist is available every day during lunch for questions and to resolve concerns.

**Health Services:** The camp is staffed by one physician, three to four physician assistants, and one dentist. The camp provides outpatient care. Local hospitals are located approximately five to ten minutes away from the institution. Inmates who wish to be seen for routine care or evaluation of a health problem must report to Health Services at 6:30am-7pm, Monday, Tuesday, Thursday and Friday for sick call. At that time, the inmate will be given an appointment slip. Any inmate with a dental emergency should report to Health Services at 6:45am, Monday, Tuesday, Thursday, and Friday. The pill line operates every day, 8am-8:30am and 3pm-3:30pm. Insulin lines are everyday at 6:10am and 2:30pm. Annual breast examination is available to all inmates. Annual breast examination and routine pregnancy screening are provided during the initial physical examination. Mammograms are suggested every three to five years for women between the age of 40 and 50, and annually for women over the age of 50. The institution does not have 24-hour health services; however, a system has been established to ensure that immediate care will be provided in emergency situations. At least one physician assistant is on call.

**Housing:** Inmates are housed in "open bay" dormitories and dormitories containing four-man to 10-man rooms. The television rooms are available for off-duty inmates Sunday throughThursday from 6am-11:30pm. On Friday, Saturday, and holidays the televisions are operational until 2am.

**Fitness/Recreation:** Outdoor recreation is open seven days a week, 6am-3:30pm and 5pm-8:30pm. Indoor recreation is open five days a week, 6:30am-3:30pm and 5pm-8:30pm. Check the schedule of exact times and days that each area is open. Outdoor activities include: softball, soccer, volleyball, jogging track and horseshoes. Pavilion activities include: basketball, ping-pong tables, weightlifting, and step aerobics. Health/fitness classes are offered for ACE credits in nutrition, women's health, anatomy, diabetes, sports injury, total fitness, AIDS awareness, disease prevention, weight management, and personal training certification. The hobby shop offers ceramics, paper jewelry making, beading, fimo clay, plastic canvas art, t-shirt painting, cross-stitching, crochet, knitting, scrapbooking, card making, and drawing.

**Religious Services:** The Religious Services Department operates a full program to respond to all spiritual and religious needs. An updated schedule with program times and chaplain schedules is available in the chapel and on chapel bulletin boards located in the unit. The camp has one full-time chaplain. Contractors and community volunteers assist in providing services for most faiths.

**Commissary:** : Commissary and validation schedules are posted on the inmate bulletin boards. Inmates may make purchases only once a week. Shopping days are determined by the last two digits of the first five numbers of her register number. The monthly commissary spending limit is currently $360.

**Telephone Policy:** Inmates can dial direct or call collect. The inmate telephone system (ITS) is utilized in the Housing Units for inmates. Telephones are available from 6am-11:30am, but use will usually be limited from 7:30am-10:30am, and 12:30pm after 4pm count. Inmates may only place calls to those on their approved telephone list. No third-party calls or credit card calls are authorized. All telephone calls are limited to 15 minutes, but should be limited further when others are waiting. Each inmate has a total of 300 calling minutes per month. Ordinarily, inmates will be allowed an extra 100 minutes per month in November and December.

**Inmate Mail:** The camp accepts mail from the U.S. Postal Service via First-Class, U.S. Priority, and Express Mail. For those interested in sending overnight mail via a private carrier (FedEx or UPS Overnight), it is recommended that you first contact the institution to find out whether the receipt of such mail is permitted. Inmates may receive soft cover publications (paperback books, etc.) from any source. Newspapers and hardcover publications may be received only from a publisher, a bookstore or a book club.

**Inmate Mail to FPC:**
INMATE NAME & REGISTER NUMBER
FPC Bryan
Federal Prison Camp
P.O. Box 2149
Bryan, TX 77805

**Visiting Hours:** Approved visitors may visit Saturday and Sunday from 8am-5pm, and on federal holidays from 8am-3pm. Attorneys must make advance arrangements to visit, and should visit during regular visiting hours. Additional visiting information can be found on the BOP website, www.bop.gov, at https://www.bop.gov/locations/institutions/bry/.

**Lodging/Accommodations:** Should visitors be spending the night, the following is a short list of accommodations that are available in Bryan, Texas:

| | |
|---|---|
| Best Western Premier Old Town Center | 979-731-5300 |
| Hampton Inn College Station | 979-846-0184 |
| Holiday Plaza Motel | 979-822-3748 |
| LaSalle Hotel | 979-822-2000 |
| Relax Inn | 979-778-1881 |

## §15:15  FMC CARSWELL

FMC Carswell
Federal Medical Center Carswell
J Street, Bldg. 3000
Fort Worth, TX 76127
CRW/ExecAssistant@bop.gov
817-782-4000
Fax: 817-782-4875

**Location:** In the northeast corner of the Naval Air Station Joint Reserve Base at Fort Worth, one mile from Highway 183 and three miles from Interstate 30. The area is served by Dallas/Fort Worth International Airport, the Fort Worth Transportation Authority, Amtrak, and commercial bus lines.

**History:** Reopened in 1994, FMC Carswell serves as a medical/psychiatric referral center for female offenders. A satellite camp provides labor support for the FMC.

**Judicial District:** Northern District of Texas.

**Security Level:** Provides specialized medical and mental health services to female offenders.

**Population:** As of 6/21/2017, the FMC inmate population is 1,201, and the camp population is 287. Weekly population figures are available on the BOP website at https://www.bop.gov/locations/institutions/crw/.

**Education:** Education programs provided to inmates include ESL, GED basic literacy, life skills, parenting classes and an apprenticeship program. Post-secondary courses are available through correspondence courses, at the inmate's expense. Parenting classes are available.

**Vocational/Apprenticeship:** FMC and the camp offer vocational training and apprenticeships, which change often.

**Library:** The law library contains a collection of legal reference materials mandated by Congress and monitored by the Bureau of Prisons. The law library is open for inmates to prepare legal documents and to do legal research. The Electronic Law Library is a search engine that contains legal reference materials from various publishers. A copying machine is available to reproduce materials needed for research. Also available on the electronic system are current Bureau of Prisons program statements. Printing legal reference materials is available for 15 cent a page when using the Electronic Law Library system. The leisure library contains a wide variety of reading material, including fiction and non-fiction books, magazines, newspapers, encyclopedias, reference books, and bilingual reading material. Reading books may be checked out with the clerks on duty. The FMC's library is open weekdays, evenings and weekends. The camp's law/leisure library provides similar services.

**UNICOR:** None.

**Counseling/Rehab Services:** Psychology Services has organized its program for female offenders into four tracks as a means of efficiently offering a wide variety of self-improvement and recovery opportunities. The track model is similar to the organization of academic course work in a college setting. Inmates, in consultation with their unit team or on referral from mental health Staff, may choose an organized series of group experiences which address their primary relevant issues. There are four tracks: Abuse Recovery; Addictions; Values; and Wellness. Each track consists of four core groups and two "electives." The core groups are each offered several times a year and the electives allow inmates to individualize their experience. The track system provides direction and a clear sense of accomplishment, as well as measurable goals. Once an inmate has completed a track, she may choose another. Inmates interested in participating in any of the tracks should send a cop-out to the psychology department referencing the title of the track. Outpatient psychiatric services are also available. The institution also offers a 500-hour residential drug abuse treatment program (RDAP).

**Health Services:** The FMC is staffed by physicians, physician assistants, nurses, psychiatrists, social workers, and dentists specifically to meet the needs of female inmates who require placement in this medical facility. The FMC consists of 264 medical, surgical, and chronic care beds, which includes a 41-bed psychiatric unit. All inmates, including camp inmates, can have a yearly pap smear and breast examination. The pharmacy operates three pill lines daily for the administration of restricted medications, and two pill lines for the dispensing of medications for self-administration. Patients who have chronic medical problems will be monitored and followed up in a chronic care specialty clinic at least every 90 days. More frequent evaluations can be established, based on clinical findings by medical staff as often as needed.

**Housing:** Inmates at the FMC are housed in individual rooms, two, four and five-man rooms, open dormitories. Inmates at the camp are housed in dormitories containing two-man cubicles. The televisions at the camp are operational until 11:30pm on weekdays. On Fridays, Saturdays, and holidays the televisions are operational until 2am.

**Fitness/Recreation:** The Recreation Department offers leisure activities such as bingo, organized and informal sports, social activities, arts and hobby crafts, physical fitness and aerobic activities; also sponsors special programs and holiday activities such as tournaments, music programs, and talent shows. Other general interest courses include health education, fitness, and wellness.

**Religious Services:** The FMC has staff chaplains, contract clergy and community volunteers to provide services. Chaplains are available for pastoral counseling. Participation in religious programs is voluntary. There are regular organized religious services in most major faiths. The schedule of regular religious activities is posted on unit bulletin boards and outside the entrance to the chapel. The department offers free religious readings and audio/visual library for inmate use.

**Commissary:** The commissary is open Monday through Friday; shopping days and times are determined by the inmate's registration number. All hospital and general population inmates are included in this schedule. The monthly commissary spending limit is currently $360.

**Telephone Policy:** Inmates at the FMC and the camp may either call collect or dial direct using the Inmate Telephone System (ITS). The following are standard features of ITS: (1) inmate calls automatically terminate after 15 minutes; (2) an inmate's calling list is limited to 30 callers; and (3) calls are charged to an inmate's debit card. Inmates are allowed a total of 300 minutes per month. There is a delay of 30 minutes between each telephone call. Telephones are located in the housing units at both the FMC and the camp and are available for use 6am-11:30pm (except during count times).

**Inmate Mail:** The camp accepts mail from the U.S. Postal Service via First-Class, U.S. Priority, and Express Mail. For those interested in sending overnight mail via a private carrier (FedEx or UPS Overnight), it is recommended that you first contact the institution to find out whether the receipt of such mail is permitted. All newspapers must be received directly from the publisher. First class letters and publications are distributed Monday through Friday (excluding holidays) immediately after the 4pm count. Inmates are required to attend mail call. Inmates may only subscribe to publications authorized by the institution. The newspaper must be of pulp-like paper stock, and/or sectioned and folded. Hard-cover books must also be received directly from the publisher, a book club, or a bookstore. Magazines must come directly from the publishers via subscriptions. Magazines may be retained for three months from the date of issue, and newspapers may be retained for seven days from the date of issue. Inmates are allowed a total of 10 personally owned books, excluding books directly relating to their educational/vocational training courses.

**Inmate Mail to FMC:**
INMATE NAME & REGISTER NUMBER
FMC Carswell
Federal Medical Center
P.O. Box 27137
Fort Worth, TX 76127

**Inmate Mail to Camp:**
INMATE NAME & REGISTER NUMBER
FMC Carswell
Federal Medical Center
Satellite Camp
P.O. Box 27137
Fort Worth, TX 76127

**Visiting Hours:** Approved visitors may visit the FMC and the camp Saturday, Sunday and federal holidays from 8am-3pm. A maximum of six adult visitors and unlimited children is allowed per inmate. Attorneys should request visits in writing in advance; however, a phone call or fax will suffice in unusual situations. Attorneys should visit during regular visiting hours. Additional visiting information can be found on the BOP website, www.bop.gov, at https://www.bop.gov/locations/institutions/crw/.

**Lodging/Accommodations:** Should visitors be spending the night, the following is a short list of accommodations that are available in Fort Worth, Texas:

| America's Best Value Inn Fort Worth | 817-244-9446 |
| Best Western Lake Worth | 817-238-1199 |
| Hampton Inn & Suites Fort Worth West I-30 | 817-732-8585 |
| Holiday Inn Express Hotel & Suites Fort Worth | 817-234-9033 |

## §15:16   FCI EL RENO

FCI El Reno
Federal Correctional Institution
4205 Highway 66 West
El Reno, OK 73036
ERE/ExecAssistant@bop.gov
405-262-4875
Fax: 405-319-7626

**Location:** 30 miles west of Oklahoma City, off Interstate 40 (Country Club Exit, two miles to Highway 66 West north to Sunset Drive, then west for two miles). The area is served by Will Rogers World Airport in Oklahoma City.

**History:** Opened in 1933 on part of the Fort Reno Military Reservation, FCI El Reno serves as a hub of inmate movement for the Federal Prison System. Inmates are male offenders from Texas and nearby states. Opened in 1980, the satellite camp houses minimum-security inmates who are employed on its farm providing beef and milk for El Reno and other Federal Prisons.

**Judicial District:** Western District of Oklahoma.

**Security Level:** Medium-security facility housing male offenders. The FCI also has an adjacent satellite camp that houses minimum-security male inmates.

**Population:** As of 6/21/2017, the FCI inmate population is 906, and the camp population is 275. Weekly population figures are available on the BOP website at www.bop.gov, https://www.bop.gov/locations/institutions/ere/.

**Education:** The FCI and the camp offer GED, ESL, adult continuing education and correspondence courses. The college program is currently sponsored by Redlands Community College and offers evening semester classes through classroom and telecourse instruction. Camp education staff conduct an open house 3pm-4pm every weekday.

**Vocational/Apprenticeship:** FCI offers advanced occupational education in business administration. Vocational training: business management, building maintenance, electrical work and welding. FCI apprenticeships are available in the following areas: dental technician, dental assistant, drafting, electrician, machinist, carpenter, millwright, painter, quality control technician, HVAC, tool and die, and welding.

**Library:** The main institution's law/leisure library is open Monday through Friday, 12:30pm-3pm (additional hours Monday through Thursday, 5:30pm-8pm); Saturday and Sunday, 7:30am-10am and 11:30am-3pm; closed on holidays. Electric typewriters and a copier are available to inmates for the preparation of legal documents. Inmates must purchase their own typewriter ribbon from the commissary. Inmates also have access to the Electronic Law Libraries (ELL). An interlibrary loan program is available through the state of Oklahoma. A book cart with a variety of reading materials is maintained by the education department. Legal materials may be requested via Inmate Request to Staff Member to the librarian. An index of available law materials is available upon request.

**UNICOR:** An industrial products factory employs approximately 256 inmates.

**Counseling/Rehab Services:** Individual counseling and other programs may be available based on the need of the inmate. A psychologist will monitor each inmate at least once each month. If a need exists, a psychologist may be reached by sending an inmate letter or requesting a referral from a staff person. The Non-Residential Drug Abuse Program (NRDAP) is provided to inmates with a substance abuse problem. Participation in the NRDAP is voluntary. This is a treatment program that covers a variety of issues related to drug abuse. Additionally, the FCI offers a 500-hour Residential Drug Abuse Program (RDAP). The RDAP is nine months in length.

**Health Services:** The main institution is staffed by physicians, physicians' assistants, dentists, an optometrist, and one to two pharmacists. General hours of operation are 6am-10pm seven days a week, with at least one physician assistant on duty or on call 24 hours a day. The FCI and the camp provide out-patient care. The pill line is open Monday, Tuesday, Thursday, and Friday from 6:45am-7:15am and 7pm-7:25pm at the main institution, and the same days from 7am-7:15am and 6:30pm-6:45pm at the camp. The sign-up sheet for sick call sign-up sheet is available at the officer station at 6am-6:30am on Monday, Tuesday, Thursday, and Friday. Inmates may request a physical examination every three years if they are under 50 years old, and may request one annually if they are over the age of 50.

**Housing:** Inmates at the FCI are primarily housed in two-man cells. Inmates at the camp are housed in dormitories in two-man and four-man cubicles. Television viewing at the camp is from 6am until 11:30pm, Sunday-Thursday, and until 2am on Friday and Saturday.

**Fitness/Recreation:** The facilities include arenas for both indoor and outdoor activities, field games, court games, table-top games, individual events, arts and crafts, and team sports. The outside recreation areas are open seven days a week from 6am or daylight, whichever occurs first to 8:30pm, except during count. A hobby shop, open Monday through Sunday and holidays, 7:30am-8:30pm except during count, is available for those inmates who want to do art or leather craft work. Inmates are permitted to have weight gloves, six handballs or racquetballs, and one tennis or racquetball racquet as long as they can be stored neatly and safely in their locker. Certain musical instruments, not to exceed a reasonable value, may be authorized to be stored in the unit by the camp administrator. An inmate may ordinarily possess only one instrument at one time.

**Religious Services:** The main institution is staffed by professional chaplains. Contract rabbi and imam services are available on a bi-monthly basis. At least one chaplain is on duty or on call to provide pastoral care at the camp. Community volunteers also assist in providing services for most faiths. If an inmate desires to see a minister of his or her religious faith, arrangements can usually be made to do so. Besides worship services and programs, the chaplains provide services in personal and family counseling, crisis intervention, and emergency contacts for/with inmates/families. Also available are Bibles and other religious reading materials.

**Commissary:** The FCI commissary is open Monday through Thursday: 6:30am-7:15am, 11am-12:25pm, and 1:55pm-3:45pm. Shopping days and hours are assigned according to an inmate's register number (odd or even). Even-numbered shoppers shop on Mondays and/or Wednesdays, while odd-numbered shoppers shop on Tuesdays and/or Thursdays. The camp trust fund sales unit hours are 10:30am-12:30pm and 2:30pm-3:45pm. The even-numbers shop on Tuesday, odd-numbers shop on Thursday. The monthly commissary spending limit is currently $360.

**Telephone Policy:** The telephones are for the purpose of allowing inmates to place collect, local, or long distance calls to family. Inmates may submit telephone number request forms for up to 30 numbers, and forms may be submitted once per month. Inmate telephones for general population are operable from 6am-10pm, seven days a week. Inmates are required to call from assigned unit only. All calls will automatically end after 15 minutes of conversation. Each inmate receives 300 calling minutes per month.

**Inmate Mail:** The FCI and the camp accept mail from the U.S. Postal Service via First-Class, U.S. Priority, and Express Mail. Overnight mail via a private carrier (FedEx or UPS Overnight) will be processed as regular mail. Inmates are permitted to subscribe to publications of their choice, with limitations. All publications must come directly from the publisher, bookstore, or book club. Inmates are permitted a total of five hard/soft books, ten magazines and four magazines at a time.

**Inmate Mail to FCI:**
> INMATE NAME & REGISTER NUMBER
> FCI El Reno
> Federal Correctional Institution
> P.O. Box 1500
> El Reno, OK 73036

**Visiting Hours:** FCI and camp visiting is permitted 8am-3pm, Thursday through Monday and federal holidays. Each inmate will be provided 32 points each month. One point is deducted for each hour of a weekday visit, and two points are deducted for each hour of a weekend/holiday visit. Inmates at the camp are only charged one point for each hour on weekends. No more than 20 of the visiting points can be used for weekend/holiday visit. Inmates can request ten additional visiting points for extraordinary circumstances. No more than five adult visitors and up to five children visitors are allowed at one time. Attorneys should visit during regular visiting hours, or must make special advance arrangements to visit at other times. Additional visiting information can be found at https://www.bop.gov/locations/institutions/ere/.

**Lodging/Accommodations:** Should visitors be spending the night, the following is a short list of accommodations that are available in El Reno, Oklahoma:

| | |
|---|---|
| Best Western Hensley's | 405-262-6490 |
| Days Inn | 405-262-8720 |
| Economy Express | 405-262-1022 |
| Budget Inn | 405-262-0242 |

## §15:17   FCC FORREST CITY

FCI Forrest City Medium
Federal Correctional Institution
1400 Dale Bumpers Road
Forrest City, AR 72335
FOM/ExecAssistant@bop.gov
870-494-4200
Fax: 870-494-4496

FCI Forrest City Low
Federal Correctional Institution
Camp: 1340 Dale Bumpers Road
Forrest City, AR 72335
FOR/ExecAssistant@bop.gov
870-630-6000
Fax: 870-494-4496

**Location:** 779 SFC 806, Forrest City, in St. Francis County, adjacent to Yocona Road, approximately 45 miles west of Memphis, Tennessee, and 85 miles east of Little Rock, Arkansas.

**History:** The Low FCI opened in 1996.

**Judicial District:** Eastern District of Arkansas.

**Security Level:** Medium-security facility housing male offenders and a low-security facility housing male offenders. A satellite prison camp adjacent to the facility houses minimum-security male offenders.

**Population:** As of 6/21/2017, the Medium FCI inmate population is 1,668; Low FCI inmate population is 1,771; and the camp population is 293. Weekly population figures are available on the BOP website at www.bop.gov, at https://www.bop.gov/locations/institutions/for/ for FCI Forrest City Low and the camp, and at https://www.bop.gov/locations/institutions/fom/ for FCI Forrest City Medium.

**Education:** The institutions offer GED, ESL, adult continuing education, post-secondary education, career counseling, parenting and correspondence courses.

**Vocational/Apprenticeship:** FCC Low and Medium offer advanced occupational education in office technology. The camp offers vocational training in drafting technology. The FCC Low offers apprenticeship programs in cooking and dental assisting.

**Library:** The law library contains a variety of legal reference materials for use in preparing legal papers. Reference materials include the United States Code Annotated, Federal Reporter, Supreme Court Reporter, Bureau of Prisons Program Statements, Institution Supplements, and other legal materials. The law library is located in the Education Department. An electronic card-operated copy machine is available in the law library for inmate use. Inmates may purchase a weekly limit of three five-dollar cards (each card makes 50 copies) from the commissary. Inmates who are without funds and can demonstrate a clear need for particular copies may request a limited amount of free duplication through their unit counselor or case manager. Electric typewriters and a copier are available to inmates for the preparation of legal documents. The leisure library contains a computer lab, language lab, and video library.

**UNICOR:** The UNICOR operation at FCC Forrest City is undergoing organizational vision with a new mission in the near future.

**Counseling/Rehab Services:** Psychology Services has programs available for the following: drug abuse programs, stress management, Emotional Awareness and personal counseling. Inmates are required to send a "cop-out" to Psychology Services requesting services, or inmates may bring a cop-out to Psychology Services during open move. In the event of emergencies, inmates need to notify staff. All inmates will be screened by Psychology Services staff during the institution's Admission and Orientation Program. Mental Health Services are offered in the areas of drug and alcohol abuse, as well as for other behavioral or emotional problems. Psychology Services also has a self-help resource library with materials available for check-out on appointment only basis. The FCI offers a 500-hour (nine-month) Residential Drug Abuse Program (RDAP).

**Health Services:** Sick call is Monday, Tuesday, Wednesday and Thursday from 7am-7:30am. Emergency services are available. Specialty clinics will be provided to those inmates identified with various chronic medical conditions as hypertension, diabetes, etc. Pill line hour at the camp are 6:15am-6:30am and 4:30pm-4:45pm on weekdays, and 7am-7:15am and 3pm-3:15pm on weekends and holidays. Pill line hours at the FCC Low are 7am-7:15am and 8pm-8:30pm on weekdays, and 9:30am-10am, 12noon-12:30pm, and 8pm-8:30pm on weekends and holidays. Pill line hours at the FCC Medium are 6:45am-7am and 7:30pm-8pm weekdays, and 8:30am-8:45am and 7:30pm-completion weekends and holidays. Contract services are provided in-house and in the community. All emergencies, requiring additional medical services will be transported to the Baptist Memorial Hospital, Forrest City. Inmates under the age of 50 may request a physical every three years, and inmates 50 years of age or older may request a physical every year. Inmates 50 years of age or older will be offered three additional tests at the time of their physical.

**Housing:** Inmates are primarily housed in "open bay" dormitories (hold up to 100 inmates) and two-man cubicles.

**Fitness/Recreation:** The hours of operation for various recreation activities and areas are at different times for the Low, Medium and camp facilities (see facility handbook at www.bop.gov for a detailed schedule). The recreation leisure center offers a fitness center and gym, recreation yard, hobby craft center, and a leisure area with music rooms, pool, foosball, and ping-pong tables, and table games. The fitness center has cardio equipment (stationary bikes, treadmills, ellipticals, etc.) and offers a wellness program. The recreation yard has areas for intramural and varsity sports such as basketball, volleyball, softball, soccer, flag football, racquetball, horseshoes, bocce ball, and a walking track. The hobby craft center has an art studio, leather craft, and a hobby tool room. There are five televisions throughout the facilities designated for sports, movies, Spanish channels, news, and general purpose. Television viewing is allowed from 6am until 10pm every day. Cards and games are allowed in the unit recreation rooms at the Low facility until 10pm. There are ten federal holidays in which activities will be offered, including: special tournaments, bingo, inmate productions, community sports participation and many other activities.

**Religious Services:** Chaplains contract clergy and community volunteers also provide assistance with services for most faiths. Religious services provide pastoral care to institutional staff and inmates. The chaplains have an open-door policy for personal counseling. If inmates need to visit with any of the chaplains, they may simply stop by the chapel. The chapel offers free greeting cards, a religious library, and free literature (newspapers, devotionals, and journals).

**Commissary:** Inmates are allowed to shop once per week on their designated shopping day, determined by their registration number. The commissary hours of operation at the FCI Low and FC Medium are 6:15am-3pm, Monday through Thursday. The commissary hours of operation at the cam are 6:15am-12:30pm, Tuesday and Wednesday. The monthly commissary spending limit is $360.

**Telephone Policy:** Inmates direct dial using the Inmate Telephone System (ITS). The following are standard features of ITS: (1) inmate calls automatically terminate after 15 minutes; (2) an inmate's calling list is limited to 30 callers; and (3) calls are charged to an inmate's debit card. There is a 30-minute waiting period between calls for each inmate. Telephones may be used from 6am-4pm and 4:30pm-10pm in the housing units (except during count times). Inmates are limited to 300 minutes per month, except during the months of November and December, when the allowance will be increased to 400 minutes per month. All phone calls are subject to being monitored and recorded, except where approval for unmonitored legal calls has been obtained. Unmonitored, unrecorded phone calls to attorneys can be arranged through the unit team with approval by the unit manager.

**Inmate Mail:** The FCI and the camp accept mail from the U.S. Postal Service via First-Class, U.S. Priority, and Express Mail. For those interested in sending overnight mail via a private carrier (FedEx or UPS Overnight), it is recommended that you first contact the institution to find out whether the receipt of such mail is permitted. Inmates may subscribe to and receive publications without prior approval, although the warden may reject publications that are determined to be detrimental to the security, good order, or discipline of the institution. An inmate at FCI Low or the camp may receive paperback books, magazines and newspaper clippings from any source, but may receive hardcover publications and newspapers directly from the publisher, bookstore, or book club. Inmates at the FCI Medium must subscribe to all publications directly from the publisher, bookstore, or book club.

### Inmate Mail to Medium:
INMATE NAME & REGISTER NUMBER
FCI Forrest City Medium
Federal Correctional Institution
P.O. Box 3000
Forrest City, AR 72336

### Inmate Mail to Low:
INMATE NAME & REGISTER NUMBER
FCI Forrest City Low
Federal Correctional Institution
P.O. Box 9000
Forrest City, AR 72336

**Inmate Mail to Camp:**
INMATE NAME & REGISTER NUMBER
FCI Forrest City Low
Federal Correctional Institution
Satellite Camp
P.O. Box 8000
Forrest City, AR 72336

**Visiting Hours:** As of June 22, 2017, visitation on mondays has been suspended indefinitely for fcc medium and fcc low. This policy may have changed by the time you read this entry.

Currently, visiting at all FCC Forrest City facilities is permitted on Saturdays, Sundays, and federal holidays from 8am-3pm. Each inmate will be permitted five visiting points per month. One point will be assessed for each visit. Each inmate is limited to four adult visitors and five children. If an inmate has more than five dependent children, they may be approved through a counselor. Each inmate is limited to four adults and five children. Attorneys should make advanced appointments for visits. You can find more visiting information at https://www.bop.gov/locations/institutions/for/ for FCI Forrest City Low and the satellite camp, and at https://www.bop.gov/locations/institutions/fom/ for FCI Forrest City Medium..

**Lodging/Accommodations:** Should visitors be spending the night, the following is a short list of accommodations that are available in Forrest City, Arkansas:

| | |
|---|---|
| America Best Value Inn | 870-633-0042 |
| Best Western Colony Inn | 870-633-0870 |
| Super 8 Motel | 870-633-0888 |
| Days Inn Suites | 870-633-6300 |
| Hampton Inn | 870-630-9000 |

## §15:18   FCI FORT WORTH

FCI Fort Worth
Federal Correctional Institution
3150 Horton Road
Fort Worth, TX 76119
FTW/ExecAssistant@bop.gov
817-534-8400
Fax: 817-413-3350

**Location:** In southeast Fort Worth, adjacent to Forest Hill and the Tarrant County College; north of Interstate 20 and east of Interstate 35. Fort Worth is served by Dallas/Fort Worth International Airport, Amtrak, and commercial bus lines.

**History:** FCI Fort Worth was obtained by the Bureau of Prisons in 1971 and provides specialized programs for inmates who have medical needs which cannot be met at a regular institution. Prior to the acquisition by the BOP, this facility was utilized as a United State Public Health Service facility.

**Judicial District:** Northern District of Texas.

**Security Level:** Low-security institution housing male offenders.

**Population:** As of 6/21/2017, the inmate population is 1,448. Weekly population figures are available on the BOP website, www.bop.gov, at https://www.bop.gov/locations/institutions/ftw/.

**Education:** Offers Adult Basic Learning Examination (ABLE), GED literacy classes, ESL classes, post-secondary education, parenting classes and social education classes. Transferable credits by a local college may be earned toward an Associate of Arts degree by correspondence. Tuition is the resp-onsibility of the inmate.

**Vocational/Apprenticeship:** FCI offers advanced occupational education in office technology, construction trades, and building service maintenance. Programs are four to eight months in length. Apprenticeship training is available in the areas of cook, plumbing, dental assistant and HVAC installer and servicer.

**Library:** The law/leisure library is open Monday through Friday (except federal holidays): 7:30am-10am, 12:30pm-3:30pm, 5:30pm-8:30pm. Saturday, Sunday, federal holidays: 12:30pm-3:30pm, 5:30pm-8:30pm. Electric typewriters and a copier are available. An inter-library loan is available. The institution library collection consists of approximately 5,000 books, both fiction and non-fiction. Books can be checked out for one week, and may be renewed for a second week. Newspapers, magazines, and reference books may be used only in the library. FCI Fort Worth has an inter-library loan agreement with the Forth Worth Public Library which allows inmates to borrow books that are not available at the institution. Video cassette recorders and audio cassette players are available to inmates for instructional purposes only. The law library contains all required legal materials and is maintained in accordance with Bureau of Prisons policy. Materials may not be removed from the library.

**UNICOR:** None.

**Counseling/Rehab Services:** Psychology services include: intellectual and/or personality evaluation, crisis intervention, brief counseling, and individual or group therapy, drug abuse program, psycho-educational groups in stress and anger management, chronic pain, smoking cessation, and weight management. The psychology department consists of full-time psychologists and psychology interns and is responsible for counseling services, coordination of testing materials and research, preparation of psychological reports for the courts, and operation of the drug treatment programs (residential and non-residential). General hours of operation for the psychology department are 7:30am-4pm, Monday through Friday. Psychological services are available 24 hours a day, every day of the year, for emergency situations. The institution also offers a 500-hour residential drug abuse treatment program (RDAP).

**Health Services:** FCI Forth Worth has a full-service, primary care medical facility. An 85-bed Health Services Unit (HSU) was constructed and dedicated in 1993. FCI is staffed by full-time physicians, physician assistants, nurses, and dentists. The FCI has long-term care beds, acute care beds, and ambulatory care services. Hours of operation are 24 hours a day. Emergency medical attention is available 24 hours a day. Sick call for medical and dental sign-up is Monday, Tuesday, Thursday, Friday 7am-7:30am in the clinic. No sick call on federal holidays. Pill line hours are posted.

**Housing:** Inmates are housed in individual rooms, two- and three-man dorm rooms, and "open bay" dormitories containing six to 30 inmates. A 102-cell Jail/ Special Housing Unit was activated in 1992. This unit operates with a population of approximately 150-160 inmates, with a maximum capacity of 204. The Jail Unit services the U.S. Marshal for Tarrant County.

**Fitness/Recreation:** The recreation department consists of outdoor and indoor facilities. The indoor facility has a large hobby craft program, fitness equipment, pool tables, ping-pong tables, card tables, music rooms, and televisions. Outdoor facilities include a running/walking track, multi-purpose courts, handball/ racquetball courts, softball fields, and a weightlifting area.

**Religious Services:** The FCI is staffed by two full-time chaplains and a religious services technician. A Native American sweat lodge is available on Thursdays from 11:30am-3:30pm, with periodic visits scheduled by a medicine man and other Native American volunteers. Community volunteers provide assistance. The chapel is open Saturday and Sunday mornings from 7:45am-10:15am; Sunday through Friday afternoons from 12:30pm-3:30pm; Saturday afternoon from 2pm-3:30pm; and Monday, Thursday and Friday evenings from 6pm-8:30pm. Bible studies, religious teachings, concerts, fellowships, discussion and prayer groups are held on a regular basis.

**Commissary:** The commissary is open for shopping Monday through Thursday 6am-7:30am and 11am-12:30pm. Shopping days are based on the first five digits of the inmate's registration number. The monthly commissary spending limit is currently $290.

**Telephone Policy:** Inmates dial direct using the Inmate Telephone System (ITS). The following are standard features of ITS: (1) inmate calls automatically terminate after 15 minutes; (2) an inmate's calling list is limited to 30 callers; and (3) calls are charged to an inmate's debit card. Each inmate has 300 minutes of calling time per month.

**Inmate Mail:** The FCI accepts mail from the U.S. Postal Service via First-Class, U.S. Priority, and Express Mail. For those interested in sending overnight mail via a private carrier (FedEx or UPS Overnight), it is recommended that you first contact the institution to find out whether the receipt of such mail is permitted.

**Inmate Mail to FCI:**
INMATE NAME & REGISTER NUMBER
FCI Fort Worth
Federal Correctional Institution
P.O. Box 15330
Fort Worth, TX 76119

**Visiting Hours:** Inmates are allowed 20 visitors on their approved visiting list. Six adults and/or children can visit at one time. Each inmate gets nine points on the first of the month for visiting. Regular visiting hours are Saturday, Sunday, Monday, and federal holidays 8am-3pm. Two points are deducted for weekends and holidays; one point is deducted for weekdays. Jail unit visiting hours are scheduled on a rotating basis according to the fifth digit of the inmate's register number. Jail unit visitation hours are 8am-11am and 12:30pm-3:30pm. During the Admission and Orientation Program, inmates may submit a list to their correctional counselor, of immediate family members with whom they wish to visit. Immediate family members are ordinarily approved without question. Friends and acquaintances having an established relationship with the inmate prior to confinement will be approved for visitation, unless such visits could reasonably create a threat to the security or good order of the institution. A given inmate can have up to six visitors at a time, including children. Attorney visits must be arranged and approved on a special basis by the inmate's unit team. For more information on visiting, visit https://www.bop.gov/locations/institutions/ftw/.

**Lodging/Accommodations:** Should visitors be spending the night, the following is a short list of accommodations that are available in Fort Worth, Texas:

| | |
|---|---|
| Comfort Inn | 817-568-9000 |
| La Quinta Inn & Suites Lake Worth | 817-237-9300 |
| Regency Inn and Suites | 817-545-1111 |
| Sunset Motel | 817-535-1171 |

## §15:19  FDC HOUSTON

FDC Houston
Federal Detention Center
1200 Texas Avenue
Houston, TX 77002
HOU/ExecAssistant@bop.gov
713-221-5400
Fax: 713-229-4200

**Location:** In the heart of downtown Houston at the intersection of Texas Avenue and San Jacinto Street. Take U.S. 45 south; exit Milam. It is approximately 195 miles from San Antonio, 246 miles from Dallas/Fort Worth, 294 miles from Texarkana, Texas, 352 miles from Brownsville, Texas, and 88 miles from Beaumont, Texas.

**History:** Opened in 2000, the FDC houses adult male and female pre-trial and sentenced holdover detainees, and has a work cadre of low/minimum-security male inmates who are serving relatively short terms.

**Judicial District:** Southern District of Texas.

**Security Level:** This is an administrative facility housing male and female pre-trial and holdover inmates.

**Population:** As of 6/22/2017, the inmate population is 895. Weekly population figures are available on the BOP website, www.bop.gov, https://www.bop.gov/locations/institutions/hou/.

**Education:** GED literacy classes, ESL, adult continuing education, and college courses on a correspondence basis. Inmates who do not possess a high school diploma or GED will be required to attend the literacy program.

**Vocational/Apprenticeship:** This institution does not offer vocational or apprenticeship training programs.

**Library:** The main law library is located on the second floor of the institution, and schedules for it are posted in the housing units. Reference materials, legal papers, legal forms, typewriters, and a copier are available. Inmates must submit an Inmate Request ("cop-out") to the Education Department in order to reproduce legal material. Legal books may not be taken off this floor.

**UNICOR:** None.

**Counseling/Rehab Services:** Psychology services staff will provide a full range of mental health services on an as-needed basis. Services include: crisis intervention, self-help groups, short-term therapy and counseling. Drug education programs are also available to inmates with a history of drug/alcohol abuse. The institution offers a non-residential drug treatment program, a residential drug treatment program, Alcoholics Anonymous and Narcotics Anonymous for Cadre Inmates. A contract psychiatrist will be available to offer treatment and medication. Psychiatric consultations will generally be made through the department and services will be made on a voluntary basis.

**Health Services:** The Health Services Unit at FDC Houston provides urgent medical and dental care evaluations, when needed. Inmates who require access to routine medical/dental health care will complete a Health Care Request Form. The forms and drop box are located in each unit. When a federal holiday is on a Monday or Friday, physical evaluations will be scheduled on Wednesday. The pill line is three times a day: 6:30am, 4:30pm and 8pm. Specialty care clinics are provided for all inmates with specific medical needs or life-long medical problems such as: high blood pressure, cardiac disabilities, diabetes, etc. Inmates with chronic or long-term medical conditions are scheduled as needed, but at least once every 90 days.

**Housing:** Inmates are housing in two-man cells and dormitories. There are four housing units; a unit is a self-contained inmate living area that includes housing sections and office space for the unit staff.

**Fitness/Recreation:** Scheduled activities are posted in inmate bulletin boards. Books, magazines, cards, board games, and television viewing are provided in each unit's activity room. Limited Spanish language television is also provided. Outdoor activities include: basketball, stationary bikes, soccer and racquetball. Television viewing is provided in the housing units.

**Religious Services:** Religious services will be provided in each unit, with a calendar posted in each unit indicating the religious services and programs available. An inmate may designate any or no religious preference at his/her initial team screening. By notifying the chaplain, in writing, an inmate may request to change this designation at any time, and the change will be made in a timely manner.

**Commissary:** Items may be purchased one day per week per submitted commissary list. The list must be submitted by 6:30am on the day prior to commissary shopping.

**Telephone Policy:** Inmates dial direct using the Inmate Telephone System (ITS). The following are standard features of ITS: (1) inmate calls automatically terminate after 15 minutes; (2) an inmate's calling list is limited to 30 callers; and (3) calls are charged to an inmate's debit card. Inmates are limited to 300 minutes per month for monitored telephone calls. Phones are available for use daily from 6am-7:30am, 9:30am-3:30pm, and 6pm-9:30pm.

**Inmate Mail:** The FDC accepts mail from the U.S. Postal Service via First-Class, U.S. Priority, and Express Mail. For those interested in sending overnight mail via a private carrier (FedEx or UPS Overnight), it is recommended that you first contact the institution to find out whether the receipt of such mail is permitted. Inmates may subscribe to publications, although magazines with sexually explicit or criminal content will be rejected. Newspapers and books must come directly from the publisher, bookstore or book club.

**Inmate Mail to FDC:**
INMATE NAME & REGISTER NUMBER
FDC Houston
Federal Detention Center
P.O. Box 526255
Houston, TX 77052

**Visiting Hours:** Visiting hours: Friday through Sunday and federal holidays, 8am-11am and 12noon-3pm; Monday and Thursday, 8am-11am, 12noon-3pm, and 5pm-8pm. There are no social visits on Tuesdays and Wednesdays. Legal visits: Friday through Saturday and federal holidays, 8am-3pm; Monday through Thursday, 8am-8pm. Inmates will ordinarily be allowed a social visit with the three-hour session designated for the inmate's assigned housing unit. The weekend and holiday visiting for work cadre and female inmates is one continuous 8am-3pm session. Inmates will be permitted to visit with four visitors at one time. Children who occupy a seat will be considered an adult. Visiting lists for pre-trial and holdover (except those in-transit) inmates are limited to immediate family. Work cadre and designated short-term female inmates may have other relatives or friends and associates added to their approved visiting list. Friends and associates must have a prior established relationship with the inmate. A maximum of ten visitors, in addition to immediate family members, may be on the Visiting list for a work cadre or designated short-term female inmate. Inmates at FDC Houston are afforded an opportunity to receive legal visits on a daily basis, during regular visiting times. Additional visiting information can be found https://www.bop.gov/locations/institutions/hou/.

**Lodging/Accommodations:** Should visitors be spending the night, the following is a short list of accommodations in Houston, Texas:

| | |
|---|---|
| Doubletree Hotel Houston Downtown | 713-759-0202 |
| Holiday Inn Express Hotel & Suites Downtown | 713-652-9400 |
| Magnolia Hotel | 713-221-0011 |
| Golden Motel | 713-748-1440 |
| Palace Inn | 713-672-8822 |
| The Sam Houston Hotel | 832-200-8800 |

## §15:20   FCI LA TUNA

FCI La Tuna
Federal Correctional Institution
8500 Doniphan Road
Anthony, TX 79821
LAT/ExecAssistant@bop.gov
915-791-9000
Fax: 915-791-9758

**Location:** On the Texas/New Mexico border adjacent to Mexico, 15 miles north of El Paso off of Interstate 10, and on State Highway 20. The Satellite Low facility (formerly FPC El Paso) is located approximately 25 miles east of Las Cruces, New Mexico and 370 miles west of Midland, Texas, FSL is located on Fort Bliss, about five miles northeast from Biggs Field.

**History:** Opened in 1932, FCI La Tuna Houses offenders primarily from Western Texas. Opened in 1978, the camp serves as a satellite minimum-security facility for male offenders. Most recently, the Federal Prison Camp (FPC) El Paso, Texas was converted from an independent minimum-security camp to a low-security satellite facility associated with FCI La Tuna.

**Judicial District:** Western District of Texas.

**Security Level:** This is a low-security facility housing male inmates (adjacent to a minimum/male camp and satellite/low male in El Paso).

**Population:** As of 6/22/2017, the FCI inmate population is 765; the camp population is 278; and the Satellite Low inmate population is 219. Weekly population figures are available on the BOP website, www.bop.gov, at https://www.bop.gov/locations/institutions/lat/.

**Education:** GED, ESL, a parenting program, correspondence courses and post-secondary education classes are offered at the facilities.

**Vocational/Apprenticeship:** In cooperation with El Paso Community College, the Education Department offers vocational training programs in air conditioning/refrigeration repair, automotive repair and office technology at the FCI and FSL, and a building trades program at the camp. These year-long programs are rewarded with certificates from El Paso Community College upon completion, and students demonstrating high levels of competency may be recommended for state or agency certifications.

**Library:** The FCI libraries are open Monday through Thursday 8:30am-10:30am, 12:30pm-3:30pm and 5:30pm-8:30pm; Friday 8:30am-10:30am and 12:30pm-3:30pm; and Saturday 7:30am-3:30pm. Sundays, the libraries are closed, but books and newspapers are available at the recreation yard from 7:30am-9:30am and 12:30pm-3:30pm. At the FSL, leisure material is located adjacent to the Franklin Unit and is available 1pm-8:30pm every day. Legal material is located in the education department, which is available 8:30am-10:30am and 12:30pm-3:30pm weekdays, and 1pm-3:30pm weekends/holidays. Legal material is also available during the evening, 5:30pm-8pm, Monday through Thursday and Sunday. The camp's administration building has a law and leisure library as well as a recreational library. These are open Monday through Friday, 5:30pm-8:30pm; weekends, 11am-3:30pm and 5:30pm-8:30pm. Libraries are closed on federal holidays. Electric typewriters and a copier are available to inmates for use in the preparation of legal documents. An inter-library loan program through El Paso Community College is also available.

**UNICOR:** The main operation at the FCI and the FPC consists of vehicle retro-fitting, which encompasses the modification of existing vehicles for use by the Department of Homeland Security, Bureau of Indian Affairs, U.S. Forest Service. At the FPC, the Warehouse operation is responsible for the receipt of goods and raw materials that will be used in the production process. The Warehouse is also responsible for the shipment of all finished goods.

**Counseling/Rehab Services:** Services include group and individual counseling, crisis intervention, and suicide companion program. A resource library is available comprised of self-help materials, audiotapes, videotapes, books and programs in English and Spanish. Drug programs offered include a 30-hour drug education program, non-residential drug counseling, and a 500-hour, nine-month residential drug abuse program. The department is comprised of three doctoral level psychologists, five drug treatment specialists and a psychology technician. Psychology Services and the DAPS building are located side by side in the low-level facility.

**Health Services:** The institution is staffed by physicians, physicians assistants, dentists, an optometrist and a pharmacist. The FCI, camp and Satellite Low provide outpatient care. The local hospital is approximately 20-30 miles away. Sick call sign-up is conducted on Mondays, Tuesdays, Thursdays and Fridays (except holidays) from 6am-6:30am at the FCI and camp. At the FSL, all inmates desiring to use sick call must sign-up at the medical dispensary at 6:30am-7:30am, Monday through Friday. The pill line at the FCI operates 6am-6:30am, 11:45am-12:15pm, 4:3pm0-4:45pm (insulin only) and 8:30pm-8:45pm daily. The pill line at the FSL operates 6am-6:30am and 1pm-1:30pm weekdays, and 8:15am-8:45am and 1pm-1:30pm weekends. The pill line at the camp operates 6:15am-6:30am and 7pm-7:15pm daily. Inmates may request a free prevention periodic visit every three years if they are under 50 years old, and may request one annually if over age 50. Medical staff is either on duty or on call 24 hours a day; urgent care is available at all times.

**Housing:** Two open dormitory units have four men cubicles. Each dormitory contains TV rooms and a game room. At all three facilities, the televisions are available Monday through Thursday, 6am-7:30am and 2:30-11pm; Friday, 6am-7:30am and 2:30pm-2am; Saturday, 6am-12am; and Sunday, 6am-11pm. Television will be allowed until 12am on the evenings preceding holidays.

**Fitness/Recreation:** The FCI has a recreation yard consisting of three handball courts, racquetball court. A basketball court, a multi-purpose court, a soccer/softball field, a volleyball courts, and a walking/running track. Indoor facilities are provided for a number of hobby craft activities, such as ceramics, leather craft, and painting. There is also a wellness program which includes aerobics, smoking cessation, and a walk/run program. Tournaments are held during the holidays, and movies are shown every weekend on Channel 49. Acoustic guitar lessons are available. Intramural sports leagues: soccer, softball, basketball, volleyball, racquetball, handball, chess and occasionally flag football. Hobby craft activities and classes: leather-work, ceramics, drawing and painting as well as other forms consistent with institution guidelines. Mail-out day is Wednesday from 1:30 p.m. – 3:30 p.m. and 4:30 p.m. – 7:30 p.m. Wellness: cardiovascular endurance (run/walk), aerobic exercise (step, spin, jump rope, yoga), body fat/flexibility and dynamic strength (one minute sit-up/push-up) test, as well as health and nutrition educational courses. Health awareness resource library is available inside the wellness office. Steel toe shoes are required in the weight pile. Rental movies are shown on weekends and holidays on channel 20. Hours are 6:30am-7:30am, 12:30pm-3:30pm, and 4:30pm-8:30pmweekdays. Weekend and holiday hours are 6:30am-9:30am, 10:30am-3:30pm, and 4:30pm-80:30pm.

The FSL has indoor and outdoor recreation facilities that are open weekdays, 8:30am-10:30am, 12:30pm-3:30pm, and 5:30pm-8:30pm; weekends, 1pm-3:30pm and 5:30-8:30pm. Activities at the FSL include weightlifting, racquetball/handball, horseshoes, ping-pong, running/walking on a track, and table games. Sports at the FSL include softball, basketball, volleyball, flag-football, and tennis. The hobby craft activities offered in the indoor recreation room include leather crafts and art/drawing. Movies are rented on a weekly basis and shown in the TV rooms within each unit.

The camp's administration building has a recreation office and a hobby shop. The recreation department at the camp offers softball, basketball, volleyball, tennis, handball, weightlifting and a walking/running track. Hours of operation are Monday-Friday 6:30am-10:30am, 11am-3:30pm, 4:30pm-8:30pm; week-ends and holidays 6:30am-9:30am, and 10:30am-3:30pm.

**Religious Services:** This institution has both Catholic and Protestant chaplains who conduct weekly services, as well as Bible study and other activities as the need or season arises. Community volunteers also provide assistance. The weekly religious services schedule includes programs for Native-American faiths, Judaism, Islam, and other religious groups represented by the inmate population. A religious diet program is available with approval of the chaplain.

**Commissary:** The FCI and FSL commissaries are open Monday through Thursday, 6:15am-7:15am and 11am-12:30pm. The camp commissary is open Monday through Thursday, 11am-12:30pm.. Inmate shopping days are assigned according to an inmate's register number. The monthly commissary spending limit is currently $360.

**Telephone Policy:** There are telephones located in the dormitories of all three facilities. Inmates can dial direct or call collect. The maximum numbers allowed on an inmate's approved list is 30. Calls automatically end after 15 minutes. Each inmate receives 300 calling minutes per month. The telephones at the camp are located in the housing units and are operational from 6am-11:30pm. Inmate access to telephones will normally be limited during the following times, Monday through Friday, not including holidays: 7:30 am until 10:30 am; and 12:30 pm until after 4:00 pm count. All calls are monitored, but inmates may request un-monitored phone calls to their attorneys.

**Inmate Mail:** The FCI accepts mail from the U.S. Postal Service via First-Class, U.S. Priority, and Express Mail. For those interested in sending overnight mail via a private carrier (FedEx or UPS Overnight), it is recommended that you first contact the institution to find out whether the receipt of such mail is permitted. An inmate may only receive hard cover publications and newspapers from the publisher, a book club, or a bookstore, but may receive softcover publications (other than newspapers) from any source.

### Inmate Mail to FCI:
INMATE NAME & REGISTER NUMBER
FCI La Tuna
Federal Correctional Institution
P.O. Box 3000
Anthony, TX 88021

### Inmate Mail to Low:
INMATE NAME & REGISTER NUMBER
FCI La Tuna
Federal Satellite Low
Federal Correctional Institution
P.O. Box 6000
Anthony, TX 88021

### Inmate Mail to Camp:
INMATE NAME & REGISTER NUMBER
FCI La Tuna
Federal Correctional Institution
Satellite Camp
P.O. Box 8000
Anthony, TX 88021

**Visiting Hours:** Regular visiting hours at FCI: Saturday, Sunday, Monday and federal holidays, 8am-3pm. Visiting hours for the camp and Federal Satellite Low: Saturday, Sunday and federal holidays, 8am-3pm. Inmates will be allowed a maximum of five adult visitors at one time, and a maximum of five children. Inmate visits are based on a point system where each inmate will receive six points per month. For weekday visits, one point will be deducted; for weekend and federal holiday visits, two points will be deducted. There is no limit to the number of family members that can be on an inmate's visiting list. A maximum of 20 friends or associates can be placed on the approved list. Attorneys should be included on the inmate's approved visiting list; once approved, the Unit Manager will arrange to have the inmate brought to the visiting room for the attorney visit. Additional visiting information can be found at https://www.bop.gov/locations/institutions/lat/.

**Lodging/Accommodations:** Should visitors be spending the night, the following is a short list of accommodations that are available in Anthony, Texas and nearby El Paso, Texas:

**Anthony, Texas:**

| | |
|---|---|
| Best Western Oasis of the Sun | 915-886-3333 |
| Hampton Inn & Suites Big Spring | 432-264-9800 |
| Super 8 Anthony/El Paso | 915-886-2888 |

**El Paso, Texas:**

| | |
|---|---|
| Days Inn El Paso West | 915-845-3500 |
| Holiday Inn Express Hotel & Suites El Paso | 915-587-5885 |
| Motel 6 El Paso West | 915-584-4030 |
| La Quinta Inn El Paso West | 915-833-2522 |

## §15:21  FCC OAKDALE I & II

FCI Oakdale I
Federal Correctional Institution
1507 East Whatley Road
Oakdale, LA 71463
OAK/ExecAssistant@bop.gov
318-335-4070
Fax: 318-215-2688

FDC Oakdale II
Federal Correctional Institution
2105 East Whatley Road
Oakdale, LA 71463
OAK/ExecAssistant@bop.gov
318-335-4466
Fax: 318-215-2185

**Location:** In central Louisiana, 35 miles south of Alexandria and 58 miles north of Lake Charles, on State Highway 165, east of Route 165 on Whatley Road. The area is served by Esler Regional Airport (50 miles from the facility), and bus service to Alexandria and Lake Charles.

**History:** Opened in 1986, FCI Oakdale I was the first facility to be operated jointly by the Federal Bureau of Prisons, the Immigration and Naturalization Service, and the Executive Office of Immigration Review. Its original purpose was to house aliens awaiting deportation proceedings. In November 1986, its mission was changed to house Cuban detainees. An inmate riot in November 1987 destroyed much of the facility, which was reconstructed and returned to full operation in January 1989, housing sentenced aliens and regularly sentenced federal inmates. In 1990, FCI Oakdale II was opened by the Federal Bureau of Prisons, the INS, and the Executive Office for Immigration Review. These facilities, and a minimum-security camp have been administratively combined to now comprise a Federal Correctional Complex (FCC).

**Judicial District:** Western District of Louisiana.

**Security Level:** FCI Oakdale is a low-security institution that houses male inmates. FDC Oakdale is an administrative Federal Detention Center (FDC) that houses male pre-trial and holdover inmates; with an adjacent satellite prison camp that houses minimum-security male inmates.

**Population:** As of 6/22/2017, the FCI I inmate population is 1,125; the FDC II population is 894; and the camp population is 164. Weekly population figures are available at https://www.bop.gov/locations/institutions/oak/ and at https://www.bop.gov/locations/institutions/oad/.

**Education:** All institutions offer a literacy program (GED), ESL, a parenting program, a keyboarding program, adult continuing education, and correspondence courses. The FCI's education department hours of operation are Monday through Thursday, 7:30am-10:30am, 12:30pm-3:30pm, and 5pm-8pm; Friday, 7:30am-3:30pm; Saturday, 7:15am-3:45pm. The FDC's education department is open 7:40am-10:30am and 12:30pm-3:30pm Monday through Friday, with extra evening hours 5pm-8pm Tuesday through Thursday.

**Vocational/Apprenticeship:** The FCI offers advanced occupational education in the following areas: industrial sewing, occupational videos, horticulture, and building maintenance. Apprenticeships are available, including fields such as HVAC, electrician, plumbing, carpentry, and landscaping. The FCI II and camp currently do not offer vocational or apprenticeship programs.

**Library:** Various reading materials such as newspapers, magazines, dictionaries and books are available in the Education Department for check out. The leisure/law library at the FDC is open Monday through Friday from 9am-10:30am and 2pm-3:30pm, with extra evening hours 6:30pm-8pm Tuesday through Thursday. The FDC law library is located in the Education Department, and contains a variety of legal reference materials for use in preparing legal papers. Electric typewriters and copiers are available to inmates for the preparation of legal documents. An inter-library loan program is available through Baton and Oak-dale Public Libraries. The schedule for the FCI and camp libraries are posted in the Education Department. Legal materials are also available to detainees in detention or in segregation status. Any materials not immediately available in detention or in segregation status can be obtained through an Inmate Request to a Staff Member ("cop-out"). Copies of legal materials for general population are free for up to 25 copies per month, with additional copies at a rate of five cents per copy (no charge for INS Forms/Applications).

**UNICOR:** UNICOR Oakdale is a textile operation manufacturing several apparel items for the Bureau of Prisons and the Defense Department and employs approx-imately 172 inmates. These items include inmate clothing and several different clothing items for the military.

**Counseling/Rehab Services:** The FCC has a professional staff that is trained in various social science fields. The staff in each unit is available for informal counseling sessions. Additionally, the staff psychologist conducts the following programs: 40-hour drug education program; stress management group; psy-chological-educational support group; and anger management group. For an appointment to see the psychologist regarding a mental health issue, inmates should send an Inmate Request to Staff Member form ("cop-out") to the Psychol-ogy Department, then watch the call-out sheet for the appointment day and time. If an inmate has an emergency mental health problem, he should request that a staff member call the Psychology Department for an immediate appointment.

**Health Services:** Health Services are provided on a 24-hour basis through routine clinic and urgent care. Inmates will be provided necessary medical, dental, and mental health services by professional staff, consistent with acceptable commu-nity standards. The institutions are staffed by physicians, physician assistants, nurses, dental department, pharmacist, x-ray technician, and lab technician. The FCC also provides outpatient care. Daily sick call sign-ups are between 6:15am-6:30am on Monday, Tuesday, Thursday and Friday. Pill line hours at the FCI and FDC are: Monday through Friday, 6:15am-6:30am; 11:30am-12noon; 5pm-5:30pm; 7:30pm-7:40pm; Saturday, Sunday, and holidays, 8am-8:30am, 12noon-12:30pm, 5pm-5:30pm and 7:30pm-7:40pm. Medication dispensed at the Camp, SHU, and A&O unit may be staggered before or after the above times. There will be no over-the-counter medications provided to the general population. Emergency medical care is available 24 hours per day. The nearest hospital is three blocks away.

**Housing:** Inmates at FCI I are housed in dormitories in two-man and four-man cubicles. The televisions may be viewed from 6am-7:15am during the weekdays, weeknights until 10:15pm and weekends and holidays until 1am. Inmates at FCI II and FPC are housed in two-man cells and multiple-occupancy rooms. Televi-sion hours at the FDC are 6:30am-9pm; 9pm-6:30am are quiet hours.

**Fitness/Recreation:** Leisure time activities and recreational programs are available in the housing units, on the recreation yard, and in the leisure center. Programs range from individualized arts and crafts programs, to team sports such as softball, soccer, basketball, volleyball and flag football. The FCI I recreation department offers intramural team sports such as softball, basketball, and volleyball, along with physical fitness and weight reduction programs. Hobby craft activities include: painting, drawing, leather craft, wood work, knitting, basket weaving, and musical instruments. The FCI II has a gym with a basketball court for league and free play, a hobby craft area in the leisure center, guitar instruction, health awareness programs, and a recreation yard. The recreation yard has an asphalt track, soccer and football fields, two handball/racquetball courts, a softball field, weight pile, and volleyball court. The hobby craft program offers leather craft, beadwork, clay, and crochet. Board games are available in the housing units and hobby craft area of all three facilities.

**Religious Services:** FCI I and FCI II are served by full-time chaplains. Contract rabbi and imam services are available on a bi-monthly basis, and a sweat lodge is available for Native American services. Contract and volunteer representatives of various faiths are available to aid in a wide range of religious programs. Special religious diets, holiday observances, and other worship activities are coordinated through the chaplain's office. Information about these programs is available in the orientation program and from the chaplains. The chaplain's office maintains a religious library of reading material, audiotapes and videotapes.

**Commissary:** The FCI commissary is open Tuesday through Thursday from 11am-12noon and immediately following the 4pm count until 6pm. The FDC commissary is open Tuesday through Thursday from 11am-12noon and 2pm-2:45pm. Inmates are assigned one shopping day per week, according to their registration number. There is a monthly spending limit of $360.

**Telephone Policy:** Inmates dial direct using the Inmate Telephone System (ITS). The following are standard features of ITS: (1) inmate calls automatically terminate after 15 minutes; (2) an inmate's calling list is limited to 30 callers; and (3) calls are charged to an inmate's debit card. A 30-minute time period is set between completed telephone calls to promote access for all inmates/detainees. There is a limit of 300 minutes per month, with 400 minutes a month available in November and December. Each contact list is limited to 100 contacts and 30 telephone numbers. Inmates can contact their unit team to make unmonitored legal calls. The telephones at the FCI are in operation daily from 6am-11:30pm. The telephones are in operation at the FDC from 6am-9pm.

**Inmate Mail:** All three facilities accept mail from the U.S. Postal Service via First-Class, U.S. Priority, and Express Mail. Mail sent by private carriers (*e.g.*, FedEx or UPS Overnight) to the FDC will be sent to the warehouse and not to the mail room, which will result in a delay of the delivery of these items. Inmates may subscribe to publications without prior approval, although the warden will reject those that depict criminal activity or pose a threat to the security, good order, or discipline of the institution. At the FCI II, a total of five magazines (no more than three months old) and two newspapers (no more than five days old) can be kept. All publications must be received directly from the publisher, bookstore, or book club. At FCI I, only newspapers and hardcover books must be received directly from the publisher, bookstore, or book club.

**Inmate Mail to FCI I:**
INMATE NAME & REGISTER NUMBER
FCI Oakdale I
Federal Correctional Institution
P.O. Box 5000
Oakdale, LA 71463

**Inmate Mail to FCI II and Camp:**
INMATE NAME & REGISTER NUMBER
FCI Oakdale II
Federal Detention Center
P.O. Box 5010
Oakdale, LA 71463

**Visiting Hours:** Visiting hours: Sunday, Saturday and federal holidays, 8:30am-3pm. Each inmate's visiting list will consist of immediate family members and no more than ten additional friends and associates. Five visitors, including children, will be allowed to visit one inmate at one time. Inmates are allowed eight visits a month. Attorney visits should be coordinated in advance and should take place during regular visiting hours if possible. Attorneys should be added to the inmates' visiting lists. An ion detection unit is located in the front entry lobbies at the FCI and FDC. Visitors will be randomly screened for traces of drugs during normal visiting hours. Additional visiting information can be found at https://www.bop.gov/locations/institutions/oak/ and at https://www.bop.gov/locations/institutions/oad/.

**Accommodations:** Should visitors be spending the night, the following is a short list of available accommodations in Oakdale, Louisiana and nearby Oberlin and Kinder, Louisiana:

**Oakdale:**
| | |
|---|---|
| Best Western Oakdale Inn | 318-335-3155 |
| Oakwood Inn | 318-335-4000 |

**Kinder:**
| | |
|---|---|
| Black Jack Inn | 337-738-7979 |
| Days Inn | 337-738-3381 |
| America Best Value Inn | 337-738-3123 |

## §15:22    FTC OKLAHOMA CITY

FTC Oklahoma City
Federal Transfer Center
7410 South MacArthur
Oklahoma City, OK 73169
OKL/ExecAssistant@bop.gov
405-682-4075
Fax: 405-680-4043

**Location:** Western edge of Will Rogers World Airport, three miles west of Interstate 44 and four miles south of Interstate 40.

**Judicial District:** Western District of Oklahoma.

**Security Level:** Administrative facility housing male and female holdover offenders.

**Population:** As of 6/22/2017, the FTC inmate population is 1,312. Weekly population figures are available the BOP website, www.bop.gov, at https://www.bop.gov/locations/institutions/okl/.

**Education:** FTC Oklahoma City offers GED, ESL, adult continuing education classes, and a two-year release preparation program.

**Library:** The electronic law library is available for access to law library materials, and it is available during open unit hours. In the leisure library, leisure reading materials are also available to the work cadre. Paperback leisure reading carts are available 24 hours per day. These books are rotated weekly. Additional reading materials are also available in both English and Spanish. A complete list of these materials is available on the basic law library cart. An inter-library loan program and a McNaughton book exchange program offers the cadre additional leisure reading opportunities.

**Counseling/Rehab Services:** Psychology staff will provide a full range of psychological services on an as-needed basis. Specialty programs such as: stress management, rational thinking, and dealing with grief will be available on an as needed basis. All psychology services programs are voluntary. Psychology services staff will also offer a 12-week "drug education class" as part of the national drug treatment initiative.

**Health Services:** Medical services are available on a 24-hour basis through routine medical programs and urgent care. Medical services are provided by FTC medical staff and community consultants. Sick call sign-up is conducted in each unit between 7:15am and 7:30am, Monday through Friday, except Wednesday and federal holidays. Dental sick call is reserved for emergency care only; routine dental care will be done only as time and resources permit. Inmates who have been incarcerated by the Bureau of Prisons for at least two years are entitled to a physical examination every two years; inmates older than 50 years of age are eligible to receive a physical examination every year.

**Housing:** The Federal Transfer Center houses approximately 174 Work Cadre inmates, and 1,440 male and female holdover inmates. Bed assignments are made by unit staff. Cell changes will occur only once every six months, or at the unit team's documentation. Further, these changes will occur only at the approval of the unit team and will take place on Sundays only. Television viewing is controlled by the unit officer, and may be watched with headphones only. Quiet hours start at 9:45pm every night.

**Fitness/Recreation:** Recreation facilities are available in each unit. There are several opportunities to maintain physical fitness with available equipment and scheduled activities (such as basketball, handball, and unit walking). During holidays, various tournaments and special activities are available. Various board games and television viewing is available in the unit. There are several hobby craft programs offered to cadre inmates.

**Religious Services:** The institution chapel and religious activities room are available to inmates with prior approval from the chaplain. Contract employees, volunteers, and other visitors assist in meeting the religious needs of those persons incarcerated at FTC. Opportunities for worship services are offered weekly. Inmates should consult the bulletin board in their housing unit area for a schedule of worship, religious activity times and authorized areas.

**Commissary:** Inmates may shop once a week. Inmates are required to submit a commissary list with a spending limit of $360 per month.

**Telephone Policy:** FTC uses the Inmate Telephone System (ITS). With this system, inmates can access up to 30 approved telephone numbers. Calls automatically terminate after 15 minutes. Each inmate gets 300 calling minutes per month. All unit telephones are monitored telephones. Legal calls can be made on a non-monitored telephone. The request for this type of phone call should be directed via an Inmate Request to Staff addressed to the unit counselor.

**Visiting Hours:** Approved visits will be allowed on Saturday, Sunday and federal holidays 8am-3pm. Visitors are not allowed during the morning count (9am-10:20am). Inmates will be given five visiting points per month. One point will be deducted on weekend visits and two points deducted on federal holidays. Visits from attorneys, minister of record, and medical services do not take away visiting points, although clergy visits will count against the total number of visits. An inmate who receives more than one visit a day and/or exits then re-enters the visiting room will have another point applied against his/her visiting points. No more than five visitors, including children, will be allowed to visit at one time. Visitors will pass through an ion detection unit, which detects traces of drugs. Additional visiting information can be found at https://www.bop.gov/locations/ institutions/okl/.

**Inmate Mail:** The FTC accepts mail from the U.S. Postal Service via First-Class, U.S. Priority, and Express Mail. Mail privileges such as overnight mail and express mail are not allowed, and will be processed as regular mail. Inmates are allowed to subscribe to publications, with the stipulation that newspapers and hardcover books should come directly from the publisher.

**Inmate Mail to FTC:**
INMATE NAME & REGISTER NUMBER
FTC Oklahoma City
Federal Transfer
P.O. Box 898801
Oklahoma City, OK 73189

**Lodging/Accommodations:** Should visitors be spending the night, the following is a short list of available accommodations in Oklahoma City:

| | |
|---|---|
| Country Inn & Suites | 405-605-8300 |
| Hampton Inn | 405-682-2080 |
| Hyatt Place | 405-682-3900 |
| Wyndham Garden Hotel | 405-685-4000 |

## §15:23   FCI POLLOCK

USP Pollock
U.S. Penitentiary
1000 Airbase Road
Pollock, LA 71467
POL/ExecAssistant@bop.gov
318-561-5300
Fax: 318-561-5391

**Location:** in Central Louisiana in southeastern Grant Parish, Louisiana. The facility is situated approximately fifteen miles north of Alexandria, Louisiana. From Baton Rouge, take expressway 10 toward Lafayette to Highway 49 North. Take the Pineville Expressway North. Take the Highway 165 Exit. Proceed seven miles through the Town of Ball. Look for sign that says USP. Make a left on Airbase Road.

**History:** Opened in 2007.

**Judicial District:** Western District of Louisiana.

**Security Level:** Medium security institution housing male offenders.

**Population:** As of 6/23/2017, the FCI inmate population is 1,326. Weekly population figures are available on the BOP website, www.bop.gov, at https://www.bop.gov/locations/institutions/pom/.

**Education:** The FCI offers GED, ESL, adult continuing education, parenting program and college correspondence courses.

**Vocational/Apprenticeship:** The FCI offers vocational programs in culinary arts, small engine repair, sewing, and building trades. There are no apprenticeship programs.

**Library:** The FCI has both leisure and law libraries, with a variety of services. Books, magazines and newspapers and an inter-library loan program are available for inmates. Legal materials are available in the law library, and inmates have access to the Electronic Legal Library (ELL). Class schedules and hours of operation for the libraries will be posted in the Education Department.

**UNICOR:** Inmates are employed and trained in textile operations producing high-quality products and services for the federal government.

**Counseling/Rehab Services:** A psychologist will be available for individual psychotherapy on an as-needed basis. The FCI offers individual therapy, Suicide Prevention Companions, non-residential drug treatment, a drug abuse education program, group counseling, crisis intervention, correctional counseling, pre-release counseling and other voluntary groups.

**Health Services:** The FCI provides outpatient care. Sick call sign-up is Monday, Tuesday, Thursday and Friday at 6:05am. Pill line times are breakfast mainline through 7:30am and during the evening.

**Housing:** Inmates are housed in one- and two-man cells.

**Fitness/Recreation:** The Recreation and Wellness Center hours of operation: Monday through Friday 8:30am-10:30am; 11am-3:30pm; 4:30pm-8:30pm. Saturday, Sunday and federal holidays 8:30am-9:30am; 10:30am-3:30pm; 4:30pm-8:30pm. Recreation includes: league play, wellness programs, health/fitness classes and cardiovascular conditioning, and music programs. The hobby craft program includes leather working and art. During weekdays, TV rooms will be designated for viewing from approximately 6am-11:30pm weekdays, and on weekends/holidays from 6am-1am.

**Religious Services:** The FCI has full-time chaplains from various religious backgrounds. They perform worship services and religious classes for inmates who are of each chaplain's faith group. Chaplains provide counseling for working through personal and religious decisions and in crisis. They also coordinate services weekly for other faith groups by using a large number of community contractors and volunteers. The Chapel has religious books, videos and literature available for many faith groups to be checked out. A religious diet and/or religious headwear may be requested through a chaplain.

**Commissary:** This institution uses a point-of-sale computerized commissary withdrawal system and gives the inmate an improved up-to-date record of all account activity. Account balances may be checked by the computerized ITS system. The commissary access time for inmates is based on their register numbers. The schedule is posted in the unit. The monthly commissary spending limit is currently $360.

**Telephone Policy:** Inmates at the USP and the camp dial direct using the Inmate Telephone System (ITS). The following are standard features of ITS: (1) inmate calls automatically terminate after 15 minutes; (2) an inmate's calling list is limited to 30 callers; and (3) calls are charged to an inmate's debit card. There are 30-minute breaks between calls. Each inmate gets 300 calling minutes per month.

**Inmate Mail:** The USP and the camp accept mail from the U.S. Postal Service via First-Class, U.S. Priority, and Express Mail. Only mail from the U.S. Postal Service will be accepted. Inmates may subscribe to publications without prior approval, although the warden will reject publications that pose a threat to the security, good order, or discipline of the institution. Publications may be received only from the publisher, bookstore, or book club. Inmates are limited to the number of publications that can be stored in their cells.

**Inmate Mail to USP:**
> INMATE NAME & REGISTER NUMBER
> FCI Pollock
> Federal Correctional Institution
> P.O. Box 2099
> Pollock, LA 71467

**Visiting Hours:** Social inmate visiting at the FCI is, Friday, Saturday, Sunday and federal holidays from 8am-3pm. Inmates will be given 12 visiting points. One point will be deducted for weekday visits and two points will be deducted for weekend and holiday visits. The visiting privilege will be extended to friends and associates having an established relationship with the inmate prior to incarceration. No more than ten friends and associates can be placed on the visiting list. Only five visitors may visit at a time. Attorney visits must be approved in advance, are encouraged to visit during regular visiting hours and will subject to visual monitoring.

**Lodging/Accommodations:** Should visitors be spending the night, the following is a short list of available accommodations in and around Pollock, Louisiana:

| | |
|---|---|
| Motel Max Pollock | 318-765-2808 |
| Country Inn & Suites Pineville | 318-641-8332 |
| Days Inn Pineville | 818-640-5818 |
| Sleep Inn & Suites | 318-640-8505 |
| La Quinta Inn | 318-442-3700 |

## §15:24   USP POLLOCK

USP Pollock
U.S. Penitentiary
1000 Airbase Road
Pollock, LA 71467
POL/ExecAssistant@bop.gov
318-561-5300
Fax: 318-561-5391

**Location:** in Central Louisiana in southeastern Grant Parish, Louisiana. The facility is situated approximately fifteen miles north of Alexandria, Louisiana. From Baton Rouge, take expressway 10 toward Lafayette to Highway 49 North. Take the Pineville Expressway North. Take the Highway 165 Exit. Proceed seven miles through the Town of Ball. Look for sign that says USP. Make a left on Airbase Road.

**History:** Opened in 2000.

**Judicial District:** Western District of Louisiana.

**Security Level:** High security institution housing male offenders; adjacent satellite prison camp housing minimum-security male offenders.

**Population:** As of 6/23/2017, the USP inmate population is 966, and the camp population is 252. Weekly population figures are available on the BOP website at www.bop.gov, https://www.bop.gov/locations/institutions/pol/.

**Education:** The USP and camp offer GED, ESL, adult continuing education, parenting program and college correspondence courses.

**Vocational/Apprenticeship:** The USP and camp offer vocational programs in culinary arts, small engine repair, sewing, and building trades.

**Library:** Both the penitentiary and camp have leisure and law libraries, with a variety of services. Books, magazines and newspapers and an inter-library loan program are available for inmates. Legal materials are available in the law library. Class schedules and hours of operation for the libraries will be posted in the Education Department.

**UNICOR:** Inmates are employed and trained in textile operations producing high-quality products and services for the federal government.

**Counseling/Rehab Services:** A psychologist will be available for individual psychotherapy on an as-needed basis. The USP and camp offer individual therapy, non-residential drug treatment, a drug abuse education program, group counseling, crisis intervention, correctional counseling, pre-release counseling and other voluntary groups.

**Health Services:** The FCI provides outpatient care. Sick call sign-up is Monday, Tuesday, Thursday and Friday at 6:05am. Pill line times are breakfast mainline through 7:30am and during the evening.

**Housing:** Inmates at the USP are housed in one- and two-man cells. Inmates at the camp are housed in open bay dormitories.

**Fitness/Recreation:** The Recreation and Wellness Center hours of operation: Monday through Friday 8:30am-10:30am; 11am-3:30pm; 4:30pm-8:30pm. Saturday, Sunday and federal holidays 8:30am-9:30am; 10:30am-3:30pm; 4:30pm-8:30pm. Recreation includes: league play, wellness programs, health/ fitness classes and cardiovascular conditioning, and music programs. The hobby craft program includes leather working and art. During weekdays, TV rooms will be designated for viewing from approximately 6am-11:30pm week- days, and on weekends/holidays from 6am-1am.

**Religious Services:** The USP has full-time chaplains from various religious backgrounds. They perform worship services and religious classes for inmates who are of each chaplain's faith group. Chaplains provide counseling for work- ing through personal and religious decisions and in crisis. They also coordinate services weekly for other faith groups by using a large number of community contractors and volunteers. The Chapel has religious books, videos and litera- ture available for many faith groups to be checked out. A religious diet and/or religious headwear may be requested through a chaplain.

**Commissary:** This institution uses a point-of-sale computerized commissary with- drawal system and gives the inmate an improved up-to-date record of all account activity. Account balances may be checked by the computerized ITS system. The commissary access time for inmates is based on their register numbers. The sched- ule is posted in the unit. The monthly commissary spending limit is currently $360.

**Telephone Policy:** Inmates at the USP and the camp dial direct using the Inmate Telephone System (ITS). The following are standard features of ITS: (1) inmate calls automatically terminate after 15 minutes; (2) an inmate's calling list is limited to 30 callers; and (3) calls are charged to an inmate's debit card. There are 30-minute breaks between calls.

**Inmate Mail:** The USP and the camp accept mail from the U.S. Postal Service via First-Class, U.S. Priority, and Express Mail. Only mail from the U.S. Postal Service will be accepted. Inmates may subscribe to publications without prior approval, although the warden will reject publications that pose a threat to the security, good order, or discipline of the institution. At the USP, hardcover publications may be received only from the publisher, bookstore, or book club, and inmates at the camp may only subscribe to softcover publications directly from the publisher, bookstore, or book club. Inmates are limited to the number of publications that can be stored in their cells, and must throw out magazines after 90 days and throw out newspapers after seven days.

**Inmate Mail to USP:**
INMATE NAME & REGISTER NUMBER
USP Pollock
United States Penitentiary
P.O. Box 2099
Pollock, LA 71467

**Inmate Mail to Camp:**
INMATE NAME & REGISTER NUMBER
USP Pollock
United States Penitentiary
Satellite Camp
P.O. Box 2099
Pollock, LA 71467

**Visiting Hours:** As of June 2017, all visiting at this facil-ity has been suspended until further notice. This policy may have changed by the time you read this entry. See https://www.Bop.Gov/locations/institutions/pol/.

Social inmate visiting at the FCI is, Friday, Saturday, Sunday and federal holidays from 8am-3pm. Inmates will be given 12 visiting points. One point will be deducted for weekday visits and two points will be deducted for weekend and holiday visits. The visiting privilege will be extended to friends and associates having an established relationship with the inmate prior to incarceration. No more than ten friends and associates can be placed on the visiting list. Only five visitors may visit at a time. Attorney visits must be approved in advance, are encouraged to visit during regular visiting hours and will subject to visual monitoring/ For additional information, see www.bop.gov, https://www.bop.gov/locations/institutions/pol/.

**Lodging/Accommodations:** See entry for § 15:23 FCI Pollock.

## §15:25   FCI SEAGOVILLE

FCI Seagoville
Federal Correctional Institution
2113 North Highway 175
Seagoville, TX 75159
SEA/ExecAssistant@bop.gov
972-287-2911
Fax: 972-287-5466

**Location:** Eleven miles southeast of Dallas, off Highway 175 (Hawn Freeway). The area is served by the Dallas-Fort Worth International Airport, Amtrak, and commercial bus lines.

**History:** FCI Seagoville was originally opened in 1940 to house female offenders. The facility served as a detention facility during World War II for Japanese, German, and Italian families. In 1945, after the war, Seagoville became a Federal Correctional Institution for male offenders who are primarily from the South Central United States, with a Federal Detention Center (FDC) for male pre-trial and holdover inmates.

**Judicial District:** Northern District of Texas.

**Security Level:** FCI Seagoville is a low-security facility housing for male offenders. The facility includes a detention center for male offenders and an adjacent satellite prison camp that houses minimum-security male offenders.

**Population:** As of 6/22/2017, the FCI/FDC inmate population is 1,807, and the camp population is 184. Weekly population figures are available on the BOP website at https://www.bop.gov/locations/institutions/sea/.

**Education:** The institution offers GED, ESL, adult continuing education, college correspondence courses, and parenting courses. Adult continuing education classes include business, commercial driving, accounting, strategies for living, are offered on a continual basis. Post-secondary scholarships are awarded semi-annually to selected inmates.

**Vocational/Apprenticeship:** FCI offers advanced occupational education in customer service and copy repair. FCI offers vocational training in the following areas: auto mechanics, HVAC, horticulture, and building trades. FCI offers apprenticeship programs in dental assisting, horticulture, paralegal, and youth development. All programs are accredited through the Dallas County Community College District. The FDC and the camp do not offer vocational training.

**Library:** Law library schedule: Monday through Friday 7:40am-8:15pm; Saturday 7:40am-5:15pm; closed Sunday, holidays, and during counts. Typewriters and a copy machine are available in the law library and are to be utilized for legal work only. Per request, legal materials which cannot be located in the basic libraries can be obtained from the main law library. Inmates will be permitted to assist other inmates in the preparation of legal documents and briefs, provided the assistance is rendered on a voluntary basis, and provided the inmate rendering assistance makes no charge for his assistance and the assistance is rendered during the free time of the inmate involved. Special time off from the inmate's work detail assignment may be given for the purpose of research and document preparation to meet an imminent court deadline. The inmate will make his request in writing and list reasons why the task cannot be accomplished during leisure time. A basic law library is available for inmates in administrative detention/ disciplinary segregation.

Leisure library schedule: Monday through Friday 7:40am-8:15pm; Saturday 7:15am-5:15pm; closed Sundays, holidays, and during counts. The leisure library provides a variety of educational videos and books on tape for inmates interested in personal enrichment. Inmates may borrow materials using their commissary card or with a pre-approved note from the library coordinator. There are electric typewriters and a copier available for the preparation of legal documents only. The leisure library contains bestseller paperback books, current magazines, and newspapers. An inter-library loan program is available through various state libraries. The FDC and camp also provide leisure/law library services.

**UNICOR:** Textile factory employs approximately 203 inmates.

**Counseling/Rehab Services:** Psychological services are available to inmates in both English and Spanish. Services include: individual consultation, counseling, and crisis intervention, drug education, non-residential drug counseling and residential drug treatment. The drug education program is 40 hours in length, and meets twice a week for ten weeks. Non-residential drug treatment counseling is available to all inmates on an individual basis. The Residential Drug Abuse Treatment Program (RDAP) is a voluntary 500-hour program, with follow-up counseling for RDAP graduates. All participation in non-residential treatment services is voluntary.

**Health Services:** The institution is staffed by physicians, physician assistants, dentist, dental assistant, and a pharmacist, with medical staff available seven days a week. The institution provides outpatient care and is also served by Mesquite Hospital approximately 15 minutes away. Sign-ups for routine medical sick call are Monday, Tuesday, Thursday and Friday from 6am-6:30am. A physician assistant shall screen all appointment requests and schedule appointment time based upon the needs of the patient. Open house for medical records: Monday through Friday 7am-7:30pm. Health service administration hours: Monday through Friday 2pm-3pm. Pill line hours: 7am-7:20am, 2:50pm-3:10pm, 7pm-7:20pm (weekdays); 8am-8:30am, 2:50pm-3:10pm and 7pm-7:20pm (weekends and holidays). Periodic age-specific preventative health examinations are available.

**Housing:** Inmates are housed in dormitories in two-man, three-man (DAP units), and five-man rooms. Inmates at the FDC are housed in two-man cells. All televisions must be turned off by 12midnight, Sunday through Thursday. On Friday, Saturday and federal holidays, televisions are turned off by 2am.

**Fitness/Recreation:** Leisure time activities are posted on the unit bulletin boards. Organized sports include: softball, flag football, soccer, volleyball, tennis, handball, racquetball and basketball. Varsity sports teams are chosen from the inmate population to compete in contests against outside teams. Weightlifting and fitness equipment are stationed within the weight area. A wellness program, auditorium and music room are available. Hours for the recreation yard, weight area and music room are weekdays, 6am-2:50pm and 4:30pm-8:20pm; weekends and holidays, 7:30am-2:50pm and 4:30pm-8:20pm (staff coverage and weather permitting). The hobby shop is open weekdays 7am-10:30am and 11:30am-2:50pm; weekends and holidays, 7:30am-2:50pm, 4:30pm-8pm. A variety of arts and crafts tools, including leather craft and painting, are available.

**Religious Services:** The institution is staffed by several full-time chaplains. Contract rabbi and imam services are also provided, and over 150 community volunteers help in providing services for most faiths. A sweat lodge is available for Native-American services. To participate in Islamic Jumah Prayer or Native-American sweat lodge ceremonies, an inmate must submit an Inmate Request to Staff Member form to the chaplains. Participation in the chapel program is on a voluntary basis; schedules are distributed at Admission and Orientation sessions then posted on the compound-side outer chapel wall, as well as inside the chapel. The chapel offers a religious library for inmates who choose to use it. Chaplains are available on an individual basis, usually seven days a week.

**Commissary:** Shopping hours are Monday through Friday 11am-12:30pm and after the 4pm count until 8pm. Inmates' commissary shopping hours are based on the fourth and fifth digits of their registration numbers. The commissary is closed the last five working days of December, March, June and September and on every federal holiday. The monthly commissary spending limit is $360.

**Telephone Policy:** Inmates at FCI and camp can dial direct or call collect. The following are standard features of ITS: (1) inmate calls automatically terminate after 15 minutes; (2) an inmate's calling list is limited to 30 callers; and (3) calls are charged to an inmate debit card. Each inmate will be issued 300 minutes a month, with the possibility of additional minutes granted with unforeseen emergencies only. Unit telephones are in operation 6am-7:30am, 10:30am-12:30pm, 3:30pm-11:30pm (except during counts), Monday through Friday. During normal working hours, only one telephone per unit is operational from 6am-11:30pm on weekdays. On weekends and federal holidays, all telephones are operational from 6am-11:30pm (except during counts). All calls are monitored, although arrangements can be made for unmonitored attorney calls.

**Inmate Mail:** The FCI accepts mail from the U.S. Postal Service via First-Class, U.S. Priority, and Express Mail. For those interested in sending overnight mail via a private carrier (FedEx or UPS Overnight), it is recommended that you first contact the institution to find out whether the receipt of such mail is permitted. Inmates may receive softcover publications (magazines, paperback books) from any source, but hardcover publications and newspapers must come directly from the publisher, bookstore, or book club.

**Inmate Mail to FCI:**
INMATE NAME & REGISTER NUMBER
FCI Seagoville
Federal Correctional Institution
P.O. Box 9000
Seagoville, TX 75159

**Inmate Mail to Camp:**
INMATE NAME & REGISTER NUMBER
FCI Seagoville
Federal Correctional Institution
Satellite Camp
P.O. Box 9000
Seagoville, TX 75159

**Visiting Hours:** FCI visiting hours: Friday 2:30pm-8:30pm; Monday, Saturday, Sunday and holidays 8:30am-3pm. FDC visiting hours: Friday, Saturday, Sunday, Monday 8:30am-3pm. SCP visiting hours: Saturday, Sunday, federal holidays 8:30am-3pm. Inmates may have up to five visitors. Inmates are limited to six visiting points per month, with two points deducted for a weekend or holiday visit, and one point deducted for a weekday visits. No more than ten friends and/or associates and unlimited family members that can be confirmed will be included on the visiting list. Inmates may request changes to their respective visiting lists at any time. Attorneys should request their visits in advance. Additional information is available at the BOP website, www.bp.gov, at https://www.bop.gov/locations/institutions/sea/.

**Lodging/Accommodations:** Should visitors be spending the night, the following is a short list of accommodations that are available in Seagoville and nearby Dallas, Texas:

| | |
|---|---|
| Best Western Executive Inn | 972-287-9100 |
| Hampton Inn & Suites Dallas-Mesquite | 972-329-3100 |
| Motel Six Balch Springs | 972-286-1010 |
| Seagoville Inn | 972-287-2600 |
| Western Skies Motel | 972-287-5521 |

## §15:26   FCI TEXARKANA

FCI Texarkana
Federal Correctional Institution
4001 Leopard Drive
Texarkana, TX 75501
TEX/ExecAssistant@bop.gov
903-838-4587
Fax: 903-223-4424

**Location:** In northeast Texas near the Arkansas border, 70 miles north of Shreveport, Louisiana, and 175 miles east of Dallas/Fort Worth, off Route 59 South, on Leopard Drive; exit 220 from I-30, to the Lake Drive/Leopard Drive Exit. Remain in the middle lane, go through the intersection, and move to the right lane. Turn right at the stop sign (Leopard Drive) and continue south on Leopard Drive to the institution (approximately one quarter mile).

**History:** Opened in 1940, FCI Texarkana houses a variety of male offenders, including inmates completing their sentences started at other institutions. Inmates are primarily from the South Central and Southeastern United States.

**Judicial District:** Eastern District of Texas.

**Security Level:** FCI Texarkana is a low-security facility housing male inmates. An adjacent satellite prison camp houses minimum-security male offenders.

**Population:** As of 6/23/2017, the FCI inmate population is 960, and the camp population is 289. Weekly population figures are available on the BOP website at https://www.bop.gov/locations/institutions/tex/.

**Education:** The FCI and the camp offer GED, ESL, Adult Continuing Education and correspondence courses.

**Vocational/Apprenticeship:** The FCI has offered vocational training in the following areas: A+ Computer Technician, Auto Mechanics, Computer Literacy, HVAC, Construction, Culinary Arts, Drafting, Upholstery, Welding. Check with the VT coordinator for a complete list of available programs and the specific eligibility criteria for each. The apprenticeship program consists of cook, electrician, air conditioning, dental assistant and dental technician.

**Library:** The inmate library houses a wide variety of books including vocational and technical books, general reference (encyclopedias, dictionaries, etc.), college and high school texts, as well as fiction and non-fiction. Several magazines and daily newspapers are also provided. The law library carries law books and case law as defined by Bureau of Prisons policy. Typewriters are available for inmates for legal material only. An Education staff member and inmate clerks are available to assist.

**UNICOR:** Electronics Recycling and Industrial Filter operations are located at both the FCI and camp.

**Counseling/Rehab Services:** The Psychology Department offers a wide range of treatment options for drug/alcohol abuse, from a 30-40 hour drug education course, to AA/NA groups, to comprehensive drug abuse interventions. Specifically, the institution offers a 500-hour residential drug abuse treatment program (RDAP). Other programs include a focus on post-release survival, anger management, values development, self-help modules, and more. Individual and group interventions are available by request. The clinicians making up the treatment staff at FCI Texarkana are all licensed in their fields of specialty.

**Health Services:** Medical staffing for FCI and FPC Texarkana includes two full-time physicians, two dentists, a health systems administrator, five mid-level practitioners, five registered nurses, three health information technicians, a pharmacist, a pharmacy technician, an infectious disease/IOP coordinator, an x-ray technician, a dental technician, a contract optometrist, and two medical secretaries. FCI and camp sick call are held on Monday, Tuesday, Thursday and Friday, excluding holidays; from 6:30am-7am, unless otherwise announced over the public address system. Pill lines takes place at 6:30-6:45 am, 12pm, 3:35pm, and 8:20pm. Inmates age 50 and over are eligible for a physical examination every year. Emergency medical care is available 24 hours a day. Local hospitals are approximately five to ten minutes away.

**Housing:** Inmates at the FCI are housed in open dormitories (contain up to 40 inmates), two-man and four-man rooms. Television rooms close at 10pm every night, except Friday and Saturday, when they close at 11:30pm. Television programs are pre-selected and the television schedules will be posted.

**Fitness/Recreation:** All inmates are encouraged to participate in recreational activities. The Recreation Department sponsors a number of exercise programs based on cardiovascular exercise, which are ten weeks in length and are available for all age groups. A small recreation yard with one tennis court, two handball courts, a covered weightlifting area, a large recreation yard which has a softball field, soccer field, running track, six handball courts, two horseshoe pits, a bocce pit, two shuffleboard decks, a basketball court, and a weightlifting area. The recreation yard's hours of operation are 6:20am-8:25pm daily. Organized teams from housing units play scheduled softball and other games. The recreation department provides league play in softball, volleyball, soccer, basketball, and flag football. Most sports equipment can be obtained at the commissary sales unit. The checkout office in the recreation shack on the large yard has golf equipment, baseball gloves, bats, soccer balls, and shuffleboard equipment (check the bulletin board for specific hours of operation).

When the weather does not permit outside activities, there is a gymnasium (not available at the Camp) with basketball, handball/racquetball, volleyball, and aerobic equipment. The modular unit (not available at the Camp) offers a place for table and board games, music, art and hobby craft. The hobby craft program offers leather craft, stick art, beads, painting, drawing, and airbrushing. There are two band rooms in the modular unit.

**Religious Services:** A full-time chaplain is available to provide worship services and group programs. Contract rabbi (monthly) and imam services are available. Many other programs are led by community volunteers. Chapel schedules are posted and supplemented on the bulletin boards at the chapel and in the housing units.

**Commissary:** The commissary is open Monday through Thursday evenings and at noon. Commissary hours and prices are posted on the bulletin board. The national monthly commissary spending limit set is $360, but the monthly spending limit per inmate for the FCI Texarkana commissary changes occasionally. A representative from the commissary will explain the current spending limit during the A&0 programs.

**Telephone Policy:** Inmates at the FCI and the camp dial direct using the Inmate Telephone System (ITS). The following are standard features of ITS: (1) inmate calls automatically terminate after 15 minutes; (2) an inmate's calling list is limited to 30 callers; and (3) calls are charged to an inmate's debit card. At the FCI, the telephones are located in each housing unit. There is a one-hour waiting period between calls. At the FCI, the telephones are located in each housing unit. The telephones are operational from 6am-10pm daily.

**Inmate Mail:** The FCI accepts mail from the U.S. Postal Service via First-Class, U.S. Priority, and Express Mail. For those interested in sending overnight mail via a private carrier (FedEx or UPS Overnight), it is recommended that you first contact the institution to find out whether the receipt of such mail is permitted. Inmates may receive softcover material (*e.g.*, paperback books, magazines) from any source, while hardcover publications and newspapers must come directly from the publisher, bookstore, or book club. Publications will be searched for contraband; packages marked "paperback books" or "magazines" will be rejected if they contain other items.

**Inmate Mail to FCI:**
    INMATE NAME & REGISTER NUMBER
    FCI Texarkana
    Federal Correctional Institution
    P.O. Box 7000
    Texarkana, TX 75505

**Inmate Mail to Camp:**
INMATE NAME & REGISTER NUMBER
FCI Texarkana
Federal Correctional Institution
Satellite Camp
P.O. Box 9300
Texarkana, TX 75505

**Visiting Hours:** Visiting hours for the FCI and camp: Saturday, Sunday and all federal holidays from 8am-3pm. Inmates are given five visiting points per month, with one point deducted on regular visiting days and two points deducted on holidays. Points may be waived for major holiday periods. Inmates are limited to four adult visitors and four minor children visiting at one time. Should more than four visitors arrive at the same time, a split visit may be arranged, with one interchange of visitors allowed. Visiting lists may include immediate family and up to 20 additional adult visitors. Attorney visits should be requested in advance and will take place during regular visiting hours. However, depending on the nature and urgency of the legal issue, such visits will not be limited by normal visiting procedures. Additional visiting information can be found on the BOP website, www.bop.gov at https://www.bop.gov/locations/institutions/tex/.

**Lodging/Accommodations:** Should visitors be spending the night, the following is a short list of accommodations that are available in Texarkana, Texas:

| | |
|---|---|
| Budget Inn | 903-838-0300 |
| Country Inn & Suites | 903-838-6955 |
| Hampton Inn & Suites | 903-832-3499 |
| Holiday Inn Express Hotel & Suites Texarkana | 903-223-0008 |
| Comfort Suites | 903-223-0951 |

## §15:27 FCI THREE RIVERS

FCI Three Rivers
Federal Correctional Institution
U.S. Highway 72 West
Three Rivers, TX 78071
TRV/ExecAssistant@bop.gov
361-786-3576
Fax: 361-786-5051

**Location:** Eight miles west of the city of Three Rivers across the highway from Choke Canyon reservoir, about 80 miles south of San Antonio and 73 miles northwest of Corpus Christi.

**History:** Opened in 1990, FCI Three Rivers houses medium- and minimum-security offenders who are primarily from the Southwestern United States.

**Judicial District:** South Texas.

**Security Level:** FCI Three Rivers is a medium-security facility housing male inmates. Adjacent satellite prison camp houses minimum-security male offenders.

**Population:** As of 6/23/2017, the FCI inmate population is 1,008, and the camp population is 308. Weekly population figures are available on the BOP website at www.bop.gov, https://www.bop.gov/locations/institutions/trv/.

**Education:** The FCI and camp offer GED, ESL, adult continuing education, parenting programs, and correspondence courses.

**Vocational/Apprenticeship:** FCI offers no certificate programs. The FCI offers vocational training in the following areas: building maintenance service, building trades, computer applications, welding, and HVAC. The camp offers vocational training as well: building trades, horticulture, waste water processing, dental assistant, and HVAC.

**Library:** The law library is now in an electronic format. An inmate library clerk is available to assist you Monday through Friday from 5pm-8:30pm; Saturday from 7am-3:30pm. The main institution's law/leisure library is open Monday through Thursday from 7:45am-10:30am, 12:30pm-3:30pm, and 5pm-8:30pm; Friday from 7:45am-10:30am and 12:30pm-3:30pm; Saturday from 7am-3:30pm; closed on holidays. The leisure library carries novels, westerns, science fiction, mysteries, and non-fiction. An inter-library loan program is available. Each inmate is allowed to check out two leisure library books and one interlibrary loan book at a time. The camp's leisure/law library is open weekdays from 7:30am-3:30pm and 4:30pm-8:30pm. The camp's law/leisure library offers resources and services similar to those found at the FCI.

**UNICOR:** UNICOR Three Rivers is an upfit operation for various DOJ law enforcement agencies. The upfit operations job skill requirements are as follows: electrical/welding/automotive experience. UNICOR Three Rivers also operates a Fleet Management Call Center, which supports a DOJ-wide mandate on record keeping of the entire motor fleet.

**Counseling/Rehab Services:** The institution has professional staff as resources that are trained in the various social science fields. Inmate participation in counseling/rehab services will be encouraged upon the staff's assessment of a prisoner's needs, but participation in such activities is voluntary. Among some of the services provided by the psychology staff are individual and group therapy, a 40-hour drug prevention program, non-residential drug abuse treatment, residential drug abuse program, relapse prevention groups, psycho-educational programs (*e.g.*, anger management, stress management, communication skills) and crisis intervention. Inmates who want an appointment to see the psychologist regarding a mental health issue should send a request to the Psychology Department, and then watch the call-out sheet for appointment day and time. The psychology department has an open house Monday and Wednesday, 8:30am-9:30am.

**Health Services:** The FCI is staffed by two physicians and nine physician assistants who function as primary health care providers. The FCI and the camp provide outpatient care. The nearest hospital is approximately 45 minutes away. Sick call sign-up at the FCI is at the Health Services Department: 7am-7:30am, Monday, Tuesday, Thursday, and Friday (except for holidays). Sick call sign-up at the camp is at the Health Services Department: 8am-8:30am, Monday, Tuesday, Thursday and Friday (except for holidays). Pill line hours at the FCI and FPC are Monday through Friday, 6:20am-6:50am and 4:50pm-5:20pm; Saturday, 6:45am-7:15am and 4:50pm-5:20pm. At least one physician assistant is on duty or on call 24 hours a day.

**Housing:** Inmates at the FCI are housed in two-man cells. Inmates at the camp are housed in "open bay" dormitories.

**Fitness/Recreation:** The recreation department offers leisure and fitness programs: walk run club, bike club, stair master club, calisthenics, yoga, and health promotion disease prevention program. These programs are open on a continued basis. Inmates are entitled to use the fitness equipment during non-business hours when they enroll in fitness programs. The leisure center has acoustic guitars, accordions, and percussion instruments available for inmate use. Beginner and intermediate acoustic guitar and art classes are available on a 12-week basis. The leisure center also has a hobby craft program, which offers inmates the opportunity to work with wood, leather, beads, crochet/knitting, and art. Intramural sports leagues are offered throughout the year: softball, basketball, flag football, soccer, and volleyball. The outdoor track at the camp is open at 6am every day.

**Religious Services:** Protestant and Catholic services are available as well as contract and volunteer representatives of other faiths. The Pastoral Care Department maintains a religious library of reading material, audiotapes and videotapes. These materials are available for distribution and to be checked out. Audio and videotapes are available for listening and viewing in the chapel area, if time and space permit. If an inmate is confined to a restricted area, the chaplains are available to visit upon request.

**Commissary:** The commissary at the FCI is open Monday through Thursday, 9:30am-12noon. Hours at the camp commissary are Tuesday through Thursday, 6:30am-7am and 10:30am-11:15am. Shopping days are based on the inmates' registration numbers. The shopping schedule is subject to change during holidays and institutional changes; the inmate population will be notified of any changes. The spending limit is set at $360 per month.

**Telephone Policy:** Telephones operate on the Inmate Telephone System II (ITS-II). The ITS-II is a direct dial/collect call, debit system, which allows inmates to place local, long distance, and international telephone calls. Inmates at the FCI and the camp can dial direct or call collect. Inmate telephones at the FCI are operational from 6:30am-9:30pm (except during counts). There are some periods where the phones are shut off, which will be detailed in the inmates' handbooks. Telephones at the camp are operational 24 hours a day, except during count times. All telephone calls, except approved legal calls, are subject to monitoring and recording.

**Inmate Mail:** The FCI and the camp accept mail from the U.S. Postal Service via First-Class, U.S. Priority, and Express Mail. For those interested in sending overnight mail via a private carrier (FedEx or UPS Overnight), it is recommended that you first contact the institution to find out whether the receipt of such mail is permitted. Inmates may subscribe to and receive publications without prior approval, although the warden will reject publications if they are determined to be detrimental to the security, good order, or discipline of the institution. Newspapers and magazines can only be received from the publisher while books can only be received from the publisher, bookstore, or book club. Accumulation of publications will be limited to ten magazines, five books, and two newspapers.

**Inmate Mail to FCI:**
INMATE NAME & REGISTER NUMBER
FCI Three Rivers
Federal Correctional Institution
P.O. Box 4200
Three Rivers, TX 78071

**Inmate Mail to Camp:**
INMATE NAME & REGISTER NUMBER
FCI Three Rivers
Federal Correctional Facility
Satellite Camp
P.O. Box 4200
Three Rivers, TX 78071

**Visiting Hours:** Visiting hours for the FCI and camp: Saturday, Sunday and federal holidays 8:15am-3pm. Social and special visits (legal or religious) for each inmate will be unlimited in accordance with the institution visiting hours and days; each inmate is authorized a minimum of four hours of visiting time a month. Inmates are limited to six visitors, including minor children at one time. Inmates are limited to no more than 20 visitors on their visiting list (including children). Attorney visits should be scheduled in advance and take place during regular visiting hours, although visits can be arranged at other times based on the circumstances of each case and availability of the staff. Additional visiting information can be found on the BOP website at https://www.bop.gov/locations/institutions/trv/.

**Lodging/Accommodations:** Should visitors be spending the night, the following is a short list of accommodations that are available in Three Rivers, Texas:

| | |
|---|---|
| Bass Inn | 361-786-3521 |
| Rodeway Inn | 361-786-3563 |
| Best Western Inn Three Rivers | 361-786-2000 |
| Live Oak Lodging | 361-786-4440 |
| Atria Inn and Suites | 361-786-1500 |

(This page intentionally left blank.)

# CHAPTER 16

---

# THE SOUTHEAST REGION

(This page intentionally left blank.)

**Central Office**
Central Office
Federal Bureau of Prisons
320 First St., NW
Washington, DC 20534
Phone: 202-307-3198

**Southeast Regional Office**
Southeast Regional Office
Federal Bureau of Prisons
3800 Camp CRK PK SW/BDG 2000
Atlanta, GA 30331
Phone: 678-686-1200

## §16:09   FCI ALICEVILLE

FCI Aliceville
Federal Correctional Institution
11070 Highway 14
Aliceville, AL 35442
ALI/ExecAssistant@bop.gov
205-373-5000
Fax: 205-373-5020

**Location:** In rural Alabama, in Pickens County, between Aliceville and Pickensville. It is 55 miles southwest of Tuscaloosa, Alabama, and 35 miles southeast of Columbus, Mississippi. Airline and taxi services are available in Tuscaloosa, but no closer.

**History:** Opened in 2013, FCI Aliceville is a medium-security prison for female inmates. A satellite prison camp for minimum-security female inmates is located outside the secure FCI compound.

**Security Level:** FCI Aliceville houses medium-security female inmates, with a satellite camp for minimum-security female inmates.

**Population:** As of 06/4/2017, the inmate population at the federal correction institution is 1,216 female offenders, and at the camp it is 258 female offenders. Weekly population figures are available on the BOP website www.bop.gov, at https://www.bop.gov/locations/institutions/ali/.

**Education:** The FCI and the camp offer GED, English as a Second Language (ESL), adult continuing education, parenting, vocational, apprenticeships, and release preparation. The vocational programs require a high school diploma or GED, and fluency in English. College correspondence programs are also available.

**Library:** The FCI and camp leisure library is open 7:30-10:30 am weekdays and 7:30 am–9:30 pm Saturday. Inmates may check books out for two-week periods. The law library is open 12:00-3:30 pm and 11:00 am–3:30 pm Saturday. The law library contains a copy machine and typewriters.

**Work:** The Facilities Operations Department employs an inmate work force of 75 in the following trade shops: Carpentry, Electric, HVAC, Landscape, Paint, Plumbing, Utility Maintenance, and General Maintenance.

**Counseling/Rehab:** Brief counseling sessions are available to address individual needs. Group counseling is available for drug and trauma treatment.

**Health Services:** Sick Call is held in Health Services 6:30 am–7:15 am Monday, Tuesday, Thursday, and Friday. A triage nurse conducts the screening, and then schedules a complete assessment by a provider. Inmates are assigned a specific pill line to receive medication not authorized to be on the compound.

**Fitness/Recreation:** The recreation yard is open 6:30 am–10:30 am Monday–Friday and 7:00 am–9:30 am weekends and holidays.

**Commissary:** Inmates are assigned one shopping day per week. Bureau of Prisons policy currently sets a monthly commissary spending limit of $360.

**Telephone Policy:** Inmates at the FCI and the camp may either call collect or dial direct using the Inmate Telephone System (ITS). The following are standard features of ITS: (1) inmate calls automatically terminate after 15 minutes; (2) an inmate's calling list is limited to 30 callers; and (3) calls are charged to an inmate's debit card. Inmates at the FCI and camp are authorized 300 minutes of call time per month to be used for direct and collect/prepaid calls. In order to make an unmonitored call to an attorney, a "Request for Legal Call Form" must be submitted to your unit team. Camp inmates have phone access Monday through Friday from 6:00 a.m. until 9:30 p.m.

**Inmate Mail:** The FCI and the camp accept mail from the U.S. Postal Service via First-Class, U.S. Priority, and Express Mail. For those interested in sending overnight mail via a private carrier (FedEx or UPS Overnight), it is recommended that you first contact the institution to find out whether the receipt of such mail is permitted. Inmates may receive publications without prior approval, although the warden will reject publications if they are determined to be detrimental to the security, good order or discipline of the institution. Hardcover publications may only come directly from the publisher or bookstore, but softcover publications may come from any source.

**Inmate Mail to FCI:**
    INMATE NAME & REGISTER NUMBER
    FCI Aliceville
    Federal Correctional Institution
    P.O. Box 4000
    Aliceville, AL 35442

**Inmate Mail to Camp:**
    INMATE NAME & REGISTER NUMBER
    FCI Aliceville
    Federal Correctional Institution
    Satellite Camp
    P.O. Box 4878
    Aliceville, AL 35442

**Visiting Hours:** Visiting hours at the FCI and camp are Friday, Saturday, Sunday, Monday, and federal holidays 8am-3pm. Visitors 18 years and older must have a current photo ID, such as a driver's license or passport. Visitors will be checked with a metal detector. Attorneys are encouraged to visit during the regular visiting hours, but can be arranged at other times. Additional visiting information can be found at https://www.bop.gov/locations/institutions/ali/.

**Lodging/Accommodations:** Here is a short list of accommodations nearby:

| | |
|---|---|
| Oak Tree Inn, Macon, MS | 662-726-4334 |
| Comfort Inn Eutaw, Eutaw, AL | 205-372-9363 |
| Days Inn, Columbus, MS | 662-329-4544 |
| Ramada Inn, Columbus, MS | 662-327-7077 |
| Best Western Catalina Inn, Northport, AL | 205-339-5200 |
| Comfort Inn, Livingston, AL | 205-652-4839 |

## §16:10   USP ATLANTA

USP Atlanta
U.S. Penitentiary
601 McDonough Blvd., S.E.
Atlanta, GA 30315
ATL/PublicInformation@bop.gov
404-635-5100
Fax: 404-331-2403

**Location:** In the southeast quadrant of Atlanta, at the junction of Boulevard and McDonough Streets. Off Interstate 75 (Exit 26), Interstate 20 (Exit 26), or Interstate 285 (Exit 39). Atlanta is served by Hartsfield International Airport, Amtrak and commercial bus lines.

**History:** Opened in 1902, USP Atlanta consists of general housing units, a detention center, and a satellite camp. It primarily held Cuban detainees from 1980-1987. It was reconstructed following the 1987 prison disturbance and currently houses male inmates of all security levels, holdovers, and pre-trail detainees. A new building houses pre-trial detainees was added in 1995.

**Judicial District:** Northern District of Georgia.

**Security Level:** USP Atlanta houses medium-security male inmates, with a detention center for pre-trial and holdover inmates and a satellite camp for minimum-security male inmates.

**Population:** As of 6/24/2017, the inmate population at the USP is 1,736, and at the camp it is 413. Weekly population figures are available on the BOP website at www.bop.gov, https://www.bop.gov/locations/institutions/atl/.

**Education:** The USP and the camp offer GED, ESL, adult education, and correspondence courses.

**Vocational/Apprenticeship:** The USP offers advanced occupational education in basic/certification custodial maintenance and building maintenance/electric. The USP offers vocational training in HVAC. The USP offers apprenticeship in: cook, electrician, and plumber. The camp offers advanced occupational education in: basic/certification custodial maintenance. The camp offers apprenticeship programs in: cook, electrician, and plumber.

**Library:** The penitentiary and camp leisure/law libraries are open during non-working hours, including weekends. There are electric typewriters available to inmates for the preparation of legal documents. A copier is also available. VCRs and audio cassette players are available to inmates in the leisure library.

**UNICOR:** A textile factory (manufactures mailbags and uniforms for the U.S. Army) employs approximately 496 inmates.

**Counseling/Rehab Services:** The penitentiary and the camp offer a non-residential drug treatment program, a drug education program, and Alcoholics Anonymous and Narcotics Anonymous groups. In addition, the penitentiary offers counseling groups in stress management, anger management, anxiety and depression, and living free. The psychology department is staffed by four to six full-time psychologists and three interns.

**Health Services:** The penitentiary is staffed by five physicians, seven to ten physician assistants, two to three dentists, and three to five dental assistants. The USP and the camp provide outpatient care. A small hospital ward is also available at the USP. The pill line at the USP is available daily from 6:30am-7am, 11:30am-12:30pm, and 5pm-5:30pm; the pill line at the camp is available from 6:30am-7am and 3pm-3:30pm. Sick call sign-up at the penitentiary is from 6:30am-7am, four times a week. At least one physician assistant is on duty or on call 24 hours a day. Preventative health screenings may be requested every three years for inmates under the age of 50, and every year for inmates over the age of 50.

**Housing:** Inmates at the USP are housed in one and two-man cells and open dormitories. Inmates at the camp are housed in dormitories in two-man cubicles.

**Fitness/Recreation:** The penitentiary's recreation department offers indoor/outdoor sports, music rooms/musical instruments, racquetball, stationary bicycles, and treadmills. The hobby craft center offers leather craft, art, beading, drawing, painting and crocheting. The camp's recreation department offers team sports, weights, bocce ball, and shuffleboard. The camp also contains an art room leather craft room, billiard room, and music room.

**Religious Services:** The penitentiary is staffed by four full-time chaplains. Community volunteers help with service for most faiths.

**Commissary:** Inmates are assigned one shopping day per week. Bureau of Prisons policy currently sets a monthly commissary spending limit of $360.

**Telephone Policy:** Inmates at the USP and the camp may either call collect or dial direct using the Inmate Telephone System (ITS). The following are standard features of ITS: (1) inmate calls automatically terminate after 15 minutes; (2) an inmate's calling list is limited to 30 callers; and (3) calls are charged to an inmate's debit card. Each inmate gets 300 call minutes per month. The telephones at the penitentiary are located in the housing units and are operational daily from 6am until 11pm. Inmates at the penitentiary may submit proposed updates/changes or corrections to their telephone list on any day, up to three times a month.

**Inmate Mail:** The USP and the camp accept mail from the U.S. Postal Service via First-Class, U.S. Priority, and Express Mail. For those interested in sending overnight mail via a private carrier (FedEx or UPS Overnight), it is recommended that you first contact the institution to find out whether the receipt of such mail is permitted. Inmates may receive publications without prior approval, although the warden will reject publications if they are determined to be detrimental to the security, good order or discipline of the institution. Hardcover publications may only come directly from the publisher or bookstore, but softcover publications may come from any source. Each inmate is limited to five magazines (no more than 60 days old) and to the amount that can be stored neatly in their room.

**Inmate Mail to USP:**
INMATE NAME & REGISTER NUMBER
USP Atlanta
U.S. Penitentiary
P.O. Box 150160
Atlanta, GA 30315

**Inmate Mail to Camp:**
INMATE NAME & REGISTER NUMBER
USP Atlanta
U.S. Penitentiary
Satellite Camp
P.O. Box 150160
Atlanta, GA 30315

**Visiting Hours:** Visiting hours at the USP and camp are Friday, Saturday, Sunday and federal holidays 8am-3pm. Extra hours for attorney visits are on Tuesday and Wednesday. Holdover and pre-trial inmates can receive social and attorney visits Saturday through Wednesday. On Saturday and Sunday an even/

odd schedule will be used for USP general population inmates only. The fifth digit of an inmate's register number is utilized when determining if he has an even or odd number. Each USP inmate is allotted five visits per calendar month. Visits on federal holidays will not count against the five allotted visits each month. No more than four adults and three children are allowed to visit at one time. Attorney visits should take place during regular visiting times, but special arrangements can be requested. Additional visiting information can be at www. bop.gov, https://www.bop.gov/locations/institutions/atl/.

**Lodging/Accommodations:** Should visitors be spending the night, the following is a short list of accommodations that are available in Atlanta, Georgia:

| | |
|---|---|
| Atlanta Airport Travelodge | 404-768-7750 |
| Country Inn & Suites Atlanta Downtown | 404-658-1961 |
| Econo Lodge Airport | 404-363-6429 |
| Grant Park Hotel | 404-658-1610 |
| New American Inn | 404-767-8020 |

## §16:11   FCI BENNETTSVILLE

FCI Bennettsville
Federal Correctional Institution
696 Muckerman Road
Bennettsville, SC 29512
BEN/ExecAssistant@bop.gov
843-454-8500
Fax: 843-454-8219

**Location:** FCI Bennettsville is located on 670 acres in the southeast region of South Carolina approximately 86 miles from Myrtle Beach in Marlboro County off Hwy 9. This area is served by Florence Regional Airport (31 miles) and Douglass International, Charlotte, NC (89 miles).

**Judicial District:** District of South Carolina.

**Security Level:** FCI Bennettsville is a medium-security facility that houses male inmates. It has an adjacent minimum-security male camp.

**Population:** As of 6/24/2017, the FCI inmate population is 1,268, and the camp population is 164. Weekly population figures are available on the BOP website, www.bop.gov at https://www.bop.gov/locations/institutions/ben/.

**Education:** The FCI offers GED, ESL, adult continuing education, and correspondence courses. Adult continuing education classes include business, public speaking, writing, Spanish, math, calligraphy and commercial driver's license (academic instruction only). Current offerings range from African-American

History to Law I. In addition, there are several self-study language courses available for enrollment, including Spanish, Arabic, French, German, and Mandarin Chinese. Debate Club and Drama Club are offered once a year. Some classes are available in Spanish.

**Vocational/Apprenticeship:** The Vocational Training Program offers a variety of work-related programs. Inmates must have a verified GED or high school credential to participate in vocational training classes. Course offerings at the FCI include the following: Automotive Chassis and Powertrain, Culinary Arts, Electrical Technology, Green Technology (NCCER), HVAC, Mechanical Maintenance and Systems, Fundamentals of Construction, Machine Shop, Microsoft 2010, NCCER Core, Safety Technology (NCCER), and Welding . The NCCER Core class is offered in English and Spanish. There are seven courses from the Green Clean Institute. The courses range from Green Janitorial Technician to Waste and Recycling Management. The students are required to pay a nominal fee for certification from the Green Clean Institute. The facility also offers two Department of Labor Apprenticeship programs: Industrial Cleaning and Electrical Offerings at the camp include NCCER Core, Welding, Culinary Arts, computer-based courses in Microsoft 2010, key-boarding, English as a Second Language, Spanish as a Second Language, and Resume Writing. There are also seven courses from the Green Clean Institute. The courses range from Green Janitorial Technician to Waste and Recycling Management. The students are required to pay a nominal fee for certification from the Green Clean Institute. Two Department of Labor Apprenticeship programs are also offered: Industrial Cleaning and Electrical.

**Library:** The law and leisure libraries at the FCI are open Monday through Thursday, 7:30am-10am, 12noon-3:30pm and 5pm-8pm; Friday and Saturday, 7:30am-10am and 12noon-3:30pm; closed Sunday and holidays. An additional leisure library is available in the Recreation Department and is open during recreation hours. The camp's library is open every day 7:30am-10am, 12noon-3:30pm and 5pm-8pm.

**UNICOR:** A heavy equipment remanufacturing plant employs approximately 250 inmates.

**Counseling/Rehab Services:** Services provided by the Psychology Department include: crisis intervention, individual counseling, group counseling and drug abuse treatment programs. These drug abuse treatment programs include the 500-hour Residential Drug Abuse Program, a non-residential drug abuse treatment, and a 40-hour drug education class.

**Health Services:** Inmates must submit a cop-out for routine medical appointment requests. For more urgent needs or concerns, inmates may attend sick call sign-up on Monday, Tuesday, Thursday and Friday from 6:30am-7am. At the camp, sick call sign-up is 6:15am-6:30am. Pill line times for both facilities: Monday through Friday, 6am-6:15am (insulin only), 6:15am-6:30am, 4:30pm-4:45pm (insulin only), 7pm-7:30pm; weekend morning hours are 7am-7:15am (insulin only) and 7:15am-7:30am, with the same evening hours.

**Housing:** FCI Bennettsville is broken up into 12 units. Televisions may be viewed in the unit activities area during established off-duty hours; all televisions will turn off at 11:30pm.

**Fitness/Recreation:** The Recreation Department's goals are to reduce personal stress and institutional tension; to keep inmates constructively occupied; and to increase physical fitness while incarcerated. Intramural sports include basketball, flag football, volleyball, softball and soccer. The yard has softball fields, racquetball, handball, and basketball courts, a walking/running track, and areas for bocce ball and horseshoes. FCI outdoor activities are open seven days a week, 7:30am-8:30pm; for the camp, the hours are Monday through Friday, 8am-8:30pm; Saturday, Sunday and holidays, 7am-8:30pm. The inside leisure center offers a fitness room, a wellness program, art, ceramics, crochet, music, board games, and guitar lessons. Movies are shown Friday, Saturday and Sunday evenings, and holidays. Indoor activities are available Monday through Friday, 8am-8:15pm; Saturday, Sunday and holidays, 7am-8:15pm.

**Religious Services:** A wide range of religious programs are offered. Staff chaplains are available, as well as contract and volunteer representatives of various faiths. Special religious diets, holiday observances, and other worship activities are coordinated through the chaplain's office. There is an 18-month residential Life Connections Program for inmates interested in deepening their spirituality. Information and schedules for religious activities are posted on the inmate and chapel bulletin boards, and inmates may contact the chaplain's office for additional information.

**Commissary:** The FCI sales Monday through Thursday from 9am-7pm, and for open house and Special Purpose Order sales Friday from 10:30am-noon. At the camp, sales are conducted on Wednesdays. Hours of the Commissary will be clearly posted. Bureau of Prisons monthly spending limit is currently $360.

**Telephone Policy:** Inmates at the FCI and the camp may call collect or dial direct using the Inmate Telephone System (ITS). The following are standard features of ITS: (1) inmate calls automatically terminate after 15 minutes; (2) an inmate's calling list is limited to 30 callers; and (3) calls are charged to an inmate's debit card. Each inmate gets 300 calling minutes per month. Telephones are available in each housing unit from 6am-9:45pm.

**Inmate Mail:** The FCI and the camp accept mail from the U.S. Postal Service via First-Class, U.S. Priority, and Express Mail. For those interested in sending overnight mail via a private carrier (FedEx or UPS Overnight), it is recommended that you first contact the institution to find out whether the receipt of such mail is permitted. Inmates may receive publications without prior approval, although the warden will reject publications if they are determined to be detrimental to the security, good order or discipline of the institution. All publications must be received directly from the publisher, bookstore or book club. Each inmate is limited to five newspapers, five magazines, and five books.

**Inmate Mail to FCI:**
INMATE NAME & REGISTER NUMBER
FCI Bennettsville
Federal Correctional Institution
P.O. Box 52020
Bennettsville, SC 29512

**Inmate Mail to Camp:**
INMATE NAME & REGISTER NUMBER
FCI Bennettsville
Federal Correctional Institution
Satellite Camp
P.O. Box 52010
Bennettsville, SC 29512

**Visiting Hours:** Visiting hours are Saturday, Sunday and holidays from 8:30pm-3pm, and Friday from 5pm-8pm. Visitors must arrive at least one hour before the the end of visiting hours. Each inmate is allowed a maximum of five visitors at a time. Attorneys should make advance appointments; they are encouraged to visit during regular hours, but visits can also be arranged at other times depending on the circumstances and availability of staff. Additional information can be found at https://www.bop.gov/locations/institutions/ben/.

**Lodging/Accommodations:** Should visitors be spending the night, the following is a short list of accommodations that are available near Bennettsville, South Carolina:

| | |
|---|---|
| Quality Inn Bennettsville | 843-479-1700 |
| Breeden Inn Bed & Breakfast | 843-479-3665 |
| Marlboro Inn | 843-479-4501 |
| Williams Motel | 843-479-6841 |

## §16:12   FCI COLEMAN—LOW

FCI Coleman Low
Federal Correctional Institution
846 N.E. 54th Terrace
Sumterville, FL 33521
COA/PublicInformation@bop.gov
352-689-4000
Fax: 352-689-4008

**Location:** In central Florida, approximately 50 miles northwest of Orlando, 60 miles northeast of Tampa, and 35 miles south of Ocala, off Highway 301 on State Road 470. The institution is located south of the town of Coleman.

**History:** Opened in 1995, it is now part of a correctional complex (FCC).

**Judicial District:** Middle District of Florida.

**Security Level:** FCI Coleman is a low-security facility housing male inmates.

**Population:** As of 6/24/2017, the inmate population is 1,906. Weekly figures are available at https://www.bop.gov/locations/institutions/col/.

**Education:** The FCI and the camp offer GED, ESL, Adult Continuing Education, parenting and correspondence courses.

**Vocational/Apprenticeship:** FCC Low offers advanced occupational education in culinary arts. FCC Low offers vocational training in computer based word processing, custodial maintenance, HVAC, and/or a comprehensive culinary arts program. FCC Low offers apprenticeship programs in: dental assistant, HVAC, maintenance mechanic plumber, maintenance mechanic electrical.

**Library:** The leisure/law library hours are Monday through Thursday, 7:30am-8pm; Friday and Saturday, 7:30am-3:30pm; closed Sunday. Law books may not be removed from the law library for any reason. Copies of documents or books may be made by using the "vending" machine balance on an inmate's card. There are ten to 12 electric typewriters available to inmates for the preparation of legal documents. A copier is available in the leisure library. Video cassette recorders and audio cassette players are available.

**UNICOR:** UNICOR at FCC Coleman consists of a furniture factory which employs approximately 1,192 inmates. There is a waiting list for UNICOR.

**Counseling/Rehab Services:** The Psychology Department is comprised of the chief psychologist, the Drug Abuse Program (DAP) coordinator, the Drug Abuse Program (DAP) psychologist, one staff psychologist, seven drug treatment specialists, and one psychology technician. A part-time psychiatrist is contracted by the Health Services Department. Services include: a residential drug abuse treatment program (RDAP), a 12-month intensive treatment program; non-residential drug treatment groups, and the Choice and Change groups (formerly drug education); transitional services for RDAP graduates); psychological screenings, individual counseling, group counseling, psychological assessment, crisis counseling, and AIDS counseling; and Alcoholics Anonymous and Narcotics Anonymous groups.

**Health Services:** The institution is staffed by two physicians, two physician assistants, two dentists, and one pharmacist. Outpatient care is provided. Local hospitals are 20 minutes away. Sick call and dental call sign-up is conducted on Monday, Tuesday, Thursday, and Friday, excluding holidays, from 6:30am-7am. Pill line times: 6am-6:30am; 11:15am-12noon; 3pm-3:40pm; and 7:45pm-8:30pm. There will be a daily schedule at the commissary for over-the-counter (OTC) medications. OTC medications will not be routinely prescribed by practitioners. It is an inmate's responsibility to keep these items available for personal use.

**Housing:** The FCC Coleman low-security facility is comprised of three general population buildings (housing units): Citrus, Lake and Sumpter. Each of these buildings has two units, one on each floor, and each floor has two wings. Inmates are housed in dormitories in two-man cubicles.

**Fitness/Recreation:** The recreation department offers team sports, fitness/wellness classes, aerobics, stationary bicycles, a music center, musical instruments (drums, guitar, accordion, piano), pool tables, bocce ball, shuffle board, horseshoes, and ping-pong tables. The hobby craft center offers beadwork, drawing, and leatherwork.

**Religious Services:** The Religious Services Department has three full-time chaplains and utilizes the services of religious contractors and community volunteers. The chaplains are responsible for conducting religious services for their religious community, and personally counseling with inmates during times of crisis. The chaplains are dedicated to assisting inmates in their spiritual development and growth. The chaplains also regularly consult with the unit teams and are very interested in the various inmate programs offered at FCC Colman Low and in assisting inmates in programs of self-help. Inmates are employed in the Religious Services Department in clerical and janitorial positions.

**Commissary:** Monday through Thursday: 1pm-3pm; 4:30pm-8:30pm. Anyone not responding after their name has been called three times will forfeit their turn to shop, and will not be allowed to shop until the following week. Bureau of Prisons policy currently sets a monthly commissary spending limit of $360.

**Telephone Policy:** Inmates at the FCI and the camp may call collect or dial direct using the Inmate Telephone System (ITS). The following are standard features of ITS: (1) inmate calls automatically terminate after 15 minutes; (2) an inmate's calling list is limited to 30 callers; and (3) calls are charged to an inmate's debit card. Each inmate gets 300 calling minutes per month.

**Inmate Mail:** The FCI and the camp accept mail from the U.S. Postal Service via First-Class, U.S. Priority, and Express Mail. For those interested in sending overnight mail via a private carrier (FedEx or UPS Overnight), it is recommended that you first contact the institution to find out whether the receipt of such mail is permitted.

**Inmate Mail to FCI:**
INMATE NAME & REGISTER NUMBER
FCI Coleman Low
P.O. Box 1031
Coleman, FL 33521

**Visiting Hours:** Sunday, Monday, Friday, Saturday, federal holidays 8am-3pm. Each inmate will receive seven points per month. Inmates will be deducted three points weekend and holiday visits and one point for all other days. Inmates are limited to four adults (no limit for children) visiting at one time. No more than ten friends or associates and 20 relatives will be allowed on an inmate's visiting list. Attorneys must be on the inmate's approved visiting list, and are encouraged to visit during regular visiting hours; special arrangements must be made for visits during other times. Additional visiting information can be found on the BOP website at https://www.bop.gov/locations/institutions/col/.

**Lodging/Accommodations:** Should visitors be spending the night, the following is a short list of accommodations that are available in Leesburg which is about nine miles from Coleman, Florida:

| | |
|---|---|
| Best Western Plus Chain of Lakes Inn & Suites | 352-460-0118 |
| Hampton Inn Leesburg | 352-310-1023 |
| Palms Motel | 352-728-8606 |
| Sleep Inn | 352-326-9002 |

## §16:13   FCI COLEMAN—MEDIUM

FCI Coleman Medium
Federal Correctional Institution
846 N.E. 54th Terrace
Sumterville, FL 33521
COA/PublicInformation@bop.gov
352-689-5000
Fax: 352-689-5027

**Location:** See §16:12 FCI Coleman-Low.

**History:** Opened in 1997, is part of a correctional complex (FCC).

**Judicial District:** Middle District of Florida.

**Security Level:** FCI Coleman is a medium-security facility housing male inmates. It is part of the Coleman Federal Correctional Complex. The FCI also has an adjacent, minimum-security satellite camp housing female offenders.

**Population:** As of 6/24/2017, the inmate population at the FCI is 1,535, and the camp population is 384. Weekly population figures are available on the BOP website at https://www.bop.gov/locations/institutions/com/.

**Education:** The FCI and the camp offer GED, ESL, adult continuing education, parenting and correspondence courses.

**Vocational/Apprenticeship:** FCC Medium and the camp offer advanced occupational education in culinary arts and marketing, as well as vocational training in business education, drafting, and HVAC and apprenticeship programs in electrical wiring, plumbing, woodworking and masonry.

**Library:** The law and leisure library is open from 7:30am-8:30pm Monday through Friday and 7:30am-3:30pm on Saturday and 7:30am-9:30am on Sunday. Typewriters and photocopiers are available in the department and inmates with legal work will have priority. Leisure books may be checked out of the library. Newspapers and magazines must remain in the leisure reading area and legal books must be requested for use in the library only and cannot be checked out. The law/leisure library at the camp is open Monday through Friday from 12noon-8pm; from 7:30am-3:30pm on Saturday; and from 12noon-3:30pm on Sunday. The camp's law/leisure library offers similar services.

**UNICOR:** A furniture factory employs approximately 1,192 inmates at FCI Low/Medium. Inmates at the FCI laminate wood surfaces.

**Counseling/Rehab Services:** In addition to conducting routine initial intake screenings on all inmates admitted to the facility, Psychology Services staff provides crisis intervention services, brief counseling, individual and group therapy, and psycho-educational groups to inmates who are interested in these programs. Other services provided to inmates include HIV counseling and segregation reviews. In addition, Psychology Services coordinates the suicide prevention program. Psychology Services offers a drug education class as well as the Non-Residential Drug Abuse Program. Specifically, the institution offers a 500-hour residential drug abuse treatment program (RDAP). Transitional services are offered for inmates who have completed a Bureau of Prisons Residential Drug Abuse Program. The main institution is staffed by three full-time psychologists. A psychologist and contract psychiatrist are available at the camp.

**Health Services:** The main institution is staffed by one to two physicians, five physician assistants, four nurses, two dentists, and one to two pharmacists. The FCI and the camp provide outpatient care. Local hospitals are twenty minutes away. The Health Services unit is available for sick call, first-aid, emergency and routine treatment, and follow-up care prescribed by the mid-level practitioners or the clinical director. Sick call sign-up is from 6:30am-6:50am, Monday, Tuesday, Thursday, and Friday. Pill line hours, seven days a week: 6am-6:30am;

11:30am-12noon; 8pm-8:15pm. At least one physician assistant is on duty or on call 24 hours a day.

**Housing:** Inmates at the FCI are primarily housed in two-man cells. There are 12 housing units. Inmates at the camp are housed in dormitories in two-man cubicles. Televisions are operational on weekdays until 11:30pm and until 2am on weekends and holidays.

**Fitness/Recreation:** The recreation department offers three levels of league team sports, depending on ability. Outdoor recreation facilities also provide bocce courts, horseshoes, handball, and racquetball. The wellness center provides stair-steppers, pull-up bars, stationary bicycles, treadmills, and a music room. The music room offers drums, piano, classical theory, and orchestral instruments. The hobby craft center offers leather craft, art room, and wellness room. The camp offers team sports, aerobics, ping-pong, a band room, individual musical practice, billiards, shuffleboard, air hockey, foosball, and table top games. The hobby craft center offers art, crocheting, and leather.

**Religious Services:** The Religious Service Department provides a full pastoral ministry to inmates of faith groups. Visitations are conducted throughout the institutions and individual/group counseling is provided to those inmates in need of spiritual counseling, crisis intervention, etc. The chaplains are available to assist inmates in their spiritual development through informal visits to the chapel area or through a scheduled appointment. The main institution is staffed by three full-time chaplains. Contract rabbi and imam services are available. There are also full-time chaplains at the camp. Community volunteers assist with services for most faiths.

**Commissary:** The commissary is open Monday through Thursday from 12:30pm-3pm; 4:30pm-8:30pm. For special purchase orders: Friday 1pm-2pm. Special Housing Unit sales: Friday 8am-4pm. Shopping days are on a quarterly rotating basis, according to the inmate's register number. The Bureau of Prisons policy currently sets a monthly commissary spending limit of $360.

**Telephone Policy:** Inmates at the FCI and the camp may call collect or dial direct using the Inmate Telephone System (ITS). The following are standard features of ITS: (1) inmate calls automatically terminate after 15 minutes; (2) an inmate's calling list is limited to 30 callers; and (3) calls are charged to an inmate's debit card. Each inmate gets 300 calling minutes per month.

**Inmate Mail:** The FCI and the camp accept mail from the U.S. Postal Service via First-Class, U.S. Priority, and Express Mail. For those interested in sending overnight mail via a private carrier (FedEx or UPS Overnight), it is recommended that you first contact the institution to find out whether the receipt of such mail is permitted.

**Inmate Mail to FCI:**
INMATE NAME & REGISTER NUMBER
FCI Coleman Medium
Federal Correctional Institution
P.O. Box 1032
Coleman, FL 33521

**Inmate Mail to Camp:**
INMATE NAME & REGISTER NUMBER
FCI Coleman Medium
Federal Correctional Institution
Satellite Camp
P.O. Box 1027
Coleman, FL 33521

**Visiting Hours:** Approved visitors may visit FCC Coleman Medium: Sunday, Monday, Thursday, Friday, Saturday and holidays 8am-3pm. FCC Satellite Camp: Saturday, Sunday, holidays 8:15am-3pm. FCC Coleman Medium inmates are allowed visits based on a point system. Inmates are given two points each month. One point is deducted on Saturday, Sunday, other days and holidays no points will be deducted. Camp does not have a point system. Inmates are limited to five adult (no limit on children) visitors at one time. Attorneys should be on the approved visitor list and are encouraged to visit during regular visiting hours. Additional visiting information can be found on the BOP website, at https://www.bop.gov/locations/institutions/com/.

**Lodging/Accommodations:** See §16:12, FCI Coleman—Low.

## §16:14   USP COLEMAN I AND II

USP Coleman I
U.S. Penitentiary I
846 N.E. 54th Terrace
Sumterville, FL 33521
COA/PublicInformation@bop.gov
352-689-6000
Fax: 352-689-6012

USP Coleman II
U.S. Penitentiary II
846 N.E. 54th Terrace
Sumterville, FL 33521
COA/PublicInformation@bop.gov
352-689-7000
Fax: 352-689-7012

**Location:** See §16:12 FCI Coleman-Low.

**History:** Opened in 2001, USP I and USP II are part of the Coleman Federal Correctional Complex (FCC).

**Judicial District:** Middle District of Florida.

**Security Level:** USP Coleman I and II are high-security facilities housing male inmates.

**Population:** As of 6/24/2014, the inmate population at USP I is 1,304, and the USP II population is 1,371. Weekly population figures are available on the BOP website at www.bop.gov, https://www.bop.gov/locations/institutions/cop/ and https://www.bop.gov/locations/institutions/clp/, respectively.

**Education:** The USPs offer GED, ESL, adult continuing education, parenting, and correspondence courses.

**Vocational/Apprenticeship:** The USP I offers advanced occupational education in computer based word processing, custodial maintenance, and culinary arts. The pre-industrial classes in manufacturing are offered to help inmates earn certification in apprenticeship programs. USP I offers apprenticeship programs in: baker, dental assistant, HVAC, maintenance mechanic plumber, and maintenance mechanic electrical. USP II offers no certificate programs. USP II offers vocational training in computer based word processing, custodial maintenance, and culinary arts. USP II offers apprenticeship programs in: cooking, cook (hotel/restaurant), HVAC, maintenance mechanic plumber and maintenance mechanic electrical.

**Library:** At both USPs, typewriters and photocopiers are available in the library, and inmates with legal work will have priority. Leisure books may be checked out of the library. Newspapers, magazines, and all law books must remain in the libraries and cannot be checked out. Library hours are Monday through Thursday 9am-8pm; and Friday and Saturday 7:30am-3:30pm.

**Counseling/Rehab Services:** In Psychology Services there are clinical psychologists who provide assessment and treatment for problems such as depression, anxiety, and interpersonal issues. Treatment is offered through individual and group psychotherapy, as well as several self-help programs which utilize self-help books. This department also offers drug abuse education, non-residential drug abuse treatment, and referrals to the residential drug abuse program. Consultations with psychiatrists are arranged through Psychology and Medical Services staff to meet the needs of inmates who may require their services. USP II also offers a 500-hour residential drug abuse treatment program (RDAP).

**Health Services:** The Health Services Unit available for sick call, first aid, emergency and routine treatment, and follow-up care provided by the clinical nurse, mid-level practitioners, staff medical officer, or clinical director. Sick call sign-up is from 6:30am-7am, Monday, Tuesday, Thursday, and Friday. Pill line hours, seven days a week: 6am-6:30am; 2:30pm-3pm; 5:30pm-6pm.

**Fitness/Recreation:** The USP I recreation yard offers basketball courts, bocce courts, horse areas, handball/racquetball courts, a softball and soccer field, and jogging. The facility also offers a leisure room, music center, game room, cards, and fitness area.

**Religious Services:** Religious Services offers a wide range of religious programs for inmates. Chaplains are available for pastoral care, counseling, or other professional services. In addition to the chaplains on staff, programs and services are supported by outside volunteers. Religious Services provides fair and equitable treatment of all faith groups. Therefore, cooperation and understanding among the different faith groups is a necessary standard maintained at all times.

**Commissary:** The commissary is open for sales Monday through Thursday from 1pm-3:30pm and after the 4pm count-8:30pm. Bureau of Prisons policy currently sets a monthly spending limit of $360.

**Telephone Policy:** Inmates may call direct or call collect. The following are standard features of ITS: (1) inmate calls automatically terminate after 15 minutes; (2) an inmate's calling list is limited to 30 callers; and (3) calls are charged to an inmate's debit card.

**Inmate Mail:** The FCI and the camp accept mail from the U.S. Postal Service via First-Class, U.S. Priority, and Express Mail. For those interested in sending overnight mail via a private carrier (FedEx or UPS Overnight), it is recommended that you first contact the institution to find out whether the receipt of such mail is permitted.

**Inmate Mail to USP I:**
> INMATE NAME & REGISTER NUMBER
> USP Coleman I
> U.S. Penitentiary
> P.O. Box 1033
> Coleman, FL 33521

**Inmate Mail to USP II:**
> INMATE NAME & REGISTER NUMBER
> USP Coleman II
> U.S. Penitentiary
> P.O. Box 1034
> Coleman, FL 33521

**Visiting Hours:** Approved visitors may visit inmates at the USP I and USP units on Saturday, Sunday, Monday, and federal holidays 8am-3pm. Inmates are allowed visits based on a point system. Inmates are given two points each month. One point is deducted on Saturday, Sunday, other days and holidays no points will be deducted. Camp does not have a point system. Inmates are limited to five adult (no limit on children) visitors at one time. Attorneys should be on the approved visitor list and are encouraged to visit during regular visiting hours. Additional visiting information can be found on the BOP website, at www.bop. gov, https://www.bop.gov/locations/institutions/cop/ and at https://www.bop. gov/locations/institutions/clp/, respectively.

**Lodging/Accommodations:** See §16:12, FCI Coleman—Low.

## §16:15   FCI EDGEFIELD

FCI Edgefield
Federal Correctional Institution
501 Gary Hill Road
Edgefield, SC 29824
EDG/ExecAssistant@bop.gov
803-637-1500
Fax: 803-637-9840

**Location:** Near the border of South Carolina and Georgia, approximately 25 miles north of Augusta, approximately 30 miles northeast of I-20, on Highway 25. The area is served by airports in Augusta, Georgia and Columbia, South Carolina.

**History:** The FCI and the satellite camp were activated in 1998.

**Judicial District:** District of South Carolina.

**Security Level:** FCI Edgefield, South Carolina, is a medium-security facility housing male offenders. The facility also has an adjacent satellite camp that houses minimum-security male offenders.

**Population:** As of 8/5/2014, the inmate population at the FCI is 1,296, and the camp population is 526. Weekly population figures are available on the BOP website at www.bop.gov, https://www.bop.gov/locations/institutions/edg/.

**Education:** The FCI and the camp offer GED, ESL, adult continuing education, and correspondence courses.

**Vocational/Apprenticeship:** The FCI offers no advanced occupational education programs. FCI offers vocational training in: culinary arts, culinary arts serve safe, and small appliance repair. FCI offers apprenticeship programs in: culinary arts, and small appliance repair.

**Library:** The FCI and camp leisure and law libraries are open Monday through Thursday 7:30am-10:30am, 1pm-3:30pm, 5:30pm-8pm; Friday 7:30am-10am, 1pm-3:30pm; Saturday 7:30am-9:30am, 11am-3:30pm. The law library contains a variety of legal reference material for use in preparing legal papers. An inmate law library clerk is available for assistance in legal research. Typewriters and a copier are also available for the preparation of legal documents. Video cassette recorders and audio cassette players are available.

**UNICOR:** A textile factory employs inmates from the FCI. A warehouse employs a small work force of inmates from the camp.

**Counseling/Rehab Services:** Qualified staff and various groups are available for the inmate's counseling needs. These groups may include drug abuse, self-image, Alcoholics Anonymous and Narcotics Anonymous. Additionally, the FCI offers a 500-hour Residential Drug Abuse Program (RDAP). The RDAP is nine months in length. The FCI also offers a non-residential drug abuse program. Psychologists are available for individual and/or group psychotherapy. Mental health services are offered in the areas of drug and alcohol abuse, and other psycho-educational interventions. The Living Free Program is designed to assist inmates to develop a more socially acceptable lifestyle through a review of their values. Program participation is voluntary.

**Health Services:** The institution medical program is enhanced with a group of outside medical consultants that provided services to special medical referral cases made by health care providers. Dental and sick call will be by appointment only: Monday, Tuesday, Thursday, and Friday, excluding holidays, 6:30am-7am. FCI pill line hours: Monday through Friday 6:15am-6:30am, 10am-11pm, 3pm-3:30pm, 4:30pm-5pm, and 7pm-8pm; weekends/holidays 7am-7:30am, 11am-11:30am, 3pm-3:30pm, 4:30pm-5pm, and 7pm-8pm. There are no over-the-counter medications given at FCI Edgefield. Limited over-the-counter medications may be purchased from the commissary. Inmates under 50 years of age may request a preventative health screening every two years, while those over 50 may request one annually.

**Housing:** There are six separate units at FCI Edgefield. Inmates at the FCI are primarily housed in two-man cells. Inmates at the camp are housed in dormitories in two-man cells.

**Fitness/Recreation:** The recreation department offers indoor and outdoor activities as well as individualized arts and crafts programs. The camp offers hobby craft programs in art and leather.

**Religious Services:** A wide range of religious programs are offered. Staff chaplains are available at the FCI and the camp, as well as contract and volunteer representatives of various faiths.

**Commissary:** The operating hours of the commissary at the FCI are from 10:30am-work call and 4pm-8pm or until last call Monday through Thursday, and at the camp from 10:30am until last call, Monday through Wednesday, and Thursday after count clears until last call. If a commissary sale day falls on a federal holiday, an alternate schedule will be posted. Inmates are allowed to shop once a week on a rotating basis according to the inmate's housing unit. This rotation schedule will rotate every 12 weeks and will be posted in the commissary and all units. Bureau of Prisons policy currently sets a monthly commissary spending limit of $360.

**Telephone Policy:** Inmates at the FCI and the camp may call collect or dial direct using the Inmate Telephone System (ITS). The following are standard features of ITS: (1) inmate calls automatically terminate after 15 minutes; (2) an inmate's calling list is limited to 30 callers; and (3) calls are charged to an inmate's debit card. Inmates get 300 calling minutes per month. Telephones at the FCI are located in the housing units and are operational 6am-10pm daily. Inmates may change their phone list up to three times a month.

**Inmate Mail:** The FCI and the camp accept mail from the U.S. Postal Service via First-Class, U.S. Priority, and Express Mail. For those interested in sending overnight mail via a private carrier (FedEx or UPS Overnight), it is recommended that you first contact the institution to find out whether the receipt of such mail is permitted. Inmates may receive publications without prior approval, although the warden will reject publications if they are determined to be detrimental to the security, good order or discipline of the institution. All publications must be received directly from the publisher or bookstore. Each inmate is limited to five magazines and five books.

**Inmate Mail to FCI:**
> INMATE NAME & REGISTER NUMBER
> FCI Edgefield
> Federal Correctional Institution
> P.O. Box 725
> Edgefield, SC 29824

**Visiting Hours:** Approved visitors may visit inmates at the FCI and camp Friday 5pm-8pm; Saturday, Sunday, federal holidays 8am-3pm. The camp utilizes an odd/even visiting system. Inmates are limited to 20 names on their visiting list. Inmates are limited to four adult visitors (no limit on children) at one time. Attorneys should be on the approved visitor list and should visit during regular visiting hours. Additional visiting information can be found on the BOP website, www.bop.gov, at https://www.bop.gov/locations/institutions/edg/.

**Lodging/Accommodations:** Should visitors be spending the night, the following is a short list of accommodations that are available in Edgefield, South Carolina, and in Augusta, Georgia, which is approximately 35 miles from Edgefield, South Carolina:

**Edgefield, SC:**
Edgefield Inn                                                       803-637-2001

**Augusta, Georgia:**
Augusta Marriott Hotel & Suites                    706-722-8900
Baymont Inn & Suites                                     706-733-5900
Candlewood Suites                                          706-733-3300
Motel One                                                        706-724-0081
Ramada Inn & Suites Augusta West              706-855-6060

## §16:16  FCI ESTILL

FCI Estill
Federal Correctional Institution
100 Prison Road
Estill, SC 29918
EST/ExecAssistant@bop.gov
803-625-4607
Fax: 803-625-5635

**Location:** Approximately 50 miles north of Savannah, Georgia, 96 miles west of Charleston, South Carolina, and three miles south of Estill city limits and 95 miles south of the state capitol, Columbia, South Carolina. The institution is accessible via U.S. 321 and South Carolina Route 3. Visitors arriving into the area via I-95 South should use Exit 38 (at Yamasee); those arriving from I-95 North should use Exit 5. Commercial airline service is available through three major airports within a 100-mile radius: Savannah, Georgia, Columbia, South Carolina; and Charleston, South Carolina. Interstate bus service and Amtrak's north-south passenger trains have regular stops in Hampton County. There are no local taxi companies to provide travel from Hampton County bus station or the rail station.

**History:** Opened in 1993.

**Judicial District:** District of South Carolina.

**Security Level:** FCI Estill, South Carolina, is a medium-security facility housing male inmates. It also has an adjacent satellite camp that houses minimum-security male inmates.

**Population:** As of 6/24/2017, the FCI inmate population is 959, and the camp population is 312. Weekly population figures are available on the BOP website at www.bop.gov, https://www.bop.gov/locations/institutions/est/.

**Education:** The FCI and the camp offer GED, ESL, adult continuing education, parenting courses and correspondence courses. Inmates must pay for books and tuition.

**Vocational/Apprenticeship:** FCI and the camp offer advanced occupational education in computer technology. There are apprenticeship programs in cooking, plumbing, dental assistant work, industrial mechanics, carpentry, HVAC, and welding. The FCI also offers vocational training in carpentry, HVAC, baking, computers, and food technology.

**Library:** The leisure and law library hours are Monday-Thursday 7am-3:30pm and 5pm-8pm; Friday 7am-3:30pm; Saturday 7am-9:30am, 10:30am-3pm. The law library contains a variety of legal reference materials for use in preparing legal papers. Reference materials include the United States Code Annotated, Federal Reporter, Supreme Court Reporter, Bureau of Prisons Program Statements, Institution Supplements, Indexes, and other legal materials. An inmate law library clerk is available for assistance in legal research. Electric typewriters and a copier are available to inmates for the preparation of legal documents.

**UNICOR:** None.

**Counseling/Rehab Services:** Psychology staff coordinates a full range of psychological treatment and consultative services. Various groups are available for counseling needs. These groups may include drug abuse, self-image, personal finance, health and nutrition, employment, personal growth and development, release preparation, parenting, and other voluntary groups. Staff is available during prescribed open house hours (3pm-3:30pm Monday-Thursday) for individual counseling on various educational issues. Other services include individual therapy, brief counseling, drug abuse treatment, and psycho-educational programs. Psychology staff develops personalized treatment plans as clinically appropriate and a psychologist is available for crisis intervention as needed. The Living Free Program is frequently offered by unit and psychology staff.

**Health Services:** The main institution is staffed by one physician, one dentist, and six to eight physician assistants. The FCI and the camp provide outpatient care. Buford Hospital and Walter Burough Hospital are 50 miles away. Sick call at FCI Estill will be conducted from 7:15am-7:45am Monday, Tuesday, Thursday, and Friday. Only acute/immediate care will be provided at sick call. Dental sick call is conducted Monday, Tuesday, Thursday, and Friday, 7:15am-7:45am. Sign-up for dental sick call is conducted by the physician assistant or nurse on duty Monday, Tuesday, Thursday, and Friday, 6:30am. Pill line at the FCI: 10:30am-11am and 7:30pm-8pm. Sick call sign-up at the camp is from 6am-6:30am. The pill line at the camp is from 7am-7:30am and 6pm-6:30pm. On site emergency medical care is available 24 hours a day. Inmates may request age-specific physical examinations.

**Housing:** Inmates at the FCI are housed in two-man and three-man cells. Inmates at the camp are housed in dormitories in two-man cubicles.

**Fitness/Recreation:** Programs include indoor and outdoor activities including individualized arts and crafts programs, music and table games, tournament and league events, and intramural team sports in softball, basketball, and volleyball. Hobby craft offers leather, art, drawing, beadwork, and crochet. Athletic and music equipment are provided and maintained by the recreation department.

**Religious Services:** The main institution is staffed by full-time chaplains, as well as contract and volunteer representatives of various faiths. Special religious diets, holiday observances, and other worship activities are coordinated through the chaplains' office. Information and schedules are posted on the inmate and chapel bulletin boards; contact the chaplains' office for additional information.

**Commissary:** The commissary at the FCI is open Monday through Wednesday 6:15am-2pm; Thursday 6:15am-1pm (SHU shopping day). Shopping days for all inmates will rotate monthly on the first Monday of the month. The rotation schedule is posted in the commissary. The camp commissary is open Monday and Tuesday 11:30am-2:30pm and reopens after the 4pm count until last call. The Bureau of Prisons policy currently sets a monthly spending limit of $360.

**Telephone Policy:** Telephones are located in the housing units and are available for daily use. Inmates at the FCI and the camp may call collect or dial direct using the Inmate Telephone System (ITS). The following are standard features of ITS: (1) inmate calls automatically terminate after 15 minutes; (2) an inmate's calling list is limited to 30 callers; and (3) calls are charged to an inmate's debit card. Each inmate gets 300 calling minutes per month.

**Inmate Mail:** The FCI and the camp accept mail from the U.S. Postal Service via First-Class, U.S. Priority, and Express Mail. For those interested in sending overnight mail via a private carrier (FedEx or UPS Overnight), it is recommended that you first contact the institution to find out whether the receipt of such mail is permitted. Inmates may receive publications without prior approval, although the warden will reject publications if they are determined to be detrimental to the security, good order or discipline of the institution. All publications must be received directly from the publisher or bookstore. Each inmate is limited to five magazines, five newspapers and five books.

**Inmate Mail to FCI:**
> INMATE NAME & REGISTER NUMBER
> FCI Estill
> Federal Correctional Institution
> P.O. Box 699
> Estill, SC 29918

**Inmate Mail to Camp:**
INMATE NAME & REGISTER NUMBER
FCI Estill
Federal Correctional Institution
Satellite Camp
P.O. Box 699
Estill, SC 29918

**Visiting Hours:** Approved visitors may visit FCI Estill Friday 5pm-8:30pm; Saturday, Sunday, holidays 8am-3pm. The camp's visiting hours are Friday 5pm-8:15pm; Saturday, Sunday, holidays 8am-3pm. Inmates are limited to four adult visitors (children under age 16 years are not limited) at one time. Inmates are not permitted to have more than 20 names on their approved visitor list. Attorneys are encouraged to visit during the regular visiting hours; however other time arrangements can be requested by the attorney. Additional visiting information can be found at https://www.bop.gov/locations/institutions/est/.

**Lodging/Accommodations:** Should visitors be spending the night, the following is a short list of accommodations that are available in Estill South Carolina and in Hampton County which is approximately 30 minutes away:

**Estill:**
Palmetto Inn                                            803-625-4322

**Hampton County:**
Carolina Lodge                                          803-943-5660
Days Inn of Hampton                                     803-398-1786
Baymont Inn and Suites Waterboro                        843-538-5473

## §16:17  MDC GUAYNABO

MDC Guaynabo
Metropolitan Detention Center
652 Carreta 28
Guaynabo, PR 00965
GUA/ExecAssistant@bop.gov
787-749-4480
Fax: 787-775-7824

**Location:** Approximately six miles west of San Juan, Puerto Rico, off Highway 22 at the Intersection of Roads 165 and 28. Luis Munoz Marin International airport is 15 miles from MDC Guaynabo. Taxi service is available.

**History:** Opened in 1992, MDC Guaynabo is the first federal prison outside the continental United States.

**Judicial District:** Puerto Rico, U.S. Virgin Islands.

**Security Level:** MDC in San Juan, Puerto Rico, is an administrative facility housing male and female inmates.

**Population:** As of 6/24/2017, the inmate population is 1,384. Weekly population figures are available on the BOP website, www.bop.gov, at https://www.bop.gov/locations/institutions/gua/.

**Education:** The MDC offers GED, ESL, and adult continuing education programs.

**Vocational/Apprenticeship:** MDC offers advanced occupational education in Bookbinding. MDC offers no vocational training or apprenticeship programs.

**Library:** Inmates must request books and legal materials from staff. Housing units are equipped with electric typewriters. Copies may be obtained by request. Legal supplies are paid for by the inmates. A very limited leisure library is available in each housing unit.

**UNICOR:** None.

**Counseling/Rehab Services:** The Psychology Services staff of MDC Guaynabo will evaluate and treat mental health problems which may surface as the result of arrest and detention. Psychology staff works closely with medical staff to provide a coordinated approach to treatment: Treatment includes psychological evaluations, crisis intervention, referral to medical services, short-term counseling, a non-residential drug treatment program, a drug education program, Alcoholics Anonymous, and Narcotics Anonymous for designated cadre inmates.

**Health Services:** Health services staff consists of one to two physicians, nurses, three to five physician assistants, one dentist, pharmacist, x-ray technician and administrative personnel. The FCI also contracts the services of specialized medical personnel as needed. Medical coverage is provided 24 hours a day. Sick call sign-up is Monday through Friday. Medication pick-up hours are between 5pm and 8pm in the inmate's housing unit. Pill line medication will be delivered to the housing unit in the morning, noon, and evening (bedtime) hours. Medical testing and services unique to females are provided, including pregnancy testing and mammography.

**Housing:** Inmates are housed in two-man cells.

**Fitness/Recreation:** The recreation department offers organized sports, pool tables, and ping-pong tables. The hobby craft center offers card making and bookbinding.

**Religious Services:** The institution is staffed by three full-time chaplains. There are additional chaplains from a variety of religious preferences who also come to assist in the institution. Inmates should contact a staff chaplain to see a representative from their religious preference, including Christian Science, Jehovah's Witnesses, Jewish, Muslim, Church of Christ, Catholic, and Protestant faith groups. Each unit chapel will have a TV tuned only to the closed circuit channel that broadcasts religious services videos. There is also a shelf in the chapel with books that can be borrowed, as well as literature and pamphlets to take. Some religious books may also be requested from the education library. The chaplains have information regarding a large number and variety of religious study correspondence courses and most are free of charge.

**Commissary:** The commissary is open in the evenings. Inmates are assigned one shopping day per week. A schedule for commissary purchasing will be posted on the unit's bulletin board. The Bureau of Prisons policy currently sets a monthly spending limit of $360.

**Telephone Policy:** Inmate telephones have been placed in each residential unit at this facility. Inmates may utilize the telephone equipment during the day and evening hours. Inmates may call collect or dial direct using the Inmate Telephone System (ITS). The following are standard features of ITS: (1) inmate calls automatically terminate after 15 minutes; (2) an inmate's calling list is limited to 30 callers; and (3) calls are charged to an inmate's debit card. Each inmate receives 300 calling minutes per month.

**Inmate Mail:** The MDC accepts mail from the U.S. Postal Service via First Class, U.S. Priority, and Express Mail. For those interested in sending overnight mail via a private carrier (FedEx or UPS Overnight), it is recommended that you first contact the institution to find out whether the receipt of such mail is permitted. Inmates may receive publications without prior approval, although the warden will reject publications if they are determined to be detrimental to the security, good order or discipline of the institution. All publications must be received directly from the publisher or bookstore. Each inmate may retain no more than 12 publications.

**Inmate Mail to MDC:**
    INMATE NAME & REGISTER NUMBER
    MDC Guaynabo
    Metropolitan Detention Center
    P.O. Box 2005
    Cataño, PR 00963

**Visiting Hours:** Visiting is on a set schedule, which rotates every 12 weeks, according to unit housing assignment. With the exception of inmates housed in Unit 1-A (cadre inmates), each inmate is allowed four visiting points per month.

Each visit counts as one point. Inmates in Unit 1-A may visit as often as the schedule permits, provided he/she has no visiting restrictions resulting from a disciplinary sanction. Inmates are allowed three adult visitors per visit. Children under age three years will not be counted as a visitor unless they occupy a seat in the visiting room. No more than ten relatives, friends and associates will be allowed on the visiting list. No points will be deducted for legal visits. Visiting hours for attorneys are from 8am-8pm, every day, except Mondays and Tuesdays, in which attorneys may visit before 11am or after 5pm. Additional visiting information can be found at https://www.bop.gov/locations/institutions/gua/.

**Lodging/Accommodations:** The following is a short list of accommodations that are available in San Juan, near Guaynabo, Puerto Rico:

| | |
|---|---|
| Hotel Milano | 787-729-9050 |
| Sofo CasaBlanca Hotel | 787-725-3436 |
| Atlantic Beach Hotel | 787-721-6900 |
| Hotel Miramar San Juan | 787-977-1000 |

## §16:18   FCI JESUP

FCI Jesup
Federal Correctional Institution
2600 Highway 301 South
Jesup, GA 31599
JES/ExecAssistant@bop.gov
912-427-0870
Fax: 912-427-1125

**Location:** Southeast Georgia on Route 301, 65 miles southwest of Savannah, 40 miles northwest of Brunswick, and 105 miles northwest of Jacksonville, Florida. The area is served by airports in Jacksonville, Savannah, and Brunswick and also by Amtrak.

**History:** Opened in 1989, the Medium FCI houses male offenders primarily form the southeastern United States. The satellite camp houses minimum-security male offenders, most of who provide services to the main institution. The Satellite Low facility opened in 2003.

**Judicial District:** Southern Georgia.

**Security Level:** Medium-security facility housing male offenders. It has two adjacent satellite facilities: a low-security facility and a minimum-security prison camp (both housing male inmates).

**Population:** As of 6/25/2017, the medium-security FCI inmate population is 949; the Satellite low-security inmate population is 354; and the camp population is

153. Weekly population figures are available on the BOP website at https://www.
bop.gov/locations/institutions/jes/.

**Education:** The FCI and the camp offer GED, ESL, adult continuing education,
parenting classes, and correspondence courses from Altamaha Technical College.
Continuing education classes include a Commercial Driver's License (CDL)
course, Legal Research, Writing, and Analysis, Spanish I, Basic Finance, and
Resume Writing. There is also a Mock Job Fair. The Education Department also
offers a Pre-Release course designed to assist the inmate with project release or
halfway house placement.

**Vocational/Apprenticeship:** The medium-security FCI offers advanced occupational education in commercial wiring, HVAC, and information technology.
FCI offers apprenticeship programs: plumber, and electrician. The FSL offers
occupation education in information technology.

**Library:** The law library is located in the Education Department and contains a
variety of legal reference materials for use in preparing legal papers. Reference
materials include the United States Code Annotated, Federal Reporter, Supreme
Court Reporter, Bureau of Prisons Program Statements and Institution Supplements, Indexes and other legal materials. The law library is open during convenient
non-working hours, including weekends and holidays. An inmate law library clerk
is available for legal research assistance. Legal materials are also available to
inmates housed in the Special Housing Unit, ordinarily via delivery system. Electric typewriters and a copier are available to inmates for the preparation of legal
documents. An inter-library loan program is available through the local public
library. Video cassette recorders and audio cassette players are also available.

**UNICOR:** A textile factory employs approximately 503 inmates.

**Counseling/Rehab Services:** The psychology department consists of four
psychologists, three drug treatment specialists, and one psychology technician.
Services offered by the psychology department include: Sexual assault education
and counseling, crisis intervention, individual counseling, medication management, psychiatric consultation, drug abuse education, court-ordered evaluation
and counseling, segregation evaluations, personal development programs
including self-help groups, smoking cessation, non-residential drug program,
and the Residential Drug Treatment Program (500-hour, nine-month program).

**Health Services:** The main institution is staffed by one physician, six to eight
physicians' assistants, and two dentists. The FCI and the camp provide outpatient
care. The institution is served by Wayne Memorial Hospital, which is four miles
away. Dental and sick call sign-up is conducted on Monday, Tuesday, Thursday,
and Friday, excluding holidays, at 6am for the camp, 11:15 for the FSL, and 7:40
for the FCI. Pill lines at the camp are 6:30am and 6:15pm; at the FSL, 6:30am and

4:30pm; and at the FCI, 6:30am, 11:30am, 5pm, and 7:30 pm. Weekends and Holidays are subject to change but will be announced on the overhead page system.

**Housing:** Inmates at the Medium FCI are housed in two-man cells and two-man dorm rooms. Inmates at FSL and camp are housed in dormitories. There are television rooms in each housing wing. The small television rooms are accessible to disabled inmates. The televisions are operational every day until 9:45pm.

**Fitness/Recreation:** FCI and FSL recreation areas are open from 6:30am-8pm on weekdays and 7am-8pm on weekends, except during institutional counts. Camp recreation areas are open from 6am-dusk. Some activities include: softball, flag football, track, soccer, handball, racquetball, volleyball and bocce ball. Hobby craft program includes: leather craft, painting, sketching, and bead work. Musical instruments are available. The music program consists of a one room set-up with music equipment for organized bands to perform; a second music room is available for individual practice or may be used as a multi-purpose room. Monday through Friday, inmates, authorized in the unit during the day, will be permitted to view the television in a posted designated area. After the announcement of work call, all other television rooms will close until after the 4pm count. All table games may be played from 7:30am until 9:45pm in the common area.

**Religious Services:** The Religious Services Department at the Medium FCI is staffed by three full-time chaplains and contract chaplains and two chaplains at the Low FCI. Community volunteers assist with services for most faiths. The chaplains are available upon request to provide pastoral care, counseling, religious education and instruction. Volunteers from the nearby communities augment and supplement the institutional religious services staff. The chapel facility does contain a religious library where inmates may use religious reference material and obtain some religious devotional and other reading material. This library also has a supply of video and audiotapes which can be used in the chapel area only. The religious program and activity schedule and chaplain's duty schedules are posted in each unit and in the chapel.

**Commissary:** The FCI commissary is open Monday through Thursday; the FSL commissary is open Tuesday through Thursday; and the camp commissary is open Monday. Shopping days are determined by an inmate's register number. Times the commissaries are open will be posted. The Bureau of Prisons policy currently sets a monthly spending limit of $360.

**Telephone Policy:** Inmates may call collect or dial direct using the Inmate Telephone System (ITS). The following are standard features of ITS: (1) inmate calls automatically terminate after 15 minutes; (2) an inmate's calling list is limited to 30 callers; and (3) calls are charged to an inmate's debit card. Each inmate gets 300 calling minutes per month. Telephones will be available between the hours of 6am and 9:30pm daily, with the exception of times during counts.

**Inmate Mail:** The FCI and the camp accept mail from the U.S. Postal Service via First-Class, U.S. Priority, and Express Mail. For those interested in sending overnight mail via a private carrier (FedEx or UPS Overnight), it is recommended that you first contact the institution to find out whether the receipt of such mail is permitted. Inmates may receive publications without prior approval, although the warden will reject publications if they are determined to be detrimental to the security, good order or discipline of the institution. At medium security, high security, and administrative institutions, all publications must be received directly from the publisher or bookstore; at minimum and low security institutions, soft-cover publications may be received from any source.

**Inmate Mail to FCI:**
INMATE NAME & REGISTER NUMBER
FCI Jesup
Federal Correctional Institution
26800 301 South
Jesup, GA 31599

**Inmate Mail to Satellite Low:**
INMATE NAME & REGISTER NUMBER
FCI Jesup
Federal Correctional Institution
Federal Satellite Low
2680 301 South
Jesup, GA 31599

**Inmate Mail to Camp:**
INMATE NAME & REGISTER NUMBER
FCI Jesup
Federal Correctional Institution
Satellite Camp
2650 301 South
Jesup, GA 31599

**Visiting Hours:** The visiting schedule for all facilities is Saturdays, Sundays, and federal holidays 8am-3pm. Inmates are given eight visiting points per month. One point will be deducted for each weekday visit and two points will be deducted for each holiday and weekend visit. Holdovers will be allowed four visiting days per month, two of which may occur on weekends. Attorney visits and clergy visits will not be deducted. The point system does not apply to FPC inmates. A maximum of four adult visitors, excluding children, may visit an inmate at one time. Attorney visits must be verified and coordinated by the unit team at least 24 hours in advance. If approved, the attorney will be permitted to visit during regular visiting hours. Additional information can be found at the BOP website at https://www.bop.gov/locations/institutions/jes/.

**Lodging/Accommodations:** Should visitors be spending the night, the following is a short list of accommodations that are available in Jesup, GA:

| | |
|---|---|
| Western Motel | 912-427-7600 |
| Motel Jesup | 912-427-2086 |
| Economy Inn | 912-427-4294 |
| Days Inn & Suites | 912-427-2980 |

## §16:19   FCI MARIANNA

FCI Marianna
Federal Correctional Institution
3625 FCI Road
Marianna, FL 32446
MNA/ExecAssistant@bop.gov
850-526-2313
Fax: 850-718-2014

**Location:** In the northern panhandle of Florida, 65 miles west of Tallahassee and five miles north of the town of Marianna, off highway 167. Marianna is served by Tallahassee Municipal Airport and Greyhound. Commercial airports also operate in Dothan (35 miles northwest of the facility), and Panama City (54 miles south).

**History:** Opened in 1988, FCI Marianna initially housed medium-security male and maximum-security female inmates in separate areas. There is no longer a maximum-security female unit. A satellite camp houses female minimum-security offenders.

**Judicial District:** Northern District of Florida.

**Security Level:** A medium-security facility housing male inmates. An adjacent satellite prison camp houses minimum-security female offenders.

**Population:** As of 6/25/2017, the FCI inmate population is 1,206, and the camp population is 212. Weekly population figures are available on the BOP website at www.bop.gov, https://www.bop.gov/locations/institutions/mna/.

**Education:** The FCI and the camp offer GED, ESL, adult continuing education, (ACE), parenting, and college correspondence courses. ACE classes include but are not limited to Parenting, Financial Management, Conversational Spanish, Health Education, Career Planning, Career Counseling, and Basic Study Skills.

**Vocational/Apprenticeship:** The FCI offers vocational training in computer applications, computer refurbishing, electrical, HVAC, plumbing, and diversified cooperative training (DCT). FCI offers apprenticeship programs in cook, dental assistant, electrician, HVAC, and plumber. The camp offers computer applications and DCT.

**Library:** The law libraries at the FCI and camp are open during non-working hours, including weekends and holidays. Reference materials include the United States Code Annotated, Federal Reporter, Supreme Court Reporter, Bureau of Prisons Program Statements, Institution Supplements, Indexes, and other legal materials. An inmate Law Library Clerk is available for assistance in legal research. Electric typewriters and copiers are available to inmates for the preparation of legal documents.

**UNICOR:** A recycling program (e-scrap) employs inmates from the Camp.

**Counseling/Rehab Services:** The Psychology Department consists of six psychologists (the Chief, the DAP Coordinator, one Resolve Program Coordinator, the SOMP Coordinator, one SOMP psychologist, and one Staff Psychologist), six Drug Treatment Specialists, three SOMP treatment specialists and one Psychology Technician. Services offered include: Alcoholics Anonymous, anger management, stress management groups and other voluntary groups. In addition, this facility has professional staff that is trained in the various social science fields. Inmate participation in these activities will be encouraged upon the staff's assessment of inmate needs, but participation in such activities is voluntary. The staff of each unit is available for informal counseling sessions and they also conduct formal group counseling activities. The Psychology Department provides three kinds of drug abuse treatment and services. A 12 to 15-hour drug education program is available to all inmates. A 500-hour, nine-month Residential Drug Treatment Program is available to male inmates in the FCI. A non-residential drug abuse group meets weekly. Psychologists are available for brief counseling, crisis intervention, individual therapy (when determined appropriate by the psychologist) and group psychotherapy. Inmates with a history of sexual offenses may be designated to the Sex Offender Management Program (SOMP). Sex Offender Treatment Program (SOTP-NR) offers inmates individualized non-residential treatment: six to eight hours a week for six months. All participation in non-residential treatment services is voluntary.

**Health Services:** Medical department personnel include administrators, physicians, mid-level practitioners, nurses, dentists, a pharmacist, and administrative support staff. Normal duty hours are 6:30 a.m., until 4:00 p.m., Monday through Friday, with the exception of weekends and holidays. The FCI and the camp offer outpatient care. Specialty medical consultants from the community provide care as needed, including specialized services for female inmates at the Camp. Local hospitals are approximately eight miles away. Medical sick call is from 6:45am-7:15am Monday, Tuesday, Thursday, and Friday. Pill line hours are clearly posted at the pharmacy window. At least one physician assistant is on duty or on call 24 hours a day. Elective female health examinations (such as pap smears or pelvic/breast examinations) may be requested every year for patients below the age of 30, and every three years for patients over the age of 30. Mammograms begin at age 40 and are performed every two years afterwards.

**Housing:** Inmates at the FCI are housed in two-man cells. Inmates at the camp are housed in dormitories in two-man cubicles.

**Fitness/Recreation:** Recreation activities include: intramural sports, art, aerobics, music, and physical fitness and health education classes. Hobby craft program offered at FCI and the camp.

**Religious Services:** The main institution is staffed by full-time chaplains, as well as contract and volunteer representatives. Special religious diets, religious holiday observances, and other worship activities are coordinated through the chaplain's office. Schedules for worship services are posted on the chapel bulletin board. In addition to group activities, individual pastoral care is available.

**Commissary:** The commissary is open Monday through Wednesday from 6:30am-3pm. Inmates are assigned one shopping day a week based on their housing unit assignment, which changes on a quarterly basis. Bureau of Prisons policy currently sets a monthly commissary spending limit of $360.

**Telephone Policy:** Inmates may call collect or dial direct using the Inmate Telephone System (ITS). The following are standard features of ITS: (1) inmate calls automatically terminate after 15 minutes; (2) an inmate's calling list is limited to 30 callers; and (3) calls are charged to an inmate's debit card. Inmates may purchase phone credits seven days a week after 4:30pm.

**Inmate Mail:** The FCI and the camp accept mail from the U.S. Postal Service via First-Class, U.S. Priority, and Express Mail. For those interested in sending overnight mail via a private carrier (FedEx or UPS Overnight), it is recommended that you first contact the institution to find out whether the receipt of such mail is permitted. Inmates may receive publications without prior approval, although the warden will reject publications if they are determined to be detrimental to the security, good order or discipline of the institution. At the FCI, all publications must be received directly from the publisher, bookstore or book club; at the camp, softcover publications may be received from any source. Each inmate is limited to five magazines (no older than three months).

**Inmate Mail to FCI:**
INMATE NAME & REGISTER NUMBER
FCI Marianna
Federal Correctional Institution
P.O. Box 7007
Marianna, FL 32447

**Inmate Mail to Camp:**
INMATE NAME & REGISTER NUMBER
FCI Marianna
Satellite Camp
Federal Correctional Institution
P.O. Box 7006
Marianna, FL 32447

**Visiting Hours:** Regular visiting hours for inmates at the FCI: Saturday, Sunday, Monday, federal holidays: 8:15am-3:15pm; the Camp: Saturday, Sunday, federal holidays 8:15am-3:15pm. Visits are conducted on a point system at the FCI. One point deducted for Monday visits, two points deducted for Saturday and three points deducted for Sunday and federal holidays. Inmates will be limited to ten points per month. A maximum of five visitors (including children) at the FCI are permitted to visit an inmate at one time. A total of five visitors (excluding children) is permitted at the Camp. The inmates approved visiting list will list no more than ten friends and associates. Attorneys should be on the inmates approved visiting list, however this does not preclude other attorneys from visiting at the inmate's request. Additional visiting information can be found at https://www.bop.gov/locations/institutions/mna/.

**Lodging/Accommodations:** Should visitors be spending the night, the following is a short list of accommodations that are available in Marianna:

| | |
|---|---|
| Quality Inn | 850-526-5600 |
| Days Inn | 850-526-1006 |
| Hinson House Bed & Breakfast | 850-526-1500 |
| America's Best Value | 850-526-5666 |
| Marianna Inn & Suites | 850-526-2900 |
| Executive Inn | 850-526-3710 |
| Super 8 Motel | 850-482-4770 |

## §16:20  FCI MIAMI

FCI Miami
Federal Correction Institution
15801 S.W. 137th Avenue
Miami, FL 33177
MIA/ExecAssistant@bop.gov
305-259-2100
Fax: 305-259-2160

**Location:** In southwest section of Dade County, 30 miles from downtown Miami, off the Florida Turnpike (Homestead Extension, 152nd Street exit, 2.5 miles to 137th Street). Miami is served by Miami International Airport, Amtrak, and commercial bus lines.

**History:** The facility returned to its original mission as an FCI as opened in 1976. The satellite camp opened in January 1992.

**Judicial District:** Southern District of Florida.

**Security Level:** A low-security facility housing male inmates. The institution also has an adjacent satellite prison camp that houses minimum-security male offenders.

**Population:** As of 6/25/2017, the FCI inmate population is 908, and the camp population is 390. Weekly population figures are available on the BOP website at www.bop.gov, https://www.bop.gov/locations/institutions/mia/.

**Education:** The FCI and the camp offer GED, ESL, adult continuing education, parenting, foreign language and correspondence courses.

**Vocational/Apprenticeship:** The FCI offers advanced occupational education in: accounting operations, business supervision and management, business management and law, data entry operations, keyboarding, as well as drafting and AutoCAD. FCI offers no vocational training. FCI offers apprenticeship programs in plumbing, electrician, heating and air conditioning, and landscape technician.

**Library:** All main and basic libraries contain a collection of legal reference materials which are required by the Federal Prison System. Main inmate law libraries are located in the Education Building. Inmates are permitted to use law library materials in the main or basic law libraries. Inmates will not be allowed to take law books and materials from the law libraries. Materials not contained in a basic law library are requested from the main law library. A complete list of available main law library materials is available for reference in each housing unit. A copier and typewriters are available to inmates. The library hours are Monday through Thursday 7:30am-8pm; Friday 7:30am-3pm; and Saturday 7:30am-3:30pm. Inmates also have access to the library on their floor. Some of the leisure library's materials include fiction and non-fiction books, specialized and general reference books, periodicals, magazines, newspapers, BOP Program Statements, Operations Memorandums, Institution Supplements, reading material in foreign languages, and educational pamphlets. Library material may be checked out for two weeks. Reference materials are provided for in-library use only. The "Book Cart Program" is established and implemented throughout the institution. Book carts are available in each housing unit, including SHU and segregation. Also available is an inter-library loan program, under which inmates can borrow up to five books from the Florida InterLibrary Loan Department. Video cassettes recorders and audio cassette players are also available. This institution has also implemented an Electronic Law Library System (ELL). Inmate law clerks are available during all ELL hours to assist with accessing the ELL, as well as to teach inmates how to use all features of this program.

**UNICOR:** A textile factory employs approximately 213 inmates within its departments: cutting, sewing, folding, packing, shipping, business office and quality assurance.

**Counseling/Rehab Services:** The Psychology Department at FDC Miami provides mental health services to those inmates who have a history of mental illness and who have difficulty adjusting to incarceration. The psychology and medical staff work closely together to provide a coordinated approach to treatment. The psychology department also conducts psychological evaluations, provides crisis consultation, makes referrals to medical services, and offers individual and group counseling. Services are provided in English and Spanish. Staff members are assigned to individual floors in order to expedite the mental health concerns of inmates. FDC Miami has a Drug Abuse Program (DAP) that is open to all inmates. There is a 40-hour drug education program for those who are initially beginning the road to recovery. There is a non-residential program for those who have completed residential programs and are in need of follow-up services. The main institution is staffed by five full-time psychologists. Additionally, the FCI offers a 500-hour Residential Drug Abuse Program (RDAP). The RDAP is nine months in length.

**Health Services:** The main institution is staffed by three physicians, eight physician assistants, two dentists, and one pharmacist. The FCI and the camp provide outpatient care. The institution is served by several local hospitals approximately 3-7 miles away. The Health Services Unit at FDC Miami functions as an ambulatory outpatient clinic. Some of the services available to inmates are: sick call, x-rays, lab, dental, pharmacy, etc. The medical staff consists of physician assistants, license practical nurses, physicians, dentists, and supporting staff. The clinic is open 24 hours daily. A staff member is always on emergency calls for any problems that develop after 4pm. At the FCI, the medication line is available three times daily, 7:15am, 3:10pm, and 7:45pm. Inmates must report to the medical annex between 6:30am and 7am on Monday, Tuesday, Wednesday, and Friday to receive a sick call appointment. Inmates housed at the satellite camp sign-up between 7am and 7:30am. At least one physician assistant is on duty or on call 24 hours a day. Inmates under the age of 50 may request a physical examination every two years, while inmates over the age of 50 may request one annually.

**Housing:** Inmates at the FCI are housed in two-man cells. Inmates at the camp are housed in open dormitories in two-man cubicles.

**Fitness/Recreation:** Leisure activities include participation in organized and informal games, wellness activities, curricular and extracurricular activities, intramural group and individual activities, movies, games, sports, social activities, art work, hobby crafts, physical fitness, table games, board games and social and cultural organizations. Recreation staff is available to provide assistance in planning and organizing recreational activities. Unit recreation decks are open seven days a week (including holidays). The recreation decks are open Monday through Friday 6:10am-8:30pm; and weekends and federal holidays 7:10am-8:30pm. Recreation decks are closed during breakfast and lunch and during all counts. The following activities/ tournaments are available: mini soccer, handball, mini volleyball, and basketball. Activities are conducted in the housing units. Since the exercises and times vary, schedules are posted on each education and recreation bulletin board. Board games: chess, checkers, dominoes, ping-pong, Monopoly, UNO, Scrabble, Risk, Parcheesi, backgammon, and spades.

Leisure activities: crocheting, step aerobics, stair-stepping machines, calisthenics, exercise bikes, chin-up bars and walking (crocheting for work cadre inmates only).

Art activities: coloring and drawing; holiday activities (special). The FDC, Miami, art work and hobby crafts programs includes a portrait drawing program, self-directed drawing, sketching and coloring program. Card design, crocheting, bead/loom program, and basket weaving are offered only to the work cadre.

Competitive tournaments conducted on a weekly basis: basketball, soccer, handball, dominoes, spades, bingo, bowling, and hula hoops.

**Religious Services:** A full-time staff chaplain coordinates the various programs. Christian, Jewish and Muslim clergy contractors are available for religious services and instruction for adherents of their respective faith traditions. Clergy and lay volunteers of various faith groups are utilized to supplement all aspects of the religious program. Religious and personal counseling is available to all inmates upon request. Religious services and activities are normally held in the individual unit religious activity areas (chapels) and are generally open to all inmates. A chaplain is on duty every day of the week. Their schedules, as well as each unit's overall religious activity schedule, are located on the chapel bulletin board.

**Commissary:** The commissary is open during weekday daytime hours and after the 4pm count, with specific shopping times determined by an inmate's work assignment. Inmates are assigned one shopping day per week, determined by the fourth and fifth digits of their inmate registration number. The rotation changes quarterly. Commissary hours are posted in the housing areas, as well as at the bulletin board in front of the commissary. The Bureau of Prisons policy currently sets a monthly spending limit of $360.

**Telephone Policy:** Inmates may call collect or dial direct using the Inmate Telephone System (ITS). The following are standard features of ITS: (1) inmate calls automatically terminate after 15 minutes; (2) an inmate's calling list is limited to 30 callers; and (3) calls are charged to an inmate's debit card. Each inmate receives 300 calling minutes per month.

**Inmate Mail:** The FCI and the camp accept mail from the U.S. Postal Service via First-Class, U.S. Priority, and Express Mail. For those interested in sending overnight mail via a private carrier (FedEx or UPS Overnight), it is recommended that you first contact the institution to find out whether the receipt of such mail is permitted. Inmates may receive publications without prior approval, although the warden will reject publications if they are determined to be detrimental to the security, good order or discipline of the institution. All publications must be received directly from the publisher or bookstore. Each inmate is limited to five books, two current magazines and one current newspaper.

**Inmate Mail to FCI:**
> INMATE NAME & REGISTER NUMBER
> FCI Miami
> Federal Correctional Institution
> P.O. Box 779800
> Miami, FL 33177

**Inmate Mail to Camp:**
> INMATE NAME & REGISTER NUMBER
> FCI Miami
> Federal Correctional Institution
> Satellite Camp
> P.O. Box 779800
> Miami, FL 33177

**Visiting Hours:** Visiting hours at the FCI are Friday through Sunday, and federal holidays, 8am-3pm. Camp visiting hours are Friday 5pm-8pm, and Sunday, and federal holidays, 8am-3pm. Visits for FCI inmates will be on a point system. Inmates will be charged one point for weekdays and two points for weekend and holidays. Weekend visitation is based on an odd/even system; and is determined by the first five digits on the inmate's registration number. Inmates are limited to five adult visitors and three children under the age of three years. Attorneys are encouraged to visit during regular visiting hours. All attorney visits for the FCI and camp must be arranged with the legal liaison. Attorneys requesting a visit must make the request at least 24 hours prior to their visit. A maximum number of eighteen persons will be placed on the inmates approved visitor list. Additional visiting information can be found at https://www.bop.gov/locations/institutions/mia/.

**Lodging/Accommodations:** Should visitors be spending the night, the following is a short list of accommodations that are available in Miami, Florida:

| | |
|---|---|
| Comfort Suites Miami Kendall | 305-220-3901 |
| Quality Inn-South | 305-251-2000 |
| The Best Miami Hotel | 305-667-6664 |
| Airport Regency | 305-441-1600 |
| River Park Hotel and Suites | 305-374-5100 |
| Hyatt Regency | 305-358-1234 |
| JW Marriott Hotel | 305-374-1224 |

## §16:21   FDC MIAMI

FDC Miami
Federal Detention Center Miami
33 N.E. 4th Street
Miami, FL 33132
MIM/ExecAssistant@bop.gov
305-577-0010
Fax: 305-536-7368

**Location:** East of Miami International Airport in downtown Miami. The institution is located at the corner of N.E. 4th Street and N. Miami Avenue. Miami is served by Miami International Airport, Amtrak, and commercial bus lines.

**History:** The FDC houses pre-trial inmates, male and female, of all security levels. In addition, it has a cadre of minimum/low-security male inmates, sentenced to relatively short-terms, who are designated to the FDC as a work detail.

**Judicial District:** Southern District of Florida.

**Security Level:** An administrative facility housing male and female inmates.

**Population:** As of 6/25/2017, the inmate population is 1,270. Weekly population figures are available on the BOP website, www.bop.gov, at https://www.bop.gov/locations/institutions/mim/.

**Education:** FDC offers GED, ESL, post-secondary education, adult continuing education, parenting and correspondence courses.

**Vocational/Apprenticeship:** The FDC offers advanced occupational education in: accounting operations, business supervision and management, business management and law, data entry operations, keyboarding, and computerized engraving. The FDC does not offer vocational or apprenticeship training programs.

**Library:** There are two main law libraries located on the 3rd and 11th floors of the FDC, and three basic law libraries located in three housing units. Access to the law libraries is determined by housing unit and designation status, and the schedules are posted in the units and are in the Admission & Orientation booklets given to all inmates. Typewriters are available in the main law libraries and in housing units. Copiers are also available in the main law libraries. Cadre (designated) inmates have direct access to the leisure library, and for other inmates book carts are taken to the housing units.

**UNICOR:** None.

**Counseling/Rehab Services:** The FDC offers a non-residential drug treatment program, a 500-hour residential drug abuse program, a drug education program, Alcoholics Anonymous and Narcotics Anonymous.

**Health Services:** The institution is staffed by one physician, four to six physician assistants, one dentist, and one pharmacist. Inmates are provided with outpatient care. The pill line times are at 6am-6:55am, 11:30am-12:30pm, and 5pm-8:30pm. Sick call sign-up is in the housing unit from 6am-2pm Monday, Tuesday, Thursday, and Friday. At least one physician assistant is on duty or on call 24 hours a day.

**Housing:** Inmates are housed in two-man rooms.

**Fitness/Recreation:** The recreation department offers stair-steppers, stationary bicycles, aerobics, board games, movies, and ping-pong tables. Outdoor recreation activities include soccer, volleyball, basketball, and handball (there are outdoor recreation decks.) The hobby craft center offers card making and crocheting.

**Religious Services:** The institution is staffed by four full-time chaplains. Christian, Jewish, and Muslim clergy contractors are available for services and instruction.

**Commissary:** The commissary is open Monday through Friday in the evenings. Inmates are assigned one shopping day per week, according to unit/floor. Bureau of Prisons policy currently sets a monthly spending limit of $360.

**Telephone Policy:** Telephones are located in each housing unit. Pre-trial and holdover inmates may use the telephones during the day and evening, and can call collect or dial direct using the Inmate Telephone System (ITS). Cadre inmates may not use the telephones during regular work hours, without special permission. The following are standard features of ITS: (1) inmate calls automatically terminate after 15 minutes; (2) an inmate's calling list is limited to 30 callers; and (3) calls are charged to an inmate's debit card. Inmates are permitted to change their existing telephone list up to three times per month. Each inmate is limited to 300 minutes per month. Attorney calls are available by special request and not made on the Inmate Telephone System.

**Inmate Mail:** The FCI and the camp accept mail from the U.S. Postal Service via First-Class, U.S. Priority, and Express Mail. For those interested in sending overnight mail via a private carrier (FedEx or UPS Overnight), it is recommended that you first contact the institution to find out whether the receipt of such mail is permitted.

**Inmate Mail to FDC:**
    INMATE NAME & REGISTER NUMBER
    FDC Miami
    Federal Detention Center
    P.O. Box 019120
    Miami, FL 33101

**Visiting Hours:** Visiting hours: Sunday-Saturday 7am-9pm. Inmates are limited to three visitors at one time. Inmates will be allowed only one social visit on a single day. Once a visit begins, no other visitors will be allowed into the visiting area. Visiting lists for pre-trial and holdover inmates will be limited to immediate family members. The approved visiting list for Cadre inmates may have up to four relatives and friends in addition to immediate family members. Attorneys must receive approval in advance of visiting, by submitting an application form to the legal liaison and will visit during regular visiting days and times. Additional visiting information can be found on the BOP website, www.bop.gov.

**Lodging/Accommodations:** See §16:20 Miami FCI.

## §16:22   FPC MONTGOMERY

FPC Montgomery
Federal Prison Camp
Maxwell Air Force Base
Montgomery, AL 36112
MON/ExecAssistant@bop.gov
334-293-2100
Fax: 334-293-2326

**Location:** On the bank of the Alabama River, at Maxwell Air Force Base, off Interstates 65 and 85. Montgomery is served by Dannelly Field Airport, Amtrak, and commercial bus lines.

**History:** Open for over 70 years, FPC Montgomery houses minimum-security inmates mainly from the southeastern United States.

**Judicial District:** Middle District of Alabama.

**Security Level:** A minimum-security facility that houses male offenders.

**Population:** As of 6/25/2014, the inmate population is 826. Weekly population figures are available on the BOP website at www.bop.gov, at https://www.bop.gov/locations/institutions/mon/.

**Education:** The camp offers GED, ESL, adult continuing education, release preparation courses, and literacy programs.

**Vocational/Apprenticeship:** Vocational training is available in the area of commercial driver's license. The FPC offers apprenticeship programs in conjunction with the U.S. Department of Labor in the following occupations: barber, plumber, horticulturist, housekeeper, HVAC, landscaper, cook, carpenter, electric technician, animal trainer, and greenskeeper. These occupational training programs are certified through the

Department of Labor. In order to participate in an apprenticeship program, inmates must have a high school diploma or GED, or be currently enrolled in the GED program.

**Library:** The electronic law library is open Monday through Friday 7:30am-3:30pm and 6pm-8pm; weekends and holidays 8am-9:30am, 12noon-3:30pm and 6pm-8:30pm. LEXISNEXUS ELL programs are available on the computers. Electronic typewriters and a copier are available. The leisure library participates in the inter-library loan program.

**UNICOR:** The majority of business at FPC Montgomery UNICOR involves processing linens, including towels, bath mats, wash cloths, sheets, and pillow cases, as well as items used at the Maxwell AFB Hospital/Medical Treatment Facility Inmates may apply for UNICOR by submitting an application. Inmates with prior UNICOR employment are given priority for UNICOR hiring.

**Counseling/Rehab Services:** The Psychology Department offers individual therapy, group therapy, and personal adjustment courses. There is a 500-hour, nine-month Residential Drug Abuse Program (RDAP). Inmates in the RDAP are housed in the Birmingham Unit. In addition, the camp offers a non-residential drug treatment program, a drug education program, smoking cessation program, and Alcoholics Anonymous and Narcotics Anonymous groups. The Drug Abuse Treatment Program staff have office hours from 2:30pm-3:30pm on weekdays.

**Health Services:** The camp is staffed by physicians, dentists, and pharmacists, with outpatient care provided. Local hospitals are approximately 10 miles away. The medication line is open from 6:15am-6:45am, 3:15pm-3:45pm, 5pm-5:30pm (weekdays), and 8:30am-9am, 3:15pm-3:45pm, and 5pm-5:30pm (weekends). Sick call sign-up is from 6am-6:20am, four days a week. At least one physician assistant is on duty or on call 24 hours a day.

**Housing:** There are three housing units at FPC Montgomery: Birmingham, Mobile, and Montgomery. Inmates are housed in dormitories in two-man cubicles.

**Fitness/Recreation:** The recreation department offers stair-steppers, exercise bicycles, weights, a music room, ping-pong tables, and pool tables. The hobby craft center offers ceramics, leather craft, and art.

**Religious Services:** The camp has one full-time chaplain, one chaplain assistant, contract clergy, volunteer clergy and lay ministers that represent various faith communities. The chaplain's normal open house hours are Monday through Thursday, 3pm-3:45pm. A sweat lodge is available for Native-American inmates. Sweat lodge ceremonies are held on Saturdays from 7:30am-3:30pm.

**Commissary:** The commissary is open for regular sales Monday through Wednesday from 9am-12noon and 1pm-3:30pm. Each inmate is allowed to shop once each week. The commissary is closed once every six months for inventory purposes. Inmates should plan for this when making purchases. Bureau of Prisons policy currently sets a monthly spending limit of $360.

**Telephone Policy:** Inmates may call collect or dial direct using the Inmate Telephone System (ITS). The following are standard features of ITS: (1) inmate calls automatically terminate after 15 minutes; (2) an inmate's calling list is limited to 30 callers; and (3) calls are charged to an inmate's debit card. Each inmate is limited to 300 minutes per month.

**Inmate Mail:** The FCI and the camp accept mail from the U.S. Postal Service via First-Class, U.S. Priority, and Express Mail. For those interested in sending overnight mail via a private carrier (FedEx or UPS Overnight), it is recommended that you first contact the institution to find out whether the receipt of such mail is permitted. Inmates may receive publications without prior approval, although the warden will reject publications if they are determined to be detrimental to the security, good order or discipline of the institution. Hardcover publications and newspapers must be received directly from the publisher, bookstore or book club; softcover publications may be received from any source.

**Inmate Mail to FDP:**
> INMATE NAME & REGISTER NUMBER
> FPC Montgomery
> Federal Prison Camp
> Maxwell Air Force Base
> Montgomery, AL 36112

**Visiting Hours:** Visiting hours: Saturday, Sunday, federal holidays 8am-3pm. An inmate's approved visiting list is limited to 25 visitors (ages 16 years and older). No more than four visitors may visit an inmate at one time. Attorneys are required to give at least 24 hours notice of their desired visit with an inmate. Additional visiting information can be found on the BOP website, www.bop.gov, at https://www.bop.gov/locations/institutions/mon/.

**Lodging/Accommodations:** Should visitors be spending the night, the following is a short list of accommodations that are available in Montgomery, Alabama:

| | |
|---|---|
| Knights Inn | 334-288-7999 |
| Country Inn & Suites Montgomery East | 334-270-3223 |
| Candlelight Inn | 334-281-1660 |
| America's Best Inn | 334-288-5740 |
| Comfort Inn & Suites | 334-532-4444 |

# §16:23 FPC PENSACOLA

FPC Pensacola
Federal Prison Camp
110 Raby Avenue
Pensacola, FL 32509
PEN/ExecAssistant@bop.gov
850-457-1911
Fax: 850-458-7291

**Location:** 175 miles west of Tallahassee and 50 miles east of Mobile, Alabama, on Saufley Field, an outlying base of the Pensacola Naval Air Station (NAS), off Interstate 10. The area is served by the Pensacola Municipal Airport and Greyhound.

**History:** Opened in 1988, FPC Pensacola houses male offenders primarily from the southeastern United States who do not have records of escape, violence, or major medical and emotional problems, and have not been convicted of sexual offenses. This site has experienced hurricanes, which has sometimes necessitated the evacuation of inmates to other prison facilities.

**Judicial District:** Northern District of Florida.

**Security Level:** A minimum-security facility houses male offenders.

**Population:** As of 6/25/2017, the FPC inmate population is 707. Weekly population figures are available on the BOP website, www.bop.gov, at https://www.bop.gov/locations/institutions/pen/.

**Education:** The camp offers GED, ESL, adult education, and correspondence courses. College courses are available through the use of computer assisted instruction. Inmates may pay for the courses or choose to audit the courses at no charge.

**Vocational/Apprenticeship:** The FPC does not offer certificate programs. The FPC offers vocational training in computer applications and A+ computer technician. The FPC offers apprenticeship programs in the following occupations: cook, baker, greenskeeper, landscape technician, horticulturist, maintenance electrician, plumber, bricklayer, HVAC, painter, small engine mechanic, welder, carpenter, cabinetmaker, and outboard motor mechanic.

**Library:** The leisure/law library is located on the first floor of building 844. It has a balanced collection of hardback and paperback fiction, non-fiction books, reference books and periodicals. Reference books and newspapers are for use in the library only. Other books may be checked out. The library hours are from 6am-9pm daily, including weekends and holidays. The law library adjoins the leisure library in building 844. Legal books and materials may not be removed or checked out of the law library. An inmate clerk is available to help find legal reference materials. Typewriters, paper and supplies are available to assist in legal writing. An inter-library loan is available.

**UNICOR:** None.

**Counseling/Rehab Services:** The psychology department offers individual and/or group psychotherapy which is available by request. Drug abuse treatment programs are available for inmates with a history of drugs/alcohol abuse or dependence. Treatment programs are voluntary. Drug abuse education, however, is required for some inmates. The FPC offers a 500-hour, nine-month Residential Drug Abuse Program (RDAP). Reading material on a variety of psychological/motivational topics is available for checkout from the Psychology Media Center. The media center also has audio and videotape material which may be used in the chapel building, which houses the Psychological Department. Materials are available on self-help topics such as relaxation, stress management, relationships, motivation, substance abuse, and smoking cessation. Weekend personal growth seminars are held approximately once each quarter. The department also sponsors L.I.F.E. Talks (Learned Insights From Experience). The psychology department is staffed by one full-time psychologist.

**Health Services:** The camp provides outpatient care and each inmate is assigned a health care provider. Local hospitals are approximately 15 miles away. The Health Services Unit is staffed from 7:30am-4pm weekdays and from 7am-5pm on weekends and holidays. After hours emergency care will be provided by Saufley Field Fire Department and the Escambia County Emergency Medical Service. Medical/dental sick call sign-up is Saturday and Sunday 12noon-12:30pm; and Tuesday and Thursday 4:30pm-5pm. Sick call screening is held four days a week: Monday, Tuesday, Thursday, Friday. Daily pill line hours are clearly posted at the pharmacy window.

**Housing:** Inmates are housed in "open bay" dormitories, two-man cubicles, and in dormitories consisting of eight-man and 10-man rooms. Television sets are located in the TV rooms in each dorm. A TV committee has been set up in each dorm to make and publish program selections.

**Fitness/Recreation:** The Recreation Department offers a wide variety of active and passive leisure time activities: intramural sports (softball, basketball, flag football, soccer, and volleyball), weight training, fitness (abs/stretching, step aerobics, presidential sports award program, and wellness), music, hobby craft (art, leather, wood), racquetball, bocce ball, and horseshoes. Program times are listed on a monthly recreation schedule. The Recreation Department sponsors movies weekly. Movie schedules are posted on bulletin boards and are frequently announced. Movies will be broadcast in either the Base Theater (sometimes referred to as the Reserve Center) or visiting room, or via the institutional channel.

**Religious Services:** FPC Pensacola has one full-time chaplain. The chaplain's office is in the Chapel Building (Bldg. 2474). The chaplain is in his office Sunday through Thursday. The audio/video room is used on a first come/first served basis. Free religious publications are available in English and Spanish in a brochure rack in the hall outside the chaplain's office. The worship area of the chapel is available for individual private prayer, when it is not scheduled for services or other activities. The chaplain is available for counseling/pastoral care.

**Commissary:** The commissary is open on Tuesdays and Wednesdays from 4:30pm-7:30pm. Shopping day is determined by the inmate's register number. The Bureau of Prisons policy currently sets spending limits at $360.

**Telephone Policy:** Inmates may dial direct or call collect. Twenty long distance telephones plus local and international phones are provided in the inmate phone room (Building 836). These are the only telephones inmates are authorized to use. Telephones are operational weekdays from 6am-7:30am, 10:30am-12:30pm, and 4pm-9:30 pm; weekends and holidays from 6am-9:30pm.

**Inmate Mail:** The FCI and the camp accept mail from the U.S. Postal Service via First-Class, U.S. Priority, and Express Mail. For those interested in sending overnight mail via a private carrier (FedEx or UPS Overnight), it is recommended that you first contact the institution to find out whether the receipt of such mail is permitted. Inmates may receive publications without prior approval, although the warden will reject publications if they are determined to be detrimental to the security, good order or discipline of the institution. Hardcover publications and newspapers must be received directly from the publisher or bookstore; softcover publications may be received from any source.

**Inmate Mail to FPC:**
> INMATE NAME & REGISTER NUMBER
> FPC Pensacola
> Federal Prison Camp
> P.O. Box 3949
> Pensacola, FL 32516

**Visiting Hours:** Visiting hours: Friday 5pm-8:30pm; Saturday, Sunday, federal holidays 8am-3pm. Each inmate is granted an unlimited amount of visiting time, during regular visiting hours. An inmate is limited to five visitors, including children, at one time. An inmates approved visitor list is limited to ten non-immediate family members, friends and associates. Attorney visits will be coordinated by the Unit Staff. Additional visiting information can be found at the BOP website, www.bop.gov, at https://www.bop.gov/locations/institutions/pen/.

**Lodging/Accommodations:** Should visitors be spending the night, the following is a short list of accommodations that are available in Pensacola, Florida:

| Hampton Inn Pensacola Airport | 850-478-1123 |
| Best Western Blue Angel Inn | 850-477-7474 |
| Homewood Suites by Hilton Pensacola Airport | 850-474-3777 |
| Residence Inn by Marriott Pensacola Downtown | 850-432-0202 |
| Red Roof Inn Pensacola West Florida Hospital | 850-476-7690 |
| Microtel Inn & Suites Fairgrounds | 850-941-8902 |

## §16:24   FCI TALLADEGA

FCI Talladega
Federal Correctional Institution
565 E. Renfroe Road
Talladega, AL 35160
TDG/ExecAssistant@bop.gov
256-315-4100
Fax: 256-315-4495

**Location:** In the foothills of northern Alabama, 50 miles east of Birmingham and 100 miles west of Atlanta, Georgia. It is situated on the west side of Talladega, off Interstate 20 on County Road 42, Renfroe Road.

**History:** Opened in 1979, FCI Talladega houses male offenders from the southeastern Unites States. Opened in 1989, the camp serves as a satellite facility to the main institutions. It houses minimum-security male offenders.

**Judicial District:** Northern District of Alabama.

**Security Level:** A medium-security level facility housing male inmates with an adjacent minimum-security satellite camp that also houses male offenders.

**Population:** As of 8/26/2017, the FCI inmate population is 816, and the camp population is 279. Weekly population figures are available on the BOP website at www.bop.gov, https://www.bop.gov/locations/institutions/tdg/.

**Education:** The FCI and the camp offer GED, ESL, parenting class and adult continuing education which may include typing, word processing, accounting, business management, creative writing/speaking, career development, and a Spanish course.

**Vocational/Apprenticeship:** The FCI offers advanced occupational education in: computer information processing. The camp offers A+ computer refurbishing hardware/software. The FCI offers vocational training in: cabinetmaking helper, cabinetmaking basic. The FCI offers vocational training in: cabinetmaking advanced, carpentry helper, carpentry basic, carpentry advanced, masonry helper, basic masonry, advanced masonry, welding helper, welding basic, and welding advanced. The camp offers CDL Class B. The FCI and the camp offer apprenticeship in electrician. FCI offers apprenticeships in: machinist wood, painter, plumber, sheet metal worker, and welding technician.

**Library:** The main institution's law library is open Monday through Sunday from 7:30am-6pm. Electric typewriters and a copier are available to inmates for the preparation of legal documents only.

**UNICOR:** A furniture factory employs approximately 211 inmates.

**Counseling/Rehab Services:** The camp offers the 500-hour Residential Drug Abuse Program (RDAP). The program is nine months in length. In addition, the FCI and the camp offer a non-residential drug treatment program, a drug education program, Alcoholics and Narcotics Anonymous groups, and individual psychotherapy. The main institution is staffed by four full-time psychologists. Services include: stop smoking seminar, stress management, drug abuse program, individualized treatment program including formal instruction and personal counseling.

**Health Services:** The main institution is staffed by two physicians, five to seven physician assistants, two dentists, and one pharmacist. The FCI and the camp provide outpatient care. A small infirmary is available. The institution is served by Citizens Hospital approximately five minutes away.

Sick call hours: Monday, Tuesday, Thursday and Friday 6am-7am. Appointments will be scheduled (excluding Wednesday) from 8am-11am and 12noon-3:15pm with certain times blocked out for other scheduled activities. A physician assistant will be available Monday through Friday, (excluding Wednesday) from 6am-7am, for initial sick call screening. Pill line for inmates with yard privileges will be at the HSU pharmacy, for prescription meds only: 6am-7am; 11am-12noon, and 5pm-5:30pm. Weekend and holiday pill line: 8am-8:30am, 12noon-12:30pm and 5pm-5:30pm. Medical staff regular duty hours: Monday through Friday 7:30am-4pm. Medical staff will be on duty 24 hours a day as staffing permits.

**Housing:** Inmates at the FCI are housed in four modern housing units (Gamma, Delta, Sigma, and Beta) in single-man and two-man cells. Beta B is designated as the 500-hour Residential Comprehensive Drug Treatment Unit. Inmates at the camp are housed in two-man cubicles.

**Fitness/Recreation:** The recreation department offers stationary bicycles, a music room (acoustic instruments), and ping-pong tables. No hobbies are offered.

**Religious Services:** The main institution is staffed by a full-time chaplain. There are a variety of faith groups represented in the chapel program such as Protestant, Catholic, Jewish, Muslim, Nation of Islam, Moorish Science Temple,

Jehovah's Witnesses and Native American. Bible studies are conducted by Prison Fellowship, Jehovah's Witnesses, and charismatic volunteers. Inmates may stop by the chapel and pick-up a copy of the religious services schedule whenever the chapel is open. Videotapes, cassette tapes, and religious books are also available.

**Commissary:** Inmates are allowed to shop once a week. The sales unit is open Monday-Thursday for sales to the general population after the 4pm count. Inmates must shop on assigned sales day, which is determined by their registration number. The camp commissary is open Tuesday through Thursday from 11am-1:30pm. The Bureau of Prisons policy currently sets a monthly spending limit of $360.

**Telephone Policy:** Inmates at the FCI and the camp call collect. At the FCI, the telephones are located on each side of the living units.

**Inmate Mail:** The FCI and the camp accept mail from the U.S. Postal Service via First-Class, U.S. Priority, and Express Mail. For those interested in sending overnight mail via a private carrier (FedEx or UPS Overnight), it is recommended that you first contact the institution to find out whether the receipt of such mail is permitted.

**Inmate Mail to FCI:**
> INMATE NAME & REGISTER NUMBER
> FCI Talladega
> Federal Correctional Institution
> P.O. Box 1000
> Talladega, AL 35160

**Inmate Mail to Camp:**
> INMATE NAME & REGISTER NUMBER
> FCI Talladega
> Federal Correctional Institution
> Satellite Camp
> P.O. Box 2000
> Talladega, AL 35160

**Visiting Hours:** FCI visiting hours: Friday, Saturday, Sunday, federal holidays 8:30am-3pm. FPC visiting hours: Friday 5pm-9pm; Saturday, Sunday, federal holidays 8am-3:30pm. FCI and FPC inmates are generally allowed an unlimited number of visits; however the number of visitors at one time is limited to six adults, not including children. Attorney visits must be directed to the respective case manager. Inmates in the Alpha Unit are allowed a maximum of four visitors, with one visit per week, scheduled Monday through Friday. No special visits will be approved for inmates in the Alpha Unit. Additional visiting information can be found at https://www.bop.gov/locations/institutions/tdg/.

**Lodging/Accommodations:** Should visitors be spending the night, the following is a short list of accommodations that are available in Talladega, Alabama:

| | |
|---|---|
| Budget Inn | 256-362-0902 |
| McCaig Motel | 256-362-6110 |
| Super 8 Motel of Talladega | 256-315-9511 |

## §16:25  FCI TALLAHASSEE

FCI Tallahassee
Federal Correctional Institution
501 Capital Circle, N.E.
Tallahassee, FL 32301
TAL/ExecAssistant@bop.gov
850-878-2173
Fax: 850-671-6105

**Location:** Three miles east of downtown Tallahassee, on Highway 319 and Conner Blvd. at the intersection of Park Avenue. The area is served by Tallahassee Regional Airport, Amtrak, and commercial bus lines.

**History:** Opened in the late 1930s, FCI Tallahassee houses designated female offenders primarily from the southeastern United States and pre-trial/holdover males of all security levels.

**Judicial District:** Northern District of Florida.

**Security Level:** A low-security facility housing female inmates with an adjacent detention center that houses administrative security level male inmates.

**Population:** As of 6/26/2017, the inmate population is 803. Weekly population figures are available at https://www.bop.gov/locations/institutions/tal/.

**Education:** The institution offers GED, ESL, adult continuing education, parenting classes and correspondence courses.

**Vocational/Apprenticeship:** FCI offers advanced occupational education in business education, building trades, cosmetology, electronics, horticulture, and custodial maintenance. FCI offers apprenticeships in the following areas: baker, horticulturist, plumber, construction, electrician, metal fabricator, landscape management, refrigeration, woodworking, housekeeper, cook, painter, butcher, and landscape technician.

**Library:** The Law Library is open during convenient non-working hours, including weekends. An inmate Law Library Clerk is available for assistance in legal research. Legal materials are also available to inmates in detention or segregation status, ordinarily via a delivery system or satellite collection. Electronic Law Library (ELL) is also available.

**UNICOR:** FCI Tallahassee employs approximately 337 inmates in contracting services. Some of the services include: data services, warehousing, distribution and fulfillment, assistance and help desk, custom printing.

**Counseling/Rehab Services:** A full range of mental health services available through the psychology department includes: acute crisis intervention, treatment of mentally ill, suicide prevention, psychological evaluations and reports, initial screening, brief counseling, psycho-educational/therapeutic groups, individual psychotherapy, staff consultation and treatment programs. All clinicians are trained in issues significant to the inmate population. A contract psychiatrist is available by appointment for consultation concerning mental health conditions that might require treatment that includes use of medication. Inmates who have a history of substance abuse and a desire to correct their patterns of abuse can seek help through the Residential Drug Abuse Program (RDAP), which coordinates long-term residential treatment, a non-residential group, and a 40-hour drug education group. Various counseling groups (including Alcoholic Anonymous) and informal counseling sessions are available.

**Health Services:** The institution is staffed by three physicians, five to eight physician assistants, three dentists, two nurses, and one to two pharmacists. Each inmate is assigned to a Primary Care Provider (Mid-Level Practitioner/PA) and a Physician. A managed health care system is used, and each inmate is assigned to a primary care provider. Outpatient and limited infirmary care are provided. The institution is served by the Tallahassee Memorial and Tallahassee Community Hospital. Both hospitals are located approximately five minutes away. Sick call is held four days a week at the Health Services Department Monday through Friday (except Wednesdays and holidays) from 6:30am-7am. Sick call at the FDC is conducted by the assigned MLP in the units four days a week from 7am-10am. Pill line and prescription pick-up hours: are posted outside of the pharmacy. Female inmates between the ages of 35 and 40 are offered an elective initial mammography. Any inmate under the age of 35 with a family history of breast cancer, tumors, or other breast related problems should make a routine sick call and arrangements will be made to schedule a baseline mammography and follow-up if medically indicated. Emergency medical care is available 24 hours a day, seven days a week.

**Housing:** Inmates are housed in open dormitories.

**Fitness/Recreation:** Leisure activities and recreation programs are supervised by the education department. Programs include indoor and outdoor activities, and range from individualized arts and crafts programs to intramural team sports such as softball, basketball, and volleyball.

**Religious Services:** A wide range of religious programs are available to inmates. Chaplains of specific faiths are available, as well as contract and volunteer representatives of other faiths.

**Commissary:** The commissary is open Monday, Tuesday, Wednesday, Thursday after the 4pm count, and will remain open past 8:30pm, until all inmates have been served. Fridays are reserved for special purchase orders. Inmate shopping days are based on the inmate's register number. The Bureau of Prisons policy currently sets a monthly spending limit of $360.

**Telephone Policy:** Inmates may call collect or dial direct using the Inmate Telephone System (ITS). The following are standard features of ITS: (1) inmate calls automatically terminate after 15 minutes; (2) an inmate's calling list is limited to 30 callers; and (3) calls are charged to an inmate's debit card. The FCI telephones are operational from 5am-12midnight. FDC phones are operative from 6:30am-8:45pm daily.

**Inmate Mail:** The institution accepts mail from the U.S. Postal Service via First-Class, U.S. Priority, and Express Mail. For those interested in sending overnight mail via a private carrier (FedEx or UPS Overnight), it is recommended that you first contact the institution to find out whether the receipt of such mail is permitted. Inmates may receive publications without prior approval, although the warden will reject publications if they are determined to be detrimental to the security, good order or discipline of the institution. All publications must be received directly from the publisher or bookstore. Each inmate is limited to five magazines, no older than three months old.

**Inmate Mail to FCI:**
> INMATE NAME & REGISTER NUMBER
> FCI Tallahassee
> Federal Correctional Institution
> 501 Capital Circle NE
> Tallahassee, FL 32301

**Visiting Hours:** FDC and FCI visiting hours: Friday-Sunday 8:30am-3pm. All holiday weekend/weekdays are open to the inmate population for visits. Inmates at the FCI are limited to four adult visitors at one time. Inmates at the FDC are limited to three adults and children visitors at one time. Attorneys should make an advanced appointment to visit and should visit during regular visiting times. Legal visits are permitted seven days a week. Additional visiting information can be found at https://www.bop.gov/locations/institutions/tal/.

**Lodging/Accommodations:** Should visitors be spending the night, the following is a short list of accommodations that are available in Tallahassee:
> Regency Inn                                                      850-385-2038

| Comfort Inn | 850-224-3200 |
| DoubleTree Hotel | 850-224-5000 |
| Baymont Inn and Suites | 850-562-4300 |
| Hilton Garden Inn | 850-385-3553 |
| Quality Inn | 850-562-2378 |

## §16:26   FCI WILLIAMSBURG

FCI Williamsburg
Federal Correctional Institution
8301 Highway 521
Salters, SC 29590
WIL/ExecAssistant@bop.gov
843-387-9400
Fax: 843-387-6961

**Location:** FCI Williamsburg is located in Williamsburg County off Highway 521 in Salters, South Carolina.

**Judicial District:** Southern District of Carolina.

**Security Level:** The Federal Correctional Institution Williamsburg is a medium-security facility that houses male inmates. It has an adjacent minimum-security male camp.

**Population:** As of 6/26/2014, the medium-security inmate population is 1,249, and the camp population is 150. Weekly population figures are available on the BOP website at https://www.bop.gov/locations/institutions/wil/.

**Education:** The institution offers GED, ESL, adult continuing education, parenting classes and college correspondence courses.

**Vocational/Apprenticeship:** The FCI offers vocational training in: introductory and advanced carpentry, introductory and advanced cabinet-making, and introductory and advanced culinary arts. The FCI and the camp offer apprenticeship programs in the following areas: electrician, HVAC, plumbing, and industrial housekeeping.

**UNICOR:** FCI Williamsburg employs approximately 216 inmates in contracting services. Some of the services include: data services, warehousing, distribution and fulfillment, assistance and help desk, custom printing.

**Counseling/Rehab Services:** The institution employs one staff psychologist. Psychology services perform a variety of functions, including classes on anger and stress management, drug education, sexual abuse/assault prevention and intervention, and programming related to the comprehensive residential drug treatment programs. Counseling activities include Alcoholics Anonymous, Narcotics Anonymous, People in Prison Entering Sobriety, self-image groups, and other voluntary groups.

**Health Services:** The Health Services unit is on duty from 7:30am-4pm, Monday through Friday. Emergency care is available 24 hours a day. Sick call is 10:30 am at the FCI and 3pm at the satellite camp. Pill line hours at the FCI are 6:45am-7:15am, 11am-12noon, and 5:30pm-8:30pm. Pill line hours at the camp are 6:45am-7:15am and 3pm-3:30pm. Age-specific preventative health examinations are available, and may be requested via cop-out.

**Fitness/Recreation:** Recreation programs include, but are not limited to, intra-mural sports, community-based sports, informal sports, physical fitness and wellness, special events, hobby craft, music, movies, and other leisure time activities. A gymnasium, softball fields, jogging track soccer field, handball, bocce ball, basketball courts, and volleyball courts are also available., along with a passive recreation area for board games.

**Religious Services:** A wide range of religious programs are available to inmates. Chaplains of specific faiths are available, as well as contract and volunteer representatives of other faiths.

**Commissary:** The commissary is open from Monday to Friday. Sales hours are posted by memorandum for both the FCI and the satellite camp in the housing units. BOP policy sets a monthly commissary spending limit of $360.

**Telephone Policy:** Inmates are allowed to dial direct or call collect using the Inmate Telephone System (ITS). The following are standard features of ITS: (1) inmate calls automatically terminate after 15 minutes; (2) an inmate's calling list is limited to 30 callers; and (3) calls are charged to an inmate's debit card. Unmonitored calls for legal purposes must be scheduled in advance. The inmate telephones will normally be activated daily from 6:45am-7:30am, 10:30am-12pm, and 4:30pm to lockdown for the count on weekdays, and 6:45pm-lockdown for the count on weekends.

**Inmate Mail:** The institution accepts mail from the U.S. Postal Service via First Class, U.S. Priority, and Express mail. For those interested in sending overnight mail via a private carrier (FedEx or UPS Overnight), it is recommended that you first contact the institution to find out whether the receipt of such mail is permitted.

**Inmate Mail to FCI:**
    INMATE NAME & REGISTER NUMBER
    Federal Correctional Institution
    P.O. Box 340
    Salters, SC 29590

**Inmate Mail to Camp:**
   INMATE NAME & REGISTER NUMBER
   FCI Williamsburg
   Federal Correctional Institution
   Satellite Camp
   P.O. Box 340
   Salters, SC 29590

**Visiting Hours:** Social visit hours for the FCI and SCP: Friday 5pm-8pm; Saturday, Sunday, and federal holidays 8am-3pm. Inmates housed in the FCI and SCP will be limited to five adult visitors at one time. Children under 16 are not limited. Attorneys must be on the approved visitor list and must visit during regular visiting hours. Additional visiting information can be found on the BOP website, www.bop.gov, https://www.bop.gov/locations/institutions/wil/.

**Directions to Facility:** FCI Williamsburg is located at Highway 521, Salters, SC. From Northeastern Areas, take interstate 95 South to Highway 521 South, FCI Williamsburg will be on your right. From the Southeastern Areas, take 95 North to Highway 521, FCI Williamsburg will be on your right. From the South Central Areas take Interstate 26, to Interstate 95 South, to Highway 521 South and FCI Williamsburg will be on your right.

**Lodging/Accommodations:** The following is a short list of accommodations that are available in Williamsburg County, South Carolina:

**Kingstree, SC 29566:**
   Signature Boutique Hotel            843-355-5888
   Deluxe Inn                          843-355-8585
   Mets Motel                          843-355-7662

**Hemingway, SC 29554:**
   Coachman Inn                        843-558-2576

## §16:27   FCI YAZOO CITY I & II

FCI Yazoo City
Federal Correctional Institution I
Federal Correctional Institution II
2225 Haley Barbour Parkway
Yazoo City, MS 39194
YAZ/PublicInformation@bop.gov
662-751-4800 (FCI Low)
662-716-1020 (FCI Medium)
Fax: 662-751-4800 (FCI Low)
Fax: 662-716-1036 (FCI Medium)

**Location:** Both FCI Yazoo City facilities are located 36 miles north of Jackson, off Highway 49. Take Highway 49 North to Yazoo City, then take Highway 3 West approximately two miles to the institution. The area is served by the Jacksonville International Airport and commercial bus lines.

**History:** The low-security FCI opened in 1996. The satellite camp opened in 2001. The medium-security FCI began receiving inmates in June 2005.

**Judicial District:** Southern District of Mississippi.

**Security Level:** A low-security facility housing male offenders an adjacent satellite prison camp houses minimum-security male offenders; and a medium-security facility housing male offenders.

**Population:** As of 6/26/2014, the low-security inmate population is 1,843; the medium-security inmate population is 1,395 and the camp population is 267. Weekly population figures are available on the BOP website, www.bop.gov at https://www.bop.gov/locations/institutions/yaz/.

**Education:** The institutions offer GED, ESL, adult continuing education, parenting and correspondence courses.

**Vocational/Apprenticeship:** FCI does not offer advanced occupational education programs. FCI offers vocational training in Microsoft Office applications, carpentry, restaurant management, drafting/AutoCAD, and HVAC. The FCI and the camp offer apprenticeship in: carpentry, HVAC, drafting, and custodial maintenance. FCI Medium offers vocational training in: drafting, HVAC. FCI Medium does not offer advanced occupational education or apprenticeship programs.

**Library:** The law library contains a variety of legal reference material for use in preparing legal papers. Reference materials include the United States Code Annotated, Federal Reporter, Supreme Court Reporter, Bureau of Prisons Program Statements, Institution Supplements, and other legal materials. The law library is located in the Education Department. A copy machine and electronic typewriters are available. The law library schedule is posted at each of the facilities and is located in the education department. An inter-library loan is available through the local public library.

**UNICOR:** A textile factory employs approximately 635 inmates.

**Counseling/Rehab Services:** Psychologists are available for individual and/or group psychotherapy. Mental health services are offered in the areas of drug and alcohol abuse, as well as for other behavioral or emotional problems. The FCI offers a 500-hour, nine-month Residential Drug Abuse Program (RDAP).

**Health Services:** The institution is staffed by physicians, physician assistants, dentists, and a pharmacist. The institution provides outpatient care. Local hospitals are five to ten minutes away. A major university hospital is 45 minutes away. Sick call will be scheduled once daily on Monday, Tuesday, Thursday and Friday from 6:30am-7:45am. Pill line hours are clearly posted at the pharmacy window. At least one physician assistant is on duty or on call 24 hours a day.

**Housing:** Inmates are housed in dormitories in two-man rooms at the low-security FCI.

**Fitness/Recreation:** The institution offers intramural and league sports in basketball, soccer, softball, and volleyball. There are also fitness/wellness classes, music room, walking/cycling club, rowing machines, yoga classes, racquetball/handball, bocce ball, horseshoes, stationary bikes, life steppers, abdominal benches, exercise mats, board games. Hobby craft offers painting, art, and leather craft.

**Religious Services:** The institution is staffed by three full-time chaplains. Contract clergy and community volunteers also provide services for most faiths. The religious services department contracts clergy from the various religious faiths. Additionally, the religious services staff will have community volunteers to assist with an inmate's particular religious needs. A religious services schedule will be updated periodically and posted in the chapel and on the unit bulletin boards. Free greeting cards; a religious library (including books and audio-visual resources); and other free religious literature (including Bibles, Koran and devotionals). The chaplains have an open-door policy for personal counseling.

**Commissary:** The commissary is open to inmates once a week. Shopping days are determined by the inmate's registration number. Hours: Monday-Thursday 1:30pm-3pm; 4:30pm-8pm. Bureau of Prisons policy currently sets a monthly commissary spending limit of $360.

**Telephone Policy:** Inmates may call collect or dial direct using the Inmate Telephone System (ITS). The following are standard features of ITS: (1) inmate calls automatically terminate after 15 minutes; (2) an inmate's calling list is limited to 30 callers; and (3) calls are charged to an inmate's debit card. Each inmate is limited to 300 minutes per month.

**Inmate Mail:** The FCI and the camp accept mail from the U.S. Postal Service via First-Class, U.S. Priority, and Express Mail. For those interested in sending overnight mail via a private carrier (FedEx or UPS Overnight), it is recommended that you first contact the institution to find out whether the receipt of such mail is permitted. Inmates may receive publications without prior approval, although the warden will reject publications if they are determined to be detrimental to the security, good order or discipline of the institution. At the medium security facility, all publications must be received directly from the publisher or bookstore; at the low and minimum-security facilities, softcover publications may be received from any source. Each inmate is limited to five magazines, five newspapers and five books.

**Inmate Mail to Low:**
INMATE NAME & REGISTER NUMBER
FCI Yazoo City Low
Federal Correctional Institution
P.O. Box 5000
Yazoo City, MS 39194

**Inmate Mail to Medium:**
INMATE NAME & REGISTER NUMBER
FCI Yazoo City Medium
Federal Correctional Institution
P.O. Box 5888
Yazoo City, MS 39194

**Inmate Mail to Camp:**
INMATE NAME & REGISTER NUMBER
FCI Yazoo City Low
Federal Correctional Institution
Satellite Camp
P.O. Box 5000
Yazoo City, MS 39194

**Visiting Hours:** Visiting hours at the low and medium-security facilities: Friday 5pm-8:30pm; Saturday, Sunday, federal holidays 8am-3pm. Camp: Saturday, Sunday, federal holidays 10am-5pm. Inmates will be given five points per calendar month. One point will be assessed for each weekend day visit. Each time the inmate enters the visiting room on a weekend, one point will be deducted. Points will not be deducted for Friday evening visits. Attorneys can visit during regular visiting hours or must make arrangements through the Unit counselor to visit at other times. An inmate's approved visiting list is limited to 25 visitors. Up to four adults and four children may visit at one time. Additional visiting information can be found on the BOP website, www.bop.gov, at https://www.bop.gov/locations/institutions/yaz/.

**Lodging/Accommodations:** Should visitors be spending the night, the following is a short list of accommodations that are available in Yazoo City, Mississippi:

| | |
|---|---|
| Best Western | 662-716-0930 |
| Days Inn | 662-746-1877 |
| Econo Lodge | 662-746-6444 |
| Hampton Inn | 662-746-3333 |

## §16:28   USP YAZOO CITY

USP Yazoo City
U.S. Penitentiary
2225 Haley Barbour Parkway Yazoo City, MS 39194
YAZ/PublicInformation@bop.gov
662-751-1241
Fax: 662-751-1255

**Location:** See §16:27 FCI Yazoo City I & II.

**History:** Unavailable.

**Judicial District:** Southern District of Mississippi.

**Security Level:** A high-security facility housing male offenders; part of the Yazoo City FCC.

**Population:** As of 6/26/2017, the low-security inmate population is 412. Weekly population figures are available on the BOP website at www.bop.gov, https://www.bop.gov/locations/institutions/yap/.

**Education:** The institution offers GED, ESL, adult continuing education, parenting and correspondence courses.

**Vocational/Apprenticeship:** FCI does not offer advanced occupational education programs. FCI offers vocational training in Microsoft Office applications, carpentry, restaurant management, drafting/AutoCAD, and HVAC. The FCI and the camp offer apprenticeship in: carpentry, HVAC, drafting, and custodial maintenance. FCI Medium offers vocational training in: drafting, HVAC. FCI Medium does not offer advanced occupational education or apprenticeship programs.

**Library:** The law library contains a variety of legal reference material for use in preparing legal papers. Reference materials include the United States Code Annotated, Federal Reporter, Supreme Court Reporter, Bureau of Prisons Program Statements, Institution Supplements, and other legal materials. The law library is located in the Education Department. A copy machine and electronic typewriters are available. The law library schedule is posted at each of the facilities and is located in the education department. An inter-library loan is available through the local public library.

**UNICOR:** A textile factory employs approximately 635 inmates.

**Counseling/Rehab Services:** Psychologists are available for individual and/or group psychotherapy. Mental health services are offered in the areas of drug and alcohol abuse, as well as for other behavioral or emotional problems. The FCI offers a 500-hour, nine-month Residential Drug Abuse Program (RDAP).

**Health Services:** The institution is staffed by physicians, physician assistants, dentists, and a pharmacist. The institution provides outpatient care. Local hospitals are five to ten minutes away. A major university hospital is 45 minutes away. Sick call will be scheduled once daily on Monday, Tuesday, Thursday and Friday from 6:30am-7:45am. Emergency dental services are available by using the same procedures as an emergency sick call. For routine dental care, inmates must submit a cop-out between 6:30am-6:45am at sick call. Specialty clinics will be provided to those inmates identified with various chronic medical conditions such as hypertension, diabetes, etc. Inmates will be placed in a specialty clinic conducted by the physician or physician assistant at least quarterly. Pill line hours are clearly posted at the pharmacy window. At least one physician assistant is on duty or on call 24 hours a day.

**Housing:** Inmates are housed in dormitories in two-man rooms at the low-security FCI.

**Fitness/Recreation:** The institution offers intramural and league sports in basketball, soccer, softball, and volleyball. Fitness/wellness classes, music room, walking/cycling club, rowing machines, yoga classes, racquetball/handball, bocce ball, horseshoes, stationary bikes, life steppers, abdominal benches, exercise mats, board games. Hobby craft offers painting, art, and leather craft.

**Religious Services:** The institution is staffed by three full-time chaplains. Contract clergy and community volunteers also provide services for most faiths. The religious services department contracts clergy from the various religious faiths. Additionally, the religious services staff will have community volunteers to assist with an inmate's particular religious needs. A religious services schedule will be updated periodically and posted in the chapel and on the unit bulletin boards. Free greeting cards; a religious library (including books and audio-visual resources); and other free religious literature (including Bibles, Koran and devotionals). The chaplains have an open-door policy for personal counseling.

**Commissary:** The commissary is open to inmates once a week. Shopping days are determined by the inmate's registration number. <u>Hours</u>: Monday-Thursday 1:30pm-3pm; 4:30pm-8pm. Bureau of Prisons policy currently sets a monthly commissary spending limit of $360.

**Telephone Policy:** Inmates may call collect or dial direct using the Inmate Telephone System (ITS). The following are standard features of ITS: (1) inmate calls automatically terminate after 15 minutes; (2) an inmate's calling list is limited to 30 callers; and (3) calls are charged to an inmate's debit card. Each inmate is limited to 300 minutes per month.

**Inmate Mail:** The FCI and the camp accept mail from the U.S. Postal Service via First-Class, U.S. Priority, and Express Mail. For those interested in sending overnight mail via a private carrier (FedEx or UPS Overnight), it is recommended that you first contact the institution to find out whether the receipt of such mail is permitted. Inmates may receive publications without prior approval, although the warden will reject publications if they are determined to be detrimental to the security, good order or discipline of the institution. At the medium security facility, all publications must be received directly from the publisher or bookstore; at the low and minimum security facilities, softcover publications may be received from any source. Each inmate is limited to five magazines, five newspapers and five books.

**Inmate Mail to Low:**
INMATE NAME & REGISTER NUMBER
USP Yazoo City
U.S. Penitentiary
P.O. Box 5000
Yazoo City, MS 39194

**Visiting Hours:** Visiting hours at USP are Saturday, Sunday, and federal holidays, 8am-3pm. Additional visiting information can be found on the BOP website, www.bop.gov, at https://www.bop.gov/locations/institutions/yap/.

**Lodging/Accommodations:** See §16:27 FCI Yazoo City.

# CHAPTER 17

# THE WESTERN REGION

(This page intentionally left blank.)

# The Western Region

## Central Office
Central Office
Federal Bureau of Prisons
320 First St., NW
Washington, DC 20534
Phone: 202-307-3198

## Western Regional Office
Western Regional Office
Federal Bureau of Prisons
7338 Shoreline Drive
Stockton, CA 95219
Phone: 209-956-9700

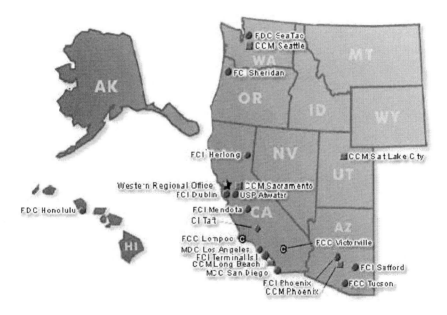

## §17:10   USP ATWATER

USP Atwater
U.S. Penitentiary
1 Federal Way
Atwater, CA 95301
ATW/ExecAssistant@bop.gov
209-386-0257
Fax: 209-386-4635

**Location:** USP Atwater is located on a former portion of Castle Air Force Base, approximately 130 miles from San Francisco.

**Judicial District:** Eastern District of California.

**Security Level:** The USP Atwater is a high-security facility housing male offenders, and also includes a minimum-security satellite camp.

**Population:** As of 6/27/2017, the USP inmate population is 1,042, and the camp population is 130. Weekly population figures are available on the BOP website at www.bop.gov, https://www.bop.gov/locations/institutions/atw/.

**Education:** The foundation of the Education Department is the Literacy Program. The USP and the camp require inmates who do not have a GED or high school diploma to attend classes for a minimum of 240 hours, unless this requirement has already been met at a prior institution.

**Vocational/Apprenticeship:** USP does not offer advanced occupational education programs. USP offers vocational training in office automation, culinary arts, and janitorial. The USP offers apprenticeship programs in cook and teacher's aide.

**UNICOR:** FCI Atwater participates in a recycling program (e-scrap) and employs approximately 100 inmates.

**Counseling/Rehab Services:** The psychology services department includes screening, assessment, and treatment of mental health or drug abuse problems, individual and/or group counseling, psycho-educational classes, self-help and supportive services, or referral to health services for medical treatment of a mental illness. USP Atwater's psychology services department is staffed by a drug abuse program coordinator, a drug treatment specialist, a Challenge program coordinator, Challenge treatment specialists, staff psychologists, and a chief psychologist. Also available are drug abuse programming, a drug abuse education course, nonresidential drug abuse treatment, and the Residential Drug Abuse Treatment Program (RDAP). RDAP is provided for a minimum of nine months.

**Health Services:** Sick call sign-up is conducted Monday, Tuesday, Thursday, and Friday, excluding holidays, from 6am-7am. Clinic hours are by appointment. Pill line times are 6am and 4:30pm Monday through Friday. Inmates under the age of 50 may request a physical examination every two years, while inmates over the age of 50 may request one annually.

**Fitness/Recreation:** The recreation department offers official sports classes for volleyball, soccer, softball, and basketball. Indoor recreation opportunities include the following: chess, checkers, spades, dominoes, pinochle, triominoes, and Scrabble. A crafts area is open to inmates interested in acrylic and watercolor painting, origami, calligraphy, and crochet. The Music Program provides guitars, trumpets, and saxophones that are to be used only in the recreation area. The Wellness Program includes the following: nutrition, aerobics, and yoga classes; a wellness center; fitness assessments; body fat testing; and cardiovascular equipment.

**Religious Services:** Full-time chaplains coordinate a wide range of religious activities. These take place on a regular basis, as well as for special events. The schedule is posted on the bulletin board of each housing unit. The chaplains are also available for individual pastoral counseling.

**Commissary:** The commissary sales unit at USP Atwater is open to the general population Tuesdays, Wednesdays, and Fridays based on a sales schedule. UNICOR will shop on Thursdays. Board of Prisons policy currently sets a monthly spending limit of $360.

**Telephone Policy:** USP Atwater uses the ITS-III Telephone System. This system allows the inmate to make either collect or direct calls. The following are standard features of ITS: (1) inmate calls automatically terminate after 15 minutes; (2) an inmate's calling list is limited to 30 callers; and (3) calls are charged to an inmate's debit card. Telephone calls are limited to 300 minutes per month.

**Inmate Mail:** The FCI and the camp accept mail from the U.S. Postal Service via First-Class, U.S. Priority, and Express Mail. For those interested in sending overnight mail via a private carrier (FedEx or UPS Overnight), it is recommended that you first contact the institution to find out whether the receipt of such mail is permitted. Inmates are permitted to receive publications without prior approval, although the warden will reject publications that are determined to be detrimental to the security, good order or discipline of the institution. Hardcover publications may only be received directly from the publisher, bookstore or book club; softcover publications may be received from any source. Accumulation of publications will be limited to 10 magazines no older than 60 days.

**Inmate Mail to USP:**
    INMATE NAME & REGISTER NUMBER
    USP Atwater

U.S. Penitentiary
P.O. Box 019001
Atwater, CA 95301

**Inmate Mail to Camp:**
INMATE NAME & REGISTER NUMBER
USP Atwater
U.S. Penitentiary
Satellite Camp
P.O. Box 019001
Atwater, CA 95301

**Visiting Hours:** USP and camp visiting hours: Saturday, Sunday, and federal holidays 8am-3pm. Inmates will be limited to three adults and three children (under age 16 years) visitors at one time. A maximum of 20 visitors will be authorized on the inmate's visiting list. Additional visiting information can be found at https://www.bop.gov/locations/institutions/atw/.

**Lodging/Accommodations:** Should visitors be spending the night, the following is a short list of accommodations that are available in Atwater, California:

| | |
|---|---|
| Applegate Inn | 209-357-0202 |
| Valley Motel | 209-358-0401 |
| Motel 6 Merced | 209-384-2181 |

**Directions to Facility:** From the north, take Route 99 South to the Buhach Road exit (left side exit). Turn left onto Buhach Road. Turn right at the second light onto Bellevue. Turn right onto Olive after crossing the railroad tracks. Turn left onto Fox Road, then left onto Federal Way. From the south, take Route 99 North to the Franklin Road exit. Continue straight ahead after passing through the intersection at Fox Road.

# §17:11   FCI DUBLIN

FCI Dublin
Federal Correctional Institution
5701 8th Street
Camp Parks Dublin, CA 94568
DUB/ExecAssistant@bop.gov
925-833-7500
Fax: 925-833-7599

**Location:** 20 miles southeast of Oakland on the Camp Parks Army Reserve Forces Training Area Military Base, off Interstate 580. The area is served by San Francisco and Oakland Airports.

**History:** Opened in 1974, FCI Dublin houses female offenders primarily from the Western United States. The FDC (opened in 1989) houses pre-trial and pre-sentence offenders in custody of the United States Marshal Service. The satellite camp, which opened in 1990, houses minimum-security female offenders and provides inmate labor to support the base.

**Judicial District:** Northern District of California.

**Security Level:** FCI Dublin is a low-security facility housing female offenders. The institution also has an adjacent administrative detention facility housing males on holdover or pre-trial status, and a minimum-security satellite camp housing female offenders.

**Population:** As of 6/27/2017, the FCI inmate population is 990, and the camp population is 197. Weekly population figures are available on the BOP website at www.bop.gov, https://www.bop.gov/locations/institutions/dub/.

**Education:** The FCI offers GED, ESL, adult continuing education, parenting, and correspondence courses.

**Vocational/Apprenticeship:** FCI and the camp offer advanced occupational education in computer graphics; and vocational training in Microsoft Office XP, computer graphics, and forklift operator's license. The FCI offers an apprenticeship in dental assistant.

**Library:** General library services are offered daily. A variety of reading materials, including newspapers, magazines, periodicals, reference sources, and audio-visual materials can be found in the leisure reading rooms. Services of the Alameda County Library Bookmobile are made available bimonthly. The law library is located in the Education Department, and contains a variety of legal reference materials for use in preparing legal papers. Reference materials include the United States Code Annotated, Federal Reporter, Supreme Court Reporter, Bureau of Prisons Program Statements, Institution Supplements, Indexes, and other legal materials. The law library is open during convenient non-working hours, including weekends and holidays. An inmate law library clerk is available for assistance in legal research.

**UNICOR:** Services and textiles are the two business areas operating at FCI Dublin. In addition, a business office supports the factories' operations. Textiles employ approximately 135 inmates, and contract services employ approximately 302 inmates.

**Counseling/Rehab Services:** Counseling services provide full-time psychologists and drug treatment specialists, and part-time psychology practicum students are available to the inmate population throughout their stay at Dublin.

They are responsible for counseling services, coordination of testing materials and monitoring of drug abuse treatment programs. These options include the following: Alcoholic Anonymous, self-image groups and other voluntary groups. In addition, Dublin has professional staff who are trained in the various social science fields. Inmate participation in these activities will be encouraged upon the staff's assessment of inmate needs, but participation in such activities is voluntary. The staff of each unit is available for informal counseling sessions and they conduct formal group counseling activities. The Psychology Services Department consists of the chief psychologist, Drug Abuse Program coordinator, staff psychologists and drug treatment specialists. The range of available programs will be discussed during the institution's A&O program and during an inmate's one-on-one screening interview with a psychology staff member. The Residential Drug Abuse Program (RDAP) is one year in duration and comprises classroom instruction and individual and group therapy; individuals must live in Unit D and have a documented history of alcohol and/or substance abuse. The Drug Education Program is classroom instruction about the social, psychological, and physical impact of substance use. The Pathways Treatment Program is a nine-month non-residential trauma and recovery program. Inmates engage in five hours of treatment per week. Groups include the following: anger management, stress management, expressive arts therapy, trauma and recovery, self-esteem, relationships, health and wellness, spiritual issues and a process group.

**Health Services:** The FCI provides outpatient care. The full-time medical staff includes the following: hospital administrative officer, clinical director, and two additional medical officers, two assistant hospital administrative officers, one dentist, 11 mid-level health care practitioners, two health information technicians and a medical secretary. The Health Services Unit (HSU) is open seven days a week. Female inmates are eligible for pregnancy tests, pap smears, pelvic examinations, and breast examinations on intake and at routine intervals. The Health Services Unit facilities include x-ray, pharmacy, laboratory, dental clinic, and examination rooms. The FCI Dental facility is in a separate building. The services of community hospitals are utilized when necessary. An inmate desiring to attend sick call for medical problems of a non-emergency nature must first report to the Health Services Center between 6:15am and 6:30am on Monday, Tuesday, Thursday, or Friday. There is no non-emergency sick call on Wednesday. Pill line hours: 6am-6:20am; 12noon-12:30pm (M-F only); 7:30pm-8:30pm (restricted pill line).

**Housing:** Male inmates in the administrative unit are housed in two-man and four-man cells. Female inmates in the low-security and minimum-security units are housed in dormitories in three-man and four-man rooms. There are four television rooms per housing unit.

**Fitness/Recreation:** Programs include indoor and outdoor activities, and range from individualized arts and crafts programs to intramural team sports such as softball and volleyball. Physical fitness and weight reduction programs are also important activities for inmates and contribute to mental health, good interpersonal relations, and stress reduction. Hobby craft offers painting, leather craft, ceramics, and copper work.

**Religious Services:** Full-time chaplains conduct religious services and coordinate religious activities for all faiths. Inmates are invited to consult with the chaplains at any time. Approximately 175 community volunteers are involved with the institution. Consultants also provide religious services to those who wish to participate in Thai Buddhist, Muslim, Native American, or Jewish worship activities. Full-time chaplains and part-time contract chaplains conduct religious services and coordinate religious activities for all faiths.

**Commissary:** The commissary, located between Units A/B and C/D, is operated for the benefit of the inmates. Inmates may shop by unit Monday through Wednesday, after the 4pm official count clears, until 8:30pm. Inmates may only shop once a week. Bureau of Prisons policy currently sets a monthly commissary spending limit of $360.

**Telephone Policy:** Inmates dial direct or collect using the Inmate Telephone System II (ITS-II). The following are standard features of ITS: (1) inmate calls automatically terminate after 15 minutes; (2) an inmate's calling list is limited to 30 callers; and (3) calls are charged to an inmate's debit card. Telephones are available for inmate use daily from 6am-11:30pm. At the FDC, each housing unit has telephones available for calls. There is a 300-minute monthly limit for non-emergency, non-legal calls.

**Inmate Mail:** The FCI and the camp accept mail from the U.S. Postal Service via First-Class, U.S. Priority, and Express Mail. For those interested in sending overnight mail via a private carrier (FedEx or UPS Overnight), it is recommended that you first contact the institution to find out whether the receipt of such mail is permitted. Inmates are permitted to receive publications without prior approval, although the warden will reject publications that are determined to be detrimental to the security, good order or discipline of the institution. Hardcover publications may only be received directly from the publisher, bookstore or book club; softcover publications may be received from any source. Accumulation of publications will be limited to five magazines no older than three months old.

**Inmate Mail to FCI:**
INMATE NAME & REGISTER NUMBER
FCI Dublin
Federal Correctional Institution
5701 8th Street—Camp Parks
Dublin, CA 94568

**Inmate Mail to Camp:**
INMATE NAME & REGISTER NUMBER
FCI Dublin
Federal Correctional Institution
Satellite Camp
5675 8th Street-Camp Parks
Dublin, CA 94568

**Visiting Hours:** Visiting hours at FCI and camp: Saturday, Sunday, and federal holidays, 8am-2pm. Inmates are limited to 25 approved visitors. Inmates are limited to five visitors at one time. Attorney visits will be coordinated and supervised by the unit staff. Attorneys should make advance appointments for each visit. Attorney hours: Monday through Friday 8am-3:30pm, excluding holidays. Additional visiting information can be found on the BOP website, https://www. bop.gov/locations/institutions/dub/.

**Lodging/Accommodations:** Should visitors be spending the night, the following is a short list of accommodations that are available in Dublin, California:

| | |
|---|---|
| Holiday Inn | 925-828-7750 |
| La Quinta Inns & Suites | 925-828-9393 |
| Hyatt Place | 925-828-9006 |
| Extended Stay America | 925-875-9556 |

**Directions to Facility:** Travel east on Highway 580 from Oakland to the Hacienda exit, turn north, and continue approximately 1/4 mile; turn left (east on Dublin Blvd.) approximately 1/4 mile and turn left onto Arnold Road. Continue approximately 1/4 mile and turn left on 8th St. Parking for the FCI is the first entrance on the right. There is a designated parking area in the southeast corner of the parking lot.

## §17:12   FCI HERLONG

FCI Herlong
Federal Correctional Institution
741-925 Access Road A-25
Herlong, CA 96113
HER/ExecAssistant@bop.gov
530-827-8000
Fax: 530-827-8024

**Location:** In the Sierra Highlands of northern California, 50 miles northwest of Reno, NV, and 30 miles southeast of Susanville, CA.

**Judicial District:** Eastern District of California.

**Security Level:** FCI Herlong is a medium-security institution housing male inmates, with a satellite camp that houses minimum-security male inmates.

**Population:** As of 6/27/2017, the inmate population is 908, and the camp population is 103. Weekly population figures are available on the BOP website at www.bop.gov, https://www.bop.gov/locations/institutions/her/.

**Vocational/Apprenticeship:** No programs offered.

**Inmate Mail:** The FCI and the camp accept mail from the U.S. Postal Service via First-Class, U.S. Priority, and Express Mail. For those interested in sending overnight mail via a private carrier (FedEx or UPS Overnight), it is recommended that you first contact the institution to find out whether the receipt of such mail is permitted.

**Inmate Mail to FCI:**
INMATE NAME & REGISTER NUMBER
FCI Herlong
Federal Correctional Institution
P.O. Box 800
Herlong, CA 96113

**Inmate Mail to Camp:**
INMATE NAME & REGISTER NUMBER
FCI Herlong
Federal Correctional Institution
Satellite Camp
P.O. Box 800
Herlong, CA 96113

**Visiting Hours:** FCI and FPC visiting hours: Saturday, Sunday, federal holidays 8am-3pm. Inmates are limited to five adult visitors at one time. Inmates are limited to 20 visitors on their approved visitor list. Attorney visits must be arranged by the unit team prior to the visit if the attorney is not on the inmate's approved visitor list. Attorney visits will ordinarily take place in the attorney/client visiting room. Additional visiting information can be found on the BOP website, www. bop.gov, https://www.bop.gov/locations/institutions/her/.

**Lodging/Accommodations:** Should visitors be spending the night, the following is a short list of accommodations that are available in Herlong, California:

| | |
|---|---|
| Apple Inn Motel and Gift Shop | 530-257-4726 |
| Best Western Trailside Inn | 530-257-4123 |
| Bieber Motel | 530-294-5454 |
| Budget Host Frontier Inn | 530-257-4141 |
| Dorado Inn | 530-284-7790 |
| High Country Inn | 530-257-3450 |

**Directions to Facility:** FCI/FPC Herlong is located approximately 30 miles northwest of Reno, NV and 35 miles south of Susanville, CA. From Reno, NV: Take U.S. Highway 395 north approximately 50 miles to the Herlong exit, Access Road A-26. Proceed approximately seven miles on A-26 to FCI/FCP Herlong. From Susanville, CA: Take U.S. Highway 395 South approximately 35 miles to Herlong Access Road A-25. Proceed approximately seven miles on A-25 to FCI/FCP Herlong.

## §17:13   FDC HONOLULU

FDC Honolulu
Federal Detention Center
351 Elliott Street
Honolulu, HI 96819
HON/ExecAssistant@bop.gov
808-838-4200
Fax: 808-838-4507

**Location:** Adjacent to Honolulu International Airport, on the Aloha/Hawaiian Airlines side.

**History:** Opened in 2001, the FDC houses pre-trial, holdover and cadre inmates; Bureau of Immigration and Customs Enforcement Detainees; and Hawaii state prisoners.

**Judicial District:** Central District of Hawaii.

**Security Level:** FDC Honolulu is an administrative facility housing male and female inmates.

**Population:** As of 6/27/2017, the FDC inmate population is 435. Weekly population figures are available on the BOP website at www.bop.gov, https://www.bop.gov/locations/institutions/hon/.

**Education:** This institution offers GED, ESL, adult continuing education, and correspondence courses.

**Vocational/Apprenticeship:** This institution does not offer vocational or apprenticeship training programs.

**Library:** The law library is maintained and coordinated by the Education Department. Legal materials will be available upon request to the Education Department through the use of an Inmate Request to Staff Member form. Removal of books or law library material is prohibited. Typewriters are located in the housing units. A copier is available.

**UNICOR:** None.

**Counseling/Rehab Services:** The Psychology Department has several psychologists. Depending upon the unit to which inmates are assigned, services include the following: intake screening, evaluations, group or individual treatment, and crisis intervention. FDC Honolulu does not offer the Residential Drug Abuse Program (RDAP). Any inmate who wishes to be considered for the RDAP at another institution must submit an Inmate Request to Staff Member ("cop-out") to the Drug Abuse Program Coordinator (DAPC). Drug abuse treatment at FDC Honolulu consists primarily of drug education groups for cadre inmates, and transitional services for cadre inmates who have completed the RDAP. The drug education course is an extensive, classroom style, comprehensive study of the physiological and psychological aspects of drug use. Any cadre inmate can volunteer to participate in drug education. Some cadre inmates may be required to participate in the drug education program. Other substance abuse programs are available to inmates who request these services including pre-trial inmates. Contact the DAPC for determination of eligibility for services and an evaluation.

**Health Services:** The Health Services Unit at FDC Honolulu will provide medical and dental care to all inmates. The Health Services Unit houses a pharmacy, dental department, laboratory, x-ray room, examination and treatment rooms, medical records and offices for staff. Pill lines will be conducted three times daily in the Housing Units and Special Housing Units. All routine medical care for the inmates will be provided in the housing unit exam room on Monday, Tuesday, Thursday and Friday. In the Special Housing Unit, routine medical care triaging will be conducted seven days a week. Medical staff will conduct routine medical and dental triaging and sign-up in the housing unit exam room on assigned days and times. Inmates requesting urgent medical or dental care will report to the Work Detail Supervisor or unit officer. They, in turn, will inform the on-duty health care staff, who will determine the urgency of the medical needs and take appropriate action. Age-specific preventative health examinations are available, and may be requested via cop-out.

**Housing:** Inmates are housed in two-man cells.

**Fitness/Recreation:** Hours and events for recreational activities/classes are posted in the housing units. Additional outdoor recreation may be considered whenever correctional staffing permits. The recreation department offers a variety of indoor and outdoor activities as well as individualized arts and crafts programs. Recreation equipment and board games are available within each housing unit.

**Religious Services:** The institution is staffed by full-time chaplains who are available to assist inmates. Clergy provide pastoral services and are available for counseling and religious consultation. They can also provide a limited amount of religious material. Weekly religious services are conducted as posted on unit bulletin boards. Community clergy volunteers visit periodically.

**Commissary:** Shopping is permitted once per week. Commissary lists are available in the units and must be completed in a legible and complete manner or the list will be returned. The monthly commissary spending limit is $360, but this limit is slightly raised in December.

**Telephone Policy:** Inmates dial direct or collect using the Inmate Telephone System (ITS). The following are standard features of ITS: (1) inmate calls automatically terminate after 15 minutes; (2) an inmate's calling list is limited to 30 callers; and (3) calls are charged to an inmate's debit card. Each inmate receives 300 calling minutes per month.

**Inmate Mail:** The institution accepts mail from the U.S. Postal Service via First-Class, U.S. Priority, and Express Mail. For those interested in sending overnight mail via a private carrier (FedEx or UPS Overnight), it is recommended that you first contact the institution to find out whether the receipt of such mail is permitted. Inmates are permitted to receive publications without prior approval, although the warden will reject publications that are determined to be detrimental to the security, good order or discipline of the institution. All publications must be received directly from the publisher, bookstore or book club. Accumulation of publications will be limited to five magazines, five newspapers, and ten books.

**Inmate Mail to FDC:**
INMATE NAME & REGISTER NUMBER
FDC Honolulu
Federal Detention Center
P.O. Box 30080
Honolulu, HI 96820

**Visiting Hours:** A visiting schedule will be posted in the front lobby and on each housing unit bulletin board. Social visits are scheduled by Unit: Monday 7:30am-1:30pm for Unit 4B, Monday 2:15pm-8:15pm for Unit 4A; Tuesday 7:30am-1:30pm for Unit 5B; Tuesday 2:15pm-8:15pm for Unit 5A; Friday 7:30am-1:30pm for Units 3B and 6B; and Friday 2:15pm-8:15pm for Unit 6A, Weekend/holiday hours are 6:15am-8:15am for Units 3B and 6B on Saturday, Unit 4A on Sunday, and Unit 5A on holidays; 8:45am -10:45am for Unit 6A on Saturday, Unit 4B on Sunday, and Unit 5B on holidays; 11:15am-1:15pm for Unit 5B on Saturday, Unit 5A on Sunday, and Unit 4A on holidays; 2:45pm -4:45pm for Unit 5A on Saturday, Unit 5B on Sunday, and Unit 6B on holidays; 5:15pm-7:15pm for Unit 4A on Saturday, Unit 6A on Sunday, and Units 3B/6B on holidays; and 7:45pm-9:45pm for Unit 4A on Saturday, Unit 3B/6B on Sunday, and Unit 4B on holidays. Inmates are limited to a total of ten adult visitors on their approved visitor list. Inmates are limited to five visitors at one time. Attorneys are encouraged to visit during regular visiting hours. Additional visiting information can be found on the BOP website, www.bop.gov, https://www.bop.gov/locations/institutions/hon/.

**Lodging/Accommodations:** Should visitors be spending the night, the following is a short list of accommodations that are available in Honolulu, Hawaii:

| | |
|---|---|
| Ala Moana Hotel | 808-955-4811 |
| Best Western Hotel | 808-836-3636 |
| Hawaii Prince Hotel Waikiki | 808-956-1111 |
| Ohana Honolulu Airport Hotel | 808-836-0661 |
| Pacific Beach Hotel | 808-922-1233 |

**Directions to Facility:** FDC Honolulu is located at 351 Elliott Street. From the airport, follow the signs that direct you to Nimitz Highway. At Nimitz Highway make a left and proceed to Elliott Street. Turn left on Elliott Street. You will see Hawaiian Airlines to your left on the outskirts of Honolulu International Airport. FDC Honolulu is the tall white building on your left past Hawaiian Airlines Air Cargo.

## §17:14  FCI LOMPOC

FCI Lompoc
Federal Correctional Institution
3600 Guard Road
Lompoc, CA 93436
LOX/ExecAssistant@bop.gov
805-736-4154
Fax: 805-736-1292

**Location:** 175 miles northwest of Los Angeles, adjacent to Vandenberg Air Force Base off Route 1. The area is served by the Santa Barbara Airport (25 miles south), Santa Maria Airport (25 miles north), and Greyhound.

**History:** Opened in 1970 as a Federal Prison Camp, FCI Lompoc was converted to a low-security facility in 1990. It houses male offenders, primarily from California, Arizona, and Nevada, many of whom are serving their first period of confinement.

**Judicial District:** Central District of California.

**Security Level:** FCI Lompoc is a low-security facility housing male inmates. It is part of the Lompoc FCC.

**Population:** As of 6/27/2014, the FCI inmate population is 1,301. Weekly population figures are available on the BOP website at www.bop.gov, https://www.bop.gov/locations/institutions/lof/.

**Education:** The FCI offers GED, ESL, adult continuing education, and correspondence courses.

**Vocational/Apprenticeship:** FCI offers advanced occupational education in Microsoft Office computer applications and industrial maintenance sanitation. The FCI offers vocational training in computer applications and computer-aided drafting. The FCI offers an apprenticeship in landscaping.

**Library:** The FCI's law library is open Monday through Sunday (closed on Wednesday) from 7:30am-8:30pm. Electric typewriters and a copier are available. Video cassette recorders and audio cassette players are also available.

**UNICOR:** A sign factory employs approximately 150 inmates.

**Counseling/Rehab Services:** The Psychology Services Department offers a full range of individual and/or group counseling and psychotherapy services: Drug abuse education (offered in English and Spanish), non-residential abuse treatment, 500-hour Residential Drug Abuse Program (RDAP), and transitional services including stress management, anger management, and relapse prevention, Alcoholics Anonymous, Narcotics Anonymous, and Rational Recovery. The Psychology Department is staffed by three full-time psychologists.

**Health Services:** Inmates who require urgent medical attention will be seen once daily on Monday, Tuesday, Thursday, Friday 6am-7am. Emergency sick call will be provided during duty and non-duty hours. Dental sick call is by appointment: 6am-6:30am during regular sick call. Pill line hours: Monday through Friday 6am-7:15am, 10:30am-12:15pm (prescription pickup only), 5pm-6pm; Saturday, Sunday, holidays 8:30am-9:30am, 5pm-6pm. Medical staff is on duty 24-hours a day, seven days a week. Inmates under the age of 50 may request a physical every two years, while those over the age of 50 may request one every year.

**Housing:** Inmates at the FCI are housed in two-man cells. Inmates at the ICC are housed in military-style barracks.

**Fitness/Recreation:** The recreation department offers weights, a music room, full gym, tennis courts, pool tables, ping-pong tables, foosball, horseshoes, and bocce. The hobby craft center offers ceramics, leather, oil painting, crocheting, and pencil art.

**Religious Services:** The FCI is staffed by two full-time chaplains. Contract rabbi and imam services are available. A community of volunteers provides services for most faiths. The primary function of the chaplain is to provide pastoral care services, such as conducting regular worship services, facilitating worship for other faith groups, providing religious literature, supervising volunteer religious activities and visiting hospitalized inmates. Check the chaplain's bulletin board for the program schedule. The chapel is open all day Saturday, Sunday and during several weekday evenings. The sweat lodge is located on the recreation yard. Inmates must obtain permission from the chaplain before using the sweat lodge.

The chaplains can counsel inmates in crises. The chaplain has a well supplied religious library with books, cassettes, videos, and equipment.

**Commissary:** The commissary is open Monday through Thursday from 2pm-3pm for UNICOR workers and after the 4pm count for the general population, 4:30pm until 8pm Monday through Thursday with the exception of special holiday schedules. Shopping days are determined by an inmate's registration number. Fridays are reserved for special purchase orders. Bureau of Prisons policy currently sets a monthly commissary spending limit of $360.

**Telephone Policy:** Telephone calls are limited to 15 minutes and require a 60-minute wait time between calls. There is a maximum of 300 minutes per month of calling time. Inmates dial direct or collect using the Inmate Telephone System (ITS). The following are standard features of ITS: (1) inmate calls automatically terminate after 15 minutes; (2) an inmate's calling list is limited to 30 callers; and (3) calls are charged to an inmate's debit card.

**Inmate Mail:** The FCI accepts mail from the U.S. Postal Service via First-Class, U.S. Priority, and Express Mail. For those interested in sending overnight mail via a private carrier (FedEx or UPS Overnight), it is recommended that you first contact the institution to find out whether the receipt of such mail is permitted. Inmates are permitted to receive publications without prior approval, although the warden will reject publications that are determined to be detrimental to the security, good order or discipline of the institution. Hardcover publications may only be received directly from the publisher, bookstore or book club; softcover publications may be received from any source. Accumulation of magazines will be limited to five, no older than three months old.

**Inmate Mail to FCI:**
INMATE NAME & REGISTER NUMBER
FCI Lompoc
Federal Correctional Institution
3600 Guard Road
Lompoc, CA 93436

**Visiting Hours:** As of June 2017, all visiting at this facility has been suspended until further notice. This policy may have changed by the time you read this entry.
Normally, visiting hours are Saturday, Sunday, federal holidays 8:30am-3:30pm. Attorney visits must be scheduled with the inmate's unit team. Inmates are given six visiting points per month. Two points deducted for visits on Saturday, Sunday and federal holidays. Camp visiting is not limited by points and no point system is in place in the camp visiting rooms. Inmates are limited to 15 people on their approved visiting list. A limit of four adults (not including children under age 16 years) will be allowed to visit at one time. Additional visiting information can be found at https://www.bop.gov/locations/institutions/lof/.

**Lodging/Accommodations:** Should visitors be spending the night, the following is a short list of accommodations that are available in Lompoc, California:

| | |
|---|---|
| Embassy Suites Hotel | 805-735-8311 |
| Holiday Inn Express | 805-736-2391 |
| Rodeway Inn | 805-735-3737 |
| O'Cairns Inn and Suites | 805-735-7731 |
| Budget Inn Motel of Lompoc | 805-736-1241 |

**Directions to Facility:** FCI Lompoc is located approximately five miles northwest of Lompoc. Visitors should drive west through the city of Lompoc on Ocean Avenue (Route 246), turn right on Floradale Avenue and proceed approximately three miles to the main entrance on the left side of the road which is clearly marked.

## §17:15   USP LOMPOC

USP Lompoc
U.S. Penitentiary
3901 Klein Blvd.
Lompoc, CA 93436
LOX/ExecAssistant@bop.gov
805-735-2771
Fax: 805-737-1292

**Location:** 175 miles northwest of Los Angeles, adjacent to Vandenberg Air Force Base off Route 1. The area is served by the Santa Barbara Airport (25 miles south), Santa Maria Airport (25 miles north), and Greyhound.

**History:** Opened in 1959, USP Lompoc houses inmates serving long sentences for sophisticated offenses. The satellite camp provides services to USP and FCI Lompoc, Vandenberg AFB, and farm and community service projects.

**Judicial District:** Central District of California.

**Security Level:** USP Lompoc is a high-security facility housing male inmates. It is part of the Lompoc FCC. Two adjacent satellite prison camps houses minimum-security male inmates.

**Population:** As of 6/27/2017, the USP inmate population is 1,028, the camp population is 279, and the Camp North population is 134. Weekly population figures are available at https://www.bop.gov/locations/institutions/lom/.

**Education:** The USP and the camp offer GED, ESL, adult continuing education, and correspondence courses.

**Vocational/Apprenticeship:** The USP does not offer advanced occupational education programs. The USP offers vocational training in barbering, business computer, and soldering. The camp offers vocational training in maintenance, woodworking, and an apprenticeship in meat cutting.

**Library:** The law library is located in the Education Department and contains a variety of legal reference materials for use in preparing legal papers. Reference materials include the United States Code Annotated, Federal Reporter, Supreme Court Reporter, Bureau of Prisons Program Statements, Institution Supplements, Indexes, and other legal materials. An inmate law library clerk is available for assistance in legal research. Legal materials are also available to inmates in detention or segregation units, ordinarily via a delivery system or satellite collection. The main institution's law library is open Monday through Friday from 8am-8:30pm, and on Saturday and Sunday from 8am-3pm. There are approximately 15-20 electric typewriters available to inmates for the preparation of legal documents. A copier is available. Copies are 15 cents and charged to an inmate's debit card. The law library at the camp is open Monday through Sunday from 7:30am-9:45pm, closed on holidays. The camp law library provides similar services.

**UNICOR:** An electronic cable factory, sign factory, print plant, and quality assurance department employ approximately 500 inmates from the penitentiary and camp.

**Counseling/Rehab Services:** See §17:14 FCI Lompoc.

**Health Services:** See §17:14 FCI Lompoc.

**Housing:** Inmates at the USP are housed in single-man and two-man cells. There are 11 housing units. Inmates at the camps are housed in "open bay" (boot camp style) dormitories. There are approximately 140 inmates per dormitory.

**Fitness/Recreation:** See §17:14 FCI Lompoc.

**Religious Services:** See §17:14 FCI Lompoc.

**Commissary:** Shopping days are determined by an inmate's registration number. Bureau of Prisons policy currently sets a monthly commissary spending limit of $360.

**Telephone Policy:** The institution uses the Inmate Telephone System (ITS-II) and calls must be dialed directly. Inmates are limited to 30 approved telephone numbers. The following are standard features of ITS: (1) inmate calls automatically terminate after 15 minutes; (2) an inmate's calling list is limited to 30 callers; and (3) calls are charged to an inmate's debit card. Inmates receive 300 calling minutes per month.

**Inmate Mail:** See §17:14 FCI Lompoc.

**Inmate Mail to USP:**
INMATE NAME & REGISTER NUMBER
USP Lompoc
U.S. Penitentiary
3901 Klein Blvd.
Lompoc, CA 93436

**Inmate Mail to Camp:**
INMATE NAME & REGISTER NUMBER
USP Lompoc
U.S. Penitentiary
Satellite Camp
3705 West Farm Road
Lompoc, CA 93436

**Visiting Hours:** As of June 2017, all visiting at this facility has been suspended until further notice. This policy may have changed by the time you read this entry.
Otherwise, see §17:14 FCI Lompoc. Additional visiting information can be found at https://www.bop.gov/locations/institutions/lom/.

**Lodging/Accommodations:** See §17:14 FCI Lompoc.

**Directions to Facility:** See §17:14 FCI Lompoc.

# §17:16  MDC LOS ANGELES

MDC Los Angeles
Metropolitan Detention Center
535 N. Alameda Street
Los Angeles, CA 90012
LOS/ExecAssistant@bop.gov
213-485-0439
Fax: 213-253-9510

**Location:** In downtown Los Angeles, off the Hollywood Freeway (Highway 101) on the corner of Alameda and Aliso Streets. The area is served by Los Angeles International Airport and Amtrak.

**History:** Opened in 1988, MDC Los Angeles houses a small work cadre, pre-trial and pre-sentence inmates from California, and holdovers from other parts of the country.

**Judicial District:** Central District of California.

**Security Level:** MDC Los Angeles is an administrative facility for male and female inmates.

**Population:** As of 6/27/2017, the MDC inmate population is 773. Weekly population figures are available on the BOP website at www.bop.gov, https://www.bop.gov/locations/institutions/los/.

**Education:** The institution offers GED, ESL, adult continuing education, and correspondence courses.

**Vocational/Apprenticeship:** The institution does not offer advanced occupational education, vocational or apprenticeship programs.

**Library:** See your Unit Officer for sign-up procedures and assigned times. The electronic law library is available in the housing units and in the education department. Reference materials are available, as well as typewriters and legal paper. Inmates can request extra law library time.

**Counseling/Rehab Services:** Full-time psychologists, psychology interns, and a contract psychiatrist provide services for mental health issues. Psychology interns are under the direct supervision of licensed staff. Mental health services are available for the following: crisis intervention, suicide prevention, limited group therapy, limited individual therapy, limited substance abuse treatment, and psychiatric medication consultation. Support groups are available for inmates who are detoxing from drugs and alcohol: comprehensive drug treatment program, education groups, Alcoholics Anonymous, Residential Drug Treatment, and non-residential treatment.

**Health Services:** The institution is staffed by three physicians, eight physician assistants, two dentists, and one pharmacist. Inmates are provided with outpatient care. A small infirmary is available. Pill line is available three times a day, seven days a week. The institution is served by a Veteran's Hospital (located next door). Medical staff is on-site 24 hours a day, seven days a week.

**Housing:** Inmates are housed in two-man cells. There are three televisions in each living unit that are controlled by the unit officer.

**Fitness/Recreation:** Each housing unit provides several types of recreation activities: cards, pool, table tennis, and games. Outdoor recreation is limited by the physical structure of the facility.

**Religious Services:** Chaplains are available seven days a week to provide pastoral care and counseling to inmates of all faiths. A schedule of religious services and activities is posted on each unit's bulletin board.

**Commissary:** Once a week, request sheets are turned in and delivery follows shortly thereafter. Unit officers will inform inmates of the times. The commissary is open Monday through Friday. Bureau of Prisons policy currently sets a monthly commissary spending limit of $360.

**Telephone Policy:** MDC Los Angeles utilizes the ITS-II telephone system. Inmates dial collect or direct. Phone calls are restricted to 15 minutes, and inmates are allowed up to 300 minutes of calls per month. Inmates are required to sign-up for a specific time with the unit officer. There are approximately four telephones per each large living unit.

**Inmate Mail:** The institution accepts mail from the U.S. Postal Service via First-Class, U.S. Priority, and Express Mail. For those interested in sending overnight mail via a private carrier (FedEx or UPS Overnight), it is recommended that you first contact the institution to find out whether the receipt of such mail is permitted.

**Inmate Mail to MDC:**
INMATE NAME & REGISTER NUMBER
MDC Los Angeles
Metropolitan Detention Center
P.O. Box 1500
Los Angeles, CA 90053

**Visiting Hours:** Visiting hours: Saturday, Sunday, and federal holidays 8am-1pm; weekdays, 2:30pm-8pm. Attorney visits are permitted daily from 8am-8pm. Inmates will be allowed visits on an odd/even basis determined by the inmate's registration number. Inmates are allowed three adult visitors at one time for up to 1.5 hours. Inmates designated to the cadre unit are limited to 10 visitors on their visiting list. Additional visiting information can be found at https://www.bop.gov/locations/institutions/los/.

**Lodging/Accommodations:** Should visitors be spending the night, the following is a short list of accommodations that are available in Los Angeles, California:

| | |
|---|---|
| Crowne Plaza Hotel LAX | 310-642-7500 |
| La Quinta Inn LAX | 310-645-2200 |
| Los Angeles Courtyard | 310-649-1400 |
| Los Angeles Embassy Suites (LAX) | 310-215-1000 |

## §17:17 FCI MENDOTA

FCI Mendota
Federal Correctional Institution
33500 West California Avenue
Mendota, CA 93640
MEN/ExecAssistant@bop.gov
559-274-4000
Fax: 559-274-4223

**Location:** FCI Mendota is located in Fresno County, 36 miles west of Fresno, California. Fresno Yosemite International Airport is located approximately 40 miles west of the FCI/Camp. Air carriers such as United, American, Alaska Airlines, Allegiant Airlines, Delta, and US Airways have flights in and out of this airport.

**History:** One of the newest FCIs, this institution was opened in 2011.

**Judicial District:** Eastern District of California.

**Security Level:** FCI Mendota is a medium security facility housing male offenders. An adjacent satellite prison camp houses minimum security male inmates.

**Population:** As of 6/28/2017, the FCI inmate population is 685, and the camp population is 75. Weekly population figures are available on the BOP website at www.bop.gov, https://www.bop.gov/locations/institutions/men/.

**Education:** The FCI and the camp offer GED, ESL, special interest classes (including parenting, languages, and career resources), and correspondence courses.

**Vocational/Apprenticeship:** Some of the programs offered include vocational training in recycling and computer literacy.

**Library:** There is a leisure library and law library at FCI Mendota. The legal library includes an electronic law library, available for inmate use. Typewriters are in the legal library and to be used for legal material only.

**Counseling/Rehab Services:** A psychologist is available for individual therapy on an as-needed basis at the camp. A drug education program and non-residential drug program are available, as well as group/individual therapy or counseling, personal development groups, Alcoholics Anonymous, and other voluntary groups.

**Fitness/Recreation:** The recreation department offers team sports, hobby craft, and structured leisure/wellness programs. The outdoor recreation yard has six handball/racquetball courts, two softball fields, five basketball courts, one soccer field, and one quarter-mile track. There is also a gymnasium for activities such as aerobics, yoga, calisthenics, and spinning. The indoor leisure center has board games, table games, treadmills, band rooms, and the hobby craft room. The music program has structured classes in guitar, drums, accordions, and music theory. The hobby craft program has leather craft, ceramics, stick art, crochet, beading, and drawing.

**Religious Services:** The Chapel comprises facilities for worship services, prayer, religious study areas, and a religious library. Worship, counseling, spiritual guidance and education services are available, and community volunteers of a variety of religious faiths periodically visit the institution. There is a Prisoner Visitation and Support Services program, which sends volunteers into the institution to visit inmates who would not ordinarily receive visits. Religious diets may be approved through the chaplain.

**Inmate Mail:** The FCI and the camp accept mail from the U.S. Postal Service via First-Class, U.S. Priority, and Express Mail. For those interested in sending overnight mail via a private carrier (FedEx or UPS Overnight), it is recommended that you first contact the institution to find out whether the receipt of such mail is permitted.

**Inmate Mail to FCI:**
INMATE NAME & REGISTER NUMBER
FCI Mendota
Federal Correctional Institution
P.O. Box 9
Mendota, CA 93640

**Inmate Mail to Satellite Camp:**
INMATE NAME & REGISTER NUMBER
FCI Mendota
Satellite Camp
P.O. Box 9
Mendota, CA 93640

**Visiting Hours:** Visiting hours for FCI and the camp are Saturday, Sunday, and federal holidays from 8:15am-3pm. Each inmate may receive up to four visitors per visit, excluding infants that can sit on adults' laps. There is a children's area; inmates are not allowed into this area. Requests for attorney visits must be made at least 24 hours in advance. Additional visiting information can be found at www.bop.gov.https://www.bop.gov/locations/institutions/men/.

**Lodging/Accommodations:** Should visitors be spending the night, the following is a short list of accommodations that are available near Mendota, California:
| | |
|---|---|
| Best Western Apricot Inn | 559-659-1444 |
| Motel 33 | 559-659-2971 |
| Hampton Inn & Suites Madera | 559-561-0910 |
| Kerman Inn Motel | 559-846-6530 |

**Directions to Facility:** From Fresno: 180 West to Panoche Road. Turn left on Panoche Road which becomes California Avenue. Turn right into the institution.

From Fresno/Yosemite International Airport: East Clinton Way to North Peach Ave. Merge onto 180 West. Turn Left on Panoche Road. Panoche Road becomes California Avenue. Turn right into the institution.

Traveling South on Highway 5: Take Exit 379, Shields Avenue towards Mendota. Turn left onto Little Panoche Road West/Shields Avenue. Turn right onto North Fairfax Avenue. Turn left onto Belmont Avenue. Turn right onto North San Diego Avenue. Turn left onto California Avenue. Turn left into the institution.

Traveling North on Highway 5: Take exit 349, Derrick Avenue/33 North. Turn right onto 33.

# §17:18  FCI PHOENIX

FCI Phoenix
Federal Correctional Institution
37900 N. 45th Avenue
Phoenix, AZ 85086
PHX/ExecAssistant@bop.gov
623-465-9757
Fax: 623-465-5199

**Location:** 25 miles north of downtown Phoenix, off Interstate 17 (Black Canyon Freeway) at the Pioneer Road exit (Exit 225). The area is served by Phoenix Sky Harbor International Airport, seven regional airports, Amtrak, and commercial bus lines. Google Maps coordinates for FCI Phoenix are available at the BOP website, https://www.bop.gov/locations/institutions/phx/.

**History:** Opened in 1985, FCI Phoenix houses male offenders primarily from the Southwestern United States. A self-contained jail unit houses holdovers in the custody of the U.S. Marshal. A special housing unit is for administrative detention and disciplinary segregation. Opened in 1989, the satellite camp houses minimum-security female offenders who do not have any significant history of violence or escape.

**Judicial District:** District of Arizona.

**Security Level:** The Federal Correctional Institution (FCI) in Phoenix, Arizona is a medium-security facility for male offenders. An adjacent satellite prison camp houses minimum-security female offenders.

**Population:** As of 6/05/2017, the FCI inmate population is 1,036, and the camp population is 300. Weekly population figures are available on the BOP website at https://www.bop.gov/locations/institutions/phx/.

**Education:** The FCI and the camp offer GED, ESL, ABLE (Adult Basic Learning Examination), adult continuing education (including typing, computer literacy, foreign languages, and business skills), and correspondence courses. Parenting classes are also available.

**Vocational/Apprenticeship:** FCI offers vocational training in HVAC, facility maintenance, and computer technology. FCI offers apprenticeship programs in the following areas: cabinet making, food service cook, electronic utility worker, and food services. The camp offers apprenticeship in food service cook and food service. The camp offers advanced occupational education in quality control technician.

**Library:** The FCI's law/leisure library is open Monday through Thursday from 7:15am-11:15am, 12:00pm-3:30pm, and 430pm-8:00pm; Friday 7:15am-11:15am and 12:00pm-3:30pm; Saturday and Sunday from 10:30am-3:30pm, and is closed on holidays. The camp's law/leisure library is open Monday through Friday 7:30am-8:30pm, Saturday and Sunday 12pm-8:30pm, and is closed on holidays. The law library is located in the Education Department with a satellite unit in the Special Housing Unit. Case law books from federal districts, circuits, and state supreme courts are available for reference. Electric typewriters are available for the preparation of legal documents, as well as a copy machine. Inmates must purchase their own typewriter ribbons from the commissary. An inmate law clerk is also available. Program Statements from the Bureau of Prisons and Institutional Supplements are available for inmate reference. Law library books, typewriters, and writing materials are available on a first-come, first-served basis.

The leisure library contains novels, fiction, non-fiction, reference materials, Spanish language materials, magazines, and newspapers. A maximum of three requests may be submitted by an inmate at one time.

**UNICOR:** FCI Phoenix operates an electronics factory that manufactures electronic connectors and electronic cable harnesses. The camp offers warehouse and quality assurance programs.

**Counseling/Rehab Services:** A psychologist is available for individual therapy on an as-needed basis at FCI and at the camp. Programs include the following: drug and alcohol abuse programs, group/individual therapy or counseling, personal development groups, correctional counseling, crisis intervention, pre-release counseling, Alcoholics Anonymous, and Narcotics Anonymous groups. The FCI offers a nine-month Residential Drug Abuse Program (RDAP). Residential substance abuse treatment is not available at the camp; however, female inmates may be referred to other institutions.

**Health Services:** The main institution is staffed by three full-time physi- cians, eight physician assistants, one dentist, two dental assistants, and two pharmacists. The FCI and the camp provide outpatient care. AIRVAC trans- portation (via helicopter) to local hospitals is available. Local hospitals are 30 minutes away. FCI Medical and Dental Sick Call is Monday, Tuesday, Thursday, and Friday, 6:30am-7am. Camp Medical Sick Call is Monday, Tuesday, Wednesday, and Friday 6:30am -7am. Camp Dental Sick Call open house is Thursday, 630am-7am. Pill line at the FCI is available Monday through Friday from 6am-7am (insulin line only), 6:30am-7am, 11am until last call, 4:20pm-4:40pm (insulin line only), and 8:15pm-8:45pm; weekends and holidays, 7:45am-8:15am, 11am until last call, 4:20pm-4:40pm (insulin line only), and 8:15pm-8:45pm. Pill line at the camp is 6:30am-6:45am and after 5:30pm daily. Outside medical care is available for medical issues beyond the scope of the camp Health Services Unit. Medical staff is on duty 24 hours, seven days. At least one physician assistant is on duty or on call 24 hours a day. Physical examinations may be requested every two years for inmates under the age of 50, and every year for inmates over the age of 50the FCI is from 6:30am-7am, four days a week. Camp sick call hours: Monday, Tuesday, Wednesday, Friday 6:30am-7am. Camp dental sick call is on Tuesdays only. Outside medical care is available for medical issues beyond the scope of the camp Health Services Unit. Medical staff is on duty 24 hours, seven days. Camp pill line is available daily from 6:30am-6:45am and after 5:30pm. At least one physician assistant is on duty or on call 24 hours a day. Physical examinations may be requested every two years for inmates under the age of 50, and every year for inmates over the age of 50.

**Housing:** Inmates at the FCI are housed in two-man and three-man cells in one of four housing units: Mojave, Pima, Navajo, and Yuma. Inmates in the Residential Drug Abuse Program (RDAP) are housed in Mojave A. Televisions are turned off from 7:30am-9:30am Monday through Friday for unit cleaning, and Monday through Thursday 12pm-2pm, except on holidays. Inmates at the camp are housed in two cubicle dormitories. The television room at the camp is operational from 6am-8:30pm daily.

**Fitness/Recreation:** The recreation department offers team sports, a weight room, a music room and instruments, board games, pool tables, and ping-pong tables. The hobby craft center offers ceramics, leather craft, knitting, painting, and drawing.

**Religious Services:** The FCI and camp have clergy and volunteers of various faith groups available to assist inmates. Pastoral care will also be provided to inmate families as needed and requested. Worship and education services are available to a variety of faith groups. A weekly schedule is posted on each of the unit bulletin boards.

**Commissary:** The commissary is open Monday through Friday from 5:30pm-8:30pm. Inmates are assigned at least one shopping day per week. Commissary price list/order blanks are available in the housing units and must be turned in to the Unit Officer prior to the 10pm count the night before shopping. The commissary schedule is as follows: Pima, Navajo, and Mojave Units report to the commissary on either Monday, Tuesday, or Thursday and rotate monthly. The Yuma Unit reports to the commissary on Wednesdays only. Bureau of Prisons policy currently sets a monthly spending limit of $320, but FCI Phoenix allows a month spending limit of $360 ($180 biweekly). The camp is limited to $160 biweekly. Commissary price list/order forms are available in the housing units. Orders must be completed prior to arrival at the sales window.

**Telephone Policy:** Inmates at the FCI and the camp dial direct using the Inmate Telephone System (ITS). The following are standard features of ITS: (1) inmate calls automatically terminate after 15 minutes; (2) an inmate's calling list is limited to 30 callers; and (3) calls are charged to an inmate's debit card. Inmates are allowed up to 300 minutes of calling time per month. It takes two to four days for phone numbers to be added to the inmate's caller-approved list. There are telephones located in each FCI Phoenix housing unit for inmate use. The telephones at the camp are operational daily from 6am-12noon.

**Inmate Mail:** The FCI and the camp accept mail from the U.S. Postal Service via First-Class, U.S. Priority, and Express Mail. For those interested in sending overnight mail via a private carrier (FedEx or UPS Overnight), it is recommended that you first contact the institution to find out whether the receipt of such mail is permitted. An inmate may receive hardcover publications only from a publisher, book club, or bookstore.

**Inmate Mail to FCI:**
INMATE NAME & REGISTER NUMBER
FCI Phoenix
Federal Correctional Institution
37910 N. 45th Avenue
Phoenix, AZ 85086

**Inmate Mail to Satellite Camp:**
INMATE NAME & REGISTER NUMBER
FCI Phoenix
Federal Correctional Institution
Satellite Camp
37930 N. 45th Avenue
Phoenix, AZ 85086

**Visiting Hours:** FCI visiting hours: Saturday, Sunday, Monday, and federal holidays, 8am-3pm. Inmates are given 10 visiting points per month. Visits on Saturday and Sunday will be deducted two points. Visits on Monday will be deducted one point. No points will be deducted on holidays. Inmates are limited to 12 visitor names on their approved visitor list. A limit of five adults can visit at one time. Attorneys will be permitted to visit during regular visiting days and hours. Camp visiting hours: Saturday, Sunday, federal holidays 8am-3pm. There is no limit to the number of visits per inmate, although due to area constraints it is limited to six visitors. Additional visiting information can be found on the BOP website, https://www.bop.gov, at https://www.bop.gov./locations/institutions/phx/.

**Lodging/Accommodations:** Should visitors be spending the night, the following is a short list of accommodations that are available in Phoenix, Arizona:

| | |
|---|---|
| Best Western Phoenix Hotel/Suites | 602-997-6285 |
| Quality Inn Phoenix Airport | 408-565-2978 |
| Intown Suites Phoenix South | 480-893-9399 |
| Phoenix Comfort Suites North | 602-861-3900 |
| Phoenix Springhill Suites North | 602-943-0010 |

**Directions to Facility:** The facility is located approximately 30 miles south of downtown Phoenix on I-17 at Exit 225 (Pioneer Road). For those traveling from the west, take I-10 East until it intersects with I-17 North. For those traveling from the east, take I-10 West until it intersects with I-17 North. Those traveling from the north should take I-17 south to exit 225. Note: in some areas, I-17 is referred to as Black Canyon Highway.

## §17:19  FCI SAFFORD

FCI Safford
Federal Correctional Institution
1529 West Highway 366
Safford, AZ 85546
SAF/ExecAssistant@bop.gov
928-428-6600
Fax: 928-348-1331

**Location:** In southwestern Arizona, 127 miles northeast of Tucson, 165 miles east of Phoenix, seven miles south of the city of Safford off Highway 191. The area is served by airports, Amtrak and commercial bus lines in Tucson and Phoenix.

**History:** Opened in 1964, FCI Safford was originally a minimum-security Federal Prison Camp. Opened in 1984 as an FCI, the institution presently houses male offenders primarily from the southwestern United States.

**Judicial District:** District of Arizona.

**Security Level:** FCI Safford is a low-security institution housing male offenders.

**Population:** As of 6/28/2017, the FCI inmate population is 862. Weekly population figures are available on the BOP website, www.bop.gov, at https://www.bop.gov/locations/institutions/saf/.

**Education:** The institution offers GED, ESL, adult continuing education, and correspondence courses. A variety of college-level courses are offered through Eastern Arizona College. The inmate must pay for his own tuition, books, and class materials.

**Vocational/Apprenticeship:** FCI offers advanced occupational education in business computer, and retail sales, FCI offers vocational training in HVAC.

**Library:** The general library includes a variety of magazines, newspapers, reference materials, and fictional and nonfiction books necessary for meeting inmates educational, cultural, and leisure needs. Inmates have the opportunity to prepare legal documents and reasonable access to legal materials via the

Electronic Law Library (LexisNexis). The law libraries contain required legal publications, general legal reference materials, and a selection of Bureau of Prisons policies. Electric typewriters are available on a first-come, first-serve basis. A copier is also available.

**UNICOR:** A textile factory employs approximately 297 inmates.

**Counseling/Rehab Services:** The institution offers a non-residential drug treatment program, a drug education program, and other groups. The FCI also offers a 500-hour residential drug abuse treatment program (RDAP).

**Health Services:** The institution is staffed by a clinical director, a health services administrator, an assistant health services administrator, and other medical professionals. Outpatient care is provided. Local hospitals are seven miles away. The pill line is available three times per day (6:30am-7am, 11am-11:30am, and 4:30pm-4:45pm) Monday through Friday, and twice per day (9:30am-10am and 4:30pm-4:45pm) Saturday, Sunday and federal holidays. Sick call sign-up is available from 6:30am-7am, four days a week. At least one physician assistant is on duty or on call 24 hours a day. Periodic health examinations are available for age-specific inmates.

**Housing:** Inmates at the FCI are housed in dormitories in 8-man cubicles. There are several television viewing areas. Inmates must purchase their own TV headphones from the commissary.

**Fitness/Recreation:** The recreation department consists of the equipment issue room, hobby shop, music room, weightlifting area, auditorium, and outdoor activities. All recreation areas are open on a daily basis from: 6am-7:30am, 8am-3:30pm, and 5pm-8:45pm. Weekend and holidays, the Rec-reation Department opens at 6:30am. the department offers organized intramural leagues throughout the calendar year to include following sports: soccer, volleyball, softball, and basketball.

**Religious Services:** The main institution is staffed by one full-time chaplain. Contract rabbi (once per month) and imam (bi-monthly) services are available. A community of volunteers provides services for most faiths.

**Commissary:** The commissary is open Monday through Thursday. The shopping rotation and times are posted on the inmate bulletin boards. Inmates are assigned to at least one shopping day per week. Assignments are made by the inmate's laundry bin number. Bureau of Prisons policy currently sets a monthly spending limit of $360.

**Telephone Policy:** Inmates may either call collect or dial direct using the Inmate Telephone System (ITS). The following are standard features of ITS: (1) inmate calls automatically terminate after 15 minutes; (2) an inmate's calling list is limited to 30 callers; and (3) calls are charged to an inmate's debit card.

**Inmate Mail:** The institution accepts mail from the U.S. Postal Service via First-Class, U.S. Priority, and Express Mail. For those interested in sending overnight mail via a private carrier (FedEx or UPS Overnight), it is recommended that you first contact the institution to find out whether the receipt of such mail is permitted.

**Inmate Mail to FCI:**
INMATE NAME & REGISTER NUMBER
FCI Safford
Federal Correctional Institution
P.O. Box 9000
Safford, AZ 85548

**Visiting Hours:** Visiting hours: Saturday, Sunday, federal holidays 8am-3pm. Inmates are limited to four adult visitors at one time. Attorneys will make prior arrangements with the unit team and will visit during regular visiting hours. Additional visiting information can be found on the BOP website, www.bop. gov, at https://www.bop.gov/locations/institutions/saf/.

**Lodging/Accommodations:** Should visitors be spending the night, the following is a short list of accommodations that are available in Safford, Arizona:

| | |
|---|---|
| Best Western Desert Inn | 928-428-0521 |
| Budget Inn | 928-428-7850 |
| Economy Inn | 928-348-0011 |
| Quality Inn & Suites | 928-428-3200 |

**Directions to Facility:** The facility is located approximately seven miles south of downtown Safford on Highway 191. It is approximately 120 miles east of Tucson, Arizona, and 180 miles southeast of Phoenix. From Tucson, visitors should travel east on Interstate 10 to Highway 191 North. Take Highway 191 North to Highway 366, then turn left. Visitors from Phoenix should travel east on Highway 60 to Highway 70, then east on Highway 70 to Highway 191. Turn south on Highway 191 to Highway 366, then turn right.

## §17:20  MCC SAN DIEGO

MCC San Diego
Metropolitan Correctional Center
808 Union Street
San Diego, CA 92101
SDC/ExecAssistant@bop.gov
619-232-4311
Fax: 619-595-0390

**Location:** In downtown San Diego, connected to the United States Court-house via a secure tunnel. San Diego is served by Lindberg Field, Amtrak, and Greyhound.

**History:** Opened in 1974, MCC San Diego was the first of the Bureau of Prisons' high-rise detention facilities. It houses male and female detainees held primarily for immigration violations, *i.e.*, illegal entry and alien smuggling. The next most common offenses for which pre-trial and pre-sentenced offenders are housed for are narcotics violations, bank robbery, and probation and parole violations. A sentenced work cadre serves as a manpower resource.

**Judicial District:** Southern District of California.

**Security Level:** MCC is an administrative facility housing male and female inmates.

**Population:** As of 6/28/2014, the MCC inmate population is 899. Weekly population figures are available on the BOP website, www.bop.gov, at https://www.bop.gov/locations/institutions/sdc/.

**Education:** The institution offers GED, ESL, adult continuing education, and correspondence courses.

**Vocational/Apprenticeship:** No advanced occupational education programs, vocational training or apprenticeship programs are offered.

**Library:** The law library is open at least five days a week. Electric typewriters are available to inmates. A coin-operated copier is also available. Copies are 10 cents. An inter-library loan is not available. The law and leisure libraries are located on the sixth floor of the Education Department.

**UNICOR:** None.

**Counseling/Rehab Services:** Psychological services are available to all inmates on a voluntary basis. Services include the following: crisis intervention, short-term therapy and counseling, and diagnostic evaluations. There is a chemical abuse program that utilizes group and individual therapy and provides drug and alcohol education. Alcoholics Anonymous and Narcotics Anonymous meetings are held weekly. The psychology department is staffed by one to two full-time psychologists.

**Health Services:** The institution is staffed by two physicians, three to four physician assistants, two dentists, and two pharmacists. The institution provides outpatient care and is served by Alvarado Hospital, which is located approximately 20 miles away. Pill line is available three times a day, seven days a week. Medical staff is available 24 hours a day for emergency care. Sick call is on Monday, Tuesday, Thursday, Friday 6pm-6:30pm. All routine medical examinations and non-emergency care will be done by a mid-level practitioner.

**Housing:** Inmates are housed in two-man cells and dormitories.

**Fitness/Recreation:** The Recreation Department offers weights, stair-steppers, stationary bicycles, a music room, pool tables, and ping-pong tables. Some art classes are available.

**Religious Services:** Staff chaplains are available seven days a week to provide pastoral care and counseling. A schedule of religious services and activities is posted at the chapel entrance and on each unit bulletin board in English and Spanish. The camp is staffed by two full-time chaplains. A community of volunteers provides services for most faiths.

**Commissary:** Inmates are allowed to shop once a week. The commissary is open Monday through Friday from 8am-3pm. Bureau of Prisons policy currently sets a monthly spending limit of $360.

**Telephone Policy:** The facility is equipped with the ITS-2 telephone system. Each housing unit has telephones for use between 6am-10pm. Calls must be made direct. Telephone calls are limited to 15 minutes. There is a maximum of 300 minutes per month of calling time.

**Inmate Mail:** The institution accepts mail from the U.S. Postal Service via First-Class, U.S. Priority, and Express Mail. For those interested in sending overnight mail via a private carrier (FedEx or UPS Overnight), it is recommended that you first contact the institution to find out whether the receipt of such mail is permitted. Inmates are not authorized to request merchandise, materials, or anything for which they would be billed.

**Inmate Mail to MCC:**
>      INMATE NAME & REGISTER NUMBER
>      MCC San Diego
>      Metropolitan Correctional Center
>      808 Union Street
>      San Diego, CA 92101

**Visiting Hours:** Visiting hours: Monday, Thursday, Friday 4:45pm-9pm; Saturday, Sunday, federal holidays 8am-3:30pm. An inmate will be allowed a single one-hour visit on each of the visiting days. Visiting days are assigned according to an inmate's register number. Inmates are given 12 visiting points per month. A weekday visit will be counted as one point. A weekend or holiday visit will count as two points. A newly admitted inmate will be given eight points for the month of arrival. Inmates will be limited to three adult visitors at one time. Additional

visiting information can be found on the BOP website, www.bop.gov, at https://
www.bop.gov/locations/institutions/sdc/.

**Lodging/Accommodations:** Should visitors be spending the night, the following
is a short list of accommodations that are available in San Diego, California:

| | |
|---|---|
| Harborview Inn and Suites | 619-233-7799 |
| Main Street Motel | 619-232-0356 |
| San Diego Courtyard Marriott Downtown | 619-446-3000 |
| Western Inn | 619-298-6888 |

# §17:21   FDC SEA TAC

FDC Sea Tac
Federal Detention Center
2425 South 200th Street
Seattle, WA 98198
SET/ExecAssistant@bop.gov
206-870-5700
Fax: 206-870-5717

**Location:** 12 miles south of Seattle and 16 miles north of Tacoma, one mile west
of Interstate F (200th Street Exit).

**History:** Opened in 1998, FDC Sea Tac houses sentenced, pre-trial, and holdover
inmates, as well as Immigration and Naturalization Service detainees. Sentenced
inmates primarily provide labor support for the institution.

**Judicial District:** Western District of Washington.

**Security Level:** FDC Sea Tac is an administrative facility housing male and
female inmates.

**Population:** As of 6/29/2017, the FDC inmate population is 761. Weekly population figures are available on the BOP website at www.bop.gov, https://www.
bop.gov/locations/institutions/set/.

**Education:** The institution offers GED, ESL, adult continuing education, and
correspondence courses. A parenting class is also offered.

**Vocational/Apprenticeship:** No advanced occupational education programs,
vocational training or apprenticeship programs are offered.

**Library:** The law library is located in the Education Department. Cadre inmates
may use the library during assigned hours. Typewriters and a copier are available
to inmates. Inmates in the Special Housing Unit cannot go to the law library, but

may request books by submitting a "cop-out" to the Department supervisor. The library contains a collection of legal reference materials mandated by Congress and monitored by the Bureau of Prisons. It also contains Program Statements and Institutional Supplements to aid in legal research.

**UNICOR:** None.

**Counseling/Rehab Services:** A psychology staff provides a full range of psychological services on an as-needed basis. Services include the following: crisis intervention, short-term therapy and counseling. Diagnostic evaluations and assessments are provided for work cadre inmates only. The chemical abuse program utilizes group and individual therapy and provides education about drugs and alcohol. Alcoholics Anonymous and Narcotics Anonymous are also available.

**Health Services:** Sick call sign-up: Monday, Tuesday, Wednesday, and Friday. Pill lines are offered twice a day. In the morning hour it begins after the 5am count has cleared and in the evening at 6pm. The insulin pill line is prior to the 4pm stand up count. At least one physician assistant is on duty or on call 24 hours a day. Female inmates receive gynecological tests in addition to their initial physical screening, and receive mammograms after the age of 40.

**Housing:** Inmates are housed in two-man cells and dormitories.

**Fitness/Recreation:** The Recreation Department offers these activities: crochet, origami, hobby craft, screen-writing classes, movies, knitting, card and board games, chess club, ping-pong, pool, aerobics, and wellness programs. Outdoor activities: volleyball, basketball, stationary bikes, treadmills, and stair-steppers.

**Religious Services:** Religious programming is provided in the main chapel and in the unit program room. Unit programs are led by staff, contractors or volunteers. Religious media, including greeting cards, is available in the chapel library. Native American smudging is permitted in the unit recreation area Tuesday 8pm-9pm.

**Commissary:** All commissary lists must be turned in prior to 6am on the inmates' scheduled commissary shopping day. Bureau of Prisons policy currently sets a monthly spending limit of $360.

**Telephone Policy:** Inmates may either call collect or dial direct using the Inmate Telephone System (ITS). The following are standard features of ITS: (1) inmate calls automatically terminate after 15 minutes; (2) an inmate's calling list is limited to 30 callers; and (3) calls are charged to an inmate's debit card. Inmates receive 300 calling minutes per month.

**Inmate Mail:** The institution accepts mail from the U.S. Postal Service via First-Class, U.S. Priority, and Express Mail. For those interested in sending overnight mail via a private carrier (FedEx or UPS Overnight), it is recommended that you first contact the institution to find out whether the receipt of such mail is permitted. Inmates are permitted to receive publications without prior approval, although the warden will reject publications that are determined to be detrimental to the security, good order or discipline of the institution. Hardcover publications may only be received directly from the publisher, bookstore or book club; softcover publications may be received from any source. Each inmate can retain up to five publications at once.

**Inmate Mail to FDC:**
   INMATE NAME & REGISTER NUMBER
   FDC Sea Tac
   Federal Correctional Center
   P.O. Box 13900
   Seattle, WA 98198

**Visiting Hours:** Visiting hours: Saturday, Sunday, federal holidays 7:30am-2:30pm; Monday and Friday 2pm-9pm. All inmates are allowed only one visit a day. Inmates will be subject to visiting on odd and even calendar days, according to their registration number. Inmates will be permitted to visit with a maximum of six visitors, including adults and children at one time. Attorney visits: Saturday, Sunday, and federal holidays 7:30am-2:30pm; Monday, Friday 7:30am-9pm; Tuesday, Wednesday, Thursday 7:30am-6pm. Attorneys should schedule 24 hours in advance with the unit team if visiting at other times. Additional visiting information can be found on the BOP website, at https://www.bop.gov/locations/institutions/set/.

**Lodging/Accommodations:** Should visitors be spending the night, the following is a short list of accommodations that are available in Seattle, Washington:

| | |
|---|---|
| Comfort Inn & Suites-Sea Tac | 206-878-1100 |
| Island Country Inn | 206-842-6861 |
| Marco Polo Motel | 206-633-4090 |
| University Motel Suites | 206-522-4724 |
| Westin Hotel Seattle | 206-728-1000 |

## §17:22   FCI SHERIDAN

FCI Sheridan
Federal Correctional Institution
27072 Ballston Road
Sheridan, OR 97378
SHE/ExecAssistant@bop.gov
503-843-4442
Fax: 503-843-6645

**Location:** In northwestern Oregon in the heart of the south Yamhill River Valley, 90 minutes south of Portland, off Highway 18 on Ballston Road. Sheridan is located 50 miles from Portland, Oregon. The area is served by Portland International Airport, Amtrak in Salem and Portland, and commercial bus lines.

**History:** Opened in 1989, FCI Sheridan houses male offenders primarily from the Western United States. Opened in 1989, the satellite camp houses minimum-security male offenders.

**Judicial District:** District of Oregon.

**Security Level:** FCI Sheridan is a medium-security facility that houses male offenders. The facility includes a detention center for male offenders and an adjacent minimum-security satellite prison camp that also houses male offenders.

**Population:** As of of 6/29/2017, the FCI inmate population is 1,171, and the camp population is 520. Weekly population figures are available on the BOP website at www.bop.gov, https://www.bop.gov/locations/institutions/she/.

**Education:** The FCI and the camp offer GED, ESL, adult continuing education, and correspondence courses.

**Vocational/Apprenticeship:** FCI and the camp offer advanced occupational education in business computer applications. FCI and the camp offer vocational training in building trades, horticulture, personal fitness trainer, and apprenticeships in HVAC technician, maintenance electrician, career center clerk and tutor. FCI offers vocational training in business computer applications, woodworking and apprenticeship in dental assistant, dental laboratory technician, and agriculture. The camp also offers vocational training in landscape design and pesticide management.

**Library:** The law library is located in the Education Department and contains a variety of legal reference materials for use in preparing legal papers. Reference materials include the United States Code Annotated, Federal Reporter, Supreme Court Reporter, Bureau of Prisons Program Statements, Institution Supplements, Indexes, and other legal materials. The law library is open Monday through Thursday 7:30am-8:15pm, excluding lunch and the 4pm count; Fridays from 7:30am-3:30pm, excluding lunch; Sundays from 11am-8:15pm, excluding the 4pm count; and is closed on Saturdays and holidays. An inmate law library clerk is available for assistance in legal research. Legal materials are also available to inmates in the Special Housing Unit via a delivery system and satellite collection. Copy machines and typewriters are available. An inter-library loan is available. Inmates may check out books from the Sheridan Public Library and the Chemeketa Cooperative Regional Library, which includes 17 libraries.

**UNICOR:** The UNICOR Furniture Factory is the single largest employer of inmates at FCI Sheridan. The facility employs approximately 65 inmates in contracting services. Some of the services are as follows: data services, warehousing, distribution and fulfillment, assistance and help desk, and custom printing.

**Counseling/Rehab Services:** The psychologist is available to inmates via open house Monday through Friday from 11am-12noon, or on emergency basis by request from staff. The Residential Drug Abuse Program (RDAP) is a 500-hour, unit-based program that takes approximately nine months to complete. Comprehensive programs are located in various federal institutions. Each program delivers a standardized treatment package in which participants program 10 to 15 hours a week in a wide variety of therapeutic modalities targeting skills acquisition. The drug education program is a 40-hour program providing general information about drug abuse and treatment options. Outpatient services, such as Alcoholics Anonymous and Narcotics Anonymous, are also provided at FCI Sheridan.

**Health Services:** The main institution is staffed by two full-time physicians, four physician assistants, and two pharmacists. The FCI and the camp provide outpatient care. Routine sick call is held Monday, Tuesday, Thursday and Friday between 6:30am-7am. On Wednesday, physical examinations and other diagnostic testing is conducted. Pill line hours: Monday through Friday 6:30am-6:55am, 4:45pm-5:10pm; weekends/holidays 8:30am-8:55am, 4:45pm-5:10pm. At least one physician assistant is on call 24 hours a day. Inmates over the age of 50 may request yearly health screenings.

**Fitness/Recreation:** There are a variety of organized sports at the facility: softball, flag football, soccer, volleyball, handball, racquetball and basketball. A gymnasium with fitness equipment is also available for use, as well as a hobby shop and various board games and ping-pong tables.

**Housing:** Inmates at the FCI are housed in four housing units in two-man cells. Inmates held in administrative detention will be housed first in a three-man cell, pending bed space in a standard two-man cell. Inmates at the camp are housed in dormitories in four-man cubicles.

**Religious Services:** The pastoral care department consists of two full-time chaplains who are also available for counseling services. Assisting the chaplains are approved volunteers and contract religious leaders. The schedule of religious activities is posted on bulletin boards in the chapel and in the units.

**Commissary:** The commissary is open for general population inmates Monday through Thursday 5:30pm-8:30pm. Hospital and special housing unit inmates will have commissary on Fridays. Inmates are assigned one shopping day per week. An inmate's shopping day is determined by the weekly rotation for the units. The monthly commissary spending limit is currently $360.

**Telephone Policy:** Inmates may dial direct using the Inmate Telephone System (ITS). The following are standard features of ITS: (1) inmate calls automatically terminate after 15 minutes; (2) an inmate's calling list is limited to 30 callers; and (3) calls are charged to an inmate's debit card. It takes two to four days for inmates to add phone numbers to their caller-approved list. Each side of the housing unit has three telephones for inmate use. Inmates receive 300 calling minutes per month.

**Inmate Mail:** The FCI and the camp accept mail from the U.S. Postal Service via First-Class, U.S. Priority, and Express Mail. For those interested in sending overnight mail via a private carrier (FedEx or UPS Overnight), it is recommended that you first contact the institution to find out whether the receipt of such mail is permitted. Inmates are permitted to receive publications without prior approval, although the warden will reject publications that are determined to be detrimental to the security, good order or discipline of the institution. All publications must be received directly from the publisher, bookstore or book club; however, at the camp, inmates may receive softcover publications from any source.

**Inmate Mail to FCI:**
> INMATE NAME & REGISTER NUMBER
> FCI Sheridan
> Federal Correctional Institution
> P.O. Box 5000
> Sheridan, OR 97378

**Inmate Mail to Camp:**
> INMATE NAME & REGISTER NUMBER
> FCI Sheridan
> Federal Correctional Institution
> Satellite Camp
> P.O. Box 6000
> Sheridan, OR 97378

**Visiting Hours:** FCI visiting hours: Friday, Saturday, Sunday, federal holidays 8:30am-3pm Camp visiting hours: Fridays, 5pm-8:30pm, and Saturday, Sunday, federal holidays 8:30am-3pm. Attorneys are encouraged to visit Monday through Friday 8am-3pm. An inmate's visiting list is limited to 10 friends and associates. Immediate family members will not be counted toward the limit. Each FCI and SCP inmate will be given 12 visiting points per month. Two points will be deducted for Saturday and Sunday visits; one point will be deducted for Friday visits. Inmates are limited to six visitors, including children, at one time. A maximum of four adult visitors will be allowed at one time. Additional visiting information can be found on the BOP website at https://www.bop.gov/locations/institutions/she/.

**Lodging/Accommodations:** Should visitors be spending the night, the following is a short list of accommodations that are available in Sheridan, Oregon or nearby McMinnville, Oregon:

**Sheridan, Oregon:**

| | |
|---|---|
| Sheridan Country Inn | 503-843-3151 |

**McMinnville, Oregon:**

| | |
|---|---|
| Red Lion Inn McMinnville | 503-472-1500 |
| Best Western Vineyard Inn | 503-472-4900 |
| Steiger Haus Bed & Breakfast | 503-472-0821 |

**Directions to Facility:** From Portland: Interstate Highway 5 South to Highway 99 West. Proceed west on Highway 99W toward McMinnville. Take the Highway 18 bypass around the town of McMinnville. Continue on State Highway 18 toward the Beach. Approximately 13 miles west on State Highway 18 take the second Sheridan exit, and turn right off the ramp. The Institution is located on the south side of the highway and is noticeable from the exit. From Salem: State Highway 22 West toward Dallas/Beach cities. Continue on State Highway 22 to the Valley Junction, turn-off to Highway 18 East. Continue on Highway 18 East to Sheridan off ramp. Turn left; the Institution is on Ballston Road.

# §17:23   TAFT CORRECTIONAL INSTITUTION (CI TAFT)

CI Taft
Taft Correctional Institution
1500 Cadet Road
Taft, CA 93268
TAF/General@bop.gov
661-763-2510
Fax: 661-765-3034

**Location:** Take Interstate 5 to Highway 119. Highway 119 will become Highway 33. Stay on Highway 33 to Cadet Road (located 4-5 miles from the Hwy 119-Hwy 33 change). Make a left on Cadet Road.

**History:** Opened in 1997. This is a privately owned and managed correctional facility, under contract with the Bureau of Prisons. As such, it is to remain in full compliance with Bureau of Prison policies concerning inmates.

**Judicial District:** Central District of California.

**Security Level:** CI Taft is a low-security prison for male deportable offenders with a minimum-security camp housing male offenders.

**Population:** As of 6/29/2017, the CI Taft federal offender population is 2,141. Weekly population figures are available on the BOP website at www.bop.gov, https://www.bop.gov/locations/ci/taf/.

**Education:** Educational opportunities include post-secondary education, correspondence courses, a wide range of occupational training programs, and leisure time activities. A variety of college courses are provided by Taft College to inmates at the main institution and the camp. The camp offers courses in basic and advanced real estate, basic and advanced commodities, stocks, public speaking, health and wellness, legal research and personal and business planning.

**Vocational/Apprenticeship:** A number of vocational training programs are available to the inmate population. Inmates are encouraged to contact the academic counselor or vocational teachers, who are located in the education and vocational training buildings. The camp offers vocational training programs in horticulture, landscape design and landscape installations. The camp does not offer apprenticeship programs.

**Library:** The law library is located in the education building. Inmate law library clerks are available to assist inmates. A schedule and hours of operation will be posted and available to all inmates. Legal reference material is available for preparation of legal documents in the law library. Reservations can be made in the law library for use of the typewriter. Inmate assistance is available in the law library. A collection of hardcover books, paperback books, magazines, and newspapers are available in the leisure library. A selection of leisure reading books in Spanish is available in the leisure library. Inmates may have copies of legal materials necessary for their research or legal matters.

**UNICOR:** Not available.

**Counseling/Rehab Services:** The institution offers Alcoholics/Narcotics Anonymous, drug abuse counseling, and other special interest groups upon request. Prison staff is trained in the various social science fields. Inmate participation in these activities will be encouraged upon staff's assessment of inmate needs. Participation in such activities can be voluntary or mandatory. The staff of each unit is available for informal counseling sessions, in addition to formal group counseling activities.

**Health Services:** CI Taft provides outpatient care. The medication line is available daily at meal times and bedtime. The times for sick call sign-up are posted in the units and in the Health Services Unit. Emergency medical services are available and provided on a 24-hour, seven day a week basis.

**Housing:** Inmates are housed in cells or open bay dormitories.

**Fitness/Recreation:** The Recreation Department provides for a comprehensive recreation program that includes leisure-time activities and outdoor exercise, operating on a prescribed schedule that is posted and available to inmates in the recreation specialist's office. There is a wide variety of organized league tournaments, classes and leisure time activities, including a television for sporting event viewing. The music room is available by schedule. A variety of craft programs are offered by the Recreation Department.

**Religious Services:** The Religious Services office at CI Taft provides programming designed to meet the religious needs of each inmate so that he may maintain and develop his spirituality while incarcerated. Worship services are provided by staff and volunteer chaplains, Catholic priest, Protestant minister, and a number of other volunteer ministers and lay persons from various area faith groups.

**Commissary:** The commissary is open five days a week and inmates are allowed to shop no more than once a day. Commissary lists are available at the commissary and in the units. The monthly spending limit is posted in each unit and is subject to change annually. Bureau of Prisons policy currently sets a monthly spending limit of $360.

**Telephone Policy:** Telephones for inmates are located at various locations in the institution. Third-party calls, credit card calls, or call forwarding are not acceptable and prohibited by the institution's phone policy. Inmates are allowed access to 120 minutes of collect calls per month. Inmates may have up to 30 approved telephone numbers on their caller approved list and may change their telephone list up to three times per month. Inmates dial direct using the Inmate Telephone System (ITS). Calls are limited to 15 minutes, an inmate's calling list is limited to 30 callers, and calls are charged to the inmate's debit card. Telephones are available for inmate use during convenient non-working hours.

**Inmate Mail:** The institution accepts mail from the U.S. Postal Service via First-Class, U.S. Priority, and Express Mail. For those interested in sending overnight mail via a private carrier (FedEx or UPS Overnight), it is recommended that you first contact the institution to find out whether the receipt of such mail is permitted.

**Inmate Mail to CI Taft:**
    INMATE NAME & REGISTER NUMBER
    CI TAFT
    Correctional Institution
    P.O. Box 7001
    Taft, CA 93268

**Visiting Hours:** Visiting hours are normally on Thursday, Friday, Saturday, Sunday and federal holidays, between the hours of 8am and 3pm (this includes the noon hour). Visitors are not processed after 1:30pm. Saturday night visitation begins at 5pm and will be processed until 7:30pm. Visitation on Saturday ends at 9pm. Inmates are allowed one visit per day. All visitors must be approved prior to the scheduled visiting day. A total of six visitors will be allowed per inmate. Attorneys are encouraged to visit inmates during the regular visiting hours. However, visits from an attorney can be arranged at other times based on the circumstance of each case and available staff. Saturdays and Sundays from 8am-3pm, with the addition of Thursdays from 8am-3pm. The inmates are on a 20-point per month system for visitation with a maximum number of six visitors at one time. Weekday visits are charged one point, while weekend visits are charged two points. Additional visiting information can be found at https://www.bop.gov/locations/ci/taf/.

**Lodging/Accommodations:** Should visitors be spending the night, the following is a short list of accommodations that are available in Taft, California:

| | |
|---|---|
| Holland Inn & Suites | 661-763-5211 |
| Caprice Motel | 661-765-2161 |
| Sunset Motel | 661-765-6214 |
| Topper's Motel | 661-765-4145 |
| Welcome Inn | 661-765-4174 |

## §17:24   FCI TERMINAL ISLAND

FCI Terminal Island
Federal Correctional Institution
1299 Seaside Avenue
San Pedro, CA 90731
TRM/ExecAssistant@bop.gov
310-831-8961
Fax: 310-732-5325

**Location:** On a pier in Los Angeles Harbor, between San Pedro and Long Beach, off Harbor Freeway to San Pedro (cross the Vincent Thomas Bridge and take Seaside Avenue to the Main Gate). The area is served by the Los Angeles International Airport, Long Beach Airport, Amtrak, and commercial bus lines.

**History:** Opened in 1938, FCI Terminal Island served as a Naval Disciplinary barracks from 1942 to 1950 and as a medical facility of the California Department of Corrections for a short time after 1950. In 1995, the institution was re-acquired by the Bureau of Prisons. It now houses male offenders and serves as a medical referral facility for the Western Region providing short-term medical care.

**Judicial District:** Central California.

**Security Level:** The FCI Terminal Island is a low-security facility housing male inmates.

**Population:** As of 6/29/2014, the FCI inmate population is 1,207. Weekly population figures are available on the BOP website at www.bop.gov, https://www.bop.gov/locations/institutions/trm/.

**Education:** The institution offers GED, ESL, adult continuing education, and correspondence courses.

**Vocational/Apprenticeship:** FCI offers advanced occupational education in AutoCAD and welding. FCI offers vocational training in the following areas: carpentry, chloro-fluoro-carbon certification, contract licensing, home wiring, home inspection, HVAC theory, HVAC troubleshooting, and plumbing. FCI also offers apprenticeship programs: baker, cabinet maker, combination welder, dental hygienist, electrician, HVAC, pipefitter maintenance, painting, plumbing, quality control, stationary engineer, tool and die, electrical maintenance, electrostatic powder paint spray operator, machine setter, materials coordinator and powder paint and coating. You must have a GED, high school diploma, or shown concurrent enrollment in GED to participate in occupational courses. Apprenticeship programs are certified through the U.S. Department of Labor.

**Library:** The law library is open Monday through Friday from 11am-9pm. Electric typewriters are available to inmates for the preparation of legal documents. Copiers are also available. Copies are 10 cents and charged to an inmate's debit card. The law library is located in the Education Department and contains a variety of legal reference materials for use in preparing legal papers. Reference material include the United States Code Annotated, Federal Reporter, Supreme Court Reporter, Bureau of Prison Program Statements, Institutional Supplements, Indexes, and other legal materials. Inmate law library clerks are available for assistance in legal research. Applications for legal assistance from the U.S.C. Law School are also available in the law library. The leisure library is very small. An inter-library loan program is available. Video cassette recorders and audio cassette recorders are available. The Education Department also regularly provides leisure reading materials such as paper books, magazines, and newspaper to SHU. Specific leisure reading materials may be requested on a cop-out to the Education Department.

**UNICOR:** A metal factory and a data processing plant employ inmates.

**Counseling/Rehab Services:** A 500-hour Residential Drug Abuse Program (RDAP) is available. The program is 9-12 months in length. Currently, the FCI Terminal Island RDAP is for the designated low-security inmates only, and not for minimum-security work cadre inmates. In addition, the institution offers a non-residential drug treatment program, a drug education program, and Alcoholics Anonymous and Narcotics Anonymous groups, as well as individual psychotherapy. The psychology department is staffed by a chief psychologist, a Care 3 coordinator, a clinical psychologist, and three psychology interns. The staff of each unit is available for informal counseling sessions. Psychology programs include initial psychology screening, crisis intervention, suicide prevention, drug abuse treatment, and individual/group psychotherapy.

**Health Services:** The institution is staffed by three physicians, nine physician assistants, one dentist, and one pharmacist. The institution provides outpatient care. A small infirmary is also available. The institution is served by San Pedro Hospital, which is approximately five minutes away. Sick call sign-up is Monday, Tuesday, Thursday, and Friday, 6:15am-6:45am. Pill line hours: 6:15am-6:30am (insulin only), 6:30am-7:15am, 11am-12noon, 4pm-4:15pm (insulin only), 5:30pm-6:30pm. On-site emergency medical care is available 24 hours a day in the institution. All inmates are eligible for age-specific periodic physical examinations.

**Housing:** Inmates are housed in open dormitories with single and two-man rooms.

**Fitness/Recreation:** Programs include indoor and outdoor activities ranging from individualized arts and crafts programs to intramural team sports, such as basketball, flag-football, baseball, and volleyball. These programs help the inmate develop an individual wellness plan; also, physical fitness and weight reduction are important for interpersonal relations and stress reduction. Hobby craft programs include knitting, crocheting, painting and leather lacing.

**Religious Services:** The institution offers a wide range of religious programs and pastoral care. Staff chaplains of specific faiths are available, as well as contract and volunteer representatives of other faiths. Special religious diets, holiday observances, and worship activities are coordinated through the chaplain's office. Information about these programs is available in the institution A&O Program and from the chaplains. Spiritual and family counseling is also available through the chaplains.

**Commissary:** Sales are conducted by Unit and are held Monday through Thursday from 11am-12:30pm and 4pm-last sale or 7pm. The schedule for shopping is based upon weekly unit sanitation scores. The commissary is closed on Fridays. Sales will be called alphabetically by unit and there will be no "last call." Inmate shopping days are determined by the unit an inmate resides in. Once a month each account is validated. Validation dates are determined by the fifth digit of the inmate register number. Bureau of Prisons policy currently sets a spending limit of $360.

**Telephone Policy:** Inmates may either call collect or dial direct using the Inmate Telephone System (ITS). The following are standard features of ITS: (1) inmate calls automatically terminate after 15 minutes; (2) an inmate's calling list is limited to 30 callers; and (3) calls are charged to an inmate's debit card. Telephone hours: Sunday through Saturday 6am-11:55pm.

**Inmate Mail:** The institution accepts mail from the U.S. Postal Service via First-Class, U.S. Priority, and Express Mail. For those interested in sending overnight mail via a private carrier (FedEx or UPS Overnight), it is recommended that you first contact the institution to find out whether the receipt of such mail is permitted. Inmates are permitted to receive publications without prior approval, although the warden will reject publications that are determined to be detrimental to the security, good order or discipline of the institution. Hardcover publications must be received directly from the publisher, bookstore or book club; softcover publications may be received from any source. Accumulation of publications will be limited to four magazines (no more than three months old) and five books.

**Inmate Mail to FCI:**
INMATE NAME & REGISTER NUMBER
FCI Terminal Island
Federal Correctional Institution
P.O. Box 3007
San Pedro, CA 90731

**Visiting Hours:** Visiting hours: Saturday, Sunday, Monday, and federal holidays 8am-3pm. Inmates have the opportunity to receive 40 visiting points each month. One hour of visiting per person is equal to one point. Up to 20 visitors can be placed on the inmate's approved visitor list. Attorneys must be on an inmate's approved visiting list prior to visiting. Attorneys will visit during regular visiting hours. However, visits from an attorney can be arranged at other times based on the circumstances of each case and available staff. Additional visiting information can be found at the BOP website at https://www.bop.gov/locations/institutions/trm/.

**Lodging/Accommodations:** Should visitors be spending the night, the following is a short list of accommodations that are available in San Pedro, California:
| | |
|---|---|
| Sunrise Hotel | 310-548-1080 |
| Royal Hotel | 310-832-5225 |
| Americas Best Value Inn | 310-519-9990 |
| Pacific Inn & Suites | 310-514-1247 |

**Directions to Facility:** <u>From Long Beach:</u> Travel west on Ocean Boulevard or south on Interstate 710 over the Gerald Desmond Bridge. After you pass through three traffic lights, you will see an exit sign indicating Ferry Street. Take that exit, which exits to the right. This is Seaside Avenue. Continue to the traffic light and make a left. This is Ferry Street. Continue to the third traffic light, which will be the intersection of Terminal Way. Turn right on Terminal Way and continue. The road will curve to the left and the name changes once again to Seaside Avenue. Continue down Seaside and the road will lead you to the entrance to the institution.

From the Harbor Freeway: Travel south on Interstate 110 toward San Pedro. Just before the highway ends, take the exit for the Vincent Thomas Bridge to Terminal Island (Route 47). After you cross the bridge, take Ferry Street exit on the right. At the traffic light turn left. This is Ferry Street. At the second traffic light, turn right on Terminal Way. Continue until the road curves to the left and the name changes to Seaside Avenue. Continue down Seaside and the road will lead you to the entrance to the institution.

# §17:25   FCI TUCSON

FCI Tucson
Federal Correctional Institution
8901 South Wilmot Road
Tucson, AZ 85706
TCN/ExecAssistant@bop.gov
520-574-7100
Fax: 520-574-4206

**Location:** In southern Arizona, 10 miles southeast of the city of Tucson near Interstate 10 and Wilmont Road. Tucson is served by Tucson International Airport, Amtrak, and Greyhound.

**History:** Opened in 1982, FCI Tucson houses male offenders, including pre-trial offenders, and those who have been sentenced and are awaiting transfer to other federal facilities. Additionally, a small pre-trial and short-term female population is housed at FCI Tucson.

**Judicial District:** District of Arizona.

**Security Level:** FCI Tucson is a medium-security facility housing male inmates with an administrative facility for male and female offenders.

**Population:** As of 6/29/2017, the FCI inmate population is 645. Weekly population figures are available on the BOP website at www.bop.gov, https://www.bop.gov/locations/institutions/tcn/.

**Education:** The institution offers GED, ESL, adult continuing education, parenting and correspondence courses.

**Vocational/Apprenticeship:** FCI offers advanced occupational education in environmental technician waste water management, culinary arts and basic baking. FCI offers apprenticeship in plumbing, HVAC, cooking/baking, and electrician. USP offers no advanced occupational education programs, vocational training or apprenticeship.

**Library:** This facility operates a law library combined with a leisure library. The law library includes a complete selection of legal reference books that contain an extensive range of information on federal legislative and case law. It also includes the Federal Prison System Policy Statements. Some typewriters are designated for inmate legal work only. The leisure library offers a varied selection of reading materials. Subjects include fiction, non-fiction, and reference materials. Some typewriters are also available for non-legal use in the library. Inmates can obtain books from the Tucson Public Library via an inter-library loan program. The law library is open Monday through Thursday, 7:30am-11:15am, 12:30pm-3:30pm, and 6pm-8:30pm; Friday, 7:30am-11:15am and 12:30pm-3:30pm; Saturday, 7:30am-9:30am and 12:30pm-3:30pm. The leisure library is open Mondays through Fridays, 12:30pm-3:30pm, and 6pm-8:30pm; Saturday, Sunday, and holidays, 7:30am-9:30am, 12:30pm-3:30pm, and 6pm-8:30pm.

**UNICOR:** FCI Tucson participates in a recycling program (e-scrap) and employs approximately 100 inmates.

**Counseling/Rehab Services:** Psychology Services is composed of two full-time psychologists and one drug treatment specialist. The Health Services Department provides contract psychiatric services three days each month. The drug abuse treatment specialist provides a drug education program to both designated and pre-trial inmates, such as a non-residential drug abuse treatment program and a 500-hour Residential Drug Abuse Program (RDAP). Other psychological program offerings: individual psychotherapy/counseling, group psychotherapy, counseling, Alcoholics Anonymous meetings, Narcotics Anonymous meetings, BOP Values Program, inmate suicide prevention companion program, anger management, coping skills & stress management, Salvation Army Relapse Prevention (Wednesday evenings), Framework to Recovery/Living Sober Program. Inmates with a history of sexual offenses may be designated to the Sex Offender Management Program (SOMP). The Sex Offender Treatment Program (SOTP-NR) offers inmates individualized non-residential treatment, for six to eight hours a week, for six months. All participation in non-residential treatment services is voluntary.

**Health Services:** Outpatient care is provided. Local hospitals are approximately 20-30 minutes away. Inmates who experience sudden illness may report to the Health Services Unit between 6:30am-7am Monday, Tuesday, Thursday or Friday (excluding holidays) for sick call sign-up. Pill line is available Monday through Friday 6am to 6:30am, 5pm-6pm, and 8pm-8:30pm; Saturday and Sunday 7am to 7:30 am, 5pm-6pm, and 8pm-8:30pm. At least one physician assistant is on duty or on call 24 hours a day. Periodic physical examinations are offered as clinically indicated. Mammograms and gynecological examinations will be offered to female inmates every year.

**Housing:** Inmates are housed in two-man cells. The housing units are wheelchair accessible. The television viewing rooms are open daily from 6am-10pm.

**Fitness/Recreation:** Various structured recreation/leisure programs are offered by the Recreation Department during the evening hours on weekdays; and during morning, afternoon and evening hours on weekends and holidays. Programs may be seasonal and available according to the availability of space and equipment. These programs include the following: league sports, varsity sports, holiday and weekend tournaments, and inmate wellness.

**Religious Services:** The Religious Services Department consists of several chaplains who are responsible for providing services for the inmate population. Religious activity schedules are published and posted on the unit bulletin boards. Religious volunteers assist the chaplains with various programs. They are selected from a large number of religious groups in the Tucson area. Pastoral visits from outside clergy may be arranged by the chaplains.

**Commissary:** The commissary is open for regular sales Tuesday through Thursday starting after the 4pm count clears. Pre-trial and pre-sentence inmates shop on Fridays. Female inmates shop Wednesday during the day. Holdovers will shop on regular sale days with the general population. The information posted on the bulletin board outside of the commissary will answer many of the questions pertaining to commissary operations. Bureau of Prisons policy currently sets a monthly commissary spending limit of $360.

**Telephone Policy:** Inmates may call collect. There are four telephones in each wing of the housing units. Telephones are operational from 6am-11:30pm daily.

**Inmate Mail:** The institution accepts mail from the U.S. Postal Service via First-Class, U.S. Priority, and Express Mail. For those interested in sending overnight mail via a private carrier (FedEx or UPS Overnight), it is recommended that you first contact the institution to find out whether the receipt of such mail is permitted. Inmates are permitted to receive publications without prior approval, although the warden will reject publications that are determined to be detrimental to the security, good order or discipline of the institution. Hardcover publications must be received directly from the publisher, bookstore or book club; softcover publications may be received from any source. Accumulation of magazines will be limited to five, no more than three months old.

**Inmate Mail to FCI:**
    INMATE NAME & REGISTER NUMBER
    FCI Tucson
    Federal Correctional Institution
    P.O. Box 23811
    Tucson, AZ 85734

**Visiting Hours:** FCI visiting hours: Monday, Tuesday 5pm-8:30pm; Saturday, Sunday, holidays 8:15am-3pm. Inmates are limited to three visitors at one time, and 12 names on their approved visitors list. Attorney, paralegal, or private investigator visits, representing an inmate client, will be arranged and approved through the unit team. Requests must be made 24 hours in advance. Additional visiting information can be found on the BOP website, www.bop.gov, https://www.bop.gov/locations/institutions/tcn/.

**Lodging/Accommodations:** Should visitors be spending the night, the following is a short list of accommodations that are available in Tucson, Arizona:

| | |
|---|---|
| Comfort Suites by Choice Hotels Airport | 520-295-4400 |
| Residence Inn Airport | 520-294-5522 |
| Best Western Inn & Suites Foothills | 520-297-8111 |
| Riverside Suites | 520-202-2210 |

**Directions to Facility:** Take I-10 exit #269 South. FCI Tucson is located approximately 1 1/2 miles south of the intersection of I-10, and Wilmot Road on the left side of the road. Tucson International Airport is located approximately seven miles west of FCC Tucson.

# §17:26   USP TUCSON

USP Tucson
U.S. Penitentiary
9300 South Wilmot Road
Tucson, AZ 85756
TCP/ExecAssistant@bop.gov
520-663-5000
Fax: 520-663-5024

**Location:** See §17:25 FCI Tucson.

**Judicial District:** District of Arizona.

**Security Level:** USP Tucson is a high-security institution housing male inmates, with a satellite camp that houses minimum-security male inmates.

**Population:** As of 6/30/2017, the USP inmate population is 1,343, and the camp population is 140. Weekly population figures are available on the BOP website at www.bop.gov, https://www.bop.gov/locations/institutions/tcp/.

**Library:** Leisure Library and Legal Resource Center hours: 8am-10am, 1pm-3:30pm Monday through Friday; 5:35pm-8:30pm Monday through Thursday; 8am-9:30am and 12noon to 3:30pm Saturday and Sunday.

**UNICOR:** FCI Tucson participates in a recycling program (e-scrap) and employs approximately 100 inmates.

**Counseling/Rehab Services:** Psychology Services is composed of two full-time psychologists and one drug treatment specialist. The Health Services Department provides contract psychiatric services three days each month.. The drug abuse treatment specialist provides a drug education program to both designated and pre-trial inmates, such as a non-residential drug abuse treatment program and a 500-hour Residential Drug Abuse Program (RDAP). Other psychological program offerings: individual psychotherapy/counseling, group psychotherapy, counseling, Alcoholics Anonymous meetings, Narcotics Anonymous meetings, BOP Values Program, inmate suicide prevention companion program, anger management, coping skills & stress management, Salvation Army Relapse Prevention (Wednesday evenings), Framework to Recovery/Living Sober Program. Inmates with a history of sexual offenses may be designated to the Sex Offender Management Program (SOMP). The Sex Offender Treatment Program (SOTP-NR) offers inmates individualized non-residential treatment, for six to eight hours a week, for six months. All participation in non-residential treatment services is voluntary.

**Health Services:** Outpatient care is provided. Local hospitals are approximately 20-30 minutes away. Inmates who experience sudden illness may report to the Health Services Unit between 6:30am-7am Monday, Tuesday, Thursday or Friday (excluding holidays) for sick call sign-up. Pill line is available Monday through Friday 6am to 6:30am, 5pm-6pm, and 8pm-8:30pm; Saturday and Sunday 7am to 7:30 am, 5pm-6pm, and 8pm-8:30pm. At least one physician assistant is on duty or on call 24 hours a day. Periodic physical examinations are offered as clinically indicated. Mammograms and gynecological examinations will be offered to female inmates every year.

**Fitness/Recreation:** Various structured recreation/leisure programs are offered by the Recreation Department during the evening hours on weekdays; and during morning, afternoon and evening hours on weekends and holidays. Programs may be seasonal and available according to the availability of space and equipment. These programs include the following: league sports, varsity sports, holiday and weekend tournaments, and inmate wellness.

**Religious Services:** The Religious Services Department consists of several chaplains who are responsible for providing services for the inmate population. Religious activity schedules are published and posted on the unit bulletin boards. Religious volunteers assist the chaplains with various programs. They are selected from a large number of religious groups in the Tucson area. Pastoral visits from outside clergy may be arranged by the chaplains.

**Commissary:** The information posted on the bulletin board outside of the commissary will answer many of the questions pertaining to commissary operations. Bureau of Prisons policy currently sets a monthly commissary spending limit of $360.

**Telephone Policy:** Inmates at the USP dial direct using the Inmate Telephone System (ITS). The following are standard features of ITS: (1) inmate calls automatically terminate after 15 minutes; (2) an inmate's calling list is limited to 30 callers; and (3) calls are charged to an inmate's debit card. Inmates receive 300 calling minutes per month.

**Inmate Mail:** The USP and the camp accept mail from the U.S. Postal Service via First-Class, U.S. Priority, and Express Mail. For those interested in sending overnight mail via a private carrier (FedEx or UPS Overnight), it is recommended that you first contact the institution to find out whether the receipt of such mail is permitted. Inmates are permitted to receive publications without prior approval, although the warden will reject publications that are determined to be detrimental to the security, good order or discipline of the institution. All publications must be received directly from the publisher, bookstore or book club.

**Inmate Mail to USP:**
INMATE NAME & REGISTER NUMBER
USP Tucson
U.S. Penitentiary
P.O. Box 24550
Tucson, AZ 85734

**Inmate Mail to Camp:**
INMATE NAME & REGISTER NUMBER
USP Tucson
U.S. Penitentiary
Federal Satellite Low
P.O. Box 24549
Tucson, AZ 85734

**Visiting Hours:** USP visiting hours: Friday 5pm-8pm; Saturday, Sunday, holidays 8:15am-3pm. SPC visiting hours: Saturday, Sunday, holidays 8:15am-3pm. Inmates must submit a special visit request to their unit team at least two weeks in advance of the visiting date. Visits from persons not on the approved list must be approved by the deputy warden. Attorney visits must be arranged and approved through the unit team. Inmates at USP will be limited to three total approved adult visitors (over the age of 16) at any one time, not to exceed six total visitors. Additional visiting information can be found on the BOP website, www.bop.gov, https://www.bop.gov/locations/institutions/tcp/.

**Lodging/Accommodations:** See §17:25 FCI Tucson.

**Directions to Facility:** See §17:25 FCI Tucson.

# §17:27  FCI VICTORVILLE I AND II

Victorville I:
FCI Victorville Medium I
Federal Correctional Institution
13777 Air Expressway Blvd.
Victorville, CA 92394
VIM/ExecAssistant@bop.gov
760-246-2400
Fax: 760-246-2461

Victorville II:
FCI Victorville II
Federal Correctional Institution
13777 Air Expressway Blvd.
Victorville, CA 92394
VIM/ExecAssistant@bop.gov
760-530-5700
Fax: 760-560-5706

**Location:** Approximately 85 miles northwest of Los Angeles on Interstate 15.

**History:** FCI Victorville I opened in 2001. FCI Victorville II opened in 2005.

**Judicial District:** Central California.

**Security Level:** FCI Victorville is a medium-security facility housing male inmates. It is part of the Victorville FCC. FCI II is a medium-security facility housing male inmates with a satellite prison camp that houses minimum-security female offenders. It is part of the Victorville FCC.

**Population:** As of 6/30/2017, the FCI inmate population is 1,334; the FCI II population is 1,093; and the FCI II camp population is 285. Weekly population figures are available on the BOP website at www.bop.gov.

**Education:** The FCI and the camp offer GED, ESL, adult continuing education, and correspondence courses. Inmates who have either a high school diploma or GED may enroll in college courses through Coastline Community College. All costs will be borne by the inmate.

**Vocational/Apprenticeship:** The Victorville FCC offers FCI Medium I offers vocational training in Automotive Service Excellence, Building Trades, Horticulture, Recycling/Solid Waste Management, Solar Panel Installation, Microsoft Office, ServSafe Food Handling, Wheels of the World and Bicycles, and Forklift. The Apprenticeship Training Program includes plumbing, HVAC, and dental assistant.

**Library:** The FCC's law library is located in the Education Department. It is open 7:30am-8:30pm Monday-Thursday, and 7:30am to 3:30pm on Friday and Sunday, and is closed on Saturday. Case law books from the federal districts, circuits, and U.S. supreme courts are available for reference during the library hours of operation. Bureau of Prisons' Program Statements and Institutional Supplements are available for inmate reference. An Electronic Law Library is also available. Law library books, typewriters, typing paper, and lift-off tape are available for inmate use. Typewriter ribbons are available for purchase from the commissary. Typewriters are available on a first-come, first-serve basis, and are only to be used for legal work. The FCI maintains a leisure library with a variety of books for reference and general interest.

**UNICOR:** UNICOR at FCC Victorville is a vehicular component factory that rebuilds and reconditions various types of motorized and non-motorized equipment such as but not limited to; trailers, forklifts, HMMWVs, 5-tons and various other Military and commercial vehicles and equipment. UNICOR provides this service for the Department of Defense, Department of Homeland Security, and the Department of United Sates Forest Service. There are two factories, one at the FCI-I and an Annex Factory at the USP, an outside Paint\Wash\Blast operation, as well as a Warehouse operation.

**Counseling/Rehab Services:** Psychologists are available for individual assistance on an as-needed basis. Psychologists will also conduct various groups and workshops for inmates in the facility. A small Inmate Resource Library of psychology-related books and tapes is also available. Individualized programs will be designed to meet each inmate's needs and may consist of one or more of the following support groups: Alcoholics Anonymous and Narcotics Anonymous; psycho-educational groups; group and/or individual therapy; biblio-therapy; pre-release counseling; and assessment and referral to a Residential Drug Abuse Program (RDAP) at another institution when appropriate.

**Health Services:** Sick call sign-up is held Monday, Tuesday, Thursday, and Friday. The times for sick call sign-up are posted in the units and in the Health Services Unit. Pill line times are posted in the units and in the Health Services Unit and will take place twice daily. Emergency medical care from qualified medical staff is available 24 hours a day. Any emergencies that occur when Health Services is closed must be reported to the unit officer, detail supervisor, or a member of the unit team.

**Housing:** Inmates at the FCIs are housed in two-man cells. Inmates at the camp are housed in open bay dormitories.

**Fitness/Recreation:** The Recreation Department offers a variety of hobby craft programs, sports programs and leagues, leisure and holiday programs, music programs, and structured exercise/wellness programs. Outdoor facilities include the following: basketball courts, handball courts, volleyball court, soccer field, softball fields, and a 1/2 mile jogging/walking dirt track. Indoor facilities:

cardiovascular room, recreation hall, music room (only acoustic equipment is available), resource room (fitness and wellness information is available), hobby craft room (water color art, leather craft, and ceramic programs) and equipment issue room (ID required to check out equipment). Hours of operation, activities schedule, and program announcements are posted on the bulletin boards in the recreation room and housing units. Trained recreation specialists are available to assist with recreation and leisure time activities.

**Religious Services:** Clergy persons are available to inmates of all faith groups. If there is a need during working hours to see a chaplain, a detail supervisor should contact the chaplain's office. Worship opportunities are available to the various faith groups. A schedule of religious services and activities is posted on unit bulletin boards as well as in the chapel area. The schedule also indicates the hours the chaplains, contractors, and volunteers are in the institution.

**Commissary:** A list with the price of each item can be obtained from the commissary. Inmates may submit a Commissary Order Form according to the schedule posted in their unit. All sales are final and there are no returns or exchanges. All items are sold on an "as is" basis with no warranty implied. Bureau of Prisons policy currently sets a monthly spending limit of $360.

**Telephone Policy:** Inmates at the FCC dial direct using the Inmate Telephone System-II (ITS-II). The following are standard features of ITS: (1) inmate calls automatically terminate after 15 minutes; (2) an inmate's calling list is limited to 30 callers; and (3) calls are charged to an inmate's debit card. Inmates receive 300 calling minutes per month.

**Inmate Mail:** The FCI and the camp accept mail from the U.S. Postal Service via First-Class, U.S. Priority, and Express Mail. For those interested in sending overnight mail via a private carrier (FedEx or UPS Overnight), it is recommended that you first contact the institution to find out whether the receipt of such mail is permitted.

**Inmate Mail to FCI:**
INMATE NAME & REGISTER NUMBER
FCI Victorville Medium I
Federal Correctional Institution
P.O. Box 3725
Adelanto, CA 92301

**Inmate Mail to FCI:**
INMATE NAME & REGISTER NUMBER
FCI Victorville Medium II
Federal Correctional Institution
P.O. Box 3850
Adelanto, CA 92301

**Inmate Mail to Satellite Camp:**
INMATE NAME & REGISTER NUMBER
FCI Victorville Medium II
Federal Correctional Institution
Satellite Camp
P.O. Box 5300
Adelanto, CA 92301

**Visiting Hours:** FCI I and II visiting hours: Saturday, Sunday, Monday, and holidays 8:30am-3pm. Camp visiting hours: Saturdays, Sundays, and all federal holidays, 8:30am-3pm. The total number of visitors is limited to four adults. The total number may be exceeded by three children when those children are under the age of 10 and will not occupy a seat during the visit. Inmates will be limited to 40 visiting points per month. One hour of visiting equals two points on weekends and holidays. One point will be deducted on weekdays and evening visits. A maximum of 20 visitor names can be on the inmate's approved visitor list. Attorney visits will be conducted during normal visiting hours. Prior to the visit, attorneys must submit a request to the inmate's unit manager, for approval of the visit. Additional visiting information can be found on the BOP website, www.bop.gov.

**Lodging/Accommodations:** Should visitors be spending the night, the following is a short list of accommodations that are available in Victorville, California:

| | |
|---|---|
| Ambassador Hotel & Conference Center | 760-245-6565 |
| Comfort Suites Hotel | 760-245-6777 |
| Extended Studio Hotel | 760-843-3800 |
| Green Spot Motel | 760-245-2101 |
| Hawthorn Suites Hotel | 760-949-4700 |
| New Budget Inn | 760-241-8010 |
| New Corral Motel | 760-245-9378 |

**Directions to Facility:** From the north: Take Interstate 15 South. Exit Mojave Dr., turn right on Mojave Dr., go to Village Dr., turn right on Village Dr., go to Air Expressway Blvd., turn left on Air Expressway Blvd., go to George Blvd., turn left to arrive at FCI Victorville.

From the south: Take Interstate 15 North. Exit Mojave Dr., turn left on Mojave Dr., go to Village Dr., turn right on Village Dr., go to Air Expressway Blvd., turn left on Air Expressway Blvd., go to George Blvd., turn left to arrive at FCI Victorville.

From the east: Take Interstate 10 West to Interstate 215 North to Interstate 15 North. Exit Mojave Dr., turn left on Mojave Dr., go to Village Dr., turn right on Village Dr., go to Air Expressway Blvd., turn left on Air Expressway Blvd., go to George Blvd., turn left to arrive at FCI Victorville.

From the west: Take Interstate 10 East to Interstate 215 North to Interstate 15 North. Exit Mojave Dr., turn left on Mojave Dr., go to Village Dr., turn right on Village Dr., go to Air Expressway Blvd., turn left on Air Expressway Blvd., go to George Blvd., turn left to arrive at FCI Victorville.

## §17:28  USP VICTORVILLE

USP Victorville
U.S. Penitentiary
13777 Air Expressway Blvd.
Victorville, CA 92394
VIM/ExecAssistant@bop.gov
760-530-5000
Fax: 760-530-5103

**Location:** Approximately 85 miles northwest of Los Angeles on Interstate 15.

**Judicial District:** Central California.

**Security Level:** USP Victorville is a high-security facility housing male inmates. It is part of the Victorville FCC.

**Population:** As of 6/29/2017, the USP inmate population is 1,128. Weekly population figures are available on the BOP website at www.bop.gov, at https://www.bop.gov/locations/institutions/vip/.

**Vocational/Apprenticeship:** See §17:26, FCI Victorville I and II.

**Telephone Policy:** Inmates dial direct using the Inmate Telephone System II (ITS-II). The following are standard features of ITS: (1) inmate calls automatically terminate after 15 minutes; (2) an inmate's calling list is limited to 30 callers; and (3) calls are charged to an inmate's debit card. Inmates receive 300 calling minutes per month.

**Inmate Mail:** The FCI and the camp accept mail from the U.S. Postal Service via First-Class, U.S. Priority, and Express Mail. For those interested in sending overnight mail via a private carrier (FedEx or UPS Overnight), it is recommended that you first contact the institution to find out whether the receipt of such mail is permitted.

**Inmate Mail to USP:**
INMATE NAME & REGISTER NUMBER
USP Victorville
U.S. Penitentiary
P.O. Box 5300
Adelanto, CA 92301

**Visiting Hours:** USP visiting hours: Saturday, Sunday, Monday, holidays 8:30am-3pm. USP inmates are given 40 visiting points. One point is deducted on weekdays, weekends and holidays. Inmates are limited to four approved visitors at one time. Children who occupy seats will be counted as an adult visitor. Attorneys should visit during regular hours. Attorneys must submit a request to visit to the inmate's unit manager, for approval of the visit. Additional visiting information can be found at https://www.bop.gov/locations/institutions/vip/.

**Lodging/Accommodations:** See §17:26, FCI Victorville I and II.

# CHAPTER 18

# PRIVATELY MANAGED FACILITIES HOUSING FEDERAL INMATES

(This page intentionally left blank.)

# §18:10  INTRODUCTION

At the time this *Guidebook* went to press, there were approximately 28,191 federal inmates housed in privately managed facilities under contract with the BOP.

Approximately 14 percent of the Bureau's inmate population is confined in secure facilities primarily operated by private corrections companies, and to a lesser extent in privately operated community correction centers. Contract facilities help the Bureau manage population and are especially useful for meeting the needs of low-security, specialized population like sentenced criminal aliens. Staff of the Correctional Programs Division in the Central Office provides oversight for privately operated facilities.

This does not include federal inmates in home confinement programs, in short-term jailed detention facilities, in juvenile facilities, or housed in privately managed secure facilities under contract with the BOP or with a state or local government that has an Intergovernmental Agreement with the BOP. That number, at the time this *Guidebook* went to press, was 42,387.

# §18:20  PRIVATELY MANAGED FACILITIES

## Adams County Correctional Institution

Physical Address
CI Adams County
Correctional Institution
20 Hobo Fork Road
Natchez, MS 39120
ACC/General@bop.gov
601-304-2500
601-446-5224 Fax

*Use the following address when sending correspondence and parcels to inmates confined at this facility.*
    INMATE NAME & REGISTER NUMBER
    CI ADAMS COUNTY
    CORRECTIONAL INSTITUTION
    P.O. Box 1600
    Washington, MS 39190

**Security Level:** Low-security facility.

**Population:** Approximately 2,159 inmates.

**Visiting Hours:** Saturdays, Sundays, federal holidays, 8am-3pm.

## Big Spring Correctional Institution

Physical Address:
CI Big Spring
Correctional Institution
1701 Apron Drive
Big Spring, TX 79720
BSC/General@bop.gov
432-264-0060
432-267-6522 Fax

*Use the following address when sending correspondence and parcels to inmates confined at this facility.*
INMATE NAME & REGISTER NUMBER
CI Big Spring
Correctional Institution
2001 Rickabaugh Drive
Big Spring, TX 79720

**Security Level:** Low-security adult males.

**Population:** Approximately 3,451 inmates.

**Education:** Educational offerings include GED, adult basic education, ESL and computer training.

**Counseling/Rehab:** Volunteers from Alcoholics Anonymous (AA) and Narcotics Anonymous (NA) provide offenders with substance abuse and addiction counseling. Offender therapy includes criminal thinking errors, rational self analysis, learning to take responsibility for crime and understanding the impact and cost of crime to the victim and community.

**Vocational/Apprenticeship:** Employment assistance and training includes resume writing, job search strategies, application assistance and interview techniques. Vocational training is offered in conjunction with Howard College and includes building trades, landscaping, computer science and commercial housekeeping.

**Religion:** Community ministers conduct religious services.

**Visiting Hours:** Visitation hours are from 8am-3pm Friday, Saturday, Sunday, and federal holidays. Visitation must be pre-approved through the inmate's Unit Manager at their facility (below). To locate an inmate, please call the Case Management Coordinator at BSCC Administration: (432) 264-0060.

## D. Ray James Correctional Institution

Physical Address
CI D. Ray James
Correctional Institution
Highway 252 East
Folkston, GA 31537
DRJ/General@bop.gov
912-496-6242
912-496-7806 Fax

*Use the following address when sending correspondence and parcels to inmates confined at this facility. Inmate funds may also be sent directly to this address.*
INMATE NAME & REGISTER NUMBER
CI D. Ray James
Correctional Institution
P.O. Box 2000
Folkston, GA 31537

**Security Level:** Low-security facility.

**Population:** Approximately 1,881 inmates.

**Education:** English as a Second Language (ESL), GED studies and testing, college-level courses and Primeria, Secundaria, Prepatoria and Universidad courses for inmates who will return to their native country of Mexico.

**Visiting Hours:** Fridays, Saturdays, Sundays and federal holidays: 8am-3pm.

## Giles W. Dalby Correctional Institution

Physical Address
CI Giles W. Dalby
Correctional Institution
805 North Avenue F
Post, TX 79356
DAL/General@bop.gov
806-495-2175
806-495-3157 Fax

*Use the following address when sending correspondence and parcels to inmates confined at this facility.*
INMATE NAME & REGISTER NUMBER
CI Giles W. Dalby
Correctional Institution

805 North Avenue F
Post, TX 79356\

**Security Level:** Low-security facility.

**Population:** Approximately 1,857 inmates.

**Education:** English as a Second Language (ESL), GED studies and testing, and Primeria and Secundaria courses for inmates who will return to their native country of Mexico.

## Great Plains Correctional Institution

Physical Address CI Great Plains
Correctional Institution
700 Sugar Creek Drive
Hinto, OK 73047
GCP/General@bop.gov
405-542-3711
405-542-3710 Fax

*Use the following address when sending correspondence and parcels to inmates confined at this facility.*
　　INMATE NAME & REGISTER NUMBER
　　Great Plains
　　Correctional Institution
　　P.O. Box 400
　　Hinton, OK 73047

**Population:** Approximately 1,893 inmates.

## McRae Correctional Institution

Physical Address
CI McRae
Correctional Institution
112 Jim Hammock Dr.
McRae, Helena GA 31055
MCA/General@bop.gov
229-868-7778
229-868-7640 Fax

*Use the following address when sending correspondence and parcels to inmates confined at this facility.*

INMATE NAME & REGISTER NUMBER
CI McRae
Correctional Institution
P.O. Drawer 55030
McRae Helena, GA 31055

**Security Level:** Male, low-security.

**Population:** Approximately 2,099 inmates.

**Education:** GED, ESL.

**Vocational:** Includes carpentry, masonry, art and electrical wiring classes, and life skills classes.

**Visiting Hours:** Saturday, Sunday and federal holidays: 8:30am-3:30pm.

**Directions:** I-16; exit 51, McRae/Dublin; Highway 441 South to second traffic signal; left onto West Oak Street, right onto Jim Hammock Drive; follow road to Facility.

### Moshannon Valley Correctional Institution

Physical Address
CI Moshannon Valley
Correctional Institution
555 Geo Drive
Philipsburg, PA 16866
MVC/General@bop.gov
814-768-1200
814-342-5900 Fax

*Use the following address when sending correspondence and parcels to inmates confined at this facility.*
INMATE NAME & REGISTER NUMBER
CI Moshannon Valley
Correctional Institution
555 Geo Drive
Philipsburg, PA 16866

**Security Level:** Low-security adult males.

**Population:** Approximately 1,680 inmates.

**Visiting Hours:** MVCC has visitation hours from 8am-3pm, Friday through Sunday and federal holidays. For additional information or to make a visitation appointment, please call the MVCC receptionist at (814) 768-1200.

**Education:** Educational offerings include GED, adult basic education, English as a Second Language (ESL) and law and general libraries.

**Vocational/Apprenticeship:** Employment assistance and training includes resume writing, job search strategies, application assistance and interview techniques. On-the-job training opportunities are available in food and laundry services, barbering, library clerk services and classroom tutoring.

**Counseling/Rehab:** Volunteers from Alcoholics Anonymous (AA) and Narcotics Anonymous (NA) provide offenders with substance abuse and addiction counseling. Life skills are taught in anger and stress management, budgeting, banking and personal finance, personal hygiene, securing housing and victim awareness and impact.

### Reeves Correctional Institution I & II

Physical Address
CI Reeves I & II
Correctional Institution
98 West County Road 204
Pecos, TX 79772
REE/General@bop.gov
432-447-2926
432-447-9224 Fax

*Use the following address when sending correspondence and parcels to inmates confined at this facility.*
INMATE NAME & REGISTER NUMBER
CI Reeves I & II
Correctional Institution
P.O. Box 1560
Pecos, TX 79772

**Security Level:** Low-security facility.

**Population:** Approximately 1,337 inmates.

**Education:** GED and English as a Second Language (ESL) classes are available, along with classes in electrical repair, typing, basic computer skills, and basic home wiring.

**Vocational/Apprenticeship:** Vocational classes are offered in areas such as auto mechanics and horticulture.

**Visiting Hours:** Friday, Saturday, Sunday and federal holidays: 8am-3pm.

## Reeves Correctional Institution III

Physical Address
CI Reeves III
Correctional Institution
100 County Road 204
RVS/General@bop.gov
Pecos, TX 79772
432-447-2909
432-447-2084 Fax

*Use the following address when sending correspondence and parcels to inmates confined at this facility.*
>    INMATE NAME & REGISTER NUMBER
>    CI Reeves III
>    Correctional Institution
>    P.O. Box 2038
>    Pecos, TX 79772

**Security Level:** Low-security facility.

**Population:** Approximately 1,217 inmates.

**Education:** GED and English as a Second Language (ESL) classes are available, along with classes in electrical repair, typing, basic computer skills, and basic home wiring.

**Vocational/Apprenticeship:** Vocational classes are offered in areas such as auto mechanics and horticulture.

**Visiting Hours:** Friday, Saturday, Sunday and federal holidays: 8am-3pm.

## Rivers Correctional Institution

Physical Address
CI Rivers
Correctional Institution
145 Parker's Fishery Rd.
Winton, NC 27986
RIV/General@bop.gov
252-358-5200
252-358-5202 Fax

*Use the following address when sending correspondence and parcels to inmates confined at this facility.*

INMATE NAME & REGISTER NUMBER
CI Rivers
Correctional Institution
P.O. Box 630
Winton, NC 27986

**Security Level:** Low-security facility.

**Population:** Approximately 1,070 inmates.

**Education:** Educational offerings include GED, adult basic education and ESL.

**Vocational/Apprenticeship:** Vocational training is offered in building construction, commercial driving and computer technology.

**Visiting Hours:** Friday, Saturday, Sunday and federal holidays: 8am-3pm.

### Taft Correctional Institution

Physical Address
CI Taft
Correctional Institution
1500 Cadet Rd.
Taft, CA 93268
TAF/General@bop.gov
661-763-2510
661-765-3034 Fax

*Use the following address when sending correspondence and parcels to inmates confined at this facility.*
INMATE NAME & REGISTER NUMBER
CI Taft
Correctional Institution
P.O. Box 7001
Taft, CA 93268

**Security Level:** Low-security facility.

**Population:** Approximately 2,331 inmates.

**Visiting Hours:** Friday, Saturday, Sunday and federal holidays: 8am-3pm.

*Please see §14:22 of the Guidebook for more information on this facility.*

# INDEX

## A

# C

# D

# E

# F

# G

# I

# J

# L

# M

Otisville
    Federal Correctional Institution, §14:25
Oxford
    Federal Correctional Institution, §13:20

# P

Pekin
    Federal Correctional Institution, §13:21
Penalty Assessments
    Fines. *See* Fines
    Payment during confinement, §4:10.4
    Sentencing guidelines, §8:18
"Special assessments." *See* "Special Assessments"
Pensacola
    Federal Prison Camp, §16:23
Personal Possessions
    What to bring, §4:10.2
Petersburg
    Federal Correctional Institution (Low-Security), §12:29
    Federal Correctional Institution (Medium-Security), §12:30
Philadelphia
    Federal detention center, §14:26
Phoenix
    Federal Correctional Institution, §17:18
Physical Examination
    New inmates, §4:10.3
Placement
    Halfway houses, §§4:10.4, 4:10.8
    Prison. *See* Prison Placement
Plea Agreements
    Lower sentences with, §8:13.12
    Post-*Booker,* §8:30.2
Pollock
    Federal Correctional Intitution, §15:23
    U.S. Penitentiary, §15:24
Post-Conviction Remedies/Rights
    *Habeas Corpus* Motions. *See* Section 2241 Motions; Section 2255
        Motions
    Waivers
        difficulties with, §10:30.2
        general considerations, §10:30.1
        stemming the tide of, §§10:30–10:30.2
Pregnant Inmates

# Q

# R

# V

# W

Written Plea Agreements. *See* Plea Agreements

# Y

Yankton
   Federal Prison Camp, §13:29
Yazoo City
   Federal Correctional Institution (I and II), §16:27
   U.S. Penitentiary, §16:28

# Z

Zimmer Amendment
   Generally, §1:10.9